## DATE DUE

| | | | |
|---|---|---|---|
| | | | |
| | | | |
| | | | |
| | | | |
| | | | |
| | | | |
| | | | |
| | | | |
| | | | |
| | | | |
| | | | |
| | | | |
| | | | |
| | | | |
| | | | |
| | | | |
| | | | |

DEMCO 38-296

# MASTERPLOTS II

## AMERICAN FICTION
## SERIES

# MASTERPLOTS II

---

# AMERICAN FICTION SERIES

## 1

A-Eig

*Edited by*

# FRANK N. MAGILL

SALEM PRESS

Englewood Cliffs, N.J.

**Library of Congress Cataloging-in-Publication Data**
Masterplots II: American fiction series.
  Includes bibliographies and index.
  Summary: Includes more than 360 interpretative
essays on works of twentieth-century fiction published in the United States and Latin America.
  1. America—Literatures—Stories, plots, etc.
2. America—Literatures—History and criticism—
Addresses, essays, lectures. 3. Fiction—20th century—Stories, plots, etc. 4. Fiction—20th century—History and criticism—Addresses, essays,
lectures. [1. America—Literatures—Stories, plots,
etc. 2. America—Literatures—History and criticism—Addresses, essays, lectures] I. Magill, Frank
Northen, 1907-    . II. Title: Masterplots 2. III.
Title: Masterplots two.
PN846.M37  1986    809.3    86-1910
ISBN 0-89356-456-7 (set)
ISBN 0-89356-457-5 (volume 1)

# PREFACE

It has been almost forty years since the first *Masterplots* set was published. While that work is still valid and still in wide use, since its appearance there have been changes in the social structure of American society, in the way teachers and students approach the Humanities, and in the emphasis placed upon style and content in creative depictions of the contemporary scene. Above all, many new and talented authors are now available for inclusion in a new reference work addressing the best in the twentieth century American novel.

The justification for *Masterplots II* is thus obvious, and though no need arises to disregard the favorites of the past, the inclusion of many new works since 1949, and indeed since 1900, in the general concept of *Masterplots* allows today's students—and researchers interested in pertinent creative development—the opportunity to observe a more inclusive evaluation of the subject.

To delineate these changes, it would be enlightening to call attention statistically to the overall contents of *Masterplots II*, American Fiction Series. There are 383 new titles that are covered in 363 special articles. There are 198 authors represented, among them fifty-three women writers (27% of the list), thirty-two black writers (16%), and thirty-four Latin American writers (17%).

In developing the list for this new series, several philosophical concerns were acknowledged and taken into account. For example, the social fabric of the United States was slow to change even after the Civil War, but with the turn of the century and our involvement in World War I that soon followed, America's narrow societal views broadened greatly and carried forward into the popular literature that reflected the mores of the period: the flapper age, the "lost generation," the Harlem Renaissance—all of which were moving forces in the new creativity. Also, changing with the times meant not merely covering more works by groups previously less well represented but also selecting competent novels that deal with the concerns and needs of these neglected areas, thus bringing them to the forefront of intellectual discussion. In addition, certain works by major authors that were formerly considered to be on the second level of the author's canon have been selected because the subject matter itself is now more in keeping with today's changing world. Thus, the titles represented in this work cover pertinent novels of the period from the dawn of the twentieth century to 1985, eight-and-a-half decades of human progress, worldwide wars, striking scientific developments, cosmic speculation, and space exploration—physical and intellectual changes the extent of which dwarf any similar period in man's history.

By including Latin American novels in the American Fiction Series of

*Masterplots II*, we have opened to our users the broad and delightful creative thrust of the Latin American literary Renaissance (the "Boom") of the 1960's and 1970's, a truly remarkable outpouring of talent that moved across South America, Central America, and much of the Caribbean.

Perhaps one should begin a discussion of late twentieth century Latin American literature with Colombia's 1982 Nobel Prize winner Gabriel García Márquez, whose *One Hundred Years of Solitude* (1967) is considered a world classic; his *The Autumn of the Patriarch* (1975), a political novel about Latin American dictators as a breed, is not far behind.

Peru is well represented with Ciro Alegría's *The Golden Serpent* (1935), an encomium of a place and a people by one of Peru's most sensitive writers, who describes the beauty and danger of life among the majestic Marañon River in Northern Peru. Alegría's *Broad and Alien Is the World* (1941) is a prizewinning effort seeking social justice for Peru's *cholos* and Indians. Another outstanding novel from Peru is Mario Vargas Llosa's *Conversation in the Cathedral* (1969), a family chronicle depicting the social history of both a prosperous Peruvian family and their less-favored servants. Vargas Llosa presents a sharp contrasting picture of the mores of two distinct social classes living daily in the same environment but under vastly different circumstances.

Readers familiar with Mexican author Carlos Fuentes' *Where the Air Is Clear* (1958) and *The Death of Artemio Cruz* (1962) will probably find his *The Good Conscience* (1959) especially interesting because its literary style varies markedly from the "cinema technique" adaptations of the author's more famous novels. Also in Central America, one should not overlook the excellent novels of Guatemala's Miguel Ángel Asturias, among which, as translated, are *The President* (1946), *Mulata* (1963), and *Men of Maize* (1949), a strong social morality study.

With Eduardo Mallea's *All Green Shall Perish* (1941), Manuel Puig's *Heartbreak Tango* (1969), *Diary of the War of the Pig* (1969), by Adolfo Bioy Casares (a somewhat neglected author), Luisa Valenzuela's *The Lizard's Tail* (1983), and many other fine examples, Argentina has contributed its share to the post-1950's "Boom," as has Brazil, with such active writers as Jorge Amado (*Jubiabá*, 1935, and *Dona Flor and Her Two Husbands*, 1966), and Rachel de Queiroz with her *Dôra, Doralina* (1975), a maturation novel in which the author raises the social issue of women's secondary status in Northeastern Brazil.

As suggested above, much early literature by blacks have been given a second look in recent years, and the *Masterplots II* staff has taken full note of this trend. Not surprisingly, much of the work is protest literature; on the contrary, an admirable theme throughout seems to center on the simple expectation of a satisfactory place in the flow of the social stream, based on the worth of the individual in human terms, and on that alone.

One of the most popular black writers today is Alice Walker, whose 1982 novel *The Color Purple* is a beautiful story depicting the spiritual and mental growth of one of life's losers. The novel won several literary prizes and was later made into a highly successful motion picture. Another significant novel by Walker is *Meridian* (1976), set in the Deep South and New York City during the Civil Rights Movement of the 1960's. Another well-established black woman writer is Toni Morrison, whose *The Bluest Eye* (1970) depicts the sad, depressing story of an eleven-year-old girl who is raped by her drunk father. *The Bluest Eye* was followed by *Sula* in 1973, by *Song of Solomon* in 1977, and by *Tar Baby* in 1981. It is not likely that either of these two talented novelists has yet reached her peak.

Black writers who achieved major publication in the United States were rather rare prior to the Harlem Renaissance in the 1920's, but this stimulant created much activity. Even before that, the 1912 publication of James Weldon Johnson's novel *The Autobiography of an Ex-Coloured Man* (1912) created quite a stir. Yet it was in the 1920's that black literary voices finally began to be heard regularly. Among these pioneers was Claude McKay, with *Home to Harlem* (1928) presenting protagonist Jake Brown, *Banjo* (1929), and *Banana Bottom* (1933). Somewhat later Arna Bontemps published *Black Thunder* (1936), a fascinating story of a black slave rebellion in 1800. In 1940, Richard Wright gained immediate critical and popular attention with his excellent *Native Son*. This novel was followed by other successes including *The Long Dream* (1958) and the posthumous *Lawd Today* (1963). Unfortunately, the career of this gifted novelist was cut short at age 52. Meanwhile, James Baldwin was active and influential on the scene with works such as *Go Tell It on the Mountain* (1953), *Another Country* (1962), and other popular novels.

Among the later outstanding works that should not be overlooked are Ernest J. Gaines's *The Autobiography of Miss Jane Pittman* (1971), the story— told in her own words— of a young girl born during slavery who lives to be a hundred and sees freedom finally gain a foothold in the 1960's. *Captain Blackman* (1972), by John A. Williams, is the story of a strange Vietnam War experience by the author of the popular 1967 novel *The Man Who Cried I Am*, and it is further evidence of this novelist's unique rapport with his readers.

In 1985, John Edgar Wideman published *The Homewood Trilogy*, consisting of *Damballah* (1981); *Hiding Place* (1981); and *Sent for You Yesterday* (1983). This outstanding work heralds a career likely to be long and fruitful.

The style of the individual articles in *Masterplots II*, American Fiction Series, is slightly different from that of the plot-summary format employed in the original *Masterplots* series. In the new work, along with a summarization of plot, narrative devices are often explored and characterization studied in more depth than before—an aspect useful for younger students. In addition, the major themes of the novel at hand are identified and analyzed, and the overall success of the author's effort is usually discussed in an interpretive summary.

I wish to thank all those who have contributed to the development of this initial four-volume element of the new analytical series, *Masterplots II*. We trust that the refined explicative techniques introduced in the new series will prove to be informative and helpful.

FRANK N. MAGILL

# CONTRIBUTING REVIEWERS

Michael Adams

Terry L. Andrews

Andrew J. Angyal

Stanley Archer

Edwin T. Arnold

Bryan Aubrey

Thomas Banks

Dan Barnett

Craig Barrow

Jane M. Barstow

Mary G. Berg

Anthony Bernardo

Thomas G. Bowie

Mark Braley

Harold Branam

Jeanie R. Brink

Mollie A. Brodsky

Keith H. Brower

Carl Brucker

Richard Butts

John Canfield

Rosemary M. Canfield

Karen Carmean

Krista Ratkowski Carmona

David A. Carpenter

John Carpenter

Susanna Castillo

Deborah Charlie

Sandra Christenson

Stella T. Clark

James W. Coleman

John J. Conlon

Linda Seidel Costic

Cecil Costilow

Joanna Courteau

Michael Crane

Virginia Crane

Jim Crawford

Lucia Guerra Cunningham

J. D. Daubs

Frank Day

John Deredita

Carolyn Dirksen

Virginia A. Duck

Gweneth A. Dunleavy

Bruce L. Edwards, Jr.

Jackie Eisen

Robert P. Ellis

Ernesto Encinas

Tom Erskine

Clara Estow

Donald M. Fiene

Edward Fiorelli

Christopher J. Forbes

Robert J. Forman

Teresa Chittenden Frary

Lawrence S. Friedman

Susan VanZanten Gallagher

Charles Ganelin

René P. Garay

Betty G. Gawthrop

Flora González

Sandra Y. Govan

James Grove

Daniel L. Guillory

Donna B. Haisty

Blair M. Hancock

Ronald M. Harmon

Natalie Harper

Terry Heller

Rosalie Hewitt

Emily Hicks

Jane Hill

Robert W. Hill

Hal Holladay

Elvin Holt

John B. Hughes

Jacquelyn L. Jackson

Mercedes Jiménez González

Ronald L. Johnson

Cynthia Lee Katona

Steven G. Kellman

Rebecca Kelly

David W. Kent

John Knowles

Glenn E. Kunkel

Deborah Lally

Naomi Lindstrom

León Lewis

William Luis

Laura Riesco Luszczynska

Len McCall

Broderick McGrady

A. L. McLeod

Marian B. McLeod

Christopher R. McRae

Carol P. Marsh

S. Elaine Marshall

Charles E. May

Laurence W. Mazzeno

Adriana Méndez Rodenas

Julia Meyers

Walter E. Meyers

Sally Mitchell

Leslie B. Mittleman

Marisa Moolick-Gutiérrez

Katharine M. Morsberger

Ann R. Morris

John M. Muste

Marshall Myers

George O'Brien

Patrick O'Donnell

Rosanne Osborne

Robert M. Otten

David B. Parsell

David Peck

Gustavo Pellón

Gustavo Pérez-Firmat

Robert C. Petersen

Mary Sanders Pollock

René Prieto

Norman Prinskey

José Promis

Jennifer L. Randisi

Thomas Rankin

Bruce D. Reeves

David Rigsbee

Danny Lee Robinson

Bernard F. Rodgers, Jr.

Mary Rohrberger

Carl E. Rollyson, Jr.

Joseph Rosenblum

Diane M. Ross

Kathleen Ross

Victor Anthony Rudowski

Susan Rusinko

Arthur M. Saltzman

Lisa M. Schwerdt

Patricia Sharpe

T. A. Shippey

R. Baird Shuman

Charles L. P. Silet

Marjorie Smelstor

Gilbert Smith

Katherine Snipes

Susan Spagna

Karen Stolley

Gerald H. Strauss

Daniel Taylor

Thomas J. Taylor

Jonathan Tittler

Rebeca Torres-Rivera

Thomas Travisano

John H. Turner

Nelson H. Vieira

Jon S. Vincent

Kathi Vosevich

Ruth Weiss

Jack Welch

Bruce Wiebe

Barbara Wiedemann

Shirley A. Williams

John Dugdale Wilson

Mark Royden Winchell

Michael Witkowski

Patrick Wright

# LIST OF TITLES IN VOLUME 1

# LIST OF TITLES IN VOLUME 1

# ACROSS THE RIVER AND INTO THE TREES

*Author:* Ernest Hemingway (1899-1961)
*Type of plot:* Realism
*Time of plot:* Winter, 1949
*Locale:* Venice, Italy, and the surrounding area
*First published:* 1950

>   *Principal characters:*
>     RICHARD CANTWELL, the protagonist, a colonel, formerly a
>       United States brigadier general, a professional soldier
>     RENATA, an Italian countess, "nearly nineteen," the colonel's
>       mistress
>     JACKSON, an army sergeant, the colonel's driver
>     THE GRAN MAESTRO, the headwaiter at the Gritti Palace Ho-
>       tel and a member of the colonel's fictitious Order of
>       Brusadelli

## The Novel

The novel opens on a cold Sunday morning with the protagonist traveling by boat to shoot ducks along a partially frozen lagoon near Venice. He assists the boatman in poling through the ice and offers to help place decoys, becoming somewhat angry at the surly boatman's responses. Taking his place in a partially submerged barrel that serves as a blind, Colonel Richard Cantwell skillfully brings down the first two ducks that fly within range.

The narrative returns in a flashback to a physical examination that the colonel took three days earlier, when a skeptical army surgeon allowed him to pass, even though both men knew the colonel to be dying of heart disease. With Jackson, his driver, the colonel sets out from Trieste, recalling along the way sites where he fought and was wounded during World War I. Arriving in Venice, he goes by boat to the Gritti Palace Hotel and, once settled there, dines with his young mistress, Countess Renata. Afterward they make love in a gondola on the way to Renata's home.

The following morning, the colonel leaves the hotel to walk through the market in the brisk winter air, returning in time for breakfast with his mistress. In his room he begins to tell her how he lost his regiment in the Hurtgen Forest. Although she finds portions of the account confusing, she listens as if knowing that it is important for him to share the experience. Even after the countess has fallen asleep, he continues his discourse—at times through an interior dialogue, at times addressing a portrait that Renata gave him.

They go to a jewelry shop where he buys Renata a moor's head brooch that she admired; he informs her that the heirloom emeralds that she gave him have been deposited for her in the hotel safe. After martinis at Harry's Bar, they return to the hotel for lunch, where the colonel and the Gran Maestro make her an honorary member of their humorous Order of Brusadelli. At their parting Renata weeps, although she has told him that she never does, and the colonel sets off for the Barone Alvarito's estate, where he will hunt the next morning.

The narrative returns abruptly to the Sunday hunt, with the colonel in the blind recalling stories told by other hunters the preceding evening. After modest success, he finds the chances for more kills diminished by unfavorable weather. Returning to his car, he sets out with Jackson back to Trieste but en route is racked by a series of attacks which convince him that he cannot live. After repeating General Stonewall Jackson's final words, "No, no, let us cross over the river and rest in the shade of the trees," he moves to the back seat of the Buick and firmly closes the door. Jackson finds him dead shortly thereafter and reads a note that the colonel had written minutes earlier, ordering that the portrait and his shotguns be sent to the hotel for Renata to claim. Continuing the journey, Jackson reflects that this request will be handled through channels.

Except for the chapter narrating the physical examination, the entire plot unfolds within a period of three days. The book opens on the day of the hunt, moves backward to Friday and Saturday, and returns to the final day at the end. In the course of three days, the hero manages to tell his life's story to those he encounters, its most important stages being the two world wars. The narrow time frame beginning *in medias res* lays heavy emphasis upon his approaching death. These final three days are narrated almost exclusively from the protagonist's point of view, although one hears the authorial voice in the introduction and in the conclusion. The plot moves inexorably toward the climactic death of the protagonist.

In presenting the colonel's interaction with other characters, Hemingway achieves an economy of narrative. Rarely does the novel focus on scenes involving more than two people. At first the colonel is with the boatman on the hunt and later, he is in the car with Jackson. Much of the remaining time he is with Renata—in a hotel or dining room, walking along the street, or riding in a gondola. Other scenes involve the colonel and barmen, waiters, or the Gran Maestro. Often a deep emotional bond exists between the hero and the other character, yet the characters serve primarily as straight men designed to facilitate the colonel's rambling discourse.

*The Characters*

The protagonist, Colonel Richard Cantwell, a fifty-one-year-old professional soldier, is dying of heart disease. A veteran of both world wars, he seeks to relive his earlier life among friends and former comrades in Venice.

He narrates his most important experiences to Renata, whose name means "reborn." A man with strong likes and dislikes and some regrets, he avoids laying blame. Aggressive, somewhat short-tempered, he struggles to keep control over a truculent nature. An existential hero who conquers despair and angst, he lives by his code and feels most strongly drawn to those like himself, wounded by war or life. He quotes William Shakespeare and Dante and appreciates great works of art, but he is no mere aesthete: He lives life to the fullest and dies courageously. Lacking illusions, he nevertheless holds strong personal values—physical exertion, comradeship, kindness toward the weak, chivalry toward women, toughness toward oneself.

Renata, an Italian countess nearly nineteen, genuinely loves Cantwell. A woman of beauty, sensitivity, and wisdom beyond her years, she attempts to keep the dying colonel optimistic and forward-looking, even as she hears the unfolding story of his past. Like him, she is somewhat guarded in the expression of emotion, but her depth of feeling is undeniable.

Jackson, a technical sergeant and the colonel's driver, has shared the military experience of war, having served in the Italian campaign. To a degree, he also shares the colonel's temper and sense of dignity. His name may suggest to the colonel the quotation from Stonewall Jackson that gives the novel its title.

The Gran Maestro, who has the dignity and reserve of a headwaiter, fought with the colonel in World War I. He now suffers from ulcers and a heart condition less serious than the colonel's. The two experience a kind of magical brotherhood when they are talking of their order, a magic that vanishes whenever the Gran Maestro returns to his duties. A complement of boatmen, barmen, and waiters, each making a brief appearance, remind the reader that the hero meets them on terms of easy familiarity. Sketched with brevity and economy, they exist primarily to reveal facets of Cantwell's character or past experience.

## Themes and Meanings

The last three days of Cantwell's life are devoted to the values he holds dear—comradeship, intensity in romantic love, a sense of power, aggressiveness, and assertiveness. The values of living life to the full, loving passionately, killing cleanly, and dying courageously predominate in the work. Earlier Hemingway heroes often had a cause or at least a calling in life to which they were devoted. Cantwell, older and facing death, seems to have grown disillusioned with all causes. He expresses ambivalent attitudes about his profession of soldiering. A kind of existential hero, he attaches no mystical significance to life or death.

Like the later work *The Old Man and the Sea* (1952), the novel incorporates Christian symbolism. The colonel's wounded hand, for example, suggests the wounds of Christ, and there are allusions to Madonnas with reference to romantic love and love of family. The three-day plot, lasting from Friday through Sunday, may well hold symbolic significance, but the symbolism does not form any consistent allegory and at best offers only tantalizing suggestions.

The hero's almost incessant traveling in the novel—in boats, in a car, in walks with Renata—symbolically suggests a journey toward death. Cantwell undergoes a kind of Dantean journey requiring him to come to terms with his past. Recalling and to some extent reliving his war experiences, he has numerous regrets—the many dead, the loss of his regiment and his general's rank, the three failed marriages—yet he does not attempt to lay blame. Though he does not achieve a satisfactory resolution of his conflicting emotions, he comes to terms stoically with his losses even as he is upholding through living the values he affirms.

*Critical Context*

From the beginning, critical estimates of Hemingway's novel have been largely unfavorable, and the book continues to rank among his least successful. However fine the narrative technique and style, the novel centers so heavily on the hero that his character and expression influence readers most strongly. Cantwell closely resembles earlier Hemingway heroes such as Frederic Henry in *A Farewell to Arms* (1929) and Robert Jordan in *For Whom the Bell Tolls* (1940). Like them he is tragic, yet he carries the machismo of the traditional hero to excess. Once, while walking at night with Renata, Cantwell bridles at insults from two sailors. When they go too far, he approaches and begins a fight, quickly knocking one out. After landing several devastating blows against the other, he smashes him above the ear and turns rapidly away so that he will not hear the sailor's head bounce against the pavement. Then, ignoring the hurt to his previously injured hand, he tells Renata that they should walk in such a way that the backs of their legs look dangerous.

In his attitudes, Cantwell resembles Hemingway and is in fact a highly autobiographical character. His blunt criticism of military and political leaders such as General George Patton, British Field Marshal Bernard Montgomery, President Harry S Truman, and President Dwight David Eisenhower embarrassed many readers at the time. The dialogue incorporates the mannerisms of earlier Hemingway heroes taken to excess—insider jokes, cryptic allusions to weapons and weapons systems, military jargon, and slangy nicknames. Cantwell refers to a martini with fifteen parts gin and one part vermouth as a Montgomery—the point being that British Field Marshal Montgomery wanted favorable odds of fifteen to one before attacking and even then moved with caution. The numerous references and allusions to the World War II era must inevitably pose more difficulty for readers as time passes. One must be rather well grounded in languages to recognize and understand all of the Italian, German, French, and Spanish phrases and sentences sprinkled throughout the book.

Although the novel reveals many of the qualities of Hemingway's art, it does not advance his previous achievement, either aesthetically or thematically. It remains among the minor achievements of a major novelist.

*Sources for Further Study*
Baker, Carlos. *Hemingway: The Writer as Artist*, 1952.
Wagner, Linda Welshimer, ed. *Ernest Hemingway: Five Decades of Criticism*, 1974.
Waldhorn, Arthur. *A Reader's Guide to Ernest Hemingway*, 1972.
Young, Philip. *Ernest Hemingway: A Reconsideration*, 1966.

*Stanley Archer*

# ADA OR ARDOR
## A Family Chronicle

*Author:* Vladimir Nabokov (1899-1977)
*Type of plot:* Romance and literary parody
*Time of plot:* 1850 to 1965
*Locale:* Antiterra or Demonia
*First published:* 1969

> *Principal characters:*
> IVAN (VAN) VEEN, the protagonist, born in 1870
> ADELAIDA (ADA) VEEN, his cousin, born in 1872
> DEMENTIY (DEMON) VEEN, Van's father
> AQUA DURMANOV, Van's mother
> MARINA DURMANOV, Ada's mother
> LUCINDA OR LUCETTE VEEN, Ada's sister

*The Novel*

If *Ada or Ardor* (most commonly known as *Ada*) is about people—it is subtitled "A Family Chronicle," and Nabokov supplies a detailed family tree that precedes the novel—it is also a book about literature, a parody. The difficulty for the reader is to judge correctly the proportions of the two. To what extent is it a book about people—above all about two lovers, Ada and Van—and to what extent is it a book about literary works and traditions? Clearly the novel is both. It is an interesting love story about two cousins who fall in love and consummate that love, when Van is fourteen and Ada twelve. The novel follows the vicissitudes of this love affair until the protagonists' old age. It is also a "chronicle" of the nineteenth and twentieth century novel, with almost as many literary references as James Joyce's *Ulysses* (1922). It is a love story and a *roman à clef*—or rather *aux clés*. It can be confidently predicted that graduate students and critics will want to write articles and books about *Ada*'s literary allusions well into the future. It is questionable, however, whether readers will also continue to come to *Ada* because of its love story and family chronicle. Interest in the novel will be generated by its literary complexity on the one hand, and by interest in its explicitly erotic passages on the other. Like Joyce scholars, Nabokov scholars will probably continue to say that the general reader cannot appreciate the novel without understanding its multiple literary references. *Ada* will probably have as few readers who enjoy it without reference to a literary tradition as *Ulysses*. The erotic passages will attract the curious, yet it is difficult to imagine such an audience reading the novel from beginning to end with satisfaction.

Nevertheless, reading *Ada* provides a unique kind of experience. The novel can be appreciated as a work of imagination about people, without reference to other books or literary traditions. There are obstacles to this, just as there are similar obstacles in *Ulysses*, but they are not insuperable. The parody can be understood on the level of personalities and word play; above all, the major imaginative act of the novel can be clearly grasped by a Russianless reader.

*Ada* does not take place on the familiar Earth; it is set neither in Russia (or the literal context of Russian literature) nor in America. The novel takes place in "Antiterra," sometimes called Demonia. Terra—our Earth—is a myth, a distant world about which the characters in the book dream; it is an unattainable Utopia. This basic premise of the novel should give pause to the seekers of literary influences. Antiterra has its own laws and its own elements, which are different from those on Terra. Consequently the novel's protagonists are also different; they are not human in the normal sense, nor is the love of Ada and Van a normal human love. It is their inhuman qualities that are central to the novel. The reader's recognition of these is central to an understanding of *Ada*.

On the planet of Antiterra, not only Van and Ada but also all other people are possessed by the fury of erotic love. To the exclusion of almost everything else, the characters are obsessed with the "dementia" of ardor. The Veens are not Demonia's only libertines; nearly every minor character in the book is either inspired or victimized by passion. As the Greeks distinguished between searing Eros and Agape—the warm affection that exists in families or among friends—so Nabokov distinguishes between Antiterra and Terra. The world of *Ada* is entirely the world of Eros, with other types of love methodically excluded. No characters in the book are left unscathed by the "ardent" practices of pederasty, nympholepsy (the novel frequently harks back to *Lolita*, 1955), lesbianism, or simple promiscuity and adultery. As the critic Ellen Pifer has remarked in *Nabokov and the Novel* (1980),

> nearly everyone, from servants to stealthy heads of state, is busy fondling someone else behind a convenient tree or in a handy corner. More often than not, the object of such ardent caresses is another man's lover or spouse, a child decades younger than her (or his) adorer, or a triptych of prostitutes who have turned up for the occasion. On Antiterra, young "whorelets," beautiful and diseased, are offered to the highest bidder by their mother or older brother.

The repellent effect of these episodes is deliberate.

As the novel proceeds, the reader quickly discovers that Van, Ada, Van's father Demon, and other characters are quite unpleasant. The reader might be legitimately puzzled by this unpleasantness, and shortly after the novel appeared in 1969 several critics attributed it to Nabokov, the author. Matthew Hodgart reviewed *Ada* for *The New York Review of Books* (May 22,

1969), assuming that Van and Ada's love affair was modeled after Nabokov's own marriage. Nabokov's indignant response to the reviewer (published July 10, 1969) was:

> I do object violently to your seeing in reunited Van and Ada (both rather horrible creatures) a picture of my married life. What the hell, Sir, do you know about my married life? I expect a prompt apology from you.

Clearly Hodgart had made a mistake. The novel is a sustained exercise in the description of "inhuman" desire that transcends or obliterates the "restraints, principles and consolations" of everyday life on the Earth. Questions of intention or consequence—of whether human life is preserved or destroyed—are irrelevant to that ecstasy; Nabokov attempts to apply this psychological principle to all the relationships in the book. It is the across-the-board premise of the fictitious world of Antiterra, which is both beautiful and cruel. The powerful and privileged practice every form of aesthetic and erotic indulgence at the expense of the weak.

What is the ultimate goal of this allegorical or fictitious world? The novel traces the passion of Van and Ada from its inception to their old age, when they are more than ninety years old. The reader is informed that when Van is eighty-seven he becomes impotent, but that does not substantially change the nature of his relationship with Ada, and Antiterra remains Antiterra. Van writes a treatise on time and space, he attempts to "caress time." As Nabokov (or rather, Van) writes, "To be eternal the Present must depend on the conscious spanning of an infinite expansure." Indeed, this conscious act is the writing of the novel *Ada* which has been composed, the reader learns, by Van himself. *Ada* is Van's "treatise on the Texture of Time, an investigation of its veily substance, with illustrative metaphors."

The novel ends with a rapid history of the world in the 1920's and 1930's, of the conquest of Rus by the Golden Horde and the rise in 1933 of "Athaulf Hindler." The narrator mentions the "L.F.T. idea," which is "leaving from Terra" in a cosmic capsule. Nabokov's "world" or allegory is consistent to the end.

Normally when irony is used in a work of art, it is signaled by a variety of devices—exaggeration, irreverent twists, understatement, or the unexpected joining of opposites. *Ada* contains an abundance of the first two devices, but there is very little of the latter two. As a result, "Antiterra" is disconcertingly a world unto itself. The parody lacks real bite, or mordancy. Is it a hypothetical world, or what the world has become? "Van" is incapable of answering this question. Nabokov declines to do so.

### The Characters

The characters define Antiterra, and they are all destructive. They might be roughly divided into victimizers and victims. Demon Veen, Van's father, is a monstrous egotist and a rake. He seems to feed on live beauty with the same appetite with which he feeds on gourmet meals. Van takes after his father—he is a younger and more robust, more spontaneous and less jaded, copy. Ada has a devastating effect on the frail mortals with whom she comes in contact. From childhood on, Van's and Ada's appetites are as prodigious as their intellectual gifts—they do not have to work for their conquests, who succumb to them without the least resistance. Nor do the men work for money, or do any drudgery; they live in a world of Swiss bank accounts, of multiple villas on the most desirable spots of the globe with "staffs" of servants filling them. It would seem that there might be an element of wish-fulfilling fantasy here, of self-indulgence bordering on privatism. The "author" (technically, Van) insists that to all of his endeavors Van applies "athletic strength of will, ironization of excessive emotion, and contempt for weepy weaklings." In this black-and-white world where extremes (incestuously) meet, the victims appear little different from their victimizers; they feel no resentment or rebellion, and no doubt victims would be victimizers if only they had the means.

These values, or antivalues, are reinforced by the narration's tone. All events are seen through the prism of Van's hyperbolic disdain, his striking metaphors, constant parody, and trilingual puns. ("Demon's former valet explained to Van that the 'dor' in the name of an adored river equalled the corruption of hydro in 'dorophone.' Van often had word dreams.") The reader is never able to escape this "nasty" tone or point of view; it produces a sense of claustrophobia from which there is no respite. This is the novel's basic flaw and greatest weakness, its Achilles' heel. The narration is often sprightly, inventive—but it cloys. It desperately needs a foil, something to be set against, another voice to give relief, or proof that Van's authorial tone is not Nabokov's. None, however, is provided.

The saving grace of Antiterra is that its inhabitants long for another "more deeply moral" world to which they might escape. They dream of a paradise called Terra "on the opposite side of the cosmic lane" where cruel appetite and pride have been dispelled. Ironically, it is when the reader encounters these longings that Antiterra seems most like our own world.

*Themes and Meanings*

The dominant theme of *Ada* is the parody of our world by means of Nabokov's construct, Antiterra. It is both Utopia and anti-Utopia combined. It has features in common with science fiction—with some of the worlds imagined by Stanisław Lem, for example—but also with books such as Aldous Huxley's *Brave New World* (1932), George Orwell's *Nineteen Eighty-Four* (1949), and Yevgeny Zamyatin's *My* (1924; *We*, 1925). Nabokov's "brave" world is, however, more elusive. It is a subtle combination of paradise and hell, without any middle ground, that is much more difficult to grasp. It is above all a parody of the world of unrestrained appetite.

The late nineteenth and twentieth centuries, Nabokov seems to say, have gradually become an Antiterra, and all that is left of Terra is our longings. The causes for this are both external and internal: the triumph of the Golden Horde and Athaulf Hindler (Joseph Stalin and Adolf Hitler) from outside, and the cruelty of our demands for gratification, for an egotistical "paradise now," from within.

*Critical Context*

When *Ada* first appeared it was hailed by some, strongly disliked by others. The dislike was not hard to understand—because the entire chronicle is suffused by Van's special tone of disdainful hyperbole from beginning to end, it is, in effect, "Van's book," and the reader has some excuse to think that Van is a stand-in for Nabokov. The reviewer for the *Times Literary Supplement* (October 2, 1969) thought that the novel was a form of "self-parody"—like *The Golden Bowl* (1904), *Sordello* (1840), *Pericles, Prince of Tyre* (c. 1607-1608), *The Kreutzer Sonata* (1890), and *Across the River and into the Trees* (1950).

Critics and scholars of Russian literature, however, and specialists of Nabokov's writings knew that this impression was partly misleading. Nabokov had always been a parodist, and the particular tone adopted for *Ada* was not identical to that of his other books. In an article, Simon Karlinsky sketched the literary allusions of *Ada*, opening the way to an interpretation of the book as a novel about literature. Antiterra proves to have a strong resemblance to nineteenth and twentieth century Russian literature. The novel's subtitle points to Sergey Aksakov's *Semeynaya khronika* (1856; *The Family Chronicle*, 1903), Demon Veen's ancestry goes back to Mikhail Lermontov's 1841 narrative poem *Demon* by way of Fyodor Sologub's *The Little Demon* (1916). Sologub's *The Created Legend* (1916) is partly situated in Russia during the revolution of 1905 and partly on a distant imaginary planet reminiscent of Antiterra. Karlinsky's article provided a preliminary "skeleton key" for the intellectual plot of *Ada*. Also, nineteenth century European diabolism and the Don Juan myth could be seen at the core of *Ada*—rightly so, as Ada herself acts in a mediocre film, *Don Juan's Last Fling*, and during the closing pages of the novel she and Van watch it half a dozen times with absorbed interest. Karlinsky, Alfred Appel, Jr., Carl Proffer, and others have pointed out other allusions in *Ada*; the novel begins with a parody of the opening of *Anna Karenina*, and there are numerous references to Alexander Pushkin, Anton Chekhov, Ivan Turgenev, Aleksandr Griboyedov, Miguel de Cervantes, John Milton, Lord Byron (again Don Juan), Chateaubriand, Marcel Proust, and many others, among them T. S. Eliot ("Solemn Kithar Sween, a banker who at sixty-five had become an avant-garde author; in the course of one miraculous year he had produced *The Waistline*, a satire in free verse on Anglo-American feeding habits").

There are three main purposes behind the allusions: high spirits in keeping with the multiple puns and plays on words in the novel, the extension of the "chronicle" of Antiterra deep into the past, and the criticism—by parody—of the only-too-familiar traits of Antiterra embodied in literary tradition. There is no question about it: An abundant literature about Antiterra already existed. It turned out to be right under our noses.

*Sources for Further Study*
Boyd, Brian. *Nabokov's Ada: The Place of Consciousness*, 1985.
Field, Andrew. *Nabokov: His Life in Part*, 1977.
Karlinsky, Simon. "Nabokov's Russian Games," in *The New York Times Book Review*. LXXVI (April 18, 1971), p. 2.
Pifer, Ellen. *Nabokov and the Novel*, 1980.
*TriQuarterly*. No. 17 (Winter, 1970). Special Nabokov issue.

*John Carpenter*

# THE AGONY AND THE ECSTASY
## A Novel of Michelangelo

*Author:* Irving Stone (1903-    )
*Type of plot:* Biographical novel
*Time of plot:* 1487-1564
*Locale:* Italy, especially Florence and Rome
*First published:* 1961

Principal characters:
> MICHELANGELO BUONARROTI, the protagonist, a sculptor,
> painter, architect, and poet
> LODOVICO DI LIONARDO BUONARROTI SIMONI, Michelangelo's
> father
> LORENZO DE' MEDICI, IL MAGNIFICO, Michelangelo's first pa-
> tron and the epitome of Renaissance humanism
> CONTESSINA DE' MEDICI, Lorenzo's daughter and
> Michelangelo's first love
> CLARISSA SAFFI, Michelangelo's other early love
> GIROLAMO SAVONAROLA, a zealous priest bent on reforming
> the Church
> VITTORIA COLONNA, the object of Michelangelo's love in later
> life
> TOMMASO DE CAVALIERI, Michelangelo's apprentice/assistant
> on St. Peter's and his other "love" in later life
> LEONARDO DA VINCI, Michelangelo's rival in painting
> BERTOLDO, Michelangelo's teacher in sculpture

*The Novel*

*The Agony and the Ecstasy,* a biographical novel, spans most of Michelangelo's life: It begins with him as a twelve-year-old and concludes with his death approximately eighty years later. Although Stone covers most of Michelangelo's life, he seems most concerned with Michelangelo's apprenticeship and early work; when Michelangelo reaches sixty, approximately two-thirds of his lifetime, the novel is practically completed. Struggle appears to be more interesting than success. Because of the mass of details, many gleaned from previously untranslated letters about Michelangelo's long life, Stone had to shape his material, to provide dramatic structure to the history of a man and his time.

As Stone presents him, Michelangelo is the complete artist: painter, sculptor, poet, architect, and, ultimately, engineer. *The Agony and the Ecstasy* depicts Michelangelo's struggle to become the embodiment of Renaissance humanism. In the course of the novel Michelangelo must overcome the interference of his family, religious dogma, political intrigue, papal patronage, military campaigns, and artistic jealousy to realize his artistic ambition.

Despite his father's opposition, twelve-year-old Michelangelo becomes an apprentice, first to painter Ghirlandaio and then to Bertoldo, a sculptor, who directs a school financed by Lorenzo de' Medici, patron of Florentine art. Michelangelo quickly wins Lorenzo's esteem, meets his children (among them two future popes, Giulio and Giovanni, and Contessina, his first love), suffers the first of several attacks by jealous colleagues (his nose is broken by Torrigiani, whose later appearances always threaten Michelangelo), and through forbidden dissection learns the anatomy and physiology he needs. Eventually Savonarola, a reform priest, comes to power, and his crusading zeal threatens Lorenzo de' Medici's family and the Florentine art world.

When Savonarola gains political, as well as religious, control, Michelangelo flees Florence and travels to Bologna, where he meets the sensuous Clarissa Saffi and carves the Bambino that attracts the attention of Leo Baglioni. In Rome for the first time, Michelangelo meets Jacopo Galli, a banker, who commissions a sculpture; Giuliano Sangallo, an architect; and Bramante, another architect and an adversary. In Rome, Michelangelo carves the *Pietà*, learns about the whims of religious patrons, and becomes interested in St. Peter's—the building of the new St. Peter's will embroil him in controversy and ultimately consume his last years.

Michelangelo returns to Florence, where he carves "the Giant," a sculpture of David which becomes the symbol of Florence. There he meets Leonardo da Vinci, his principal rival, and Raphael, the painter—the three become the triumvirate of Renaissance Italian art. Jealous of Leonardo, Michelangelo competes with him as the two artists paint frescoes for the rulers of Florence. Word of Michelangelo's work reaches Pope Julius, who forces Michelangelo to work in bronze, rather than his beloved marble, and to paint the Sistine Chapel ceiling. It is Julius who resolves to build a new St. Peter's.

Julius is followed by two Medici popes who only add to Michelangelo's problems: Giovanni, by forcing him to work with marble from Pietrasanta, an almost inaccessible region, thereby making Michelangelo an engineer, and Giulio, against whose forces Michelangelo must use his engineering talents to fortify the city of Florence. The Medici popes are followed by Pope Paul III, who commissions Michelangelo to paint the Last Judgment and who, after bitter disputes about the ongoing building of St. Peter's, appoints him as architect for the cathedral. The dome, Michelangelo's last creation, is the appropriate capstone for his creative efforts. In addition to achieving artistic acclaim, he finds an assistant, Tommaso de Cavalieri, who is to complete St. Peter's, and Vittoria Colonna, the female epitome of Renaissance humanism and his last great love.

*The Characters*

Stone presents Michelangelo as the idealized Renaissance humanist, the artist whose commitment to his work becomes a religion and whose creative efforts are no less than godlike. In fact, his commitment to art is such that it alienates him from society, makes him a misunderstood recluse, and, in becoming the outlet for his passion, prevents him from finding love. Because art becomes religion, art cannot be commercialized; the artist is not a businessman. Overly generous to his parasitic family and deaf to the warnings of his banker/agent Galli, he lives in relative poverty, unlike Leonardo and Raphael. Also unlike them, he works alone, refusing to compromise his work by using, even in the Sistine Chapel, other painters. Leonardo da Vinci and Raphael, despite their stature, exist in Stone's novel primarily as foils, artists whose deficiencies help define Michelangelo's greatness.

Other characters serve to demonstrate the plight of the artist whose superior work is often prey to the jealousy of less talented colleagues. Torrigiani breaks Michelangelo's nose, itself part of a work of art, as Stone carefully points out in the first paragraph of the novel. Later Vincenzo, an inferior sculptor in Bologna, defaces Michelangelo's *St. Petronius* because of jealousy. Perugino's vicious attack on Michelangelo's work is motivated, according to Raphael, by envy and despair: Michelangelo has made Perugino's work obsolete. Another act of "desecration" is committed by Bandinelli, who breaks into Michelangelo's studio during the attack on Florence. These examples attest the validity of Lorenzo de' Medici's words: "The forces of destruction march on the heels of creativity."

Despite the obstacles posed by such critics, Michelangelo succeeds because of his own talent, which is shaped by his mentors: Ghirlandaio, who instructs him in painting; Bertoldo, who instructs him in sculpture; Prior Bichiellini, who instructs him in life; and, most important, Lorenzo de' Medici, Il Magnifico, whose Platonic Academy instructs him in poetry and in the blending of classical and Christian cultures that characterizes his work. Even after his death, Lorenzo's ideas and influence inform Michelangelo's art.

The women in the novel serve primarily as symbols which ultimately are related to Michelangelo's work. Contessina, Lorenzo's daughter, is inaccessible, because of her exalted position, and pure; Michelangelo is bound to her aesthetically, spiritually, and mystically. Clarissa Saffi, a fictional rather than historical character, represents the emotional and physical side of love, and she is accessible. According to Michelangelo, she is the female form "already carved" and is the incarnation of love in its "ultimate female form." During the Florentine War he thinks of both women, and when their images merge, they become one, "the figure of love itself." This blending is analogous to the blending of classical and Christian in his work.

*The Agony and the Ecstasy* is a lengthy, sprawling novel, a large canvas peopled with characters from all walks of life. The historical characters serve to provide a cultural and intellectual milieu, a background for Michelangelo. Many of the fictional characters are from the lower classes, which tend to be sentimentalized and contrasted with the corrupt and ambitious upper classes. Nowhere is this conflict of values more apparent than in the juxtaposition of the Topolinos, the stonecutters, and the denizens of Rome.

## Themes and Meanings

In *The Agony and the Ecstasy*, Stone uses Michelangelo as a working definition of the idealized artist, a creation who is, simultaneously, a godlike creator. Early in the novel Michelangelo refers to God as the "first sculptor" and as the "supreme carver"; later, he refers to artists as the species "apart" who will speak for God. "To draw is to be like God," asserts Michelangelo, who claims elsewhere that sculpture is "my faith." As he gazes at his Sistine Chapel, Michelangelo recalls Genesis, and Stone has him, in analogous terms, see all that he has made and "find it very good."

This extraordinary analogy is extended when Michelangelo sees himself as not only God the Father, but as "God the Mother," source of a "noble breed, half man, half god"; as God the Mother, he inseminates himself with his "creative fertility." Stone thus incorporates sexuality within religiosity and provides his readers with a new metaphor involving the equation of sex with sculpture. In its coarsest terms, the relationship is described by Beppe: "What you put into the ladies at night, you can't put into the marble in the morning." In more elevated terms, the conflict between art and sexuality is akin to the traditional opposition between the body (sex) and spirit (art). Given that conflict, the sculptor expresses his relationship to marble in sexual terms; having expended himself on the marble, he has no creative energy for personal relationships. For Michelangelo, the act of creation involves the "thrust, the penetration, the beating and pulsing" toward climax. Blocks of marble are seen as "virginal"; the chisel penetrates and seeds its female form. Conversely, when he makes love to Clarissa, the sexual act is expressed in terms of sculpture: He uses a "chisel" on the "warm living marble" of Clarissa's body, which had been earlier described as being "already carved." Through the use of the analogy Stone explains Michelangelo's relative lack of sexual interest in women (Clarissa is a fictional character), but Stone avoids dealing with his subject's bisexuality.

Stone also addresses the incompatibility of art and business. During most of his life, Michelangelo is totally dependent on the patronage of the wealthy, especially the papacy, and their whims and eccentricities prevent him from expressing himself in his beloved marble. Although a creative god in theory, the artist is, as Michelangelo ruefully acknowledges, a "hireling," below a tradesman in status. Rather than financing the artist and allowing freedom of expression, the patrons exercise their vanity and force artists to work on inappropriate projects. Running throughout the novel is the notion that the artist exists only to be exploited both artistically and financially. Lodovico may not approve of his son's vocation, but he extorts money from him. Michelangelo is, in truth, his father's "quarry." Finally, he recognizes that both his Holy Fathers and his earthly one have exploited him.

It is only the committed artist who can survive, even thrive, in the midst of such materialism. Michelangelo's commitment allows no distractions and necessitates mastery of every phase of art: painting, poetry, sculpture—he masters them all. Like the amateur film director who wishes to control all phases of the filmmaking process, the sculptor wants to control the marble from the time it is cut from the quarry until the carved statue is safely installed. Therefore, readers learn that Michelangelo can cut stone, that he can build roads to the quarry, that he can protect his work from the ravages of war. According to Bertoldo, the stone "works with" a sculptor like Michelangelo.

*Critical Context*

*The Agony and the Ecstasy*, perhaps Stone's most acclaimed novel, is a worthy successor to *Lust for Life* (1934), his first venture into the artistic world, and the two novels contain many of the same themes. Stone's other novels concern, for the most part, political figures as diverse as Eugene V. Debs and Mary Todd Lincoln; he returned to the world of art in *Depths of Glory* (1985), a novel about the Impressionist painter Camille Pissarro. In his genre, the biographical novel, Stone has no American equal in quality or quantity, though Andre Maurois is a worthy foreign rival.

The lack of competition is understandable, given the demands of the genre and the lack of critical appreciation for it, despite its popular acceptance. First, the research is formidable, for the biographical novelist must know not only his subject but also his times, including history, religion, politics, science, and the arts. Second, because they believe that less imagination and creativity are required in "history," critics value fiction over fact. As Stone points out, however, a biographical novel is not simply history or biography; a biographical novelist must select and shape his material to give it dramatic structure and theme. In *The Agony and the Ecstasy*, Stone eliminates historical characters, alters them, adds fictional ones, and has them reappear so as to give unity, focus, and theme to his novel. Given the massive amount of material that was at his disposal, Stone's novel is a significant achievement.

*Sources for Further Study*

Clements, Robert J. "The Artist as Hero," in *Saturday Review*. XLIV (March 18, 1961), p. 18.

Stone, Irving. "The Biographical Novel," in *The Writer*. LXXV (January, 1962), pp. 9-13.

*Tom Erskine*

# THE ALBANY CYCLE

*Author:* William Kennedy (1928-      )
*Type of plot:* Regional chronicle
*Time of plot:* The 1920's and the 1930's
*Locale:* Albany, New York
*First published:* 1985: *Legs*, 1975; *Billy Phelan's Greatest Game*, 1978;
   *Ironweed*, 1983

> *Principal characters:*
> JACK (LEGS) DIAMOND, a gangster
> MARCUS GORMAN, Diamond's attorney
> KIKI ROBERTS, Diamond's mistress
> BILLY PHELAN, a bookmaker and pool hustler
> MARTIN DAUGHERTY, a newspaper columnist
> FRANCIS PHELAN, Billy's father, a hobo and former profes-
>    sional baseball player
> HELEN ARCHER, Francis' companion, a hobo

*The Novel*

Although each is a highly individual work, the three novels that comprise William Kennedy's Albany Cycle are interrelated and can be read as one continuous story. The books are linked by characters, by plot events, and, above all, by locale: They are all set in Albany, New York, and that city's history, geography, and ambience inform their every aspect. Like William Faulkner's Yoknapatawpha County, William Kennedy's Albany is a semimythological realm inhabited by characters whose speech, actions, lives, and deaths are inextricably linked to the region in which they live. Kennedy's Albany is the Irish Catholic underworld of the Depression and Prohibition eras, a netherworld of organized crime and machine politics, peopled by saints and sinners of heroic dimensions.

*Legs*, the first of the cycle, is loosely based on the real-life Prohibition-era gangster, Jack (Legs) Diamond, who was killed in Albany in 1931. Narrated by Marcus Gorman, Diamond's Irish-Catholic lawyer, *Legs* is episodic in structure, concerned more with evoking an era and creating a character than with telling a carefully plotted story. The book opens decades after Diamond's death: Gorman, who intends to write a book about Diamond, has convened three of the outlaw's former associates to tell what they remember about him. As the four elderly reprobates reminisce, the scene changes to Albany in 1930, when Gorman became Diamond's attorney and a minor operative in his syndicate. The remainder of the novel consists of Gorman's account of Diamond, arranged into chapters that form a rough chronology of the last year and a half of Diamond's life.

Gorman views Diamond through almost worshipful eyes. Bored with his career as a criminal lawyer, Gorman eagerly seizes the opportunity to go to work for Diamond, and his life is changed overnight from that of a promising but unfulfilled public servant to that of a legal adviser to a much publicized mobster. Though careful to distance himself from Diamond's more sinister dealings, he becomes Diamond's staff lawyer and close personal friend. For Gorman, Diamond is a mythic figure (the gangster's favorite book is François Rabelais' *Gargantua and Pantagruel*), a man far removed from the ethical and moral codes that govern lesser mortals. He lives by his own ethic, wiping out enemies and rewarding friends with a zest and a style that leave Gorman dazzled. Gorman lives vicariously through Legs Diamond, unable to resist the glamour that surrounds this underworld superstar.

Gorman's is not the only interpretation of Diamond, however; other characters (an elderly black caretaker, for example, and a former prostitute and dance-hall singer) are allowed to tell their own stories, and those often unsympathetic narratives serve to temper Gorman's sometimes irritatingly steadfast devotion to his boss. Newspaper clippings, real and fictitious, are also presented as evidence, and what emerges is a remarkably complex work of portraiture. The reader must draw his own conclusions about the dutiful Catholic husband who keeps a show-girl mistress; the bootlegger who cold-bloodedly tortures an elderly farmer, but whose eyes fill with tears at the mention of his dead brother; the darling of the press and public who is hated and reviled by lesser mobsters. *Legs* brilliantly evokes not only a personality but also a dangerous and exciting era as Gorman follows Diamond from New York to Albany, through the Catskills and the capital cities of Europe in the heady days before the repeal of Prohibition.

Though the plot is built largely around the two kidnaping trials in which Gorman is directly involved, Diamond's truly gargantuan sins and virtues are frequently recounted by characters less intelligent than Gorman but more at home than he is in Diamond's world of larger-than-life criminal behavior. Marcus Gorman's hero worship of Legs Diamond has possibly cost him a congressional seat, but years after that gangster's unglamorous death, Gorman is still obsessed with his former boss, peering from the outside in at a life lived perilously close to the brink.

*Billy Phelan's Greatest Game* tells the story of an underworld kidnaping from the vastly different perspectives of the novel's two main characters: Martin Daugherty, a middle-aged newspaper columnist, and Billy Phelan, a small-time pool hustler and gambler. Both men are natives of Colonie Street, the Irish-Catholic neighborhood that is still home to the McCall brothers, kingpins of the Albany political machine, and both are tangentially involved in freeing Charlie Boy McCall, the scion of the McCall dynasty, who is kidnaped shortly after the novel opens.

Billy Phelan's small-time bookmaking operation is indirectly dependent on the largess of the McCalls, as is almost everything else in Albany. This all-powerful family controls not only Albany's political machinery, but also the gambling and drinking establishments that make up Billy's world. Though he lives with his sister, Peg, and her husband, George Quinn, Billy's real home is Broadway, site of the theaters, restaurants, pool halls, and saloons that he haunts night and day. Billy is proud of his ability always to earn a living at pool, at poker, or at bowling. He always pays his debts, but soon after the novel opens, his personal code is seriously threatened: On a hunch, Martin Daugherty has placed an unlikely bet with Billy and has won. Billy must now cover it, but doing so will ruin him financially. One of the novel's story lines follows Billy's search for the winning game that will end his financial difficulties and enable him to pay off his seven-hundred-dollar debt.

Ironically, Martin Daugherty is one of the few characters in the novel for whom money and its uses are not a preoccupation. Distant, mystic, and ever philosophical, Martin is an unlikely product of Colonie Street, a man who frequents the Albany underworld but is never entirely of it. Haunted by the fame and notoriety of his now senile father, who was an internationally famous playwright early in the century, Martin is a lapsed Catholic who has recently lost his only son to the priesthood. When Charlie Boy McCall is kidnaped, the McCall family, whom Martin has known since childhood, call upon Martin to keep the story from leaking to the press; he later serves as a liaison between the McCalls and the kidnapers. Meanwhile, the actress Melissa Spencer, a former lover of both Martin and his father, is in Albany appearing in the play that the senior Daugherty wrote about their affair in 1913, twenty-five years before the action of the novel takes place.

As the novel progresses, both the visionary Martin Daugherty and the practical Billy Phelan become ever more involved in the McCall kidnaping. Billy, flat broke and desperate to win enough money to pay his debt to Martin, finds his very existence threatened when he refuses to act as an informant for the McCalls and they, in turn, bar him from nearly every drinking and gaming establishment in town. This banishment, combined with the unexpected reappearance of his long-lost father, Francis, forces Billy to reassess his life as he has never before done. Martin, too, is compelled to reconsider his professional and familial commitments as Melissa's visit and Charlie Boy McCall's incarceration come to acquire a common meaning for him. In the end, Billy's good name is restored, largely because of favorable sentiment aroused by Martin's column. Charlie Boy is free, and Billy and Martin, though changed, return to the kind of lives they led before the kidnaping.

Francis Phelan, Billy's father, is the principal character in *Ironweed*, which takes place only a few weeks after the McCall kidnaping in October, 1938. Back in Albany after a three-year absence, Francis has recently become a local celebrity and figure of fun by illegally registering to vote twenty-one times (he was paid to do so by the McCalls, who still owe him fifty-five dollars). Once one of Albany's most famous sons, Francis is now destitute and homeless, reduced to wandering through the streets with his common-law wife, Helen Archer.

Francis has been on the run for most of his adult life. After killing a scab laborer during a trolley strike in 1901, Francis fled to Dayton, where he became a famous professional baseball player before returning to Albany, marrying, and fathering three children. In 1916, guilt-ridden after the accidental death of his infant son, he abandoned his wife and children. Now, in 1938, Francis finds himself surrounded by reminders of his past. The novel opens, appropriately, on Halloween, and much of it is given over to Francis' real or imaginary encounters with the spirits of the dead, among them the two men whom Francis has killed, one whose life he has tried to save, and Katrina Daugherty, Martin Daugherty's mother and Francis' first lover.

The splendid first chapter, set in the cemetery where the Phelans are buried, is typical of the novel's technique of juxtaposing fantasy with harsh realism. Though decidedly unsentimental, Francis encounters his past at every turn, and the ghosts with whom he communicates are as real to him as are his wife and his living children. Helen, too, is visionary, prone to reliving her short-lived term at Vassar and fantasizing about her abortive career as a classical musician. Yet their life together is anything but a dream, and their hobo milieu is described with an antiromantic honesty. Francis and Helen move through a world of vacant lots, abandoned cars, and charity missions; their friends are tramps like themselves who spend what money they have on cheap muscatel and seedy lodgings. *Ironweed* is set in an Albany that makes the Broadway of *Billy Phelan's Greatest Game* seem unimaginably glamorous by comparison.

*Ironweed* is a fitting summation to the Albany Cycle, covering as it does much of the ground covered by the two earlier novels. Characters and plot events from the first two books make a final appearance: The Daughertys are here, but Francis' abiding interest is in Katrina, who receives little mention in *Billy Phelan's Greatest Game*. Billy himself is very much an offstage figure in *Ironweed*, an embodiment of the guilt from which Francis seems unable to escape. The McCall family, consequential forces in both earlier novels, affect Francis only to the extent that they owe him money. The members of the Phelan family are reunited in *Ironweed*, but the brevity of the reunion tells the reader much about Billy Phelan, about Colonie Street, and about William Kennedy's fictional Albany in the years between the two world wars.

## The Characters

From the rich and world-renowned mobster to the down-at-the-heels tramp, each major character in these Albany novels is supplied with a personality and a personal history of striking depth. Even such relatively minor characters as Katrina Daugherty and Jake Berman, the radical Jewish political activist in *Billy Phelan's Greatest Game*, are given complete and carefully developed backgrounds, while such major figures as Francis Phelan and Legs Diamond are analyzed, described, and observed from many different perspectives and appear in more than one novel. Further, each character's chronology is observed with great accuracy: Though his story is not told chronologically, Francis Phelan's life, for example, can be charted very precisely through the repeated mention of dates and events in both *Billy Phelan's Greatest Game* and *Ironweed*. This almost obsessive attention to detail is more than simply an attempt at verisimilitude: In that such thoroughness weaves the three novels together into one multiplotted narrative, it raises the Albany Cycle to the level of epic and its characters to the stature of heroes.

Augmenting this epic sense is the manner in which individual characters come, through repetition, to take on symbolic and archetypal associations: Kiki Roberts, for example, is the quintessential gold-digging chorus girl, while Alice Diamond is the long-suffering Roman Catholic wife. The characterization of these two women is representative also of Kennedy's method of undermining stereotypes when he chooses: The respectable Alice is gunned down by Legs's enemies, while Kiki disappears into a fog of rumor, hearsay, and uncertainty. Highly individualized behavior (Helen Archer's constant biting of the hand that feeds her) combines with archetype (Billy Phelan's literal and metaphoric search for the perfect "game") to make for quirky and unforgettable characters.

Kennedy's approach to characterization is especially impressive in the light of his easy blending of the real, the partially real, and the totally fictitious. The story of Legs Diamond, a real-life gangster murdered in Albany in 1931, is made to conform to the known facts of Diamond's life, yet in Kennedy's hands, he becomes not only a name in the headlines, but also an embodiment of the Prohibition era and, through his interaction with Marcus Gorman, a character of depth and intricacy. The McCall family is based on the real-life O'Connells of Albany, whose heir, John, Jr., was kidnaped in 1933; in this case, Kennedy changes the name and moves the date forward five years. Fictitious characters such as the Phelans and the Daughertys rub elbows with historical personages: The legendary journalist Damon Runyon publishes Martin Daugherty's defense of Billy Phelan, and Edward Daugherty recalls an encounter with the novelist Henry James. Perhaps only E. L. Doctorow among modern American novelists shares with Kennedy this bold and refreshing capacity for blending fiction, history, and journalism to create a realm where such distinctions seem of little importance.

Any discussion of Kennedy's method of character development must mention his inspired use of dialogue. Through conversations that often go uninterrupted by the narrator for pages, the uninitiated reader learns hobo lingo from Francis Phelan, mob lingo from Legs Diamond, and gambling jargon from Billy Phelan and Martin Daugherty. Kennedy's sure grasp of his characters' speech patterns lends the Albany novels humor, sharpness, and a documentary-like realism.

## Themes and Meanings

In an age of transience, William Kennedy seems intent on restoring the notion of eternity; and in a nation given to ignoring its history, Kennedy's fiction serves as a reminder of the inescapability of the past. All three of the Albany novels insist that some things never die. The guilt that tortures Francis Phelan is embodied in the restless spirits of the dead—Francis is literally haunted by the mistakes of his past. Melissa Spencer reenters Martin Daugherty's life, and her visit activates a long overdue Oedipal trauma in Martin, causing him imaginatively to relive the moment of his own conception. Francis Phelan, while working for a junk dealer in Arbor Hill, has a vision of his dead parents as newlyweds. Such bizarre visitations are not uncommon in the Albany Cycle, in which the past is coexistent with the present. Legs Diamond's final words to Marcus Gorman—recounted in a brief epilogue whose sole purpose seems to be to establish Diamond's immortality—deny the possibility of his own death.

Each of Kennedy's characters is the sum total of that character's past, and these Albany novels call for an understanding of the experiences that make people behave as they do. Helen Archer correctly observes that the employed and the sober deprive hobos of their individuality; Kennedy forces the reader to see that every Francis Phelan has a story, very possibly a tragic one. Every mobster has a motivation, whether it is acceptable to the mainstream of law-abiding society. Like the city of Albany itself, in whose history and folklore these novels are steeped, each of Kennedy's characters is the product of a complicated past that goes far toward explaining his present.

While the most interesting of Kennedy's characters are lapsed rather than orthodox Roman Catholics, nearly all of them have been reared in the Church and know its language and its rites. Liturgical metaphors abound in these novels, and frequently they occur in a humanistic rather than a conventionally Christian context. Each character must experience a purgatory of sorts before finding salvation; each is caught up in a personal quest for grace. William Kennedy can hardly be called a religious novelist, but one finds in even the most downtrodden of his characters the outline of a human soul.

*Critical Context*

William Kennedy grew up in the North End of Albany, the only child of working-class Irish-Catholic parents. His father was a lower-level dependent of the O'Connell political machine, and Kennedy was exposed early to the smoke-filled rooms and the gambling establishments described so masterfully in *Billy Phelan's Greatest Game*. A newspaper reporter and editor for most of his life (he twice worked for the *Albany Times-Union*, the paper for which Martin Daugherty writes), Kennedy never received wide attention as a novelist until *Ironweed* received both the Pulitzer Prize and the National Book Critics Circle Award in 1984. Neither his first novel, *The Ink Truck* (1969)—an account of a newspaper strike—nor the first two novels in the Albany Cycle had brought him fame, though each had been favorably reviewed. Among the first of Kennedy's admirers was the novelist Saul Bellow, from whom Kennedy took a creative writing course in the early 1960's. With Bellow, Kennedy shares an unmistakably affirmative bias in an age of literary pessimism; like Bellow's, Kennedy's strong characters are frequently able to survive adversity through sheer force of will. The Phelans stumble, but they never fall so far that they cannot somehow steady themselves. Though Catholicism colors every element of his work, Kennedy is at base a humanist whose characters locate solutions within themselves.

Kennedy's mythological ambitions and his complex layering of past and present have brought inevitable comparisons with James Joyce and William Faulkner, and with the latter he shares the capacity for elevating local history to the level of American myth. In an age still dominated by the short sentences and uncluttered syntax of Ernest Hemingway, William Kennedy is a Baroque presence, his language as gaudy and figurative as the lost world about which he writes.

*Sources for Further Study*

Hunt, G. W. "William Kennedy's Albany Trilogy," in *America*. CL (May 19, 1984), pp. 373-375.
"Kennedy, William," in *Current Biography*. XLVI (May, 1985), pp. 25-28.
Mitgang, H. "Inexhaustible Albany," in *The New York Times Book Review*. LXXXVIII (November 13, 1983), p. 35.

*J. D. Daubs*

# ALL GREEN SHALL PERISH

*Author:* Eduardo Mallea (1903-1983)
*Type of plot:* Existential psychodrama
*Time of plot:* The 1930's and early 1940's, prior to the rise to power of Juan
   Perón
*Locale:* Ingeniero White, Bahía Blanca, and Nicanor Cruz's *estancia* (ranch)
   on the southern pampa near Bahía Blanca, Argentina
*First published: Todo verdor perecerá*, 1941 (English translation, 1966)

> *Principal characters:*
> ÁGATA CRUZ, the protagonist, an intense and withdrawn
>    young woman who is in search of herself
> NICANOR CRUZ, her husband, an *estanciero* (rancher)
> DOCTOR REBA, Ágata's father, a Swiss immigrant who settled
>    in Ingeniero White
> SOTERO, a lawyer and Ágata's lover in Bahía Blanca after
>    Nicanor's death
> EMA DE VOLPE, a self-styled courtesan and Ágata's compan-
>    ion in Bahía Blanca

## The Novel

*All Green Shall Perish* is divided into two parts. Each depicts a crucial period in the life of Ágata Cruz, and virtually all the action of the novel takes place within Ágata's anguished consciousness. The theme and tone are established in the somber description of the desolate landscape of Nicanor Cruz's *estancia* at the beginning of part 1. The drought suffered by the barren land is mirrored in the barren relationship of Nicanor and Ágata Cruz, who remain childless after fifteen years of marriage and estranged from each other by their inability to communicate and by an ever growing sense of isolation and resentment. Nicanor has lost his battle with the sterile land, although he stubbornly refuses to admit the defeat which has transformed him into a withdrawn and bitter man. Ágata, more sensitive and intelligent than her husband, asks more from life than he does and would have liked to help him during the early years, but Nicanor's pride would not allow him to accept her help. Ágata is suffering from depression and resents being condemned to live out a life that she would never have chosen.

From this vantage point in time, Ágata reexperiences her past life in a series of flashbacks: first, the lonely childhood with her alienated father in the small port of Ingeniero White; then, her precipitous decision to marry Nicanor Cruz, a limited and taciturn man whom she did not love but who provided her with an escape from the stifling atmosphere of her childhood and the dreary prospect of life with her widower father, whom she loved but with whom she had never been able to communicate; finally, a series of grim and ever worsening incidents from her fifteen years with Nicanor. The cumulative effect of this introspection only deepens Ágata's depression.

In his unrelenting struggle with the land, Nicanor contracts pneumonia. While nursing him, Ágata reaches a crisis of desperation. Hoping to destroy herself and end her unhappiness, Ágata opens all the windows to let in the cold. Nicanor dies, but Ágata is found unconscious on the porch at the end of part 1.

The second part of the novel begins in the southern metropolis of Bahía Blanca, where Ágata has moved following the sale of the *estancia*. Through the intervention of Ema de Volpe, a predatory and superficial woman who insists on taking Ágata under her wing, Ágata meets the lawyer Sotero. Ágata passively allows Sotero to seduce her, and, to her own surprise, she enjoys a brief period of happiness with this charming but shallow opportunist. Sotero, however, is incapable of committing himself to anyone for long, and he coldly abandons Ágata, leaving her with a note as he departs for Buenos Aires on business. His desertion confirms Ágata's worst fears, as she is again thrown back upon herself. After her happiness with Sotero, Ágata finds solitude even more difficult to bear, and she gradually withdraws still further into her own consciousness, caring nothing for those around her or for her surroundings. In her desperate obsession to understand what is happening to her, she is drawn irresistibly back to the Ingeniero White of her childhood. Having lost all sense of time, wandering the streets of Ingeniero White like a madwoman, she is attacked by a gang of vicious children, who taunt and chase her. At the end of the novel, Ágata has lost all contact with reality except for the increasing intensity of her suffering. Her plight is poignantly captured in the last sentence of the novel: "It was very late when she got up suddenly, as if called by a scream, and, without direction or discernment, started running against the darkness."

*The Characters*

Mallea excels in portraying "closed" characters who are at war with themselves or somehow imprisoned within the confines of their own consciousness. The inner drama of Ágata Cruz is revealed and symbolized in her name (which translates literally as "agate cross"). What is cold and hard in Ágata is in conflict with her passion and her need for sacrifice. Ágata's passivity, her limited emotional development, her narrowness of perspective, and, above all, her awkwardness and shyness, are at war with the intensity of her need to live life to the utmost and to make life meaningful. The grim circumstances of her life and the predisposition of her own nature doom her to defeat, but Mallea succeeds in making the reader identify with Ágata's struggle and emphathize with her. In spite of the melodramatic contrast between Ágata's "extraordinary beauty" and her withdrawn and pessimistic character, Mallea succeeds in making Ágata a believable heroine.

Ágata is described in terms of death, recalling the parched landscape of the beginning: "While in bed, her slender body at rest, her face white against a bedspread a thousand years old, her eyes devoid of inner scenery, her limp fingers relaxed over the material they rested on, everything in her suggested a corpse, with the exception of that knot which from the depth of her being still insisted on having hidden rights." In a conversation with Sotero, Ágata inadvertently reveals her inner awareness of futility: "I thought the world was an enormous flight of birds and that I had only to stretch out my hand to stop the one I wanted. Then one sees that the bird is oneself, and that the world is the hand that claims one." Finally, according to Ágata, "each being is not like the water or the wind, subject to the influences and change. Each being is a single unmodified tendency. Each being *is* its tendency." Thus, Ágata, as do characters in other Mallea novels, condemns herself with the bias of her own perspective.

While the author's concentration on Ágata does not leave much room for the development of the other figures of the novel, these characters are clearly and believably drawn. The best realized is the taciturn but authentic Nicanor (the name means "without song") Cruz, whose stubbornness and brutish stoicism invest him with a perverse integrity. The brazen and manipulative mediocrity of Ema de Volpe is convincing, as is the blatant inauthenticity and duplicity of Sotero and the ratlike slyness of his sinister friend Romo. Doctor Reba, Ágata's pathetic father, is at best a shadowy figure, and Estaurófilo the imbecile was conceived as a symbol for the thwarted expression inherent in the human condition.

### Themes and Meanings

Theme, language, tone, and mood are the controlling elements of *All Green Shall Perish*. Mallea is essentially a lyric writer, a poet, who conceives the human, novelistic material of all his works in musical terms that he controls thematically, like an essayist. In structure, the novel's division into two parts allows for greater intensity and control in each. Indeed, the two halves can be read as interrelated novellas; the only link is the tortured self-awareness of Ágata, which informs the whole. She is the sole survivor of part 1. In part 2, Ágata is given what amounts to a chance for a new life in Bahía Blanca with a new cast of characters. Unfortunately, Ágata remains the same. She cannot forget her past, which colors her present and foreshadows her future.

In *All Green Shall Perish*, character cannot be separated from theme. This is ritual narration in which the central character is offered as a sacrifice to the universe. The near consummation of part 1 is fulfilled in part 2. The rite is complete.

In *La vida blanca* (1960; the sterile life), Mallea describes what he calls the "inner war": "A sweet immanent charity illumines the lives of men; all the rest is uncertainty, pettiness and betrayal." This sentence beautifully synthesizes the theme, tone, and message of *All Green Shall Perish*. In spite of the somber conclusion, never in doubt, what draws and holds the reader's attention is the defenseless lyric affirmation of the human condition that is sensed throughout Mallea's requiem for Ágata Cruz.

Another theme, secondary in *All Green Shall Perish* but central to Mallea, is the search for authenticity in a specifically Argentine context. In *Historia de una pasión argentina* (1937; history of an Argentine passion) and other essays which probe the Argentine national character, Mallea advocates a spiritually authentic Argentina as opposed to a shadowy and successful materialism. In this context, it is clear that Ágata and, to a lesser extent, Nicanor, represent aspects of the "invisible Argentina" as opposed to the inauthentic "visible Argentina" of Sotero, Romo, and Ema de Volpe.

Yet it is in universal terms that *All Green Shall Perish* is best understood. The capacity to struggle against one's fate and to suffer is equated with authenticity and emerges as the supreme human value of Mallea's fiction.

*Critical Context*

*All Green Shall Perish* has been Mallea's most popular single work of fiction, as well as the novel that received the greatest critical acclaim. It was written at the peak of Mallea's creative powers along with the autobiographical essay *Historia de una pasión argentina* and the novels *Fiesta en noviembre* (1938; *Fiesta in November*, 1942) and *La bahía de silencio* (1940; *The Bay of Silence*, 1944).

Mallea was an extremely prolific writer who continued to publish novels, short stories, essays, and plays up to his death. He enjoyed his greatest popularity during the 1930's, 1940's, and 1950's, anticipating the "Boom" of the Latin American novel in the 1960's and 1970's. Mallea did not share the preoccupation with technical innovation of such novelists as Julio Cortázar, Carlos Fuentes, and Mario Vargas Llosa, although several of his works are innovative and experimental, most notably *La ciudad junto al río inmóvil* (1936; the city on the motionless river), *Fiesta in November*, and *All Green Shall Perish*. The themes of Mallea's fiction did not change significantly in the course of his career, and, in general, his work has fallen from fashion since the 1950's. Nevertheless, the titles cited in this article continue to enjoy a wide readership and are the subject of many critical studies.

*Sources for Further Study*
Lewald, H. Ernest. *Eduardo Mallea*, 1977.
Lichtblau, Myron I. *El arte estilístico de Eduardo Mallea*, 1967.
Polt, John H. R. *The Writings of Eduardo Mallea*, 1959.

*John B. Hughes*

# AN AMERICAN DREAM

*Author:* Norman Mailer (1923-    )
*Type of plot:* Symbolic and melodramatic romance
*Time of plot:* 1962
*Locale:* New York City
*First published:* 1965

>*Principal characters:*
>    STEPHEN RICHARD ROJACK, the narrator and protagonist, a
>        war hero, former congressman, professor of existential
>        psychology, television personality, and murderer
>    DEBORAH, his wife, a wealthy socialite whom Rojack sees
>        both as a bitch and a witch and whom he kills in the first
>        chapter
>    BARNEY KELLY, Deborah's politically powerful millionaire
>        father
>    RUTA, the Rojacks' German maid
>    CHERRY, a nightclub singer with whom Rojack has an affair
>    ROBERTS, a detective who investigates Deborah's murder
>    SHAGO MARTIN, a black man with sexual prowess who has
>        been Cherry's lover and who becomes a television replace-
>        ment for Rojack

*The Novel*

The unrealistic nature of *An American Dream* is signaled in the novel's first sentence, in which Stephen Richard Rojack, who is both the narrator and the protagonist, says that he met John F. Kennedy in 1946 and that they double-dated one night during which Rojack seduced Deborah Caughlin Mangaravidi Kelly, who later became his wife. By way of comparing his heroism with Kennedy's, Rojack then tells of a war experience during which he single-handedly wiped out a German machine-gun nest and became a hero. Although this event, narrated in the tough-guy idiom of Mailer's literary hero, Ernest Hemingway, catapults Rojack into social success—resulting in his election to Congress, his marriage to the rich socialite Deborah, and his becoming an academic and television celebrity—Rojack believes that he failed in that encounter because he did not charge the final German soldier's bayonet, for "it was gone, the clean presence of *it*, the grace, *it* had deserted me." Rojack's efforts to regain this sense of grace—a Hemingway brand of cool and simple macho identity—is what dominates the rest of the novel.

At the beginning of the present action (a nightmarish three-day period following his wife's death), Rojack contemplates suicide, although he also accepts that he has murder within him, for murder, he thinks, offers power and release; "it is never unsexual." While at a party, he flirts with suicide by walking the balustrade of a high balcony, feeling that the moon is luring him to death. It is the murderous urge, however, that dominates when he confronts his estranged wife, Deborah, whom he sees as both the great American Bitch and as a mythic, demonic, witchlike figure. When he strangles her as a result of her taunting him with stories of her sexual escapades, the murder is described in erotic terms, and he seems to take on some of her magical power as her own life ends.

The murder/sex/power complex does not end there, but extends to Rojack's immediately following encounter with Ruta, the German maid, with whom he has both anal and vaginal sex while Deborah's body lies in the next room. Although the sexual encounter is described in graphic detail, it is transformed from a merely physical act to one with metaphysical importance in which the female vagina is described as a chapel and the anus is identified as the place of the Devil.

The remainder, and therefore the bulk, of the novel follows Rojack's journey through a mythic underground world of New York City in which he must engage in a number of threatening tasks to assure his salvation: deceive the police; fall in love with the nightclub singer Cherry; defeat her black lover, Shago Martin; and confront Deborah's powerful father, Barney Kelly. All these events are described in terms of gaining metaphysical power and thus are less realistic than they are hallucinatory—mythic adventures on the way to Rojack's becoming a true hero. Rojack's sexual encounter with Cherry takes on cosmic importance, as he is the first man to "give" her an orgasm; his defeat of Shago Martin is described as a reversal of roles, in which Shago becomes increasingly white in his value system and perception, while Rojack becomes the hipster with almost supernatural power.

Finally, Rojack's encounter with Barney Kelly is one in which Kelly is presented as a satanic figure, perhaps even the Devil himself. Kelly is a man who, like Rojack, has violated social taboos and thus has become powerful as a result. Whereas Rojack's energizing crime is murder, Kelly's has been incest with his daughter Deborah. In the meeting with Kelly, Rojack once again walks the balustrade of a high balcony, flirting with death; he defeats Kelly, who tries to push him off. Although his walk once around the balcony is sufficient to save himself, he fails to walk it a second time and thus, either from his own psychotic point of view or within the supernatural conventions of the novel, fails to save Cherry and Shago, who are beaten to death.

At the end of the novel, Rojack heads west, to Las Vegas (the ultimate corruption of the American dream), wins a large sum of money, and then decides to go to Guatemala and the Yucatán. Like that classic American hero Huck Finn, he leaves civilization to find himself in the primitive wilderness.

*The Characters*

There is only one "real" character in the book—Rojack himself, and he is less a fully rounded figure than a modern-day equivalent of the mythic hero who seeks some kind of primitive or existential freedom and, thus, self-identity. The problem of responding to Rojack's character is that one can either see him as heroic figure, bravely daring to break social taboos and combat the demonic forces of political power, coming out of it clean and pure—in other words, as the possessor of grace and power—or as a psychopath with grandiose delusions about both himself and the nature of reality. Either the book is a mythic journey into the dark night of the evil of which man is capable, or it is the dramatization of a journey into the dark night of the unconscious self. Perhaps it is both.

In Mailer's psycho-aesthetic realm of reality, the quest is always for some primitive state of elemental or medieval magic perception. Rojack is indeed a psychopath, but as the primitive state and the psychotic state are the same, the way of the psychopath is the way to salvation. Thus, in *The American Dream*, social and personal complexities are eradicated by a system of simple and elemental macho values of power, grace under pressure, and thus, finally, sex and violence. Mailer couches all of this within the seemingly conflicting idioms of, on the one hand, the pop-art world of detective fiction and spy thrillers and, on the other, the popularizing of Martin Heidegger's existential philosophy of dread. Rojack parrots many of the values that Mailer has expressed elsewhere about the need to face death in order to achieve authenticity, about the power of the orgasm, about cancer as the result of the denial of self, and about the power of a return to the world of magic. As Rojack believes, "magic, dread, and the perception of death" are the roots of motivation. Rojack is indeed a psychopath, but he is presented as a philosophic psychopath in the tradition of the murderous figures of Fyodor Dostoevski's Raskolnikov and Joseph Conrad's Kurtz.

The other characters in the novel embody the challenges that Rojack must face. Deborah is not only the bitch of Hemingway's fiction; she is also the magical witch of folklore and myth. Barney Kelly is not only the robber baron who pulls the strings of politics and power but also the satanic tempter of legend. Shago Martin is the "white Negro," the stereotypical black "stud," who sells out by exchanging values with the socially successful Rojack. Cherry is the untouched beautiful female whom the hero must make his own. They have little else to do in the novel except to perform their respective functions. In typical allegorical fashion, this modern romance presents characters only as reflectors of and foils for the dominant figure who hacks his way through the nightmare jungle to find himself.

*Themes and Meanings*

Unless one reads this novel as a hallucinatory allegory of the American

Dream, as a philosophical parable of one man's quest for meaning and value in a corrupt social world, it is likely to strike one as completely absurd; not only do the events seem unrealistic and ridiculous, but Rojack's own perceptions, beliefs, and language often seem childish and sophomoric. This is not to say that Rojack's (and Mailer's) belief in the power of the primitive is childish, or that his understanding of the link between the mythic and the psychotic is in error. Rather, this particular novel never seems to manage to fuse these legitimate views profoundly. Moreover, Heidegger's sense of existential dread and the need to face death to achieve authenticity seem vulgar and pretentious oversimplifications coming from the mouth of the melodramatic Rojack.

Mailer has attempted to write an allegorical satire of the American Dream, as it seemingly must be played out in a fallen and corrupt world, and indeed the novel has a disquieting surreal effect, but his use of the conventions of detective fiction, the gothic novel, and the spy thriller do not transcend their sources. Thus, this novel often reads like the writing of an amateur philosopher taking himself too seriously. In its self-important reduction of everything to macho values, it equates the instinctual with the merely self-serving and brutal. Mailer laments the loss of the medieval miracle and criticizes modern society for its empiricism and antisupernatural mode of perception; he emphasizes the need for a return to the mystical side of experience; he wishes to present Rojack as a man who yearns for a dissolution of the ego, a transformation of the self, a return to primitive wholeness. Yet either *An American Dream* is not the vehicle for such a vision, or else Mailer is simply not a sufficiently profound thinker to achieve such a synthesis.

*Critical Context*

When *An American Dream* was first published, it was harshly criticized by many critics who, expecting the realism of Mailer's earlier novels, lambasted it for the absurdity of its plot and the pop-art pretentiousness of its style. More recently, however, its genre has been determined to be, as one critic puts it, "romance, allegory, satire, dream vision." The problem of the novel is that it attempts to combine both the conventions of fantasy and the conventions of realism; it hovers uneasily in a realm between fantasy and fact, in which objective and subjective reality cannot be distinguished. Consequently, there are those who misread it at first as pure realism and thus dismiss it as a "dirty" book in which Rojack is only a vulgar alter ego of Mailer himself.

Critics have pointed out the autobiographical similarities between Rojack and Mailer, both in philosophical point of view and in certain events (for example, Mailer stabbed his wife but did not kill her), and thus the book has contributed strongly to the polarization of the literary community about the works of Mailer. On the one hand, there are those who see him as a posturing pop-art phenomenon, combating his own insecurity with efforts to become a cultural presence and force, manufacturing books which bolster his own ego and present his own adolescent fantasies and philosophies. On the other hand, there are those who see Mailer as one of the most profound novelists of the twentieth century, a man who, like Hemingway, has an un- canny ability to cut through hypocrisy and social conventions to present a genuine vision of the plight of modern man. *An American Dream* is at the very center of this debate, embodying all the virtues and the vices of Mail- er's art and thought.

*Sources for Further Study*

Begiebing, Robert J. *Acts of Regeneration: Allegory and Archetype in the Works of Norman Mailer*, 1980.

Erlich, Robert. *Norman Mailer: The Radical as Hipster*, 1978.

Gordon, Andrew. *An American Dreamer: A Psychoanalytic Study of the Fiction of Norman Mailer*, 1980.

Gutman, Stanley T. *Mankind in Barbary: The Individual and Society in the Novels of Norman Mailer*, 1975.

Poirier, Richard. *Norman Mailer*, 1972.

*Charles E. May*

# THE ANDROMEDA STRAIN

*Author:* Michael Crichton (1942-    )
*Type of plot:* Scientific adventure
*Time of plot:* 1967
*Locale:* Flatrock, Nevada
*First published:* 1969

#### Principal characters:

DR. JEREMY STONE, a bacteriologist and leader of the Wildfire
   Project
DR. PETER LEAVITT, a clinical microbiologist
DR. CHARLES BURTON, a pathologist
DR. MARK HALL, a surgeon
MAJOR ARTHUR MANCHEK, a senior officer of the Scoop
   mission

## The Novel

Michael Crichton's enormously popular novel *The Andromeda Strain* generated much of its appeal first by dramatizing the anxieties of its audience—playing on the "man was never meant to know" fears about space and science—and second by laying those fears to rest by demonstrating that the American doctor is equal to any emergency. The novel was one of the first to use "secret government research projects" as a villain, a device that has been used many times since. The premise of *The Andromeda Strain* is that a space satellite, the Scoop, has been sent into space by the United States to search for and to bring back to Earth samples of viruses and bacteria for study. Although scientists call for the study to protect both astronauts and the Earth from contagion by an alien bacteria, the government has quite another purpose: to bring back bacteria that might be used in germ warfare.

Under the pretense that its purpose is to discover new ways to prevent disease, the project is begun. After several failures, Scoop VII is sent into orbit in February, 1967. In the space flight, the Scoop is hit by something, a meteor perhaps, and begins to wobble. When the Scoop is brought to Earth, it lands in a small, isolated Arizona town. As the novel opens, the two men sent to recover the vehicle find all but two of the townspeople dead, and within a few seconds the soldiers themselves lie dead in their van.

The survivors, Peter Jackson, a sixty-nine-year-old drinker, and a two-month-old baby, are brought to Wildfire, a five-level underground laboratory hidden in the deserts of Nevada. A crew of scientists is hastily assembled to discover what factor has protected two so dissimilar people from the mysterious disease carried by the Scoop.

The novel is arranged in the form of a scientific report on the efforts that follow and contains numerous charts, graphs, and computer printouts. The narrator, speaking as an omniscient observer, comments on the work of the scientists during the four days of feverish activity following the disaster. The plot of the novel is arranged in strict chronological form, with background information on the characters interspersed from time to time. The book even adds a fictional bibliography including articles purportedly written by the characters.

## The Characters

The brilliant but contentious Dr. Jeremy Stone, the thirty-six-year-old leader of the research project to find the source of the mysterious disease and its cure, has recently won the Nobel Prize for his work on bacteria. Stone was one of the scientists responsible for the Scoop project; he is ironically chosen to solve the problems that his brainchild originated. Stone is a tireless worker and is devoted to his team members and to the project.

Dr. Peter Leavitt is a man with a secret. Even though the scientists have to pass rigorous physical examinations before beginning work, Leavitt successfully hides his epilepsy. Finally, exhaustion and the blinking lights of the computer console bring on a seizure. Leavitt is left with the guilty knowledge that his duplicity might have caused the research project to fail. This seizure, incidentally, prevents Leavitt from noticing the one way in which the bacteria are vulnerable. The incident is only one of several unfortunate coincidences on which the plot entirely depends. Had Leavitt not gone into seizure, he would have discovered the weak spot of the bacteria and the menace would have been ended.

Just as Leavitt is wrong in trying to hide his condition, Dr. Charles Burton is careless in his scientific method. As the narrator observes, if Burton had only thought to perform an autopsy on the brains of certain research animals being exposed to the bacteria, perhaps the answer to the puzzle would have come more rapidly.

The most clearly drawn and likable character is young Dr. Mark Hall, a surgeon chosen for the project not only for his credentials but also for the fact that he is the "odd man out"—the only one of the four who is unmarried. Crichton presents a fictional psychological study supporting the very dubious premise that single men are more likely to blow themselves up when ordered to do so. Thus, only Hall is given the ability to stop the explosion of an atomic device which will detonate automatically if the security of the laboratory is breached. Perhaps the fact that Hall is the most likable and most intelligent of the group is explained by noting that Crichton is a doctor himself. Whatever the cause of Hall's talents, the success of the project depends on him. Indeed, it is Hall's research and his insight into the problem that provide the answer to the puzzle. At the climax of the story, Hall makes his heroic climb through the core of the underground laboratory to save his colleagues and the building from atomic destruction.

Of all the "characters," the reader's attention keeps returning to the microscopic bit of life that is brought back on the Scoop. It is a character without a name and with a structure unlike that of any known Earth entity. This bacterium is made of hydrogen, oxygen, carbon, and nitrogen, but lacks amino acids. It therefore contains no proteins, the building blocks of all earthly life. By all the scientists' reckonings, it cannot be alive, yet it divides, respires, and changes in form—all marks of life.

The science in the novel and the pace of the adventure must maintain the reader's interest because the characters show little individuality. For example, Stone's personality has supposedly caused four of his marriages to fail, yet in the laboratory he is even-tempered, gentle, and considerate. Despite Crichton's effort to tailor carefully each character's background, they behave much alike.

*Themes and Meanings*

The most obvious theme of the novel is the necessity for the human mind to use technology to solve mankind's problems. Neither the scientists with their human mistakes nor the machines with their mechanical problems are able alone to find the source of the disease; neither alone can cure it. Moreover, both parties are fallible: Human error—a misspelling—causes one prospective member of the team to be notified too late to participate; machines are not entirely dependable either—a stray piece of paper clogs a teletypewriter, preventing an important message from being received. When man and machine join together, however, the scientists are free to use their intuition while the machines shorten the hours which it takes to do the innumerable computations needed to solve the puzzle of the bacteria from space.

The novel offers a fascinating glimpse into the world of scientific research and manages to teach much about microbiology in the course of telling a fast-paced adventure. Crichton himself worked at the Salk Institute after receiving his M.D. degree from Harvard University, and his technical competence informs the novel. The reader learns about genetics, studies the treatment of infectious diseases, reads of the history of bacteriology, and discovers some of what is known about the ability of bacteria to survive and multiply in a hostile environment. In addition, the reader comes to see the world as a place filled with bacteria, ninety-seven percent of which are helpful and necessary to man. The most pointed example of the book is the human body, which is covered and filled with bacteria: Its complete "cleansing" is neither possible nor desirable, for to sterilize it would be to kill it.

One theme notable by its absence is any moral judgment on the action of the government in lying to the scientists about the purpose of the research on which they are engaged. The plot is not so much resolved as stopped:

The bacteria magically become harmless, all the survivors recover, and the scientists return to their lives, apparently unchanged or unenlightened by the events.

## Critical Context

Crichton is noted for rapid pacing and a considerable amount of scientific fact in his works. Using the pseudonym Jeffrey Hudson, Crichton wrote *A Case of Need* (1968), which won the Edgar Award from the Mystery Writers of America for the year's best mystery novel. Using the pseudonym John Lange, he wrote several novels, including *Drug of Choice* (1970) and *Binary* (1972), which was made into a film for television. Crichton also wrote *The Terminal Man* (1972) and *Eaters of the Dead* (1976), a retelling of the *Beowulf* story. He ventured into another creative field in 1973, writing the script for and directing the film *Westworld*. He also directed Robin Cook's *Coma* in 1978.

## Source for Further Study

Bova, Ben. "The Role of Science Fiction," in *Science Fiction, Today and Tomorrow*, 1974. Edited by Reginald Bretnor.

*Julia Meyers*

# ANGLE OF REPOSE

*Author:* Wallace Stegner (1909-    )
*Type of plot:* Realistic narrative
*Time of plot:* 1860-1970
*Locale:* California, the Dakotas, Colorado, Idaho, and Mexico
*First published:* 1971

> *Principal characters:*
> LYMAN WARD, the protagonist and narrator, a retired history
>     professor with a debilitating disease
> SUSAN BURLING WARD, his grandmother
> OLIVER WARD, his grandfather
> ADA HAWKES, Lyman's housekeeper
> SHELLY RASMUSSEN, Lyman's typist

*The Novel*

Angle of Repose, a sprawling novel in both time and place, is narrated by
Lyman Ward, the protagonist, whose life has turned so bitter that he has no
recourse but to plunge himself into the past. He is a fifty-eight-year-old
retired history professor stricken with a degenerative disease and confined
to a wheelchair. One leg has been amputated and his wife has run off with
the surgeon. (This comic-tragic event is reminiscent of some scenes from
John Irving's *The World According to Garp*, 1978.)

Lyman's son wants him to go to a nursing home, but Lyman will not submit to this final degradation and defeat. He is determined to prove that he
can care for himself, and he does so in spite of his handicaps and his pain.
He has necessary adjustments made to his living quarters, and with the aid
of a loyal family housekeeper, Ada Hawkes, he manages to create for himself a comfortable life. Above all, however, he has a mission—to piece
together the life of his grandmother, Susan Burling Ward, a Victorian lady
who lived through the days of the Old West and who has left behind a
wealth of material almost as a legacy. It is his intention to tell her story in
the form of a novel. Against this backdrop the drama unfolds, seesawing
back and forth between Lyman Ward's present and his grandmother's past.

Susan Burling was a talented, cultured young lady reared in the East—
the quintessence of breeding and gentility. These traits were sorely tested
upon her marriage to Oliver Ward, a mining engineer whose heart and work
led them to many unexplored territories in the Old West. She was forced to
live and move from one crude mining camp to another, constantly uprooting
herself and her children. Oliver Ward, chasing the American Dream, failed
repeatedly as a result of his honesty and his refusal to compromise his values. Even when he was confronted with betrayal, he said, "What kind of life

is it when you can't trust?"

A strand of continuity develops, linking the past with the present. It seems that the very things that sustained Lyman Ward's grandmother, Susan Ward, are now his sustenance as well. Lyman pores over the letters to her intimate friend Augusta (which were returned to his grandmother after Augusta's death), filling in with his imagination the unsaid parts of her story: her strivings, hopes, and despair. Augusta, the dear friend she left behind, was living the kind of life, cultivated and wealthy, that Susan had always dreamed about living herself. Lyman realizes the debt she owes to her influential Eastern friends for the encouragement of her talents as a writer and illustrator and also in helping her publish and sell her work. Her earnings were often the only money coming in to support her family. In addition to old magazines with his grandmother's work in it, there are old newspapers hinting of scandal.

Organizing the material is a monumental task that Lyman nevertheless relishes—indeed, it becomes the focus of his life. Lyman could very well echo the sentiments his grandmother expressed in a letter, that she felt "limited in a limited world."

To fill in the gaps in his grandmother's story, Lyman obtains from the Idaho Historical Society newspapers covering the period during which his grandparents lived there. Two significant dates—July 7 and July 11, 1890— mark the collapse of Susan Burling Ward's world.

On July 7, Agnes Ward, daughter of the chief engineer, drowned after becoming separated from her mother while taking a walk. On July 11, Frank Sargent committed suicide. The two events seem unrelated until it is revealed that Frank was the best and most loyal friend of Susan and Oliver Ward, and that Susan wrote glowingly of Frank. The fine print of the July 7 story reports that Frank Sargent was the first one on the scene trying to save little Agnes Ward. The events that followed speak for themselves. Oliver Ward was never able to forgive Susan for her affair with Sargent and its terrible consequence, and he left her. They reunited later only to spend the remainder of their long lives together in a cold truce.

Lyman Ward's sympathies are, oddly enough, with his grandmother (living in her skin, so to speak, has had that effect). At the end of the novel, he wonders whether he can forgive his wife for her infidelity, whether "I am man enough to be a bigger man than my grandfather."

## The Characters

Lyman Ward, the protagonist and the first-person narrator of *Angle of Repose*, is one of the most fully developed characters in American fiction. Lyman is a fifty-eight-year-old history professor, forced into retirement by a deteriorating, crippling disease. He has had one leg amputated and is confined to a wheelchair. His wife, Ellen, has abandoned him for the surgeon who amputated his leg.

It would appear that Stegner has given his main character more physical, emotional, and spiritual challenges than one person could possibly manage. Despite this, Lyman emerges as a strong, human, and likable, if irascible, character. Lyman's situation is such that the reader's sympathy is instantly won. He is bitter, but his bitterness is understandable in view of his circumstances. Lyman is determined to prove to his son (to whom he refers as a Berkeley radical) that he can fend for himself and does not need a nursing home. Establishing himself in the old family cottage where he spent his childhood, he has it arranged to suit his needs. With some assistance from Ada Hawkes, who for many years was the family housekeeper, he manages amazingly well. The focus of his life becomes his grandmother's papers and mementos. He throws himself into this work wholeheartedly. Stegner has set Lyman Ward a worthy goal; from his grandmother he will learn much. The past can teach us, Stegner seems to say, and indeed it does. As Lyman uncovers his grandmother's story, he softens. He becomes very sympathetic to all the trials and hardships that she endured in the old frontier West. Moreover, the analogy between his situation and that of his grandparents is not lost upon him; seeing a similar circumstance from the past and its terrible consequence has an effect on him. He remembers quite clearly from his childhood that when his grandparents were together they were enshrouded in icy silence or remote politeness. In this way, Stegner prepares his protagonist to give up his bitter stand against the wife who has betrayed him.

Lyman Ward is Puritan-like in his morals. He believes there is not simply a gap between the generations, but a gulf. Stegner makes it clear that the one thing Lyman Ward does not have is a deteriorating moral fiber. In spite of all his handicaps, he manages to eke out a creditable life that has its share of daily conquests, victories, chores, and even small pleasures. He walks painfully but determinedly every day, using canes, in order to slow the progress of his deadly disease; he maneuvers himself in his wheelchair to get to the breakfast table; he immerses himself in his grandmother's papers in the afternoons; and at the end of the day, Ada Hawkes lifts him like a child for his bath and afterward shares a nightcap with him. It is indeed hard not to admire Lyman Ward.

Shelly Rasmussen is a welcome addition to *Angle of Repose*. She opens wide the door to refreshing dialogue with Lyman Ward and forces him to shed his somewhat moldy belief system and face up to the existence of a counterculture—the generation of the 1960's. After all, she points out, his wife of twenty-five years succumbed to its influence. It is time he came out of hiding and faced the opposition, and so Stegner presents him with Shelly.

Shelly is young, sexy, and sassy. She is also his typist and his housekeeper's daughter, hiding from her so-called liberated husband. Since she is privy to the story of Susan Burling Ward and has no compunctions about expressing her views frankly, she criticizes Lyman's reticence for not making the love scenes involving his grandmother more explicit. Lyman is annoyed. It is no use explaining that the Victorians were private about their sex— Shelly is merely amused at the notion. In spite of the fact that they are worlds apart in their views, however, there grows a genuine fondness between them.

### Themes and Meanings

*Angle of Repose* concerns not only Lyman Ward's story but also the story of his grandmother Susan, which parallels it. This parallel plot device enables Stegner to explore the past and its effect on the present, and to convey one of the novel's primary themes: that it is possible to learn from the past. Lyman Ward, in delving into the history of his grandparents to look for some continuity and meaning that can be applied to his own life, gains valuable insights.

The underlying structure of the novel is hinted at in the title itself: The geological meaning of the phrase "angle of repose" is the slope at which rocks cease to roll. The protagonist, Lyman Ward, discovers that his grandmother, married to an engineer, was familiar with the phrase and used it in one of her published articles. Lyman Ward (Stegner) projects the possibility of a more symbolic meaning: the angle at which a man and woman finally resolve their differences.

### Critical Context

Stegner has devoted a long career to the living history of the American West, which he has chronicled both in fiction and nonfiction. In part, *Angle of Repose* is a tribute to one of his predecessors, the novelist and memoirist Mary Hallock Foote (1847-1938), on whom the character of Susan Burling Ward is based. *Angle of Repose* was awarded the Pulitzer Prize in 1972 and was both a critical and a popular success; in 1976, it was adapted as an opera by Oakley Hall and Andrew Imbrie. Among many other honors, Stegner has also received a National Book Award, for his novel *The Spectator Bird* (1976), and a Robert Kirsch Award for lifetime achievement.

The latter award, which recognizes a significant body of work that draws its inspiration at least in part from the West, is a particularly fitting tribute. Both in his books and as the longtime director of Stanford University's creative writing program, Stegner has provided a powerful example of the Western writer—regional but in no sense parochial.

### Sources for Further Study

Robinson, Forrest, and Margaret Robinson. *Wallace Stegner*, 1977.
*The New York Times Book Review*. Review. August 29, 1971, p. 31.

*Publishers Weekly*. Review. CXCIX (February 15, 1971), p. 71.
*Saturday Review*. Review. LIV (March 20, 1971), p. 29.

                                                                              *Ruth Weiss*

# ANOTHER COUNTRY

*Author:* James Baldwin (1924-
*Type of plot:* Social realism
*Time of plot:* The 1950's
*Locale:* New York City
*First published:* 1962

> *Principal characters:*
> RUFUS SCOTT, a pivotal character in the novel, although he
> dies at the end of the first chapter
> VIVALDO MOORE, a friend of Rufus who refuses to acknowl-
> edge Rufus as a mirror of himself
> ERIC JONES, whose love is ultimately refused by Rufus but is
> accepted by Vivaldo
> IDA SCOTT, Rufus' sister, who forms a tense relationship with
> Vivaldo
> LEONA, Rufus' lover, who is beaten and rejected by him
> CASS SILENSKI, who is married to Richard Silenski but driven
> by her frustrations to an affair with Eric
> YVES, Eric's French lover

*The Novel*

In *Another Country*, Baldwin's choice of a third-person narrative point of view allows him to enter the minds of all of the characters to explore their inner lives as well as to chronicle exterior events. The novel is broken into several large blocks, each devoted primarily to a major character, though all of the major characters weave their way through the narrative. Baldwin's purpose seems to be to explore as many variations in racial, social, geographical, and sexual perspective as can be credibly presented in a single novel. Thus, Rufus is a black man from New York City who takes as a mistress Leona, a white woman from the American South, after he has rejected Eric, a white man of wealthy Southern parentage. Vivaldo, a poor Irish Italian from the American North, forms a liaison with Rufus' sister, Ida, after breaking up with Jane, a middle-aged artist. Vivaldo is tortured by the idea that, had he offered physical solace to Rufus, Rufus might not have committed suicide; Vivaldo accepts Eric's sexual advances, though Vivaldo realizes that he prefers women. Eric finds in Yves, a Frenchman, a replacement for Rufus, but Eric accepts as a lover Cass, a white woman from a middle-class New England background, though Eric comes to realize that he prefers men. Only Richard Silenski seems separate from this sexual game of musical chairs, but Richard is rigidly bound by middle-class American bourgeois values, biases, and stereotypes.

At the end of the novel, Rufus is dead, and Leona is in a sanatorium in the South; Vivaldo and Ida have arranged what is likely to be a temporary truce in the battle between the sexes and races; Cass and Richard may find it possible to mend their broken marriage; and Eric and Yves look forward to at least a short time of happiness with each other.

A problem with all of these relationships is that the characters tend to confuse sex and love, identifying one with the other and then confusing the complex of feelings related to sex and love with myriad other factors bearing on problems of identity. Rufus destroys Leona and himself not only because he finds that he cannot trust a white woman but also because he cannot trust women in general, not knowing what it is that they want or expect. He violently rejects Leona because he believes that he has become for her simply a means of sexual gratification in a relationship in which, he fears, she really has the upper hand. Vivaldo fears that he may be entangled with Ida because of his feelings of guilt over Rufus, and Ida fears that she may be taking out on Vivaldo her hostility against white men. Cass turns to Eric because she believes that her husband has denigrated her by prostituting his talents for money. Eric turns to Cass as a sort of last resort to test his preference for men. All use the word "love" for strong sexual feelings and then find themselves in utter distress because life, they believe, must have more to offer than sexual gratification.

Before he dies, Rufus asks Vivaldo the crucial question: "What *do* two people want from each other... when they get together... ?" Vivaldo, however, will not face the problem. He passes the question off with a facile reference to sex while at the same time he fights the feeling of panic threatening to overwhelm him. His refusal to face the existential issues results in his inability to confront Ida with his suspicions; he is afraid to lose her.

The historical relationship of the sexes in a patriarchal society is at the root of many of the problems that bedevil Baldwin's characters. Rufus uses sex to dominate Leona and to subdue her. Until he meets Ida, Vivaldo finds it difficult to think of women except in sexual terms, and he conceives of his male role as unlocking for maidens the mysterious doors of sex and life. At first with Ida, Vivaldo is concerned not so much with her gratification as with bringing her "over the edge" and into his possession. Yet Ida is not willing simply to be possessed. She also wants to dominate, to punish.

The relationship that forms between Eric and Vivaldo is the only one in which both partners exist on an equal plane. Making love with Eric, Vivaldo thinks, is strangely double-edged, like interacting in the midst of mirrors: "This was as far removed as anything could be from the necessary war one underwent with women." Vivaldo's single experience with Eric acts as a kind of catharsis, freeing him to return to Ida and freeing Eric finally to accept his preference for men and welcome Yves from France. Still, a happily-ever-after ending is not implied. The reader knows, if Vivaldo does not, that Ida will never marry him, and Eric knows that Yves will not stay with him. What is left is the hope that the characters have learned enough to allow them to continue movement away from misunderstandings about what motivates their own behavior.

### The Characters

Rufus Scott, a once-famous black jazz musician, is, at the beginning of *Another Country*, broke, hungry, and without a home. His affair with Leona ended when her brother took her back to the South. Since Rufus and Leona were not married, Rufus had no legal say in what happened to Leona, and since Leona is white, her relatives and, indeed, the hospital officials, move with alacrity to get her away from Rufus. Forced to confront his own motivation in his brutal treatment of Leona, Rufus comes to the brink of existential terror and chooses death over life.

Acting as a kind of mirror for the dark powers of the soul reflected in all of the other characters, Rufus, in choosing death over life, represents death as alternative to life. In choosing to live, the other characters face the need to examine their motivations, their lusts, their cupidities, and their biases, so as to adopt such accommodations in life-style and belief patterns as make living possible. Except for Leona, who is ruined before she can try, and Richard Silenski, who is too obtuse to learn, each character comes to some greater understanding of self.

Ida, Rufus' sister, a beautiful black woman filled with anger over not only her brother's suicide but also the plight of all American blacks in a racist society, is out to get even and in so doing not only to strike a blow for herself but also to avenge her brother's death. Finally she comes to understand something of the tremendous conflict of emotional forces motivating her, and she knows that to marry Vivaldo would only destroy them both.

Vivaldo, a kind of white counterpart to Rufus, has to make extraordinary efforts to try to understand how black people feel and why Rufus and Ida cannot simply accept Vivaldo's love at face value. He must, moreover, come to terms with his own urges and reconcile himself to an innate bisexuality.

Cass is a counterpart to Ida. Small and blonde, inexperienced in sexual matters, never mired in poverty or used by the racist society, Cass has accepted her role as wife and mother, considering herself as simply a helpmate and not realizing until her marriage is on the point of collapse that she has created the intolerable situation herself by forcing Richard to play a role in which he was never comfortable. She will try to retrieve the marriage if she can, but her straying from it is what gives her the strength to consider trying it again.

### Themes and Meanings

Baldwin believes that as an artist he is not responsible for fully delineating solutions to social problems: The artist's role is to clarify the issues, to present the social ills, not to cure them. Baldwin's scathing indictments of American society are, therefore, not meant to be destructive. Rather, he means to observe, analyze, and question. Not hatred but love must underlie the search for solutions. Hatred is vitiating and ultimately destructive. Love, on the other hand, can act in constructive ways, ultimately connecting all people and uniting them by means of their own humanity. Loving is directed outward. It means exposing oneself to others, removing the masks that cover one and facing the truths, whatever they are.

The problems that Baldwin presents generally revolve around certain central issues involving racial prejudice, sex and sexist attitudes, poverty, alienation from family and especially men from their fathers, hostile environments, and bisexual relationships between men. The latter issue has caused some critics to describe Baldwin's world as essentially a man's world because of a homosexual principle operating within it. Baldwin, on the other hand, apparently sees bisexuality as one aspect of a larger consciousness of dualities such as life-death, hate-love, male-female, with which men must learn to deal if maturity is to be achieved and identity found.

*Critical Context*

James Baldwin is one of the most popular American black writers; more than four million copies of *Another Country* have been sold—a remarkable number for a serious novel. Although *Another Country* generally received unfavorable reviews upon first publication, later critics and scholars have evaluated Baldwin's achievements within a larger context, including his relationship not only with other black writers (Ralph Ellison, Richard Wright, Amiri Baraka, and Eldridge Cleaver) but also with his white contemporaries. Within the black establishment there is a difference of opinion regarding the role of art and of the black artist. Baldwin's view, similar to Ellison's, is that people are human first and different colors second. This view is praised by some critics who speak to Baldwin's artistic achievements as well as to his social commentary and denigrated by other critics who believe that black writers should hold themselves aloof from the majority culture.

Time, however, is likely to vindicate the views held by Baldwin and Ellison. Universality is a trait central to all literature that lasts beyond its immediate time to speak to future generations of readers. Baldwin's ultimate concern is with the future and with the great American Dream, never realized but never elsewhere articulated so fully. The dream is still a potent one, filled with so much moral force and vigor that contemplation of failure in any of its aspects must lead to despair. Perhaps Baldwin is really American first, since the dream defines what it means to be human and since Baldwin apparently cannot live for too long in this country but cannot leave it either. If so, his use of *Another Country* as the title is an ironic reflection on the fact that these United States are, in terms of the dream, another country.

*Sources for Further Study*
Eckman, Fern Marja. *The Furious Passage of James Baldwin*, 1966.
Grier, William H., and Price M. Cobbs. *Black Rage*, 1968.
Kinnamon, Keneth. *James Baldwin: A Collection of Critical Essays*, 1974.
Macebah, Stanley. *James Baldwin: A Critical Study*, 1973.
O'Daniel, Therman B., ed. *James Baldwin: A Critical Evaluation*, 1977.

*Mary Rohrberger*

# THE APPLE IN THE DARK

*Author:* Clarice Lispector (1925-1977)
*Type of plot:* Mythic quest
*Time of plot:* The late 1950's
*Locale:* A remote, desolate farming region of Brazil
*First published: A maçã no escuro,* 1961 (English translation, 1967)

*Principal characters:*
MARTIM, the protagonist, who is on the run from the law
VITÓRIA, the owner-manager of the farm where Martim
    comes to stay
ERMELINDA, a young, widowed cousin of Vitória

*The Novel*
On the surface, the story in *The Apple in the Dark* could not be simpler. A man commits a crime, flees into the desolate interior of Brazil, arrives at a remote farm, is taken on as a farmhand, is reported to the authorities, and is arrested and returned to face the law. It is not the minimal action of the plot which intrigues the reader but rather the process of searching for some meaning in life, for some definition of the world and of one's place in it, that provides the interest of the novel.

Primarily, it is Martim's quest for self-awareness that forms the core of the story. The mythic nature of his quest is straightforwardly indicated by the titles of the three sections into which the book is divided: "How a Man Is Made," "The Birth of the Hero," and "The Apple in the Dark." Indeed, the author, in a stroke of brilliance, has managed to combine parallels to at least two major, complementary views of man's existence in the unfolding of Martim's symbolic journey: the biblical story of the Garden of Eden and the Darwinian theory of evolution. From the beginning of the book, the reader is alerted to these two viewpoints. Martim awakes from sleep "on a night as dark as night can get," immediately after fleeing from a crime which he will come to see as an act that frees him to start all over again in life. His flight takes him first through total darkness over unknown terrain, which permits him to focus exclusively on his sensual feelings and to ignore the burden of civilization behind him. As the sun comes up, he begins to appreciate an even closer identity with nature in its most primitive forms: stones, dirt, searing heat, silence. Bereft of language, he discovers a great joy in repeating meaningless statements to the flora and fauna around him. By the time, early in the novel, that he comes upon the farmhouse where most of the story takes place, he has duplicated a sort of climb up the evolutionary ladder. Having shed the trappings of a man, he has begun to learn what it is to be like "a creature [who] does not think and does not get involved, and is still completely there."

The farm is owned and run by Vitória, an unmarried woman in her fifties who appears to be a tower of strength and self-reliance. Staying with her is her cousin Ermelinda, a dreamy, ethereal woman recently widowed, whose rather poetic manner of approaching life is a constant source of uneasiness for Vitória. The bulk of the novel consists in observing, through the eyes of the three principal characters, the slow process of change in Martim and the effect that he has on Vitória and Ermelinda. By the novel's end, however, the reader cannot be sure that the two women have experienced any genuine enlightenment, although it is probable that the protagonist now at least realizes that he has missed gaining a firm grip on the meaning of existence. In the last paragraph of the book, Martim finally understands that "we are not so guilty after all; we are more stupid than guilty." The quest for knowledge, he learns too late, is like "reaching for an apple in the dark—and trying not to drop it."

## The Characters

The principal characters differ from one another radically, but they are similar in that each has a terrible fear particular to himself or herself. For Martim, it is the fear of acting—a fear which explains why the crime that he committed, one which he cherishes as an *act*, is essential to his survival. The crime, the nature of which is revealed only toward the end of the story, represents Martim's symbolic banishment from Eden. Yet to Martim, a man who was in his former life a statistician—whose life depended on the most abstract of occupations—the crime is the impetus that sets him on the road to salvation, or so he believes. Martim is destined to be disillusioned, however, as he goes from rocks to plants to vermin to cattle to children and eventually to adults once again. Having abandoned his wife, son, job, and friends and fled into this wilderness, he nevertheless falls back into an involvement with complex human beings.

Vitória has spent much of her life caring for her dying father, and as a result, she has never had or at least has never reached for, a love of her own. She now fears love and has hardened herself against all possibility of it. The confrontation with Martim finally forces her to face her empty and near-tragic existence. At the climax of the novel, which occurs rather melodramatically during a rare and violent rainstorm, Vitória, unable to bear her dearth of love, races to the woodshed where Martim sleeps. Martim, however, has fled into the woods during the storm, like King Lear, distraught and seeking cleansing and purification in nature. It is not long after this episode that Vitória calls for the authorities to come pick up Martim.

Ermelinda has an elliptical way of talking to people. Unlike her cousin, she embraces love; in fact, she falls in love with Martim almost at first sight, and before long they have become lovers. Yet her way of expressing her feeling for him is strangely indirect. She explains that if she comes up and says to him, "Look at that fern!" she is really saying, "I love you." Indeed, Ermelinda is so frightened of death that she has retreated into a world of private symbolism.

## Themes and Meanings

Clarice Lispector read her existentialists closely. One can pick up veiled allusions to novels by Jean-Paul Sartre and Albert Camus in *The Apple in the Dark*. The character of Martim contains elements of both Meursault in Camus' *The Stranger* (1942) and Roquentin in Sartre's *Nausea* (1938). Though unaware of the existentialist's dictum, "Existence precedes Essence," the protagonist has, in fact, set out in search of his own essence. What Martim fails to realize, and what will ultimately bring him up short in his quest for a new Eden, is that he has deluded himself from the beginning. It is almost as if he is telling the reader that his crime was necessary as a means of escaping from a banal and deadening existence into a chance for true, human essence. His error lies in thinking that the initial act will not color subsequent events; indeed, it will determine them.

## Critical Context

Clarice Lispector achieved her first general acclaim for the collection of stories *Laços de familia* (1960; *Family Ties*, 1972), in which many of the protagonists, like Martim, struggle—often unsuccessfully—for a sense of self and harmony with the outside world. This concern with what John Gledson has called an "intense, almost exclusive interest in the subjective world," which receives its most complex articulation in *The Apple in the Dark*, is also examined in *A paixão segundo G. H.* (1964; the passion according to G. H.) and *Água viva* (1973; sparkling water), and places Lispector among the Brazilian revisionists: those postwar writers whose move away from the regionalism of the 1920's and 1930's and whose focus on more universal themes has been a major force in mainstreaming Brazilian literature. Indeed, Gregory Rabassa, in the introduction to his translation of *The Apple in the Dark*, includes Lispector among those contemporary Brazilian novelists who are "in tune with . . . international currents."

## Sources for Further Study

Fitz, Earl E. *Clarice Lispector*, 1985.
Gledson, John. Review in *The Times Literary Supplement*. January 25, 1985.
Johnson, Harvey L., and Philip B. Taylor, Jr., eds. *Contemporary Latin American Literature*, 1973.

*Christopher R. McRae*

# THE ARMIES OF THE NIGHT
## History as a Novel, the Novel as History

*Author:* Norman Mailer (1923-     )
*Type of plot:* Social chronicle
*Time of plot:* 1967
*Locale:* Washington, D.C., the Pentagon
*First published:* 1968

*Principal characters:*

NORMAN MAILER, a novelist and a participant in the march on the Pentagon

ROBERT LOWELL, a poet and a participant in the march

DWIGHT MACDONALD, a literary critic and a participant in the march

PAUL GOODMAN, a social critic

WILLIAM SLOANE COFFIN, JR., the chaplain at Yale and a participant in the march

DAVE DELLINGER, an organizer of the march

JERRY RUBIN, an organizer of the march

ED DE GRAZIA, the attorney for the arrested marchers

DR. BENJAMIN SPOCK, a speaker at the march

*The Novel*

Norman Mailer's subtitle for his book, "History as a Novel, the Novel as History," aptly defines both its structure and its style. Part 1 narrates the history of the march on the Pentagon to protest the Vietnam War from the novelist's point of view; that is, Mailer describes himself and his perceptions of the march in the third person, as though he were writing a fiction about a character over whom he exercises considerable objectivity. Part 2 is a more formal history, in the sense that the author relies much more heavily on others' points of view because history is a kind of "collective novel" written by all of the participants in and witnesses to the event.

The march assembled thousands of people who planned to shut down the war machine in the Pentagon by invading the premises, staging teach-ins, burning draft cards, and disrupting business as usual. Many different peace groups, reflecting various opinions on how the war should be stopped, agreed to form a coalition that would afford the participants in the march the maximum amount of publicity. Public figures such as Mailer, Robert Lowell, and Dr. Benjamin Spock agreed not only to speak in favor of the march but also to engage in acts of civil disobedience that would emphasize their principled opposition to the war. The arrests of prominent figures, it was hoped, would demonstrate the commitment of the peace groups to forcing the United States to leave Vietnam.

While basically in sympathy with the marchers, Mailer proves to be a reluctant partisan and participant in the history of the march. As a self-described "left-conservative," he expresses nearly as many criticisms of the marchers as he does of the government and of the institutions that support the war. The arguments he advances for pulling out of Vietnam are unorthodox and paradoxical. He suggests, for example, that the United States should risk allowing Southeast Asia to be taken over by Communists because only in the expansion of Communism will its internal contradictions become apparent, so that in its very growth will be found the seeds of its own destruction.

The very elaborateness of his ideas—in contrast to the simple and often unexplored premises of Vietnam hawks and doves—suggests Mailer's value as an interpreter of history. He is frankly speculative, and he honestly shows the process by which he has arrived as his suppositions. He lays bare the roots of his thinking in a way that hawks and doves would not dare, since neither side wants to concede that it has gaps and ambiguities in its position. Mailer, on the other hand, inspires confidence precisely because he eloquently exposes the limitations of his political analysis while offering an original alternative to the clichéd ideas of others.

*The Characters*

The author's handling of characters justifies calling his book a novel. First, there is Mailer himself, middle-aged and eager to get on with his writing rather than risk an uncertain confrontation in a cause he believes he can best promote by remaining a novelist. Yet he is called into action by his friend, Mitchell Goodman, who convinces him that the march will be an unusual political event that Mailer (given his sympathy for dissenters) cannot pass up.

The drama of the novel develops as Mailer tries to fit his idiosyncratic character into the program of the marchers. The various titles he gives himself ("the Historian," "the Beast," the "Prince of Bourbon," "the Existentialist," "the Novelist," "the Participant," "the Ruminant," the "nice Jewish boy from Brooklyn") reflect the variety of roles he plays, each of which corresponds to some part of the reality upon which he builds his fiction. As part 2 proves, he has an impressive historical sensibility that provokes him to collate and shrewdly analyze conflicting views of the march. At the same time, as a character in his own novel, he can be erratic, foolish, insulting, and a boor.

The point of dwelling on these conflicting sides of his character, however, is to show that the author is capable of absorbing and distilling, as a whole, the march on the Pentagon, for the march had its silly as well as its serious aspects. There were profoundly dedicated peace activists and there were opportunists using the event for a variety of political purposes; many individuals partook in both the important and the frivolous activities Mailer attended. As philosopher and fool, he is in the best position to understand the sublime and ridiculous qualities of his allies and adversaries. If he is critical of the totalitarian war machine, he is also condemnatory of liberal college professors who adopt an antihuman, technology-based life-style that is part of what they profess to oppose. At the same time, Mailer associates with such people, knows that as individuals they do not neatly fit his generalizations about them, and recognizes that he is only one step removed from their way of life. He never forgets, in other words, how deeply implicated he is in the very conditions that he deplores.

The author's keen concentration on other characters, particularly on Robert Lowell, keeps his narrative in part 1 from becoming too self-absorbed even as it measures Mailer's power as narrator and participant. Lowell is treated as a great poet and a fixture on the American scene. He apparently shares none of Mailer's self-doubt, and he exhibits a moral rectitude that Mailer envies in other New England Ivy Leaguers such as William Sloane Coffin, Jr., of Yale. There is a solidity to the poet's identity which the novelist attributes to his Eastern ancestry. When Lowell compliments Mailer on being the best journalist in America, the novelist bristles, because journalism is not his idea of fine writing, and he replies to a disconcerted Lowell by suggesting that sometimes he thinks of himself as the best writer in America.

Like Lowell, figures such as Dwight Macdonald, Paul Goodman, and Dr. Spock seem to feel secure about their place in the march and about their authority as speakers against the status quo. Mailer, on the other hand, is never certain of his powers of persuasion, although his ambition to move people is obviously greater than that of any other character in the book. He worries over slights to his reputation and is vain enough to preen himself on his achievements. He battles for the reader's regard by showing, for example, the defects in Paul Goodman's prose and by demonstrating his ability to appreciate some of Lowell's finest lines.

*Themes and Meanings*

The theme of *The Armies of the Night* is that history and the interpretation of history go hand in hand. Part 2 clearly proves that there is no such thing as "the facts" without someone to give them a meaning. Indeed, the search for meaning is often what creates the facts. Was the march on the Pentagon a significant historical event? Mailer answers in part 2 as both a historian and a novelist.

As historian, he evaluates the evidence. How many people participated in the march? The estimates, from newspaper accounts, differ greatly, from fifty thousand to 250,000 people. Mailer allows for bias, on the Right and on the Left, and usually settles for figures approximately halfway between the two extremes. He takes a similar approach in evaluating reports of brutality and violence, conceding that both sides resorted to physical abuse and presenting a plausible case for reports of police beatings of protestors when the press was not present.

By one significant measure, Mailer concludes, the march was a failure. It did not stop the war; indeed, it may have produced a public reaction against the demonstrators and boosted President Lyndon Baines Johnson's popularity. On the other hand, the march succeeded in mobilizing masses of people in spite of the government's best efforts to discourage the marchers. As Mailer astutely points out, organizers such as Jerry Rubin and Dave Dellinger succeeded in getting the government to negotiate a protest against itself even as it sought every means of disabling it. It is an impressive achievement of *The Armies of the Night* that it maintains an evenhanded approach to the "armies" representing authority and dissent.

Of crucial importance to the book's balance is Mailer's role as novelist and historian. He never forsakes the facts that were available to him or discounts data that do not fit into his view of the march; on the other hand, he shows the limitations of data. Finally, facts cannot tell the story; only the imagination of the novelist can grasp the true significance of the march. It was not a rigidly planned, step-by-step revolutionary program; it was a social movement that did not have a final logical goal, an existential action that did not rely on either the Marxist or capitalist understanding of cause and effect. The march was "a new style of revolution—revolution by theater and without a script."

*Critical Context*

   *The Armies of the Night* is arguably the most important novel of Mailer's career. After the astonishing success of his first novel, *The Naked and the Dead* (1948), his subsequent work received mixed reviews, and many critics, perhaps mistakenly, perceived him as failing to fulfill his early promise. Twenty years later, his account of the march on the Pentagon was regarded by many reviewers as the culmination of his ambition, expressed in *Advertisements for Myself* (1959), to make "*a revolution in the consciousness of our time.*"

   It hardly seems to be an accident that Mailer made good on his ambition by re-creating an event which itself had a revolutionary aim. In other words, the march was a perfect match for his own existential politics, a brand of activism that rejected, as he puts it in *The Armies of the Night*, "the logic of the next step" that leftists had used for generations in plotting revolutionary change. In all of his work from *Barbary Shore* (1951) onward, Mailer suggests that there is nothing rational about revolutionary change, that "the logic of the next step" is stultifying because it locks the revolutionary into a model of change that may well be outmoded by the very actions he takes to make it become real.

In *The Armies of the Night*, Mailer aligns the nature of literary and political creation:

> Just as the truth of his material was revealed to a good writer by the cutting edge of his style . . . so a revolutionary began to uncover the nature of his true situation by trying to ride the beast of his revolution. The idea behind these ideas was then obviously that the future of the revolution existed in the nerves and cells of the people who created it and lived with it, rather than in the sanctity of the original idea.

Mailer's ideas of literature, of politics, of human identity, and of history itself come together dynamically and dramatically in a work that has been accorded almost universal recognition as a classic of its time.

*Sources for Further Study*
Bailey, Jennifer. *Norman Mailer: Quick-Change Artist*, 1980.
Lucid, Robert F. *Norman Mailer: The Man and His Work*, 1971.
Merrill, Robert. *Norman Mailer*, 1978.
Poirier, Richard. *Norman Mailer*, 1972.
Solotaroff, Theodore. *Down Mailer's Way*, 1974.

*Carl E. Rollyson, Jr.*

# THE ASIATICS

*Author:* Frederic Prokosch (1908-    )
*Type of plot:* Picaresque romance
*Time of plot:* The 1920's
*Locale:* Asia, from Beirut to Hong Kong
*First published:* 1935

> *Principal characters:*
> THE NARRATOR, a nameless twenty-two-year-old American
> ANTOINE SAMAZEUILH, an unreliable French rogue and the
>     temporary companion of the narrator
> FEODOR KRUSNAYASKOV, a Communist and fellow prisoner
>     with the narrator in Turkey
> HANS DE HAHN, a Dutch adventurer
> DR. AINGER, a cynical doctor in Penang

*The Novel*

   *The Asiatics* has no plot. It is a tale of an aimless vagabondage from Beirut to Hong Kong, a pilgrimage to experience made by—and told by—a nameless young American. The narrator-hero is not a rogue, but in most other respects *The Asiatics* is a picaresque romance, studded with incident and peopled by faithless opportunists and outright scoundrels. Nothing is explained of the hero's background, and the inference to be made is that he is making this long trip simply because that is what young men do. He has but little money most of the way, and he is innocent (but alert) in a way that is identified with Americans. *The Asiatics* is, in fact, partly a fable of cultural contrasts.

   The hero leaves Beirut by bus, catching a ride to Damascus, where the first of his many initiation experiences occurs when he is befriended by a faintly sinister Syrian named M. Aractingi. Their journey to Turkey ends abruptly when M. Aractingi's car breaks down, and two mysterious men come along and pursue him into the fields on foot. The hero flees in another direction, finding shelter with a hospitable peasant.

   Walking toward Homs the next day, the hero falls in with another vagrant, a young Frenchman named Antoine Samazeuilh. Their companionship endures for several days, strengthened by the company of a pretty girl, until Samazeuilh inexplicably disappears. The hero pushes on alone into Turkey, meeting new friends and dropping them, and in Istanbul a Mr. Suleiman petitions him to deliver a small package on his boat trip to Trebizond. He delivers the parcel—he suspects that it is opium—and soon takes up with an enigmatic Russian, Feodor Krusnayaskov, with whom he continues his travels. No sooner do they reach the city of Erzerum than they are arrested by the Turkish police and confined in a cell with twenty-eight political prisoners, thus beginning one of the more notable episodes of the novel.

The hero suffers through two wretched months in prison during the coldest months of winter, witnessing the extreme sexual corruption of his fellow inmates. During his incarceration he meets Hans de Hahn, a genial Dutchman whom he will encounter again much farther east. The necessary *deus ex machina* comes in the person of a friendly guard, and, with his help, the hero and Krusnayaskov escape and flee to Krusnayaskov's home in Tiflis. The hero, however, learns that Krusnayaskov is a dedicated Communist and flees into the night when fears of betrayal overcome him.

Soon the hero is in Persia, falling in step here and there with Nestorian priests and other patriarchs of the Asian sensibility. He takes his ease for several days in Teheran at the salon of a Mme de Chamellis, and through her agency he is able to fly to Meshed with Dr. Ainger, one of her other guests, but the plane crashes and the two walk different paths, the hero finding a short-term home in Meshed with the sophisticated Prince Ghuraguzlu. He is soon en route again, this time with a treacherous young epicene named Ahmed, who abandons him to the predations of a gang of mountain bandits.

In Peshawar, the hero reencounters his old cell-mate, the Dutchman de Hahn, who is now traveling with a lovely mistress, Ursule. They improvise a hasty *menage à trois* until sexual infidelities break them up, leaving the hero free for his next adventure, an extended stay with the Maharajah of Badrapur. Various complications end his respite with the maharajah, and soon he arrives in Calcutta, a mere stopover on his way to Kandy, Ceylon. He soon takes a boat to Rangoon and rejoins Mme de Chamellis, his former hostess in Teheran. This new liaison is fruitful with incident: a weeklong excursion up the Irrawaddy River and a joining of fortunes in Mandalay with a mercenary Mr. Maung, owner of the boat in which they go aground in a reed jungle on the upper Irrawaddy. This misadventure concludes with their kidnaping by river marauders, Mme de Chamellis' death, and the hero's release and return to Rangoon.

The hero rejoins Dr. Ainger—last seen walking away from the plane wreck in Persia—in his outpost near Panang, where he administers medical aid to the natives. The hero witnesses, in scenes that suggest Joseph Conrad's *Heart of Darkness* (1902), the degeneration of Dr. Ainger in a debilitating physical setting of heat, insect life, and disease. After Ainger's death, the hero travels via Bangkok to Pnom-Penh, where, improbably, he is reunited with the rascally Samazeuilh. They drift together to Saigon, meet (even more improbably) the lovely Ursule, former mistress of de Hahn, and proceed, the three of them, to Huë. There, in a final blaze of coincidence, de Hahn reappears. The novel ends inconclusively when de Hahn dies,

Samazeuilh vanishes for a final time, and the hero goes on to Hong Kong. In the novel's last lines, the initiation ends joyously as the hero, enjoying the sunlight on his naked body after taking a cool swim, exults in the great hedonism of youth: "Yes, there was no denying it, I was feeling very happy."

*The Characters*

   The hero-narrator at one point explains to an interrogator that he is going to Japan. "I have an uncle in Japan. He is very rich, and if I behave nicely to him I may some day have more money than I have now." This answer displeases Mostafa, the Persian bandit to whom it is addressed. He tells the hero, "Yes, you are an American. I am very disappointed in you. I thought you had a soul, but now I see that you have no soul, after all." Mostafa goes on to explain that fewer and fewer are happy. The world is too full of things to do, and people have no time to cultivate the loneliness that nurtures a soul. Mostafa originally mistakes the hero for an Asiatic like himself; that is, he thinks that he is an American Indian. "You watch and watch; no one ever knows what you think; you look strong and passionate and sly." This original sizing-up of the hero thus makes Mostafa's disappointment doubly sharp, and it underscores the differences both in culture and in temperament that distinguish the hero from the people among whom he passes.

   Whatever the health of his soul, the hero benefits from his rich experiences because he keeps himself courageously open to the events that overtake him. On one occasion he is worn down by "bits of irritability, splinters of suspicion, of jealousy, of detestation, of loneliness, of wicked understanding." This condition moves him to withdraw from all people: "Don't let them toy with you, don't let them wriggle their way into that part of you that matters. Be alone. Be strong. Be proud." Yet the urge soon passes, and he decides that "to understand anything at all" he must be "fragile" and "tender" and he must humiliate himself. Only through this vulnerability can he ever know himself and remain healthy.

   The hero seems to succeed in his struggle to achieve knowledge through experience. He remains in all situations a passive bystander, one who never disturbs the universe but on whom all things are registered. Yet at the end he appears as fresh a product of the New World as he was in the beginning. He is neither coarsened by his worldly initiation nor made cynical and despairing.

   Most of the other characters go by in a blur. Androgynous ephebes come and go at the author's bidding, as do princes and potentates—none of any interest as a character study. Of the cynical Europeans—de Hahn, Samazeuilh, Dr. Ainger—Ainger is the most provocative for the misanthropy he expresses in his deep loathing for modern civilization. For him, all that civilization means is "making money and making things easier for those who've made it and killing the spirit in themselves as well as in everybody else." His death from plague in a rotting jungle seems an appropriate close to a life that has moved so far away from humanity.

## Themes and Meanings

*The Asiatics* exploits one of the oldest of plot devices—the journey—and makes the appeal of geography a basic part of the story. The exotic place names roll on in an onomastic litany; Prokosch frequently has recourse to the pathetic fallacy (Damascus is "sad" and its fields are "desolate"), but his limpid poetic prose evokes climate and brings landscapes to life with great economy of description. His towns and byways are peopled with figures who blend naturally into the whole shifting panorama. In Meshed during the month of mourning, "they prostrated themselves on the dry rutted alleyways, they scratched aimlessly and absent-mindedly at their flesh until they bled and had to weep with pain and excitement." The Irrawaddy River is "dotted with houseboats full of short-legged sloe-eyed natives," and on the bank can be seen "small young priests dressed in yellow hovering on the green bank like so many dandelions."

*The Asiatics* is also, like that famous travel novel Samuel Johnson's *Rasselas, The Prince of Abissinia* (1759), in many respects a search for happiness. For most of the figures milling around in the exotic locales, a search for happiness means a search for some form of love. Mme de Chamellis concludes that the search is futile. In her cynical appraisal, no two lovers love each other equally strongly, and "wretchedness grows, little by little." For the hero-narrator, love is "any of a million different streams leading to some unguessed ocean, some unexplainable meeting-place." The need for love is a constant hunger. When an ugly eunuch comes to Dr. Ainger, digging at an open wound and seeking pity, the narrator's judgment is quick: "It was the only way he could get any attention. It was his way of asking for love." The search for love in *The Asiatics* is a fever, an ever-present seething in the blood that keeps humanity in motion.

The most compelling theme of the novel is suggested by its title, which draws attention to the narrator's quest for the meaning of Asia. Something of this meaning is suggested in a shocking metaphor in which a dead rat represents the Oriental: "There it lay, sloe-eyed, slim-fingered, yellow-toothed. A real Oriental with a growing look of uncontrollable evil in its posture." In another formulation, Prince Ghuraguzlu finds the essence of Asia to be in its "long and terrible ennui," its "vagueness." The prince explains that Asiatics have "woven" death straight into their lives and that "death's right there, running like a silver thread through the pattern." The Dutchman de Hahn expresses similar thoughts vividly. For him, Asia is "the land of death," and "we're all Asiatics." De Hahn envisions a dying race faced with eternal darkness, a humanity that is doomed for having replaced reason with instinct: "And do you know what instinct is?" he asks. "It's a wild lion roaming through the jungle with blood on his tongue." In de Hahn's words lies perhaps the most resonant of the meanings behind the title of *The Asiatics*.

*Critical Context*

*The Asiatics* was Prokosch's first novel, and it has always had an audience of prestigious admirers, such as Albert Camus and Thomas Mann. Prokosch's virtuoso descriptive powers, his renderings of settings and moods, account for much of the praise. Not every reader, however, could be expected to enjoy the faintly iridescent sheen of sexual corruption that clings to much of the description, especially in the novel's elicitation of androgynous youths, and there is a sameness to its dreamy descriptiveness that eventually diminishes interest in the story despite Prokosch's talent for metaphor and epithet. As a specimen of the novel of the imaginary journey, however, it deserves high rank in American literature.

*Sources for Further Study*
Said, Edward W. *Orientalism*, 1978.
Squires, Radcliffe. *Frederic Prokosch*, 1964.

*Frank Day*

# THE ASSISTANT

*Author:* Bernard Malamud (1914-1986)
*Type of plot:* Domestic realism
*Time of plot:* Mid-twentieth century
*Locale:* Brooklyn, New York
*First published:* 1957

> *Principal characters:*
> MORRIS BOBER, a sixty-year-old Russian-Jewish immigrant
>   who runs a small, failing grocery store
> IDA BOBER, his nagging wife
> HELEN BOBER, their twenty-three-year-old daughter, who still
>   lives at home
> FRANK ALPINE, a young drifter who saves the grocery from
>   bankruptcy

*The Novel*

The evolving relationships among Morris Bober, Frank Alpine, Helen Bober, and Ida Bober comprise the bulk of the action in *The Assistant*. All are failures in the eyes of the world, but through the example of Morris' honesty, faith, and love for his fellowman, Frank learns how to use his own suffering to redeem himself from himself.

Frank has always lost or driven away that which he most wanted. After becoming involved with robbing Morris, he feels guilty over hurting the old man and returns to the failing grocery, trying to expiate his guilt by helping around the store. Although he can ill afford it, Morris' characteristic kindness allows him to take the drifter on as his assistant, paying him by providing room and board, not knowing of his part in the robbery. The relationship quickly becomes successful—business in the store picks up, Morris enjoys his new apprentice and surrogate son (his own had died young), Frank basks in the kindness and warmth of the family, Ida worries over having a non-Jew in the house but is glad Morris can relax, and Helen comes to see a kindred spirit bent on improving his lot in life.

Denied love and security as an orphan, shunted from home to home, Frank begins to feel increasingly guilty over the robbery of the receptive family and tries to confess to the accepting Morris, but he cannot. He is wracked by his past life of pain and deprivation, occasionally pocketing money from the register, then berating himself and deciding to pay it all back. When Helen starts to return some of the interest he has in her, Frank begins to think that finally he may be turning his unlucky life around. When, however, Morris sees him take money from the register and fires him, his dreams of happiness are shattered. Again, Frank has made a wrong choice that has cost him the pleasure he has found.

As Helen innocently waits for him in the park that night, she is attacked by Ward Minogue, the one who set up the robbery of Morris' grocery. Frank rescues her and, unable to control himself, afraid he has now lost Helen forever by being fired, forces himself on her. He is soon consumed by remorse, seeing his action as another in a long string of mistakes. When Morris' illness creates an opportunity for him to continue at the store, he makes the most of his reprieve, even taking on another job to help the store stay afloat. Still looking for forgiveness, he finally tells Morris about the robbery but is turned out. The old man dies soon after, but Frank reappears, first at the funeral and then at the store, again taking over the business for no reward. He scrapes for the money to give Helen her dream of attending college, trying to make up for his mistake with her. He starts using the Yiddish phrases and mannerisms of the dead grocer, even converting to Morris' Judaism. Through the example of the compassionate, long-suffering Morris, Frank has learned the self-satisfaction of sacrificing for another, of extracting meaning from suffering; his moral education is complete.

### The Characters

Bernard Malamud's characters are developed primarily through narration, interior monologue, and dialogue. Morris Bober is a Job figure who values being a good man. His actions reflect his largess of heart, and he tells Frank that what is most important is "to do what is right, to be honest, to be good." Morris is the moral center of the novel, the failure no one can laugh at because of his honesty and goodness. Through his interactions with his customers and his acceptance of Frank, he teaches Frank that to suffer in order to do good for others is to claim one's individuality and humanity. Clearly, Malamud admires Morris' character, although he is careful not to present him as an unattainable ideal but simply as a man with frailties who acts to the fullest of his abilities.

Frank Alpine is different. He is unable to discipline himself and is continuously resolving to break one bad habit or another, then berating himself for being unable to do so. Sympathy for Frank is elicited primarily through his self-recriminations and flashbacks to his past. His attempt to better himself and to break from his cycle of failure supplies the essential plot of the novel, and it is his moral education that is depicted.

Ida Bober is largely a unidimensional stereotype: an overprotective Jewish mother who constantly nags at her husband. Her character seems to exist primarily to complete the domestic setting and to create opportunities for dialogue that establishes the ethnicity and social class of the couple; the two of them use the Yiddish vocabulary and slightly skewed syntax of the immigrant.

Helen Bober is linguistically more sophisticated and emotionally more complicated. She is no prude, but, although beginning to worry about becoming a spinster at twenty-three, she refuses to continue a possible romance because the boy forced her into sex. She wants better for herself—a commitment from him and an education for herself. Helen parallels Frank in her desire to improve herself, but her hurdles have been raised much more by financial circumstances than Frank's have and by her desire to do what is right for her parents; that is, to help support them, as the store is failing. Unlike Frank, Helen never lost a chance through a mistake—she simply never had the chance.

The minor characters in the novel exist to help move the plot, flesh out the neighborhood, and emphasize Morris' isolation in the store. None is developed in any detail because Morris knows them only on the surface. Helen's first lover, Nat Pearl, has some depth, which parallels the slightly more involved relationship between them.

### Themes and Meanings

The most prominent theme in the novel is that which is reflected so unrelentingly—the quality and purpose of suffering. Malamud illustrates how hardships and bad luck can be transcended through making suffering meaningful. Morris is a failure if measured by the American dream of wealth, but he is a success as a man because his example and love have turned Frank into an honest, compassionate, and responsible individual. The religious theme of the book rests on the presentation of redemptive suffering, but the human theme is the tale of a man becoming a *mensch*.

Malamud firmly anchors his religious theme in life and people. He develops his tale through the use of doubles who share similar characteristics, or the same qualities are presented in different ways and thus reinforced; through understatement, allowing the characters to exist as Everyman and creating gentle humor; and through numerous ironic reversals through which the idea of ill fate is conveyed. The primary style is realistic, but there are several impressionistic segments and symbolic scenes. Perhaps the most pronounced is the association of Frank with Saint Francis, the man who gave away all of his possessions to live happily in poverty. Frank also comes to live happily in poverty and in so choosing finds his true self—the good, responsible man he had tried so many times to be.

### Critical Context

*The Assistant*, although Malamud's second novel, was responsible for establishing him as a major writer, a popular as well as a critical success. The novel is somewhat more naturalistic than Malamud's usual work; it is representative, with its emphasis on the Jewish experience, of the Jewish approach to life. Some critics believe, in fact, that the Jewish element is not as well integrated as it could be, that it stands out too blatantly, detracting from and obscuring the universality of man's struggle to endure and to evolve. Despite the oppressive gloom and unrelenting images of imprisonment, *The Assistant* is positive in its outlook. The novel is typical of Malamud's work in its belief that life is made meaningful only when the individual has a connection beyond himself. Malamud suggests that only through a right relationship with God, through obeying The Law of helping others, will one realize one's connection with man and find one's own core.

*Sources for Further Study*

Baumbach, Jonathan. *The Landscape of Nightmare: Studies in the Contemporary American Novel*, 1965.
Field, Leslie A., and Joyce W. Field. *Bernard Malamud: A Collection of Critical Essays*, 1975.
_____ . *Bernard Malamud and the Critics*, 1970.
Hershinow, Sheldon J. *Bernard Malamud*, 1980.
Richman, Sidney. *Bernard Malamud*, 1966.

*Lisa M. Schwerdt*

# AT PLAY IN THE FIELDS OF THE LORD

*Author:* Peter Matthiessen (1927-    )
*Type of plot:* Naturalistic adventure
*Time of plot:* The early 1960's
*Locale:* Oriente State, a fictional province in an unnamed South American country in the Amazon jungle
*First published:* 1965

*Principal characters:*
BORONAI, the chief of the Niaruna Indian tribe
LES HUBEN, a Protestant missionary from the United States who wishes to convert the Niaruna
ANDY HUBEN, his wife
MARTIN QUARRIER, Huben's assistant missionary
HAZEL QUARRIER, his wife
BILLY QUARRIER, his nine-year-old son
COMMANDANTE GUZMÁN, the military governor of Oriente, who plans to attack the Niaruna
LEWIS MOON, a mercenary soldier and a Cheyenne Indian
WOLFIE, Moon's fellow mercenary
PINDI, Moon's Niaruna lover
AEORE, a Niaruna shaman and rival of Boronai
UYUYU (YOYO), a Niaruna converted to Christianity

*The Novel*

*At Play in the Fields of the Lord* has the plot elements of stereotypical nineteenth century colonial novels and twentieth century Hollywood adventure films. The discovery of a savage Indian tribe, living in a remote and dangerous jungle, brings a handful of whites to a decrepit town on the edge of *terra incognita*. An ambitious and ruthless military commander competes with ne'er-do-well mercenaries and intrepid missionaries to establish first contact with the savages. All must battle the elements—oppressive heat and an unhealthy jungle—as well as resist the temptations of drink, which relieves boredom, and of forbidden passion, which eases loneliness.

The novel is not, however, a typical adventure tale. Matthiessen employs these romantic elements only to invert them. The Indians of this novel, the Niaruna, may be primitive by modern standards, but they are not savage, especially in comparison to the whites who would bring them "civilization." The outcome of the adventure will not be typical: These whites will discover, not some lost treasure, forgotten city, or secret of life, but the dark reality of their own hearts. One fortunate intruder will discover a small light amid the darkness.

Matthiessen constructs the tale around two contrasting protagonists, Martin Quarrier and Lewis Moon. Quarrier is a missionary, Moon a mercenary soldier. Quarrier is a white Anglo-Saxon Protestant, Moon a Cheyenne Indian. Quarrier comes to Oriente to propagate the Gospel, Moon to bomb the inhabitants into submission. Though they start the novel with opposite intentions, the plot leads them to one moment of common purpose and understanding before they discover their destinies.

The first half of the novel prepares the protagonists to meet the Niaruna. When Quarrier arrives at the capital city of Madre de Dios, he is anxious to begin his missionary work. He seems well supported by his wife, Hazel, and son, Billy, as well as by his coworkers, Les and Andy Huben. From the start, however, Quarrier is uneasy. Hazel quickly grows lethargic and fearful. Les Huben's idea of conversion seems superficial. Andy Huben unwittingly arouses Quarrier's sexual interest. No one except Billy seems as anxious to learn about the Niaruna's culture and language as does Martin Quarrier.

Madre de Dios is no more hospitable to Lewis Moon. His employer, Commandante Guzmán, is imperious but stupid. His partner Wolfie attends to—and is content with—the alcohol and whores of the town. The presence of missionaries fills Moon with uneasy memories of the proselytizers who controlled the Cheyenne reservation where he spent an unhappy, degraded youth. When a Niaruna shoots an arrow at the airplane during a reconnaissance flight, Moon is awed by the Indian's bravery. That night, Moon steals away from Madre de Dios.

In the second half of the novel, Quarrier and Moon contact the Niaruna. Quarrier reopens an abandoned station along the river, and Moon parachutes into the Indian village. Quarrier intends to preach; Moon plans to help the Niaruna resist.

Quarrier's efforts are futile. The Niaruna, except for a handful of the timid and weak, avoid the missionary's enticements. Hazel becomes virtually catatonic with fear. Billy dies of a fever, but Les interprets Quarrier's loss by declaring it God's means to convert the heathen. Quarrier begins to despair: At best, he attracts "rice Christians," converts who profess Christianity to gain tools, food, and trinkets.

Moon fits in surprisingly easily with the Niaruna. He becomes Kisu-Mu, a being descended from heaven, a god-man with inexplicable links to the divine. Boronai, the Niaruna's headman, befriends Moon and teaches him the ways of the tribe, even allowing his woman Pindi to become Moon's lover. A jungle diet and strenuous activity soon harden Moon's body. Most Niaruna quickly accept Kisu-Mu as part of their world—all except Aeore, who shot the arrow at Moon's plane earlier. Aeore quietly awaits the chance to show that Kisu-Mu is not a god.

At the climax of the novel, the paths of Moon and Quarrier intersect.

When Boronai dies of an influenza, Aeore persuades the Niaruna to destroy the mission, and he plans a confederation with other tribes to resist the intruders. Moon risks his life to bring a warning. Huben calls for military intervention by Guzmán, but Quarrier seeks out the Niaruna to head off violence. The Indians spare his life, but during Guzmán's attack on the village, Quarrier is murdered by Uyuyu, a converted Indian among the attackers.

Moon, now outcast from two societies, hides in Boronai's funeral canoe and escapes into an incredible isolation: "He did not know within a thousand miles where he might be, nor on what river, nor in what country."

## The Characters

Just as the plot does not fulfill the romantic expectations of the adventure story, so too the characters of *At Play in the Fields of the Lord* belie the stereotypes and idealizations of romantic characters. Matthiessen's characters are naturalistic creatures whose behavior is usually determined by environment.

The environment in which the characters move, the jungle and the river towns upon its fringes, are overwhelming and hostile physical presences. This description of Madre de Dios typifies the difficult stage upon which these actors must play out their fates: It "formed a yellow scar in the green waste. With its litter of rust and rotting thatch and mud, the capital of Oriente State resembled a great trash heap, smoking sullenly in the monotony of rivers." The landscape is the antagonist of everyone in the novel; it constantly assaults the senses and the spirits of these characters. Ultimately the landscape triumphs over both the indigenous and the intruders.

The Niaruna are creatures of the rain forest who resist easy labeling. They are not noble savages inhabiting some remote and primeval Eden: The jungle is too harsh to be a garden. By hunting and cultivating, the Niaruna find enough to live on, but no surplus. The Indians are constantly alert to combat the dangers from animals, poisonous plants, and rival tribes. Their humanity is fragile: As Aeore points out to Moon, the Niaruna paint their bodies because, in the jungle, how else can human beings distinguish themselves from the animals?

On the other hand, though primitive in technology and social organization by the intruders' standards, the Niaruna are neither ignorant barbarians nor Satan worshipers. They have adapted ingeniously to the rhythm of the jungle, knowledgeably working the land in both dry season and rainy season, cunningly harvesting the river in its rising and falling stages. The Niaruna possess a stoic philosophy that enables them to accept privation, injury, and death without self-pity. Moon marvels, for example, at the quiet dignity of the Indians as Boronai, on his deathbed, receives a last respectful visit from each tribesman.

The citizens of Madre de Dios also reflect their environment. As unpleasant as the jungle, the town is at least less dangerous, but the lack of danger seems to foster inertia and decay. Freed from the necessity to wrest a daily living from the jungle, the townspeople are content to get drunk and to fornicate. Guzmán and Father Xantes, its leading citizens, possess more energy but are no less degenerate: Guzmán uses his energy to tyrannize over the townspeople; Xantes abstains from grosser pleasures, yet he abstains, too, from active pastoral care. He is content to bear silent witness to the sufferings of humanity.

The North American missionaries, who have come to transform the Niaruna, find themselves transformed by the jungle and the Indians. Utterly repelled by the constant physical realities of procreation and death, Hazel retreats into sullen passivity. Stung by resistance to his energetic pastoral work, Les hypocritically interprets misery and failure as happiness and progress: In his newsletters, he conjures unwarranted hope from the senseless death of Billy and the accidental martyrdom of Quarrier. Quarrier learns that the jungle accentuates his physical limitations (clumsiness, poor sight, low stamina) even as it challenges his assumptions about conversion. Only Andy seems little affected; she pays more attention to consoling the others as the environment's demands drain them.

Of the missionaries, only Andy Huben and Martin Quarrier engage the reader's interest. They show some capacity to learn and some humility in abandoning the prejudices with which they arrived. They alone express some sympathy with the Niaruna and antipathy for the fate they help to bring upon the Indians. Andy is an underdeveloped character, however, and Quarrier is physically unattractive; neither gains much sympathy with readers. Quarrier is something of a tragic figure, a man doomed to suffer by his own limitations as well as fate. He is an admirable man, capable of transcendence, but events overwhelm him before he can act on his insight. The reader feels a sense of loss at his death because someone valuable, some ultimately (though not thoroughly) good has been defeated.

The soldiers of fortune, as dissolute as the missionaries are respectable, are more interesting and adaptable characters. Wolfie is unkempt, uncouth, and likable, a Falstaffian type who is admirable despite his qualities. He is at least honest about his ignoble ambitions.

Initially Moon is as unsavory as Wolfie, but he grows as the novel proceeds. Moon becomes the center of the novel because he bridges the worlds of North and South and because, like Quarrier, his encounter with the Niaruna leads him to abandon the goal which brought him to Oriente. Like Quarrier, too, Moon wins more of the reader's sympathy as he loses the sympathy of the other characters in the story. Moon moves closer to the Niaruna than any other character by becoming one of them and accepting the discipline of the jungle.

An Indian at heart, Moon alone lives well in isolation; he alone can sense the harmony which exists between man and a harsh environment. The novel ends with Moon transfigured: "Laid naked to the sun, he felt himself open like an enormous flower. Soon he slept. At dark he built an enormous fire, in celebration of the only man beneath the eye of heaven." Moon is a comic figure, in the classic sense, who defeats his antagonists and finds his place in the scheme of things.

### Themes and Meanings

Many of the novel's initial reviewers noted its similarities to the works of Joseph Conrad. It seemed to echo *Nostromo* (1904) and *Heart of Darkness* (1902) in its evocation of the encounter between white Europeans and primitive societies or hostile environments. Certainly there is something Conradian about the dark atmosphere of the book, its depiction of a gloomy, sullen landscape inhabited by moral wretches. Les, Quarrier, Andy, Xantes, and Guzmán are Conradian characters whose glimpses into the dark jungle are glimpses—for the reader if not for themselves—into the dark world of their own hearts.

*At Play in the Fields of the Lord* goes beyond Conrad, however, in its presentation of the Niaruna and in its character of Moon. The Niaruna are presented with an anthropologist's goal of objectivity and a naturalist's instinct for appreciation more than with a novelist's eye toward symbolism. Though primitive, the Niaruna are clearly superior to the societies (the town, faraway North America) which Guzmán, the Hubens, and the Quarriers represent. The Niaruna are not ideal: Pindi, after she bears twins, buries the female so that the male will have a better chance of survival. At the same time, however, the Niaruna lack the imperialistic impulses of the Commandante as well as the equally imperialistic religious vision of the missionaries.

Though the novel could be read as an attack on the cultural egotism of missionary work, its central theme is the irreconcilable nature of the cultures which fatally interact. The worlds of the Niaruna and of the intruders are immediately separated by language (the missionaries never do learn much of Niaruna speech) and geography. More important, they are separated by ethics, theology, and morality. Most important, they look across a gulf of thinking and feeling. The oneness with nature that Moon experiences at the conclusion is not a philosophical insight but an immersion in a way of being. Symbolically Moon is alone: Even if he had sympathetic company, he could no more explain how he feels as an Indian than he could explain aerodynamics to Aeore, challenger of planes.

The thematic function of the influenza which kills Boronai and infects the tribe (with apparent fatal effects past the time of the novel) is to express this unbridgeable gap. Ironically, the influenza was carried to the tribe by Moon, the man most eager to help. He in turn caught it from Andy, the missionary who meant no one harm. Even biology seems determined to oppose intermeshing the primitive and the civilized.

*Critical Context*

*At Play in the Fields of the Lord* signaled the coming together of Matthiessen's two interest, the literary and the anthropological. Before 1965, he had published three novels on themes and in styles typical of a postwar novelist: a coming-of-age tale in *Race Rock* (1954), the making of a young revolutionary in *Partisans* (1955), and a study of human evil in *Raditzer* (1961). Beginning with *Wild Life in America* (1959), Matthiessen wrote several anthropological works on remote areas on the globe; the major ones before 1965 concern South America in *The Cloud Forest: Chronicle of the South American Wilderness* (1961) and New Guinea in *Under the Mountain Wall: A Chronicle of Two Seasons in the Stone Age* (1962).

The themes of the anthropological books echo the themes of *At Play in the Fields of the Lord*. Matthiessen chronicles the disappearance of primitive ways of life as well as primitive ways of apprehending reality and understanding experience. Civilization's thought patterns, as well as its technology and bureaucracy, threaten prior ways of enacting the natural harmony of man and nature.

The attempt to portray this conflict of ways of thinking has led Matthiessen to technical experiments in *At Play in the Fields of the Lord* and in a later book *Far Tortuga* (1975). Both books use surrealistic devices (the abandonment of traditional grammar, synesthesia, the depiction of impression rather than sequential events) to immerse readers in new patterns of perception. *Far Tortuga* is much more surrealistic; in *At Play in the Fields of the Lord*, the experimental passages treat Moon's consciousness, the imagery of the landscapes, and the Niaruna's sense of experience.

*Sources for Further Study*

Cobbs, John L. "Peter Matthiessen," in *Critical Survey of Long Fiction*, 1983.

Karl, Frederick. *American Fictions, 1940-1980: A Comprehensive History and Critical Evaluation*, 1983.

*Robert M. Otten*

# AUNT JULIA AND THE SCRIPTWRITER

*Author:* Mario Vargas Llosa (1936-      )
*Type of plot:* Comic realism
*Time of plot:* The 1950's
*Locale:* Lima, Peru
*First published: La tía Julia y el escribidor*, 1977 (English translation, 1982)

*Principal characters:*
MARIO, the protagonist, partial narrator, radio journalist, and
   writer
AUNT JULIA, Mario's aunt by marriage, a divorcée who is
   fourteen years Mario's senior, and whom he finally marries
PEDRO CAMACHO, the Bolivian scriptwriter, a "one-man in-
   dustry," whose scripts form a second pattern of narration

*The Novel*

*Aunt Julia and the Scriptwriter* is a comedic novel about the education of young Mario (called variously Marito and Varguitas) that combines numerous elements of Vargas Llosa's own life with the fictional relationship with Aunt Julia and Pedro Camacho in Lima in the 1950's to form an autobiographical fable of identity that is neither autobiography nor history but rather an artistically rendered portrait of the artist as a young man. The primary narrator of the work, Mario, recounts, from a distance of at least twelve years later, his youthful love for his aunt by marriage, their improbable courtship and hilarious attempts to circumvent the law to get married, and his own life as a law student, radio newswriter, and would-be short-story writer. Each of the novel's twenty chapters, except the last two, which conclude Mario's narrative, are arranged so that the odd-numbered ones are Mario's attempts to describe his life and fortunes and the even-numbered ones are actual scripts of soap operas by Pedro Camacho, the indefatigable and prolific Bolivian scriptwriter.

The work begins with a semiserious Mario introducing himself as a student and news director of Radio Panamerica, the lesser of Lima's two radio stations owned by the Genaro family, with the importation of Pedro Camacho from Bolivia to write original radio serials to replace those which the Genaros brought from Cuba, and with the arrival of the newly divorced Aunt Julia, also from Bolivia. Mario's initial encounters with Camacho and Julia are equally unpromising but turn out, in true melodramatic fashion, to be important first steps in forming a professional bond between Mario and the scriptwriter and a very personal one with Aunt Julia.

The story of the furtive courtship between Mario and Julia is the central portion of Mario's narrative, as the two fall quite hopelessly, passionately, and madly in love with each other. Their love, when it is finally discovered after their ill-starred elopement, brings down upon them a family catastrophe that competes, in all of its absurdity and odd manifestations, with elements of Camacho's soap operas, the stories which are recounted antiphonally throughout the novel. Indeed, the comedy of errors of their elopement—they dash about the countryside to find a mayor who will, for a bribe, marry the underage Mario without parental consent—has exactly enough improbability about it to make it truly resemble the vicissitudes of real life. So does life often resemble bad literature and B-pictures.

Meanwhile, Pedro Camacho's soap operas make him the toast of Lima: The stories and the fortunes of their characters are on everyone's lips when Camacho begins to evidence signs of fatigue and then madness. His villains all turn out to be Argentines or Peruvians with Argentinian proclivities. Despite official protests to Radio Panamerica by the Argentine ambassador, Camacho persists in vilifying Argentina and its people. Far more serious is the growing bewilderment among his listeners: Characters who died in one serial are resurrected in another, sometimes with different professions; other characters move in and out of several serials; still others change their names in mid-script. Public confusion and dismay grow as, one by one, the principal continuing characters are killed off in one catastrophe after another until, after a series of disasters, each worse than the one before, all of fictional Lima is destroyed cataclysmically, and Camacho is finally committed to an insane asylum.

The work's final chapter serves as a neat conclusion to all the cliff-hanger questions about Mario's narrative and explains what has happened, over a twelve-year period, to Mario, Julia, Pedro Camacho, and lesser characters such as Pascual, Javier, and Big Pablito. In so doing, it serves both to provide a neat summary of much of the novel's action and to mark a decidedly new phase in Mario's fortunes.

*The Characters*

Mario is, despite the title, the principal focus of interest in the novel, which covers a brief period in his life and examines the widely different effects that both Julia and the scriptwriter have upon him. This novel of the education of a young man focuses not only upon his sensations and ideas but also upon his improbable actions and their sometimes hilarious consequences for him. Although several of the minor characters, chiefly his relatives and his companions at the radio station, do, in fact, have their own existences and concerns, one sees them predominantly through Mario's eyes and in relation to his own growth, concerns, and aspirations. In his painstaking characterization of his friends and relatives and in his precise details of the urban geography of Lima, Mario the narrator consistently views his environment personally, in relation to his sense of it and its meaning for him. In this sense, he is as much "the scriptwriter" of his own life, times, and place as Pedro Camacho is the scriptwriter of dozens of domestic and civil tragedies and melodramas of his contemporary Lima. Further, both Camacho and Mario are the creations of Mario the novelist.

As the young Mario makes his way through these few weeks and months of this extraordinary period in his life, he examines his journalistic apprenticeship at Radio Panamerica and the disparate writing assignments that he undertakes to help support Julia and himself as prologues to his Stephen Dedalus-like flight to the artistic Mecca where he aspires to work: Paris.

Pedro Camacho, the celebrated Bolivian scriptwriter who soon becomes a household word in Lima, is a prime example of one who creates his art for its own sake. Steeped in a devotion to his work that would have done credit to such prodigious creators of fictional worlds as Honoré de Balzac, Émile Zola, and Charles Dickens, Camacho finds his characters moving away from him, assuming independent lives of their own, jumping from one serial to another, and finally ending in chaotic and apocalyptic episodes that evidence the deterioration and madness of their creator. Camacho is a highly comic character whose outrageous characters complement his own absurdly melodramatic view of himself and of life. It comes as an amusing but somewhat shocking revelation to Mario that Camacho begins to dress like his characters, male and female, so that he can better interpret them in his stories. It is a darker and more sober revelation that Camacho has a wife who is Argentine and who keeps food on their table through utterly unromantic prostitution.

Of great interest, at times of greater interest than Mario, is the wonderful Aunt Julia, as perfect a foil to the numerous stereotypes of Spanish American Princesses (SAP's) as can be found in Latin American fiction written by men. Independent, witty, beautiful, intelligent, resourceful, charming, arch, and eminently commonsensical, the thirty-two-year-old Julia entirely captivates the young Mario, concedes to a marriage on the condition that it will last at least five years, and shares his dreams, hardships, difficulties, and ultimately his achievement of the goal to live the life of a writer. In the wry final chapter one learns that the marriage really was a success and lasted longer than "all the parents and even she herself had feared, wished or predicted: eight years." At this point Julia fades, her function in the work now accomplished. With her fades a time of hope and joy in Mario's narrative; the remainder is the "real" world of his present in a new and ostensibly confining marriage and in a sentimental journey back to Lima and the reacquaintance with former friends and the much altered scriptwriter.

## Themes and Meanings

The central theme of the work, clearly a *Bildungsroman* in nature, is the act of writing, of telling one's story and a succession of stories. The novel's

epigraph, from Salvador Elizondo's *El grafógrafo* (1972), is a perfect introduction to the work and a classical statement of the metaphysical and epis-
temological state of contemporary literature in which writers write about
writing about writing and invite readers to imagine them imagining themselves writing about writing. Surely an invitation to formalist and decon-
structive critical interpretation, the epigraph reinforces the perfect Viconian
circularity of the novel, in which Mario the narrator is a character of Mario
the novelist and in which both are writing about being writers and about
one notorious writer, the tireless but insane scriptwriter, whose creations are
also those of Mario the novelist.

All other elements of the novel—the themes of romance, uproariously
amusing misadventures, accidental meetings, amorous assignations, love unrequited and gloriously requited, ambition and entertainment—are subservient to the overmastering passions of Mario, Pedro, and the novelist to me-
morialize experience, fictionalize life, and artfully reinvent identity. The
final chapter is, again, supremely important in setting several records as
straight as they can be in Mario's narrative, in the supposed events and motives of Pedro Camacho's life and works, and in the ultimately enigmatic life
and adventures of the ineluctable Aunt Julia.

*Critical Context*

*Aunt Julia and the Scriptwriter* has been variously hailed as a "ribald classic," a pure example of the "literature of exhaustion" that reflects upon itself, and a postmodern novel that ratifies Vargas Llosa's early preeminence
in *el boom latino americano* of the 1960's and 1970's. It is likely to become
an international classic and one of the basic works upon which Vargas
Llosa's literary reputation will ultimately rest. Unlike most of his previous
and subsequent novels (especially *La guerra del fin del mundo,* 1981; *The
War of the End of the World,* 1984), it is a distinctly comic work, handled
with a light touch, testimony to his versatile imagination.

Indeed, Vargas Llosa has produced a consistently first-rate series of
works in the fields of criticism, journalism, fiction, and drama, explicating
and elucidating the varied facets of Latin American life and culture both to
fellow Latin Americans and to an increasing number of European and
North American readers. While he shares, surely and clearly, the "magical
realism" of such pioneering figures as Gabriel García Márquez and Julio
Cortázar, he has transmuted this technique into a more immediately accessible form of fiction that has been widely accepted in the last half of the
twentieth century.

*Sources for Further Study*
*America.* CXLVII (October 23, 1982), pp. 237-238.
*Newsweek.* C (August 30, 1982), pp. 65-66.

"Peruvian Soap Opera," in *The New York Times Book Review*. LXXXVII,
   no. 15 (August 1, 1982), p. 1.
Prieto, René. "The Two Voices in Mario Vargas Llosa's *Aunt Julia and the
   Scriptwriter*," in *Latin American Literary Review*. XI, no. 22 (Spring /
   Summer, 1983), pp. 15-25.
Ruas, C. "A Talk with Mario Vargas Llosa," in *The New York Times Book
   Review*. LXXXVII (August 1, 1982), p. 15.

*John J. Conlon*

# AURA

*Author:* Carlos Fuentes (1928-      )
*Type of plot:* Gothic fantasy
*Time of plot:* The early 1960's
*Locale:* Mexico City
*First published:* 1962 (English translation, 1965)

> *Principal characters:*
> FELIPE MONTERO, a young historian
> CONSUELO LLORENTE, an extremely old woman
> AURA, her beautiful young niece

*The Novel*

The fantastic nature of this short novel is indicated at its very beginning when Felipe Montero, an indigent young man, reads a newspaper advertisement requesting the services of a historian. The advertisement is so suited to his own experience, needs, and skills that it seems to be addressed to him and to no one else; all that is missing is his name. This sense of Montero's being especially summoned by the advertisement is further emphasized when he arrives at an ancient mansion in the old section of town where no one lives. As he enters the door, he takes one last look to try to "retain some single image of that indifferent outside world," before entering a realm of magic and imagination.

Although the incredibly old Consuelo Llorente ostensibly wishes Montero to edit the memoirs of her dead husband for publication, one suspects that she has other, more profound plans for the young historian. Indeed, with the appearance of her beautiful young niece, Aura, who immediately exerts a hypnotic hold on Montero, the reader's suspicion that this is a sort of modern fairy tale or parable is confirmed. The mysterious, old, witchlike crone, the quietly beautiful young girl, and the summoned young man establish an archetypal fairy-tale situation.

The house itself is typically gothic and always in darkness; the old woman's room is filled with religious relics and lighted only with votive candles; in private she engages in occult rituals and makes entreaties to Gabriel to sound his trumpet. She continually caresses a pet rabbit, whose name is Saga, and the trunk which contains her dead husband's papers seems always covered with rats. Montero feels a pleasure in the house that he has never felt before, a feeling that he always knew was a part of him but that has never been set free. He decides that the old woman has some secret power over her niece, and he is obsessed with the desire not only to set her free but also to possess her himself. Consuelo's witchlike nature is further emphasized when, as Montero studies her husband's papers, he discovers that she must be at least 109 years old.

The mystery of the relationship between Consuelo and her niece deepens when Montero sees Aura skinning a young goat in the kitchen and then goes to the old woman's room to find her performing the same skinning action in mime. When he dreams of Aura, he sees the old lady's image superimposed on the image of Aura. Although Montero believes that Aura is kept in the house to preserve the illusion of youth for the old woman, the truth of the matter is even more occult and mysterious. Aura seems to age each day. One day, she appears to be a girl of twenty, the next, a woman of forty. When Montero makes love to her, the act is prefaced by Aura's rubbing a wafer against her thighs and offering him half of it to eat. He falls upon her naked arms, which are stretched out on the side of the bed like the crucifix on the wall: "Aura opens up like an altar." To complete this carnal communion, she makes him promise to love her forever, even if she grows old and dies.

As the actions of Consuelo and Aura become more and more blended, as if one is an echo of the other, Montero realizes that the "sterile conception" of their lovemaking has created another double, his own other half which he now seeks. He finally discovers the secret of the old woman's relationship to Aura on the last page of old General Llorente's papers, where he reads of Consuelo's growing herbs which will perform the magic of creating Aura as an image of her own youth. Moreover, he discovers portraits of the young couple and realizes that the old woman is Aura, and that the old general is himself. Montero fears that the hand of the past will wipe away his own features, "the cardboard features that hid your true face, your real appearance, the appearance you once had but then forgot." He rejects the human vanity of clock time and accepts what seems fated to happen to him.

In the final scene of the novel, Montero goes to Consuelo's room and calls for Aura. The voice he hears from the darkness tells him that she is gone and will not come back: "I'm exhausted. She's already exhausted. I've never been able to keep her with me for more than three days." Montero tears off Aura's robe and embraces and kisses her. As the moonlight falls on her face, he discovers it to be as brittle and yellowed as the memoirs—to be the body and face of the old Consuelo. He accepts this, however, for he has promised to love Aura even when she is old. He embraces her and waits until the cloud covers the moon, when the "memory of youth, of youth reembodied, rules the darkness." In the last line of the story, Consuelo promises that Aura will come back again: "We'll bring her back together."

### The Characters

Because *Aura* is essentially a modern gothic romance, the characters of the story are not intended to be realistic, but rather representative. They are psychic archetypes in a parable of youth, love, age, and imagination.

Montero is the fairy-tale protagonist who is magically summoned to fulfill old Consuelo's desire—to recapture not only her own past, but also the past of her husband and of their love. Consuelo herself is one of Fuentes' witchlike women with the magical power of imaginative creation. The head-note to the novel, from Jules Michelet, emphasizes the power of female imaginative creation embodied in the story: "*Man hunts and struggles. Woman intrigues and dreams; she is the mother of fantasy, the mother of the gods. She has second sight, the wings that enable her to fly to the infinite of desire and the imagination.*" Aura is a self-created image of Consuelo, an imaginative projection of her own youth.

Essentially there are only two characters in the story: Aura/Consuelo and Montero/General Llorente, and neither is so much a character in the conventional sense of the term as an embodiment of an archetype—the former embodying Carl Jung's anima, or archetypal female, the latter the questing male figure who yearns to unite with, and know the secret of, the mysterious woman. Montero is drawn out of the world of external reality and into the unconscious world of the imagination and thus becomes one with the occult reality of Aura/Consuelo. This basic nature of the characters explains the mysterious blend of the occult and the erotic which dominates the story. The same character configuration and the same union of the sexual and the supernatural can be seen in the works of Henry James, Edgar Allan Poe, Alexander Pushkin, and Sir M. Rider Haggard. The basic dichotomy between the male and the female principle which *Aura* embodies is that whereas man hunts and struggles in the profane world of everyday reality, always questing for the answers to metaphysical mysteries, woman is the passive dreamer, the creator, who achieves the fulfillment of her desires by imaginative creation.

## Themes and Meanings

There are several levels of meaning in the novel. On one level, it is a love story in which the desires of youth and beauty triumph over the reality of old age and death. In a basic sense, this is a story of the power of pure desire to overcome the limitations of external reality. On the unconscious level, it is an archetypal parable about the male who is seduced into the loss of the ego, which enables him to enter completely into the world of the woman, for it is indeed the imaginative reality of the female which constitutes both erotic and supernatural transcendence over the external world. Culturally, the story suggests a theme that Fuentes has explored in other works, the simultaneous existence of the old Mexico superimposed upon the new. In fact, "superimposition" is probably the key word for all of these themes, as, gradually, Aura is superimposed on Consuelo and Montero is superimposed on Consuelo's dead husband.

The novel is narrated in the second person, in the present tense, as if

Montero were recounting the events as they occur. For example, as he looks into the eyes of Aura for the first time, he sees them surge and change: "You look into them and tell yourself it isn't true. . . . But you can't deceive yourself: those eyes do surge, do change, as if offering you a landscape that only you can see and desire." This unusual narrative strategy not only creates a sense of gradually engulfing mystery, much like that in a detective novel, but also effectively eradicates Montero's own personal past and creates a sense of the presentness of the past. Moreover, the second-person narrative stance emphasizes both the concrete detail of Montero's experience and his growing sense of being lost in a dream reality. As he becomes engulfed in the eerie atmosphere of the old house, the reader becomes absorbed in the eerie tone of the novel itself.

As a historian, accustomed to studying the past as it is preserved in documents—a past, that is, kept at a certain distance—Montero finds himself drawn into a past that is maintained in the present by the imaginative creation of the old Consuelo—a past that is not preserved in historical texts but which lives in the mind and the reality of the other. Although he desires to take Aura outside the occult and hermetically sealed world of the old woman, the imagination and the realm of the sacred prove more powerful than external, profane reality.

The action of the novel hovers uneasily between reality and fantasy, as both Montero and the reader search futilely for realistic explanations for the mystery of Aura and the old Consuelo. Just as Montero is caught up in an increasingly occult reality, so also is the reader, who finally must accept the magical nature of the events and the ultimate reality of the imagination. The sense that the novel has of existing somewhere in between the real world and the world of the imagination is emphasized not only by the gothic house, the occult Aura, and the old Consuelo, but also by Montero's being caught up in obsessive dreams which become so blended with the fantastic nature of his actual experience that the two realms cannot be distinguished.

*Critical Context*

Although many of Fuentes' novels have been concerned with political and social reality, his short stories and novellas, or short novels, have more often been mythic and symbolic. *Aura* is perhaps his best-known work in which magic, the occult, and particularly the witch archetype are of central importance. In an earlier collection of short stories, *Los días enmascarados* (1954), the same witch figure appears, as does the prevailing theme developed in *Aura* of the dominance of the past over the present.

Various sources for the story have been noted by critics. Perhaps the most commonly mentioned are Henry James's *The Aspern Papers* (1888), Pushkin's *Pikovaya dama* (1934; *The Queen of Spades*, 1896), and Haggard's *She* (1887). The single most important source, however, as Fuentes himself has noted, is Jules Michelet's *La Sorcière* (1862; *The Witch of the Middle Ages*, 1863), in which a woman is depicted as a witch who has the ability to give birth to a being identical to herself.

*Aura* was practically ignored by reviewers when first published because it appeared almost at the same time as Fuentes' best-known and most controversial novel, *La muerte de Artemio Cruz* (1962; *The Death of Artemio Cruz*, 1964). Now, however, *Aura* is recognized as a central text in Fuentes' continuing exploration of history, myth, and the anima archetype, as well as a particularly fine example of the genre of the fantastic.

*Sources for Further Study*

Brody, Robert, and Charles Rossman, eds. *Carlos Fuentes: A Critical View*, 1982.
De Guzman, Daniel. *Carlos Fuentes*, 1972
Duran, Gloria B. *The Archetypes of Carlos Fuentes*, 1980.
Sommers, Joseph. *After the Storm*, 1968.

*Charles E. May*

# THE AUTOBIOGRAPHY OF AN EX-COLOURED MAN

*Author:* James Weldon Johnson (1871-1938)
*Type of plot:* Pseudoautobiography
*Time of plot:* Between the Civil War and World War I
*Locale:* Georgia, Connecticut, Florida, New York, Europe, and the rural
    South
*First published:* 1912

> *Principal characters:*
> THE ANONYMOUS PROTAGONIST, a scholar, musician, cigar
>     roller, gambler, traveling companion, and composer
> THE PROTAGONIST'S MOTHER
> RED and
> SHINEY, the protagonist's boyhood friends
> THE MILLIONAIRE, his benefactor

*The Novel*

*The Autobiography of an Ex-Coloured Man* is the psychological and literal odyssey of an anonymous protagonist as he discovers the fact and meaning of his blackness and ultimately decides to "pass." The facts of the narrative are those of James Weldon Johnson's own life, but the story is punctuated with long passages discussing the "Negro Question" as it was viewed in 1912, and the opinions expressed are undoubtedly those of the author. By writing the novel as an autobiography, the author attained a personal intensity which might have been lost in another form, but by inventing the protagonist and the plot, he allowed himself to include a panorama of black life in the early 1900's.

As a child in rural Georgia, the protagonist and his mother lead an idyllic life which is suddenly terminated by a move to Connecticut. Here, he abruptly learns from his teacher that he is black, a fact which his genteel upbringing and pale skin have hidden from him. As he adjusts to this information, he plunges himself into literature and music to find his identity and heritage. At a crucial point, his handsome white father comes to see him. The meeting greatly disturbs him, but it opens communication between him and his mother, who becomes a valuable source of information about black life and about his personal history. During his boyhood, he is influenced by two friends, "Red," a none-too-intelligent white boy, and "Shiney," a brilliant black boy who inspires pride in his ethnic heritage and encourages him to work for the betterment of his people.

With the death of his mother just before his high school graduation, he determines to return to the South to study at Atlanta University, but on his way, he is robbed of his carefully saved tuition. He goes on to Jacksonville,

Florida, where he becomes a cigar roller, learns Spanish, and makes insightful observations on black social life. Johnson surveys three classes of blacks—the menial laborers, who hate whites; the servants, who are affectionate toward whites and are treated with affection by them; and the professionals who are ignored by whites. In these passages, he foresees the turmoil of later generations and predicts the divisions which would later become apparent among blacks themselves.

After three years in the cigar factory, he makes his way to New York City, where he is quickly initiated into the "under life" of the gambling casinos. Indeed, gambling becomes his sole livelihood, and while immersed in the life of the club where he shoots craps nightly, he masters ragtime piano and meets a millionaire who becomes a patron of his music. While Johnson describes black life in New York through the eyes of a protagonist who is enchanted by the easy money of the crap table and the sophistication of the city's nightlife, he is careful to point out the dark side of the glittering surface, noting that many promising young blacks were beguiled by this lifestyle and never returned to productive lives.

The protagonist is rescued from this fate when he witnesses a murder and is taken to Europe by his millionaire benefactor. In Europe, he soaks in continental culture, languages, and art and becomes a polished gentleman, almost forgetting his black heritage until he glimpses his father in a Paris theater with a beautiful young girl—his half sister, he concludes. The tragedy of his separation from his family overwhelms him, and he once again begins to consider what contribution he might make, as a black man, to right this injustice. In Germany, he plays some ragtime for a group of musicians who immediately take the melodies and perform them in a classical style. This inspires him to return to the United States and become a composer, collecting black folk songs, spirituals, and slave songs.

Back home, he visits wealthy black families in Boston, Washington, and Atlanta, then ventures to Macon, Georgia, where he sets off on foot, ox cart, and mule to become acquainted with rural Southern blacks and to learn about their lives and music. This odyssey leads him to unexpected poverty and ignorance and causes him to question his attitudes towards blacks and Southern whites. Johnson writes relatively little about this adventure, claiming that the stereotype of the rural black in the log cabin is already the dominant image of blacks. He does give fascinating detail to his account of a religious meeting and his description of the song leader and preacher. The cadence and imagery of these passages foretell his later work, *God's Trombones* (1927).

In one seemingly typical village, the protagonist is awakened by the angry cries of a lynch mob. By dawn they have captured their black suspect, and mob psychology overwhelms them. As the protagonist looks on, they burn the man at the stake. The protagonist is appalled by this act of brutality and is ashamed to be associated with a race which can be treated worse than animals. In response, he denounces his blackness and returns immediately to New York to assume a new identity. He marries a white woman and dismisses his plan to make a contribution as a black musician. He has second thoughts only once, when he inadvertently encounters Shiney in a New York museum and learns that he has devoted his life to the advancement of blacks. He feels that he has sacrificed his place in history and concludes, "I cannot repress the thought that, after all, I have chosen the lesser part, that I have sold my birthright for a mess of pottage." Because the story is an odyssey, it has numerous climaxes, but the protagonist's final decision to become a white man is the real turning point and underscores Johnson's theme that the degradation of American blacks encouraged them to feign an Anglo-Saxon heritage.

### The Characters

The protagonist is the only fully drawn character in this unusual book. Introduced as an idealistic adolescent, he develops to some extent, and the novel traces his journey to an adulthood which brings a kind of success, yet a success tinged with doubt. Like Joe Christmas in William Faulkner's *Light in August* (1932), he confronts the fact of his mixed racial identity, but—although Johnson spends almost a chapter probing his adjustment—the passage lacks intensity and complexity. Throughout the novel, the protagonist passes a bit too easily between black and white identities, a facility which makes him lack the depth of a great character of fiction.

Given three-quarters of a century of hindsight, modern readers might also find it perplexing that the protagonist considers himself to be black because his mother is black even though his father is white. When he chooses to "pass," he seems to disguise himself as white rather than to accept the white part of his heritage. Culturally, he seems more white than black until his sojourn in the Florida cigar factory, where he learns, as he says, the "free masonry" of his race. Although the characterization lacks the depth of great fiction and the ideas are often dated, there is much in the life of the protagonist which is universal and much in the life of black America which is unchanged.

The protagonist's mother plays a major role in the early chapters and is a model of the long-suffering black mistress. Despite her submission to a white male, Johnson portrays her as a courageous, cultured, and loving woman without the sharp edge of someone fighting discrimination. She accepts her destiny and—at least in her son's eyes—seems not to be dissatisfied. Red and Shiney are mere caricatures placed in the novel as foils for the protagonist. Red because he cannot answer questions in class, asks for help from the protagonist, who thus is given the chance to demonstrate both his intelligence and his compassion. Shiney is the true black whose intelligence and rhetorical skills give the protagonist his first surges of racial identity and pride. Although he reappears near the end of the novel, he remains a stereotype, a symbol to the protagonist of the "road not taken."

The only other character that stands out in the odyssey is the millionaire, who—as his nameless title implies—is also undeveloped and whose function is to recognize the protagonist's musical ability and give him his first enticement to become (or actually to remain) white. Other characters, such as the porter who steals the protagonist's money, his cigar-rolling comrades, and even his wife, are scenery in the ongoing saga. Like any episodic novel, *The Autobiography of an Ex-Coloured Man* introduces far more characters than it develops; nevertheless, it gives a comprehensive introduction to the variety of black life-styles that existed in 1912, and this is a significant contribution.

*Themes and Meanings*

Some of the themes of *The Autobiography of an Ex-Coloured Man* seem like truisms today but were, no doubt, remarkable revelations in 1912. One purpose of the novel is to depict the wide variety of life-styles of American blacks—to illustrate the concept that not all blacks are alike. To accomplish this, Johnson takes his character to an unprejudiced yet somewhat uncaring New England, to the inner city of Atlanta, to a prosperous and robust Jacksonville, to the darkly glamorous New York, and to the dangerous and romantic heart of the rural South. He examines black life among manual laborers and vagrants; among servants, porters, and seamstresses; and among a newly emerging professional class. Through his survey, he shows blacks working for survival, for the good life of easy money, and for acceptance as professionals, demonstrating that the variety of humankind exists within the black race.

Johnson also examines relations between blacks and whites in a variety of contexts. During his Connecticut childhood, he experiences very little prejudice. In Atlanta, he learns the reality of segregation, and in New York, he experiences the phenomenon of being a kind of entertainment for well-to-do whites. His best friends in the novel—Red and the millionaire—are white, yet he also graphically describes the lynching of a black man by a white mob. In the short span of the novel, he portrays the complex gamut of race relations which still exist, from the camaraderie of friends who know nothing about ethnic barriers, to the affection between white master and black servant, to the hatred of individual blacks by Northerners and the hatred of the race by Southerners. Johnson probes each of these relationships, and it is in this probing that his book has its greatness.

A final theme presented by Johnson, but with less interest to modern readers, is the phenomenon of "passing." In the "Preface to the Original Edition of 1912," the publisher (Sherman, French and Co.) comments,

"These pages . . . reveal the unsuspected fact that prejudice against the Negro is exerting a pressure which, in New York and other large cities where the opportunity is open, is actually and constantly forcing an unascertainable number of fair-complexioned coloured people over into the white race." With the resurgence of black pride, "passing" has become much less an issue than it might have been in 1912. Nevertheless, the guilt and doubt surrounding the protagonist's decision to become white provide much of the drama and lasting emotional appeal of the book. The fact that he is motivated by his shame over the lynching rather than by personal desire for success or fear also give the book more intensity and interest.

*Critical Context*

The *Autobiography of an Ex-Coloured Man*, James Weldon Johnson's first book, was published anonymously, perhaps to add to the sense that it was truly an autobiography of someone who had passed into white society. At the time of its publication, it was virtually the only account of black Americans' attitudes toward whites and toward one another. Johnson's book was preceded, it is true, by *Up from Slavery* (1900) and *The Souls of Black Folks* (1903), yet neither of these classics scans as broad a panorama of black life as does *The Autobiography of an Ex-Coloured Man*. As pointed out by Carl Van Vechten in the introduction to the 1927 edition, it was the first book by any novelist to touch on such topics as miscegenation, black uses of humor, facets of the black personality, black reactions to Jim Crow laws, color snobbery among blacks themselves, black rhetoric, and ragtime.

Woven throughout the novel are statements of Johnson's belief that blacks have made a significant contribution to American culture, a theme he was to pursue in subsequent books. Unlike his protagonist, Johnson did compile information about spirituals and, with his brother, published two volumes. He also captured the rhythm of black oratory in his well-known book *God's Trombones*, and he collected the works of other black poets in *The Book of American Negro Poetry* (1922). He also became a spokesman for the validity of the black aesthetic, a theme which he introduced in *The Autobiography of an Ex-Coloured Man*. In short, this novel was a monumental achievement for a black writer at the turn of the century; it broke new ground for topics in literature, began to establish black writers of fiction, and laid the groundwork for Johnson's championship of the black aesthetic which flowered during the Harlem Renaissance. At the time of its publication, *The Autobiography of an Ex-Coloured Man* pulled aside a veil and gave the reader "a view of the inner life of the Negro in America." Behind that veil, contemporary readers can still find truth and meaning.

*Sources for Further Study*

Collier, Eugenia. "The Endless Journey of an Ex-Coloured Man," in

*Phylon.* XXXII (Winter, 1971), pp. 365-373.

Fleming, Robert E. "Contemporary Themes in Johnson's *The Autobiography of an Ex-Coloured Man*," in *Negro American Literature Forum.* IV (Winter, 1970), pp. 120-124, 141.

Garret, Marvin P. "Early Recollections and Structural Irony in *The Autobiography of an Ex-Coloured Man*," in *Critique: Studies in Modern Fiction.* December, 1971, pp. 5-14.

"Irony As a Key to Johnson's *The Autobiography of an Ex-Coloured Man*," in *American Literature.* XLIII (March, 1971), pp. 83-96.

Ross, Stephen. "Audience and Irony in Johnson's *The Autobiography of an Ex-Coloured Man*," in *College Language Association Journal.* XVIII (December, 1974), pp. 198-210.

*Carolyn Dirksen*

# THE AUTOBIOGRAPHY OF MISS JANE PITTMAN

*Author:* Ernest J. Gaines (1933-    )
*Type of plot:* Historical novel
*Time of plot:* The mid-1860's to the early 1960's
*Locale:* Rural Louisiana
*First published:* 1971

*Principal characters:*
MISS JANE PITTMAN, the protagonist, a black farm worker
COLONEL BROWN, a Yankee soldier who gives Jane her first name
NED, Jane's adopted son, a militant follower of Frederick Douglass
ALBERT CLUVEAU, A Cajun hit man, who kills Ned
JOE PITTMAN, Jane's husband, a horse trainer, who is killed by a wild stallion
ROBERT SAMSON, the owner of the plantation where Jane works during her later years
TEE BOB, Robert's son, who kills himself for love of a partially black girl
MARY AGNES LE FABRE, a schoolteacher on the Samson plantation, the girl whom Tee Bob loves
JIMMY, a young civil rights leader on the Samson plantation, who is killed by white racists
THE NARRATOR, a black high school history teacher

*The Novel*

  *The Autobiography of Miss Jane Pittman* was first published in 1971 when the racial turmoil of the 1960's was still fresh in the minds of American readers. Like many writers of historical fiction, Ernest J. Gaines sought not only to illuminate the past but also to use it to comment on the present. To accomplish these twin goals, he structures his novel around the life of a black woman who is born into slavery and lives to see the dawning of the civil rights movement a hundred years later. Although the story line is episodic, it is held together by the personality and voice of Miss Jane herself.

  The ostensible narrator of the novel is a black high school teacher who interviews Miss Jane, now well past one hundred years old, for an oral history project. (During the time that Gaines was writing this novel, there was much discussion of the need for black history.) After the first few pages, however, the narrator fades from the scene and Miss Jane takes over. With an amazing ear for dialect and the cadences of spoken language, Gaines creates a compelling storyteller in the person of Miss Jane.

When the reader first meets Gaines's protagonist, she is a slave girl named Ticey working on a Louisiana plantation in the waning days of the Civil War. A Yankee soldier named Brown stops for a drink of water, befriends her, and tells her that she should discard the name of Ticey and replace it with a more attractive one such as Jane. From that time on, she calls herself Jane Brown. (This prompts her mistress to beat her in an effort to get her to respond to her slave name, a motif that Alex Haley would later "borrow" in his depiction of Kunta Kinte in *Roots*.) After the Emancipation, all the former slaves begin changing their names. Readers in the early 1970's would have seen a parallel between this and the predilection of many contemporaneous blacks to adopt Islamic or African names.

Whereas Ticey was a mischievous slave girl who resembled the impish Topsy in Harriet Beecher Stowe's novel *Uncle Tom's Cabin* (1852), Jane becomes—at an early age—a self-reliant young woman. Not only does she assume responsibility for herself, but she also cares for a young boy named Ned, whose mother is beaten to death by racist vigilantes. As Jane becomes a foster mother to Ned, she ceases to resemble Topsy and reminds the reader more of Stowe's Eliza, the mother who grabs her child and flees North to freedom. Like Eliza, Jane is headed toward Ohio (where Colonel Brown lives), but unlike the mother in *Uncle Tom's Cabin*, she eventually abandons the illusion that the North is a promised land and spends the balance of her life in Louisiana. The catalyst for her disillusionment with Yankee benevolence is the withdrawal of Northern soldiers and bureaucrats from the South. If Confederate apologists such as Thomas Dixon, Jr., and Margaret Mitchell saw Reconstruction as a rape of the glorious Southland, Gaines depicts it as the one brief moment of freedom and prosperity for Southern blacks. When it is over, the Yankees prove themselves not saviors but opportunists.

Jane also has a more personal reason for remaining in the South. She has met and fallen in love with a horse trainer named Joe Pittman. She becomes his common-law wife and keeps his name for the rest of her life. When Joe brings in a menacing wild stallion one day, Jane goes to a conjure woman to find out if the horse will kill Joe. In an effort to protect her husband, Jane opens the corral and lets the horse go. Like the characters in Greek tragedy (for example *Oedipus Rex*), Jane ironically accomplishes what she tries to prevent. It should also be noted that in this episode Gaines is forthright and respectful in his treatment of black superstition and folk magic. What a sophisticated black writer of an earlier generation might have concealed or minimized had become a valued part of the ethnic identity blacks of the 1960's and 1970's were seeking to assert.

Of Jane's many other experiences, the most crucial are probably the deaths of two other men. After the Spanish-American War, Ned returns to Louisiana to preach the gospel of Frederick Douglass. (Years before, the

Ku Klux Klan had run him out of the region because of his efforts to educate poor blacks.) When he gives a fiery speech about racial dignity and assertiveness, the local powers hire Albert Cluveau (a Cajun hit man) to murder Ned. Then, more than a half century later, a young man named Jimmy emerges as a civil rights leader and follower of Martin Luther King, Jr. He is a native of the Samson plantation (where Jane has worked since shortly after Ned's death), and all there sense that he will be the leader destined to set his people free. When he, like Ned, is murdered by white racists, the 110-year-old Jane Pittman takes up Jimmy's cause. The novel closes as she is heading to town to drink from a "whites-only" water fountain.

## The Characters

In commenting on earlier Southern novels, Gaines has said:

Whenever a black person was mentioned in these novels, either she was a Mammy, or he was a Tom; and if he was young, he was a potential Tom, a good nigger, or he was not a potential Tom, a bad nigger. When a black woman character was young, she was either a potential mammy or a nigger wench. For most of these writers, choosing something between was unheard of.

One of Gaines's purposes in *The Autobiography of Miss Jane Pittman* was to create the sort of three-dimensional black character who, with the possible exception of William Faulkner's Dilsey, is missing from the fiction of white Southern writers.

Miss Jane is clearly neither a mammy nor a wench. Although she gets along reasonably well with certain whites, her maternal feelings are reserved for members of her own race. (Unlike Mammy in Margaret Mitchell's *Gone with the Wind*, she feels no loyalty to the Confederacy and leaves her former owners as soon as Emancipation is announced.) Although no wench, she loved Joe Pittman and casually mentions having lived with two or three lesser men during her 110 years. She is a realist and a survivor, but she is also willing to take risks when her dignity is at stake. It is perhaps significant that the black men she admires most are sports heroes such as Joe Louis and Jackie Robinson. The only white public figure of whom she speaks approvingly is Louisiana governor Huey P. Long. As Miss Jane puts it: "When he said nigger he said, 'Here a book, nigger. Go read your name.' When the other ones said nigger, they said, 'Here a sack, nigger. Go pick that cotton.'"

Throughout the late 1960's (when Gaines was writing this book), blacks debated the proper stance to take toward the white power structure. Some counseled accommodation, other defiance. Gaines comments on this issue through the character of Miss Jane's adopted son, Ned. Siding with Frederick Douglass against Booker T. Washington, Ned argues that accommodation does not always guarantee survival and that blacks cannot ultimately respect themselves if they settle for less than full social equality. In his sermon by the river (which leads directly to his death), Ned even argues that as a last resort violence is sometimes necessary and justified.

The major white character in the novel is Robert Samson, the owner of the plantation on which Miss Jane works during her later years. On the surface, he appears to be the sort of gruff, paternalistic white Southerner who can deal with blacks because he knows and understands them. His racial conceit and sexual duplicity, however, prevent him from acknowledging his liaisons with black women or the children spawned by those liaisons. (When his son Tee Bob thinks that a white man might publicly love a less than purely white woman, his naïveté proves his undoing.) His implacable opposition to civil rights for blacks leads to a rift with Miss Jane that appears to be getting wider as the novel closes.

*Themes and Meanings*

In a variety of ways (some already suggested) Gaines is seeking to rewrite the Southern experience from a black perspective. One of the most intriguing episodes in the novel, however, examines the negative effects of white racism on nonracist whites. In American novels of race, one of the recurring motifs is that of interethnic rape. In *Uncle Tom's Cabin* and Alex Haley's *Roots* (1976), the aggressors are white males and the victims black women. In Thomas Dixon's *The Clansman* (1905) and Margaret Mitchell's *Gone with the Wind* (1936), it is black males who lust after white women. Hardly ever is interracial sex depicted as voluntary and normal. In the subplot concerning Tee Bob and Mary Agnes, Gaines forces the reader to reexamine this convention.

The son and heir of Robert Samson, Tee Bob commits the fatal error of falling in love with Mary Agnes Le Fabre, a partially black woman who teaches school on the Samson plantation. The other white men in the community are unable to persuade Tee Bob that black women exist for white men to seduce or to rape—but not to marry. Even the blacks (Mary Agnes included) realize the limits of what is socially acceptable. So much in love with Mary Agnes that he is unable to live without her, Tee Bob takes his own life—a white victim of white racism.

*Critical Context*

Although the significance of *The Autobiography of Miss Jane Pittman* has been somewhat obscured by the even more phenomenal success of *Roots*, Gaines's tale was the first rendering of the black experience to appeal to a wide biracial American audience. (For Gaines, as for Haley, this audience was reached primarily through a television adaptation. The initial existence of a popular book, however, was crucial—it is difficult to imagine a black epic conceived originally for television.) After the turmoil and acrimony of the 1960's, it was a time for racial healing in the United States.

In describing his black character Dilsey (and by implication her race in general), William Faulkner wrote: "They endured." In his Nobel Prize speech, Faulkner expressed his belief that man would not only endure but prevail. In Miss Jane Pittman, Ernest J. Gaines has created a character who does both. Whereas Dilsey was an adjunct to the story of the white Compson family in *The Sound and the Fury* (1929), Jane Pittman is her own woman with her own story. She may also be the most fully realized black character in American literature.

*Source for Further Study*
Callahan, John. "Image-Making: Tradition and the Two Versions of *The Autobiography of Miss Jane Pittman*," in *Chicago Review*. XXIX (Autumn, 1977), pp. 45-62.

*Mark Royden Winchell*

# THE AUTUMN OF THE PATRIARCH

*Author:* Gabriel García Márquez (1928-    )
*Type of plot:* Episodic fantasy parable
*Time of plot:* The late nineteenth and early twentieth centuries
*Locale:* An unnamed Caribbean country
*First published: El otoño del patriarca,* 1975 (English translation, 1975)

Principal characters:
THE PATRIARCH, an unnamed Latin American dictator who is
  somewhere between the ages of 107 and 232
BENDICIÓN ALVARADO, his mother, a former prostitute
PATRICIO ARAGONÉS, his double, who is assassinated
LETICIA NAZARENO, his wife, a former nun
EMANUEL, their infant son
GENERAL RODRIGO DE AGUILAR, the chief of national security
MANUELA SÁNCHEZ, a beauty queen who vanishes during a
  solar eclipse
JOSÉ IGNACIO SAENZ DE LA BARRA, a sadistic torturer

*The Novel*

 · *The Autumn of the Patriarch*, published eight years after Gabriel García Márquez' highly praised *Cien años de soledad* (1967; *One Hundred Years of Solitude*, 1970), was a novel for which both general readers and critics had waited. It was, however, a project that García Márquez had put aside earlier to write *One Hundred Years of Solitude* because, as he has commented, he was writing it at first without any clear idea of what he was doing. García Márquez has said that he got the idea for writing the work two or three days after the fall of the dictator Marcos Pérez Jiménez, when the ruling junta met. He was in the anteroom of the presidential office with other journalists when an officer in battle fatigues came out walking backward with a machine gun in his hand and mud on his boots. It was at that moment, García Márquez reveals, that he had a sudden insight into the mystery of power.

Consequently, he wanted to write a "poem on the solitude of power," in which a mythical Latin American dictator would be used as an embodiment of many such dictators, from "Papa Doc" Duvalier of Haiti to Juan Vicente Gómez of Venezuela. His first attempt at the structure of the book—a long monologue by the aged dictator as he is waiting to be executed—he abandoned for the existing polyphonic structure of a multitude of blending voices in six sections that make the book begin and end in a spiral fashion with the discovery of the patriarch's body. The result is a difficult book to read, for each of the six episodes of which it is composed is a single paragraph. There are no other breaks in the novel, and many of the sentences go on for several pages in a run-on, seemingly rambling and disconnected fashion, much like some of the novels of William Faulkner or the stream-of-consciousness works of James Joyce. The stylistic experiment of the book goes even further than Faulkner or Joyce, however, for the point of view of the work shifts constantly, sometimes even within a single line, from first-person participant to third-person author to first-person-plural choral response. García Márquez has called *The Autumn of the Patriarch* the most experimental of his novels and the one that interests him most as a poetic adventure; it is, he says, a book that he wrote like a poem, word by word, sometimes spending weeks on a few lines.

The novel begins with the discovery of the body of the aged patriarch pecked at by vultures and sprouting parasitic animals. Yet because he has not been seen by anyone in many years, and because this is the second time he has been found dead (the first time was with the death of Patricio Aragonés, his exact double), those who find him are not sure if he indeed is the dictator. Although the patriarch's entire life—from birth, to ascendancy to power, to marriage, to suspected coups, to examples of his autocratic and magical rule—is recounted in the six chapters of the work, the primary plot line (if that is possible in such a multifaceted novel as this) focuses on the twenty-four-hour period from the discovery of the body to the final celebration and jubilation at the end of the book.

There is no real sense of chronological time in the novel, for the various voices which recount the events that characterize the patriarch's life blend into a kind of grotesque tone-poem in which time becomes a mythical cycle, ranging throughout the supposed two centuries of the patriarch's mythic life and even beyond to one scene when the patriarch looks out the window and sees the ships of Columbus beside a battleship of modern-day marines. Yet this world of mythic reality, like the world of many of García Márquez' other works, is a world of violence and grotesquely brutal events. A few examples should be sufficient to indicate the nature of the details of the novel and to show the mythically mad world that the patriarch creates around him.

There is, for example, the execution of General Rodrigo de Aguilar after he is suspected of instigating an attempt on the patriarch's life. On the night when he is to be the honored guest at a banquet for the palace guards, he makes his entrance on a silver platter decorated with cauliflower and laurel branches, marinated in spices, browned in the oven, then carved and served up with the order to eat heartily. There is the death of Bendición Alvarado, the patriarch's mother, who rots away of some mysterious disease but whose body is preserved and displayed throughout the country, revived and, according to some, still alive as the patriarch attempts to have her canonized as a saint. There is the death of Leticia Nazareno, the patriarch's wife, and his small son, Emanuel, devoured piece by piece by a pack of trained dogs.

After this murder, José Ignacio Saenz de la Barra, who is hired to find the killers, sends the patriarch numerous bags of what appear to be coconuts but which really contain the heads of some of his enemies, until, finally, 918 heads are delivered, many of which decay in a filing cabinet. There are the two thousand children who have been used by the patriarch as a way to cheat on the national lottery and who, because of their innocent complicity, must all be killed—an atrocity that is achieved by placing them in a ship filled with concrete which is then exploded. The list of absurd and grotesque events goes on and on—countless horrors that become so numerous that the reader can no longer take them completely seriously but must allow them to blend together in a kind of lyrically maintained mythical world of madness and extremity.

### The Characters

The central character, the figure for whom the entire novel exists, is the patriarch himself. Yet he is less a unified character than a pastiche of the idea of the dictator: one who has ultimate power to create his own world and to manipulate other human beings as though they were dispensable pieces in an elaborate, self-indulgent game. If the patriarch were to be taken as a real person, he could be dismissed simply as mad. Since, however, he is an embodiment of the horrors of ultimate power that corrupts absolutely, he suggests the madness of power itself, which is a much more horrifying concept.

He is given all the attributes of the magical personage—one who can change the weather, who is invulnerable to bullets, who fathers hundreds of children, who is destined to live forever, who rules so absolutely that when he asks what time it is, the answer is whatever time he wishes it to be. At the same time, however, he is also seen as weak, fearful of assassination, often sexually impotent, at the mercy of those around him, and generally in a state of aging decay. His gigantic herniated testicle, which he must carry about in a leather case, is a central symbol of this double image: Even as it suggests the magnitude of his sexual organs and thus his power, it also is like a hump on his back, a burden that limits him. Moreover, his seemingly unrestrained power is made ridiculous by the various ruses that his followers must employ to maintain the illusion of power; for example, the young virginal schoolgirls whom he sexually accosts on their way home are really prostitutes hired by his men, and the soap operas he watches are created for his eyes only, because he insists on happy endings.

The other named characters in the novel (there are hundreds who are not named) are similarly extreme and grotesque images rather than real people. The patriarch's mother insists on living in the servants' quarters and paints birds to make them more colorful for sale, seemingly unaware of her great wealth. At one point, during an official parade, she hands a basket of empty bottles in the window of her son's car and asks him to drop them off at the store, Leticia Nazareno, the patriarch's wife, continually goes to the marketplace and buys numerous useless items with the order to "send the bill to the government"—bills which never get paid. During the wedding itself, when she is seven months pregnant, she squats in the "steamy puddle of her own water" and brings "out from among the tangle of muslin the premature infant."

## Themes and Meanings

Certainly *The Autumn of the Patriarch* is a political novel concerning the nature of the paradigmatic Latin American dictator. Yet it is less a novel that focuses on particular political realities than it is about the most universal truth that underlies the nature of all political reality: the truth of absolute power. Moreover, it is about the need of the people to create a supernatural leader, a kind of demigod who, although his decisions are often arbitrary, still represents a sense of destiny and a source of control or responsibility for all the seemingly unpredictable absurdities that dominate life. It is a book about power and the ultimate solitude of power: He is ultimately alone, less in control than controlled by the demands and expectations of those who created him to fulfill their own needs.

Although there are indeed social themes in this novel—where petty corruption is magnified to the gigantic, where there are dark hints at the threat of American imperialism, and where the fundamental unjustness of the rigid economic and class distinctions in Latin America are revealed— *The Autumn of the Patriarch* is ultimately not a political novel. Rather, it is a grotesque lyric poem, a richly metaphoric and mythical experience that overpowers the reader who has the fortitude and the dedication required to read it and become lost in its comic absurdity and its horrific reality. Reading the book is like being caught up in an obsession of the invisible presence that has created it, for the reader who allows the rhythm of the poetic prose of the work to engulf him becomes carried away by the continuous and unrelenting assault on his sense of reality. *The Autumn of the Patriarch* is a book so richly and completely imaginative that it seems to be a palpable embodiment of the mind of García Márquez; indeed, the author has called it an autobiography in code, a confession, "the only book I always wanted to write and never could."

## Critical Context

García Márquez has admitted that his primary literary debts are to the lyric, stream-of-consciousness style of William Faulkner, the restrained and stylized realism of Ernest Hemingway, and the nightmarishly concrete world of Franz Kafka. After the publication of *One Hundred Years of Solitude*, a work which astonished the critics and the reading public with its fantastically realized world of myth and magic, many wondered how García Márquez could go beyond the experimental narrative style of that work. *The Autumn of the Patriarch* did not disappoint them, although many found it much less readable than his earlier works. As might be expected, professional critics have had a field day with the book, for it is surely ripe for explication. Indeed, they have itemized the obsessively repeated symbolic motifs of the novel, have suggested historical sources for the patriarch himself, and have generally delighted in demonstrating their ability to "read" and then to clarify what seems to be an extremely demanding book. Although the book has been generally praised, it has also been criticized for being too long, often too self-indulgent, and too stylistically idiosyncratic to be widely read.

Still, although it is a book more often referred to than actually read, it reaffirms García Márquez' place as the most famous and respected figure of the Latin American literary renaissance—an elite group that includes Julio Cortázar, Carlos Fuentes, and José Donoso, all of whom share García Márquez' narrative worldview of a reality that is much more fictional and absurd than our common sense and our sense of common decency will allow us to accept.

*Sources for Further Study*
Guibert, Rita. *Seven Voices*, 1973.
Janes, Regina. *Gabriel García Márquez: Revolutions in Wonderland*, 1981.
McMurray, George R. *Gabriel García Márquez*, 1977.
Mendoza, Plinio Apuleyo, and Gabriel García Márquez. *The Fragrance of Guava*, 1983.
Sims, Robert Lewis. *The Evolution of Myth in Gabriel García Márquez*, 1981.

                                                                                    *Charles E. May*

# AVALOVARA

*Author:* Osman Lins (1924-1978)
*Type of plot:* Existential quest
*Time of plot:* 200 B.C., 1908-1940, and 1938-1970
*Locale:* Pompeii, France, Holland, Italy, Germany, England, São Paulo,
    Recife, and Rio Grande do Sul, Brazil
*First published:* 1973 (English translation, 1980)

> *Principal characters:*
> ABEL, the protagonist, a Brazilian writer in his early thirties
> ANNELIESE ROOS, his German lover
> CECÍLIA, his Brazilian lover in Recife
> ☿, his Brazilian lover in São Paulo
> PUBLIUS UBONIUS, a Pompeiian businessman
> LOREIUS, a slave of Publius Ubonius
> JULIUS HECKETHORN, a German clockmaker
> OLAVO HAYANO, the husband of ☿

## The Novel

The structure of Osman Lins's *Avalovara* is at once astonishingly complex
and altogether transparent. The sequence of events is predetermined by a
geometric design which appears before the first page of text, consisting of a
Latin palindrome of five five-letter words with a spiral superimposed on it.
To visualize this palindrome here, draw a large square subdivided into
twenty-five smaller squares—five across and five down. In the first row of
squares place the letters S-A-T-O-R; in the second, A-R-E-P-O; in the
third, T-E-N-E-T; in the fourth, O-P-E-R-A; and in the fifth, R-O-T-A-S.
The entire square is centered over a fourteen-ring spiral.

Each letter of the palindrome represents one plot line, and when the spiral touches a letter, a passage of that plot line appears. Since some letters
are more frequent than others, plot segments vary in number of episodes
from twenty-four (letter "O") to two (letter "N," which is in the center of
the design). In addition, episodes increase in length each time that particular plot line reappears—most are ten lines long in the first episode, twenty
lines long in the second, and so on. Exceptions are the themes corresponding to the letters "P" and "T," whose first episodes are twelve and twenty
lines long, respectively.

Such a contrived structure would make *Avalovara*'s plot seem to be an extremely easy one to recount, but in fact the reading experience is nearly
impossible to describe, because the reader is simultaneously witnessing a
dazzling display of literary legerdemain and being led in and out of eight
very different but interrelated plot lines. Plots of such visible artifice often

turn out to be admirable failures, but Lins never sacrifices his fiction to the contrivances that order its unfolding, and the novel betrays none of the self-centeredness many cleverly concocted novels have.

Though there are eight plot divisions, six of them involve the protagonist Abel directly, two dealing with his love affairs with Roos (largely set in Europe) and Cecília (largely set in Recife). The other four are all in some way concerned with the enigmatic ℧, with whom Abel lives a consuming passion and in whose arms he dies, at the hands of Olavo Hayano. One of the other remaining plot lines deals with the Pompeiian Publius Ubonius, who offers to free his slave Loreius if the slave can construct a magic sentence which reflects the mobility of the universe and the immutability of the divine. The sentence Loreius invents is "Sator arepo tenet opera rotas" ("The farmer carefully maintains his plow in the furrows"); the square in which it lies is space; the spiral superimposed on it is time. The final subplot is the story of the obsessed clockmaker Julius Heckethorn, who early in the twentieth century attempts to devise a clock unencumbered by the bothersome ticks of ordinary clocks. He abandons the scheme but does design a clock with a complex triple sound system which will some day play Domenico Scarlatti's Sonata in F Minor.

As the reader approaches the end of the book, the spiral approaches the center of the square, and the various narratives, separated in time and space, draw together as Abel approaches something like an erotic transcendence in the arms of his mysterious and oddly polymorphous lover. The moment of this epiphany coincides with the beginning of a solar eclipse, which is precisely the second that the intricate clock, now in the same room with Abel, begins the sonata.

*The Characters*

Each of the characters in *Avalovara* is identified with a particular notion, either abstract or concrete, which contributes to an understanding of the character in the context of the whole. Abel's German lover Roos, for example, is identified with cities, and part of her function appears to be to suggest the mobility, even random movement, of people and objects in the space of the cosmos. Cecília, his first Brazilian lover, is identified with a series of animals but has as a salient characteristic not some animal trait but a complex of non-traits, which contribute to her ambiguity—she is neither woman nor animal, woman nor man, and she is surrounded by characters who similarly have interchangeable or indeterminate names. Abel himself is most clearly identified with water, a traditional symbol of some richness, but he is the seeker of truth, not an embodiment of it. Undoubtedly the most interesting, and the most difficult, character is ℧, a woman "twice-born" whose behavior makes her seem more mythic than human but who is at the same time the object of Abel's almost hallucinatory erotic obsession. Even

Olavo Hayano, who is important in the action only at the climax and who remains a sketchy figure throughout, is likely to be associated in the reader's mind with the "Yolyp," an imaginary creature of great destructive power.

Avalovara is not really a character here, but it is most closely associated with ☉, and many of its attributes are hers. The name derives from the Buddhist *Avalokitesvara*, a male Bodhisattva, one who has attained enlightenment but who postpones Nirvana in order to help others attain enlightenment. ☉ is not only magical but also double, because there is within her another set of eyes, another life, another self.

One of the most interesting characterization devices in *Avalovara* is found in the use of names. Novelists have long used suggestive names to hint at the configuration of soul of a character, but Lins seems to have been determined to force readers into a more active role in determining a character's goodness or badness. Most of the principal characters here have no last name—one of the two principals has no name at all, but rather a symbol.

## Themes and Meanings

*Avalovara* is clearly a very ambitious work. Two themes—time and space—are suggested by the geometric design at the front of the text, and the entire structure of the novel is determined by the relationship of the physical space of the squares and the progression of the spiral of time over that space. Julius Heckethorn's clock is a variation on the theme, since he decides to set the device in motion at the exact second that will cause its musical culmination to coincide with Abel's moment of fruition. That moment of fruition is a contrary one, since in the process of attaining paradise (Nirvana, knowledge, awareness) he must die, a conceit which is only partially in harmony with any orthodoxy, at least any Western orthodoxy. The title itself suggests that the philosophical framework for Abel's quest is rooted in a mysticism more encompassing than can be found in Roman Catholicism, though there are also allusions to Western notions of transcendence, which might indicate that the substructure of the inquiry is not exclusively Buddhist but eclectic.

The interrelationship of time and space is, then, the overriding conceit in *Avalovara*, but numerous other kinds of questions are included in this central quest. Each major theme is elaborated contrapuntally by secondary ones: The cities embodied in Roos are part of the search for Absolute City; the names and non-names of the characters suggest a search for *the* name, the Word; the spiral reappears in the shape of a unicorn's horn and in the spiraling descent of a vulture; time is viewed both as the linear progression marked by the ticks of a clock and as a (spiral) flow toward fruition. The geometric design itself suggests two different views of the cosmos, one rooted in symmetry and cosmic order, the other based on the unforeseen and unforeseeable chance meeting of the spiral on one of the squares.

Yet time and space are really only the setting for the central theme, which is contained in the metaphor of a fish which leaps from the water and is devoured—at the moment of its plenitude. Abel's route to plenitude is through the sexual act, and his fruition is a cosmic orgasm and the moment of death and knowing, counterpointed by the eclipse and the chiming of the clock.

Finally, it is useful to note that one-to-one relationships are not easily established in a work of such scope. The palindrome itself is ambiguous, and the structure of the novel is based on two opposing numerical systems, one based on the magical number three, the other based on the symmetrical ordering number ten.

*Critical Context*

Osman Lins published his first novel, *O visitante*, in 1955, and his second, *O fiel e a pedra*, in 1961. His first novel won for him several literary prizes, and two of his books of short stories, *Os gestos* (1957) and *Nove, novena* (1966), contributed substantially to his reputation as a serious and very talented writer. His works also enjoyed notable success abroad, especially the French translation of *Nove, novena*. *Avalovara* itself was ready for publication in Italian, French, and German before the Brazilian edition appeared.

Lins has not been a "popular" writer in Brazil because his works are all, like *Avalovara*, intellectually and philosophically challenging. He does, however, have a solid reputation as one of Brazil's most accomplished, as well as one of its most difficult, authors. *Avalovara* is legitimately regarded as the culmination of a brilliant writer's career. Though he published one more novel before his death in 1978, *Avalovara* had obviously been germinating in its author's mind for some time, since some tentative suggestions of it appeared in earlier works, notably the short stories. Brazilian critics have consistently admired his works, though there have been reservations expressed about some of his technical innovations, occasionally so complex as to produce not much more than perplexity in his readers.

Consistent with such perplexities, *Avalovara* can be seen as belonging to two important but apparently contradictory literary traditions: apocalyptic fiction and Utopian fiction. It is in some ways comparable to such apocalyptic works as Thomas Pynchon's *Gravity's Rainbow* (1973)—there is even a symbolically suggestive Nike rocket launch in *Avalovara*, reminiscent of Pynchon's symbolic V-2's—but it also fits into the more established Utopian tradition. What is unusual about *Avalovara* is that it presents the apocalypse as the means of achieving the utopian state.

*Avalovara* is also a distinguished example of yet another literary fashion, one which has had particular importance in the twentieth century: the self-referential novel. In fact, it is so intensely self-referential that some are reluctant to call it a novel at all, preferring to see it more as a tour de force of fiction about writing fiction than as a story about characters. There is some validity to this point, since few novels obey such a rigid and elaborate predetermined structure, but the only episodes which belabor this premeditation are the sections of the geometric design itself (the ten episodes corresponding to the letter "S"), and the rest of the stories are so densely evocative and so symbolically suggestive that readers become so involved as to overlook the artifice. Even those who do not are likely to remember *Avalovara* as an incomparable reading experience.

*Sources for Further Study*

Brushwood, John S. "Recent Translations of Latin American Fiction," in *The Missouri Review*. XCVII (1981), pp. 97-108.

Daniel, Mary L. "Through the Looking Glass: Mirror Play in Two Works of João Guimarães Rosa and Osman Lins," in *Luso-Brazilian Review*. XIII (1976), pp. 19-34.

Delos, Katherine. "*Avalovara*," in *Latin American Literary Review*. XII (1982), pp. 81-83.

Rabassa, Gregory. "Osman Lins and *Avalovara*: The Shape and Shaping of the Novel," in *World Literature Today*. LIII (1979), pp. 30-35.

Stern, Irwin. "Brazilian Literature," in *Review*. XXVIII (1981), pp. 69-72.

*Jon S. Vincent*

# BABEL-17

*Author:* Samuel R. Delany (1942-       )
*Type of plot:* Science fiction
*Time of plot:* The distant future
*Locale:* Aboard various spaceships and on several planets of the Alliance
*First published:* 1966

> *Principal characters:*
> RYDRA WONG, a renowned poet, cryptographer, and linguist
> THE BUTCHER, a linguistically handicapped crew member and
>     a figure of mystery
> JEBEL, the pirate captain of the spaceship *Jebel Tarik*
> DR. MARKUS T'MWARBA (MOCKY), a psychologist, teacher,
>     and patron of Rydra
> MOLLYA,
> CALLI, and
> RON, crew members of Rydra's spaceship *Rimbaud*
> DANIL D. APPLEBY, a customs official who helps Rydra
>     assemble the *Rimbaud* crew

*The Novel*

*Babel-17* is much more a spy story set centuries in the future than a space adventure of the Flash Gordon kind. The novel takes its name from the central mystery of the plot: A group of planets—the Alliance—is under attack by forces called the Invaders. The Alliance is hampered in the struggle by sabotage attempts on their defense installations, and the only clue is that each attack has been preceded by a radio transmission in an unknown language, a language that the Alliance has called "Babel-17." Alliance general Forester consults Rydra Wong, a famous poet and a superlative student of language, and asks for her help in breaking the code.

Rydra agrees to help, and to pursue the saboteurs she immediately begins enlisting a crew for her spaceship. Much of Delany's inventiveness is shown in the recruiting scenes of the story. The demands of galactic navigation make it impossible for normal humans to carry out some necessary tasks, so these duties are handled by "discorporates," beings who are essentially ghosts. Rydra finds one such, Mollya, to add to her crew.

During the voyage of her spaceship *Rimbaud*, Rydra suspects one of her crew of being an Invader agent. She survives one sabotage attempt and, after a landing at a defense installation, returns to the ship only to have it blast off under someone else's control. When she regains her senses after blacking out, she finds herself imprisoned in a web, on a strange ship. At this point, she makes her first use of the fragments of Babel-17 that she has managed to learn. She has intuited that the structure of words in Babel-17 models the structure of the things the words name. When she thinks of the word for "web" in Babel-17, she understands the structure of the web that holds her and is able to release herself and her crew from it.

The group is rescued by the arrival of the *Jebel Tarik*, a privateer whose captain is sympathetic to the Alliance. Aboard the ship, Rydra meets an intriguing character, called only the Butcher, who has no memory. The Butcher, whose affection for Rydra lends romance to the story, suffers from a strange affliction: He has no concept of self, the reader is told, because he has no first-person pronouns in his speech. Rydra succeeds in teaching him the words "I," "me," "mine," and their definitions.

After entering the Butcher's mind, Rydra proceeds from solution to solution: first, that the Butcher, originally an Alliance agent, was captured, brainwashed, and trained as a saboteur by the Invaders; then, that the messages in Babel-17 held both the instructions for the sabotage and the programming that directed the saboteurs. With this knowledge, Rydra is able to foresee both a quick end to the war and the development of yet another language, Babel-18: one that will contain both the information about reality that Babel-17 offers and the personal pronouns that allow a sense of identity and therefore responsibility.

*The Characters*

Rydra Wong, supremely competent as a linguist, as a poet, as a polyglot, and as a spaceship captain, seems almost overburdened with talent. If she has a flaw as a character, it is that she never seems seriously threatened: In any situation, she will think of something. She must also be one of the most loved and respected characters in the genre: General Forester is in love with her, as is the Butcher; her mentor, Dr. Markus T'Mwarba, has a deep affection for her; even her poetry is universally admired.

The Butcher is much more interesting as a character because of his vulnerability. At some time in his past, he has been inhumanly treated and left with his strange defect. Rydra succeeds in giving the Butcher a sense of self in one of the most touching (and affectionate) scenes in science fiction.

The minor characters serve well to supply the novel with the sense of strangeness, of the exotic, that science fiction must have. These touches of the unusual are illustrated in realms ranging from unconventional sexual groupings (a common theme in Delany's work) to the altering of the human form. In that future time, bodies may be surgically changed, both for practical purposes, such as the adding of extra limbs, and for the cosmetic whim of the patient—perhaps the addition of retractable claws and a mane.

*Themes and Meanings*

Throughout his career, Delany has been intensely interested in problems of communication and theories about it. He is obviously a man of both wide and deep reading, much of which shows up in his fiction. In *Babel-17*, one finds the speculations about language of several linguists, all of whom share a common theme. Alfred Korzybski, a Polish aristocrat and émigré, published *Science and Sanity: An Introduction to Non-Aristotelian Systems and General Semantics* in 1933. This turgid and cranky book attracted many admirers both in and out of science fiction by its thesis that if one clearly distinguished words from the things that they represent, one could free oneself from many misunderstandings and follies.

Korzybski's principal advocate in the United States was S. I. Hayakawa, who promoted the ideas of general semantics in a much more readable form. Some of Korzybski's ideas resembled those of Benjamin Lee Whorf, a noted American linguist of the 1930's, after whom the Whorfian hypothesis was named—the idea that the language one speaks controls the way one experiences reality. According to the Whorf hypothesis, to control someone's language is to control his behavior.

This notion had been explored in science fiction before *Babel-17*, most notably in Jack Vance's *The Languages of Pao* (1957), but Vance's work dealt with the action of language on the mass of people, while Delany's is concerned with the control of language over the individual. One of Delany's characters specifically argues that if one does not know the word, one cannot know the idea for which the word stands. This is precisely the control used to manipulate the Butcher (and the Invader saboteurs) in *Babel-17*: Since the Butcher has no word for "I," he does not understand the concept, and only superb teaching by Rydra remedies that lack.

Linguistics is the science in the science fiction of *Babel-17*, but one must not forget that the generic label also includes the word "fiction." Delany uses the Whorfian hypothesis in the novel because of his general interest in communication, much as he was later to use other theories from the realm of semantics and linguistic philosophy.

For that reason, one should not read *Babel-17* as a textbook on linguistics—it is not—but one who reads the novel with the general theme of communication in mind cannot help but be impressed with the degree to which we are all creatures of our speech, an idea copiously illustrated by comments that show Delany's wide range of interest in language.

*Critical Context*

*Babel-17* was one of nine novels that Delany published in a burst of creativity at the beginning of his career between 1962 and 1968. It was chronologically the seventh, after *The Jewels of Aptor* (1962), *Captives of the Flame* (1963), *The Towers of Toron* (1964), *City of a Thousand Suns* (1965), *The Ballad of Beta-2* (1965), and *Empire Star* (1968), this last written after *Babel-17* but published earlier in the same year. *Babel-17*, though, was the work that clinched Delany's reputation in the science-fiction community: It was his first work to win a Nebula Award by ballot of the Science Fiction Writers of America.

His writing up to that time, although often showing as high a quality as his later works, and the same interest in communication, had not reached as wide a readership as it would later. *The Ballad of Beta-2*, for example, was published by Ace as half of a paperback "double-novel," one novel piggybacked with another, each having its own cover, each upside down with respect to the other. *Empire Star* and *Babel-17* had been written with that sort of publication in mind, a lowly form, subject to the ephemeral life of a genre paperback, on the shelf for a few months and then never seen again. After *Babel-17*, however, Delany began to gather critical attention and praise with almost every novel, and his later works especially became longer and much more philosophically ambitious.

Finally, no study of Delany's fiction should overlook his own criticism, especially his collection of essays on writing science fiction, *The Jewel-Hinged Jaw* (1977), in order to understand and appreciate one of the most thoughtful and articulate of today's authors.

*Sources for Further Study*
Barbour, Douglas. *Worlds out of Words: The SF Novels of Samuel R. Delany*, 1979.
Slusser, George Edgar. *The Delany Intersection: Samuel R. Delany Considered as a Writer of Semi-Precious Words*, 1977.

*Walter E. Meyers*

# BANANA BOTTOM

*Author:* Claude McKay (1889-1948)
*Type of plot:* Regional romance
*Time of plot:* The early 1900's
*Locale:* The country town of Jubilee and the village of Banana Bottom in Jamaica
*First published:* 1933

*Principal characters:*

TABITHA PLANT (BITA), the protagonist, a Jamaican girl adopted by the Craigs and educated abroad, age twenty-two

MALCOLM CRAIG, an ordained Calvinist minister of a mission church in Jubilee

PRISCILLA CRAIG, an ordained Calvinist minister, the wife of Malcolm and the mother of a deformed child, Patou

CRAZY BOW ADAIR, the descendant of a Scots settler and landowner, Bita's first lover

HOPPING DICK, a wild, sensual, fine-strutting dandy who is interested in Bita

HERALD NEWTON DAY, a black trainee minister intended by the Craigs as Bita's future husband

SQUIRE GENSIR, a freethinking British aristocratic settler who studies black culture and promotes black self-esteem

JUBBAN, a black laborer whom Bita later marries

*The Novel*

In a series of flashbacks the reader learns that Bita Plant was "seduced" by Crazy Bow Adair (actually, it was a willing sexual union, but the social niceties of Banana Bottom required that a twelve-year-old had to be an unwilling victim); that she was adopted by the Reverends Malcolm and Priscilla Craig, who wanted to demonstrate their ability to transform a wayward black girl into a cultured Christian; that she was educated in England and had visited Europe before returning to Jubilee seven years later.

The Craigs have planned that Bita marry a local black theological student, Herald Newton Day, who is egotistical, ashamed of his blackness, and a perfect example of the transformation that the Craigs would like to effect in all the villagers; Bita immediately discovers that she has little in common with him, although she agrees to an engagement. Soon after her return, she meets Hopping Dick at a local market and is attracted by his undisguised sensuality and even by his reputation for being "wild." She discovers his skill in dancing and romancing, and she learns that he is the antithesis of the

Craigs' ideal, Herald. Squire Gensir accompanies Bita to a "tea-meeting" at which the locals enjoy themselves with dancing, singing, and merriment; she dances enthusiastically and recognizes her affinity with the village folk. When Mrs. Craig learns of Bita's behavior from Sister Phibby Patroll (the local midwife and gossip), she is apprehensive about "saving" the atavistic Bita.

Bita escapes from Jubilee and visits her own village, Banana Bottom, for a weekend. Here she notices Jubban, her father's drayman, who is a stalwart, self-confident, and absolutely admirable black laborer of fine physique and natural dignity: Their mutual attraction is obvious. Bita visits the swimming hole where, as a child, she had many delightful moments: In the Edenic situation her sexuality is aroused (and described in truly poetic prose). In this situation she realizes that her roots lie in the rural countryside with the folk rather than with the Westernized and Christian converts.

On her return to Jubilee and at a harvest festival, Bita introduces Herald and Hopping Dick; Herald's pomposity repels her and his superficiality impresses Squire Gensir. (Discovered in an act of bestiality, Herald is dispatched to Panama.) Yet when Bita decides to marry Hopping Dick, he backs out and converts to Christianity, forsaking his unrestrained folkways.

Bita attends a revival meeting with Squire Gensir, but when it becomes a non-Christian religious orgy, she succumbs, dancing wildly and surrendering to masochistic flagellation. She is rescued by Jubban—who also subsequently rescues her from the sexual advances of Arthur Glengley, a wealthy near-white, and later marries her.

During a hurricane and flood, Malcolm Craig and Jordan Plant, Bita's father, are drowned returning from a church meeting. Mrs. Craig dies shortly after, "worried to death by disappointment": Her speechless adult son is dead, Herald has disgraced both the Craigs and their whole little world, and Bita has forsaken the values and life-style of the white community.

Squire Gensir returns to England, dies, and leaves his Jamaican property and house to Bita, who is rearing her son, Jordan, in an environment that represents an amalgam of the best of West Indian rural values modified by some of those of European society. Thus, the reader sees the significance of Bita's full name, Tabitha, which is also the name of a free-spirited gazelle, a coarse-woven silk (taffeta), and (in the form "tabby") a cat of variegated color.

*The Characters*

Bita Plant is without doubt McKay's most skillfully drawn character, and she embodies all those traits that McKay admired: freedom from the hypocrisy that all too frequently accompanies religiosity, unrestrained enthusiasm for the arts and entertainments of the folk, pride in black institutions and heritage, independence in thought and behavior, and discernment in the choice of competing ideologies. Whether the choice is between Christianity and God or Obeah and the Devil, between village society or rural isolation, between cantatas or digging *jammas* (songs), Bita is seldom persuaded by others' opinions: She exercises her independent judgment, which had been developed during her European schooling. In some ways she exhibits the characteristics of the Pankhursts, the British liberals with whom McKay worked in his early years while contributing to the *Workers' Dreadnought*: They were liberal, independent, indefatigable—though not given to the free expression of sexuality that characterizes Bita's life.

The Craigs, determined Christians and well-intentioned as they are, are nevertheless unforgiving, confining, and sexually repressed; their generosity in adopting and educating Bita is negated by their inability to grant her freedom to develop in her own way; their goal is conversion to middle-class Christian ways and the expunging of natural, instinctive, emotional behavior—especially as it is manifest in physical attraction and consummation. Theirs is a battle against sin that is equated with the folkways of their black congregation and neighbors, and their ideal—before his fall—is the convert Herald.

Herald Newton Day and Hopping Dick are carefully balanced as foils: One is the sanctimonious missionary trainee intent upon succeeding to the leadership of the local church, yet unable to repress his base sexuality; the other is the profligate ne'er-do-well and womanizer who is unable to accept the responsibility that is part of mature interpersonal relationships, including marriage, and escapes from the consequences of his enticements by retreating into a convenient conversion to Christianity. To both of them, Jubban is an ideal contrast: He is thoughtful, not overly intellectual, hardworking, and an emotional, responsive, and responsible lover.

Most of the characters in *Banana Bottom* have names that are meaningful if not necessarily symbolic or emblematic; in a novel that is clearly intended to portray the sexual emancipation of the central character, many have sexual overtones. The Plants, as the name implies, are rooted in the soil, and Bita is growing into full womanhood; Herald Newton Day is the herald of the new town and new day for which the Craigs work; Sister Phibby Patroll is a sister (in both the British sense of nurse and the black sense), a "fibber" (or storyteller, or liar), and a patrol member, constantly on the watch for others' misdeeds; Hopping Dick and Yoni Legge (a sexually unrepressed village girl) have names that indicate their predispositions.

*Themes and Meanings*

In this more than in his other fiction, Claude McKay concurrently develops a number of themes: Principal among them are the merging of intellect and instinct (or emotion and reason, the physical and the mental) in the younger members of an agricultural, colonial community to the end that a characteristic, natural, local personality will develop; also that in the maturation of the "natural" self, one has to choose between hypocrisy and instinct. Bita's discarding her clothes to have a swim in her favorite mountain pool is symbolic of her casting off the veneer of acquired tastes and values: She displays her body and admires those of the bathing boys nearby without embarrassment or shame; likewise, she is not ashamed to display her inner self, her natural instincts.

In addition, McKay shows the debilitating effects of traditional Christian morality: The Craigs' denial of sexuality has resulted in an only child who is unable to speak (and is therefore named Patou, dialect for "screech-owl"), and who dies of "knot-guts" just when he reaches adulthood; they try to hide any sign of their intimacy from their housekeeper; they denigrate affection and reproduction. By way of contrast, McKay imbues the rural folk with a sense of joy, sharing, and wholesomeness that is admirable. Ultimately, these themes coalesce into praise for the distinctive, unrepressed behavior of the Jamaican (and hence Third World) peasants and disdain for the paternalistic and dampening influence of Western, Eurocentric civilization. Primitive positiveness survives, though it benefits from training, cultivation, and hybridization, no matter where it is planted.

*Critical Context*

While McKay's first novels, *Home to Harlem* (1928) and *Banjo* (1929), depict the world of men (mainly Caribbean) in distant urban centers (New York and Marseilles), *Banana Bottom* presents a Jamaican woman returning to her native land after having been introduced to urban life in England and Europe and attempting to find a middle way between the spontaneous expression of natural emotion that McKay always presents as the norm in Caribbean rural communities and the carefully measured (and often hypocritical), socially acceptable behavior that he sees as typical of urban life. Bita's reading Blaise Pascal's *Pensées* while enjoying the property that she inherited from Squire Gensir suggests that she has, in fact, managed to bridge the two cultures. Her husband, Jubban, has provided her with a child who constantly affirms her blackness; her benefactor has provided her with a home and culture that is a continual reminder of the white culture that she has absorbed and valued. Her characteristic openness, honesty, and independence of judgment reveal her to be an admirable person. She is perhaps the best-drawn character in McKay's fiction: Though she never expounds a philosophy in the propagandistic fashion of Jake and Ray in the earlier novels, she nevertheless represents a way of life that is inescapably the one that McKay would have his readers accept. She is also dynamic: She returns from England a "made-over" islander, a brown-skinned Briton, as it were; she quickly evaluates the life-style of her own people and that represented by the Craigs and sees that neither is ideal, that each can contribute to the creation of something better than each alone. She is McKay's best symbol of his philosophy of cultural dualism—even pluralism. At times extravagant with her emotions and sympathies, she is also, from time to time, pensive, articulate, intellectual, and considerate. She is never mean-spirited, cruel, niggardly, or wanton.

Perhaps because he was writing about the leisurely life in the West Indies, McKay's prose in *Banana Bottom* is much less agitated and frenetic than that of *Home to Harlem* and *Banjo*: There are fewer short, simple declarative sentences and sentence fragments; there are many long, descriptive sentences, frequently marked by parenthetical elements and polysyllables. There are also a dozen or more songs and poems that help to impart a general air of tranquillity to the novel even when it carries a message of less than tranquil content. This adaptation of style to content is especially effective: Had McKay continued the Hemingwayesque, reportorial prose of the urban, man's-world novels, *Banana Bottom* would not have succeeded as it does.

It is not unreasonable to suggest—as some critics have done—that *Banana Bottom* is the first truly mature novel by a West Indian writing in English: The occasional dialect is no impediment to comprehension (and is mastered with the use of the glossary that the author provided) and provides a measure of authenticity; the characters comprise almost the entire range of those encountered in a colonial environment (black and white, religious and secular, master and servant, illiterate and savant); the exotic and erotic, both true-to-life, are never overdone.

The explanation of McKay's success in this novel is not easily located, but it may be that (as with his poetry) his best writing was usually evinced by his reminiscing about his homeland, about his green hills of Clarendon in Jamaica. Twenty years after having left Jamaica, he returned symbolically in the character of Bita Plant, a fine representation of his ideal woman, his ideal Caribbean.

*Sources for Further Study*
Bone, Robert A. *The Negro Novel in America*, 1958.
Cooper, Wayne F., ed. *The Passion of Claude McKay*, 1973.
Giles, James R. *Claude McKay*, 1976.
Ramchand, Kenneth. *The West Indian Novel and Its Background*, 1970.

*Marian B. McLeod*

# BANG THE DRUM SLOWLY

*Author:* Mark Harris (1922-     )
*Type of plot:* Tragicomedy
*Time of plot:* 1955
*Locale:* Perkinsville, New York; Rochester, Minnesota; Bainbridge, Georgia;
  and New York City
*First published:* 1956

> *Principal characters:*
> HENRY W. WIGGEN, the unlettered narrator, a pitcher for the
> New York Mammoths
> BRUCE PEARSON, the third-string catcher for the Mammoths
> and Henry's roommate
> HOLLY WEBSTER WIGGEN, Henry's wife
> KATIE, an expensive prostitute with whom Bruce is in love
> DUTCH SCHNELL, the team manager, whose principal aim is to
> win baseball games
> RED TRAPHAGEN, a catcher and a college professor
> GOOSE, an aging catcher, who rags Bruce
> LESTER T. MOORS, JR., the wealthy owner of the Mammoths
> PATRICIA MOORS, his daughter
> PINEY WOODS, the catcher for the Mammoths and a motorcy-
> cle enthusiast

## The Novel

*Bang the Drum Slowly* is not a sequel to *The Southpaw* (1953), even though many of the characters in Mark Harris' earlier novel reappear in this second novel narrated by Henry W. Wiggen (the full title is *Bang the Drum Slowly by Henry W. Wiggen: Certain of His Enthusiasms Restrained by Mark Harris*). When references are made to *The Southpaw*, those passages are reprinted in *Bang the Drum Slowly*. Henry Wiggen, who tells the story, is a star pitcher for the New York Mammoths. Bruce Pearson, his roommate and the third-string catcher for the Mammoths, is dying of Hodgkin's disease. The novel begins as Bruce calls Henry from the Mayo Clinic in Rochester, Minnesota, to tell him that he must come to see him, and it ends with a winning season for the Mammoths and Bruce's death.

After Bruce checks out of the hospital, Henry and Bruce drive to Bruce's hometown of Bainbridge, Georgia. The principal activities in Bainbridge are waiting for the mail and swatting flies on the front porch. The high point of the visit for Bruce is learning to play Tegwar, a game in which the rules change all the time and the object is to keep a straight face.

Bruce wants to continue to play ball as long as he can. Realizing that

Lester T. Moors, Jr., the owner, and Dutch Schnell, the manager, would release Bruce if they knew of his illness, Henry and Bruce decide to keep it a secret. When Henry negotiates his contract for the year, he includes a clause stating that he and Bruce must be treated as a package: "[I]f he is traded I must be traded the same place. Wherever he goes I must go." Humor is introduced in this very poignant scene, when Henry is asked if Bruce Pearson owes him money. When he says no, Dutch considers, but then discards the idea that the two men are "fairies."

Long after most of the team knows about Bruce's illness, the management finds out but has to keep Pearson with the team because of the clause in Henry Wiggen's contract. The knowledge of Bruce's illness draws the team together. As Henry puts it, "It was a club, like it should of been all year but never was but all of a sudden become." Bruce stays with the team and dresses for every game. He leaves after the Mammoths are assured of winning the World Series. Henry is one of the pallbearers at Bruce's funeral, but no one else from the Mammoths attends.

*The Characters*

Mark Harris' characterization of Bruce Pearson is brilliantly successful. Bruce is not a charming, intelligent, valuable player whose fellow players love him. Bruce is a third-string catcher who laughs at his teammates jokes in order to belong. When he sends postcards to his family, he manages to write only three words on the card: Pearson, Mill, Georgia; the rest is left blank. Bruce is a natural athlete, but not very bright. He sits at the window of the room that he shares with Henry, spitting and watching to see if the spit curves in or out.

The team players amuse themselves by taunting and ridiculing Bruce. Henry tries to protect Bruce from their ragging without revealing his roommate's approaching death. After Henry tries to stop the ridicule of Bruce, Perry, who was the first black man on the Mammoths, alludes to Bruce's Southern background and sneers, "Pearson would not give me the time of day if I was dying." Henry replies: "He does not know it himself half the time."

Harris juxtaposes the cocky, talented, and successful Henry Wiggen, who writes books and sells insurance, with the simpleminded Bruce Pearson. Henry is nicknamed "Author" by his teammates, and Bruce thinks that they are saying "Arthur," which becomes his name for Henry. Bruce gets drunk once a year every spring before training begins because he is a third-string catcher and has little to do other than assist pitchers in warming up.

After Henry becomes Bruce's roommate, the two men become friends, although they have little in common other than their friendship. Henry comments, "We hit it off pretty good once I got used to the stink of shaving lotion and this filthy chewing tobacco called Days O Work and spitting incurves and outcurves out the window and urinating in the sink and calling me 'Arthur.'" When Henry and Holly are given a place in which to live, Bruce spends all of his time with them, but Henry cannot tell him to stay away because Bruce is always so happy to see them.

Bruce falls in love with Katie, a successful prostitute who is fond of dining at expensive restaurants. Katie agrees to marry him, after she learns that he is dying, if he makes her the beneficiary of his insurance. Henry, who sold Bruce his insurance policy, stalls about changing the beneficiary until Katie finally attempts unsuccessfully to bribe him. Katie's affection for money is handled lightly; she is not censored for her greed.

Even minor characters in *Bang the Drum Slowly* are carefully drawn. Goose, the aging catcher who has not saved for his old age and who abuses his wife, comes alive when Henry confides to him the truth about Bruce. Goose is an excellent catcher, but he is not in the same class as Red Traphagen. His position on the team affects his sense of self and his marriage: "But there was Traphagen and all, and finally the only person that loved me I bashed her in the eye now and then to keep up my spirit."

Harris views ragging teammates and bashing loved ones as needless cruelty. On the other hand, he very sensitively describes why Goose, the aging second-string catcher with debts, or Perry, the black player who has had to withstand verbal abuse from fans, want to rag Bruce in order to make themselves feel better. It is human nature to take out anger and frustration on those weaker than oneself.

Piney Woods, a brash young catcher who adores his motorcycle, remarks when he is being sent back to the minor leagues, "Well, maybe somebody will drop dead soon and open up a slot for me." Bruce will die by the end of the novel, necessitating Piney's return to the Mammoths. Harris consistently uses the clichés and slang with which the characters habitually express themselves to generate ironic wit. The dialogue is amusing, even comic, but its implications are serious.

*Themes and Meanings*

The title of *Bang the Drum Slowly* is adapted from a line in "The Streets of Laredo," a song about a cowboy who dies young. That the novel is not about baseball is suggested by the epigram taken from Wright Morris' *The Huge Season* (1954) that "a book can have Chicago in it, and not be about Chicago. It can have a tennis player in it without being about a tennis player." *Bang the Drum Slowly* is not about baseball, nor is it really about the friendship which develops between Henry Wiggen and Bruce Pearson. Red Traphagen, the catcher and college professor, reads part of *Bang the Drum Slowly* in manuscript and comments that few people will read the book and that "even the people that read it will think it is about baseball or some such stupidity as that, for baseball is stupid, Author, and I hope you put it in your book, a game rigged by rich idiots to keep poor idiots from wising up to how poor they are." Red tells Henry to "stick to death and Pearson." Ironically, Mark Harris has done precisely that. Whatever Henry Wiggen sees or says, the knowledge of Bruce Pearson's death is ingrained in his consciousness. Every chance reference to death, from the lyrics of a cowboy song to the jeer of a cab driver, resounds in Henry's mind and reminds the reader of human mortality.

When Bruce becomes ill and Henry sends Goose for the doctor, Bruce accuses Henry of having told Goose that he is dying. He realizes that people are likely to be nice to a dying person. Reassuringly, Henry says, "Everybody knows everybody is dying. . . . That is why people are nice. You all die soon enough, so why not be nice to each other." What Henry has said is not true, but the reader wishes that it were.

*Bang the Drum Slowly* was made into a touching film which some critics have described as sentimental; the novel is not sentimental. Harris concludes the story of Bruce Pearson's death by having Henry forget to send him the scorecard from the World Series: "Wouldn't it been simple instead of writing a page on my book to shoved it in the mail? How long would it of took? Could I not afford the stamps?"

Henry acts as Bruce's pallbearer; flowers are sent, but "no *person*" comes from the Mammoths. The novel concludes with his epitaph for Bruce and the moral he draws from it: "He was not a bad fellow, no worse than most and probably better than some, and not a bad ballplayer neither when they give him a chance, when they laid off him long enough. From here on in I rag nobody." Henry intends to remember that everyone is dying.

*Critical Context*

*Bang the Drum Slowly* is a deceptively simple book, which, like *The Southpaw*, has suffered from being assessed as a "baseball book." Even in the clichés and slang of the ballplayers, the word "death" is repeated with telling irony. The reader shares Henry Wiggen's sensitivity to the word and gradually comes to realize that Bruce's death foreshadows that of everyone. The understatement of the dialogue accentuates the impact of *Bang the Drum Slowly*. The characters are inarticulate, most of all Bruce, but their very lack of sophistication is skillfully used by Harris to engage the reader's emotions.

*Bang the Drum Slowly* merits comparison with some of Ernest Hemingway's best short stores. As a work of art, it is better written than Hemingway's story of Colonel Cantwell's death in *Across the River and into the Trees* (1950).

At the end of the novel, when Henry forgets to send Bruce a copy of the winning scorecard, Harris resists the temptation to sentimentalize the relationship of Henry and Bruce. Henry Wiggen quite nobly works out his contract so that Bruce will remain with the Mammoths throughout the season, but he forgets to send the scorecard. Ironically, too, Harris makes a point of the fact that Henry Wiggen has been writing the book about Bruce's death while Bruce is dying. At one point, Henry even wonders if the book will have an audience if Bruce lives. Though Harris resists any hint of sentimentality, he resists the pressure on contemporary artists to depict the world as valueless and empty. The owners and manager would sever Bruce's relationship with the Mammoths if they knew of his illness, but the men on the team are united and inspired by the fact of his approaching death.

Few novels with such a serious theme manage to be so amusing. *The Southpaw* had great energy and charm; *Bang the Drum Slowly* ought to be regarded as a minor classic. Perhaps because it has baseball as its setting, this important novel has not received the careful scrutiny that it deserves.

*Sources for Further Study*

Cort, David. "Ball Players," in *The Nation*. CLXXXII (May 12, 1956), p. 413.

Daley, Robert. "Henry Was a Southpaw," in *The New York Times Book Review*. March 18, 1956, p. 5.

Gottlieb, Robin. "Who Said a Southpaw Has to Be Crazy?" in *New York Herald Tribune Book Review*. XXXII (March 18, 1956), p. 6.

Lavers, Norman. *Mark Harris*, 1978.

Munson, Gorham. "Doomed Ballplayer," in *Saturday Review*. XXXIX (March 31, 1956), p. 14.

*Jeanie R. Brink*

# BANJO
## A Story Without a Plot

*Author:* Claude McKay (1889-1948)
*Type of plot:* Social criticism
*Time of plot:* The early 1920's
*Locale:* Marseilles
*First published:* 1929

> *Principal characters:*
> LINCOLN AGRIPPA DAILY (BANJO), a vagabond from the South
> RAY, a West Indian would-be writer and a beachboy
> LATNAH, a woman of mixed blood who befriends Banjo
> BUGSY, small, wiry, aggressive boy who is antiwhite
> TALOUFA, a young Nigerian who has been in Wales and the
> United States and supports the Back-to-Africa cause
> GOOSEY, a flute-playing mulatto and an exponent of the uplift
> philosophy of the Harlem Renaissance intellectuals
> BUCHANAN MALT AVIS (MALTY), a West Indian drummer and
> beachboy
> GINGER, a long-term beachboy, former seaman, and ex-
> convict
> DENGEL, a Senegalese

*The Novel*

*Banjo* is subtitled "A Story Without a Plot," but it is not a novel in the manner of Virginia Woolf—although it is conversational and at times even dialectical. Rather, it is an episodic narrative involving a small group of relatively permanent residents of the Vieux Port section of Marseilles and a larger cast of incidental characters who are encountered briefly in the varied but fundamentally routine activities of unemployed black seamen trying to maintain a sense of camaraderie and well-being. It is, therefore, basically a picaresque fiction that offers a measure of social criticism (sometimes at considerable length, at other times with considerable force); this social message, however, is extraneous to the novel and is a structural weakness.

Except for occasional excursions to Aix-en-Provence and other nearby locations in the Midi for seasonal employment or diversion, the characters spend their time frequenting the bars, nightclubs, and restaurants of the Ditch, Boody Lane, and Bum Square—names that they have given to the Quartier Réservé, rue de la Bouterie, and Place Victor Gelu in Marseilles.

Some chapters introduce Arabs, Orientals, and Europeans, who are shown less favorably than the motley assortment of blacks who constitute McKay's principal concern; other chapters present hospitals, rooming-houses, bordellos, gambling rooms, and pornographic movie houses. Both people and places sample the exotic as well as the erotic, and Marseilles becomes an overseas replica of the New York City of *Home to Harlem* (1928).

The book is divided into three sections. The first introduces Lincoln Agrippa Daily (Banjo), strolling along the breakwater and encountering Malty, Ginger, Dengel, and Bugsy, who have arrived in the boxcars of a train. All are seeking "the joy stuff of life" and believe that they can find it by playing as a black band in the cafés and "love spots." In the second part, Ray (who has left Harlem to become a seaman) appears and joins Banjo's little group, becoming a somewhat sobering influence through his incessant philosophizing, though participating in the life of the Monkey Bar, the Anglo-American Bar, and similar establishments. Yet times are changing: White crews are replacing black ones on ships, and work is scarce; foreigners are being subjected to irritations. The beachboys are broke and scatter: Banjo accompanies a group of Europeans to Nice and Monte Carlo; Ray and Malty (in company with Latnah) go to the vineyards; Goosey and Bugsy are sent by a municipal agency to an up-country factory; only Ginger and Dengel remain, taking their chances on the docks of Marseilles: "Now that Banjo was gone and the group dispersed, the spell was broken."

The third section of the novel opens with Ray, Malty, and Latnah (enjoying a beer on the waterfront after their return from bringing in the vintage) spotting Banjo working as a coal handler. He has been tricked out of his banjo and has undergone a complete metamorphosis: "Even the wine he drank afforded him little pleasure," and Ray finds him "exasperatingly melancholy." To Ray, the life of the Ditch has become "gray," and he decides to move on. Banjo dreams of reuniting his musicians (instrumentless and without rehearsals) in a band. Bugsy dies; Banjo is hospitalized and then cared for by Latnah; the boys are beaten by the police, sign on as crew for a voyage to the West Indies, and foresee a new life-style. Banjo, however, influenced by Ray's outlook and arguments, takes his advance of a month's pay and skips ship before sailing, in order to continue the vagabond existence. The novel concludes with Banjo addressing Ray: "Come on, pardner. Wese got enough between us to beat it a long ways from here." Though the goal of a band has disappeared, Banjo clearly has a new goal: conjunction (the word he uses in referring to women, particularly Latnah) of the physical and the intellectual.

## The Characters

As in any eponymous work, the author's principal focus is on Banjo, whose name receives special notice from McKay: "The banjo dominates the other instruments. . . . And Banjo's face shows that he feels that his instrument is first . . . the banjo is preeminently the musical instrument of the

American Negro." Yet Goosey, the "yellow" exponent of the philosophy of uplift, a thoughtful and at times philosophic character who can be thought of as a representative of the W. E. B. DuBois–Alain Locke school of thought, counters that the banjo is a symbol of Dixie, of bondage, of slavery; and he advocates blacks' playing the violin, the piano. He and Taloufa refuse to play "any of that black-face coon stuff," he says, to which Banjo replies that he likes the instrument and sees "saxophone-jazzing" as "the money stuff today." His liking for the banjo is clearly the effect of his being a "child of the Cotton Belt." His enthusiasm for the ukulele and mandolin likewise reveals an attachment to the old days and ways of the South, but wherever he goes in Marseilles he finds that though people are amused by the banjo, they are more often entertained by the piano. The beachboys are therefore clearly identified with a musical tradition and technology that have been superseded, and when Banjo and Ray set off together at the end of the story, they do so as itinerant workers rather than as poets or troubadours, regardless of their spiritual state of mind and predilections. Ray is an unsuccessful writer; Banjo is an unsuccessful musician; the arts are merely accompaniments to their lives.

The beachboys of the Ditch are a polyglot group: They represent the broad spectrum of blacks: West Indian, African, and American. Yet they have a cohesion that is admirable, and overall Banjo represents the hegemony of blackness: He deprecates both racial inferiority and "passing."

Yet none of the black characters is an exclusivist: They all share a common sympathy toward and appreciation of Latnah, who is olive-toned, of mixed race, and "not young and far from old, with an amorous charm." She suggests an Earth Mother who comprises every admirable trait: sensuality, practicality, compassion, energy, and adaptability among them. She is, however, unique in the novel: The other women are prostitutes, minor criminals, European ruins, and jaded drifters. It is instructive when Ray laments that it would have been good if he and Banjo had been able to take Latnah with them as they left Marseilles. "Don't get soft ovah any one wimmens, pardner" is Banjo's response. One wonders just how they will fare without her love and care.

The remainder of the central group of characters are not well limned, yet they do develop sufficient individuality to become discernible. Bugsy is consistently antiwhite; his complexion is described as dull black, but this might as well have been used to describe his mental type; he is fittingly small, wiry, and aggressive. Taloufa, the Nigerian who was born in the bush, is young, well-traveled (he has been in Wales, the United States, and Europe), and an advocate of Marcus Garvey's Back-to-Africa movement. When he landed in England, the authorities wanted to deport him to West Africa, but "Taloufa did not want to go there. Christian missionaries had educated him out of his native life." When he returned to Marseilles (with his guitar), he was "broke, but unbroken." In many ways he is an interesting and absorbing—though minor—character, since he represents the great mass of present-day Africans who are cut off from traditional village life and not integrated into contemporary urban and industrial society. Malty, the West Indian drummer and guitarist, is ebullient and indefatigable: He is reminiscent of the type of person whom McKay admired and remembered from his Jamaican days. Each of these (and the score of minor characters such as the Arab taxi-driver-cum-tout and Chère Blanche, the prostitute) is memorably drawn in colorful vignettes.

*Themes and Meanings*

By placing the story in Marseilles, McKay is able to draw together a variety of blacks, just as he had done in *Home to Harlem*. Yet because all of the blacks in Marseilles are expatriates, mere temporary residents, and beachboys, there is a smaller and less interesting range with which to work. Nevertheless, the novel reiterates McKay's constant themes: that the folk rather than the black intelligentsia represent the best in the race; that blacks should have a high regard for their heritage and hence a racial self-esteem; that the ideal life is one of vagabondage, of natural gusto and emotional response, allowing one to "laugh and love and jazz and fight." The breakup of the beachboys at the end of parts 2 and 3 suggests that cohesiveness is less powerful among McKay's favorite people than individualism—the very characteristic of the materialistic, commercial class that Ray inveighs against in his numerous diatribes and asides. Ironically, it is this assertion of individuality (which is, however, always punctuated by examples of group concern for others in distress) that plays into the arms of those classes and attitudes that Ray sees as inimical to racial betterment.

Ray is the mouthpiece for an unrelenting indictment of white civilization. In his eyes, its chief shortcomings are crass commercialism (one shipping line is called the Dollar Line); an unwarranted sense of racial superiority; hypocrisy (white Europeans assert that they make the best pornographic films, yet they condemn the uninhibited—even justifiable—sexuality of the blacks); nauseous patriotism, rather than internationalism; standardization; and Calvinist attitudes toward sex, alcohol, music, and entertainment.

Yet the behavior of Banjo and the other denizens of the Ditch is far from admirable—if one excepts Ray, who is moderate, literate, and emotional. When he arrives in port, Banjo has 12,525 francs—a considerable sum— but he quickly spends it on a girl who leaves him as soon as he is broke. He is wholly improvident and far from admirable: "He was a type that was never sober, even when he was not drinking." Accordingly, it is difficult to maintain any sympathy for him and to feel that he is anything more than a wastrel, a womanizer, a loafer, and an impractical dreamer. His word is seldom binding. When he leaves with Ray, it is with the advance in wages that he has received from the shipping line: He breaks a contract to pursue a drifter's dream in the company of a husband and father who has apparently turned his back on his social responsibilities.

Yet if McKay means *Banjo* to be a paean to the free life, the life of the spirit and the emotions untrammeled by responsibilites, he seems to be suggesting that his motley sybarites are enviable models. They most certainly are not: They are irresponsible and without any admirable ambition. Their parallels are the Europeans who attend the "blue" cinema, who are rootless, affected, and suffering from ennui. (Their Satanism and sexual aberrations have cut them off from their cultural bearings.) It is hard to understand how any reader could come away from the novel believing that the beachboys—and Banjo in particular—are to be admired for their instinctive, spontaneous, sensual behavior. Moreover, at the end most of them express their dissatisfaction with pointless drifting, with unemployment, with poverty, and with temporary liaisons dependent on money alone. It is little wonder, then, that *Banjo* has been subjected to criticism on the basis of its not having a clearly defined and defensible theme. Similarly, one can see a weakness in Banjo's saying that his instrument is his "buddy," that it is more than a "gal, moh than a pal; it's mahself." The Jazz Age had not ended, but the banjo was a symbol of a past era, and its owner, who places a thing above persons, seems to be disoriented. Banjo has become an anachronism.

*Critical Context*

In essence, *Banjo* is a continuation of *Home to Harlem*: The location has been shifted from the United States to France, but the *dramatis personae* are remarkably similar, and their exploits differ only insofar as Harlem and Marseilles differ. Naturally, the problem then became what to do with a third novel. The answer was to shift from the urban world of men to the rural world of men and women, families and children, teachers and preachers in Jamaica, and remarkably, *Banana Bottom* (1933), with its balance of sense and sensuality, showed that McKay could combine emotional and social realism, propaganda and polemics, characterization and plot. It seems that he recognized the limitations of *Banjo* and that it did not enhance his growing reputation as poet and fiction writer.

One of the most frequently cited weaknesses in *Banjo* is the tendency for Ray's comments to overwhelm the story and change the balance from fiction to propagandist tract, and when Goosey adds his philosophical—and at times sophomoric—musings, the novel is endangered. Yet the inclusion of discussion on major matters of the day (such as race, capitalism, socialism, and xenophobia) should not be condemned per se: The unemployed and discriminated against are often voluble critics of social policy and not infrequently have some well-informed, first-class exponents of their causes as spokesmen.

While advocating the cause of the black masses, McKay leaves the reader confused at times about his social policy. Latnah, the quintessential black mother-figure, is deserted by Banjo for Chère Blanche, the "pink sow"; and after loving and nursing, feeding and housing him, she is unceremoniously left in the Ditch while he and Ray head off on their continuing odyssey. In his fiction, as in his personal life, McKay was unable (until *Banana Bottom*) to develop a lasting black married relationship. Ironically, it is Latnah who criticizes Banjo for his lack of race pride—the one thing that he thought that he exemplified.

In his unpublished "Romance in Marseilles" and "Harlem Glory" (both written some time after 1935, when he was already in declining health, fortune, and reputation as a Harlem Renaissance writer), McKay tried to recapture the spirit of the two cities and their black communities, but he was too far from his sources in time and geography, and the novellas lack the qualities of the earlier works. One short story, "Dinner at Douarnenez," which was first published in 1985, conveys McKay's deep attachment to France and his belief that blacks have generally been more welcome there than in other countries. Most of the social and political topics that Ray addresses are the subjects of articles in *The Liberator* and *Amsterdam News*, for which McKay worked as a journalist; many of them were treated also in *The Negroes in America* (1979), which McKay wrote when he visited the Soviet Union in 1922-1923 but which remained unpublished until its discovery decades later among some materials in the New York Public Library.

*Sources for Further Study*
Bone, Robert A. *The Negro Novel in America*, 1958.
Giles, James R. *Claude McKay*, 1976.
Kaye, Jacqueline. "Claude McKay's *Banjo*," in *Présence africaine*. LXXIII (1970), pp. 165-169.

A. L. McLeod

# THE BEAUTIFUL AND DAMNED

*Author:* F. Scott Fitzgerald (1896-1940)
*Type of plot:* Romantic satire
*Time of plot:* 1913-1921
*Locale:* New York City and environs, and the vicinity of a military training camp in South Carolina
*First published:* 1922

> *Principal characters:*
> ANTHONY PATCH, the protagonist, a young man with great expectations of wealth
> GLORIA GILBERT PATCH, a beautiful young woman from the Midwest who marries Anthony
> ADAM PATCH, an aging millionaire and philanthropist, Anthony's grandfather
> RICHARD CARAMEL, Gloria's cousin and Anthony's best friend, a successful novelist
> MAURY NOBLE, Anthony's friend
> DOROTHY RAYCROFT, Anthony's mistress during World War I

*The Novel*

Originally called "The Flight of the Rocket," *The Beautiful and Damned* is the story of Anthony Patch's life between his twenty-fifth and thirty-third years. The novel follows the progression of his intense love for the dazzlingly beautiful Gloria Gilbert. It traces their attachment through their courtship and marriage, through their apparently endless round of parties and gaiety, to their eventual financial difficulties, and finally to their triumphant achievement of Anthony's "great expectations." The victory comes too late, however, and the conclusion is more bitter than sweet.

As the novel opens, Anthony Patch, handsome, intelligent, and moderately well educated, wants only to live a life of luxury. When he inherits his grandfather's many millions, he will be able to do exactly that. Until then, he has enough money to continue to live comfortably although without any particular goal. Someday, he tells his family and friends, he may write, but in actuality he lacks both the discipline and the ambition of his friend Richard Caramel.

When Anthony meets the incredibly beautiful Gloria Gilbert, his life changes. He pursues her, eventually marries her, and believes that he has everything that he needs to be happy—except his grandfather's money. The years that follow, however, gradually take Anthony and Gloria from blissful romantic happiness to alcoholic boredom. The novel becomes the story of how a lack of purpose and discipline can undermine everything else in life.

Fitzgerald saw *The Beautiful and Damned* as the story of a man with the tastes and weaknesses of an artist, but with no creative inspiration. While this outline suggests that Fitzgerald himself had a rather romantic idea of what makes an artist, the pertinence of the novel's diagnosis is not confined to the artist manqué. Anthony's weaknesses are those of a rootless generation writ large. He has no focus to his life beyond Gloria's beauty and his grandfather's millions. Similarly, Gloria sees herself as a beautiful flower that needs only to be displayed to full advantage. The void at the center of their lives is soon filled with liquor.

Anthony and Gloria buy a car, rent a summer home, give endless parties, all the while living beyond Anthony's income. Soon, they are dipping into their capital in order to pay their bills. As they become more desperate financially, they quarrel more and more frequently. When Adam Patch surprises them during a wild party at their summer home, he disinherits Anthony. When the old man dies, he leaves his millions to his secretary. To recover the fortune, Anthony begins a suit that drags on for years.

The world of illusion in which both Gloria and Anthony have been living is emphasized when Anthony is drafted in World War I and is sent to the South for training. Gloria has always been told that she is beautiful enough for a career in films, but now, when she finally tries to do it to earn a little money, she discovers that—at twenty-nine—she is too old. With despair, she realizes that her beauty is fading.

Anthony's friends, Richard Caramel and Maury Noble, have made successes in literature and business, but when Anthony returns to New York after the war, he discovers that his financial situation is worse than he thought. He and Gloria barely have enough to survive, and that money is running out. They become desperate to win the lawsuit. Finally, they do win, but it is too late. Anthony has been broken, both mentally and physically.

## The Characters

Anthony Patch was intended by Fitzgerald to be a tragic character, but Anthony does not have enough substance for his fate to be tragic. At times, Fitzgerald treats Anthony satirically, as if Anthony is not to be taken seriously. Yet the moments of poignancy—especially in the love affair of Anthony and Gloria—undermine any satirical intent. At the end, the reader has confused feelings about Anthony, pitying him but believing that, after all, he brought about his own destruction.

Gloria Gilbert Patch is, in some ways, more sympathetic than Anthony. Gloria believes above all in the rights and privileges of her beauty. She believes in this with a passion that is lacking in Anthony's supposed belief in his own undemonstrated intellectual and moral superiority. When she is forced, brutally, to recognize that her beauty is fading, she accepts it with a dignity of sorts. She is not crushed, as Anthony finally is.

Richard Caramel, who enjoys the kind of early literary success that Fitzgerald himself experienced, is too heedless to realize that he is compromising his talent as he churns out one popular book after another. He is incapable of recognizing that the success which he has achieved through compromise is not worth having. The character is, in some ways, a warning from Fitzgerald to himself, of what he feared he might become.

Maury Noble, supposedly based on the contemporary wit George Jean Nathan, is cynical enough to compromise with full awareness of what he is doing, although he knows the worthlessness of what he thereby achieves. His wit and philosophy are shallow, and Fitzgerald devotes all too much space to his orations. Yet his success, along with that of Caramel, forms a counterpoint to Anthony's decline and fall.

Dorothy Raycroft, the nineteen-year-old South Carolina girl whom Anthony makes his mistress while he is stationed at the army camp, is sharply distinct from the other characters. Warmhearted, realistic, and sensible, she accepts her life with the ingrained stoicism of those who have no illusions. It is easy to see how Anthony becomes involved with her, although she possesses none of Gloria's beauty or glamour.

### Themes and Meanings

On the surface a study in failure, *The Beautiful and Damned* might more accurately be said to be a study of the atmosphere of failure. Through chapter after chapter, one finds Anthony and Gloria overwhelmed by nothing more substantial than the depressing, claustrophobic ambience of the world in which they find themselves. They are constantly fleeing *places*—their apartment, their summer house, parties—trying to escape their own emotions and sense of frustration. Similarly, they escape into alcohol, fleeing the *sense* of desperation and failure that surrounds them like an ever-growing shroud.

The thrust of the novel is blunted by Fitzgerald's ambivalence. At times, Anthony is portrayed as an admonitory example of the man without purpose, a representative figure of his generation. At other times, he is more sympathetically portrayed as a man who will not compromise with a brutal and meretricious world. The focus of Fitzgerald's criticism shifts correspondingly. In the end, the reader is moved by Anthony and Gloria's pathos rather than by their tragedy, and the moral message of the novel is shortchanged by the frailty of its underlying sentiment.

### Critical Context

Coming only two years after Fitzgerald's first novel, *This Side of Paradise* (1920), *The Beautiful and Damned* was a much more literary and thought-out book. Yet although it was in most respects a superior and more controlled performance, it was far short of the advance in craftsmanship and in maturity of perception that Fitzgerald would demonstrate only three years later in *The Great Gatsby* (1925). Although *The Beautiful and Damned* was not as popular with the readers or with the critics as was Fitzgerald's first novel, the novelty of its subject matter helped its sales and consolidated his position as the spokesman of the Jazz Age.

*Sources for Further Study*

Canby, Henry Seidel. "The Beautiful and Damned: The Flapper's Tragedy," in *F. Scott Fitzgerald in His Own Time: A Miscellany*, 1971. Edited by Matthew J. Bruccoli and Jackson R. Bryer.

Field, Louise Maunsell. Review, in *The New York Times Book Review and Magazine*. March 5, 1922, p. 16.

Shaw, Virginia. "This Side of Innocence," in *The Dial*. LXXII, no. 4 (April, 1922), pp. 419-422.

Van Doren, Carl. "The Roving Critic," in *The Nation*. CXIV, no. 2,958 (March 15, 1922), p. 318.

Wilson, Edmund. "F. Scott Fitzgerald," in *The Shores of Light: A Literary Chronicle of the Twenties and Thirties*, 1952.

*Bruce D. Reeves*

# BEETLECREEK

*Author:* William Demby (1922-     )
*Type of plot:* Existential realism
*Time of plot:* The American Depression era
*Locale:* Beetlecreek, West Virginia
*First published:* 1950

> *Principal characters:*
>     BILL TRAPP, a white recluse who lives close to the black
>         community
>     JOHNNY JOHNSON, a teenage black boy from Pittsburgh,
>         Pennsylvania, who develops an acquaintanceship with Bill
>     DAVID DIGGS, Johnny's uncle, a black man who develops an
>         acquaintanceship with Bill
>     MARY DIGGS, David's wife
>     EDITH JOHNSON, a former resident of Beetlecreek who re-
>         turns to the town and renews an old relationship with
>         David

*The Novel*

The plot of *Beetlecreek* develops chronologically, in four parts focusing on three different sets of human circumstances, actions, and events that converge at the end.

Part 1 introduces four of the five main characters. In chapter 1, Bill Trapp, a white hermit feared by a large number of the black people who live nearby, chases four young black boys from under a fruit tree in his yard and discovers that there is one young black boy up in the tree. Bill, whose reputation is unjustified, invites young Johnny Johnson to come down out of the tree and into his house. After Johnny and Bill talk and drink cider together, Johnny's uncle, David Diggs, arrives looking for him, the other boys having reported that the strange white man has caught Johnny up in the tree. Trapp also invites David to have some wine, and the two men become acquainted and later go to Telrico's Bar and get drunk together. The budding relationship carries a sense of heightened expectancy for Johnny and David, because they are stepping across racial lines, violating black and white community conventions by associating with the ostracized white recluse. For Bill, the potential relationship is exciting because it represents his coming out of seclusion, the end of his isolation from both blacks and whites.

The last chapter of part 1 focuses on David's wife, Mary Diggs, as she immerses herself in the trivial social activities and church events that define her life. Throughout the novel, Mary's actions and activities remain on the level of the petty. The events of Mary's life are one of the three sets of events that are important in the novel; her actions suggest all the negative possibilities in life.

Part 2 centers on the attempts of Bill and Johnny to develop the sense of rich possibility which they had when they first met. Bill comes out of seclusion, associates with both black and white people, and actively tries to win community favor by doing kind deeds. Johnny, who is visiting Beetlecreek from Pittsburgh, Pennsylvania, struggles to reconcile his friendship with Bill with his need, as a newcomer to the community, to prove himself to the local black youth gang. The gang attempts to force Johnny into behavior that is callous and insensitive and that interferes with his deepest responses to Bill. The connection between Bill and Johnny is the catalyst for a second group of events, which allow Demby to examine the possibility that two people can interact with each other on a spontaneous, human level that is above societal insensitivity.

In part 3, Bill, with the intention of continuing his pursuit of a meaningful life through significant human interaction, has a picnic that brings together young black and white girls. His good intentions, however, have negative consequences: The black girls feel intimidated by the white girls, and more important, one of the white girls steals a picture of a naked human body from Bill's anatomy book and takes it to her parents, who start the rumor that Bill has molested the girls. The community rejects Bill even more strongly than before and with great pleasure spreads and magnifies rumors of what happened at the picnic. Although Johnny knows what really happened, he allows peer pressure from the gang to stop him from revealing the truth and also renounces Bill. Johnny decides that he wants to be a member of the gang more than anything else.

Edith Johnson enters the novel in part 3 and renews an old romance with David. After his encounter with Bill, which has awakened his desire to escape what he calls the "death grip" of the average human life, David is ready to leave his wife, Beetlecreek, and their pettiness. He agrees to go away with Edith to Detroit, hoping to draw from her the strength to live as a self-determined, independent person, free of society's death grip. The situation in which Demby places David by means of this relationship provides the impetus for the third major set of circumstances in the novel, circumstances that hold forth the possibility of true freedom and fresh, authentic living.

In part 4, as part of his initiation into the gang, Johnny agrees to burn down Bill's shack to punish him for molesting the girls, but when he starts the fire and is confronted by Bill, he hits Bill over the head with the gasoline can. The blow apparently seriously injures Bill or kills him, and Johnny runs away. David leaves for Detroit on the bus with Edith: The tone and atmosphere of the last chapter are suggestive of his negative future. To the tragic end of the relationship between Bill and Johnny, Demby adds the strong implication that David, too, will fail to escape the meaningless death trap that life is for most people.

### The Characters

It is through the three major male characters—Bill, Johnny, and David—that Demby conveys his concern in *Beetlecreek*: the pursuit of a significant life experience. These three characters and the relationships between them form three perspectives from which to view this concern.

Bill, an orphan, has always had to struggle against his sense of being alone and outside the human community. Before coming to Beetlecreek, he tried to live a meaningful life among other people, but he became frustrated and eventually retired to the seclusion of a farm in Beetlecreek. At the time of the novel, he has lived there for fifteen years. Now an old man, his encounter with Johnny at the beginning of the novel rekindles in him a desire to pursue a significant life through relationships with others. Bill's character incorporates a broad range of qualities with which readers can identify: When inspired, he can be almost heroic, devoting energy, patience, and tolerance to others in an attempt to get them to see him for the compassionate human being that he is; on the other hand, he can be small, weak, pathetic, and ineffectual as he gropes for his identity in seclusion.

Johnny, a teenager adrift in the world, is trying to find the most significant pattern for the life ahead of him. He is perceptive enough to know that it is important to respond spontaneously and humanely to Bill; moreover, his soul instinctively revolts when he sees acts of wanton cruelty, such as those practiced by the gang members in an attempt to prove their manhood as dictated by society. Despite this revulsion, however, Johnny, like many teenagers, is highly vulnerable to peer pressure, and his desire to be accepted by the gang—to become what he calls the "new Johnny"—is so strong that he is willing to burn down Bill's shack to gain that acceptance. Johnny is adrift, with no landmarks but his own emotions. His precarious position shows how easy it is to slip from achieving true personhood, which is based on spontaneous human emotion as demonstrated in his warm response to Bill, to "achieving" a shallow, insensitive version of manhood as touted by the gang.

David, at thirty-two, knows that it is "necessary for himself to act for himself"—that is, to move beyond what other individuals or society in general prescribes for him—but this nevertheless frightens him. He has spent much time in pursuit of pleasure, as well as in the mundane activities of his life with Mary—all socially sanctioned behaviors—despite his knowledge of the importance of independence. David believes that when he first married Mary, he was, for a time—before he settled into Beetlecreek's superficial community patterns—actually beyond the clutches of life's death grip. He has the opportunity to live beyond that death grip again with Edith, yet he suspects (indeed, knows) that the same thing will happen in his relationship with Edith that happened with Mary. His challenge is to renew his struggle for meaning constantly, without falling into negative patterns. The reader can identify with David because his crisis—the crisis of maintaining meaning and relevance in one's life—is one that many people face.

Mary and Edith are less well developed than are the male characters of *Beetlecreek*; rather, they serve symbolic functions. Mary is a totally one-dimensional character. Although the narrative is related from her point of view several times in the novel, Demby never shows her as having a thought that is not selfish or narrow. Her stereotyped characterization therefore serves as a mundane standard against which the reader can judge the strivings of Bill, Johnny, and David.

Edith is somewhat less easily defined. Since Demby never narrates the novel from her point of view, as he does for the other major characters, it is difficult to tell exactly what he intends to achieve through her. At times, Edith seems to be the character who has attained the individual freedom for which David is searching; she appears to do whatever she wants and to answer to no one. On the other hand, she is limited by her lack of compassion—for the woman who adopted and reared her, for poor people, and for people in general. It is clear that she is seductive and alluring and will probably place David in another death grip after he has been with her for a while. From one perspective, she represents the extreme of the carefree life of sensual pleasure, the opposite of Mary's overly structured life. Yet, from another perspective, Edith, like Mary, represents a conventional approach to life that David needs to avoid. Her characterization, then, is almost as one-dimensional as that of Mary.

## Themes and Meanings

The novel focuses on the idea that there is the ever-present challenge to make something of one's life, no matter what stage of life in which one may be—Bill's, Johnny's, or David's. This quest for meaning is one that transcends race—racial concerns and mores being factors that aid in keeping people locked in superficial interactions—and it also transcends the routine religious activities, in which Mary and the Beetlecreek community are very much involved.

Finding human connection briefly, as the three main male characters do, is important, but being trapped in a meaningless existence is inevitable, Demby suggests. One can accept the challenge to escape, as these characters do, and that attempt to escape can be courageous, humane, and heartwarming, but it is ultimately doomed to failure. The most that man can do is accept the terrible responsibility of acting for himself, although he will certainly fail. Thus, in this context, the human experience is tragic, and the tragedy is not diminished by the fact that the novel suggests an unachievable, ideal life. That ideal is an existence that is fresh, humane, independent, sensitive, spontaneous, and free—somewhere between the structured but mindless triviality of Mary and the careless, insensitive abandon of Edith.

*Critical Context*

Perhaps, the best way to see *Beetlecreek* is in the context of the literary "mainstreaming" which was popular among some black writers and scholars during the time that Demby wrote the novel. Black literary mainstreamers believed, in part at least, that black writing would mature when it lost its distinctive identity, as manifested in a focus on concerns that were specifically black and merged thematically with the general body of American and world literature. In *Beetlecreek*, some readers may find that Demby is too easily and too summarily rising above racial concerns in his attempt to produce the mainstream, universal novel that depicts broadly the problems of human existence. Perhaps Ralph Ellison's *Invisible Man* (1952), another work by a black author that aims to enter the mainstream, is more successful in the manner in which it works through to the universal by concerning itself first with specifically racial themes. Yet one must remember that *Beetlecreek* preceded *Invisible Man* by two years and, at least in the context of literary history, achieved very early something that a number of black writers and intellectuals were trying to achieve.

It is also important to note that Demby's approach to his existential theme (the idea that man is cast alone into a meaningless universe in which he has to determine his own meaning) is more like the approach of Ellison, who followed him, and less like that of the French existentialist Albert Camus, for example. Camus not only assumed that man's search for meaning was doomed to failure, but he also failed to stress that the values of sensitivity and humanity were important in the search. For Demby and Ellison, the values of humanity and sensitivity are important in this quest. Demby's fiction is thus an example of one important direction that literary existentialism took in the mid-twentieth century.

*Sources for Further Study*

Bayliss, John F. "Beetlecreek: Existential or Human Document?" in *Negro Digest*. XIX (November, 1969).
Bone, Robert. *The Negro Novel in America*, 1958.
Connely, Joseph F. "William Demby's Fiction: The Pursuit of the Muse," in *Negro American Literature Forum*. X (1976).
Margolies, Edward. *Native Sons*, 1968
O'Brien, John. *Interviews with Black Writers*, 1973.

*James W. Coleman*

# THE BELL JAR

*Author:* Sylvia Plath (1932-1963)
*Type of plot:* Psychological realism
*Time of plot:* 1953
*Locale:* New York City and suburban Boston
*First published:* 1963

> *Principal characters:*
> ESTHER GREENWOOD, a bright college student undergoing a
> mental breakdown
> MRS. GREENWOOD, her widowed mother, a business-English
> teacher at a city college in Boston
> BUDDY WILLARD, a medical student whom Esther has been
> dating
> DR. NOLAN, a woman psychiatrist who helps Esther to
> recover

*The Novel*

The Bell Jar describes a young woman's descent into a private, schizophrenic hell, and the first steps of her recovery. Like Esther Greenwood, its protagonist, the novel itself is split into two uneven parts. In the first half, Esther describes her frantic month in New York City as one of twelve student editors for a special college issue of a leading women's magazine, *Ladies' Day*. Like J. D. Salinger's *The Catcher in the Rye* (1951), this first half of *The Bell Jar* has a particular 1950's taste of humor, pathos, and naïveté. Like Holden Caulfield, Esther Greenwood is slowly falling apart in New York City as she rushes through the frenetic magazine life of lunches, meetings, and dances. On her last night in Manhattan, Esther stands on the roof of the Amazon hotel, calmly feeding her new wardrobe to the night wind.

At this point, where Holden ended *The Catcher in the Rye*, Esther begins her frightening descent into the nightmare world of schizophrenia, and the second half of *The Bell Jar* is a second, almost unrelated novel. Back home in Boston, with no job or friends in this summer before her last year of college, Esther wanders the city seeking her identity and contemplating suicide. She is hospitalized after swallowing a bottle of pills and begins the slow, painful process of recovery. Through a combination of treatments (including shock therapy) and the wise and sensitive care of Dr. Nolan, Esther begins to gain her own identity, and the "bell jar" under which she feels she has been trapped finally begins to lift.

Yet what is Esther's problem? In part, it is the difficulty of being a bright and self-conscious young woman in the restricted 1950's, and not a little of the novel's power, like that of *The Catcher in the Rye*, lies in its ability to suggest the limitations to human possibility in this Eisenhower world. Yet at a deeper level, the problem is Esther's sexual identity, or lack of it. As Esther says, "pureness" is a big issue in the 1950's, and it is even a bigger issue for a sheltered young woman whose father died when she was a child and whose mother seems to spend her whole life working to survive. Esther has never been able to work out her own sexual identity in her partial family in this parochial, 1950's world. Whenever she thinks about sex, she thinks about babies, and especially about the fetuses in bottles that she has seen in a visit to Buddy Willard at medical school the year before. Esther herself is like a baby in a bottle—or bell jar—stopped or arrested in her own psychosexual development and unable to move into the adult world of heterosexuality.

Her recovery is marked by two significant events. She meets and seduces Irwin, a young Boston math professor, but she hemorrhages badly and must get a friend, Joan Gilling, to take her to a local hospital, where the doctor tells her, "it's one in a million it happens to like this." It should be, for, in the psychological symbolism of the novel, Esther is in effect giving birth to herself, to her first adult identity. There ought to be "a ritual for being born twice," she says. Later, Joan kills herself, but, as Dr. Nolan tells her, Esther cannot be responsible for the death of another, only for herself. Esther survives both these events and, in the last scene, is walking alone into her final interview with the hospital board before her release. She will recover. Actually, as clues at the beginning of the novel tell the reader, she is married, and has a baby as she is narrating this novel.

*The Characters*

The central character in this initiation novel is Esther Greenwood, but other characters play important roles in her passage into adulthood. In some ways, characterization in *The Bell Jar* resembles a fictional Rorschach test, in which Esther is being forced to choose among various 1950's roles. As she describes it early in the novel, her life is like a fig tree in a story that she read, and from "every branch, like a fat purple fig, a wonderful future beckoned and winked." Yet Esther can imagine herself sitting only "in the crotch of this fig tree, starving to death, just because I couldn't make up my mind which of the figs I would choose." Part of her problem is that each sexual role is restrictive. Esther's mother works so hard to support her family that she has nothing left for herself. Buddy Willard's mother, in perhaps the best metaphor of all, braids rugs that her family immediately walks on, and Esther's neighbor Dodo Conway produces babies year by year. Yet career women here are limited, too. JayCee, Esther's editor at *Ladies' Day*, is hard and aggressive, and Esther cannot imagine her married life. Esther's patron at college is the popular women's novelist Philomena Guinea, who will not help Esther in the hospital if there is "a boy in the case." Other choices are more sexual, from the promiscuous Doreen in New York City to the lesbian Joan in Boston. Esther believes that she must choose among these limited 1950's roles for her own future, but, by the end of the novel— and with the help of the only whole person present, Dr. Nolan—Esther has discovered and is choosing herself instead.

The roles for men in this world are not much wider. Buddy Willard is a rigid and repressed young man whose sexual innocence almost matches Esther's. In New York City, Esther meets Lenny, Doreen's hypersexual boyfriend; Marco, a woman hater; and Constantin, a simultaneous interpreter at the United Nations who is apparently asexual. In Boston there are Dr. Gordon, Esther's first psychiatrist and the successful family man, who is insensitive to his patients' real needs, and Irwin, precocious but sexually immature. In spite of the fact that some of these characters are types, Plath's rich poetic style breathes life into them, fleshes them out beyond the caricatures that they might have become in another author's hands.

### Themes and Meanings

*The Bell Jar* has multiple layers of meaning. On one level, it is an initiation novel, a book about growing up female in America, with all the role restrictions and psychological hurdles that a woman may face. At the same time, it is a novel about the dead ends of the 1950's, when anti-Communist hysteria contrasted so sharply with the blandness of American cultural life. A symbolic echo of that period is the execution of the Rosenbergs, which Esther mentions in her first paragraph and which recurs, metaphorically, at least, in Esther's shock treatments in the hospital.

At its deepest level, *The Bell Jar* describes the world of the schizophrenic from the inside, and Sylvia Plath's poetic language renders this complex psychological story realistically but with reverberations. Images of babies in bottles, fetuses and figs, bell jars and scenes of electroshock and drowning—all help carry the reader through Esther's descent, hospitalization, and beginning recovery.

In the end, the major themes of the novel are inextricably intertwined: the psychosexual story of Esther's faltering attempts, in spite of her illness, to gain her own identity, and the peculiar 1950's version of this story which, like Salinger's *Catcher in the Rye*, captures a world of conformity and hypocrisy. Few first novels have the thematic depth or the rich poetic language of *The Bell Jar*. Unfortunately, the split in the narrative structure of the novel keeps it from becoming the masterpiece that it might otherwise have been.

### Critical Context

*The Bell Jar* was first published in January of 1963 in England, where Sylvia Plath was then living, under the pseudonym Victoria Lucas. Less than a month later, as Lois Ames writes in her biographical afterword to the

1971 American edition, Plath took her own life. The novel was first published in the United States eight years later, under Plath's own name, and has known popular and critical acclaim ever since that second publication.

Had Plath been alive when *The Bell Jar* was published in the United States, she might have solved the problem of the split in the novel. Certainly, she recognized its limitations. "I've tried to picture my world and the people in it as seen through the distorting lens of a bell jar," she wrote to her mother in 1962. "My second book will show that same world as seen through the eyes of health." Yet, as Esther Greenwood says toward the end of the novel, "To the person in the bell jar, blank and stopped as a dead baby, the world itself is the bad dream." From that dream, Plath herself never awoke, and, ever since the publication of the novel, critics have not been able to discuss it without knowledge of the tragic early death of its author.

Yet in other ways as well, Plath created the critical framework within which the book is discussed. Perhaps because its history has paralleled the growth of the women's movement in the United States, *The Bell Jar* has become a feminist touchstone. Certainly, there were psychological novels about women before *The Bell Jar*, such as Mary Jane Ward's *The Snake Pit* (1946), but Sylvia Plath wrote an initiation novel that coincided with the emergence of feminist literary consciousness in the United States and, since its publication, the novel has stood at the top of a long and growing list of works by women writing about themselves in that society. Whenever the feminist initiation novel is discussed, from Hannah Green's *I Never Promised You a Rose Garden* (1964) through Lisa Alther's *Kinflicks* (1976) to a slew of contemporary novels, *The Bell Jar* is cited as a beginning. In a number of ways, the novel captures the experience of growing up female in America. The tragic story of its poet-author says something about the difficulties of the literary life for women in America. For the feminist critic, furthermore, the novel has become a weapon in the fight to bring the discussion of literature back into the context of the lives out of which it has grown. The emotional power of *The Bell Jar*, such critics argue, cannot finally be separated from the life and death of Sylvia Plath.

Yet *The Bell Jar* also represents a number of other novels to come out of the changing sociopolitical energy of the 1960's, from Ken Kesey's *One Flew over the Cuckoo's Nest* (1962) and Joseph Heller's *Catch-22* (1961) through Jerzy Kosinski's *The Painted Bird* (1965) to Kurt Vonnegut's *Slaughterhouse-Five* (1969). In these and other essentially 1960's works, the focus is on the relationship between the individual and society, and war and madness become metaphors for the human condition, as hospitals (or the army) become both microcosms of and escapes from the insanity of society. Like a number of novels that followed it, *The Bell Jar* focuses concern on the individual lost in a society that can no longer respond to individual needs, and where institutions no longer work.

Finally, *The Bell Jar* is often discussed in analyses of Plath's important work as a poet, particularly of the collections of poetry in *The Colossus and Other Poems* (1960) and *Ariel* (1965): The language of the novel has been examined numerous times in connection with Plath's work as a poet and an image-maker.

*Sources for Further Study*
Aird, Eileen M. *Sylvia Plath*, 1973.
Barnard, Caroline King. *Sylvia Plath*, 1978.
Newman, Charles, ed. *The Art of Sylvia Plath*, 1970.

*David Peck*

# BELLEFLEUR

*Author:* Joyce Carol Oates (1938-    )
*Type of plot:* Allegory, gothic satire
*Time of plot:* Five years in the 1930's, and from 1806 to 1826
*Locale:* A mythical region not unlike the Adirondacks on the shores of Lake
    Noir, also Mount Blanc
*First published:* 1980

> *Principal characters:*
> LEAH BELLEFLEUR, the female protagonist, a heroine of sorts
> GIDEON BELLEFLEUR, her husband, the male protagonist, a
>     villain of sorts
> JEDEDIAH BELLEFLEUR, their great-great-grandfather, a her-
>     mit searching for God on Mount Blanc
> GERMAINE, their daughter, who may or may not possess magi-
>     cal powers

*The Novel*

   *Bellefleur* is a big, baggy novel filled with suspense, graphic sexual scenes, and a mix of realistic and fanciful atrocities. The novel begins with the arrival of an apparently portentous beast, the cat Mahalaleel, and ends with Gideon's suicide bombing of the Bellefleur manor five days after Mahalaleel's sudden disappearance. The many comic and frightening episodes that fill the intervening five hundred pages relate the history of the infamous and wealthy Bellefleur clan and its fall—the rise and fall set against a backdrop of real and imagined incidents from American history. It is even rumored that Abraham Lincoln once slept in the Bellefleur home.

   The family's fate is attributed to both the presumed Bellefleur curse and a psychological ailment, the "Bellefleur temperament, an unfortunate combination of passion and melancholy." The castle itself seems the victim of deferred maintenance as well as a third-floor ghost. Moreover, there is the enmity of neighboring families plus an assortment of other creatures—a beast of a man who turns into a bear, a half-wit who turns into a mangy dog, grotesque and cruel mountain gnomes, and the rapacious Noir Vulture—to blame for the maiming, abduction, and murder of Bellefleur children.

   Mahalaleel arrives at the castle one stormy night in the middle of a marital quarrel between Leah and Gideon. Leah cradles in her arms the "begrimed starving contemptible rainsoaked ugly thing" despite her husband's plea that it be chased away or killed. The next morning the sinister cat appears transformed into a magnificent creature, a peacock of a cat with an "immense plume of a tail, in which hairs of myriad colors meshed." Soon after, Leah is pregnant and apparently endowed with miraculous powers which enable her to win all card games and ultimately regain Bellefleur lands and fortune.

Out of Leah's womb, in the most teasingly symbolic chapter, comes a baby and a half: "a single melon-sized head, two scrawny shoulders and at the torso something hideous that resembled . . . part of another embryo . . . rubbery-red slippery male genitalia, possibly oversized . . . growing out of the abdomen of what appeared to be a perfectly well-formed, though somewhat large, baby girl." The grandmother's solution—"three skillful chops of the knife"—occurs before Leah has a chance to save still another monstrous creature.

The novel proceeds episodically with occasional flashbacks to earlier Bellefleur generations and, in particular, to the story of Jedediah, the first generation's would-be saint. Jedediah, Germaine's great-great-great-grandfather, by dropping out to search for God atop Mount Blanc, might in effect have obliterated the entire Bellefleur line at the start.

In a kind of epilogue to Gideon's bombing of the manor, Jedediah receives a messenger from below who informs him that his entire family has been murdered with the exception of his sister-in-law, who now calls for his return. It was, in fact, his incestuous love for this first Germaine which had sent him on his quest for God twenty years earlier. The novel comes full circle as the reader realizes Jedediah will marry Germaine, a union germinating four generations later in a namesake who too survives a second devastation of the Bellefleur clan.

## The Characters

Oates described Leah, the most prominent character in the novel, as "an exceptionally tall woman, tall and strong and full bodied, her long legs superbly muscled, her neck columnar, her thick braid of dark, burnished-red hair falling between her shoulder blades, heavily to the very small of her back: a beautiful giantess." She is a Bellefleur twice over, having married her cousin. In one of the novel's most amusing allegories, the narrator describes how Leah as an adolescent kept a very large spider named Love for a pet. All of her suitors were intimidated by Love except for Gideon who killed it "just by . . . gripping it fast and squeezing." Years later, after she has succeeded in restoring the Bellefleur family and manor to its past glory, Leah takes on a human pet, Nightshade, a grotesque, humpbacked dwarf who, like Mahalaleel, is magically transformed into a prince of sorts under her loving care.

Gideon, with his great muscular chest and dark mane of hair, seems the stereotypic gothic male, the fitting mate for this giantess, yet he is driven out of his home by his own uncontrollable passions and the rising dominance of his wife. The story of his many and increasingly brutal affairs parallels the central plot of power achieved and lost. Apparently maddened from the moment of Mahalaleel's arrival, Gideon sinks deeper and deeper into self-destruction as he seeks to lose himself in typical masculine pleasures—horse racing, gambling, hunting, and ultimately flying. In the end, reduced literally to "skin and bones," with a limp, a maimed right hand, but still a "hot, glaring half-crazy eye for women," he moves his daughter Germaine to safety at her aunt Mitilde's house, says his proud farewell to the earth itself, and flies his Hawker Tempest into the massive stone of Bellefleur manor.

Jedediah also seeks to escape the earth or, at least, his family. He has been living on Mount Blanc three years when conflicting rumors reach his brother. One report describes him aging with a beard to his knees, another sees him lean, muscular, bare-chested, dark as an Indian, still another has him living with a full-blooded Iroquois squaw. A family spy is sent to keep track of him as Jedediah, like so many of Oates's would-be saints, sinks further and further into despair at his failure to find God and his inability to suppress his own erotic dreams. Finally, in one of the novel's most graphic and ironic scenes, when hour after hour Jedediah is seized by such ferocious diarrhetic spasms that "his pelvic bones jutted through his skin. . . . God showed His face to His servant Jedediah, and forever afterward kept His distance." Soon after, the messenger arrives to summon him home.

Germaine is apparently born with the clairvoyance Jedediah hoped to achieve. On her first birthday she is described as a "sturdy toddler, large for her age . . . with amazing green-bronze eyes, whose fabled luminosity varied: in the candlelight . . . they frequently glowed with a discomforting intensity, but in the ordinary glare of midmorning sun they appeared no more striking" than any other child's. Though given to "queer prolonged spells of 'knowingness,'" she also likes to play with cats and dolls. Ultimately, she refuses the prophetic role her mother wanted for her as Oates seems to undercut her own symbolism; at the age of four she is safe at her Aunt's, safe from being a "witness," a role she believes was forced upon her.

In addition to these main characters are a large number of Bellefleur relatives, each with his own tale. Of the children, Vernon the poet and Raphael the introspective dreamer receive the most attention. Both die "interesting" deaths true to the Bellefleur curse; Vernon is drowned by poet-hating rednecks in a barroom quarrel and Raphael simply disappears as does the magic pond which had once saved him.

The most important outsider is Garnet, one of Gideon's women, who is taken in by Leah's mother, whose bastard child is adopted by Leah before being abducted by the Noir Vulture, and who ultimately leaves the manor to marry the kindly Lord Dunraven. Her story is a good example of the web of coincidences and fantastic events Oates weaves to tie together the seemingly separate episodes of the novel.

*Themes and Meanings*

The novel seems to be about American naïveté and arrogance. In building the Bellefleur manor the family had sought to obliterate the past and dissociate itself from "that rotting graveyard Europe." "We are all Americans now," Raphael I states, launching a history of political intrigue, materialism, and greed marked by alternating periods of good and bad fortune. Later generations divide between those who insist on their Bellefleur identity and those who seek to flee it. Vernon, for example, considers himself a poet, not a Bellefleur, yet his murderers curse him for being both. Leah becomes obsessed with clearing the Bellefleur name by proving the innocence of the "Innisfail Butcher," alias Jean-Pierre Bellefleur II, long imprisoned for a mass murder he clearly committed.

The novel also seems to be about violence itself, about the ways in which normal life can suddenly turn monstrous and the ways in which human brutality can imitate the most grotesque literary fantasies. When Leah snatches Garnet's baby from her she enacts on a literal level the later metaphoric action of the Noir Vulture. The beastly man may be a bear or the Bellefleur clan may see him as such to justify their own brutal execution of him. Violence in the novel seems invested with an archetypal or biblical significance (most of the characters have biblical names). Bromwell, the most intellectual of the Bellefleurs, explains, "Our universe began with an explosion of immeasurable violence . . . so it's natural for the human species to *rest*, so to speak in violence." Volume one ends with the violent solution to Germaine's monstrous birth—a half murder; following this event each subsequent chapter ends with more numerous and brutal murders than the preceding one.

These themes are common to the bulk of Oates's fiction, yet there is a danger here in taking them too seriously. It may be that Oates is spoofing gothic novels in general as well as her own earlier work. Though other Oates novels and stories have blurred the border between reality and fantasy, the symbolism in *Bellefleur* appears intentionally outrageous. Mahalaleel's transformation, Germaine's hermaphrodite birth, the half-wit boy who turns into a dog, the pond that breathes and later disappears—all these apparent symbols and portents mock themselves and those who would invest them with meaning. Perhaps seriousness itself is a function of perspective. Take as an example the decision of Raphael I to have himself skinned so that his hide could be treated and stretched across a Civil War cavalry drum. When his doctor asked why he wished to mock himself in such a bizarre way, he replied, "*Is* it mockery? . . . I had thought, rather, it was a kind of immortality." Oates's style—its elaborate, long-winded sentences, heaped up modifiers and clauses, and countless parenthetical statements—adds to the comic deflation and makes the novel read as if written at breathtaking speed.

*Critical Context*

*Bellefleur* is one of Joyce Carol Oates's most popular and most controversial novels. Oates has been publishing prolifically at the rate of several volumes of short stories, poetry, novels, and literary criticism per year since her first collection of short stories, *By the Northern Gate*, appeared in 1963. With *Bellefleur* in 1980, Oates, at the age of forty-two, had published more than thirty-five books and also found time to teach at the universities of Detroit and Windsor, and Princeton University.

Two equally important novels precede and follow *Bellefleur* and suggest a progression in Oates's writing from serious allegory to satire. *Son of the Morning* (1978) has as its hero a fanatical evangelist preacher. Nathan, the product of a gang-rape (the symbolic antithesis of the virgin birth), is reared by his grandmother in a world steeped in fundamentalist religion. The novel is at once a study of an obsessive and disturbed consciousness (Jedediah is a minor version of the same theme) and of a particularly American phenomenon, Pentecostal religious fanaticism viewed in the larger context of American naïveté and violence. The novel is ironic and powerful, the language biblical and intense.

*A Bloodsmoor Romance* (1982) begins with the abduction of sixteen-year-old Deirdre Zinn by "an outlaw balloon of sinister hue." The novel then examines the fate of each of the six Zinn daughters and their various suitors and husbands (several Bellefleur daughters have similar stories) in a humorous feminist revision of Victorian and gothic romances. Zinn women are apparently to be feared rather than victimized. Their father, unlike most Oates men, is a bumbling inventor, obsessive but not intense. The novel as a whole is enlivened by much seemingly authentic detail about nineteenth century American life; the style is as labyrinthine as usual but in the service of comedy rather than passion.

*Bellefleur* shares elements of both these books: the historical backdrop, the psychological study of violence, obsession, and their roots, the large cast of characters, each with his separate story, the mix of realism and fantasy. Some critics complain that the novel has no humor at all and too much gratuitous violence; others love its nonsense and find it a joy to read.

Despite disagreement about how *Bellefleur* should be read, critics tend to agree that Oates's work in general might benefit from more compression; most distrust her extraordinary fluency and her very popularity. There is no doubt that the suspense, the violence, the sex, and the flamboyant style keep her readers reading. As these are the ingredients of popular fiction, the question raised is whether Oates's work also achieves the large vision and thematic seriousness which would earn for her a permanent slot in the American literary canon, or whether she might even emerge as a successful satirist. As a pivotal work, *Bellefleur* will play an important role in whatever conclusions are ultimately drawn on Oates's complete oeuvre.

*Sources for Further Study*

Banks, Russell. "Joyce Carol Oates: In a Gothic Manor," in *Book World*. X
   (August 17, 1980), p. 4.
Batchelor, John Calvin. "Hot News: Funny Oates," in *The Village Voice*.
   XXV, no. 31 (July 30, 1980), p. 34.
Gardner, John. "The Strange Real World," in *The New York Times Book
   Review*. LXXXV (July 20, 1980), p. 1.
Leonard, John. " '*Bellefleur*,'" in *The New York Times*. CXXV (July 21,
   1980), sec. III, p. C15.

*Jane M. Barstow*

# BEND SINISTER

*Author:* Vladimir Nabokov (1899-1977)
*Type of plot:* Surrealistic tragicomedy
*Time of plot:* Sometime during the first half of the twentieth century
*Locale:* An unnamed European country where the people speak a language
that blends Slavic and Germanic elements
*First published:* 1947

> *Principal characters:*
> ADAM KRUG, the protagonist, an internationally known
> philosopher
> DAVID KRUG. his young son
> PADUK, the leader of the Party of the Average Man, which is
> in control of the government

## The Novel

*Bend Sinister* is the story of a philosopher who tries to keep himself remote from the politics of his country by reasoning that he is too well-known a figure to be hurt. He watches his friends disappear and seems to have little concern for what happens to them. Finally, government forces remove Krug and his son from their apartment and separate father and son. Only now does Krug realize that he will do or say anything to save his son. Unfortunately, the son is mistakenly, pointlessly killed, and Krug takes refuge in madness to remove himself from a world become absurd.

A simple summary of the plot of the novel, however, misses most of its thematic and structural complexities and its creation of a surreal, fictional realm where cosmic tragedy and comedy mesh (Vladimir Nabokov once said that the trouble with the "cosmic" was that it was always threatening to lose its "s") and where protagonist and narrator/author are reflections of each other in a drama in which the terror of dreams intertwines with nightmarish reality.

The novel begins and ends with images reflected in a rain puddle situated in the middle of an asphalt road. Krug sees the puddle first at the beginning of the novel as he looks into the street from the window of a hospital, where his wife has just died unexpectedly. The narrator/author sees the same puddle at the end of the novel as he wonders whether people leave an imprint in the texture of space similar to the imprint made by the depression in the ground that is filled with rainwater. Nabokov himself, in a 1963 introduction to the novel, points out how the puddle reappears in various guises throughout the book. The puddle becomes an ink blot in chapter 4, an ink stain in chapter 5, spilled milk in chapter 11, a ciliated thought in chapter 12, and a footprint in chapter 18.

Such recurring images are representative of the many rhetorical devices that Nabokov uses in the course of the novel to provide the intricate patterning and stylistic play with words that are the basis of his style and the essence of his perennial theme—that it is not reality that matters but what one makes of it. The emphasis on artifice with its concomitant factors—imagination and memory—provides the rationale for Nabokov's characteristic use of point of view, which allows an omniscient author to show himself through certain tears in the narrative fabric in ways peculiar to Nabokov's fiction.

In *Bend Sinister*, an omniscient narrator begins to reveal his presence in the first chapter, where a reader must wonder about the identity of the "I" who reports what is seen and felt. Soon the "I" becomes a character whose wife has died, changing brightly dappled surfaces into dull, liquid-white traversed by dead-black and then becoming inky black. In chapter 2, the first person changes to the third person, and the "I" becomes Krug, but a Krug with a shadow-double—the throbbing one and the one who looked on, "the last stronghold of the dualism he abhorred," Krug thinks. "The square root of I is I." In every mask that he tries on, Krug believes, there are slits for his shadow's eyes. In chapter 5, an omniscient narrator separates himself from Krug again and appears as "a nameless, mysterious genius," author of a "dream-code" which permeates the entire novel.

The dreamlike experience on the bridge, where Krug finds himself doomed, he believes, to walk back and forth with neither bank attainable, is a microcosm encapsulating every event of the novel, each of which is a replay of the first. References to stage plays and motion pictures intertwine with Krug's dreams to provide a network of images at the interstices of which creator and created are revealed as one. Thus it comes as no surprise to a reader when the author/narrator emerges at last in his own person to remove Krug from the action the instant before he is to be killed; thus, the artist dismantles the props that he has created.

## The Characters

Adam Krug is a supreme individualist. The name "Adam" suggests the archetypal individuation that occurred in the Garden of Eden with the naming of the first humans. "Krug" is Russian for "circle," suggesting a whole, a unity that circles back upon itself. Yet with Krug's wife, Olga, dead, the Garden is under attack; evil has entered and must be confronted. This Krug refuses to do, believing that he cannot be hurt by anyone in government, feeling arrogantly secure in his international reputation. The nether side of Krug, his mirror image ("bend sinister" is a term from heraldry, denoting a diagonal band that divides a shield from upper left to lower right), is Gurk, "Krug" spelled backward. Gurk is an Ekwilist soldier who wants his share of the brutalizing fun. Yet Gurk and all the soldiers, like all the citizens of

Padukgrad, are, Nabokov says, merely anagrams of everybody else. Thus, the leader Paduk is simply a slightly brighter Gurk and, at the same time, the inverse side of Krug, the brutalizing side, the selfish side. In their youth, Krug had tormented Paduk. "I was something of a bully," Krug says, "and I used to trip him up and sit upon his face . . . every blessed day for about five school years."

As a philosopher, Krug works with words, attempting to come to rational conclusions about the nature of the universe, but, although he has been successful in demolishing the theories of other philosophers, he has not posited one of his own. In the end, he is unable to comprehend the stupidly excessive and senselessly brutal behavior of the Ekwilists. Madness is an appropriate response to the all too literal nightmare of history. Madness allows escape from the prison of space and time.

Paduk, known to Krug as "Toad," is pictured, like all of Nabokov's tyrants, as stupid, coarse, brutal, unhealthy, sadistic, grotesque, and mechanical. Within the Party of the Average Man, all Ekwilists, as replicas of one another, are the lowest common denominator of human potential. The concluding scenes, in which Ekwilists foolishly kill the wrong child and then show Krug motion pictures of what happens to captured children, are an absurd foreshadowing of the grotesque "shoot 'em up" conclusion, which seems a nightmarish replay of the obligatory showdown in Westerns and crime and spy films, raised to preposterous and bizarre proportions.

Krug's son David plays a small role in the novel. He is an object of love, as his mother was, and he is a throwaway in the society, the tick of a clock already moved ahead, as Olga is, present only in memory, and then only as long as Krug is rational and lives (or *Bend Sinister* stays in print).

## Themes and Meanings

Nabokov's basic theme in everything that he writes is human imprisonment in space and time where there is infinite foretime before birth and infinite aftertime, one would assume, after death. Krug cannot make up his mind with regard to death. Intelligence will not "accept the transformation of physical discontinuity into the permanent continuity of a nonphysical element . . . nor can it accept the inanity of accumulating treasures of thought" and sensation to lose them all at once in black "nausea followed by infinite nothingness."

John Shade, the poet in Nabokov's novel *Pale Fire* (1962), makes precisely the same point:

> And I'll turn down eternity unless
> The melancholy and the tenderness
> Of mortal life; the passion and the pain;
>
> Are formed in Heaven by the newly dead.

The only redemption from the horror of mortal existence is the metaphoric, thematic, and structural harmony of art. Art is a repository of the joy of existence expressed by Nabokov in his loving presentation of minute detail, his passionate concern for pattern, and his delight in style. Thus, at the end of *Bend Sinister*, the author/narrator removes Krug from the action, commenting that his death is "but a question of style."

### Critical Context

*Bend Sinister* was Nabokov's second novel written in English, the first being *The Real Life of Sebastian Knight* (1941). Before publishing books in the English language, Nabokov published ten others in his native Russian. It was not until the publication of his best-selling *Lolita* (1955), however, that Nabokov began to receive worldwide attention and acclaim as one of the most important literary figures of the century. Major novels following *Lolita* are *Pnin* (1957), *Pale Fire*, and *Ada or Ardor: A Family Chronicle* (1969). Besides novels, Nabokov published short stories, poems, essays, memoirs, and critical works.

Often called the last of the great modernists, the peer of such masters as Marcel Proust, James Joyce, and William Faulkner, Nabokov has just as often been hailed as one of the pioneers of metafiction, the father of such postmodernists as John Fowles, Robert Coover, Donald Barthelme, and Gabriel García Márquez. Nabokov's work has been the subject of numerous books and articles, which have been increasing in number steadily since his death.

### Sources for Further Study

Dembo, L. S., ed. *Nabokov: The Man and His Work*, 1967.
Field, Andrew. *Nabokov: His Life and Art*, 1967.
Hyde, G. M. *Vladimir Nabokov: America's Russian Novelist*, 1977.
Lee, L. L. *Vladimir Nabokov*, 1976.
Stegner, Page. *Escape into Aesthetics: The Art of Vladimir Nabokov*, 1966.

*Mary Rohrberger*

# BETRAYED BY RITA HAYWORTH

*Author:* Manuel Puig (1932-    )
*Type of plot:* Bildungsroman
*Time of plot:* 1933-1948
*Locale:* Vallejos, a provincial town in Argentina
*First published: La traición de Rita Hayworth*, 1968 (English translation, 1971)

Principal characters:
> José Casals (Toto), the central character of the novel, which
> follows him from infancy to adolescence
> Mita, his mother, educated as a pharmacist but devoting her
> life primarily to her family
> Berto, his father, a businessman
> Héctor, Berto's nephew, several years older than Toto; he
> lives with his uncle's family
> Paquita, a promiscuous young girl of Vallejos
> Cobito, a schoolmate of Toto, rough and vulgar
> Esther, a schoolmate of Toto, infatuated with Héctor

*The Novel*

Although *Betrayed by Rita Hayworth* does not resemble a traditional novel in form, its subject matter is highly conventional: the maturation and education of a sensitive young man. Because this is Puig's first novel, and because he shares the birth date of his protagonist, most readers suspect that *Betrayed by Rita Hayworth* is autobiographical to some degree. The novel reveals the world of young José Casals, nicknamed Toto, by exploring not only his fantasies and daydreams but also those of his parents, aunts, cousins, schoolmates, and teachers. Through this sometimes indirect method, the reader absorbs the multitude of influences that shape Toto's life. At the same time, Puig delineates the spectrum of provincial life in Argentina, providing insight into such facets of that culture as the meaning of machismo, the importance attached to education, and the pervasive influence of romantic fiction and Hollywood films.

Most of the novel's sixteen chapters are internal monologues of the major and minor characters. A few chapters are made up of dialogues (consisting mostly of revealing gossip) between female characters; the novel also includes excerpts from diaries, two letters, and a school essay by Toto on the topic, "The Movie I Liked Best."

A minimal plot emerges from this collage of material, although it may be difficult to discern on a first reading. Toto's mother, Mita, marries Berto even though he has less education than she, because he resembles a film star. As a consequence of the marriage, she leaves her large family in a busy town and moves to sleepy Vallejos. During the early years of her marriage she works, to Berto's discomfort, but increasingly becomes absorbed in her children and in going to films. Instead of bedtime stories, she recites to Toto the plots of films such as *Romeo and Juliet* and *The Great Ziegfield*. As soon as he is old enough, Toto also becomes a cinema buff, especially enjoying those with beautiful female stars such as Rita Hayworth. The first half of the novel revolves around the female characters who make up Mita and Toto's world.

As Toto gets older, he naturally grows curious about sex and is given many opportunities to hear about its mysteries from his older playmates and cousins. A neighborhood girl, Paquita, teases him with salacious stories. One of his teachers, helping him to draw a model of the digestive and reproductive systems, explains the biological processes to the confused nine-year-old. Even at this early stage of his life, Toto is perceived by others as small for his age and effeminate. He prefers to play with girls, does not like sports, and spends much time with his mother. Eventually, Toto is sent away to school where, as revealed by the sexually knowledgeable Héctor and the rough Cobito, he becomes the target of sadistic older boys. The savage voices of Héctor and Cobito provide a marked contrast to the predominantly female voices of the earlier chapters.

When the novel ends, Toto is still only fifteen years old, and thus no final word can be said about his development either sexually or socially. He remains immersed in the world of books, film, and music, and like a typical sensitive adolescent has begun to be scornful of the lowbrow tastes of others and of the pieties of religion. Almost the last word, however, is given to Toto's music teacher, who writes in her commonplace book that "Toto reminds me more and more of that unfriendly homosexual."

The final chapter of the novel consists of a letter written by Berto to his brother shortly after Toto's birth. This is the only chapter that is not placed in chronological sequence, and it poignantly reveals an unexpectedly tender side of Berto. Particularly emphasized is his love for his son, and his hope to educate him to a proud place in society. Berto, like many of the other characters, has been in some fashion betrayed, not by Rita Hayworth, as the novel's title suggests, but by the gap between his dreams and reality. He had hoped to get a good education; instead, he left school at fifteen to work for his brother.

Berto's disillusionment, as revealed in his letter, is typical of the loss of innocence exhibited in many of the chapters in the second half of the book. In this generally depressing litany, the one note of romantic hope is suggested by Toto's essay on "The Movie I Liked Best." Toto's favorite film appears to be a version of *The Great Waltz*, the life of Johann Strauss. Toto's retelling emphasizes not only Strauss's musical genius, but also his passionate love affair with a brilliant soprano. Although the love affair ends sadly, the film goes on to detail Strauss's ultimate triumph as an artist, ending in a scene in which the emperor leads him onto a balcony before the cheering crowds of Vienna. Near death now, Strauss has a vision of his lost beloved, and he is torn between the agony of dying without real knowledge of love's meaning and the ecstasy of remembering his beloved's beauty. Thus ends Toto's version of the film. In its extreme romanticism and emphasis on exquisite variations of feeling, Toto's favorite film provides a strong counterpoint to the brutality and discouragement glimpsed elsewhere in the novel.

## The Characters

The process of characterization is central to *Betrayed by Rita Hayworth*. Each of the main characters (and some of the minor ones) is alloted his or her own chapter (Toto is given three, counting his essay on the films) and also is more fully presented through the eyes of the others. For example, Héctor is mentioned frequently by Mita, Toto, and others, creating an image for the reader which then must be tested against Héctor's own monologue in the ninth chapter. His rampant sexuality is later ironically contrasted to Esther's perception of him in chapter 12. Esther, a scholarship student at the school Héctor and Toto attend, writes her diary in a style imitated from romantic magazines and imagines Héctor to be the kind of "gentlemanly" date she has long desired. Interestingly, it is Toto who perceives Esther's danger and calls off the rendezvous he had been helping to arrange. Esther resigns herself to her loss and goes back to dreams of helping mankind through a career in medicine.

In the stories of most of the characters certain emphases recur; in particular, each character meditates on sexuality, and most of them reveal, directly or indirectly, how their education has affected their lives. These traits are equally true in men and women, although Puig certainly presents men, particularly Héctor and Cobito, as more voracious, predatory, and impulsive with regard to sex. Even Paquita, presented earlier in the novel as promiscuous, is revealed in her monologue in chapter 10 as surprisingly cultured, reading, for example, Victor Hugo's *Les Misérables*. By the end of the novel, the reader learns that she is about to marry a good man and receive her certification as a teacher.

Although men and women in this novel can be seen to share the same concerns, there can be no doubt that Puig perceives a great deal of difference in the way the two sexes react to cultural pressures about education and sexuality. The women, more inclined to romantic fantasies, nevertheless consistently finish school and have a chance at careers with intellectual aspirations. The men, more caught up by economic concerns, find themselves out of school at an early age, perhaps, like Berto, looking back regretfully at lost opportunities. In this regard it appears that Toto is, again, more like a woman, holding on to romantic ideals and yet continuing to develop intellectually.

## Themes and Meanings

In *Betrayed by Rita Hayworth*, the method is part of the meaning. By presenting each of his characters from such a variety of perspectives, Puig underscores the complexity of human personality, both in its development and in the effort to understand any individual. Part of this complexity, he asserts, is the struggle between the raw impulses and factors which bring man down and those which can uplift. Puig shows suffering in the form of illness, death of loved ones, economic hardship, and spiritual poverty and suggests redemption through art, intellectual sensitivity, and meaningful work. The triumph of good over evil is by no means clear as the novel ends, however, even for Toto, who still has many years to develop before his fate will be certain.

## Critical Context

Puig's first novel, *Betrayed by Rita Hayworth*, established themes that would be evident in later works including *Boquitas pintadas* (1969; *Heartbreak Tango: A Serial*, 1973) and *El beso de la mujer araña* (1976; *Kiss of the Spider Woman*, 1979): the rough-and-tumble world of political and economic survival versus the sensuous dream of art, often symbolized in lushly filmed Hollywood motion pictures. In his exploration of these themes, as well as his experimentation with the form of the novel, Puig is working in concert with other important Latin American writers such as Gabriel García Marquéz, Julio Cortázar, and Mario Vargas Llosa. Puig also repeatedly explores the traditional social understanding of sexuality, with a particular interest in the development of the homosexual personality. In *Betrayed by Rita Hayworth*, he indirectly explores this theme through the composite portrait of the somewhat effeminate Toto. In *Kiss of the Spider Woman* the subject of homosexuality is directly addressed through a series of scholarly footnotes.

*Betrayed by Rita Hayworth* also shows the beginnings of Puig's characteristic experimentation with the use of dialogue as a replacement for conventional narration. The opening chapter consists of a conversation between a group of women at Mita's parents' house; another chapter consists entirely of the conversation of two maids; still another shows the reader one side of a telephone call. Always the speaker must be determined from context; no explicit attributions are given. Puig's use of this stylistic device increases in his later fiction and indicates his desire to reduce authorial intrusion: in other words, to permit the characters to speak for themselves, and to make the reader work to reconstruct the world of the characters.

*Sources for Further Study*

Brushwood, John S. *The Spanish American Novel: A Twentieth-Century Study*, 1975.

Foster, David William. *Modern Latin American Literature*, 1975.

Rodríguez-Monégal, Emir. "A Literary Myth Exploded," in *Review*. LXXII, nos. 4-5 (Winter, 1971/Spring, 1972), pp. 56-64.

Tittler, Jonathan. "Order, Chaos, and Re-Order: The Novels of Manuel Puig," in *Kentucky Romance Quarterly*. 1983, pp. 187-201.

*Diane M. Ross*

# THE BEULAH QUINTET

*Author:* Mary Lee Settle (1918-    )
*Type of plot:* Historical realism
*Time of plot:* Prisons, 1634-1649; *O Beulah Land*, 1754-1774; *Know Nothing*, 1837-1861; *The Scapegoat*, June 7, 1912; *The Killing Ground*, 1978-1980
*Locale:* England, Virginia, and the western frontier of Virginia, later the state of West Virginia
*First published:* Prisons, 1973; *O Beulah Land*, 1956; *Know Nothing*, 1960; *The Scapegoat*, 1980; *The Killing Ground*, 1982

*Principal characters:*

*Prisons*
JONATHAN CHURCH, the protagonist, a young volunteer in the Parliament army
THANKFUL PERKINS, a friend and fellow soldier of Jonathan
GIDEON MACKARKLE, an old soldier and a friend of Jonathan
NELL COCKBURN LACY, the aunt of Jonathan and wife of Sir Valentine Lacy
OLIVER CROMWELL, the shrewd, ambitious leader of the Parliament forces

*O Beulah Land*
HANNAH BRIDEWELL, a transported felon and escaped Indian captive
JEREMIAH CATLETT, a solitary squatter in western Virginia
"SQUIRE" JOSIAH DEVOTION RAGLAN, Hannah's fellow prisoner in England, who is transported and bought by a young dandy, Peregrine Cockburn
JONATHAN LACEY, a Provincial captain and planter
SALLY LACEY, his young and frivolous wife
JARCEY PENTACOST, a Virginia printer
EZEKIEL CATLETT, the son of Hannah and Jeremiah Catlett
SARA LACEY, the strong-willed daughter of Jonathan and Sally Lacey

*Know Nothing*
JOHNNY CATLETT, the protagonist, the son of Peregrine Lacey Catlett and Leah Catlett
PEREGRINE LACEY CATLETT, a wealthy slave owner
LEAH CATLETT, Peregrine's Methodist-reared wife
LEWIS CATLETT, Johnny's cruel, obsessive brother

MELINDA LACEY, Johnny's penniless orphan cousin

BRANDON LACEY, a wealthy cousin of the Catletts, who finds himself land-poor and desperate for cash

SALLY LACEY, Brandon Lacey's "frail" wife

SARA LACEY, the pampered but tenderhearted daughter of Brandon and Sally Lacey

ANNIE BRANDON, the cousin of Peregrine Lacey Catlett who lives with the Catletts, embittered because she had hoped to marry Peregrine

BIG DAN O'NEILL, a "Black Irish" laborer

### The Scapegoat

LILY ELLEN LACEY, the protagonist, an idealistic college student, the daughter of Beverley and Ann Eldridge Lacey

BEVERLEY LACEY, a well-meaning but weak mine owner

ANN ELDRIDGE LACEY, the wife of Beverley Lacey

MARY ROSE LACEY, Lily's youngest sister

ANN ALTHEA LACEY, Lily's boy-crazy sister

JAKE CATLETT, the head of a union local but also a friend of Beverley Lacey

CAPTAIN DANIEL CHESTER NEILL, a mine detective who loves violence

ANNUNZIATA PAGANO, an Italian matriarch

EDUARDO (EDDIE) PAGANO, the son of Annunziata and a friend of Lily

CARLO MICHELE, a new immigrant, the "scapegoat" of the title

NEVILLE ROUNDTREE, an English employee of the mine owners

### The Killing Ground

HANNAH McKARKLE, the protagonist, a middle-aged writer

JOHNNY McKARKLE, the brother of Hannah, who was killed in jail

KITTY PUSS BASEHEART, formerly a mistress of Johnny McKarkle

CHARLIE BLAND, a womanizer and model for Johnny

THELMA LEFTWICH, a spinster devoted to Johnny McKarkle

ANN ALTHEA LACEY NEILL, Hannah McKarkle's aunt and the widow of Daniel Chester Neill of *The Scapegoat*

JAKE CATLETT, Johnny's killer, the youngest son of Jake Catlett of *The Scapegoat*

The Beulah Quintet has had a complicated genesis. At first, Mary Lee Settle projected a trilogy set in what is now West Virginia. She published the eighteenth century story *O Beulah Land* in 1956, followed in 1960 by a novel taking descendants of the characters in the earlier work up to the Civil War. After *Know Nothing* came a contemporary novel entitled *Fight Night on a Sweet Saturday* (1964). Settle was not happy with the published version of the third novel, however, and furthermore, she wished to take her story back another century in time, as well as across the Atlantic to England, in order to set up the themes that pervaded the trilogy already written. The result was *Prisons* (1973), whose very title emphasizes the dichotomy between freedom and captivity, which had been important throughout the Beulah novels written earlier. In 1980, Settle published *The Scapegoat*, which is set immediately before World War I and which, because it involves the battle between landless workers and the owners of land which is being mined, nicely bridges the gap between the three earlier works, with their emphasis on land as a source of wealth, and *Fight Night on a Sweet Saturday*, a contemporary novel of business and industrial wealth, rewritten and published in 1982 with a new title, *The Killing Ground*. With this final novel, the Beulah Quintet was complete. The four later books in the series are all set in the same area, and all five of the novels shared the same family and Christian names, in varying conjunctions; the same character traits, appearing in men and in women; the same conflicts; and the same themes, embodied in the changing face of history.

## The Novel

The first novel of the quintet, *Prisons*, is set in mid-seventeenth century England. From babyhood, Jonathan Church has been torn between his loyalty to his mother's dour Puritanism and the appealing warmth of his young aunt, Nell Cockburn Lacy, who presides over a Royalist festival atmosphere at Lacy House. Jonathan's mother has married a self-made man who has no love for the aristocracy; her younger sister, Jonathan's aunt, married Sir Valentine Lacy, who does not question the right of his kind to govern an unchanging England. When Jonathan is sixteen, he discovers that his father can be heartless. He self-righteously judges and defies his father and leaves his home. Taking refuge at Lacy House, he encounters Nell, who is weeping over her elderly, dying husband. Her grief for Sir Valentine, her pity for young Jonathan, and the love she and her nephew have always felt for each other combine in some unforgettable hours, which result in Jonathan's only descendant, a supposed son of Sir Valentine.

The narrative begins as a confession at the point of death by Jonathan, now twenty, and the main story line traces his disillusionment as he learns that the Parliament forces, ostensibly fighting for freedom, are themselves as repressive as the Royalists and that the ambitious men who rule them are not only as tyrannical as the king's men but hypocritical as well, mouthing prayers as they use and discard, sacrifice and execute the ordinary men who follow them in fear or in hope. To break the democratic spirit which the ordinary soldiers have developed, Oliver Cromwell, the leader of the Parliament forces, and his subordinates resolve to execute a number of ringleaders, Jonathan among them. Because of Jonathan's youth and his substantial family, however, Cromwell is willing to spare the boy if he will agree to influence the troops as the leaders wish. Jonathan cannot desert his friends or his principles. He and his friend Thankful Perkins are among the young men with dreams who are murdered by the old men who have only ambitions.

Like *Prisons*, *O Beulah Land* places its characters in the midst of violent conflict—in this case, the French and Indian War and the continuing Indian resistance against the settlers. In the prologue, Hannah Bridewell, a transported thief and prostitute, survives capture by the Indians and a long period in the wilderness, to appear at last at the cabin of the squatter Jeremiah Catlett, who saves her life and eventually marries her in the informal manner of a frontier to which the law and the church have not yet come.

Moving backward in time, the novel follows Hannah and "Squire" Josiah Devotion Raglan from crime and prison in England to what amounts to sale in Virginia, a colony ruled by wealthy planters such as Jonathan Lacey, who leaves his young wife, Sally, to march toward Fort Duquesne with his own Provincial forces and with the British regulars. Hannah and Squire Raglan accompany their new masters on this venture, and the Squire's theft of a tomahawk, along with the arrogant bad manners of the English commander, so anger the Indians that an ambush and a massacre result. After her captivity, Hannah escapes, as the prologue revealed. The Squire's final act of rascality, some years later, results in his quite justifiable murder by Jeremiah Catlett.

Jonathan Lacey and his spoiled young wife Sally venture west, along with Jarcey Pentacost, a printer whose passion for freedom has cost him his shop. Sally refuses to adjust to frontier life, treating her neighbors with contempt, and Jonathan begins to regard her as a stranger instead of the friend and wife for whom he had wished. Finally, a rough frontier prank at the wedding of the gently reared daughter of Jonathan and Sally, Sara Lacey, results in Sally's madness. At the end of the novel, however, Sara evidences not only great love for her husband, Ezekiel, the son of the lower-class Catletts, but also great courage. Unlike her mother, she is worthy of Beulah Land.

Like *O Beulah Land*, *Know Nothing* traces the social and financial histories of various family units in a society still in flux—in this case, torn by differences on the issue of slavery as well as by differences between the values of the frontier in western Virginia and the values of the settled East. To prosperous Peregrine Lacey Catlett come Brandon and Sally Lacey, who are rich in land and slaves but unable to meet their obligations. When Brandon takes the gentleman's way out, Sally becomes a permanent fixture, glorying in her heredity. Other women who need the social status only a man can provide must compromise. Bitter Annie Brandon sleeps with Big Dan O'Neill, becomes pregnant, marries him, and spends years attempting to civilize him. Melinda Lacey, rejected as a wife for Peregrine's son, Johnny Catlett, by Johnny's mother, Leah Catlett, marries a wealthy man but finds life without Johnny so unhappy that she wills her own death. Without her, Johnny takes a slave girl and unwittingly causes the death of the girl's husband, Johnny's devoted servant.

As aristocrats and new immigrants, rich and poor, become involved in this mating dance, the differences on the issue of slavery split existing families. Peregrine Lacey Catlett comes to despise his son Lewis, an abolitionist like his mother Leah. In her pity for him, Sara Lacey marries Lewis, who stifles her sweet and happy personality with his grim preoccupations. Returning from his escape to the West, Johnny takes up his father's duties as farmer, slave owner, and protector of women and in the final pages of the book joins the Confederate army to fight in a war that he knows will be lost, hoping only that he will not have to kill his unionist brother Lewis.

The next novel in the quintet, *The Scapegoat*, traces the defeat of friendship and decency in the conflict between mine operators and workers. In the middle of the conflict are Beverley and Ann Eldridge Lacey, decent people who hope that their mine can avoid the violence being urged by the operators of British-owned mines and their hired detectives and thugs on one hand and union agitators on the other. The presence of their daughters Lily Ellen Lacey, Mary Rose Lacey, and Ann Althea Lacey prevents an attack on their home, and for a time it seems that Beverley's friendship with Jake Catlett, on whose property the strikers are living, will prevent the threatened violence. Yet those who hunger for a confrontation take advantage of the idealism of Lily, whose friendship with Eduardo Pagano, a young Italian striker, is deliberately misinterpreted by the war lover Captain Daniel Chester Neill and made the excuse for an attack on the strikers' camp, to the delight of the union agitator, who will use the event for her own purposes. To protect her son Eddie, Annunziata Pagano permits the new immigrant Carlo Michele to be killed in Eddie's place. Even the conspiracy between the well-intentioned Neville Roundtree, Lily, and Beverley to rescue Eddie is tainted by the fact that a human scapegoat makes Eddie's escape possible.

*The Killing Ground*, the final novel in the quintet, brings the middle-aged writer Hannah McKarkle to her home, Canona, West Virginia, so that she can at last understand the life and death of her brother Johnny McKarkle. (At the beginning of the book, set eighteen years after Johnny's death, Hannah has returned to Canona for a lecture.) There is no mystery about the facts; in 1960, Hannah had been called home by Johnny and had learned immediately after his death that it was the result of a brawl in a jail cell where he had been thrown with other drunks. That Jake Catlett knocked him down Hannah has known ever since the event; that the death resulted from Johnny's hitting his head against a bench in the fall makes it clear that there was no premeditation. The central section of the book details these events.

In the first section, set in 1978, Hannah is seeking more complex answers to much deeper questions. As she talks to clubwomen such as Kitty Puss Baseheart, as she gossips about meaningless lives such as that of the womanizer Charlie Bland, as she sees dried-up Thelma Leftwich, a "good" woman who found no happiness in her hopeless love for Johnny, and as she visits the old family home with her aunt, Ann Althea Lacey Neill, the widow of the war-lover Captain Neill of *The Scapegoat*, Hannah tries to find a pattern in human history. Because Hannah McKarkle is Mary Settle's alter ego (Hannah is referred to in the novel as the author of the four previous books of the Beulah Quintet), it is logical that in the two years after her 1978 visit to Canona she would visit all the places of quintet significance, including the churchyard where Jonathan Church was shot in 1649. Her conclusions come in the epilogue, set in 1980.

*The Characters*

At the end of *The Killing Ground*, Settle suggests that there are repetitions of character-types throughout history. In that human motivations are certainly limited in number, though unlimited in particular combinations, this point seems logical. One strain which she sees throughout history is that of rebellion against the status quo. In *Prisons*, Jonathan Church left his home rather than submit to his father, then died rather than submit to Cromwell and his henchmen. In *The Killing Ground*, Jake Catlett struck out at Johnny McKarkle because Johnny represented rule by wealth and social position. At the end of *The Killing Ground*, Settle includes among these restless spirits Hannah Bridewell of *O Beulah Land*, the Provincial captain Jonathan Lacey, troubled Johnny Catlett of *Know Nothing*, the Italian scapegoat Carlo Michele and intelligent Eddie Pagano from *The Scapegoat*, and idealistic Lily from the same book. At the end of *The Killing Ground*, Hannah McKarkle realizes that she is like those characters in her independent spirit and in her need for freedom. Throughout the novels, such characters are contrasted with other types—the unprincipled, such as Cromwell and Charlie Bland; the cruel, such as Lewis Catlett and Captain Daniel Chester Neill; the pampered and petty, such as Sally Lacey in *O Beulah Land*, Sally Lacey in *Know Nothing*, and the clubwomen in the final novel; and the weak, such as Beverley Lacey in *The Scapegoat* and Brandon Lacey in *Know Nothing*. Although none of her characters is exactly like another, Settle's repetition of types suggests that human qualities, as well as human choices, are repeated again and again in history.

Settle reveals the inner lives of her characters by skillful shifts in point of view. Even in *Prisons* and *The Killing Ground*, the two works which are primarily written in the first person and concentrate on the perceptions of a single character, there are sections that move to other characters. *The Scapegoat* begins with Mary Rose Lacey, speaking in the first person with childish candor. Just as the reader has begun to accept Mary Rose's vision of reality as certainly more accurate than that of the adults around her, however, Settle switches to limited omniscience, moving from one character to another, and later once again has a first-person account, this time from Mary Rose's sister Ann Althea Lacey, who says that Mary Rose never tells the truth but invents and believes her own reality. The complex handling of point of view is a characteristic of Settle's fiction. It is a tribute to her craftsmanship that the reader is not confused as to whose mind is being exposed, whether in the first or in the third person, and the changes of perspective, like the repetition of character-types, produce a richness of texture like that of a Gobelin tapestry.

## Themes and Meanings

The fact that the most important characters of the Beulah Quintet are the rebels points to the dominant theme of the novels: that throughout history freedom must be won again and again from varying kinds of enslavement. There is, first, enslavement by authority. In *Prisons*, Gideon Mac-Karkle is pressed into military service first by one side, then by the other, and Robbie Lokyar, who joined the Parliament forces to fight for freedom, is executed because he agitated for freedom of speech, which was more freedom than Cromwell and his subordinates wished to permit. In *O Beulah Land*, the transported criminals are sold as servants, and Jeremiah Catlett kills a blackmailer who threatens to put him and his wife Hannah once more into that bondage from which they have escaped. In *Know Nothing*, the emphasis is on the slavery of the blacks, and there, as throughout the other novels, those who have power over others are oblivious to the resentment which that power engenders. Because of the lack of knowledge which seems to accompany power, those in authority are vulnerable to the loss of their power.

A second kind of enslavement arises from an accepted social hierarchy. Although often the men and women of the upper classes are well-intentioned, like Sir Valentine Lacy in *Prisons* or slave-owning Johnny Catlett in *Know Nothing*, those of lesser rank harbor a bitterness, spawned by injustice and nourished by pride, which often erupts in violence. Sometimes the upper classes realize the menace of those for whom they have contempt; thus, the Catletts in *Know Nothing* retreat from the anger of "Black

Irish" Big Dan O'Neill. Often, however, the anger is unrecognized. Yet in *The Killing Ground*, Jake Catlett, member of a family now low in the social scale, strikes out at Johnny McKarkle because Johnny has been acting superior all of his life. On the frontier, the less-educated, the unpolished, strike out at the educated and the polished; yet as the frontier recedes and established society moves westward, the hierarchical system follows, and the inevitable anger of those who are treated as inferiors is suppressed until an explosion occurs. The biblical epigraph to *Know Nothing* suggests that the powerful are themselves victims of their power.

Sometimes enslavement is rooted in the social and economic system. In *Know Nothing*, Brandon Lacey, who is wealthy in land and slaves, is ruined financially because he cannot find cash to pay his obligations. In the same novel, Melinda Lacey and Johnny Catlett cannot marry because she is penniless, and Johnny's mother expects him to marry money. Women must marry or live as subordinates in other women's households; if they err, there is no way out. In *Know Nothing*, Brandon's wife, Sally, is doomed to dependency by her husband's ruin; their daughter will be destroyed by her marriage to the cruel, intolerant Lewis Catlett, and Annie Brandon, pushed by passion into marriage with Big Dan O'Neill, will never be able to make him into a gentleman.

Finally, enslavement may come from an obsession, which blinds one to reality. For Lily in *The Scapegoat*, the obsession is her college-learned idealism; because she does not think before she acts, she endangers the very people which she intends to help. In *Know Nothing*, Lewis Catlett is so obsessed by abolitionism and religious fanaticism that he strikes out at everyone and everything around him—his father, his brother, his wife, even an affectionate kitten, whom he kills with a kick. Lewis' family comments on the fact that Lewis, who defies his father and his community for his cause, has never done a kindness to a black. It is clear that the obsession is rooted in Lewis' love of his mother and hatred of his father, not in pity or in principle.

Whatever the source of enslavement, it is battled by Settle's most sympathetic characters, and the external struggle finally becomes less important than the internal struggle. A real triumph is generally achieved through knowledge, both of the real situation and of the self. Jonathan Church's final defiance of Cromwell is far more significant than his defiance of his father. In the first case, Jonathan did not understand the degree to which his father was shaped by his past and by his society, and Jonathan's refusal to accept his father's authority was based on his own feelings of religious superiority, his own stiff-necked pride. At the end of *Prisons*, however, Jonathan has come to understand that there is no freedom on either side in the English Civil War and that he himself is imperfect. Knowing that his death will be futile, he nevertheless speaks and dies for freedom. In *Know*

*Nothing*, Johnny Catlett goes off to war as a loyal son, knowing that the South will not win, knowing that without evil intention he has participated in the evil inherent in the institution of slavery. His triumph is in his compassion, his self-knowledge, and his courage. Similarly, in *The Scapegoat*, Lily Ellen Lacey must come to realize that her well-meaning idealism has worsened the struggle between mine owners and workers. Her death in World War I is an expiation for the lack of knowledge which, like Johnny Catlett's, was rooted in a kind of upper-class innocence; like Johnny, however, in her attainment of knowledge and her acceptance of duty, Lily triumphs. In the final book of the quintet, Hannah McKarkle says that unlike the clubwomen, who hide themselves from themselves, she must reject her training as a "know-nothing" woman. Like Antigone, she must bury a brother who was not admirable, and she must seek the full knowledge of what he was so that the burial will be complete. Those characters in Mary Lee Settle's novels who quest, who wander, and who question all desire the internal triumph which comes with freedom through knowledge.

### Critical Context

It is surprising that Mary Lee Settle is not better known. In 1978, when she received the National Book Award for Fiction for *Blood Tie* (1977), there were many critics who questioned the decision. Even since the completion of the Beulah Quintet, critical articles about her have been few. Yet her longtime admirer, George Garrett, himself an outstanding historical novelist, continues to point out Settle's scope, the depth of her vision, the proficiency of her technique. In even one historical novel, to handle varied points of view and a multitude of characters so deftly and so clearly is a notable achievement. To juggle families, characters, themes, motifs, and historical details in five related novels without departures from a high level of craftsmanship and the consistent search for truth, clearly expressed, is a task at which few other contemporary writers could succeed.

As a Southern writer, Settle is typically conscious of the burden of the past, of the anti-intellectualism and jubilant boorishness which are the inheritance from the frontier, of the stagnant smugness which accompanied the elevation in a new social hierarchy of those who had been inferior in an older hierarchy. Without family, wonders a lady in *Know Nothing*, what could the Yankee women at Egeria Springs find to talk about? Settle's use of eastern Virginia-western Virginia setting is particularly useful in illustrating the social changes which accompanied the movement of established traditions into the resistant frontier. Yet with all of her regional and historical accuracy, Settle transcends mere local color and, like the best writers of the continuing Southern Renaissance, achieves universality in characterization and in theme.

*Sources for Further Study*

Kibler, James, ed. *American Novelists Since World War II*, 1980.

Madden, David, ed. *Rediscoveries*, 1971.

Prenshaw, Peggy Whitman. *Women Writers of the Contemporary South*, 1984.

Rubin, Louis D., et al., eds. *The History of Southern Literature*, 1985.

Shattuck, Roger. "A Talk with Mary Lee Settle," in *The New York Times Book Review*. October 26, 1980, pp. 43-46.

*Rosemary M. Canfield*

# BEYOND THE BEDROOM WALL
## A Family Album

*Author:* Larry Woiwode (1941-    )
*Type of plot:* Domestic chronicle
*Time of plot:* From 1935 to the mid-1960's
*Locale:* North Dakota, Illinois, and New York City
*First published:* 1975

> *Principal characters:*
> CHARLES NEUMILLER, a carpenter and the nominal head of
>     the Neumiller family
> MARTIN, the protagonist, Charles's son, a teacher, plumber,
>     insurance salesman, and, above all, father
> ALPHA JONES, Martin's first wife
> CHARLES, an actor, the eldest son of Martin and Alpha
> JEROME, a student doctor, the second son of Martin and
>     Alpha
> TIM, a teacher, the third son of Martin and Alpha
> MARIE, the eldest daughter of Martin and Alpha
> SUSAN, the second daughter of Martin and Alpha
> LAURA, Martin's second wife

*The Novel*

A sprawling, episodic family history, *Beyond the Bedroom Wall* conveys with extraordinary fidelity and an enlightening sense of wonder the lives of ordinary people. It focuses on the Neumiller family, originally of North Dakota, but ranges over their extended families, their antecedents, and their communities. In doing so, the novel succeeds at times, without particularly attempting to, in surpassing the conventions of its genre. It attains an idiosyncratic, though nevertheless authentic, eminence as an anthropology of the affections.

The protagonist is Martin Neumiller, a sensitive, awkward, God-fearing son of the Midwest. Such story as the novel contains derives from him, his achievements and his disappointments. The latter outnumber the former. Virtually all of his significant experiences take place within the rigid frame of the here and now. His failures and attainments, therefore, are no greater and no less than those of any ordinary man.

Martin has, however, one important, distinguishing feature: his Catholicism. His faith creates some problems as he attempts to establish his teaching career—predictably, given that he lives in North Dakota. Yet again, these difficulties are not given a decisive dramatic influence in the novel's development. They are, like everything else in Martin's world, part of the varied tapestry of which his life consists. Moreover, as though to compensate for professional frustration, Martin is able to marry Alpha, although she is not a Catholic and her family objects.

Martin is a firm believer in hard work, and in addition to his work at school, he takes on extra employment, restlessly attempting to satisfy himself by pursuing a dream of material adequacy for his growing family. As his family expands, and Martin is seen through the eyes of some of its members, it becomes clear that his restlessness is more illustrative of his nature than is his capacity for satisfaction. As though to confirm this view, Martin decides to move to Illinois—ostensibly to be near his father—just when circumstances seem to be about as good as they are going to get in North Dakota.

Life in Illinois begins disastrously and only slowly improves. By this time, however, it is Martin's children—Charles, Jerome, and Tim, particularly—who command attention. In a strictly unsentimental manner, the novel succeeds in conveying all the moodiness, irrationality, and idiosyncrasy of childhood. Collisions between the different children's private worlds are as lovingly recalled as are bouts of extemporaneous harmony. By keeping the small world of childish concerns to the fore here, the author is able to increase the shock value of adult problems when they intrude. Intrude they do: Alpha dies of uremia, Martin's father dies, floods almost destroy everything, Martin remarries.

Eventually, the Neumiller children begin to go their different ways. Charles goes first and goes farthest—from the University of Illinois to New York City and, at length, a modest acting career. Much of Charles's history away from the family deals with his sojourn in Greenwich Village and his encounters with various Bohemian types there. Charles's experiences here are portrayed in the exhaustive detail characteristic of the novel. Yet whereas this approach brings the unfamiliar American heartland authentically to life, it succeeds merely in depicting the sterility of the metropolis. Charles himself recognizes this sterility only when he and his wife return to Illinois for the funeral of Martin's second wife, Laura.

With this funeral, the novel ends. The family is both wounded and reunited. The novel has also come full circle, for its opening and most powerful sequence depicts Martin's father, also named Charles, making a coffin and burying *his* father. Those two deaths are, in effect, the dark covers of the document referred to in the novel's subtitle, "A Family Album." Such a subtitle is an appropriately but unnecessarily modest indication of the celebration of the everyday enacted in *Beyond the Bedroom Wall*.

## The Characters

Since *Beyond the Bedroom Wall* is a novel of condition rather than a novel of character, it contains very little sense of character development. In addition, Woiwode treats doing as a form of being. Therefore, the novel contains little investigation of motive, not very much introspection, and seems, in general, to be resistant to the concept of the psychological man. As though to make the resistance explicit, a feature of Charles's alienated life as a newlywed in New York is that he is "deep in analysis."

On the other hand, Woiwode also resists the depiction of his characters as stereotyped pillars of society. The characters' personalities are too quirky and require too many outlets of expression to be pigeonholed: Variety and idiosyncrasy are their middle names, and it is one of the author's most impressive achievements that the novel is too densely populated with clearly visible, diverting, and widely differing characters.

The Neumillers are the predominant representatives of character conceived as erratic, copious, and different. Martin is the model upon which his wife and family are based. In his longings, his impatience, his kindness, and his energy, he embodies a wonderful zest for life, without in any sense being presented as a superman or even as a conventional hero. Martin is all the more impressive because he has little awareness of, or interest in, his own uniqueness. Moreover, his distinctiveness is most readily appreciated by observing what he does, and how he responds, rather than what he thinks.

A paradoxical feature of Martin's character is that it never amounts to anything definitive. Despite his energy and capacity for involvement and thoroughness, the world seems to resist his best efforts. His authenticity is measured most accurately in terms of his failures. His stature is most clearly visible in his ability to sustain loss. It may be that, as Martin remarks, "A man should be grateful for what he gets and not expect to get one thing more." Yet his appeal lies in the fact that his experience, in effect, restates that sentiment as a question rather than as an assertion.

Martin is a dominant influence on the novel's sense of character, but the author allows Alpha and Tim as well to make their own distinctive contributions to the narrative: Alpha's takes the form of a diary covering her courtship and the early years of her marriage, while Tim documents his childhood in a first-person narrative. Both of these resources, however, are used intermittently and arbitrarily.

In addition, Martin disappears at times while the author constructs a community in which the family can live. The community is constructed by means of a series of thumbnail sketches of its citizens, a procedure which, because of repetition, comes to have a weary air of obligation about it. For all the fascinating peripheral characters which the novel contains, notably the members of Alpha's family, Martin looms over all, an archetype of adequacy.

*Themes and Meanings*

Superficially, it seems that *Beyond the Bedroom Wall* serves no greater ambition than to live up to its subtitle. Its formal preoccupations deal fundamentally with chronicling, documenting, and remembering. Its central meaning seems contained in a need to keep faith with real life, reality in this case being synonymous with family intimacy and small towns.

Yet Woiwode resists the temptation to create a mere inventory of the past. The dream with which the novel opens places the narrator in the position of seeing again and seeing afresh, and throughout the novel there are numerous reminders that the activity of seeing is as important as the thing seen.

As though to confirm the significance of sight, moments in the novel are sometimes graced by light. The night that the family arrives in Illinois and finds itself unwelcome, Martin catches sight of "the celestial geometry of the children around Alpha's waiting face." Yet such moments do not occur predictably and do not provide a dependable means of perceiving the world. Rather, they are part of the total reality which the human experiences of the characters embrace.

Martin confirms that the family album of the novel's subtitle is the most fitting. He says, "My life is like a book. . . . There is one chapter, there is one story after another." A book does seem to be the most suitable means of embodying the character of experience as described in the novel's epigraph. The epigraph is a statement by Erik H. Erikson: "'Reality,' of course, is man's most powerful illusion; but while he attends to this world, it must outbalance the total enigma of being in it at all."

This novel's objective is to denote the quality of the illusion, to keep faith with the warmth and familiarity within the bedroom wall, as well as with the mystery and difficulty of life beyond the bedroom wall.

### Critical Context

Although *Beyond the Bedroom Wall* uses some modernist technical devices, largely in varying point of view, it is essentially an old-fashioned family history. In fact, it might seem to owe its artistic lineage to more primitive sources such as the saga, or as the quotations at the beginning from an early traveler's account of the Dakotas suggest, the voyage-narrative. As such, it suffers from some artistic limitations. The author over-indulges his powers of recall. Apart from death and threatened death, the novel lacks dramatic incident. It is too diffuse.

Nevertheless, it is the best of the author's three novels. Nominated for a National Book Award and a National Book Critics Circle Award in 1976, it enjoyed both a critical and commercial success. Moreover, it is a significant landmark in an important struggle which continues to characterize a recent important trend in American fiction.

This struggle is between the city and the soil, between metropolitan styles and rural values, between individual freedom and family obligations.

*Beyond the Bedroom Wall* not only reflects such cultural tensions but also attempts to articulate their sources and their human urgency. Despite its technical deficiencies, therefore, this novel goes beyond being an admirable act of homage to everyday life. It is also an important chapter in the sociology of the contemporary American novel and a meditation on the culture of Middle America in mid-century.

*Source for Further Study*
Gardner, John. Review in *The New York Times Book Review*. CXXV (September 28, 1975), pp. 1-2.

*George O'Brien*

# THE BIG SLEEP

*Author:* Raymond Chandler (1888-1959)
*Type of plot:* Detective
*Time of plot:* The 1930's, after the end of Prohibition
*Locale:* Hollywood
*First published:* 1939

*Principal characters:*
PHILIP MARLOWE, the private detective narrator, a former
    D. A. investigator who was fired for insubordination
GENERAL GUY STERNWOOD, Marlowe's client, the aged but
    tough last male of an oil-rich military family.
CARMEN STERNWOOD, Sternwood's twenty-year-old daughter,
    a mad, sexual predator
VIVIAN STERNWOOD REGAN, Carmen's protective older sister
EDDIE MARS, the boss of the Hollywood underworld
MONA MARS, his loyal wife
LASH CANINO, Mars's most vicious gunman

*The Novel*

Though *The Big Sleep* is clearly an example of the "hard-boiled" detective genre, it rises above the crowd and approaches the standard set by Ernest Hemingway in *The Sun Also Rises* (1926). Philip Marlowe, the narrator and hero of the novel, tells a gripping story of crime and detection, but he also records a spiritual encounter with a crumbling nation as he manages to protect one representative of the old American values from the depredations of a new, nihilistic materialism.

General Guy Sternwood hires private detective Marlowe to learn why a Mr. Geiger is trying to blackmail him with his daughter Carmen's supposed gambling debts. Marlowe soon ends the immediate blackmail threat but does not get the answer he wants. Crimes of passion eliminate Geiger and neutralize a second blackmail attempt: Carmen's current boyfriend kills Geiger because Geiger is using her to make pornographic photographs. Before the boyfriend dies—perhaps a suicide, perhaps a homicide—he allows another minor criminal, Brody, to get the photographic plates of the naked Carmen. Believing that Brody killed Geiger, Geiger's homosexual lover kills Brody. Marlowe bends the law as he traces these crimes and recovers the photographic plates. His purpose is to bring the criminals to justice while protecting Sternwood from detailed knowledge of Carmen's activities and the humiliation of exposure in the press.

In solving these crimes, Marlowe comes to feel a kind of family loyalty to General Sternwood, and when Sternwood overpays him for the job, perhaps testing his integrity, he decides to go ahead on his own to learn what his client really wants to know. Sternwood has told Marlowe that his son-in-law, Rusty Regan, the husband of Carmen's older sister Vivian, has disappeared without a word. This deeply disturbs Sternwood, because Rusty, a former I.R.A. guerrilla and bootlegger, has been the closest friend of his old age. Sternwood really wants to know what happened to Rusty.

As Marlowe begins to discover the truth about Rusty's disappearance, he also begins to see how Eddie Mars, Hollywood crime boss, is involved in all the crimes on which Marlowe has been working. Carmen murdered Rusty because he refused to go to bed with her. To protect her father from the pain and publicity of Carmen's exposure, Vivian has gone to the most powerful man in Hollywood to cover up her sister's crime. Mars and Canino, his gunman, have helped her and are now looking for ways to use what they know to get at some of Sternwood's four million dollars. Geiger's blackmail attempt is actually a test to see if Sternwood knows of Carmen's crime and if he can be blackmailed. When the attempt fails, Mars knows he will have to wait until Vivian inherits, and then blackmail her.

In order to keep Rusty's disappearance out of the public eye, Mars has fabricated the story that Rusty ran off with Mona, Mars's wife. Mars is keeping Mona in hiding under Canino's guard. Marlowe's encounters with Mona and Canino result from his attempts to learn what has happened to Rusty. When Marlowe is captured by Canino, Mona frees him, risking her own life to prevent Mars from becoming responsible for Marlowe's murder. Admiring this loyalty, Marlowe remains to fight the deadly Canino rather than leave Mona to his wrath.

By finding and killing Canino, Marlowe solves another crime, the murder of another minor criminal, who had discovered Mona's hiding place and was trying to sell the information. Marlowe, however, still has not learned what happened to Rusty Regan. He uncovers the truth by reasoning about the strangely intimate relationship between Vivian and Mars and about Vivian's attempts to distract him from the scent. Once again, he bends the law, but this time at greater sacrifice of his principles. To protect Sternwood from the knowledge that his crazy daughter has killed his best friend, Marlowe helps Vivian continue to conceal the murder. Marlowe is willing to sacrifice pure justice in the name of friendship and loyalty, to protect the last of an old aristocracy from fully understanding the depths to which his family has fallen. As a result, the main criminals, Carmen and Mars, remain free while their instruments die or are punished. Marlowe is never able to tell Sternwood what has become of Rusty. Though he feels himself compromised, he does not doubt the rightness of his actions.

## The Characters

Philip Marlowe is deservedly one of the most famous of the hard-boiled detectives. He is a man of principle in a world where principles seem to have disappeared. He hates vice, especially sexual vice, because he sees sex as one of the main tools by which the most ruthless criminals gain power over others. The natural viciousness of ordinary people causes them to abandon the virtues necessary for a civilized life; in so doing, they subject themselves to figures such as Eddie Mars.

Carmen exemplifies the depths of such vice. She apparently lives only for sexual gratification. She will pay any price for a thrill, and her rage at being denied what she wants is boundless. Though Marlowe can show a small amount of grudging admiration for a homosexual who kills his lover's murderer, his contempt for Carmen is absolute. When she invades his bachelor's apartment to try to seduce him, he can barely restrain himself as he expels her, and when she is gone, he rips his bed apart to get rid of the odor of corruption she has left.

He feels almost as much contempt for Vivian when she attempts to use sex to divert him from his pursuit of Rusty Regan. Vivian, however, is more complex; Marlowe sees through her surface cynicism, which is somewhat like his own, and he comes to believe that she is acting on behalf of some value system. When he discovers that she cares not about the money but rather about protecting her father, he joins with her in the attempt.

Even more than vice, Marlowe hates the empty materialism of Eddie Mars, a man who loves nothing but money and power. Mars is a hollow man, committed to nothing, a man driven neither by love nor by principles. Marlowe despises Mars and all he stands for—in part because Mars preys on the vices of ordinary people in order to achieve power and wealth. Mars's power extends even into law enforcement: Because the police cannot hope to stop vice, they enter into an unholy alliance with Mars to control it. Vice makes the syndicate strong, so the syndicate controls and limits vice. The police in turn attempt to keep the syndicate within limits. Mars is free to make money and accumulate power in open defiance of laws against vice as long as publicity is kept to a minimum and the right people are not directly harmed. This alliance between crime and law enforcement inevitably corrupts the law and, therefore, leads to Marlowe's insubordination, his inability to continue working for the district attorney.

Marlowe admires people who are loyal, who live by principles, even when these principles lead to mistakes. He admires Mona Mars, because she will sacrifice herself for the man she loves, even if that man is Eddie Mars. He admires the integrity of the friendship between Rusty and Sternwood. He admires the minor criminal who refuses to betray his girlfriend to Canino. He admires Vivian for her self-sacrificing attempt to cover up Carmen's crime in order to protect the general. Finally, he admires some people at the police and district attorney's offices because they manage to preserve some integrity and sense of justice in the midst of compromise and corruption.

## Themes and Meanings

The main theme of *The Big Sleep* emerges from the contrast between Eddie Mars and General Sternwood. Both are successful businessmen who have built or are building vast fortunes. Mars is a hollow man, soulless, heartless, and completely ruthless beneath his respectable exterior. Sternwood is not, however, a complete contrast to Mars. Next to Sternwood's gorgeous and orderly estate is the grimy wasteland of an abandoned oil field, the source of his wealth—unknown to the general—the site of Rusty Regan's concealed grave. Sternwood has not managed, either, to control his daughters. He has given them vast power without a set of values to which that power might be subordinated, perhaps because he has expected the world to teach those values. Because Sternwood believes in those values, because he is genuinely hurt by Rusty's disappearance, and because he and Marlowe develop an understanding, Marlowe believes that he stands for the old values of principled action. The most important principles are commitment and loyalty to loved ones.

Marlowe, then, is a defender of affectionate loyalty, wherever he finds it. Vice and corruption threaten such loyalty at several levels. He works as a private eye in order to fight these evils and preserve this good in a way which the public and organized law enforcement agencies cannot. Modern organizations depend on the absolute integrity of their members, but such integrity is impossible. Law enforcement depends on the relative freedom from vice of ordinary people, but ordinary people seek vice in uncontrollable numbers. The police work in public; whatever they discover is liable to become public knowledge. Only the individual, depending mainly on himself, can keep the private private while preserving values and obtaining justice. In a society so unsure of itself as his, Marlowe cannot produce absolute justice, but as long as he maintains his own integrity, works hard, and stays lucky, and as long as there are still some people who have hearts and really care about one another, he can help to preserve some humane order despite the almost overwhelming forces of moral chaos at large in his world.

## Critical Context

*The Big Sleep* was Chandler's first novel. When it was published, Chandler was already well established as a writer of short detective fiction, but he was not widely known outside the readership of such magazines as *Black Mask*. With the appearance of *The Big Sleep*, which received generally excellent reviews both in the United States and in England, he began to reach a much larger audience.

Frank MacShane, Chandler's biographer, says that Chandler wanted to write something new in detective fiction. Chandler was acidly critical of the "classic" mysteries popularized by authors such as Agatha Christie, Dorothy Sayers, and, earlier, Sir Arthur Conan Doyle; he regarded them as snobbish, unrealistic, and painfully contrived, burdened with conventions that were utterly remote from modern American life. Chandler's principal contributions to the detective novel include fully drawn and interesting characters (as opposed to the rather stereotyped figures of the classic mystery), a gritty naturalism of setting and situation, and a lively, passionate style that is marked by striking similes and an outsider's zest for the American idiom. (Although he was born in the United States, Chandler was reared and educated in England.) Indeed, critics often compare Chandler's works with Joseph Conrad's *Heart of Darkness* (1902) and F. Scott Fitzgerald's *The Great Gatsby* (1925) as well as Hemingway's novels; *The Big Sleep* is remarkably similar in characterization and in the use of setting to William Faulkner's *Sanctuary* (1931).

The Big Sleep's secure place in the American imagination was further assured in 1946, when Howard Hawks directed a film adaptation starring the popular team of Humphrey Bogart and Lauren Bacall.

*Sources for Further Study*
Cawelti, John G. *Adventure, Mystery, and Romance*, 1976.
Durham, Philip. *Down These Mean Streets a Man Must Go: Raymond Chandler's Knight*, 1963.
MacShane, Frank. *The Life of Raymond Chandler*, 1976.
Pendo, Stephen. *Raymond Chandler on Screen: His Novels into Film*, 1976.
Speir, Jerry. *Raymond Chandler*, 1981.

*Terry Heller*

# BLACK THUNDER

*Author:* Arna Bontemps (1902-1973)
*Type of plot:* Historical chronicle
*Time of plot:* 1800
*Locale:* Richmond, Virginia, and the surrounding countryside
*First published:* 1936

> *Principal characters:*
> GABRIEL PROSSER, the slave leader of a rebellion in 1800
> MOSELEY SHEPPARD, a Virginia gentleman
> BEN, a slave owned by Moseley Sheppard
> JUBA, a slave girl in love with Gabriel Prosser
> MELODY, a mulatto courtesan living near Richmond
> PHARAOH, a slave who wishes to lead a contingent of the rebelling slaves
> CRIDDLE, one of the slave leaders
> MINGO, a free black who befriends the rebelling slaves
> ALEXANDER BIDDLEHURST, an abolitionist from Philadelphia
> MONSIEUR CREUZOT, a Richmond printer who sympathizes with the slaves

*The Novel*

*Black Thunder* is the story of the abortive slave rebellion led by Gabriel Prosser in 1800. This historical chronicle presents a vivid portrait of the principal figures in the rebellion and explores the rationale for Gabriel's revolt.

Richmond and the surrounding Virginia countryside appear calm and peaceful in 1800, but beneath the calm façade there is brewing a storm that will break over the white population and shake their faith in the system by which their society is organized. Portraits of slave owners and their "property" illustrate the dehumanizing characteristics of the South's "peculiar institution." Owners such as Moseley Sheppard treat slaves such as Ben as if they were pieces of furniture or favorite cats; other whites beat their slaves with no more concern than they would show for an unruly horse or dog.

In this atmosphere, the slave leader Gabriel Prosser plots with a small group of disgruntled colleagues to overthrow the yoke of slavery and gain the freedom that all slaves dream about. Mingo, a free black living in Richmond, aids his cause and finds in the Bible a rationale for the revolt. Other blacks, still tied to African traditions, look for signs in nature and seek ways to conjure against evil spirits to ensure success. Aiding the slaves from a distance is a group of white sympathizers, who wish to extend the notion of liberty, equality, and fraternity to all men in America.

Gabriel's plan is simple enough: He will lead three columns of slaves into Richmond, seize the arsenal, arm his followers, and secure a base from which to gather in other blacks. Simultaneously, a few trusted lieutenants will carry word of the rebellion to nearby cities, where they will encourage slaves to join the movement. More than a thousand followers join Gabriel on the night appointed for their attack, but a driving rainstorm makes progress through the woods and streams difficult. By the time the force approaches Richmond, it has dwindled to a number too small to be effective, and Gabriel calls off the attack. Unfortunately, some of those whom Gabriel has trusted suffer a failure of nerve: Pharaoh reveals to white masters the rudiments of the plot, and Ben, under pressure from a magistrate's court, identifies the principals in the scheme.

For weeks after the word has been leaked, whites live in fear. Blacks are rounded up and executed, often after sham trials based on perfunctory evidence. The ringleaders remain free for a time, but, one by one, they are captured. Under prodding from Melody, a girl who holds sway over many men, Gabriel attempts an escape via ship to Norfolk. There he surrenders, tired of running and ashamed of having fled the cause in which he believed. He is returned to Richmond and eventually hanged.

*The Characters*

Many authors have attempted to capture the language, attitudes, and dialogue of the men and women who suffered under the yoke of slavery. Only a few have succeeded; Arna Bontemps is one of them. His portrait of the slave community around Richmond rings true.

Gabriel Prosser is the kind of hero who seems to lack all the qualities that mark men who attempt to shape history. Bontemps makes no attempt to give him any more credit than he is due. This hero is not more intelligent than his fellow slaves, not particularly brilliant at military or political tactics; rather, he is a man driven by a passion: His desire for freedom motivates his actions, and the force of his personality makes him a magnet for others with similar yearnings. He is often confused by those who rely on book learning, though he is willing to listen to them and turns to those he considers wiser than himself for advice. This willingness to heed the advice of others proves partly to be his downfall, but it seems inappropriate to ridicule him for trusting in others as he does.

The other blacks fulfill stereotypical roles without being themselves stereotypes. Through careful selection of characters, Bontemps creates a microcosm of the slave world of the early 1800's. Farm laborers, house servants, and free blacks populate the pages of *Black Thunder*. Some are good, others bad; Bontemps does not try to make the slaves better than they were. The reader will respond with indignation to the self-serving actions of Melody, who plays her black and white lovers against one another to ensure her own security. On the other hand, even those sympathetic to the slaves' cause will find it difficult to condemn old Ben, who cracks under the pressure of a magistrate's court and reveals the names of all the ringleaders in Gabriel's plot. Men such as General John and Criddle, and women such as Juba, dedicated in varying degrees to the cause of freedom, are presented with balance and restraint.

Yet the whites in this book are not presented with the same degree of verisimilitude. While not all of them are written off as evil, most appear to be either selfish or hopelessly naïve. Few appear to be more than types; little attempt seems to have been made to individualize them in the way that the black principals have been portrayed. This failure is especially noticeable in the whites' dialogue: Most of their conversations seem lifted from seventeenth century heroic plays or nineteenth century melodrama.

Despite this flaw, the overriding strength of Bontemps' characterization should not be dismissed. Too often books such as this offer little more than political rhetoric disguised thinly as fiction, and characterization is subordinated to other aims. This is not the case in *Black Thunder*; the characters in this novel, especially the black people, appeal to the reader in their own right, and Bontemps achieves a level of realism with his characters that is seldom reached in historical chronicles.

## Themes and Meanings

Bontemps' main concern in this novel is the plight of men and women of his own race who were once the victims of the most severe and demeaning form of discrimination. The implication that runs throughout as a subtext of the novel is that, while the *de jure* situation had changed (slavery had been outlawed), the demeaning status of blacks and other minorities still existed in the United States at the time of the book's publication.

Hence, the novel is really about political and social problems, and Bontemps constructs his plot and creates his characters with an eye toward highlighting those problems. Throughout the book, the reader is struck with the mindlessness of men and women of both races. Almost no whites appear to realize the unnatural predicament in which blacks find themselves. Some blacks even find the situation "normal." Herein lies part of the tragedy that Bontemps wishes to illustrate: Acceptance of one's fate, coupled with blind loyalty to social codes regardless of the justice of those codes, can be the source of untold humiliation and degradation for those against whom institutional prejudice is aimed.

While Bontemps' major aim is to show the oppressive nature of a society which practices discrimination, an important minor note is struck in his portrait of whites. None is a hero. All have a fault of some kind: arrogance, vanity, or (equally bad) a naïve desire to help the blacks without the commitment to fight and die for the cause. Ultimately, Bontemps judges white society as selfish, even in its best attempts to help oppressed minorities rise above their state of bondage.

*Critical Context*

*Black Thunder* was Bontemps' second novel and was praised by the few reviewers who bothered to notice it when it was first published in 1936. The problem was not with the novel itself, but with its subject, its author's race, and the time in which it was published. Few black authors received national recognition for their work during this period; Bontemps barely made back the advance royalties on his book. Nevertheless, the novel was reprinted in 1968, after black American literature enjoyed a renascence in the wake of intensified interest in the plight of minorities in America.

Not surprisingly, critics have compared *Black Thunder* with William Styron's best-selling novel *The Confessions of Nat Turner* (1967). That criticism has largely been divided along racial and political lines. Black critics attack Styron for sensationalizing the plight of the black slave and representing falsely the aspirations of those who had been held in bondage. Bontemps' novel is viewed as a more accurate historical portrait. White critics, and those not tied closely to the movement to promote the importance of black American literature, counter with arguments that Styron is writing fiction, and that his prose is substantially more polished than Bontemps'.

This novel does not need to rely on such comparisons; it can stand on its own merits as a well-written, sensitive account of a universal theme: man's desire to be free to choose his own destiny. The assessment must be tempered by the fact that Bontemps has chosen to write about an actual event from the past. Any historical novelist opens himself up to criticism about the accuracy of details and about his ability to capture the details of the past as they really existed. Bontemps has done so; as a result, *Black Thunder* is a novel of first-rate proportions about an issue that American contemporary readers must confront if they are to understand the world in which they live.

*Sources for Furthur Study*

Davis, Arthur P. *From the Dark Tower: Afro-American Writers, 1900 to 1960*, 1974.

Nichols, Charles H., ed. *Arna Bontemps-Langston Hughes Letters, 1925-1967*, 1980.

O'Brien, John. *Interviews with Black Writers*, 1973.

Weil, Dorothy. "Folklore Motifs in Arna Bontemps' *Black Thunder*," in *Southern Folklore Quarterly*. XXXV (March, 1971), pp. 1-14.

Whitlow, Roger. *Black American Literature*, 1974.

*Laurence W. Mazzeno*

# THE BLACKER THE BERRY
## A Novel of Negro Life

*Author:* Wallace Thurman (1902-1934)
*Type of plot:* Satiric realism
*Time of plot:* The 1920's, during the Harlem Renaissance
*Locale:* Boise, Idaho; Los Angeles; and Harlem
*First published:* 1929

> *Principal characters:*
> EMMA LOU MORGAN, the protagonist, a college student, maid,
> and teacher
> ALVA, Emma Lou's lover in Harlem
> GERALDINE, Alva's wife and mother of his son
> MARIA LIGHTFOOT, Emma Lou's grandmother, leader of
> Boise's blue veins
> JANE LIGHTFOOT MORGAN, Emma Lou's mother
> GWENDOLYN JOHNSON, a close friend of Emma Lou in
> Harlem

*The Novel*

The main action of *The Blacker the Berry: A Novel of Negro Life* focuses upon the protagonist's struggle to be accepted by light-skinned blacks. In the opening scene of the book, Emma Lou is sitting with members of her high school graduating class, waiting to receive her diploma. Emma Lou, who is a very dark-skinned girl, is also the only black student in her class. She feels self-conscious about her appearance onstage, dressed in white, surrounded by her white classmates. As the ceremony draws to a close, Emma Lou ponders the value of a high school diploma and decides that it will mean nothing to her. She would gladly trade her diploma for an "effective bleaching agent, a magic cream that would remove this unwelcome black mask from her face and make her more like her fellow men." From her mother's family of color-conscious mulattoes, she has learned to despise her dark skin and to expect few opportunities for success and happiness.

After Emma Lou is graduated from high school, her mother persuades her to enroll at the University of Southern California in a teacher education program, as no one in her family thinks she will find a husband. Encouraged by a sympathetic uncle's assurance that color-prejudice is largely confined to small towns such as Boise, Emma Lou looks forward to her studies at the University of Southern California and to the possibility of making friends with her mulatto schoolmates, for mulattoes and light-brown-skinned blacks are, in her view, "the people who really mattered." Shortly after her arrival on the USC campus, Emma Lou sets out to meet people with whom she would like to associate socially. Yet, despite sincere attempts to gain admission to the exclusive mulatto circles, Emma Lou finds these students aloof, polite, but steadfastly unwilling to accept her. During her two years at USC, she tries to ignore the indications of color-prejudice. When she finds herself repeatedly excluded from activities sponsored by the mulattoes, however, Emma Lou, discouraged and depressed, abandons her studies and moves to Harlem, seeking a job and, most important for her, a congenial mulatto community.

In Harlem, Emma Lou quickly discovers that color-prejudice plays a major role in the lives of blacks. This becomes evident to her when landlords in mulatto neighborhoods refuse to rent her a room. Although she is qualified to fill clerical positions, black businessmen will not hire her because they prefer light-complexioned female employees. She finds work as a maid, however, and subsequently becomes romantically involved with a mulatto who exploits her sexually and financially. Her relationship with Alva, the hustler, ultimately forces her to reexamine the myth of mulatto superiority which has shaped her sense of self and opens the door to a crucial confrontation with her negative self-image.

In the novel's conclusion, Emma Lou summons the courage to leave Alva, even though she still loves him. As she reorders her priorities, she determines that "what she needed to do now was to accept her black skin as being real and unchangeable...." With this new awareness, Emma Lou moves toward a positive self-image and achieves a victory over the terrible interracial color-prejudice that has dominated her life and undermined her self-esteem, causing her tremendous emotional pain and suffering.

*The Characters*

Emma Lou Morgan is one of the most skillfully drawn characters in Afro-American fiction. Born in Boise, Idaho, to a mulatto mother and a dark-skinned father, Emma Lou inherits her father's dark color, broad nose, and thick lips, much to the chagrin of her mother's color-conscious family. Rebuffed by his in-laws because of his color, Emma Lou's father soon deserts his wife and baby daughter, never to be heard from again. Consequently, Emma Lou grows up under the influence of a family whose motto is "whiter and whiter every generation." Maria Lightfoot, Emma Lou's maternal grandmother and the leader of Boise's exclusive mulatto society, abhors dark-skinned blacks, her granddaughter included. Even Emma Lou's mother loathes dark-skinned people, terming her marriage to Emma Lou's father a silly mistake. Not surprisingly, Emma Lou develops an intense color-prejudice herself; she, too, detests dark skin and African features. She, therefore, decides to choose her friends among mulattoes and light-brown-skinned blacks. She underestimates the depth of the mulattoes' commitment to maintaining the status quo, however, to holding themselves above and apart from their darker brothers. She suffers great emotional distress when she fails to gain admission to the closed circles of mulattoes and light-complexioned blacks in Los Angeles and in Harlem. Despite her obvious flaws, color-prejudice, self-hatred, Emma Lou displays a sincere, compassionate heart, a remarkable capacity for love and forgiveness. These qualities are particularly evident in her relationship with Alva and his sick baby. Like all well-conceived, multidimensional characters, Emma Lou is a complex mixture of good and bad traits. During the course of her struggles, the reader learns to understand her faults and to admire her strengths.

While staying at the YWCA in Harlem, Emma Lou meets Gwendolyn Johnson, an amiable, light-brown-skinned girl whose mother has taught her to value relationships with dark-skinned blacks and to avoid contacts with light-complexioned blacks. In short, Gwendolyn is Emma Lou in reverse. As one would expect, these two color-conscious women are immediately attracted to each other and become friends. Given their color preferences, theirs would seem to be an ideal friendship. Yet Gwendolyn's unceasing condemnation of light-skinned blacks does nothing but make Emma Lou more sensitive about her dark skin. Indeed, Gwendolyn's glorification of dark skin intensifies Emma Lou's desire to be transformed into a pretty, light-brown-skinned woman. Gwendolyn dates only dark-skinned men and tries to persuade Emma Lou to follow her example. Therefore, she is extremely irritated when Emma Lou decides to resume her relationship with Alva, her mulatto lover. In her angry response to Emma Lou's decision, Gwendolyn reveals her suppressed color-prejudice. She tells Emma Lou: "There's probably something in this stuff about black people being different and more low than other colored people. You're just a common ordinary nigger." Gwendolyn's unintentional revelation casts a new light upon her alleged preference for dark-skinned blacks.

Of the several male characters in the novel, Alva (who is given no surname) is the most fully developed. The son of an American mulatto and her Filipino husband, Alva possesses the physical attributes that Emma Lou finds attractive—skin color between yellow and brown, finely textured hair. Seeing Emma Lou in a Harlem cabaret with her white employer, Alva notices that no one has asked her to dance, so he takes pity on her and asks her to dance. She is flattered and pursues him, hoping to establish a serious romantic relationship with him. As an experienced hustler, Alva quickly recognizes the potential advantages of a discreet affair with a lonely, employed woman, and so he encourages Emma Lou's advances. Through the force of his charm and tact, he manipulates her into sharing her income with him. His scheme is so clever that Emma Lou, his naïve victim, "never realized just how she had first begun giving him money." Although he is ashamed to take Emma Lou among his light-skinned friends, he is nevertheless polite and attentive when they are together. Ironically, he breaks off the relationship when he can no longer tolerate her complaints that he intentionally subjects her to situations in which her color is ridiculed. Alva denies the charges and allows Geraldine, his mulatto girlfriend, to move in with him.

Geraldine gives birth to a sickly, retarded baby boy. The baby's handicap has a profound effect upon Alva. He loses interest in Geraldine, and "he hated that silent, staring idiot infant of his. . . ." Seeking an escape from his unhappy home life, Alva turns to alcohol for solace. His heavy drinking, despite his doctor's warnings against it, undermines his health, activating a self-destructive impulse. Fearful that Alva will succeed in drinking himself to death, leaving her alone to care for the baby, Geraldine deserts him and the baby. Determined to reestablish her relationship with Alva, Emma Lou returns to his room, nurses him back to health, and introduces Alva Junior to love and affection. While her rescue of Alva seems, for a time, to be successful, he resumes his excessive drinking and treats Emma Lou with contempt and disrespect. Alva is not only conceited and hypocritical, he also lacks moral courage; with Emma Lou's help, he could have developed strategies for coping with his son's disability, but he chose to be consumed by despair.

*Themes and Meanings*

The novel's major themes concern self-hatred and the dynamics of color-prejudice among black Americans. The novel's title, taken from the familiar black folk saying, "the blacker the berry, the sweeter the juice," is bitterly ironic, for although many blacks have traditionally embraced the notion that dark-skinned women are attractive and desirable, a significant segment of the black community has treated dark skin and other African physical features with disdain, while venerating Caucasian physical features. With this preference for white skin and values comes a clash or conflict of identities. Thurman comments on this shift of identity in his portrayal of Arline Strange, the white actress who plays the part of a mulatto in a melodrama of black life in Harlem. With make-up, the actress effects a superficial, temporary shift in identity, but unlike the mulattoes who confuse their imaginary or assumed identity with their true self, the actress shifts easily between her fictional and real identity, never losing sight of who she is.

The ultimate goal of mulattoes such as Emma Lou's mother and grandmother, however, is to achieve a complete and permanent shift of identity by eradicating all physical traces of their African ancestry through selective marriage and by assimilating the attitudes and values of the white society. Total assimilation into the white society, many color-conscious mulattoes reasoned, would free them from the limitations of interracial prejudice. Yet the inevitable result of this denial of the authentic self was a deep-seated self-hatred, as well as alienation from those blacks whose dark skin was viewed as an emblem of dishonor and inferiority. Emma Lou is the brilliant embodiment of both these penalities associated with denial of the self. She experiences self-hatred and alienation from other blacks. Thus, the novel traces Emma Lou's painful journey toward self-acceptance. As the novel closes, the end of her journey is near. Emma Lou wisely realizes that she must "begin life anew, always fighting, not so much for acceptance by other people, but for acceptance of herself by herself."

## Critical Context

When *The Blacker the Berry* was published in 1929, the Harlem Renaissance was nearing its end. Extending from the 1920's to the early 1930's, the Harlem Renaissance was a period of previously unparalleled literary productivity among black writers. Readers, both black and white, exhibited an almost insatiable appetite for books written by and about blacks. Publishers anxious to profit from this fascination with black life and culture sought out promising black writers. Wallace Thurman was one of those talented young artists. In his first novel, he set out to expose and condemn what he perceived as a disturbing contradiction in black life; he noticed blacks enthusiastically proclaiming the value and uniqueness of their African heritage, while displaying a decided preference for light skin and Caucasian features.

Moreover, many blacks routinely attacked interracial prejudice, but they remained silent on the equally reprehensible practice of intraracial prejudice. This was a sensitive topic that many of Thurman's image-conscious black readers did not care to confront in their literature. Claude McKay had touched on the issue in his controversial novel, *Home to Harlem* (1928), but Thurman was the first black writer to make the color-prejudice directed against black women by other blacks the main subject of a novel. Not surprisingly, the novel aroused a flood of criticism from black readers, many of whom denounced it as being overly harsh in its treatment of the topic. Other blacks complained that the novel did a disservice to those blacks trying to upgrade their image in the larger American society. Nevertheless, *The Blacker the Berry* became one of the most widely read and most frequently discussed novels of the Harlem Renaissance.

Thurman's novel is significant because it focused much needed attention upon the undue emphasis that many blacks of the 1920's and 1930's placed on skin color, and it encouraged other black writers to explore the issue. For example, George Samuel Schuyler, one of Thurman's contemporaries, published *Black No More* (1931), an alternately satiric and humorous novel that describes what happens in America when a black scientist discovers a way to transform black people into white people. Thurman published two other novels during his brief career, *Infants of the Spring* (1932) and *The Interne* (1932), which he wrote in collaboration with a white author, Abraham L. Furman, but his first novel, *The Blacker the Berry*, remains his most important contribution to Afro-American literature.

*Sources for Further Study*

Bone, Robert A. *The Negro Novel in America*, 1958.

Davis, Arthur P. *From the Dark Tower: Afro-American Writers, 1900 to 1960*, 1974.

Gayle, Addison. *The Way of the New World: The Black Novel in America*, 1975.

*Elvin Holt*

# THE BLOOD OF THE LAMB

*Author:* Peter De Vries (1910-      )
*Type of plot:* Comic realism
*Time of plot:* 1920's-1950's
*Locale:* Chicago and New York City
*First published:* 1962

> *Principal characters:*
> DON WANDERHOPE, the narrator, the son of a Dutch im-
> migrant in Chicago; he becomes an advertising executive
> in New York
> BEN WANDERHOPE, his father, an immigrant garbage collector
> LOUIE WANDERHOPE, his brother, a medical student who dies
> of pneumonia
> GRETA WIGBALDY, Don's girlfriend, later his wife; she even-
> tually commits suicide
> CAROL, their daughter, who contracts leukemia
> RENA BAKER, the tubercular girl with whom Don falls in love
> in the sanatorium

*The Novel*

Peter De Vries' *The Blood of the Lamb* is a deeply religious novel, although the religious sensibility is often expressed in unconventional ways:
through the comic, the grotesque, the mundane, and the tragic. The novel's
protagonist, Don Wanderhope, whose name suggests a religious quest,
grows up in a strict Dutch Calvinist immigrant family in Chicago and later
tries to escape from the confines of his immigrant background and become
more fully Americanized. Yet he finds his aspirations to the good life
thwarted by a series of unhappy circumstances as baffling in their own way
as the Calvinistic God whom he has eschewed. The novel is written as
Wanderhope's autobiography, with the first section presenting the rather
conventional, albeit comic story of an ambitious young man, but the last
part of the book, the heart of the novel, deals with the religious crisis
brought on by Wanderhope's discovery that his daughter Carol has leukemia. "What people believe is a measure of what they suffer," Wanderhope
remarks early in the novel, and his daughter's illness tests his faith and spiritual resources.

The novel opens in the Wanderhope apartment in Chicago with Don's
father, Ben, his uncle, and other relatives arguing over the infallibility of the
Bible and trying to coax Ben back to orthodoxy, while his son Louie inter-
jects wisecracks as he dresses for a date. Understandably, Don and Louie
are more interested in the secular world of Chicago than in Calvinistic

Dutch Reformed theology. Don idolizes his older brother for his freethinking and worldliness, but Louie, the golden-haired, healthy boy, dies of pneumonia at the age of nineteen. After his death, Louie remains a model for his younger brother, who strives to escape from the provincialism of his Dutch immigrant background.

Eventually Don meets a Dutch Reformed girl, Greta Wigbaldy, the daughter of a successful builder, who encourages him in his worldly quest. She obtains a key to one of her father's model homes, which they use for their rendezvous until they are caught while making love one evening when her parents arrive with buyers. Don soon finds himself committed to marry Greta.

Around this time, he contracts a slight case of tuberculosis, which requires him to go to a sanatorium near Denver for rest and recuperation. His marriage postponed indefinitely, Don finds himself bedridden and bored. He becomes a member of a small Thursday night literary group which gathers at the home of Dr. and Mrs. Simpson, but his reprieve comes when he meets Rena Baker, a lovely, demure girl who has just been moved from the infirmary to the ambulatory section. The two fall in love, although Rena is still quite ill and does not survive the winter. The pathos of Rena's death foreshadows that of Don's daughter Carol later, as does Dr. Simpson's confession that he had a son, Stevie, who died of leukemia. Rena's death further erodes Don's faith, as he reflects, "Perfect love did not quite cast out fear, but rage did grief, or nearly so."

Don returns to Chicago to find both his father and Greta Wigbaldy hospitalized in the same psychiatric institution, his father for depressive symptoms, and Greta for brooding over a child she had conceived out of wedlock with a married man at her office. When Greta's parents discover that Don is back, they railroad him into marrying their daughter. Unfortunately, Greta's emotional instability only worsens after they move to New York with Don's advertising firm. Alcoholic binges and an extramarital affair mark the progress of her self-destructive behavior, which culminates in a suicide attempt that sends her to the hospital for six months. In the meantime, their daughter Carol has become a child of extraordinary grace and charm, and her father shifts his love and affection to her as Greta succeeds in her second suicide attempt.

The heart of the novel presents Don Wanderhope's intense love and affection for his daughter, as he learns to cherish the joy of the ordinary, which, rather than suffering, best nourishes the soul. Having suffered so much already, Don is determined to enjoy every moment with his daughter, especially after a puzzling extended illness sends her to the hospital for a series of diagnostic tests. The novel deepens in religious significance as Wanderhope confronts the meaning of human suffering and death. He becomes a kind of modern, secular Job, buffeted by sorrow and loss, culminating in the last and greatest test of his faith, the discovery that his daughter has leukemia.

Through the final year that he spends with Carol, Wanderhope alternates between hope and despair as his daughter's condition temporarily improves or worsens. The spectacle of other parents living through the agony of their children's illness is enough to test anyone's faith, as the novel confronts the theological issue of why the innocent suffer. Another parent, Stein, is driven to cynicism and bitterness by the tacit assumption among the hospital staff that "everything was fine." Stein's daughter, Rachel, and Carol become fast friends as he and Wanderhope share a fellowship of parental misery. They often commiserate during their long weekends on the children's ward.

Carol becomes more thoughtful and mature as her disease worsens, actually helping to comfort her father. Birthday parties and weekend outings become great events during her temporary remissions, but the "beast" always returns. Wanderhope contemplates a statue of Christ near the hospital, which comes to represent for him the suffering servant. He prays to St. Jude, the patron saint of hopeless cases, to give them but one more year, but as Carol's leukemia slips into remission, a drug reaction destroys her immune system and leaves her vulnerable to staph infection, which runs throughout the children's ward. The blood of the lamb is sacrificed, meaninglessly, to the foul disease, which has come back to strike in disguised form. In his dignity as a suffering parent, Wanderhope achieves a kind of holiness akin to that of his brave child, who slips away as he watches over her one afternoon. He takes her unused birthday cake and flings it at the statue of the suffering Christ, the comedian who takes a pie in the face for all human suffering.

## The Characters

Though De Vries is skilled at creating comic caricatures, Don Wanderhope is clearly at the center of the novel. An immigrant's son from a poor and unpromising Dutch family, his principal motivation is to become successful enough to enjoy some of the benefits of the good life. Yet he is thwarted by a series of personal and family calamities. Wanderhope, as his name suggests, is born to wander (away from his childhood religion, in search of other consolations) and to hope (for some respite from the suffering meted out to himself and those he loves). A secular pilgrim, he chooses the comfortable path of an advertising career, but he is still beset by heartaches in his private life—Louie's and Rena Baker's deaths, his wife's suicide, and finally, Carol's death from leukemia.

A modern Job, he faces many temptations to his faith, and like Job, he is too honest to accept the easy answers of orthodoxy; but unlike Job, suffering does not deepen but diminishes his faith. For as Wanderhope comments at one point, "there seems to be little support in reality for the popular view that we are mellowed by suffering. Happiness mellows us, not troubles; pleasure, perhaps, even more than happiness."

Carol Wanderhope, his daughter, is depicted as a graceful, charming, and vibrant girl, with blue eyes and straight blonde hair, an impish grin, and re- markable courage and fortitude. She is no doubt modeled after De Vries' own daughter Emily, who also died of leukemia. Carol becomes the center of her father's life after Greta's suicide, and he lavishes such intense love upon her that one almost senses a foreboding of loss. She also becomes the focal point of her father's faith and belief. Once her disease is diagnosed, she courageously endures the long and painful treatment for leukemia, and when her death finally comes, it is a shock, though not unexpected. Carol shows a wisdom beyond her years in her understanding of her father, espe- cially in the tape-recorded message that she leaves for him after her death, and in her ability to bring joy and happiness to others despite her affliction. De Vries captures all the charm of her girlish mannerisms with great affec- tion and care in making her an unforgettable character.

Greta Wanderhope, Don's wife, on the other hand, is in many ways an unsatisfactory character. One is never given any credible motivation for her depression, alcoholism, or affairs, especially after her daughter's birth, nor for her suicide. She seems to function primarily as a plot convenience, to be discarded when no longer needed. Rena Baker, though briefly presented, is a far more appealing character than Greta.

Some of De Vries' minor characters are unforgettable comic types, such as Ben Wanderhope, Don's immigrant Dutch father, with his insomnia and religious doubts; the quack Doc Berkenbosch; the organ-grinder, Mr. Italia; his voluptuous daughter Maria; the cynical Dr. Simpson at the sanatorium; the bitter unbeliever, Stein, whose daughter Rachel also has leukemia; and Mrs. Brodhag, Wanderhope's sturdy New England housekeeper.

*Themes and Meanings*

The thematic significance of De Vries' novel may best be expressed in a credo that Don Wanderhope drafts for his college newspaper in response to their request. In it, he writes,

I believe that man must learn to live without those consolations called reli- gious, which his own intelligence must by now have told him belong to the childhood of the race. Philosophy can give us nothing permanent to believe either; it is too rich in answers, each canceling out the rest. The quest for Meaning is foredoomed. Human life "means" nothing. What does a Debussy *Arabesque* "mean," or a rainbow, or a rose? A man delights in all of these, knowing himself to be no more—a wisp of music and a haze of dreams dissolving against the sun. Man has only his own two feet to stand on, his own human trinity to see him through: Reason, Courage, and Grace. And the first plus the second equals the third.

This may seem like too easy a denial of God, and too evasive a response to the problem of gratuitous pain and suffering, but what Don is actually denying is the Calvinistic concept of a Deity who is directly responsible for human suffering, who metes out punishment to those who deserve it. Wanderhope rejects this God of his childhood and accepts instead a humanistic ethic that values love and intimacy and cherishes these moments in his relationship with his daughter. Life becomes meaningful through shared intimacy with others, not through any transcendent beliefs. After Carol's death, Don finds through his recollections of their shared life together the courage to continue, even if, as he remarks, "time heals nothing."

*Critical Context*

Many critics regard *The Blood of the Lamb*, published midway in De Vries' career, as his finest as well as his most serious novel. Basically a comic novelist, De Vries has often dealt with religious issues in a circumspect manner, but here he allows his seriousness of purpose to become more apparent. He employs a confessional format as a way of placing his narrator in a grotesque, bewildering world in which his characters have little control over events. His response to that world has been comic, as if to say that our only defense is to laugh at the tragic absurdity or grotesqueness of life. This tragicomic note is best illustrated by the birthday party in the hospital for the children suffering from leukemia. There is nothing more pathetic than the death of a child, and De Vries registers that pathos in the cynicism of Stein and the impulsive anger of Wanderhope, who flings his daughter's birthday cake at the statue of Christ.

In *The Blood of the Lamb*, De Vries employs his comic genius to serious purpose in confronting the contemporary meaning of suffering. If the tone of the novel seems mixed, that is intentional, since the grotesque is "a blend of the tragic and the comic." De Vries does not escape into nihilism in his rejection of traditional religious views but affirms, in his narrator's credo, a clear set of humanistic values. In refusing to hold God responsible for the death of his daughter, Wanderhope dignifies himself in his suffering and affirms a compassionate Deity, worthy of worship, who shares the burden of human sorrow.

*Sources for Further Study*

Bowden, J. H. *Peter De Vries*, 1983.

Hasley, Louis. "The Hamlet of Peter De Vries: To Wit or Not to Wit," in *South Atlantic Quarterly*. LXX, no. 4 (Autumn, 1971), pp. 467-476.

Jellema, Roderick. *Peter De Vries: A Critical Essay*, 1966.

Kort, Wesley. *Shriven Selves*, 1972.

*Andrew J. Angyal*

# A BLOODSMOOR ROMANCE

*Author:* Joyce Carol Oates (1938-    )
*Type of plot:* Historical romance fantasy
*Time of plot:* 1879-1900
*Locale:* Bloodsmoor, a valley in Eastern Pennsylvania
*First published:* 1982

> *Principal characters:*
> JOHN QUINCEY ZINN, a gentleman-inventor and the father of
>     a large family
> PRUDENCE KIDDEMASTER ZINN, his wife, mother of the Zinn
>     daughters
> CONSTANCE PHILIPPA, their oldest daughter who later
>     becomes a son
> MALVINIA, another daughter, later a famous actress
> OCTAVIA, another daughter, later a wife and mother
> SAMANTHA, another daughter who serves as her father's lab-
>     oratory assistant
> DEIRDRE, an adopted daughter and spiritualist

*The Novel*

Joyce Carol Oates's book *A Bloodsmoor Romance* is not a kind of fiction that is easily named, although it is not hard to recognize. The work combines both realism and fantasy in a display of authorial skill: Oates uses several techniques to achieve this effect. First, she sets her romance in a past that closely resembles the historical past; in that setting one finds both fictional characters and characters who bear the names of figures from history. In addition, the characters of the work are interested in many of the things that interested the real nineteenth century: spiritualism, the theater, the westward movement, experimental science, abnormal psychology, female sexuality, and the nature of marriage.

It is Oates's second technique that sets the work apart from historical romances per se: She freely manipulates the order of historical events and even adds events that could not possibly occur. John Quincey Zinn demonstrates both of these intrusions of fantasy: He invents the ballpoint pen and solar heating but dismisses them as useless. He invents an operating time machine, but he destroys it after he uses it to misplace one of his pupils. Similarly, Zinn's daughter Constance combines fantasy with history. Reared for marriage, Constance spends her early life accumulating household linens, but when the wedding night comes, she panics, and placing in her groom's bed the dress form used to fit her trousseau, she runs away. Disguising herself as a man, she heads west and tries her hand at being a cowboy, an outlaw, a deputy sheriff, and a gambler. During her masquerade, she turns physically into a man as well, and when she returns to the family home at Bloodsmoor, she poses as Philippe Fox, Constance's agent. Eventually, "he" apparently elopes with a childhood girlfriend.

The plot of the book unfolds by following the lives of the daughters as they grow up. In their adventures, the reader meets several characters drawn from history. For example, Deirdre, the Zinns' adopted daughter, is kidnaped by a mysterious stranger in a black balloon who deposits her on the lawn of a character named Madame Elena Blavatsky. This Madame Blavatsky shares the quirks of the historical Madame Blavatsky, cofounder of the American Theosophical Society. Recognizing Deirdre's talents, Oates's Blavatsky teaches Deirdre to become a medium, contacting spirits beyond the grave, and takes her on a world tour. The reader meets other fictional characters with real counterparts as well: Mark Twain, for one.

As may be inferred from the events recounted above, *A Bloodsmoor Romance* is an often hilariously comic work, yet one that at the same time attempts to capture some of the boundless enthusiasm of the late nineteenth century, an enthusiasm that was often as undiscriminating as it was energetic.

*The Characters*
Each of the characters seems specially chosen to exemplify many of the attitudes and interests—both common and bizarre—of the nineteenth century.

Deirdre, as has been seen, illustrates the fascination of the time with the occult, but the century had an equal passion for the stage. This love is shown through Malvinia, who runs away as a girl to join a troupe of actors. She becomes a star, attracts her leading man, and, in the first turning point of her life, discovers a horrible secret: She likes sex. Malvinia, like many people of the nineteenth century, thinks that women are too fine and high-minded to possess sexual feelings. Thus she is caught in the ironic situation in which she delights in her sexuality while despising herself for having zest for what she calls "the beast." Although she regards her lustiness as unwomanly, she is unable, as she puts it, to "control herself." Only later, when she reforms and marries a clergyman, is she freed from her "burden." She then becomes the kind of obedient and pure wife celebrated in nineteenth century domestic literature.

Her sister Octavia, on the other hand, from her earliest age wants only to be a wife and mother and through her story shows the century's commitment to a stern duty and an almost equally stern religion. The taboos of the time prevent frank instruction in reproduction, and she searches unsuccessfully for the facts of life in books. Even her mother is worse than useless: Mrs. Zinn, clearly uncomfortable at the question, scolds Octavia and tells her simply to do whatever her husband wants. This advice has unforeseen consequences when an older man, a jaded deviant, becomes Octavia's husband. He ties her up; he puts a bag over her head; he does strange things to her. Octavia, however, is rewarded: She bears two babies, whom she cherishes. When they and her husband die, she is then freed for what she calls a "higher calling," giving herself over to prayer, good works, and the care of her aged parents.

Two of the family members show the optimism of the age, an enthusiastic conquest of nature through both exploration and understanding. In Constance Philippa and her adoption of the advice to go west, the reader sees the work of the nation in consolidating its continent-wide borders and its taming of a wild environment. In her father, the reader sees the gentleman-scientist, the chief actor in the drama of scientific discovery in the time before Thomas Edison established the research laboratory. Even here, though, one finds the tendency of the age to be lured from its path by golden yet quirky goals. Despite inventing myriad useful devices, Zinn quests for one grail only—the perpetual motion machine (and only his daughter Samantha believes that he can do it).

One last character deserves description—Oates's narrator. She is the filter through which the reader sees the story, an elderly and sheltered virgin, self-effacing and innocent. She happily absorbs every piece of received wisdom of the time: For example, she is never happier than when describing Octavia or the converted Malvinia in their roles of traditional wife and mother. If the Zinn daughters try to escape from the roles society has decreed for them, they find little sympathy from the narrator. Indeed, she is so much of a type that the reader never even learns her name.

### Themes and Meanings

Some of the themes of the book are clear and straightforward: In her history of a family with five daughters, Oates has ample opportunity to explore the beginnings of feminism as those daughters react against the strictures of their times. There is a clear picture of the century's attitudes toward female sexuality, for example, in the lives of Octavia and Malvinia. Neither seems to illustrate either a desirable or natural response to natural stimuli. The awkwardness of the time in explaining sex—an awkwardness that produced actual books such as Katherine Lee Bates's euphemistic *The Wedding Day Book* (1882)—hampers rather than helps Octavia. Without guidance she has no standard of comparison.

Malvinia, on the other hand, cannot simply enjoy her sensual nature, even in marriage. She despises herself for being what she is, regarding her sexual enjoyment as a perversion rather than a reward. A character as physically satisfied in marriage as, say, Geoffrey Chaucer's Wife of Bath would be incomprehensible to either Octavia or Malvinia. Few of the daughters seem to find an accommodation with sex. It is the thought of what must occur on her wedding night, after all, that sends Constance fleeing to the West. Only with Samantha is there no suggestion of neurotic sexuality. In her role as scientist and later as a woman who freely chooses her own husband, Samantha portrays the new woman that the new century would call into being. The most modern-seeming of the sisters, Samantha is also the most satisfied. Perhaps in the pictures of these sisters is there the strongest condemnation of the century's treatment of women.

Closely connected with the theme of sexuality is that of religion. Many of the characters seem to regard spirituality as a medicine for sexuality. Even those who, like Octavia or Malvinia, find genuine fulfillment in charitable work seem to be in retreat from the urgings of their flesh. Religion makes Malvinia meek and compliant, a change made more, rather than less, dramatic because it is a change that she desires. The less pleasant underside of religion is illustrated by Deirdre. The spiritism that she practices is worse than a hoax. Under the control of the spirits, the unwitting Deirdre sometimes says vicious things. The spirits themselves become stronger through their association with her, strong enough to kill a team of doubters attempting to test the reality of Deirdre's powers.

Another theme of dark destruction is displayed in the work of the father. Nineteenth century science is naturally the foundation of twentieth century science, and the bending of scientific means to perverted ends is explored in the story of John Quincey Zinn. The quiet of the Zinn household ends when Zinn is interviewed by a reporter from the *Atlantic*. As a result of the notoriety that follows the publication of the article, Zinn's talents come to the attention of Congress. In a parody of congressional appropriation of contemporary times, the government funds Zinn's research on the condition that he direct his efforts toward finding a new method of execution. The ever-creative inventor then builds the first electric chair. Until this point, Samantha has been her father's faithful assistant and disciple, but she regards his latest work as a prostitution of his talent. She can no longer stay, but ironically when she runs away, it is with another younger inventor.

*Critical Context*

*A Bloodsmoor Romance* attempts to re-create a period novel form that no longer exists. Contemporary fiction is generally either realistic or fantastic. In the nineteenth century, however, fantasy and reality could mix freely in what was known as the romance. Contemporary novelists who try to insert fantasy in reality are often misunderstood or scolded by critics for mixing their genres. When British novelist Nevil Shute added some fantasy to one of his novels, the critics advised him to stick to the type of realism that his readers had come to expect in his works.

Joyce Carol Oates, by calling her novel a romance, is clearly signaling her readers that there will be certain elements of fantasy in addition to the real-seeming story that she is trying to tell. Some of the fantasy includes the mysterious balloonist who kidnaps Deirdre Zinn, the time machine invented and destroyed by Mr. Zinn, and the mysterious change by which Constance Philippa becomes a man in body as she becomes more masculine and assertive in character.

The realistic story line includes the poor but loving family, the real inventions of an age of inventiveness, as well as the enthusiasm with which the nation moved from the innocence of a primarily agrarian culture into the somewhat jaded technological realities of the twentieth century.

Of all the writers who might try to create a romance, Oates is one of the ablest. She is a prolific writer of more than thirteen novels, including *them* (1969), the winner of the National Book Award. In addition, she has published volumes of short stories, poems, and essays, as well as several plays.

Besides being a writer, Oates is a teacher, too, with credentials in literature. She has written much criticism in which she often takes male writers to task for their limited views on women's potential, both intellectual and sexual. She portrays in her own intellectual life the sorts of honors that gifted women can accomplish. Oates is the winner of awards from the Guggenheim Foundation, the National Institute of Arts and Letters, and the Lotos Club.

*Sources for Further Study*
Blake, P. Review in *Time*. CXX (October 4, 1982), pp. 78-79.
Johnson, Diane. Review in *The New York Times Book Review*. LXXXVII (September 5, 1982), p. 1.
Mitchell, Sally. Review in *Library Journal*. CVII (August, 1982), p. 1482.
*The New Yorker*. LVI (September 27, 1982), pp. 145-146.
Wolcott, James. "Stop Me Before I Write Again: Six Hundred More Pages by Joyce Carol Oates," in *Harper's Magazine*. CCLXV (September, 1982), pp. 67-69.

*Walter E. Meyers*

# THE BLUEST EYE

*Author:* Toni Morrison (1931-      )
*Type of plot:* Psychological realism
*Time of plot:* 1940-1941
*Locale:* Lorain, Ohio
*First published:* 1970

> *Principal characters:*
> CLAUDIA MACTEER, the narrator, a nine-year-old black girl
> PECOLA BREEDLOVE, the protagonist, Claudia's eleven-year-old friend
> PAULINE (POLLY) BREEDLOVE, her mother, a maid
> CHOLLY BREEDLOVE, her father and the father of her baby
> FRIEDA MACTEER, Claudia's ten-year-old sister
> MICAH ELIHUE WHITCOMB (SOAPHEAD CHURCH), a West Indian and a self-proclaimed psychic and spiritual adviser

*The Novel*

The events in *The Bluest Eye* are seen from the point of view of Claudia MacTeer. As the novel begins, Claudia is looking back at the year when she was nine and when her friend Pecola Breedlove, then eleven, became pregnant, having been raped by her own father, Cholly Breedlove. In the summer of 1941, Claudia and her sister, Frieda, planted marigold seeds in the childish belief that if the marigolds survived, so would Pecola's baby. Even as the novel opens, however, the reader knows that the seeds never germinated and that the baby died. Years later, it is still impossible for Claudia to explain why the events of that year happened, so the novel becomes instead her account of how they happened.

*The Bluest Eye* has two structuring devices. One is the four seasons, which provide the four major divisions of the book. Claudia begins her account with the fall of 1940, when Pecola is placed temporarily in the MacTeer home because her father has tried to burn down the storefront apartment that serves as the Breedloves' home. In the spring, Pecola is raped by her father, and by summer, her increasingly obvious pregnancy is the subject of gossip all over town, and Pecola herself has retreated into madness, kept company in the fantasy world of her own mind by an imaginary friend.

Also giving structure to the novel is a passage that imitates the Dick-and-Jane readers once so popular in elementary schools. The picture that the passage presents of the perfect white family—Mother and Father, Dick and Jane, the dog and the cat, all living happily in their pretty green and white house—contrasts sharply with the world of the Breedloves and the

MacTeers, the world of poor blacks. To show the contrast, Morrison repeats the passage three times: first, as it would normally appear on the printed page; then, with all punctuation removed; and finally, with even the spaces between words removed. The Dick-and-Jane story degenerates on the page into a jumble of letters; lines from the storybook-perfect account of its characters' lives are interspersed throughout the Breedloves' story to emphasize the contrasting ugliness and disorder of theirs. A few run-together sentences describe Dick and Jane's pretty house. The Breedloves' home is a converted store with beaverboard panels providing the only inner walls. The mother from the world of Dick and Jane is laughing and playful. Pecola's mother, Pauline Breedlove, has seen all of her dreams fade into nothingness. She finds escape from the ugliness of the storefront and her life there as a maid in a white family's home as clean and orderly as the world in which Dick and Jane live. Her own family is an intrusion into that orderly world, and she returns from that world each day to fight with her husband and to beat her children into respectability. The father, too, unlike the smiling father of Dick and Jane, has seen his dreams shattered and has suffered the humiliation associated with growing up black in a white-dominated world. He has responded to the mistreatment he has received with violence. Ironically, even the love that he wants to express to his daughter takes a violent form when he returns home drunk one afternoon and rapes her.

Early in the novel, Pecola lies in bed listening to her parents go through the mechanical but painful ritual that their fights with each other have become. She longs to make herself disappear, and in her mind she does make her whole body cease to exist, except for her eyes. She can never make her eyes go away. Eyes become the center of Pecola's life and of her constant search for love. She believes that if only she had beautiful blue eyes, the world would look prettier—that even her parents would be hesitant to fight in front of such pretty blue eyes.

After the rape and the resulting pregnancy and suspension from school, Pecola goes to Lorain's "Spiritual and Psychic Reader," Soaphead Church, to ask him to give her blue eyes. Fraud that he is, he does in a sense grant her wish. Soaphead knows that from that day on, Pecola will have blue eyes, but only in her own mind. Before she leaves the house, Soaphead uses Pecola to rid himself of a nuisance: a mangy old dog that spends its days on his doorstep. He gives Pecola poisoned meat to feed the dog, telling her that the dog's response will be a sign to her whether she will get her wish. Pecola watches in horror as the dog stumbles around the yard and dies. This episode, combined with the earlier rape as well as a second assault on her by her father, drives Pecola over the edge into insanity. In her madness, Pecola does have blue eyes, although no one sees them except for her and the imaginary friend that she invents to reassure her constantly that her eyes are indeed the bluest in the world.

## The Characters

Although the eleven-year-old Pecola is the most obvious victim in the novel, most of the black characters are presented as victims of white society. In her childish innocence, Pecola really believes that the world would be better if viewed through the blue eyes so highly valued according to the white standard of beauty. Pecola has been made to feel ugly because she is black. Her quest for blue eyes is symbolic of her quest for the attention and love that she has missed during her bleak childhood.

Claudia feels loved by her family, yet she also feels rejected by society in general because of her blackness. By having Claudia narrate the events of the novel, Morrison (who herself was born in Lorain, Ohio, in 1931) presents them with some of the naïveté of the child but also with the clarity of vision that prejudiced adults have lost. Claudia is too young to accept without question what everyone else seems to assume: that little black girls are somehow lesser beings because of their blackness. She hates white baby dolls and the little white girls (including Shirley Temple) on whom they are modeled. She would like to tear both apart to find their secret: What is it that makes all adults, black and white, prize little white girls so much and little black girls so little? Claudia and her sister, Frieda, seem to be the only people who believe that Pecola's baby deserves to live and be loved. The older Claudia who tells the story, however, knows that she has lost her innocence and her idealism. By the time she looks back on 1941 from the perspective of later years, she has transformed her hatred for the Shirley Temples of the world into a type of fraudulent love.

While the young Claudia can still look upon the inequities of life as the injustices that they are, her parents have long since accepted the roles in which society has cast them. If the white world has declared them ugly, then ugly they will be. Early in the Breedloves' marriage, Cholly makes Pauline, with her one lame foot, feel beautiful for a time, but she later comes to believe the films and billboards which tell her constantly that white is beautiful and black is ugly: She accepts the mantle of her own ugliness. Cholly shows his ugliness through his actions. As a boy, he was surprised in the middle of his first sexual encounter by three white hunters and forced to conclude the act under the glow of their lights and their laughter. Too young and small to strike out at his tormentors then, he has been striking out ever since. Ironically, he makes his own daughter's first sexual experience as painful as his own.

Soaphead Church, the fraudulent spiritualist, provides another perspective on the issue of race. For generations, his family has tried to marry "up" and nurture its white blood. Marriage between relatives, however, has also weakened the faculties of certain family members, including Soaphead. He occupies himself by promising his clients the impossible and molesting little girls. He is wise enough in his own mad way, though, to recognize the pathos of Pecola's situation. He writes a letter to God chastising Him for failing to answer Pecola's prayer and thus forcing Soaphead to do God's work for Him.

## Themes and Meanings

The principal themes of the novel are summed up in the spring section, when the narrator speaks of the ideas of physical beauty and romantic love as "probably the most destructive ideas in the history of human thought." In this novel with no single major white character, white ideas about beauty still exert their power upon the lives of blacks, creating within the black community a strict caste system based on shades of blackness. Black adults and children alike, with the exception of Frieda and Claudia it seems, admire the "high-yellow dream child" Maureen Peal. The minor character Geraldine teaches her light-skinned son that there is a line between colored people and niggers, a line that must be carefully guarded against attempts to erode it. At the opposite extreme from Maureen Peal is Pecola, whose own mother knew from the moment of Pecola's birth that her very black baby was ugly. At both the beginning and the end of the novel, Pecola is identified with a certain type of seed that the soil will not nurture. Pecola is described at the beginning as the plot of black dirt into which her father had dropped his seed. By the end, Cholly, Pecola, and their baby are all dead, and Claudia tries to explain why:

> This soil is bad for certain kinds of flowers. Certain seeds it will not nurture, certain fruit it will not bear, and when the land kills of its own volition, we acquiesce and say the victim had no right to live. We are wrong, of course, but it doesn't matter. It's too late.

If ideas of physical beauty are destructive, so are ideas of romantic love. Once Pecola starts to menstruate, she knows that physically she is ready to have a child, but Frieda tells her that first she must get someone to love her. Pecola's tragedy is that she does not know how to do that. She is aware of the choking sounds and silence of her parents' lovemaking and the commercial sex of the three prostitutes—China, Poland, and Marie—who live upstairs, but her father's attempt to show his love for her gives her a painful initiation into sex as devastating as his own was. In trying to express his love for her, Cholly destroys her: "He, at any rate, was the one who loved her enough to touch her, envelop her, give something of himself to her. But his touch was fatal, and the something he gave her filled the matrix of her agony with death. Love is never any better than the lover."

## Critical Context

*The Bluest Eye* is significant as the first novel of a writer whose succeeding works have built upon the strength and the promise of the first to establish Morrison as one of the most respected of contemporary black novelists. In the three novels that closely followed *The Bluest Eye—Sula* (1973), *Song of Solomon* (1977), and *Tar Baby* (1981)—Morrison expanded her fictional world beyond the limited black community of Lorain, Ohio, where she herself grew up, to encompass other American cities and towns and, in *Tar Baby*, the Caribbean. She also expanded her range of characters, focusing in *Sula* on the black female both as child and as adult, in *Song of Solomon* on the young black male, and in *Tar Baby* on the young black woman who has achieved success even by white standards.

The publication of *Song of Solomon* brought Morrison immediate and immense popular success. Even as early as *The Bluest Eye*, however, she was acclaimed for her poetic language, the mythic scope of her vision, and the fresh perspective from which she presented the black community and the relationships among its members. In presenting the separate but unequal world of blacks from the point of view of a child and in focusing on the child as victim, she gave the literary world a new look at a world of injustice and oppression that in itself was hardly new.

*Sources for Further Study*

Christian, Barbara. "The Contemporary Fables of Toni Morrison," in *Black Women Novelists: The Development of a Tradition, 1892-1976*, 1980.

Davis, Cynthia A. "Self, Society, and Myth in Toni Morrison's Fiction," in *Contemporary Literature*. XXIII (1982), pp. 321-342.

Ogunyemi, Chikwenye O. "Order and Disorder in Toni Morrison's *The Bluest Eye*," in *Critique: Studies in Modern Fiction*. XIX (1977), pp. 112-120.

Pullin, Faith. "Landscapes of Reality: The Fiction of Contemporary Afro-American Women," in *Black Fiction: New Studies in the Afro-American Novel Since 1945*, 1980.

Tate, Claudia. "Toni Morrison," in *Black Women Writers at Work*, 1983.

*Donna B. Haisty*

# THE BOOK OF BEBB

*Author:* Frederick Buechner (1926-    )
*Type of plot:* Religious satire
*Time of plot:* The early 1970's
*Locale:* Florida, Houston, South Carolina, New York, New Jersey, Connecticut, and other New England locales
*First published:* 1979: *Lion Country*, 1971; *Open Heart*, 1972; *Love Feast*, 1974; *Treasure Hunt*, 1977

> *Principal characters:*
> ANTONIO PARR, Bebb's son-in-law and the narrator of the story
> LEO BEBB, the protagonist, the shady evangelist of the Church of Holy Love and Gospel Faith College
> SHARON BEBB, Bebb's adopted daughter, who eventually marries Antonio Parr
> LUCILLE BEBB, Bebb's wife
> BABE BEBB, Bebb's twin brother
> BROWNIE, Bebb's assistant, whom he resurrected

## The Novel

In the 1970's, Frederick Buechner published four novels centered on his most animated and most fully realized character, Leo Bebb: *Lion Country* (1971), *Open Heart* (1972), *Love Feast* (1974), and *Treasure Hunt* (1977). These four novels form the tetralogy which was reissued as one volume entitled *The Book of Bebb* (1979). Buechner took advantage of this reissuing to make some slight revisions, none of which materially altered the structure, characterization, or tone of his raucously comic creation.

Though the incorporation of these four novels in one volume results in some repetition, in reading *The Book of Bebb*, one has the sense of following a single continuous narrative. This is a remarkable achievement by Buechner, considering the fact that the four novels were written over a six-year period without an initial design for a tetralogy. Buechner accounts for the unity of the four works by reference to the ease with which the characters came to him. In regard to its eventual expansion into a tetralogy, Buechner explains that when he wrote the last sentence of *Lion Country*, his first Bebb novel, "I thought I had finished with them all for good but soon found that they were not finished with me."

*The Book of Bebb* is not easy to summarize without making its characters and plot sound pretentiously eccentric and quirky. Its multileveled plot, however, basically chronicles the bawdy, hilarious life of Leo Bebb, "rogue preacher," founder of Gospel Faith College, and pastor of the

Church of Holy Love. His story is told by Antonio Parr, a listless man in search of a cause to which he can dedicate himself. Parr originally visits Bebb in order to expose him as a religious fraud, a charlatan who operates a shameless diploma mill. Parr becomes instead Bebb's follower—and son-in-law—fascinated by Bebb's eccentric "parish" of outcasts and nobodies. Parr is not, however, easily won to Bebb's outlandish, decidedly anachronistic gospel of miracles and prophecy.

Parr's encounter with Bebb and the trail of sorrows, joys, paradoxes, and incongruities that follow them illustrate the winding path a believer's life may take, fraught with peril and adventure at every turn. In these four comic novels of great religious fervor, Buechner underscores the fact that faith in God is always difficult—"Hard as hell," in Bebb's words—but ultimately the only foundation on which to stand in a secularized world.

The first entry in the revised tetralogy, *Lion Country*, introduces the reader to all the main characters in Bebb's entourage: his adopted daughter, Sharon; his alcoholic wife, Lucille; Brownie, a Christian whom Bebb has apparently resurrected from the dead; and Parr, the narrator and Bebb's reluctant convert. *Lion Country* is a broad satire of religion, church life, and clergy, but rooted in a serious examination of what it means to believe in God in an age where He has been ruled out of court.

Ordained by mail, Parr journeys to Armadillo, Florida, to expose Bebb's Gospel Faith College for the diploma mill it is. He finds, however, that Bebb is a sincere, down-to-earth believer with no illusions about himself or the world. Parr soon finds himself caught up in a new web of relationships that liberates him from the pretensions of modern life into the freedom of faith.

*Open Heart*, the second novel in the tetralogy, continues the Bebb chronicle two years later, employing Parr again as narrator, now married to Bebb's adopted daughter Sharon and teaching at a Connecticut high school. *Open Heart* introduces a new assortment of eccentric characters, including Gertrude Conover, a rich Princeton Theosophist whose beliefs in reincarnation preview events to occur in the last volume of the tetralogy. The story opens with Bebb in Houston and concerns the outlandish events surrounding the death of Herman Redpath, an Indian millionaire whom Bebb had healed of impotence. Redpath leaves a small fortune for Bebb; with this new bounty, Bebb moves northward (where "the Great Whore is . . . holding a golden cup in her hand full of the abominations and filthiness of her fornications"). Now in New York City, he tries another of his peculiar adventures in evangelism, attempting to establish his new Open Heart church. Attendance, however, is poor at his revival meetings, and he decides to turn aside to the "Pepsi Generation" to lead them to "Beulah Land." The disappearance of his wife and the discovery of her suicide, the emergence of the mysterious Mr. Golden out of his past, and the imperiled marriage of

Sharon and Antonio all militate against the success and buoyancy of Bebb's endeavors, and *Open Heart* ends ambiguously enough to permit a sequel.

The third novel in the series, *Love Feast*, picks up the narrative where *Open Heart* ends, retelling several episodes from the previous volumes, including Parr's crumbling marriage, Lucille Bebb's death, and Bebb's encounters with his circle of patrons: his paramour, Gertrude Conover, his former cellmate Clarence Golden, and a number of oil-rich Indians. Bebb attempts to recover his ministry despite having no church and having lost his companion by evangelizing the Pepsi Generation on the campus of Princeton University. His "Love Feast movement" is poised "to set up the Supper of the Lamb in groves of Academe."

Bebb and his clan are eventually prohibited by the authorities from saving souls on campus, and in a last act of defiance, Princeton becomes the scene of a "sacramental orgy." The rest of *Love Feast* is anticlimactic except for the death and funeral of Bebb, who apparently dies in a fiery plane crash while buzzing through the skies of Princeton with streamers advertising "Here's to Jesus . . . here's to you!" Leo Bebb, dying in a blaze of balloons and glory, is memorialized in a potato field north of Princeton, and the Bebb saga presumably has ended.

The final novel in the volume, *Treasure Hunt*, ties up remaining loose ends of the narrative, revealing essential biographical facts about Bebb and his twin brother, Babe. As Antonio and Sharon pick up the pieces of their marriage, Sharon discovers that Leo Bebb and Babe's wife, Bert, had been adulterous lovers and that she is the offspring of Leo and Bert. Leo Bebb, as far as anyone knows, went up in flames at the end of *Love Feast*.

The setting is now Poinsett, South Carolina, where a cassette recording of Bebb explains that he has left a home to his daughter Sharon, suggesting that she and Antonio "do something nice with that old place . . . for Jesus." The reader quickly gets a strong suspicion that Bebb has been reincarnated—and in, of all places, the body of a blind, one-year-old son of food-stamp parents in Poinsett. *Treasure Hunt* contains the kind of grotesquerie and carnival humor found in the three previous works, but finally settles into a serious contemplation of the demands of true faith on the believer. Bebb's legacy, ultimately, is an uncompromising determination to live life fully, through to its end, refusing to concede anything to the darkness and hatred of memory or past failure. The God of Bebb, and of Buechner as well, is a God of redemption and forgiveness, and a God of limitless beginnings.

### The Characters

Buechner's narrative techniques place most of the weight of his novels on plot and theme; characterization is designed to exemplify those basic themes of grace and faith that Buechner sees as the fundamental principles by which mankind can work its way through the world. In *The Book of Bebb*, Buechner has thus given the reader a gallery of eccentric characters, all of whom must confront the basic issues of faith and despair, physical life and spiritual death. Their various reactions to this challenge confirm Buechner's belief that life is indeed a matter of choices among the mundane affairs of life and not in hearing voices or seeing miracles. In most cases, Buechner's characters are shrewdly drawn caricatures who appear onstage in fleeting moments, dramatizing those choices. Buechner creates Leo Bebb as the supreme example of grace operating through the least likely channel; Bebb is profane, earthy, sometimes blasphemous in the way he "preaches the gospel." Nevertheless, he is but one more reminder that all men have feet of clay, that God loves His creatures in spite of their shortcomings, and that the evidence of God's grace is all around for all to see.

Bebb is the fulcrum on which the tetralogy balances—even after his death, one is not quite done with Bebb, since he is reincarnated as Jinny Bob in the fourth and final volume in the tetralogy, *Treasure Hunt*. In many ways, however, the tetralogy is really the "Book of Parr," the private journey of Antonio Parr, the tracing of one man's sacred journey. It is through the eyes of Antonio Parr that the reader "sees"; all is filtered through the consciousness of one whose original mission was to strip away the religious veneer of fraud and who becomes instead a witting accomplice in his "victim's" exploits.

The female characters, principally Lucille Bebb and Sharon Bebb, serve as foils to the central male characters, Bebb and Parr, establishing their fallibility, which is to say their humanness. Lucille withdraws into herself, unable to reach contentment or hope, retreating behind dark glasses and drinking herself into a stupor, until one day she summons up enough strength to do away with herself. With the loss of Lucille, Bebb is unable to retain the joy of his ministry and is revived only by his later fleshly indulgence. Sharon, Bebb's illegitimate daughter, is compelled by her husband's absence and general neglect to seek warmth and affection in the arms of her nephew, Tony. Parr's complicity in the adultery is thus magnified, and his realization comes nearly too late to save the relationship.

Each Buechner character is neither saint nor sinner, but a hybrid of both; the man or woman of God is not free from temptation or doubt. The triumph of faith is achieved by working through worldly lusts to restore balance and hope, not by denying their existence and retreating into false piety.

## Themes and Meanings

The Bebb novels well illustrate the wry comment of one critic, who suggested that Buechner's art is too religious for the secular reader and too secular for the religious reader. Secular readers, in the end, find the religion of Bebb and Parr preposterous; religious readers, in the end, find the bawdy and profane life-style of Bebb and his followers equally reprehensible. In *The Book of Bebb*, Buechner thus portrays the paradox of "holiness"; Bebb is every would-be religious person: part hypocrite, part devotee, part human, part divine. The novelist's task is thus to hold these seeming dichotomies in tension, demonstrating how each can be true in a single person.

Buechner's view of narrative is evangelistic; he believes that storytelling reveals the form of human life, its direction and its meaning. Each human life contains a hidden agenda, a pattern of events that bears close attention. As most people are blind to it, it is up to the storyteller to reveal that agenda. *The Book of Bebb* is intended by Buechner to offer such a revelation, a "love letter" to that "beloved stranger," his reader, who might, for a moment, entertain the reality of the author's colorful cast of characters and recognize in their oddness and in their ordinariness that life's meaning is mediated and God's presence is confirmed. The principal themes of *The Book of Bebb* are those which undergird most of Buechner's fiction as well as his theological works: the religious nature of all human endeavor, the ability of God to speak to mankind in the ordinary, mundane affairs of human existence, and the necessity of faith and vision against the despair of the modern world.

*Critical Context*

Buechner's best-selling first novel, *A Long Day's Dying* (1950), a rarefied and intellectual treatment of the ethical malaise of modern life, was highly praised as an impressive debut for a new "modernist storyteller." Buechner's subsequent work, from 1952 to 1969, while attracting a dedicated and enthusiastic audience, failed to achieve the acclaim evoked by his first novel. *The Book of Bebb*, however, comprising as it does his four most successful works of fiction in one volume, has returned Buechner to critical favor. *The Book of Bebb* is a pivotal work in his career, representing the maturity of a comic narrative style which began to evolve in Buechner's first explicitly religious novel, *The Final Beast* (1965). In *The Final Beast*, Buechner had made a sharp break from the baroque, Jamesian narrative technique of his earlier novels, moving from mannered "drawing room" characters and brooding narrators to more ordinary people speaking in direct and unpretentious dialogue.

Suddenly, it seemed, Buechner had developed a sense of humor, and he had. Both the style and substance of his fiction became much lighter and more joyful, celebrating the inexplicable meaningfulness of human life discovered in the most mundane of circumstances.

An ordained Presbyterian minister, Buechner remains the most skillful contemporary chronicler of mankind's search for faith in a secular age.

Impressive in his control of diverse fictional and nonfictional modes of discourse, he is at once a leading Christian apologist, writer of meditations, novelist, and memoirist. The common strain through all of Buechner's works is his conviction that life is, in the end, a story: a story to be celebrated, a story to be endured, but above all, a story to be told. No one who reads Buechner's prose can come away from it knowing less of himself; his readers become, finally, the parish of this minister without a church, a minister turned master storyteller.

## Sources for Further Study

Davies, Horton. "Frederick Buechner and the Strange Work of Grace," in *Theology Today*. XXXVI (July, 1979), pp. 186-193.

Davies, Marie-Helène. *Laughter in a Genevan Gown: The Works of Frederick Buechner, 1970-1980*, 1983.

Myers, Nancy B. *Sanctifying the Profane: Religious Themes in the Fiction of Frederick Buechner*, 1980 (dissertation).

Riley, Carolyn, ed. *Contemporary Literary Criticism*. IV (1975), pp. 79-80.

Thompson, Stacey Webb. *The Rediscovery of Wonder: A Critical Introduction to the Novels of Frederick Buechner*, 1984 (dissertation).

*Bruce L. Edwards, Jr.*

# THE BOOK OF LIGHTS

*Author:* Chaim Potok (1929-    )
*Type of plot:* Psychological realism
*Time of plot:* 1950-1957
*Locale:* Brooklyn, Manhattan, Boston, Philadelphia, Korea, Japan, and
    Jerusalem
*First published:* 1981

> *Principal characters:*
> GERSHON LORAN, the protagonist, a Jewish chaplain in Korea
> ARTHUR LEIDEN, his roommate in seminary
> JACOB KETER, a professor of Jewish mysticism

## The Novel

The Book of Lights is divided into three sections. The first details the
seminary days of Gershon Loran and Arthur Leiden at Riverside Hebrew
Institute in Manhattan. The second section follows Gershon in his year of
chaplaincy duty in Korea right after the war. The third is a moving account
of the visit to Kyoto and Hiroshima by Gershon and Arthur who are now
reunited.

After his parents were killed in terrorist cross fire in Palestine in 1937,
Gershon was taken in by his aunt and uncle. His aging uncle, afflicted with
emphysema, attempts to run the decaying apartment house in which they
live. The surrounding Brooklyn neighborhood is itself decaying, and there
are frequent fires. Gershon is reared in pious Judaism but chooses to attend
the nonorthodox Riverside Hebrew Institute. There he is introduced to the
academic study of Jewish mysticism by one of his professors, Jacob Keter.
Gershon's plodding, unorganized ways as a student give way to a fervency in
his exploration of what Keter called the feeling side of Judaism.

Arthur Leiden becomes Gershon's roommate at the institute. Arthur, a
Harvard graduate, had fled his studies in physics for the rabbinate. He is
disorganized, taciturn, with something strange inside waiting to explode.
Arthur comes to depend on "dear Gershon" for help in his studies.

Gershon comes to the institute at the outbreak of the Korean war; even
after the war has ended, there remains a great need for chaplains for
American military personnel stationed in Korea and elsewhere. Indeed, as a
condition of graduation, those in the institute are required to make themselves available to the chaplaincy corps. Gershon, without understanding
why, volunteers to serve the army. Nevertheless, his entrance into the service is delayed a year because the institute awards him the first Leiden
prize.

The award is named after Arthur's brother, who was killed during World

War II. Gershon learns that Arthur's father, Charles Leiden, had worked closely with Albert Einstein and other scientists in the development and testing of the first atomic bomb. In retrospect, Gershon realizes that during their seminary days together, Arthur had been haunted by the destructive death light which his father had helped unleash. Arthur had recommended to his parents that Gershon be the first recipient of the Leiden prize.

The award provides a year's deferment from the service, and Gershon spends the time in study of the Jewish cabala with Jacob Keter. Central to that collection of mystical writings is the Zohar, a series of books describing God and his creation in terms of emanations, the pure radiance of God.

Gershon, after his year of study with Keter, becomes the only Jewish chaplain in Korea, for a time assigned to a medical unit north of Seoul. The debilitating snow and intense heat of Korea provide stark contrast to the sheltered environment of the institute, but for Gershon the experience is a transforming one. Though he continues to study cabala and frequently visits with Keter in visions, his chaplaincy is an active one. He becomes sensitive to his men and is well liked. His management skills and frequent trips to serve other units result in front page write-ups in *Stars and Stripes*, a boost in the morale of the medical unit, and Gershon's eventual transfer to division headquarters. There, he learns that chaplain Arthur Leiden has arrived in Korea.

Arthur is desperate to get to Japan, to visit Kyoto and Hiroshima. When the navy refused to provide Arthur with a security clearance (he had signed some left-wing petitions in college), he managed to get accepted by the army. Arthur prevails upon Gershon, and early in 1957 they travel together to Hong Kong and Japan. Arthur is struck by the beauty of Kyoto, its temples and gardens, yet he is filled with darkness when the two enter Hiroshima and stand before the saddlelike monument to those killed in the blast. Arthur searches for words, something to say to atone for the destruction which his father's work helped bring about. One morning, Arthur stands before the monument and reads from the Psalms, reading of forsakenness and pleading for God's restoration.

Events move rapidly. Both men return to Korea, but soon Arthur is on board another plane bound for Japan. The plane crashes on takeoff, and Arthur is killed. Later, as Gershon ends his tour of duty in Korea, he visits Arthur's parents in Boston. They are thankful for Gershon's friendship with Arthur, and seem themselves to be haunted by the death light. It is here that Gershon learns the secret of Arthur's love of Kyoto: His mother, an art historian, had indirectly persuaded the government to spare Kyoto, the first intended target of the atomic bomb.

Soon Gershon finds himself in another garden, this time in Jerusalem. He has flown to the home of Jacob Keter, there to study with one of the giants, there to encounter the God of lights.

*The Characters*

*The Book of Lights* is the story of two young men and their navigation through an evil and crumbling world. Indeed, when author Chaim Potok brings Albert Einstein onstage to honor the first recipient of the (fictitious) Leiden award, Einstein observes that "loran" has something to do with navigation (it is an acronym for Long Range Navigation) and that in his studies Gershon Loran has set an example for others to follow.

Gershon has long sought the Light that could somehow encompass the death light. At sixteen, he witnesses a dog giving birth on the roof of the family's old apartment building. Such fecundity triggers an ecstatic vision: Gershon feels for a moment as if he could touch the sky, the very stars. The promise of this moment is fulfilled when he begins to study cabala in seminary; his mystical visions are given legitimacy within the Jewish tradition.

Korea changes him further. His feelings of abandonment, of the randomness of events, are no less strong, but he returns from the service with a new strength. He has learned and suffered much in Korea, but he has survived. His studies in the Zohar, he realizes, provided a curious refuge for gathering the resources within himself needed for facing a demanding chaplaincy. Inwardly, he had done battle with the voices from the other side, the voices that called for him to give up hope and dreams in a broken century.

Gershon finally understands that those voices are not foreign to the Jewish mystical tradition; somehow the voices of despair and the voices of hope are all intertwined. This realization does not explain away evil, yet it means that in the midst of conflict and contradiction, God's radiance still shines. Personal choices can still be significant.

Jacob Keter, a widower, one of the giants of Jewish mysticism, is Gershon's mentor. Keter, over six feet tall, mostly bald, incisive, humorless (like Gershon), is a secular Zionist. He explains to Gershon that while the Talmud shows Jews how to act, it is the cabala that tells how Judaism feels, how the world is to be perceived. In one of Gershon's visions, Keter talks with a Talmud teacher, explaining that cabala was full of poetry and contradiction, giving Judaism its drive and creative genius. It is significant that in the Zohar there are ten emanations of God; the first is called "Keter," the Crown, from which all other emanations flow.

Arthur Leiden is consumed by his past. He abandons a brilliant career in physics because he is afraid that any advances he might make would only lead to more destruction. His Boston accent, his suaveness and handsomeness, all belie the struggle in Arthur to atone for that in which his parents participated. Mysticism is not for him; cabala is nothing but magic charms and numerology. He seeks a solution in political activism—from signing petitions to trying to organize Korean students to protest the militarization of their country. Yet Arthur is stalked by a vision of his own: the vision of the death light when the bomb was tested at Alamogordo, New Mexico. Arthur calls himself the offspring of killers. He insists that those who died are owed something by those who produced the bomb, but he can discover nothing in himself to bequeath. Arthur's death merely quiets his frantic voice; it does not atone for the evil.

## Themes and Meanings

There is light everywhere. In reportorial style, Potok writes of sunlight, fire, the death light, and the emanations of God. Gershon frequently studies the Zohar, the compendium of Jewish mysticism from the fifteenth century. It is a book of radiance, of enlightenment, and details the ten emanations of God through which the mystic must ascend to encounter his Creator. *The Book of Lights* contains ten chapters, each reminiscent of the corresponding emanation (or *sefirah*).

The novel is an attempt to come to terms with evil through means of the Jewish mystical tradition. Gershon is the navigator who sees "creation as a vast error; the world broken and dense with evil; everything a bewildering puzzle; . . . I especially like the ambiguities. . . . You can't pin most of it down the way you can a passage of Talmud. I can live with ambiguity, I think, better than I can with certainty. Doubt is all that's left to us. . . . Doubt and desperate deeds." This is not only Potok's legacy for contemporary Jews, but also his gift to the modern world as well: We must navigate by our deepest visions, with fear and trembling, understanding that God encompasses the evil as well as the good; God himself is found in the very feeling of abandonment, of in-betweenness, of being a stranger in the land.

## Critical Context

*The Book of Lights* grew out of Potok's experiences as an army chaplain in Korea in the late 1950's. Though the author originally intended to trace the boyhood of his protagonist in flashbacks, other books intervened to tell the stories: *The Chosen* (1967), *The Promise* (1969), and *In the Beginning* (1975). Earlier themes developed in those novels appear in *The Book of Lights*, such as anti-Semitism, textual criticism and Jewish tradition, and narrow fundamentalism's inability to come to grips with the modern world. Yet here Potok goes beyond controversies within various Jewish traditions to confront the death light that has been let loose upon the world. Real world events no longer filter into the story from newscasts in the background; now the players themselves are brought onstage. Albert Einstein and former president Harry S Truman visit Riverside Hebrew Institute. If this device is not entirely successful (the two men appear larger than life in a kind of television walk-on), nevertheless Potok has avoided a simple formula piece. His descriptions of life as a Korean chaplain are sympathetic and detailed, as are his pictures of academic and Asian cultures.

Potok has written a moving story of the way of practical mysticism. It might perhaps be noted that the author's father was a Polish émigré, and that Potok's previous novels have dealt with the conflict of Orthodox Hasidic Judaism and modern Jewish scholarship. According to a noted cabala scholar, in eighteenth century Poland one man provided a link between the development of the Hasidic tradition and that of the cabala: one Abraham Gershon. Gershon Loran is perhaps the fruit of that marriage.

*Sources for Further Study*
Reed, J. D. "Illuminations," in *Time*. CXVIII (October 19, 1981), p. 102.
Wisse, R. R. Review in *Commentary*. LXX (March, 1982), pp. 45-48.

*Dan Barnett*

# BREAD GIVERS

*Author:* Anzia Yezierska (1885-1970)
*Type of plot:* Cultural realism
*Time of plot:* The early twentieth century
*Locale:* New York City's Lower East Side
*First published:* 1925

> *Principal characters:*
> SARA SMOLINSKY, a Polish-born Jewish immigrant
> MR. SMOLINSKY, Sara's Old World father
> BESSIE SMOLINSKY, Sara's oldest sister who supports the
>    family
> MASHA SMOLINSKY, Sara's beautiful sister, who is ruined by an
>    arranged marriage
> FANIA SMOLINSKY, Sara's sister who is forced to wed a gambler
> HUGO SEELIG, Sara's American, educated fiancé

*The Novel*

Hester Street, heart of Jewish immigrant life on New York's Lower East Side in the early twentieth century, with its blend of poverty, dirt, and religious fervor, is the colorful milieu of Sara Smolinsky, *Bread Givers*' main character. The youngest of four daughters born to a Polish Judaic scholar and his wife, Sara personifies the clash between the demands of tradition and the beckoning opportunities of a new land—America.

Sara's first-person narration recollects those incidents of her childhood and young adult life which shape her ambition. Sara's journey to independence is obstructed by the conditions of poverty and the traditional expectations of Jewish women, yet she fights the often bitter battle to, as she says, "make myself for a person," with determination. At age ten, she earns money by peddling herring in the street. Along with the sweatshop earnings of her three older sisters and her mother, who takes in boarders, Sara shares the burden of her father's household. The contrast between the apparent luxury of Mr. Smolinsky's time, spent in prayer, spiritual contemplation, and religious study, and the unending toil which falls to the women, is decreed by the holy law of the Torah. As Mr. Smolinsky is quick to remind his family, "women get into heaven because they were the wives and daughters of men. Women had no brains for the study of God's Torah, but they could be the servants of men who studied the Torah."

As she sees her sisters bargained away into arranged marriages which make Mr. Smolinsky's reputation as a professional matchmaker, Sara's will hardens against him and the law that he represents. Although the three older daughters all have suitors of their own, Mr. Smolinsky forbids these relationships, preferring to exercise his absolute control by forcing the girls into loveless unions with men he chooses. When Masha's "great catch" turns out to be an unemployed salesman, and not the diamond dealer her father believed him to be, Mr. Smolinsky blames the situation on his daughter's ill luck.

Sara, refusing to be cowed like her sisters, rebels against her father. After a bitter confrontation with him, Sara runs away, choosing to live for herself instead of under his domination. Living in squalor, always hungry, Sara sustains herself with night-school lessons and dreams of college and a teaching career. Suspect for living alone instead of with her family and working to help support them, she is ostracized by the other sweatshop girls with whom she works. The grim reality of her sisters' lives, coupled with dreams of the future, supports her choice.

Sara manages to complete night school and attend college in New England. An outcast among the people on Hester Street, she is truly an outsider in the middle-class college community. Realizing her dream of becoming an educated woman eases the pain of not belonging, and returning to the Lower East Side as a teacher helps heal the wounds of Sara's displacement and ease her guilt over shirking family responsibility. Still, she does not win her father's approval, for which she yearns, although she knows that it would require the self-sacrifice that she refuses to make—her compliance with the idea of innate female inferiority.

Mr. Smolinsky's remarriage almost immediately after the death of Sara's mother reinforces her determination not to succumb to his self-centered will. Yet, ultimately, she cannot refuse his needs, and, encouraged by her fiancé, Hugo Seelig, she agrees to help support him and his new wife. Hugo, also a teacher and the child of immigrants, tries to uphold the continuity of tradition by learning Hebrew from Mr. Smolinsky. Sara, still unsure of how to negotiate between her own and her father's needs, is finally able to accept that inextricable part of her nature which can only be fulfilled through the culture that Mr. Smolinsky represents: "It wasn't just my father, but the generations who made my father whose weight was still upon me."

*The Characters*

The characters in *Bread Givers*, from coarse pushcart clothing to their speech peppered with Yiddish expressions, are faithfully modeled upon the real immigrants of Yezierska's own acquaintance. Some, such as Zalmon the fish peddler, are literary memorials to the people whom Yezierska cherished for their inspiration. Other characters, such as Sara and Mr. Smolinsky, replicate the struggle that Yezierska herself experienced between the demands of traditional culture and the opportunities of contemporary American society. The Smolinsky family illustrates the gender arrangements which constrained Yezierska, even as she celebrated the culture which created them.

Many of the details of Yezierska's life coincide with those of her character, Sara Smolinsky (both are children of poor, Jewish immigrants, both helped support their families while still children, and both sacrificed much to earn an education). Yet as a literary character, Sara is able to act out conflicts in a manner both dramatic and satisfying. Sara is a model of resourcefulness at fighting the hostile influences of family and culture. As a child, Sara's character is largely formed by reacting to the example set by her three older sisters—Bessie, Masha, and Fania.

Like their mother, the three older girls do not question female submission. Mrs. Smolinsky, once the petted daughter of well-to-do parents in a Polish *shtetl*, considers herself blessed by the honor of marriage to Mr. Smolinsky, a highly esteemed scholar. In Poland, Mr. Smolinsky's devotion to study is a sign of the inherited wealth which supports it. Even when financial reverses force them to emigrate and face great changes, Mrs. Smolinsky still believes in her husband's godliness and her responsibility to enable him to study. She wavers only when Mr. Smolinsky, taking matters into his own hands, makes their financial situation worse. Even though he gives much of the women's earning away to charity and is swindled out of the small savings which might have made them comfortable, Mrs. Smolinsky never fails to see the light of God shining in her husband's eyes.

Mrs. Smolinsky's acceptance of her husband's spiritual, and hence essential, superiority, is solidly reinforced in the minds of the three older daughters. Bessie, the oldest, is famous for being the burden-bearer of her father's house. Working long hours in a sweatshop and bringing home piecework makes her more valuable to him. Her father turns the one suitor she has out of the house because he refuses to pay a dowry. She knows that she has been broken to her father's will, and the loss of her lover increases her despair. True to her self-sacrificing nature, she marries a widower who willingly pays Mr. Smolinsky's price, rationalizing her lot by concern for the man's wild, unkempt children. Like their sister Bessie, Masha and Fania are unable to overcome the injunction of submissiveness to the father's will. Masha and Fania watch helplessly as their father bans the men they love from the house as well for what he calls their godlessness and inability to support his daughters adequately. When Mr. Smolinsky arranges marriages for the two girls with truly unsuitable men, they are forced to accept their situations. Believing that the unhappiness and poverty which marriage has brought them is the norm, and unable to see beyond the cultural pattern which determines their lives, they even encourage Sara to marry a man, selected by her father, whom she dislikes.

Supported by tradition, Mr. Smolinsky assumes the right to make a profit from his daughters. Sara, demanding the right to live her own life, confronts her father, who is ensconced among the holy books that the women are not allowed to touch. Backed up by the law of patriarchy that has blinded him to the rights and worldly needs of his wife and children, he justifies her duty to him: "Now, when I begin to have a little use from you, you want to run away and live for yourself?" Fueled by years of internalized anger at her father's absolute control, Sara saves herself from a life of submission.

Starving herself to save money for school, Sara's desire to realize the American Dream is marked by ambivalence. The childhood nickname "blood and iron," bestowed on her by her father, signifies her opposition as well as likeness to him. Hating his tyranny, yet yearning to express their shared love of study and knowledge, Sara finds in secular education a spiritual bridge to the Jewish tradition of learning which shuts out women. Disdaining arranged marriage, she still wants her father's approval of the man she chooses for herself. Sara's attempt to reconcile her heritage with American culture, she realizes, places her "between two worlds," but she accepts that uncomfortable position as the only possible one.

*Themes and Meanings*

Yezierska does not romanticize the poverty of Hester Street, but she does make apparent the wisdom of the ages used to make conditions there tolerable. As Mr. Smolinsky says, "The God that feeds the worms under the stone, and the fishes in the sea, will he not feed us?" In trying to express both the beauty of Jewish culture and its incompatibility with early twentieth century urban life, Yezierska shows that Sara's success in meeting modern challenges is founded upon her realism.

While following the traditions of ritual law, Mr. Smolinsky's opportunism illustrates the inherent hypocrisy of having one foot in the Old World and the other in the New: "I want to get into some quick money-making thing that will not take up too many hours a day, so I could get most of my time for learning." Not wanting to disown the cultural identity which venerates scholarship but also realizing that, as a woman, she is excluded from that tradition, Sara's ambivalence is the result of being caught between contradictory ideals. The promise of America—individual success—can turn the subordination of women under patriarchal Judaism on its ear. Essential as such self-definition is for survival, however, the loss of cultural place creates a lack which cannot be denied.

Overcoming that lack by synthesizing personal need and cultural identity is the message of *Bread Givers*. Sara returns to the Lower East Side as a schoolteacher, believing that she has a debt to pay to the past she once thought had no claims on her. "Once I had been elated at the thought that a man wanted me. How much more thrilling to feel that I had made my work wanted!" The rewards of love may come second to career, but it is no less important. Securely independent prior to romantic involvement, Sara uses marriage to affirm culture, instead of being destroyed by it. Sara's engagement to a man of like background and ambition helps close the gap between herself and her culture. As her fiancé recognizes, "You and I, we are of one blood." Together they give life to Yezierska's hope of preserving culture without sacrificing either independence or romantic desire.

*Critical Context*

By the time she wrote *Bread Givers*, Yezierska had undergone the pivotal experience of her literary career. The success of *Hungry Hearts* (1920), her collected short stories, brought her fame and a contract as a Hollywood scriptwriter. Away from the ghetto which was both the setting and inspiration for her creative efforts, Yezierska suffered from writer's block and a painful sense of dissociation. The experience confirmed Yezierska's cultural identity, and her resolve to return to Hester Street was marked by the awareness that with financial success, "I could buy everything I wanted except the driving force I had to inspire my work."

Faithfully reproducing the battle Yezierska waged against poverty and cultural taboo, the romantic plot which gives *Bread Givers* a conventional sense of closure solves another dilemma that Yezierska faced: How can one establish independence without giving up the notion of romantic happiness? Variation on the themes of her own life was deliberately cathartic; as she wrote, "I thought by writing out what I don't know and can't understand it will stop hurting me."

The clear poignancy of her literary style does not belie the hardships Yezierska endured to learn English from a janitor's daughter, but instead transports the reader into her world without pretense or self-effacement. As one contemporary critic noted of her writing, "One does not seem to read, one is too completely inside."

Approaching middle age, Yezierska stopped writing novels and stories, and her popularity waned. In *Red Ribbon on a White Horse* (1950), her autobiography, she voices the belief that sacrificing cultural roots was too high a price for the recognition she had once craved. The mid-1970's republication of *Bread Givers* and other out-of-print books by Yezierska has fortunately made her work widely available. The returning popularity of her work testifies to the universal emotional appeal and unique voice which first established her literary reputation.

*Sources for Further Study*

Inglehart, Babette. "Daughters of Loneliness: Anzia Yezierska and the Immigrant Woman Writer," in *Studies in American Jewish Literature*. Winter, 1975.

Yezierska, Anzia. *Red Ribbon on a White Horse*, 1950.

*Mollie A. Brodsky*

# A BRIEF LIFE

*Author:* Juan Carlos Onetti (1909-     )
*Type of plot:* Psychological novel
*Time of plot:* The twentieth century
*Locale:* Buenos Aires and Santa María
*First published: La vida breve*, 1950 (English translation, 1976)

> *Principal characters:*
>    JUAN MARÍA BRAUSEN, the protagonist, a publicist
>    JUAN MARÍA ARCE, his other self
>    DR. DÍAZ GREY, a creation of Brausen's imagination
>    GERTRUDIS, Brausen's wife
>    QUECA, Arce's lover, a prostitute
>    ELENA SALAS, Díaz Grey's patient and love

*The Novel*

   *A Brief Life* presents the inner conflict of a man who, after suffering a traumatizing experience, feels lost and seeks an identity. He splits into two selves, and, at the same time, he finds refuge in his own fantasy.

   Juan María Brausen is about to fired from his job. His wife, Gertrudis, has undergone surgery on her left breast, and her scarred body is so repulsive to him that it has become an obsession. He begins to realize that he is not the same person he thought he was and suffers a crisis of identity: "I understood that I had been aware for weeks that I, Juan María Brausen and my life were nothing but empty molds, pure representations of an old meaning kept out of indolence, of a being dragging himself among the people, the streets, and the time of the city, routine acts."

   Through the wall of his apartment, Brausen can listen to the incidents that take place in the world of Queca, a prostitute. He decides to enter this adjacent world as an alternative to his tortured existence. In his imagination, Brausen becomes Juan María Arce, a new man who will exist simultaneously but apart from Brausen. Arce will live "a brief life in which time could not be enough to engage him, to make him repent, or grow older."

   The agency for which Brausen works has ordered him to write a screenplay. For that purpose, he has invented the imaginary world of Santa María at the shores of the Río de la Plata. There, an imaginary alter ego, the mediocre forty-year-old Dr. Díaz Grey, spends his life selling morphine to Elena Salas, the woman with whom he is in love. Brausen repeatedly escapes to this world and projects himself into the doctor.

   These "brief lives" exist primarily in Brausen's consciousness, rather than in the real world. The conclusion of the novel completes the image of failure presented at the beginning: Brausen has been fired from his job and has been abandoned by his wife. Queca has been killed, and Elena Salas also has died. The novel ends with Brausen walking along the streets of Santa María, integrated into his own fantasy.

### The Characters

Onetti presents in *A Brief Life* an interesting, three-dimensional protagonist. By splitting the character's personality, the author is able to make a more profound study of human identity.

Onetti concentrates on Brausen's psychological problems, fears, and fantasies, rather than on a narrative description of his life. For this reason, Brausen's internal life, depicted through his reflections and through passages of stream of consciousness, predominates over action in the book.

Juan María Brausen, like many of Onetti's protagonists, is an imaginative man who refuses to develop the practical qualities that his world demands of him. Brausen is an alienated, existentially tortured man, an outsider. He knows that the world in which he lives is full of falsehood, but he does not fight it. He adopts a skeptical and resigned attitude. He invents new lies, new identities. Brausen creates other selves through which he evades his anxiety, taking refuge in his fantasy as a self-defense mechanism, but he does not undergo change in the course of the novel. His life has changed with his wife's surgery and the consequent trauma, but Brausen has the same wandering attitude from the beginning to the end. He is consistently a failure.

The noises and voices to which Brausen listens through the wall of his room invite him to enter the world of sex, a world from which his wife's scars have separated him. Brausen transformed into Arce will visit Queca, the prostitute, to overcome the impotence that he feels with his wife. Arce can live with Queca a life that is "without memories and without foreknowledge." Arce becomes Brausen's strongest persona.

In his attempt at salvation, Brausen has also invented Dr. Díaz Grey. This fictitious doctor is based on Brausen's monotonous life and on the revulsion that his wife's scarred body provokes in him.

Brausen projects himself into Arce and Díaz Grey, all three sharing a life of failure and lies. They incarnate the fatalism in which Onetti seems to believe. They accept their colorless lives without attempting to change them. Indeed, they seem unwilling to attempt external change.

The protagonist's sense of alienation is underlined by the fact that most of the secondary characters belong to a marginal world—the world inhabited by prostitutes and pimps. Onetti does not even place his hero (or antihero) in a historical context, or in a clearly defined place. Brausen lives in some obscure part of Buenos Aires that contaminates him with its dullness and mediocrity.

The other characters are presented through Brausen's eyes and are totally dependent on Brausen-Arce-Díaz Grey. Gertrudis, a character who rarely speaks, represents Brausen's past. Queca passively accepts Arce's love and Arce's beatings. It seems that she has been created to be abused by others; this is her role, she knows, and she merely plays it. Elena Salas is a projection of Gertrudis. These three women, the foundation of Brausen-Arce-Díaz Grey's life, will have to disappear before Brausen can find his real identity.

### Themes and Meanings

*A Brief Life*, with its complex narrative structure, suggests that man is one and many, a multiple being made of a series of distinct and alienated selves. As the title of the book indicates, a man can live many short lives.

Fatalism and failure govern Brausen's world. It is a world in which man is surrounded by deception which makes futile any fight against the natural obstacles of life. (The book begins and ends symbolically during carnival; life is a masquerade.) There is no way to succeed. The only possibility of salvation is in oneiric inventions, in fantasy: "I had in my hands the paper, the blotter, and the fountain pen necessary for my salvation. . . . I would be saved if I began to write the plot. . . . If I wrote only one phrase." Salvation through the act of imagination is a recurring theme in Onetti's work.

### Critical Context

Onetti belongs to a group of writers, born in Uruguay and Argentina, who reached maturity during the politically tumultuous 1930's and who became known as "the lost generation." They share a nihilist vision of the world, expressed through the solitary, alienated characters they create. These writers practice a kind of existentialism; their conflict with society is reflected in the deliberately fragmentary quality of their fiction. A good example of such fragmentation can be seen in Onetti's *A Brief Life*.

*A Brief Life* is considered to be a pivotal work in Onetti's career. His previous works—*El pozo* (1939), *Tierra de nadie* (1941), and *Para esta noche* (1943)—sketch the psychological conflicts that are fully developed in *A Brief Life*. Many of the works that follow—*Los adioses* (1954), *Para una tumba sin nombre* (1959), *Juntacadáveres* (1964), and *La muerte y la niña* (1973)—base their plots on the inventions created in Juan María Brausen's mind.

Indeed, the world of Santa María, first introduced in *A Brief Life*, appears as a constant in Onetti's following works. Santa María, like Macondo in Gabriel García Márquez' books, becomes a mythical place. Onetti succeeds in transporting the reader to his character's fantasy world, because, although nonexistent, it seems perfectly real.

*A Brief Life* explores man's search for an answer to his existence. "People believe they are condemned to one life until death. But they are only condemned to one soul, to one identity. One can live many times, many lives, shorter or longer." By creating an imaginary world, and imaginary selves, Brausen can enjoy several lives, although he remains the same person, the same soul.

*Sources for Further Study*
Amisa, Fernando. *Las trampas de Onetti*, 1970.
Benedetti, Mario. *Juan Carlos Onetti y la aventura del hombre*, 1969.
Kadir, Djelal. *Juan Carlos Onetti*, 1977.
Rama, Angel. *Origen de un novelista y de una generación literaria*, 1966.

*Mercedes Jiménez González*

# BULLET PARK

*Author:* John Cheever (1912-1982)
*Type of plot:* Realistic fantasy
*Time of plot:* The late 1960's, with ample flashbacks to the earlier lives of the characters
*Locale:* Primarily Bullet Park, a mythical suburb in Connecticut
*First published:* 1969

*Principal characters:*
> ELIOT NAILLES, a former chemist turned advertising man who now pushes "Spang" mouthwash
> PAUL HAMMER, a neighbor of Nailles, independently wealthy but crazy
> TONY NAILLES, Nailles's son, a second-string high school football player and a victim of a mysterious disease
> NELLIE NAILLES, Eliot's wife and a stabilizing force in the Nailles's household
> SWAMI RUTUOLA, a self-proclaimed messiah and Jamaican black
> MRS. HUBBARD, a war widow, and, for a brief time, Tony's lover

## The Novel

*Bullet Park* is divided into three sections or parts. The first introduces Eliot Nailles and his family and the suburban world in which he lives. During this part, his son Tony becomes depressed and takes to his bed with a malady undetectable by the local doctor and outside specialists, only to be rather mysteriously cured some weeks later by a self-styled swami, Rutuola. The second part of the novel, related throughout the diary of Nailles's neighbor, Paul Hammer, tells of Hammer's eccentric family and his unorthodox upbringing as the bastard son of a wealthy Socialist and his secretary. This part concludes with Hammer resolved to follow his demented mother's suggestion that he crucify a resident of some suburb in order to proclaim the moral bankruptcy of the capitalist system. The final part traces Hammer's murderous obsession as he determines first to kill Nailles and then, instead, Tony. The novel and this part conclude with Nailles saving his son from immolation on the altar of Christ Church at the hands of the now totally unhinged Hammer, who is hauled off to the state hospital for the criminally insane. Tony goes back to school, seemingly untouched by his experiences, and Nailles, now addicted to a morphine-based tranquilizer, returns to the daily routine of his suburban world.

Although the setting of *Bullet Park* would seem to be the familiar suburban one used before by John Cheever, this time it is deceptive; one critic has called it a "lethal Eden." Beneath the surface of the sunny days and green lawns and social conviviality lurks an evil capable of destroying the rural innocence after which the suburbanites so desperately search. The world of Bullet Park is conventional enough and comfortable enough to allow Cheever to introduce a series of coincidences, potential tragedies, and madness without lapsing into fantasy or the grotesque. If, as one critic has asserted, the book is a philosophical novel and not a novel of manners about American suburbia, the unexceptional locale aids the reader by providing a secure and verisimilar world. The stability and order and familiarity of the setting of the first part also provide a contrast with the often bizarre world introduced in the second part when Hammer describes his life.

The accident of Hammer's birth, the strangeness of his youth amid a family of withdrawn and eccentric adults, and finally the growing insanity of his search for an escape from his personal *cafard*—a palpable melancholy or despair—create for him an increasingly unstable world ruled by chance. The intersection of these two worlds, one seemingly ordered and conventional and the other erratic and extraordinary, comes to a climax in the third section, in which Hammer's violence intersects with Nailles's innocence, leaving both men irrevocably changed at the end. As Hammer acts out the logic of his irrationalities, Nailles plunges into the depths of his decencies to save both his son and himself from succumbing to the chaos that has invaded his Eden.

## The Characters

The apparent cuteness of having the two central characters of *Bullet Park* called Hammer and Nailles masks a more serious intent. Even though the two men seem to represent the opposites of irrationality and stability, they also suggest complementary sides of the same personality and in so doing work together, as hammer and nails, to unite the contraries of the human psyche.

Eliot Nailles appears to represent all that is right with the sunny world of the suburbs. His naïve and trusting acceptance of people, his love of nature and the simple pleasures of fishing, and his domesticity, especially his comfortable relationship with his wife and passionate, if guarded, attachment to his son, would seem to place him among those for whom the retreat from the city has provided a balm for the tensions and conflicts of modern life. Certainly all of these characteristics are found in the personality of Nailles, but he also retains a somewhat hidden, if no less determining, side of himself, a dark and destructive element which causes him to have occasional thoughts of homicide (thoughts which he almost acts out against his son), ambivalent sexual feelings about his wife, and irrational fears which overwhelm him, shattering his outward appearance of calm and driving him to the dependence on drugs of which he is in the grip at the end of the novel.

Although outwardly Paul Hammer represents all of those things disruptive and chaotic which would shatter the tranquillity of the suburban, green world of *Bullet Park*, he, too, contains a mixture of characteristics which make him kin rather than simple opposite to his neighbor Nailles. If Hammer openly acts out the suppressed violence and confusion which under the surface rule Nailles's life, he also yearns for the tranquillity which Bullet Park promises. Uncomfortable in nature and with children and dogs, he lacks the socially accepted means for diffusing his mental confusion, and throughout the novel he is obsessed with destroying the world he little understands and increasingly comes to hate. Like Nailles, who is too simple to understand the dark forces which increasingly direct his life, Hammer plunges ever more deeply into the madness which envelops him. Hammer becomes an uncontrolled version of what Nailles discovers lies within himself and will emerge if social restraints are released. He provides a chance interruption of Nailles's happy and orderly life and provides Nailles with a vision of shattering and unexpected violence and evil.

If Hammer and Nailles are less opposites than alter egos, their positions are secured in part by their relationships with the novel's other characters. Nellie Nailles proves to be as emotionally opaque to the reader as she is to her husband. Seemingly always smiling and tranquil, obedient sexually, a good mother and wife, she proves to be as ineffectual against the irrationalities which are visited on the couple as does Nailles. Although driven by desperation, she at least is willing to seek out the swami who proves to provide the cure to their son's emotional immobilization. Pitted against Hammer's wife, Mariette, with her alcoholism and outbursts of vindictive behavior, Nellie keeps within herself something untouchable, something which Nailles's conventional manners and attitudes block him from discovering. Made more manifest in his relationship with his son, Tony, this loss of contact between human beings, even family members, forms a tragic leitmotif which undergirds the narrative of the fiction.

Just as Nellie and Tony form an unreachable emotional center for Nailles, so Hammer's wacky mother and distant father provide only elusive human connections. The midwestern girl, Gretchen Schurz, who once was Hammer's father's secretary, has become an insane woman who lives in genteel poverty amid the watering holes of Europe. She is the one who gives to her son the idea that he should crucify some suburbanite as a protest against the capitalist system. Since his father and mother were never married, there is a kind of crazy logic which connects suburban Connecticut with Hammer's loss of his parents. Like Nailles, Hammer wants to have life whole, but neither man can achieve tranquillity. Grace, for Cheever, does not come from an act of will but rather through the often serendipitous and accidental—for example, in the ministrations of the swami who cures Tony.

## Themes and Meanings

The central concern of the novel is the presence of evil as part of the human condition. It is an evil, moreover, that is undirected and random, dropping by chance into the orderly lives of average people who live seemingly purposeful and contented lives within the new Eden of the suburbs. It would be incorrect, however, to see *Bullet Park* as one more facile attack against suburban living; the focus of the fiction is not on where the characters live but rather on their attempts to escape evil through the rituals and events of their lives. Indeed, it is the very opportunity offered by the wealth and comfort of Bullet Park which makes the fact of evil so threatening and at the same time so inexplicable. The suggestion is that if there is a failing of the suburban world it is that therein dwells too much hope and trust, especially in the reliance on the rituals and rites, which, if followed conscientiously, seem to promise order, morality, and decorum. If Nailles has a fault, it is that he is a true believer, one who subscribes to the myth totally; if the novel has a positive ending, Nailles triumphing over Hammer, however clumsily, this may suggest that an optimistic man is able to absorb tragedy and suffering without being totally destroyed. Thus, Nailles emerges as an affirmer of survival if not of transcendence. The message seems clear: In this imperfect modern world, surviving is all that can be expected.

## Critical Context

*Bullet Park* was John Cheever's third novel and was received with mixed reviews. Some of the critics considered the novel a failure because of its flawed structure, falling into three separate parts, unconnected and disjointed. Another criticism was that the fiction was far too dark for the sunny prose style of its telling. Such concerns with a fragmented form and disjunctive style have largely been laid to rest by later accounts of the novel's achievements. The all too sunny style has been seen as a lyric embracing of the natural world, an affirmation that transcends the chaos and oddity of experience. The three parts of the novel appear on closer reflection to be more tightly connected and to reflect a unity of theme and purpose. Admittedly, *Bullet Park* is a much darker novel than the Wapshot books before it. Perhaps it would be more accurate to say that the dark side of the previous books was allowed greater sway in the latter one. This seems logical, given that the later Wapshot works lack the geographical and historical connections which provided Cheever's earlier characters with whatever grounding they required against the forces of chaos and modernism. Given what he has to draw upon, Eliot Nailles succeeds quite well in his search for meaning amid the tranquillity and treachery of his lethal Eden.

## Sources for Further Study

Cheever, Susan. *Home Before Dark*, 1984.

Coale, Samuel. *John Cheever*, 1977.
Hunt, George W. *John Cheever: The Hobgoblin Company of Love*, 1983.
Waldeland, Lynne. *John Cheever*, 1979.

*Charles L. P. Silet*

# BURR

*Author:* Gore Vidal (1925-     )
*Type of plot:* Historical chronicle
*Time of plot:* 1776-1840
*Locale:* New York, Washington, D.C., and the Western states and territories
*First published:* 1973

*Principal characters:*

AARON BURR, Vice President of the United States under
    Thomas Jefferson, killer of Alexander Hamilton in a duel
    (July 11, 1984), tried for treason (March 30, 1807)

ELIZA BOWEN JUMEL, Burr's second wife

CHARLES SCHUYLER, Burr's biographer and a journalist and
    law student

HELEN JEWETT, Schuyler's mistress

WILLIAM CULLEN BRYANT, editor of the New York *Evening
    Post*

WILLIAM LEGGETT, Schuyler's editor at the *Evening Post*

WASHINGTON IRVING, a famous American writer, diplomat,
    and adviser to Schuyler

GEORGE WASHINGTON, Burr's commanding officer during the
    American Revolution

ALEXANDER HAMILTON, Washington's aide, later Secretary of
    the Treasury and Burr's political foe

ANDREW JACKSON, friendly to Burr, hostile to the
    Jeffersonians

JAMES MADISON, Jefferson's protégé and part of what Burr
    calls the "Virginia junto"

JOHN MARSHALL, Supreme Court Justice, disaffected cousin
    to Jefferson, who presided over Burr's treason trial

JOHN RANDOLPH, a Virginia politician who is cool to Jefferson
    and a significant factor in Burr's acquittal

JAMES WILKINSON, at first Burr's ally in an effort to conquer
    Mexico, then Jefferson's tool in the treason trial

## The Novel

*Burr* begins on July 1, 1833, with a special dispatch from the New York
*Evening Post* announcing the marriage of "Colonel Aaron Burr, aged sev-
enty-seven" to "Eliza Jumel, born Bowen fifty-eight years ago (more likely
sixty-five but remember: she is prone to litigation!)." The author of the dispatch, and narrator of the novel, is Charles Schuyler, who is studying law
under Burr, an attorney still active in the affairs of love and politics.

Schuyler's narrative intended to resolve some of the confusion and the conflicting claims that mark historical accounts of Burr's controversial career, while not pretending to offer the ultimate truth about the man. As Burr himself will suggest, the printed history of his affairs has been unreliable; the point of Schuyler's dispatch is that even at this late stage in his subject's life, accurate information is difficult to obtain and to publish on a figure who refers to the legend of himself as "the hellish Aaron Burr [who] meant single-handedly to disband the United States."

Vidal has wisely chosen not to present Burr's life in strict chronological order. The most fascinating and historically significant period of the protagonist's life is over by his fiftieth year, and while Burr's personality remains intriguing, his last thirty years are of minor importance and are telescoped into a few pages of Schuyler's speculations about how Burr has coped with his infamous past.

Like many historical novels, *Burr* puts one historical period inside of another, so that one acts as a frame for the other, and the reader's sense of history, of how one period develops into the next, is superbly enriched. The novel's past covers the years of the Revolution and the first three presidential administrations by presenting Burr's point of view in twenty-one autobiographical installments that Schuyler edits and that are inserted into the ongoing narrative.

The novel's present, 1833-1836, is the era of the second administration of Andrew Jackson, in which political maneuvering has already begun to ensure that Vice President Martin Van Buren will succeed to the nation's highest office. Schuyler is employed by William Leggett (bent on discrediting Van Buren) to write about Burr in the hope of proving that Van Buren is Burr's illegitimate son. Yet Schuyler finds Burr admirable because he is free of the usual cant and hypocrisy associated with politicians and generously admits his errors. Schuyler proves to be the perfect narrator, since he is forced to explore all sides of Burr and is unaware, until the last page of the novel, of his true relation to his subject. In other words, Schuyler is the classic hero of historical fiction as it was first developed by Sir Walter Scott. He is part of the action but also removed from it; he is connected to a losing cause (the Burrites who still think their chief was correct in trying to liberate Mexico and the West), but he is also very much a man of the present, somewhat aloof from politics but nevertheless drawn into political intrigue.

By giving his novel a double time frame, Vidal is able to demonstrate that Burr's forthright opportunism is hardly what makes him a unique figure in American history. On the contrary, Burr and the other founding fathers set up a factionalized political system that was responsible for the scheming that Schuyler cannot avoid. Burr was not extraordinary for his faults but was necessary as a scapegoat for Thomas Jefferson and others who wanted to mask their own motivations in building an American empire.

## The Characters

The character studies in *Burr* are extraordinarily vivid and often amusing. George Washington is portrayed as an inept military commander but an astute politician who realized at an early age that he would have to play the aloof, austere, American "god." Thomas Jefferson is a canting hypocrite of the highest order, who nevertheless earns Burr's accolade as the greatest politician and empire builder of his age. James Madison, aware of Jefferson's duplicity, is treated as a complex figure doggedly loyal to his mentor and most impressive in his subtle construction of constitutional principles. John Marshall appears as a titanic figure in support of the Constitution, yet he is not immune to fears of his cousin Jefferson's efforts to undermine the chief justice and the United States Supreme Court. Alexander Hamilton, fiercely ambitious and contentious, finally goes too far (perhaps sensing his political failure in New York, which leads to Burr's leadership of the Federalists) in accusing Burr, not of political impropriety, but of incest with his beloved daughter Theodosia.

In *Burr*, politics and personalities are finely fused, so that it is not certain whether Hamilton and Burr fight over personal or political insults. Both men, it is clear, are deeply disappointed when they do not achieve their highest ambitions. While the novel is dominated by Burr's obviously partisan view of his opponents, it is clear from the dialogue between Burr and other political figures and from the questions that Schuyler asks him that Burr's central failing has been his inability to articulate his understanding of the Constitution and of his country's future. What puts Jefferson ahead of Burr is not simply his superior maneuvering for power; rather, Jefferson enunciates, however ambiguously, a national purpose that transcends his own person. Burr, on the other hand, has depended throughout his life on the personal loyalty of his followers. In his own words, Burr has been too frank in admitting that he is "equivocal" on the Constitution.

## Themes and Meanings

The theme of *Burr* centers on the meaning of the Constitution. Is it a document that will endure, or is it subject to changes brought about by the exploration of a vast continent composed of many different peoples who may seek many different forms of government which the Constitution cannot absorb? Vidal shrewdly shows that with the exception of Madison and Washington, most of the founding fathers, at one time or another, undermined the authority of the Constitution. Jefferson, when it was convenient for his politics, argued for nullification, the right of any state to reject a federal law deemed injurious to its interests. Hamilton favored a government closer in structure to the British parliamentary system. John Adams suppressed dissent and took, in some respects, a far more authoritarian view of his powers than the Constitution permitted.

Burr, in line with many other young men of his day, entertained the idea of a separate country west of the Mississippi and dreamed as well of liberating Mexico. Whether in this atmosphere his views were treasonous has never been clear in spite of Jefferson's best efforts to demonstrate that Burr's Western expedition was for the purpose of seizing territory and declaring a new nation.

What is clear is that Burr is the perfect tool for Vidal's debunking of several of America's revered national figures. The novelist does not deny their greatness, but he shows that it was of a different kind from that commonly celebrated. It is political craft, not political principle, that Vidal lauds and criticizes. Figures such as William Cullen Bryant and Washington Irving, discreet upholders of pious maxims and diplomatic versions of American history, would like to remove Schuyler from the fluid political realities that enmeshed Burr and Jefferson and in which politicians today, Vidal implies, are still trapped.

*Critical Context*

*Burr* is one of a series of novels by Vidal providing a lively and incisive history of the American republic. Considered by many critics to be the finest of his historical fictions, *Burr* was followed by *1876* (1976) and *Lincoln* (1984). An earlier novel, *Washington, D.C.* (1967), centers on politics in the era of Franklin D. Roosevelt and Harry Truman. Of these novels, *Burr* has the most complex narrative structure and the smoothest integration of fictional and historical characters.

Charles Schuyler is fictional, and his own story, involving an intricate balancing of private and political life, is the Burr story in a minor key. Historical novelists often have difficulty making their passive heroes, who are usually devoted to domestic life and unwillingly involved in historical epochs, sufficiently interesting, but Schuyler is like a more modest Burr in his adventuring, in his sad affair with Helen Jewett, a prostitute whom he tries to live with and marry. Schuyler has almost betrayed Burr, as did James Wilkinson, who turned into Jefferson's stooge, and Schuyler almost becomes William Leggett's lackey in the plot to bring down Van Buren, who is Burr's protégé.

For the most part, Vidal has stuck to the facts and to the chronology of history, since it is his purpose not only to entertain but also to advance provocative notions concerning the motivations of historical figures, notions of a kind that historians, relying only on data and guarding their professional reputation, are reluctant to venture. Extrapolating from the known personalities of historical figures, he creates dialogue and description that capture history in the making.

*Sources for Further Study*

Dick, Bernard F. *The Apostate Angel: A Critical Study of Gore Vidal*, 1974.

Kiernan, Robert F. *Gore Vidal*, 1982.

Stanton, Robert, ed. *Gore Vidal: A Primary and Secondary Bibliography*, 1978.

Stanton, Robert, and Gore Vidal. *Views from a Window: Conversations with Gore Vidal*, 1980.

*Carl E. Rollyson, Jr.*

# BY LOVE POSSESSED

*Author:* James Gould Cozzens (1903-1978)
*Type of plot:* Social realism
*Time of plot:* Around 1950
*Locale:* The New England town of Brocton
*First published:* 1957

*Principal characters:*
> ARTHUR WINNER, JR., the protagonist, a lawyer who struggles with a moral dilemma
> NOAH TUTTLE, also a lawyer, accused of misappropriation of funds
> JULIUS PENROSE, the husband of Winner's lover and the third partner in the law firm
> HELEN DETWEILER, the secretary to Tuttle, Winner, and Penrose

*The Novel*

Set in a small Northeastern community, *By Love Possessed* chronicles forty-nine hours in the life of Arthur Winner, Jr., a respected lawyer and citizen of Brocton. The title refers to the different types of love—sexual love, parental love, friendship, love for community and church—which play a part in Winner's life as a man and as a lawyer. The novel opens as Winner contemplates the clock in his mother's house with the inscription *omnia vincit amor*. Winner has patterned himself after his deceased father, the "Man of Reason," and the conflict between love or passion and reason dominates the action.

As the defense attorney in a rape case against eighteen-year-old Ralph Detweiler, the much younger brother of Helen Detweiler, a legal secretary in the firm of Winner, Tuttle, and Penrose, Winner attempts to apply reason and logic to the emotionally charged situation. The case is complicated by the fact that, although Ralph admits having had intimate relations with Veronica Kovacs, a young woman with a tarnished reputation, he also admits being involved with Joan Moore, whom he has gotten pregnant. Winner assures Ralph that the charge of rape will almost certainly be dropped, but the immature, spoiled Ralph panics at the thought of facing a trial and a pregnant girlfriend. He jumps bail and in the process steals money from one of the boarders in Helen's rooming house. Helen, having reared Ralph since their parents' death in a tragic boating accident, sees all of her plans for Ralph's future collapse, and she commits suicide. Winner's reasoned approach is thwarted by people tangled in passions, and he is unable to prevent tragedy.

After Helen Detweiler's death, Winner visits the law office to obtain her will and accidentally uncovers evidence that sets another conflict in motion. Noah Tuttle, the eighty-year-old senior partner of the law firm and a man of unquestioned integrity, has been misappropriating funds over a number of years to protect local investors from financial ruin as a result of the collapse of the Brocton Rapid Transit Company, which he had recommended as an investment. When Winner presents Julius Penrose with this discovery, he learns that Penrose has been aware of the situation for more than ten years and has chosen to keep silent and give Tuttle the chance to replace the money. The Orcutt trust, a fund designated for use by the Episcopal Church of Brocton (where Winner is a prominent layman), is also involved.

Winner knows that his father, the "Man of Reason," would have immediately done the "right thing" and turned Noah over to the authorities, thus destroying all the members of the firm professionally as well as financially. Penrose persuades Winner that Noah has acted out of love: "He would betray himself, sacrifice himself, before he let down, sacrificed, those who had put faith in him." During this tense discussion, Winner makes another discovery. Although he prides himself on his ability to act on reason, shortly after the death of his first wife he succumbed to passion during a brief, but intense, affair with Penrose's wife, Marjorie, and—Winner now realizes—Penrose has been aware of this affair since its inception.

Winner's simplistic moral code is challenged by Penrose's deeper understanding of moral complexity; Penrose persuades him that the strict honesty which would demand revealing Tuttle's deeds is not the best policy but only the easiest one. Their duty, like Tuttle's, lies in doing what is necessary to protect their community. Winner learns that what seems a clear choice, with freedom to act, is often no choice at all but merely the acceptance of a fate that has been predetermined. He recognizes the truth in his brother-in-law Fred Dealcy's words: "Freedom is the knowledge of necessity." Winner's faith in reason has been tempered by the effects of passion, and he now asserts that "Victory is not in reaching certainties or solving mysteries; victory is in making do with uncertainties, in supporting mysteries."

## The Characters

Arthur Winner, Jr., a middle-class, middle-aged, dispassionate man, has tried to live his life in the light of reason, patterned after his father—"the nearly unique individual; the Man, if not perfectly, at least predominantly, of Reason." Ruled by a strong sense of duty and responsibility, he serves his community, law practice, church, and family. In the space of an afternoon, he deals with the problems of his distressed secretary, Helen, her brother Ralph's rape case and bail jumping, court opinion imputing ineptness by his law partner Noah Tuttle, a cherished tree struck by lightning, a lesbian Catholic proselytizer, the discovery that his love affair with his partner Julius

Penrose's wife is no secret, and a disgruntled choir director. Winner's brother-in-law Fred Dealey remarks: "You're really a kind of universal fall guy, Arthur! They all come to you! Philosophy and religion assure me that 'fall guy' is the righteous man's other name." Winner is proud of his ability to order other people's lives and problems, and his sense of security and complacency in his power in his personal life is an extension of his professional life. He is a product of his profession. Only through deep contemplation of his failure as a father with his son Warren and his weakness in participating in a passionate affair does his sense of complacency become shaken. He is further humbled by his inability to prevent Helen Detweiler's suicide and his realization of Noah Tuttle's unethical professional activities. The Arthur Winner at the end of the novel is no longer secure in his power to rule by reason.

Noah Tuttle has reached the age of senility, and his brilliant law career is coming to a sad end with his secretary and partners covering for his lapses of memory—at least that is what Arthur Winner thinks until he discovers the misappropriation of funds that was prompted by Tuttle's magnanimous concern for the investors whom he had advised. Until this discovery, Winner has been unaware of Noah's "occasional propensity to act emotionally, of Noah's sometimes sentimental sensibilities," and therefore his assessment of Tuttle's possible range of actions has been faulty.

Julius Penrose is not blinded by reason, and his powers of perception and understanding are the catalysts for Winner's revelation. As a young man, Penrose was a powerfully built, handsome athlete, but he was crippled by polio at age forty, and now his shriveled, useless legs are encased in heavy braces. Possibly as a result of this incongruous tragedy, being struck by a childhood disease in the prime of his life, Penrose has developed great insights into the human condition. Penrose's compassion for his wife's infidelity with Winner, and his deeper understanding of the implications of Noah Tuttle's indiscretions, cause Winner to reevaluate his philosophy. Penrose, however, is not ruled by passion or feeling. He decries the overt sentimentality he sees around him. "Yes; the spirit of the age! We're in an age preeminently of capital F feeling—a century of the gulp, the lump in the throat, the good cry. . . . We've made sentimentality of the respected essence. . . . The grave and learned are no whit behind the cheap and stupid in their love of it." Penrose is wise enough to recognize the motivating power of passion in people's lives and to make decisions in the light of both reason and feeling. When Winner gives in to feelings of guilt about Helen Detweiler's suicide, Penrose admonishes him: "Regrets of that kind are unreasonable, unrealistic. *It might have been*—not so much the saddest as the silliest words of tongue or pen. Let us face it. What happens to people is simply what was always going to happen to them. To think otherwise is vain visioning." Penrose shakes Winner out of his inclination to "play God" by his pragmatic assessment. Winner is forced to face the fact that he is not as omnipotent or omniscient as he had once thought.

Helen Detweiler, the conscientious, responsible, nervous secretary of the Tuttle, Winner, Penrose law firm, has been robbed of her youth by willingly assuming the duty of rearing her younger brother Ralph. She has felt too strongly her responsibility for him, has loved him too dearly, acting on the basis of feeling rather than reason. Overindulged by Helen in her admirable attempts to compensate for the loss of their parents, Ralph is "rather spiritless and spineless." Julius Penrose's harsh judgment of Helen's suicide appears to be Cozzens' own, finding in Helen's final act "a want of principle, which is to say, too much feeling." Penrose's conclusion is that she was "possessed by love."

## Themes and Meanings

Cozzens often places at the center of his novels a mature professional man whose success demands that he accept responsibility for his community. These men have considerable authority and power over others, and the exercise of this power and their duty to wield it justly prompt most of the action. His characters are molded by their professions, and the world is presented through their eyes. Cozzens is a social realist in that he presents things as they are and does not prescribe simple resolutions for his conflicts. Moral dilemmas are explored in all their complexity: There are choices where no alternative is ideal. Indeed, Cozzens often suggests that the power to choose is an illusion, that men are the victims of fate. This Calvinist sense of predestination places Cozzens squarely in the tradition of such "dark" American novelists as Nathaniel Hawthorne and William Faulkner.

Many conflicts develop out of the conflicts between love and reason. Cozzens manifests a great respect for the traditions and established social order of the middle classes, whose virtues of rationality, self-discipline, and stability are contrasted with the irrational, undisciplined, impassioned actions of other members of the community, usually of a lower social class. Man is seen as a product of his past and as consciously influenced by it: Events from the past continually force themselves into present moments. The implication is that although time passes, man never really changes, and there is no natural progression toward perfectibility.

## Critical Context

*By Love Possessed*, an enormously successful best-seller, provoked virulent critical attacks following an interview with Cozzens in *Time* magazine, in which he expressed unfashionable opinions with aristocratic disdain. The consequences of this affair were long-lasting, but since the late 1970's there has been a renewal of critical appreciation of his work.

Cozzens' style is often elaborate, filled with allusions and choked with subordination often to the point of obscurity. His habit of referring to his characters by their full names is indicative of his self-consciously formal style, one that distances him from his characters and, to a certain extent, from his readers. Independent of the literary mainstream, Cozzens successfully introduced a substance and a style counter to contemporary fashions.

*Sources for Further Study*
Bracher, Frederick. *The Novels of James Gould Cozzens*, 1959.
Bruccoli, Matthew J., ed. *James Gould Cozzens: New Acquist of True Experience*, 1979.
Michel, Pierre. *James Gould Cozzens*, 1974.
Mooney, Harry John, Jr. *James Gould Cozzens: Novelist of Intellect*, 1963.

*Len McCall*

# THE CAINE MUTINY

*Author:* Herman Wouk (1915-    )
*Type of plot:* Historical novel
*Time of plot:* 1943 to 1945
*Locale:* New York, the West Coast of the United States, Hawaii, and the Pacific Ocean
*First published:* 1951

> *Principal characters:*
> WILLIE KEITH, a rich young New Yorker who is commissioned an officer in the Navy during World War II and assigned to duty aboard the U.S.S. *Caine*
> LIEUTENANT COMMANDER PHILIP QUEEG, the captain of the *Caine*
> LIEUTENANT STEVE MARYK, the executive officer of the *Caine*
> LIEUTENANT THOMAS KEEFER, an officer aboard the *Caine* and an aspiring novelist
> MAY WYNN (MARIE MINOTTI), Willie Keith's girlfriend

*The Novel*

Herman Wouk's novel chronicles the wartime adventures of Willie Keith aboard the U.S.S. *Caine*, a destroyer-minesweeper in the Pacific Fleet. A Princeton graduate from an affluent Long Island family, Keith works as a piano player in New York, where he meets May Wynn. Love must wait while duty calls, however, and Keith seeks an opportunity to join the Navy. His life of luxury has not prepared him for the service regimen. After barely making it through Officer Candidate School, he receives assignment orders for the *Caine*. The remaining action of the novel centers on Keith's duty aboard the *Caine* and his attempt to continue his romance with May.

On the *Caine*, Keith finds life under Captain DeVreis almost unbearable. He finds strength in the camaraderie of other officers who, like him, are in the service only because the United States is at war. Keith greets DeVreis' reassignment with pleasure and is certain that the new skipper, Lieutenant Commander Philip Queeg, will bring good fortune to the *Caine*. Others are less sanguine: Lieutenant Steve Maryk loyally supports the new captain, but Lieutenant Thomas Keefer, Keith's boss, lumps Queeg together with all other regular Navy officers as being too stupid or too lazy to make their way in civilian life. Initially Keith is impressed with Queeg's effort to bring some spit-and-polish discipline to the ship. Soon, however, it becomes apparent that Queeg is more concerned about keeping headquarters satisfied than taking care of those who serve under him. Furthermore, he appears to devote more time to harassing those who violate minor regulations than he

does to larger issues. During a target-towing exercise, while berating a
sailor for having his shirttail out, Queeg allows the ship to sail in a circle,
thus cutting the towline and losing the valuable target.

That incident is the first of several to cause a rift between captain and
crew. Similar incidents reinforce the belief among officers and men that
Queeg is overcautious, perhaps even a coward. In the ship's first real
engagement under his command, he refuses to escort a group of small landing craft close in to the shore, choosing instead to drop a yellow dye marker
at a spot where the boats can assemble and make their way in to shore
alone. Later, he becomes enraged when members of the crew drop a case of
whiskey (which Queeg was bringing back illegally into the United States)
into the ocean. He conducts a personal vendetta against one of the crewmen
and insists on court-martialing him for fabricating evidence to get an emergency leave. When the court-martial board administers a light sentence,
Queeg turns on his officers.

Maryk, the executive officer, supports Queeg; but at Keefer's prompting
he begins to doubt the captain's sanity. After Queeg orders a complete
search of the ship for a key to the food locker from which he is convinced a
quart of strawberries has been pilfered, Maryk believes that the crew should
seek to have Queeg relieved of his command. Maryk has kept a log
documenting Queeg's behavior, but Keefer convinces him that they lack
sufficient evidence to convince the naval authorities of Queeg's unfitness.

Finally, however, Maryk is left with no choice. In a raging typhoon,
Queeg becomes incapable of issuing coherent orders, and Maryk relieves
him on the bridge of the *Caine*. Keith, the officer of the deck, supports
Maryk. This mutinous action results in a trial for Maryk, at which Queeg's
abnormal behavior is revealed to a skeptical board of senior officers.
Maryk's lawyer, who uses a series of ploys to get Queeg to reveal his idio-
syncrasies, manages to get an acquittal. After the trial, Keith returns to sea
until, when the war is finally over, he ends his brief naval career as the
*Caine*'s last captain, taking her to New York for decommissioning.

*The Characters*

The Caine Mutiny is foremost a study in character, and the men who sail
aboard the *Caine* represent all walks of life.

The central character around whom the entire story revolves is Willie
Keith; much of the action of the novel centers on the conflicts that accompany his maturation both as a officer and as a man. A spoiled New Yorker
who has had all the advantages of growing up rich, Keith is introduced to
the hazards and challenges of the real world through his career in the Navy.
His mistakes are sometimes costly, but he learns that, by standing up for
what he perceives to be right, he earns the trust of his peers and subordinates and comes to feel proud of himself. That knowledge does not come

without great difficulty, and on more than one occasion Keith suffers at the hands of Queeg for siding with the crew against the captain. Keith's passage from bumbling midshipman to captain of a major combatant ship provides an exciting story with a welcome happy ending. Through Keith, Wouk shows how the war affects personal relationships as well as professional ones. Both at home and at sea, Keith struggles with his feelings for May Wynn, whom he believes he loves; yet her Catholic, working-class background makes it difficult for him to think of her as an acceptable wife. While his naval career concludes on a happy note (he ends up a hero aboard the *Caine* and finally commands the ship), the reader is left wondering if Keith will ever succeed in convincing May that she should abandon her career to marry him.

Much of this romantic conflict stems from the differences in background between the young hero and his sweetheart. May Wynn, whose real name is Marie Minotti, is a nightclub singer whose parents run a grocery in Brooklyn. While May is not as carefully drawn as many of the other characters, Wouk does manage to give her certain believable qualities so that the reader is not lulled into viewing this part of the novel as mere romantic fantasy.

The real strength of characterization in the novel, though, is in Wouk's depiction of the three men with whom Keith deals most frequently aboard the *Caine*. Each represents a type of American who has been caught up in the war, and who reacts to it in his distinctive way. Steve Maryk is a personification of working-class America, a fisherman in civilian life who does all the dirty jobs required of him out of a strong sense of duty. With stronger common sense than intelligence, Maryk always acts in the interests of the Navy and of those with whom he serves. He is a man not easily convinced, but once he makes up his mind about something, he acts with strong conviction. That trait eventually leads him to relieve Queeg of command and bring upon himself charges of mutiny.

At the other extreme is Tom Keefer, intellectual, disdainful of the military service, a man who recognizes the need to serve his country but who despises the professionals who man the force in peacetime. Wouk is careful to make Keefer an attractive figure, one who beguiles not only Keith but also the reader into believing that he sees through the sham that Queeg represents. Keefer does have insight, but he lacks courage, and ultimately he is found out for the coward he is. Ironically, he is working on a novel; Wouk suggests strongly that it is men such as Keefer who usually write about warfare and therefore do not do justice to the heroes who give of themselves for their country.

Wouk's villain, Lieutenant Commander Philip Queeg, is a genuine enigma. On the surface, he appears exactly as Keefer paints him to be: a psychopath, fearful of others, paranoid to the extreme, a coward bent on preserving his reputation and willing to bend the truth to his purposes.

Wouk, however, carefully avoids shifting the point of view to allow the reader inside Queeg's head; while almost every other major character is seen alone through interior monologue at one time, Queeg is seen only as other characters see him. His actions suggest that he is unfit to command, however, and the reader feels little remorse over his fate until, at the end of the novel, he is broken by the officers who had been sworn to serve under him. Even for Queeg, then, Wouk is able to raise in the reader a certain degree of sympathy.

## Themes and Meanings

On the surface, *The Caine Mutiny* is a fast-paced adventure novel, the story of a young American officer told with some concern for the accuracy of the historical setting. It is clear that Wouk is more concerned with character than with event, however, and that he has carefully structured his plot so that the key incidents reveal to the reader something about Willie Keith's developing sense of himself and his role both as an officer and as a man. On this level, then, the novel belongs to the genre of the *Bildungsroman*, a story chiefly involved in investigating the maturation process. His experiences in the war change Keith from a self-centered, uncertain young man into a seasoned, confident citizen who knows what he wants from life and is willing to make the sacrifices necessary to achieve his goals.

The novel, however, is more than that. It belongs in the tradition of the historical novel as well. Wouk is concerned about dramatizing the impact of World War II on America. His characters aboard the *Caine* are a microcosm of the country: From all walks of life, possessing a variety of skills, they are thrown together by a common cause and learn to put aside differences to defeat a common enemy. Wouk wants the reader to come away with a sense of the magnitude of the war and of the different ways war can affect men. Conservative in his outlook on both politics and warfare, Wouk is nevertheless careful to present without prejudice a variety of opinions about his subject. In *The Caine Mutiny*, Wouk appears to be more concerned with studying the effects of such conflicts upon men than with examining the causes of war.

*The Caine Mutiny* is also a novel about the sea, and as such it belongs to a long line of great works on that subject. For centuries, authors have attempted to use the sea as a metaphor for the universe: The life of men aboard ship is representative of mankind's journey through life itself. Wouk plants several clues to make his readers aware of the parallels. Numerous references to other novels, especially those of Herman Melville and Joseph Conrad, help establish the links. The plausibility of these references is enhanced by the backgrounds of Willie Keith (a comparative literature major) and Tom Keefer (a novelist and philosopher), but at times the allusions are heavy-handed. Through these allusions, Wouk seeks to create additional depth for his story; the reader familiar with sea literature will see the struggles of the men aboard the *Caine* as similar to those dramatized in such classics as *Moby Dick* (1851), *Billy Budd* (1924), and *Lord Jim* (1900), all of which are specifically mentioned in the narrative.

Finally, Wouk is concerned with the problem of investigating character beneath the surface levels. What motivates men to act as they do in certain situations, especially under stress? How do people really know about others? The novel is filled with passages about psychology and psychoanalysis; much of the character study is done for the reader by characters within the novel, as they offer clinical explanations for the behavior of men such as Queeg. It should not be surprising, however, to find such concern in a novel whose major focus is on the analysis of the central character's development and maturation.

### Critical Context

*The Caine Mutiny* is Wouk's most famous novel, and still his best. During the years immediately after its publication, the novel was translated into several languages and adapted into a major Broadway play. Some time shortly thereafter, it was made into a motion picture, with the legendary film actor Humphrey Bogart as Lieutenant Commander Philip Queeg and Van Johnson as Steve Maryk. The story of the *Caine* mutiny, and the strange habit of its psychotic captain rolling little steel balls in his hand, became well-known throughout the country; it is now a part of American popular culture.

Judged on its merits as a historical novel, *The Caine Mutiny* scores well. It ranks with Norman Mailer's *The Naked and the Dead* (1948) as one of the most significant works about the American experience in World War II. Although Wouk admits in the preface to the novel that he willfully distorted history to achieve dramatic effect, the book is generally faithful to events of the period, and Wouk provides meticulous detail of shipboard life.

*The Caine Mutiny* was not Wouk's first published work, but it established him as a major popular novelist. Though Wouk has not produced at the same pace as contemporaries such as Norman Mailer, John Updike, or James Michener, he has managed to remain in the eye of the reading public. Among his best later works, *The Winds of War* (1971) and *War and Remembrance* (1978) are, like *The Caine Mutiny*, centered on the American experience in World War II, and focus on naval figures. It is clear that Wouk owes his popular success in large part to *The Caine Mutiny*, which first brought him international fame. As is the case with many novelists who aim their work at a wide reading public, Wouk has not received significant attention from scholars; as a result, few systematic studies of the structure, themes, imagery, characters, and symbolism of *The Caine Mutiny* are available.

*Sources for Further Study*

Geismar, Maxwell. *American Moderns from Rebellion to Conformity*, 1958.
McElderry, B. R. "The Conservative as Novelist: Herman Wouk," in *Arizona Quarterly*. XV (1959), pp. 128-136.

*Laurence W. Mazzeno*

# THE CALL

*Author:* John Hersey (1914-    )
*Type of plot:* Historical chronicle
*Time of plot:* 1878-1981
*Locale:* Upstate New York and northeast China
*First published:* 1985

*Principal characters:*
DAVID TREADUP (T'AO TU HSIEN-SHENG), an American
   missionary in China
EMILY TREADUP, his wife
JAMES B. TODD, the charismatic leader of the Student Volun-
   teer Movement for Foreign Missions

*The Novel*

*The Call* follows the dedicated life of David Treadup, who leaves rural New York as a young man of twenty-seven and devotes his life to the welfare of the Chinese people. In the background of Treadup's career are the tumultuous events that have changed Chinese life drastically in the twentieth century, and *The Call* is thus also an impressionistic history of modern China through the Communist Revolution. John Hersey divides his seven-hundred-page narrative into ten sections, each focusing on an important phase of Treadup's life. Sketches of Treadup's pioneer forebears give the story additional historical sweep, as does the account of the futile efforts of Treadup's oldest son, Philip, to get his father's ashes buried in Shanghai in 1981.

David Treadup is born in 1878 in Salt Branch, New York, in Onondagan country, and after an erratic beginning, he is graduated from Syracuse University. The call to missionary work comes to him in his last year in college, and in 1905—after courting Emily Kean, who will join him in China a year later as his wife—he arrives in Tientsin as a YMCA missionary under the sponsorship of Syracuse University. Through 1910, Treadup teaches and develops his literati campaign, a program to introduce modern science to China's educated elite with the expectation that knowledge will then trickle down the cultural scale. His favorite teaching aid is a gyroscope he has had shipped to him, and with its properties he fascinates and charms large audiences.

Treadup's lecture program gets new strength in 1911, when his New York boss, the eloquent James B. Todd, visits China and the two give a series of talks together, Treadup expounding science and Todd preaching the Gospel. This two-pronged approach becomes the standard format for Treadup's endeavors to educate and convert the Chinese, but his work is interrupted during World War I by his duties in France as an overseer of Chinese coolies sent to Europe as manual laborers. Treadup is pleased by efforts to teach the homesick coolies simple reading and writing while they are in France, and he returns to China in 1921 with serious doubts about his theory that education should be directed toward the elite. He then undertakes his own literacy campaign in the Chinese villages west of Tientsin.

Civil war shakes China in the 1920's, and the Japanese invasion of Manchuria in 1931 intensifies the country's distress. By 1937, China is in chaos and the missionary organization is retrenching with a much-diminished budget. Treadup is himself recalled by his New York office, but he vows to stay in China on his own since he has made a commitment to a life's work. In 1937, Paoting, his home, is captured by the Japanese; in 1940, Emily returns to New York (their three sons are already in the United States), and Treadup "lives Chinese" under Japanese occupation. When Pearl Harbor is bombed, Treadup is interned but finds the closest friend of his life in Dr. Phinneas Cunningham. Camp life humiliates Treadup and leads to his loss of faith in God.

Treadup returns to New York in 1943 to find Emily much aged and infirm. Their oldest son, Philip, is successful and dull; the second son, Absolom, lives in eccentric estrangement in Maine; and the third son, Paul, has become an entrepreneur in a double-breasted pinstripe suit. When Emily dies in 1945, never having learned of Treadup's apostasy, he returns to China as part of the postwar reconstruction effort. The corruption he finds dismays him, the Red Chinese mortify him in a public castigation aimed at him as an abstract symbol of Western capitalist exploitation, and he returns to New York in 1950 and dies shortly afterward.

*The Characters*

As a child growing up in rural New York, David Treadup reveals no special abilities, but when he is seventeen he falls severely ill with osteomyelitis, and with nothing to do but read books, he experiences a new insight into the life of the intellect. He is guided in this revelation by a perceptive, kind teacher, Maud Chase. Thus he is enthusiastic when a year later he is allowed to attend the Enderby Institute, where he studies under Absolom Carter, an inspired teacher who is ultimately the greatest influence on his life. As a role model of the "all-around thinker-athlete," Carter is to Treadup a paradigm of what the naïve youth knows he wants to become. Carter tutors Treadup in Benjamin Franklin, Plato, Xenophon, and Plutarch, treating him to a secular education that forms his thinking for good. So "the agnostic Carter's instinct in giving David this extracurricular course in ethics was to bear fruit: Something skeptical, temporal, and sophisticated would stay with David all his life—and would give him difficulties as a missionary."

Treadup's conversion to Christianity comes when he is a twenty-five-year-old sophomore at Syracuse and provides him with great relief. He is freed from the terrible aimlessness that has bedeviled him and is given moral support in his struggle with carnal desire. His new purpose in life so enriches his spirit that his vague hypochondriacal complaints fade away. This spiritual confidence stays with him for forty years until, sick and despairing in a Japanese camp, he undergoes a "counterconversion" prefigured by a flare-up of his old osteomyelitis. He finds his loss of faith cathartic in an ironic way:

> *I feel as if my hands and feet had been tied for a long time, and that the knots have suddenly been undone. This has been an eerie experience. I don't think I am going to be quite so afraid any more. If there is a God, I must be a disappointment to him.*

At this stage of his life, Treadup stands quite alone, severed from the allegiance that powered his efforts for four decades.

For most of his life, Treadup goes without close relationships, his need for friendship subsumed under striving in God's service and in his deep love for his wife. His strong sexual appetite is satisfied by Emily, and she is a rock of support for him, but they are separated for long periods and she clearly takes second place to the call in his life. She never quite emerges distinctly, consigned in her fictional life to the role of patient, helpful missionary wife. Without Treadup, she apparently has no identity. When he returns to New York in 1943, he finds her wan and wasted for no discernible reason other than her separation from him. Her own call—to his service—appears finally as a miserable duping. It is not surprising that Treadup dares not confess to her his loss of faith, for the knowledge would show her what a cruel and pointless sacrifice her own life has been.

Treadup's only close adult friendship comes late in his life when he shares the stresses of Japanese internment with the British Dr. Phinneas Cunningham. Cunningham is an adamantly secular thinker, an avatar in many ways of Treadup's old teacher Absolom Carter. His library sustains Treadup through the long gloomy spell of life under surveillance. Cunningham operates successfully on Treadup's left arm, curing him of his debilitating osteomyelitis. Cunningham's dedicated humanism smooths Treadup's counterconversion and frees him finally from the powerful hold Todd has exerted on him for years.

Todd is a strong presence in *The Call*. He is a physically imposing man, and his rhetoric appeals to thousands. Yet despite the sincerity of his conviction, he always comes off as arrogant and vainglorious, even lacking in charity, although he speaks in the tongues of men and of angels. His mission is clear: to save souls. He is, then, often suspicious of the humanistic impulses of Treadup, the former pupil of Absolom Carter. When Todd and Treadup lecture together in China, Treadup's science demonstrations always draw larger audiences than Todd's evangelistic preachings.

Letitia Selden and Helen Demestrie live together in their own house in the missionary compound at Paoting. Treadup is close to them both, especially to Miss Selden. In one of the most dramatic scenes in the novel, Miss Demestrie goes mad and, naked to the waist, runs through the compound waving a sword and screaming lines in Greek from *Lysistrata*. She seems to have lost control of her emotions under the pressures of isolation, work, and unexpressed sexual desire for Treadup. This mad scene appears unexpectedly, and Hersey sketches it movingly.

The Chinese characters seldom appear in clear focus. Actual historical persons (such as Chiang Kai-shek and Mao Tse-tung) appear in the novel briefly but remain in the historical background. Hersey explains that several characters were suggested by real people (he instances Y. C. James Yen) but adds that "their names, like their selves, have been changed."

*Themes and Meanings*

Hersey blocks out Treadup's life in ten large narrative chunks, each suggestively titled (for example, "The Test"), and then divides and subdivides so that the story is told in a great many, usually brief episodes. He interlards his conventional third-person omniscient exposition with passages from Treadup's letters and diaries to create an effective historical panorama from the mesh of viewpoints.

The story of the YMCA's Student Volunteer Movement for Foreign Missions is important in *The Call*. Hersey notes that the movement, founded in 1888, became "the most influential student movement in the country, analogous, in its feverish growth and widespread appeal, to the student radical and pacifist movements of the 1930's and to the organizations of the New Left in the 1960's." Between 1888 and 1919, more than half of the North American Protestant missionaries were SVM volunteers.

Hersey also tells well the history of Chinese workers assigned to the Allies in Europe during World War I. In February, 1917, about 140,000 Chinese coolies were working in France. Hersey's summation is blunt: "It is not surprising that the historians of the Allied cause in the First World War have played down, to the point of disappearance, the suggestion that the Allies used slave labor to relieve the manpower shortage which followed the gruesome carnage of young men in the first years of that conflict."

Hersey repeatedly notes the many times that missionary cultural advances were adapted by the Communists after the revolution. For example, putting great numbers of people to work on public projects was "one of the many innovations of the missionaries which the Communists would later take up and magnify in their transformation of China."

The most powerful theme of the novel, overshadowing all else, must be the irony to which the title is reduced by Treadup's loss of faith. Even his postwar years are frustrating, and he leaves China permanently with an admittedly broken heart. Treadup dies an atheist, virtually estranged from two of his three sons by extreme differences in temperament. What comfort that can be found in *The Call* must come from the trick of history that made the missionaries into groundbreakers and innovators for the Communists.

*Critical Context*

Hersey's connections to China are strong and personal. His father, Roscoe M. Hersey, Sr., was himself a missionary to China, and Hersey was born in Tientsin and lived there until he was eleven. Nothing suggests, however, that *The Call* should be read as a chronicle of his father's experience. Indeed, Hersey notes that "all characters are fictional except recognizable historical figures, who bear their own names." *The Call* is a rigorously researched novel of a man's life and an impressionistic reconstruction of an important period in modern history.

*Sources for Further Study*

Fairbank, John K., ed. *The Missionary Enterprise in China and America*, 1974.

Latourette, Kenneth Scott. *World Service: A History of the Foreign Work and World Service of the Young Men's Christian Associations of the United States and Canada*, 1957.

Varg, Paul A. *Missionaries, Chinese, and Diplomats: The American Protestant Missionary Movement in China, 1890-1952*, 1958.

*Frank Day*

# CANNERY ROW

*Author:* John Steinbeck (1902-1968)
*Type of plot:* Sentimental realism
*Time of plot:* About 1940
*Locale:* "The Row," a sleepy fishing village near Monterey, California
*First published:* 1945

>*Principal characters:*
>    Doc, a poor, sensitive marine biologist, the most respected
>        man in Cannery Row
>    Mack, the leader of a ragtag crew of derelicts who wish only
>        to be let alone, to enjoy life, and to live contentedly in the
>        Palace Flophouse
>    Dora Flood, the local madam, a woman with a sharp busi-
>        ness sense and a heart of gold
>    Hazel,
>    Hughie,
>    Jones,
>    Gay, and
>    Eddie, "the boys" of Cannery Row

*The Novel*

*Cannery Row* is a sentimental, nostalgic portrayal of the lazy, the shift-less, the good-natured lowlifes who survive at the fringes of a fishing and canning community outside Monterey, California. Working only when they must, preferring drinking, fighting, and indolence,"the boys" of Cannery Row are somewhat akin to the old picaresque heroes of the seventeenth and eighteenth century novel. The picaro of these early novels was something of a rogue who lived by his or her wits, and who, despite poverty and social os-tracism, displayed a basic goodness and a sense of practical wisdom.

Like their picaro predecessors, Mack and the boys have little or no money; they live off the vagaries of chance and opportunity; they engage in low-key bargaining with tightfisted Lee Chong, owner of the Row's grocery store; some of them occasionally land in jail. They are not above working when they absolutely have to, but more often than not they borrow, barter, or somehow "find" what they need. Indeed, the essential difference between the picaro and Steinbeck's modern rascals is that the latter lack a sense of purpose or ambition. Where a Lazarillo de Tormes or a Moll Flan-ders proceeds from one adventure to another in a purposeful, strategic direction, from less to more, from outsider to member of the establishment, Mack and his fellows simply drift, taking one day at a time, indifferent to the possibilities of their own social reformation, of the progress from dereliction to responsibility.

The plot of *Cannery Row* reflects this drift, this flaccid indifference to significant social action. It centers on the boys' only goal—that of giving Doc a party. A marine biologist who ekes out a living collecting specimens and supplying them to commercial houses, Doc is a quiet, sensitive fellow who enjoys listening to Monteverdi arias, drinking beer in his laboratory/ residence, and entertaining female guests, during which visits he pulls down the shades and turns up the music. To Mack and the boys he is something of a role model, intelligent, kind, and usually solvent, yet mysteriously one of them, a sort of virtuous bum.

After a false start, the boys begin their arrangements for a surprise birth-day party. One of them even gets a job tending bar for a few weeks in order to syphon off the dregs from the patrons' glasses and eventually collects a few gallons of some alcoholic mixture. The core of the plot is their determi-nation to give Doc a suitable present at his party: They will themselves col-lect all the frogs, cats, and other specimens that Doc could use, saving him time, money, and labor. Like latter-day knights-errant, they successfully carry out their expedition and execute the party, to which all the good peo-ple of Cannery Row are invited, including Dora, the good-hearted madam, and her girls. The party concludes with a drunken brawl between intruding fishermen and the locals, a fight that puts everybody into benign spirits.

The brawl is an appropriate climax to the novel, suggesting that the pas-sive indolence of the characters is relieved only by physical violence, which, though personally cleansing, is nevertheless socially self-destructive. Thus, unlike traditional picaresque novels, *Cannery Row* ends with the characters' remaining in the relatively same social position in which they had begun. Poor but happy, they survive as outcasts, their social reclamation thwarted by their indolence, their indifference to ambition.

Such a plot is hardly sustained by tragic seriousness, but rather by comic whimsy. Whimsy, in fact, is a key ingredient in the novel's design. Using a technique that he made famous in *The Grapes of Wrath* (1939), Steinbeck broadens the main plot with interpolated chapters, virtually self-contained units which relate to the main plot largely through tone, atmosphere, and thematic consistency. Such chapters include those dealing with the Malloys, who live in an abandoned boiler, and the lyric "prose poems" describing the good life and the decent though often eccentric people of the Row. These chapters flesh out an otherwise thin, almost anemic narrative action and at their best also provide the book with a sentimental charm, a quiet, rhap-sodic nostalgia amounting to an idyllic myth about a sort of California peasantry.

## The Characters

The characters of *Cannery Row* are mostly stereotypes, simplifications which illustrate Steinbeck's fondness for the vagrant, the eccentric, the genial pariah. Only Doc has the complexity of a major character. Educated enough to know marine biology, sensitive enough to surround his laboratory with reproductions of works of art and to enjoy classical music, shrewd enough to know how to deal with the schemes and cons of the boys, gentle enough to befriend the simpleminded, he is at heart a loafer, a drifter, "concupiscent as a rabbit," fond of beer and company, yet a loner.

He is, too, literary kin to earlier Steinbeck heroes. Tom Joad from *The Grapes of Wrath*, for example, who was also a sensitive though politically astute individual whose natural bent seemed to be centifugal rather than centripetal: His temperament drove him away from the family unit and toward a self-imposed isolation. George Milton in *Of Mice and Men* (1937) was an even earlier antecedent of Doc, clearly the same sensitive yet isolated being, whose care and love for Lenny, the gentle but brutish misfit, keeps him apart from the mainstream of society. Doc's befriending of Hazel, the simple, slow-witted boy-man of the group, is indicative both of his role as leader and of his isolated position. Doc's compassion allows him to care for Hazel, to give him a job as laboratory assistant, but at the same time, Hazel allows Doc the opportunity to remain a private person, uncommunicative about the things that really matter, just as an adult plays with a child, keeping his real personality hidden in the game. It is this ambivalence, this need for companionship in counterpoint to his solitary nature, that gives Doc a poignancy which elevates him to the central character of the novel.

Mack is the putative leader of the boys, the angelic bums, the "beauties," the "Virtues," as Steinbeck rather sentimentally calls them. Like the boys, Mack is irresponsible, as unreliable in the conduct of social affairs as he is loyal and generous of spirit. Mack always means well, but his good intentions are often foiled by a shiftlessness and an ambition limited to the demands of the hour rather than of the future. He presides genially over the group in the Palace Flophouse, an abandoned storage shack made habitable with the discarded flotsam of the village. Yet Mack is canny when the occasion warrants. He is a born manipulator of people. For years he has been "negotiating" with Lee Chong for groceries and other staples.

In a key scene illustrating his genius, Mack and the boys are caught in a frog pond by the owner of the property. They are busily engaged in catching frogs as a present for Doc, but the irate owner, gun and shotgun poised, wants them off the grounds at once. Mack apologizes, amiably cajoles, praises the dog, and in the end heals its long-standing illness, receiving from the grateful owner a puppy, all the frogs Mack wants, and a few hours of friendly drinking at the owner's house. Crucial in appreciating the scene is the knowledge that Mack is not being hypocritical. He genuinely likes the owner and simply lets his own amiability and honesty work for him.

Dora Flood, the town madam, is of the same good-hearted nature as the others. Ironically, she is as much a success as the boys are failures. She runs "a good house," has remarkable business instincts, but treats her girls with dignity, compassion, and generosity. Her good-naturedness is proven when the town is infected with influenza and Dora and her girls nurse back to health the poor, the infirm, and the young. She is, nevertheless, not as interesting a character as Doc or Mack because she is so thoroughly stereotypical. The whore with the heart of gold was a common figure in the post-Romantic literature of the twentieth century, particularly during the Depression of the 1930's, when "good" girls sold their bodies but kept pure their souls.

## Themes and Meanings

For a novel with so slight a plot, *Cannery Row* is nevertheless engaging as a social document, a record of a state of mind, of attitudes about society and behavior during the "have-not" era of the 1930's. For although the novel was published at the end of World War II, it is suggestive both in tone and spirit of a Depression mentality. The "good" people are the unemployed, the dispossessed, or, like Doc, the marginally solvent. Some, like Dora, are successful in spite of legal sanctions and social mores. As in *The Grapes of Wrath*, Steinbeck's definitive treatment of the Depression, there are really no "bad" people, either: only those who tightly clutch the things they have and who, like Lee Chong, leer distrustfully at those who have not. Yet the socioeconomic situation is treated comically in *Cannery Row*. Already behind him, the Depression for Steinbeck was no longer a grim consequence of social pathology or a crucible of heroic despair. Instead, it had become a subject for pleasant reminiscence about a time when men survived without money, on companionship, good intentions, and kindness; a simpler time, before the postwar boom, when people were valued not for the quantity of their goods but for the quality of their hearts.

## Critical Context

Many critics are quick to belittle *Cannery Row* as a silly, trivial book, suitable more as a frothy mid-century film musical than as a serious contribution from the author of *In Dubious Battle* (1936), *The Grapes of Wrath*, and the later *East of Eden* (1952). Judged by these monuments, *Cannery Row* is justifiably consigned to the second rank of Steinbeck's work, yet the novel is interesting in its own right. Discounting *The Moon Is Down* (1942), a novella with propagandistic intentions, *Cannery Row* is Steinbeck's first major work after his Depression masterpiece. It shows his renewed interest in the comic portrayal of the simple, uncomplicated life-styles of the lovably dispossessed, a subject already treated a decade earlier in *Tortilla Flat* (1935), a picaresque novel written in mock-heroic style about the "paisanos" of Southern California, quixotic latter-day knights who are, in fact, the true literary forebears of Doc and the boys of Cannery Row. *Tortilla Flat* was Steinbeck's first major success, his first book to be bought by Hollywood, and the first in which he found his characteristic subject matter.

Ten years after *Cannery Row*, Steinbeck again returned to the treatment of the lovable bums in *Sweet Thursday* (1954), a novel far below the quality of *Cannery Row* but one which nevertheless served as the basis for a (short-lived) Broadway musical entitled *Pipe Dream*. *Cannery Row* is thus the central book in a triumvirate of novels, the first near the beginning of Steinbeck's career and the last near the end of it. *Cannery Row* balances the two. If it lacks the innocence and promise of *Tortilla Flat*, it recapitulates much of the earlier novel's spirit while evoking a more genuine nostalgia, a more tranquil whimsy. At the same time, *Cannery Row* looks ahead to the trivial entertainment of *Sweet Thursday*, a book that tries too hard at reprising an already played out tune. *Cannery Row* is thus the final effective evocation of one of Steinbeck's most enduring subjects.

*Sources for Further Study*

Benson, Jackson J. *The True Adventures of John Steinbeck, Writer: A Biography*, 1984.
French, Warren. *John Steinbeck*, 1961, 1975.
Lisca, Peter. *The Wide World of John Steinbeck*, 1958.
Owens, L. *John Steinbeck's Re-Vision of America*, 1985.
Tedlock, E. W., and C. V. Wicker, eds. *Steinbeck and His Critics*, 1957.

*Edward Fiorelli*

# A CANTICLE FOR LEIBOWITZ

*Author:* Walter M. Miller, Jr. (1923-    )
*Type of plot:* Science fiction
*Time of plot:* Around the year 2500, A.D. 3174, and A.D. 3781
*Locale:* The monastery of the Blessed Leibowitz, somewhere between Salt Lake City and El Paso
*First published:* 1959

*Principal characters:*
BENJAMIN ELEAZAR, perhaps the Wandering Jew
BROTHER FRANCIS OF UTAH, the discoverer of the Leibowitzian relics
ABBOT ARKOS, the person responsible for the sanctification of Leibowitz
THON TADDEO, a scientific inquirer, the illegitimate son of Hannegan II of Texarkana
ABBOT PAULO, the preserver of the monastery from Hannegan's ambitions
MRS. GRALES/RACHEL, a two-headed mutant, perhaps the new Messiah or new Mary
ABBOT ZERCHI, the last abbot of the monastery of Saint Leibowitz

## The Novel

The Leibowitz of this novel's title was, the reader is told, a technician engaged in weapons development at the time of the nuclear war which destroyed all civilization in America and in the rest of the world. A natural reaction of the survivors of this holocaust was to turn on all scientists, on all fragments of science, and to destroy them for being in some degree responsible for the devastation that had taken place. Leibowitz, however, though repentant of his past, received permission from the pope to form a new monastic order of Albertus Magnus, whose role would be to save books and manuscripts from the "simpleton" mobs. The order's formation was successful, but Leibowitz himself was caught in the act of "booklegging" and was martyred by simultaneous strangulation and burning.

Leibowitz himself never appears in the novel, but its three separate parts follow the affairs of his order at roughly six-century intervals into the future. In "Fiat Homo," relics of the Blessed Leibowitz are discovered by chance in a fallout shelter and are skillfully used by the abbot of his monastery to have the order's founder elevated to sainthood. In "Fiat Lux," the books so carefully preserved by Leibowitz' followers are at last read by a man capable of making some sense of them, as a scientific civilization begins once more to develop and North America takes a few steps toward reunification. In "Fiat Voluntas Tua," scientific progress makes a deadly full circle, back again to rockets, satellites, and nuclear war, and the then abbot of the monastery at Sanly Bowitts finds himself dealing once more with problems of radiation, civilian casualties, and euthanasia.

The novel is distinguished, in spite of its division into three parts, by many devices working for unity. One is that in each section an abbot of the same monastery is confronted with a problem and responds to it with a similar mixture of wisdom, guile, and principle; there is a strong sense that the role is greater and more permanent than the man. In the background, meanwhile, is the tradition of the Catholic Church, presented as immutable, whatever the changes of time and circumstance; any one of the three abbots could immediately have communicated with and understood any of the others, even if they had had to talk to one another in the Church language of Latin. A further connecting feature is the one character who appears in each section, the seemingly immortal Benjamin Eleazer, known also as "the Old Jew," or "the pilgrim." Finally, there are many objects which reappear, often unrecognized by the characters in the novel, from one section to another: the glass eyeball of the poet, the skull of Brother Francis, the carving of Brother Fingo. The first two sections end with the same image of buzzards circling: The suggestion that image contains of life arising out of death, if only by the activity of the carrion eaters, is spelled out and made clear also at the end of the novel. It is a challenge for the reader to relate the three sections of this novel to one another, yet the sections are scattered thickly with clues that make such a reading both possible and enjoyable.

*The Characters*

The most perplexing character of the novel must certainly be the immortal Benjamin Eleazer. Since he is called different names by different people, it is perhaps conceivable that the novel contains three similar but different old Jews, but the reader is much more strongly pointed to a mythological meaning for his character. He seems in fact to be the "Wandering Jew" of popular legend, who struck and mocked Jesus Christ on His way to crucifixion and was told by Christ: "I go, but you will wait till I return." Since then, the story goes, the Wandering Jew has traveled the earth waiting for the Second Coming of the Messiah. This legend is strongly suggested in one scene in which Benjamin looks into the face of a newcomer, only to say in disappointment "It's still not Him." A second legend is equally strongly suggested in the third section, when children shout at an old tramp, "he be old Lazar, same one 'ut the Lor' Hesus raise up." Could Benjamin Eleazar be the Lazarus of John 11, raised from the dead by Jesus—and then, in legend, not permitted to die again?

The answer is not clear. Yet the role of "the Old Jew" within the novel certainly is. His function is to present a kind of detachment from the follies of humanity, as one who has literally "seen it all before," and as one who realizes that the truly significant events are not scientific, or political, or historical, but are those concerned with the salvation that he himself cannot reach. In the end, in an irony characteristic of the book, it seems that the new Messiah comes without Benjamin's awareness. Nor is the Messiah male, or even immediately recognizable as human. In a minor theme of section three, an illiterate old tomato-woman has been pestering Abbot Zerchi to baptize the rudimentary head she has growing from her shoulder (a result of the mutation-inducing radiation of the previous war). Zerchi refuses, thinking that the head has no soul. As the bombs go off a second time, however, the head comes to life and starts to take over and rejuvenate the body of old Mrs. Grales, while the Grales head dies. Zerchi, dying himself, sees this as a new Immaculate Conception and recognizes the head as needing no baptism from him. Conceivably Benjamin, who is not far off, will recognize his savior in Rachel, if both somehow survive the second nuclear holocaust.

*A Canticle for Leibowitz* also contains an enormous gallery of mortal characters: the three abbots, Arkos, Paulo, and Zerchi; Thon Taddeo, who in section 2 is seen reinventing basic concepts of electricity with the doubtful aid of the Leibowitzian Memorabilia; Hongan Os, or Mad Bear, chief of the blood-drinking nomads of the future Midwest; and many servants or dignitaries of the Church. Perhaps the most endearing is Brother Francis, who, in section 1, discovers the fallout shelter, guided by Benjamin, and spends most of the rest of his life working on an illuminated copy of the (ironically valueless) Leibowitz-signed blueprint he finds there.

### Themes and Meanings

There can be little doubt as to the central theme of *A Canticle for Leibowitz*. The novel is an inquiry into the value of secular knowledge as opposed to spiritual knowledge, and, on the face of it, secular knowledge, or science, is given a very low rating. It leads with seeming inevitability to war, nuclear weapons, and racial suicide. While human beings seem to have an innate propensity toward collecting knowledge of this kind, as dramatized by Thon Taddeo and his eventual collaborator Brother Kornhoer, this seems only a proof of their fallen nature. Even the smallest dabbling with science carries ominous overtones, as in the scene in which the Leibowitzian monks are preparing to use their newly invented generator to light an arc lamp—for which they have, significantly, moved a Crucifix. As Brother Kornhoer touches the contacts, a spark snaps, and he lets out the mild monastic oath of "Lucifer!" Lucifer, however, means "light-bearer" (which is what Kornhoer himself is); it is furthermore a name for the devil and, in section 3, is strongly linked with new nuclear explosions. Kornhoer, then, kind and honest man that he is, is on the road from Satan to nuclear destruction; not even electric lights, seemingly, are sinless.

This apparent blanket condemnation of science and secularity is tempered, however, by a surprising feature of this novel—namely, its unwaveringly comic tone. The comedy is often, indeed usually, wry. Poor Brother Francis devotes his life to gilding and decorating a copy of a blueprint of which he knows nothing; all of his attitudes to the past are furthermore ludicrously false, as all readers immediately recognize. He thinks, for example, having little knowledge of archaic English, that a "fallout shelter" is a shelter for fallouts, a thought which frightens him almost to death, since he further thinks that a fallout is a demonic mix of incubus and salamander. He knows very little, what he knows is mostly wrong, and no reader can avoid regarding him with a mixture of condescension, amusement—and pity, for Francis is good-hearted and is killed in the end entirely blamelessly trying to stick to the letter of a totally unjust bargain. The reader's attitude toward him, however, is only a strengthened form of the attitude which one is encouraged to take toward most of the novel's characters. They are seen as ignorant or deluded, rather than actively wicked; the sin in which all humanity appears involved cannot accordingly be taken entirely seriously. Finally, the book is, in the end, technically and in the old sense a "comedy," even a "divine comedy." It has a happy ending of sorts, through Rachel and through the escape of a human nucleus to the stars. One is asked to believe, with Benjamin, that grace and salvation are more important than any petty turmoil, however violent, on Earth.

One further theme of importance in the novel is that of change and stability. The long perspective of the novel's three parts throws up all kinds of change in language: English evolves into separate dialects, the monastery of Saint Leibowitz becomes the city of Sanly Bowitts, the venerable monk Boedullus, who discovers an "intercontinental launching pad," turns into Bo'dollos, the giant catfish who broods in the waters of the deep crater he created. Against this, though, the Latin liturgy of Catholicism remains unaltered. Similarly, the morals of the Church remain unmoved by circumstance. There is a strong irony in the care with which successive abbots stick to seemingly trivial rules. Behind this, though, is the thought that such rules are binding on eternity, and so are not lightly to be changed. English, politics, and progress, one might say, are set against the less attractive but stronger powers of Latin, religion, and faith.

*Critical Context*

*A Canticle for Leibowitz* falls into a well-known subgenre of science fiction, the "post-disaster" story, like John Wyndham's *The Chrysalids* (1955), Algis Budrys' *Some Will Not Die* (1961), and many more. The use of nuclear weapons to end World War II naturally set many writers speculating on the possibilities of future war, mutation, and rebirth.

Walter M. Miller, Jr.'s novel is remarkable, however, for the strength of its commitment to Catholicism and the thoroughness with which it insists that all knowledge not guided by faith is potentially disastrous, however well-meaning its possessors. It could even be said that *A Canticle for Leibowitz* is an example of antiscience fiction, though if this were claimed, one would also have to say that Miller shows more understanding of and sympathy for science than most proreligious and antiscientific writers, while the fans of science-fiction had no hesitation in voting him the Hugo Award for best science fiction novel in 1961.

Miller's work contains a symbolic depth which is not easily penetrated and is informed throughout by an unusual spirit of charity. Many cruel events take place in *A Canticle for Leibowitz*. None, however, viewed close up, is entirely without excuse or sympathy for its perpetrators. That is the danger of sin, Abbot Zerchi reflects: Even Satan may have been totally sincere. *A Canticle for Leibowitz* forces its readers to reconsider the basic distinction between good and evil.

*Sources for Further Study*

Scholes, Robert, and Eric S. Rabkin. *Science Fiction: History, Science, Vision*, 1977.
Wolfe, Gary K. *The Known and the Unknown: An Iconography of Science Fiction*, 1979.

*T. A. Shippey*

# CAPTAIN BLACKMAN

*Author:* John A. Williams (1925-     )
*Type of plot:* Social criticism
*Time of plot:* 1971, alternating with dream sequences that progress over the
    length of the novel from 1775 to 2001
*Locale:* Every theater of important American military action—from the
    Revolutionary War to the Vietnam War
*First published:* 1972

> *Principal characters:*
>
> ABRAHAM BLACKMAN, the black titular hero, physically and
>     intellectually prepossessing, a career soldier in the U.S.
>     Army with the rank of captain; often of low rank in his
>     historical military dream sequence incarnations
> MIMOSA ROGERS, Blackman's tall and attractive black sweet-
>     heart, a career worker in the U.S. foreign service, who
>     appears in various incarnations in most of Blackman's
>     historical dream sequences
> DAVID HARRISON (LITTLE DAVID), small in stature, a black ser-
>     geant in Blackman's Vietnam squad and a staunch best
>     friend in the Civil War and U.S. Cavalry sequences
> BELMONT, the black radio operator in Blackman's Vietnam
>     squad, whose grandfather was a celebrated World War I
>     aviator
> WOODCOCK, the black medic in Blackman's Vietnam squad,
>     an officer and a close friend in the World War I dream
>     sequence; representative of "the new black"
> ROBERT DOCTOROW, a white soldier of Jewish descent in
>     Blackman's Vietnam squad; an ideologically committed
>     intellectual as well as a would-be writer, appearing in both
>     the Vietnam and Spanish Civil War sequences—in the lat-
>     ter, as Blackman's close friend and fellow social worker-
>     turned-volunteer-soldier
> ISHMAEL WHITTMAN, Blackman's implacable, flaxen-haired,
>     blue-eyed, white antagonist, always a superior officer,
>     whether major (Vietnam), aide to General Schuyler
>     (Revolutionary War), Union officer (Civil War), or aide to
>     an anonymous aging World War II general

## The Novel

The novel opens tensely and excitingly with Captain Blackman pinned
down, perhaps fatally, by enemy AK-47 machine-gun fire in Vietnam. When

his squad blunderingly attempts a rescue, Blackman heroically "thrust[s] his six-four frame skyward" to fire his own weapon and warn his men away from ambush, a gesture that is contradictory (since he has forbidden his own troops such actions) and, ironically, futile (since, as he notes much later in the book, several of the squad die anyway in a subsequent rocket attack back at base camp).

Wounded severely, if not mortally, Blackman finds himself "as in a dream" transported to revolutionary times in America, in an authorial parallel to Mark Twain's Connecticut Yankee in King Arthur's court. Williams surpasses Twain in historical scope, however, for Blackman, who has been a diligent student of black military history (even instituting a seminar on it in his company), as he fades in and out of consciousness, proceeds through virtually every significant military action involving Americans, from the Revolutionary War to a racial military apocalypse which occurs, with fitting symbolism, at the turn of the second millennium. Interwoven with and counterpointing the historically based fantasies is the fate of the modern-day Blackman, his sweetheart, friends, and enemies in 1971 Vietnam. With additional complexity, most of these persons are incorporated and fitted into the fantasies as well.

As with the author's *The Man Who Cried I Am* (1967), the chapters in this novel have been divided into main sections, each concluding with an important climax. Expressive of the author's criticism of white society's unjust treatment of blacks throughout history is that almost every high point, achievement, or joyous moment in the action is followed and counterbalanced by some harsh disappointment or deflation. For example, in the first six chapters that compose section 1, Blackman moves through the Revolutionary War, the War of 1812, and the Civil War, encountering (or nearly encountering) many famous historical figures (Crispus Attucks, George Washington, Andrew Jackson, Ulysses S. Grant) and rejoicing in his race's splendid deeds, which culminate in the black division's bravery at Petersburg, Virginia, which shames the white soldiers for their cowardice. Yet this triumph is undermined by false face-saving reports of the action, as the sheer number of blacks now armed in the Twenty-fifth Army Corps is negated by official refusal to use the unit.

In section 2, crossing the paths of General Custer, Teddy Roosevelt, and "Blackjack" Pershing, the seasoned Civil War veteran Blackman rises to sergeant major in the U.S. Cavalry, protecting settlers and battling Indians, then fights in the Spanish-American War, finally leaving the cavalry to become a machine gunner in the infantry, where, he perceptively foresees, the military future lies. The exuberant and humorous tone of section 1 gives way to somberness in section 2, as Blackman's boon companion in both sections, Little David Harrison, is murdered in a Western saloon by white soldiers disguised as cowboys. Equally dismal is the unjust and mass dishonorable discharge of 167 black soldiers of the Twenty-fifth Infantry, with which the section concludes.

The tone swings back to optimism (though always qualified, as by the unfair thwarting of Blackman's promotion) in section 3, which deals with black American regiments' almost universally acclaimed exploits in World War I, when they were seconded to the French army, which used them to fight rather than to unload cargo, as originally planned by white American commanders. The section concludes on two jubilant notes. First, Blackman miraculously survives, unscratched, a direct hit by an artillery shell, though all are killed around him (foreshadowing his survival of his Vietnam wounds while also symbolizing his race's indestructibility). Second, with Woodcock (his companion and superior officer through much of the section), he strides victorious into Germany.

The mood of the second half of the novel oscillates from buoyant, to bleak, and back to exuberant. In section 4, dealing with the Spanish Civil War, Blackman, in the youngest and most idealistic of his incarnations (befitting this war, the author implies), at first is optimistic about his cause and the international and racial integration of his military unit, significantly named The Abraham Lincoln Brigade; but he is quickly disillusioned by the disintegration of the soldiers' concern for their own race's and nation's wounded, his discovery of the fear and impetus to survive that override ideology, and the defeat of his side. While section 5, which deals with World War II, opens on the cheerful note of Blackman demonstrating his superiority by scoring in the top grade of the army's placement test, it quickly gives way to the gloom of his sweetheart's infidelity, the loss of his chance for becoming an officer by being caught in one of the epidemic army-base race riots, his wounds from a mortar hit in the Solomon Islands (unlike the World War I artillery shell incident, Blackman does not escape unscathed this time), his forced duty as observer of the massacre of a rebel black unit in the Italian swamps outside Tombolo, and finally the official, racial blocking of his volunteer combat in the Battle of the Bulge.

Section 6, covering the Korean and Vietnam conflicts, gradually ascends from the convalescing of Blackman's Vietnam wounds (amputation of part of one leg, loss of a lung, and consequent lifelong respiratory troubles) to Blackman's optimistic decision to survive and revenge himself on Major Whittman (who had treacherously sent him into an ambush) and all he stands for, all paralleled by the accounts of his victories over Whittman in Korea (constantly demonstrating his superior skill), Vietnam (conducting his Black military history seminar), and a final prophetic dream sequence. Set in the year 2001, when Blackman will be seventy, this last episode, which closes the book, shows the novel's only unmitigated triumph, when Blackman and his race take over the U.S. military and its nuclear forces, conclusively gaining power over their white oppressors in the United States.

## The Characters

The author is capable of supplying the odd detail that provides fully rounded characters—the manner in which Johnny Griot (in Blackman's Vietnam squad) carries his M-60 like a film soldier, the priapic talk and antics of Big Dick (a soldier in Blackman's segregated World War II barracks), or the way in which Woodcock wears the biggest afro in the company, possibly to compensate for his light skin. Yet, as with his preceding novels, Williams' main purposes in characterization are didactic and doctrinal: Characters symbolize or are spokespersons for (or both) social positions or points of view in a society that is, overall, racist. Characters are sympathetic toward the black cause, hostile, or somewhere in between. This symbolic or allegorical aspect produces a flattening effect even on the most fully realized and alive character in the book, the hero. For though animating details such as his shoe size (twelve) and preference in wine (Meursault) are provided, what is important about the hero is his embodiment of the indomitable black spirit and the hope for leaders like him who will give blacks the opportunity to live lives of the fullest potential. His allegorical significance is markedly suggested by his name, reinforced by the World War I version of Mimosa's speculation about it, in the middle of the book: "She thought his name: Abraham. A man you trust. Kind. Like a father?" Besides all these and other connotations of the name "Abraham" by way of Abraham Lincoln, including Lincoln's reputation as the Great Emancipator (Blackman has fought in the Civil War, as well as in the Abraham Lincoln Brigade in the Spanish Civil War), the biblical Abraham is also evoked as another great spiritual leader—and warrior or soldier—in an episode not often remembered, when to liberate his nephew Lot, he takes a small band of 318 to fight against the armies of four kings. The last name of the hero, "Blackman," combines "black" and "man," to suggest that he embodies the spirit and yearning of all his people.

The character and name of Blackman's chief antagonist in most sequences are similarly allegorical. The surname "Whittman" is distinctly a combination of "white" and "man," which is added to his main physical features repeatedly mentioned throughout the novel—his blond hair (the word "flaxen" is used twice) and blue eyes. Whittman is thus archetypally and exaggeratedly white, corresponding to the extremism of his racist attitudes and views. Ishmael, Whittman's first name, which is revealed only toward the end of the novel, helps express both the sources of Whittman's hostility and the irony of that hostility. Just as the novel's Whittman has been constantly made aware of Blackman's superior abilities (and thus the unfairness of the latter's inferior rank), so the biblical Ishmael was made to feel inferior and second-class by being cast off by Abraham's family, and just as Whittman's guilt generates hostility, so the biblical Ishmaelites were renowned for their ferocity (and often antagonism to the Israelites, Abraham's descendants). Ironically, though, the biblical Ishmael is Abraham's son, which recalls the current theory of some anthropologists that humanity's earliest origins were in Africa—Whittman is Blackman's "son" in this sense.

Not all whites in the novel are malevolent, by any means. For example, Robert Doctorow admires Captain Blackman, has attended the black military history seminars (enduring the initial animosity of the black auditors), and is sympathetic to the blacks' cause. Likewise, his Spanish Civil War incarnation is Blackman's closest friend—about whom Blackman thinks, after learning that Doctorow has been wounded (just as his Vietnam incarnation has): "Somehow Doctorow's life was tied to his and now that his friend lived, Blackman knew that he would, too." Doctorow's Jewish heritage, pointedly referred to in the novel, links him not only with the biblical Abraham but also with another minority that has been oppressed (a motif also to be found in Williams' *The Man Who Cried I Am*).

Finally, a complexity in the author's characterization is created by Williams' technique of the multiple versions, and thus multiple perspectives, of the characters in different eras. The seasoned, professional veteran in the U.S. Cavalry in Indian territory is different from the Spanish Civil War Blackman, who is a young, idealistic amateur. Nor are these versions identical to the young, urban New York-born Blackman who enlists in the army after World War II to find a better way of life for himself. Similarly, Blackman's sweetheart, Mimosa, also varies: a young, uneducated slave in the Civil War; a wholesome, somewhat parochial small-town girl during World War I; a married yet adulterously adventurous woman during World War II, who finally jilts Blackman for a sailor; a poised, sophisticated career woman in the Vietnam episode, devoted and faithful to Blackman. Human beings are not merely allegorical symbols, the author seems to be suggesting, and are importantly affected by their environment.

### Themes and Meanings

As with Williams' novels *Night Song* (1961) and *The Man Who Cried I Am*, the central themes of *Captain Blackman* are the oppression, injustices, and indignities suffered by blacks in a white society, and the necessity of revolt and retribution to overcome these. The function of the numerous surrealistic sections entitled "Cadences" and set off by italics, as well as of the sections entitled "Drumtaps," is to show that such oppression is conscious and intentional, not merely unthinkingly *de facto*. The "Cadences" sections usually introduce chapters or parts of the novel, and the structural placement of these conspiratorial planning sessions by white power brokers, as well as their content, implies how historical events have been directed from their inception, as does the military sense of the term "cadences," denoting the underlying measure or beat which directs the marching soldiers. The "Drumtaps" sections usually conclude chapters, in harmony with the military sense of this term, and quote actual military documents that substantiate white injustice.

A number of motifs are woven through the novel, in accord with the interweaving of historical sequences. One motif that expresses the overall racial theme is the recurrent, consciousness-robbing blow to the head that Blackman receives in the revolutionary war, Civil War, and World War II episodes, and that is always delivered by whites (and usually associated with Whittman). Blackman's revolt and retribution during the Civil War for a clubbing he receives and for the raping of Mimosa is achieved by tracking down Whittman and his white mistress, binding them after clubbing Whittman, and then raping Whittman's woman before his eyes. The simile that compares Blackman's undressing of the woman to the cleaning of a rifle suggests the dimension in such acts of war or battle that Williams sees as necessary for blacks' ultimate self-realization.

Yet salvation in the novel comes from love as well as anger. The continual circling of the plot back to versions of Mimosa helps express how important, how central, she is to Blackman, as does his very last thought—of her— just before springing up to make his sacrifice for his Vietnam squad in the novel's opening. In each historical sequence prior to Vietnam their love has been thwarted or frustrated by the climate produced by white society. Only at the conclusion of the novel, when Blackman decides to make a concerted effort at revolutionary change, are the two united; and Blackman explicitly tells Mimosa that she is the key to not only his happiness, but also his success.

*Critical Context*

In some respects, John A. Williams' corpus is remarkably homogeneous. Many of the obsessive themes and concerns of his previous novels *Night Song* and *The Man Who Cried I Am* recur in *Captain Blackman*. The conspiratorial view of events in society can be found in the enigmatic death of Richie Stokes (Eagle) in *Night Song* and the apocalyptic King Alfred document in *The Man Who Cried I Am*. The need to strike back is glimpsed in a remark by Eagle about getting money to buy weapons (*Night Song*) and in protagonist Max Reddick's purchase of a veritable arsenal in *The Man Who Cried I Am*. Further, the centrality of love is expressed by the relationships between the main characters Keel and Della in *Night Song* and Max Reddick and Margrit in *The Man Who Cried I Am* (indeed, Max dies saying Margrit's name, similar to Blackman's utterance of Mimosa's before firing at the Vietnamese enemy).

Also, *Captain Blackman* is in some respects adumbrated by *The Man Who Cried I Am*. The apocalyptic plan for racial genocide of blacks in the latter is answered in the former by Blackman's counterconspiracy; Max

Reddick's military experience and his vow to a Kennedy aide that he could recite to him a documented history of maltreatment of blacks in the military and elsewhere are elaborated in *Captain Blackman*.

This novel is, however, an advance over the others. While as socially conscious and didactic as Williams' preceding works, it is not marred by long, repeated speeches by characters about white injustice. Characters are portrayed more deftly, with more interest shown in them, and there is a greater mustering of vivid and memorable minor characters (such as Flag Sergeant Anselmas Plancianois, Old Man Flood, black frontier scout Brit Johnson, Lieutenant Buck Himes, Richard Boston, Gummidge, Linkey, and "The Gold Dust Twins"—Flash and Tisdale). Moreover, while humor is repeatedly referred to in *Night Song* and *The Man Who Cried I Am*, this novel genuinely possesses humor, in the form of Blackman's flatulent outburst used to comment on General Schuyler's revolutionary war racism, the historical joke about Blackman and Peter Salem not clearly hearing at Breed's Hill the now enshrined remark, "Don't fire until you see the whites of their eyes" ("What did he say?" "I think he said to shoot them in the eyes"), and the ingenious way that British soldiers escape death in the hopeless charge in the Battle of New Orleans.

Perhaps his most artistically finished work, *Captain Blackman* in its scope and marvelous interweaving of different times in a single story compares favorably with John Dos Passos' *U.S.A.* (which is recalled by the "Cadences" and "Drumtaps" sections) and with Tim O'Brien's complex, more-than-Vietnam novel, *Going After Cacciato* (1978), winner of the National Book Award.

*Sources for Further Study*

Bryant, Jerry H. "John A. Williams: The Political Use of the Novel," in *Criticism*. XVI (1975), pp. 81-100.

Cash, Earl A. *John A. Williams: The Evolution of a Black Writer*, 1974.

Lee, Robert, ed. *Black Fiction: New Studies in the Afro-American Novel Since 1945*, 1980.

Muller, Gilbert H. *John A. Williams*, 1984.

Munro, C. Lynn. "Culture and Quest in the Fiction of John A. Williams," in *College Language Association Journal*. XXII (1978), pp. 71-100.

*Norman Prinsky*

# THE CATCHER IN THE RYE

*Author:* J. D. Salinger (1919-      )
*Type of plot: Bildungsroman* (rite-of-passage novel)
*Time of plot:* Just before a Christmas shortly after World War II
*Locale:* Agerstown, Pennsylvania, New York City, and an unlocated
   sanatorium
*First published:* 1951

> *Principal characters:*
> HOLDEN CAULFIELD, a sixteen-year-old preparatory school
>    student, recently suspended
> PHOEBE CAULFIELD, his ten-year-old sister, living with her
>    parents in New York City
> MR. ANTOLINI, Holden's favorite teacher at Elkton Hills
>    School
> SALLY HAYES, a slightly older friend of Holden who is his date
> ROBERT ACKLEY, Holden's dorm mate at Pencey
> WARD STRADLATER, Holden's roommate, a senior

## The Novel

In an unnamed sanatorium, talking to a silent psychiatrist, Holden Caulfield retells the events of the few days just before Christmas vacation from his preparatory school, Pencey. As he recalls the events leading up to the physical and mental collapse that has brought him to the sanatorium, Caulfield selects certain details that, taken together, draw a picture of bleak indifference, stupidity, and general "phoniness" on the part of everyone with whom he has come in contact. His dormitory neighbor Robert Ackley has disgusting habits and unacceptable hygienic standards. His roommate, Ward Stradlater, dates Caulfield's old girlfriend and then punches him in the nose when Caulfield strikes out at Stradlater in frustration and inarticulate anger. Leaving Pencey three days early, with some spending money in his pocket, Caulfield wanders the streets of New York City in a series of aborted attempts to find companionship from strangers and old acquaintances. Sally Hayes, a girl for whom Caulfield once felt a kinship and affection, has grown to womanhood with all its self-consciousness; when Caulfield asks her to run away with him, she erupts with indignation and leaves him at Rockefeller Plaza.

A brief encounter with a prostitute gets Caulfield another beating, this time by her pimp. Two nuns in a restaurant are kind to him; he gives them all his spending money. The only haven Caulfield finds in his odyssey is his own home with his parents away; his little sister Phoebe, tucked cozily in her brother D.B.'s bed, offers Caulfield the unspoken understanding he craves. In a touching scene, Caulfield finally reveals his one goal in life: to stand in a field of rye and catch playing children in danger of running over a cliff.

What seems to be another island in the sea of perversion is the apartment of Mr. Antolini, his favorite teacher from another school, but when Caulfield falls asleep on the couch, he is awakened by the teacher's hand on his head, stroking his hair. Caulfield rushes from the apartment and determines to "go West," a form of retreat rather than revival for him. When he informs Phoebe of his plans, she packs her bags, intending to accompany him, but Caulfield realizes his impotence at her insistence and his salvation in her eyes. Promising not to leave her, Caulfield takes Phoebe to Central Park, and his last clear memory is sitting in the rain in the park, watching Phoebe happily riding round and round on an old brown carousel horse. Remembering the events that led to his collapse, Caulfield remembers only his earlier conviction that the world smells of urine, unbrushed teeth, vomit, or a combination of these, that people all have habits of speech that reveal their fundamental stupidity, and that every wall has an obscenity written on it or carved into it somewhere.

*The Characters*

In a sense there is only one character in the novel, the first-person narrative voice of Holden Caulfield. The external details of Caulfield's life are never so important as the full-length portrait of the character as revealed by his own observations of the "phony" world around him. The distinct quality of Holden Caulfield that earns for him his special place in literature is his ability to spot phoniness, insensitivity, self-indulgence, bad hygiene, and stupidity in others without noting those same imperfections in himself. Salinger captures the relentlessly egocentric psyche of every adolescent by going inside Caulfield's head, so that nothing is observed except through Caulfield's eyes.

From what can be pieced together from Caulfield's narrative, he is one of four children, one of whom is dead and one of whom lives in a fairly decent section of New York, with all the amenities of affluence: prep school in Pennsylvania, spending money, and familiarity with the cultural centers of the city. The character feature that separates Caulfield from his classmates is his hypersensitivity to the various devices people use to survive the day: social masks, habits of speech, polite dismissals of inferiors, and the less refined behaviors of indifference and class consciousness. Without philosophizing in the abstract, Caulfield expresses his general opinion of the imperfections of the species, notably through a marked self-centeredness that excludes sympathy for those, like himself, who need to be understood despite their inarticulate behavior.

The other characters in the novel are two-dimensional if Caulfield's descriptions are taken at face value, but because he is relating the story in a way that reveals his own character, it remains for the reader to redeem the characters by observing, *past* Caulfield, to the real person underneath. Sally Hayes, for example, is by no means a heartless shrew; rather, she is a delightful person, full of life, happy to accommodate Caulfield's impulsive behavior, up to a point. She is no more "phony" than anyone her age; on the contrary, she is more socially graceful than most, certainly more than a match for Caulfield in manners and politeness. Despite Caulfield's perception of her, Sally is a courageous spirit—willing to try skating, willing to defend Caulfield's classmates against his accusation, and hardly to be blamed for refusing his offer to run away with him to the woods.

The one character of whom Caulfield approves, his sister Phoebe, is on the brink of becoming his female equivalent; her disdain of others, her insistence on doing things her way, her rush to judgment, even her attraction to Caulfield's hat, are softened only to a point by the naïveté of her limited experience in a sheltered world. She will become very much like Caulfield when she reaches prep school age; both of them are already romantically fantasizing about the death of a brother, and both of them are already intolerant critics of others' imperfections. Their relationship, however, offers the reader a glimpse of Caulfield's only hope: to be accepted without question by someone who can love him.

Until the introduction of Mr. Antolini, the long line of characters in Caulfield's visit to Hades serves to underscore his private prejudices regarding all mankind, because, seen from his own perspective only, they are not three-dimensional characters but rather projections of his critical opinion of the entire species called "not-Holden." Mr. Antolini, however—expansive, eccentric in his late-night habits, intuitively generous, a born teacher, and a borderline alcoholic who accepts Caulfield without question, even at a late hour—comes closest to what Caulfield wishes all people could be like. The suggestion of an underlying perversity, however—hidden like swear words in a dark corridor—ruins Caulfield's only chance to find adult compassion. Caulfield interprets (or misinterprets) Mr. Antolini's affectionate stroking as perversity in a quick judgment that is emblematic of Caulfield's destructively self-protective attitude against human contact. Another character, Caulfield's brother Allie, now dead, stands behind Caulfield throughout the novel—a figure foreshadowing Salinger's long-term project, the fictitious Glass family stories.

### Themes and Meanings

On one level, *The Catcher in the Rye* is a simple narrative by a young man at a turning point in his life, presenting the events of his recent past in a language uniquely his own. His perceptions are both specific and universal, and it is no accident that the portrait of Holden Caulfield which the reader gleans from his narrative is not much different from that of his own classmates. What separates this *Bildungsroman* from others, such as Thomas Wolfe's *Look Homeward, Angel* (1929), is that Salinger chooses to recall his adolescence not in the mature language of the author looking backward, but in the actual voice-rhythms of the adolescent. On another level, however, there is considerable evidence that a larger idea is superimposed on the deceptively simple narrative. The names given to the characters and places ("Pencey" suggests the French *pensée*, meaning "thought"), the parallels to a Ulysses-like journey into an underworld, even the three-day Christian interval between the Crucifixion and the Resurrection, are all provocative suggestions that Salinger is dealing thematically with a universal pattern of cyclic behavior, of which adolescent truancy is only one manifestation. The novel's appeal lies in its invitation to symbolic interpretation, as well as in its realistic portrait of Everyman in his teens.

The suicide theme that can be detected even in a first reading of the novel is most strongly manifested in the anecdote of the young man who threw himself from the bathroom window at another school, where Caulfield heard the sound: "I just thought something fell out the window, a radio or a desk or something, not a boy or anything." This reduction of a human being to a physical object is integral to the novel.

Throughout the journey in the streets of New York, Caulfield fails to be impressed by slick performance; neither an unctuous pianist nor the Radio City Rockettes impress him. He is, however, suddenly touched by accidental events, such as the child absentmindedly singing "Coming Through the Rye." Details of this kind reinforce the central theme of the entire novel, that self-consciousness accompanies the loss of innocence. The reader watches Holden Caulfield as he undergoes this most painful of transitions. Like the broken record that his sister cherishes, Caulfield prefers accident to design.

*Critical Context*

Many of Salinger's critics contend that the awesome popularity of *Catcher in the Rye* is attributable to a misinterpretation on the part of adolescents like Holden Caulfield, who erroneously saw in the book a justification for and an understanding of the very behavior they themselves suffered through as teenagers. The young reader, thinking that the depiction of adolescence was a sympathetic one, failed to see the similarities between Caulfield's actions and the actions of the classmates he was criticizing. All kinds of previously unspoken notions—sadness at the death of siblings, extraordinary affection for a younger sister, fear of suicidal tendencies, awkwardness with the opposite sex, developing hygienic habits—were (by the standards of the time) daringly discussed, and the young readers who embraced this book for other than its more realistic qualities as a novel did so from a sense that Salinger had finally told their story. They failed to note that Salinger himself was well past the age of the adolescent Caulfield, had written excerpts of the novel for *The New Yorker*, and was himself beginning a very reclusive writing career in a cabin not unlike the one Caulfield describes to Sally.

As the Glass family stories developed in Salinger's career, critics were tempted to place Caulfield somewhere in the large panorama of the epic, and a second wave of interest followed the first. As the details of Salinger's canon are examined for possible mythological and classical references, allusions to Christian dogma, hidden suggestions of a structure of epic proportions akin to a history of Western man, and similar excursions beyond the simple storytelling impulse that Salinger acknowledges, the novel that began his fame will always be viewed as a secret code to the truths about adults, a code decipherable only by hormonally imbalanced, "unphony" descendants of Holden Caulfield or his spirit.

*Sources for Further Study*
Belcher, William F., and James W. Lee, eds. *J. D. Salinger and the Critics*, 1962.
Lettis, Richard. *J. D. Salinger: The Catcher in the Rye*, 1964.
Marsden, Malcolm M., comp. *If You Really Want to Know: A Catcher Casebook*, 1963.
Simonson, Harold Peter. *Salinger's "Catcher in the Rye": Clamor vs. Criticism*, 1963.

*Thomas J. Taylor*

# CAT'S CRADLE

*Author:* Kurt Vonnegut, Jr. (1922-    )
*Type of plot:* Science-fiction fable
*Time of plot:* The early 1960's
*Locale:* Ilium, New York, and the Caribbean republic of San Lorenzo
*First published:* 1963

> *Principal characters:*
> JOHN, surname unknown, the narrator of the novel
> DR. FELIX HOENIKKER, an atomic scientist and the creator of *ice-nine*
> NEWT HOENIKKER, a midget, his son
> ANGELA HOENIKKER, later MRS. HARRISON C. CONNERS, Newt's sister
> FRANKLIN HOENIKKER, Major General and Minister of Science and Progress in San Lorenzo
> "PAPA" MONZANO, the dictatorial president of San Lorenzo
> LIONEL BOYD JOHNSON, BOKONON, philosopher and opponent of Monzano

## The Novel

*Cat's Cradle* is a remarkably discursive book, full of loose ends, unexplained events, and characters who appear in focus for a moment only to vanish without apology. It does center, however, on one single object: the sliver of *ice-nine* created by Dr. Felix Hoenikker and divided after his death by his three children, only to bring about the end of the world almost simultaneously with the end of the book.

In Vonnegut's theory, ice is only one of the many possible ways in which water can crystallize. If there were other ways, ice of different kinds would be created, including a kind which would melt not at 32 degrees Fahrenheit but at as high as one hundred degrees or 130 degrees—in the case of *ice-nine*, at 114.4 degrees. Furthermore a single seed of this ice, introduced to ordinary water in crystalline form, could act as a catalyst, instantly freezing the entire body of water with which it came in contact. The purpose of such an object (a Marine Corps general suggests) would be to eliminate mud, and allow the United States Marines to fight in relatively congenial circumstances. The side effects, however, would be that anyone who touched *ice-nine* would freeze solid instantly; while, furthermore, any crystal not scrupulously isolated could, in one single chain reaction, freeze solid all the oceans of Earth and bring life almost immediately to an end. The basic plot of *Cat's Cradle* is that a journalist researching a book on Dr. Hoenikker, "the father of the atom bomb," discovers that the latter has created *ice-nine*, finds himself (as a result of a chain of improbable coincidences) on a plane bound for the island republic of San Lorenzo with two of Hoenikker's children, there to meet the third, and in the process of becoming the president of San Lorenzo releases crystalline *ice-nine* into the ocean (in the form of the frozen body of a previous president), thus precipitating, literally, the end of the world. One very minor irony is that the book on which the journalist-narrator was working was to have been called *The Day the World Ended* and was supposed to have been about events on the day that the first atomic bomb was dropped on Hiroshima. In a sense, though, *Cat's Cradle* is about the day the world ended; yet this was caused by *ice-nine*, not atomic bombs, and it would conceivably not have happened at all if the narrator had not started research on the book that he never wrote.

Such ironies, coincidences, and elements of humor are best treated by the philosophy of Bokonon, to which the narrator is converted, and which he spends much of the novel expounding.

### The Characters

It is entirely characteristic of the wry tone of *Cat's Cradle* that its two most important characters should either never appear or appear only on the last page, to utter a total of twenty-three words in direct speech. The two characters are antithetical. The one who never appears is Dr. Hoenikker, though he is pervasively present all through the book in the form of memories of him recounted by his children, associates, and enemies (he has no friends), all obsessively recorded by the narrator. These recollections present Hoenikker, in brief, as a monster of scientific curiosity and human detachment: He tips his wife thirty-eight cents for giving him coffee as he leaves to collect his Nobel Prize, having forgotten who she is. Only once, the reader is told, does he ever try to play with one of his children—the game is cat's cradle—and then he terrifies the child into flight. Hoenikker is in a way a devil of the modern mythological imagination: a scientist whose curiosity has entirely devoured his conscience. People, the reader is told, were not "his speciality."

Bokonon, by contrast, is an idealized guru-figure, present almost entirely by way of his recorded sayings. His philosophy defies summary but is in essence gentle, humorous, anarchic, and skeptical. To the Bokononist, only man is sacred; there is no such thing as coincidence; the Communist Party, the General Electric Company, the notion of a "Hoosier," all rank with all nation states as examples of the *granfalloon*, in other words, something that looks like a unit but is in fact completely meaningless "in terms of the ways God gets things done." Bokonon, one learns, is not by any means a nihilist. He is, however, no admirer of organization or of convention.

The action of *Cat's Cradle* could be described as a movement from Hoenikker to Bokonon, though this would be partly misleading in that the narrator is a Bokononist by the time he starts writing. This narrator, however, is the most prominent character actually present in *Cat's Cradle*; though once more, with typical paradox, he is relatively characterless, seeming at times to be a projection of the author (both were born in Indianapolis, both went to Cornell University), at others to represent the doubts and incredulity of the reader.

Around him, finally, there orbits a gallery of grotesques: Newt, Hoenikker's midget son; Angela, Newt's gigantic sister; "Papa" Monzano, the lunatic president of San Lorenzo, given to impaling opponents on hooks; H. Lowe Crosby, a bicycle manufacturer from Illinois; and many others. Logical connection between these characters is almost always rejected: They form (according to the philosophy of Bokonon) a *karass*—in other words, the opposite of a *granfalloon*, a team designed to do God's will without ever knowing exactly what they are doing or, in many cases, so much as recognizing one another. The oddity and eccentricity of his linked characters are very much part of Vonnegut's overall design.

*Themes and Meanings*

It could be argued that the meaning of *Cat's Cradle* is to prove that life is completely without meaning or purpose. Though the narrator, quoting Bokonon, often speaks of "God's will," the last advice he receives from Bokonon himself is to go to the top of the highest mountain in San Lorenzo, lie on his back, thumb his nose at God, and in that position touch his lips with a crystal of *ice-nine*—at which moment the narrator will freeze into an everlasting statue of rejection and defiance. This gesture sums up a feeling always present in the book, that in reality (as in fantasy) human aspirations are continually thwarted both by a seemingly hostile fate and also by the poor qualities of humanity itself, summed up in people such as Hoenikker—or indeed Crosby the bicycle manufacturer and his "Hoosier"-obsessed wife.

The theme of meaninglessness is further reinforced by the image of the cat's cradle. This was the game that Dr. Hoenikker was playing on the day that the atom bomb was dropped. It has also become to some anthropologists (Vonnegut studied anthropology at the University of Chicago) a model in miniature of human culture: Both are complex, absorbing, and passed on from one generation to another. Both also, it could be said, lack any immediate point except to entertain the people whose time they occupy. Newt Hoenikker, whose father tried to show him the game when he was six, takes this connection further. Cat's cradle, he says, like most aspects of human culture, is a cheat. There is no cat, and no cradle; it is all merely string. Adults tell children what to look for in what they call cat's cradle, and impressionable children believe them. Exactly the same is true, he says, of religion, marriage, human relationships, and most of what people teach one another. One might sum up by saying that Newt Hoenikker believes that human culture not only is a game but also is a very dull one, and that most human institutions grossly abuse the confidence which people place in them.

There is, however, a strongly affirmative streak also present in *Cat's Cradle*, to which many readers have responded—so much so, indeed, that certain Bokononist concepts have enjoyed some slight currency even outside the world of the book. If one sees the institutions of State and Church as being so much string, Bokonon suggests, there are still useful ways for people to live. They can love one another without sexual exploitation, for example, by the Bokononist rite of *boko-maru*, a sort of foot massage. They can form relationships with people of different races, ages, sexes, and incomes, as it were, against the grain of organized society. They can tell one another stories or write calypsos. They could accomplish much, in short—if it were not for *ice-nine*.

*Ice-nine* is a clearly symbolic concept. It destroys the world. It is the product of Dr. Felix Hoenikker. It also sprang from the desire of a general to abolish mud. Mud, though, is a traditional image of humanity—though English Bibles prefer the more dignified word "clay." Nevertheless, when Dr. Schlicter von Koenigswald (once a physician in Auschwitz, with centuries of kind deeds to do to balance his account) offers the last rites of Bokonon to the dying dictator·Monzano, he begins with the words "God made mud." In the Bokononist liturgy, the "mud" then sits up and appreciates its moment of consciousness before lying down again, content, having rehearsed a little playlet of the good life and death. The equation is absolutely clear. Humanity is only mud, but harmless mud, and mud with some potential. *Ice-nine* destroys mud, but at the cost of destroying everything else as well. *Ice-nine* becomes, then, an image of destructive science, weapons technology, contempt for humanity, and perhaps above all of the overorganization and wholly false complexity which Vonnegut sees in much of his own society. Perhaps the most telling point in *Cat's Cradle* is Vonnegut's skillful connection of such impossible figures as Dr. Hoenikker with perfectly recognizable and mildly comic ones such as H. Lowe Crosby. Both share the same intellectual errors. The spirit of *ice-nine* is real.

## Critical Context

*Cat's Cradle* has faint connections, through places and named characters, with Vonnegut's earlier works *Player Piano* (1952) and *The Sirens of Titan* (1959). In *Cat's Cradle*, however, Vonnegut may be seen approaching the theme which obsessed him from 1945 onward, but which he was only to articulate freely in *Slaughterhouse-Five* (1969). This is his own gruesome experience as a prisoner of war caught in the firebombing of Dresden, one of the most appalling, if least intended, atrocities of this or any century. It could be said that the question which Vonnegut had to ask again and again was simply: How do people manage to do such things to one another? The answer is a complex mixture of carelessness, thoughtlessness, and a channeled curiosity—a mixture that contains surprisingly little in the way of deliberate cruelty.

*Cat's Cradle* is thus one of many works written in direct response to the problem of human behavior as revealed in World War II: One could compare, for example, William Golding's *Lord of the Flies* (1954) or Walter M. Miller's *A Canticle for Leibowitz* (1960). The special achievement of *Cat's Cradle*, however, lies in its style. The arch flippancy of Vonnegut's writing, with its short paragraphs, ambiguous sayings, snippets of nursery rhyme, and rejection of all intellectualizing, had a powerful effect on the youth movement of the late 1960's, in which Vonnegut had a considerable following. Vonnegut's novels have, however, withstood the test of time much better than have those of many 1960's gurus. There are two main reasons for this enduring appeal: an evident sincerity in attempting to get to the bottom of real events, both personal and historical, and a concern with intellectual issues that remains perfectly perceptible beneath a surface of fantasy, detachment, and humor.

*Sources for Further Study*
Klinkowitz, Jerome. *Kurt Vonnegut*, 1982.
Klinkowitz, Jerome, and John Somer, eds. *The Vonnegut Statement*, 1973.
May, John R. *Toward a New Earth: Apocalypse in the American Novel*, 1972.
Mayo, Clark. *Kurt Vonnegut: The Gospel from Outer Space: Or, Yes We Have No Nirvanas*, 1977.
Reed, Peter J. *Kurt Vonnegut, Jr.*, 1972.

*T. A. Shippey*

# THE CENTAUR

*Author:* John Updike (1932-    )
*Type of plot:* Mythic novel
*Time of plot:* Monday morning to Thursday morning during the second week of January, 1947
*Locale:* Olinger, Pennsylvania, and a farm outside Olinger near Firetown
*First published:* 1963

> *Principal characters:*
> GEORGE CALDWELL (CHIRON), a general science teacher at Olinger High School
> PETER CALDWELL (PROMETHEUS), his son and the artist who tells the story
> CASSIE CALDWELL (CERES), George's wife
> POP CRAMER (KRONOS), Cassie's father
> AL HUMMEL (HEPHAESTUS), a local garageman
> LOUIS M. ZIMMERMAN (ZEUS), the Olinger High School principal
> DOC APPLETON (APOLLO), a local doctor
> VERA HUMMEL (VENUS), Al's wife and the girls' gym teacher at Olinger High School

*The Novel*

In an interview in the *Paris Review*, John Updike confessed that *The Centaur* seemed his truest and liveliest book, a book which he was prompted to write in order to publicize the myth of Chiron, one of the few instances of self-sacrifice from the classical world. The novel contains an interesting, if at times rather disturbing, mixture of classical figures amid a realistic setting. The purpose of the actual presence of the mythological figures was to expand the significance of Peter Caldwell's nostalgia and to counterpoint an ideal with a drab level of reality.

The story is told by Peter Caldwell, who describes himself as a mediocre abstract expressionist painter. In the course of the novel, Peter, who lives in Greenwich Village with his black girlfriend, re-creates a three-day period immediately after World War II, when he was a teenager. Through his recollection, Peter is able to understand his father, George, with a clarity denied him as a younger man, and he recognizes the self-sacrifice that his father made in order to enable his son to pursue his career as an artist.

The novel opens abruptly within the mode of the mythological by introducing Chiron—disguised as a high school science teacher—who has been wounded in the ankle by an arrow in accordance with the Greek myth. He limps out of the classroom on his remaining three hooves to Al Hummel's garage to have the arrow removed. Chiron returns to his classroom by way of the school basement to avoid the principal, who hectors him throughout the novel. In keeping with the mythological setting of the first chapter, the centaur recalls meeting Al Hummel's wife, Vera, in the guise of Venus, once before in the school basement. The image of her emerging from the steam of the girls' locker room suggests both her desire for and rejection of the half-man, half-stallion. Back upstairs, Chiron finds that Louis M. Zimmerman, the principal, has taken over his class in his absence. Chiron concludes this chapter by delivering a lecture on the origins of the universe to his increasingly restive class.

The second chapter, written entirely in realistic terms, begins the action of the plot by having Peter remember a wintry morning when he was fifteen years old: He overhears a conversation between his parents in which George/Chiron confesses his fear that he has cancer. Peter wonders about disease and mortality and his psoriasis, the curse that he hides from others. Peter and his father leave for school in their converted Buick hearse, stopping along the way to pick up a hitchhiker, who makes them late when George accedes to his demands to be driven to a place that is out of their way.

The remainder of the narrative traces, for the most part, the adventures of Peter and his father as they visit the doctor's office for an examination and a set of X rays, attend a high school swimming meet, spend the night in a cheap hotel after their car fails to start, go to a high school basketball game the next evening, get stuck in the snow and spend the night with the Hummels, and finally return home, where they discover that the X rays did not reveal any disease. The next morning, Peter, sick with a fever and a cold, watches as his father once more returns to his teaching duties at the high school. The novel is brought full circle when in the final chapter the narrative returns to the mythological setting and Chiron accepts his own death, although he has been given a momentary reprieve.

The novel is one of discovery for Peter, who in recalling this brief three days of his adolescence has the opportunity to reflect on the life that he took for granted and on the people whom he also accepted without reflection. The novel is not, however, elegiac in the vein of Updike's next extended fiction, *Of the Farm* (1965), the third of the Olinger novels. In the epilogue to *The Centaur*, Zeus expresses his love for his old friend Chiron by setting him among the stars as the constellation Sagittarius, who still assists in regulating human destinies, in spite of the fact, Updike notes, that in these later days few look to the heavens and fewer still are students of the stars.

## The Characters

That Updike wants his readers to make the comparisons between his

characters and their mythological analogues is apparent by the presence of
the mythological index which, at his wife's suggestion, he appended to the
novel. Matching up various figures of the fiction with their ancient proto-
types is not merely a parlor game, however, but yields a broadening significance to the fictional characters of the novel. To see George Caldwell as
Chiron, Peter as Prometheus, Al Hummel as Hephaestus, and his wife,
Vera, as Venus, elevates the work and ties it to the classical literary tradition
of Western civilization. Such a fictional device, perhaps better called a
trope, also figures in Updike's other novels, especially *The Poorhouse Fair*
(1959), *Couples* (1968), and the Rabbit Angstrom books.

Updike's pantheon is fairly widespread in *The Centaur*. George Caldwell
is Chiron, the centaur, who is sacrificed in order to protect the fire-bringer
and legendary creator/artist, Prometheus, here associated with George's
son, Peter, the painter. George's wife, Cassie, the keeper of the home fire
and the one character linked to the land and fertility not only through her
son, Peter, but also through her savage attachment to the farm that she co-
erced her husband to buy, is Ceres. Vera and Al Hummel make a good Venus and Hephaestus. The goddess of love and of the erotic, Venus seeks her
fulfillment through flirtations at the basketball game and as the object of
Chiron's lust and of George's wishful thinking. She is also responsible for
arousing Peter's sense of manhood during their stay with the Hummels after
the storm. Al is the owner of the local garage, and, through his prowess as a
mechanic, he brings the mythical blacksmith up to date. Zimmerman, the
principal of the high school, is Zeus, who, as an authority figure, rep-
rimands George as Zeus did Chiron and provides a force against which
George can rebel. Doc Appleton is Apollo but is also Asclepius, and Pop
Kramer, Peter's maternal grandfather, becomes associated with Kronos
through his connections with clocks and time.

Although most of the main characters relate to their mythological models
in a number of ways, the minor figures are usually linked in only a single
way. A female teacher at the high school who sticks yellow pencils in her
hair recalls Medusa, and the janitor, Heller, who inhabits the Hades of the
basement, at one point finds some seeds and asks the Caldwells, father and
son, how the seeds came to be there, which recalls the story of Persephone.
Such notations have been seen by some of Updike's critics as a bit over-
ingenious, symptomatic of the book's tilt toward cleverness rather than
profundity.

The characterizations and the links with mythology were drawn by
Updike from a variety of sources, including Josephine Preston Peabody's
*Old Greek Folks Stories Told Anew* (1897) and Herbert J. Rose's *A Hand-
book of Greek Mythology* (1928). He also made ample use of Hesiod, both
*The Works and Days* (c. 700 B.C.) and *Theogony* (c. 700 B.C.), and of Pliny
the Elder's *Natural History* (first century A.D.). Finally, whether or

not the reader makes the various mythic connections, the presence of such background material immeasurably enriches an already complex and profound story.

## Themes and Meanings

The central theme of the book is Peter's discovery of the meaning behind his father's sacrifice, especially in a world where the very idea of sacrifice holds no religious or cultural relevance. The teacher/father has relinquished his own ambitions for the good of the artist/son; the intellect has prepared the way for the integrating effects of the artist. Yet, and it is a large proviso, Peter, who now is guardian of the imagination, has not been able to profit from his inheritance. It is in the fiction which unfolds that Peter rummages back through his memories, in search of a new starting point for the creation of a meaningful future for himself.

It is at this juncture that the Chiron myth clearly becomes of value. In the original story, Chiron, accidentally wounded by a poisoned arrow, gives up his immortality for the sake of Prometheus, while Prometheus provides Chiron with an opportunity to escape from an eternity of pain. Stripped of this mythological base, *The Centaur* revolves on the ancient notion that the old order must give way to a new one—in this case, that the scientific man must succumb to the liberating imagination of the artist. Peter's dilemma is that he cannot justify his father's sacrifice merely through his works. He has already admitted to being a second-rate painter, but he can atone for his own guilt by a combination of work and faith, a faith that is present in the portrait of George Caldwell presented in the thoughts of his son. In some ways, Peter's task is to recall or recapture the real teaching of his father through nostalgia, through memory.

Perhaps it will be through the tension exerted between work and faith, between past and present, between imagination and intellect that Peter will at last be able to fashion a life without guilt over his father, a life that allows a mature growth toward personal meaning. The novel as reminiscence provides Peter with the first step toward a full maturity, however belated, in which he can truly begin the process of refashioning himself.

## Critical Context

*The Centaur*, Updike's third novel, won for him not only the National Book Award for 1964 but also serious consideration as a writer of important fiction. Despite the quibbling of the daily reviewers over what they perceived as the book's excessive ingeniousness and its confusing interweaving of classical and realistic elements, its critical stature has risen steadily with Updike's reputation. The book has been accorded various readings: Christian, mythological, pastoral, mock-epic, antipastoral. Critics have agonized over its mixed form or praised its stylistic inventiveness. Whatever the critical view of the novel, however, it is now perceived as providing Updike with a grounding for much of his later fiction. Echoes of stylistic experimentation as well as mythic overtones have characterized his work since the early 1960's.

If Updike is correct in believing that his generation was not reared on the Bible and therefore turned to the Greek stories as the source of a more meaningful past, perhaps in *The Centaur* he not only has fashioned a novel but also has opened a fruitful new way to explore the complexity and tenuousness of modern life and discovered a unique link between past and present, providing a ground for meaning that is free from the inhibiting effects of religious and political connections.

*Sources for Further Study*
Detweiler, Robert. *John Updike*, 1972.
Greiner, Donald J. *John Updike's Novels*, 1984.
Markle, Joyce B. *Fighters and Lovers: Themes in the Novels of John Updike*, 1973.
Taylor, Larry E. *Pastoral and Anti-Pastoral Patterns in John Updike's Fiction*, 1971.
Uphaus, Suzanne Henning. *John Updike*, 1980.

*Charles L. P. Silet*

# THE CHANEYSVILLE INCIDENT

*Author:* David Bradley (1950-    )
*Type of plot:* Historical neorealism
*Time of plot:* The late 1970's, 1930-1965, and precolonial days to the twentieth
century
*Locale:* Philadelphia, the mountains of central Pennsylvania, and some areas
southward, near Virginia and Maryland
*First published:* 1981

> *Principal characters:*
> JOHN WASHINGTON, the narrator/protagonist, a professor of
> history and a historical scholar
> MOSES WASHINGTON, his father
> JUDITH POWELL, his best friend and the woman with whom he
> is living
> "UNCLE" JOSH (SNAKEBELLY) WHITE and
> "OLD" JACK CRAWLEY, close friends of Moses Washington
> and surrogate fathers to John Washington

### The Novel

John Washington, the protagonist of Bradley's *The Chaneysville Incident*,
is a successful young historian living in Philadelphia and teaching at a large
urban university in that city. Adept at his profession and comfortable in the
academic world, he seems to be almost a paragon of achievement, an exem-
plar of the kind of life an industrious, intelligent black man might lead in
the latter part of the twentieth century in the United States. Still, Washington is at a critical point in his life. He is becoming increasingly aware of
some compelling questions about himself and his past—questions that he
knows he has been avoiding—and he realizes that he is on the threshold of
psychic chaos which can only be controlled if he stops suppressing them.
The narrative thread of the novel involves Washington's efforts to discover
the meaning of his past, to understand the significance of his "home
ground," and to establish a spiritual foundation that will permit another person to share his existence. The course of the novel takes Washington back
toward his origins in the wilderness of the Pennsylvania mountain country,
west of Philadelphia, and concurrently, back through time in an examination
of records, documents, personal and oral histories, and geographical relics.
His search for what he suspects in the "true" self which he has kept hidden
beneath the veneer of the competent academic leads him to a series of
discoveries which enable him to grow toward a kind of maturity of
completeness. The goal of his dual journey in space and time is to become a
man who is capable of using every aspect of himself without the need to

conceal weakness, to suppress emotion, or to maintain a hard edge of coldness to resist the harder edge of hate.

As the novel begins, Washington is summoned back into the country of
his youth by the urgent message that "Old" Jack Crawley, one of the three
men who reared him, and the only one still living, is near death in a cabin
close to his old hometown. Jack Crawley and "Uncle" Josh (Snakebelly)
White were his father's best friends, and Washington does not feel ready to
consider all the implications of the lives of these three men. Nevertheless,
he knows that he cannot deny the claim of love and kinship that Jack
makes, and he begins a voyage of return which carries him into the heart of
the many mysteries that he has chosen to ignore. Essentially, his journey is a
quest for knowledge; an attempt to understand the power and composed
madness of his extraordinary father Moses Washington; to appreciate the
endurance, determination, and resignation of his mother Yvette Franklin
Stanton; to look clearly at the subtly interlocked white and black communities of his childhood; and finally, to understand the ways of the natural
world, which he has never had to face in his artificially secure academic
urbanity. As he uses the methods of the trained historian to uncover layer
upon layer of "facts," and then arrange these "facts" in a form that will
reveal meaning, Washington gradually realizes the richness of his heritage.
This becomes the true source of his strength as a man and enables him to
cultivate qualities of character that will make it possible for him to share his
life with the woman he is learning to love and to solve the mystery of his
father's suicide—to understand how it is connected to the eponymous "incident" which is the key to all the other mysteries in the novel.

The events of the novel take place between March 3 and March 12, 1979,
but they actually encompass a time frame that covers almost 250 years as
Washington travels, mentally and physically, back and forth between the
mountains and the coast. His travels are set against a background of a developing late winter storm: In this trial by elemental force, the turmoil in the
natural world parallels the chaotic strife-torn state of his psychic landscape,
and to deal with both "storms," he must demonstrate his ability to use not
only his rational intelligence, which he has developed to the detriment of his
other attributes, but also his instinctual and emotional powers, which have
previously been dormant. By the end of the book, he has come to terms
with those strengths of his father which he can share but never match and is
reconciled to the ways of Moses Washington's severe love which he has
never understood. Also, he is ready to share every part of his inner life with
Judith Powell, and in a sense, his level of maturity has gone beyond that of
his father, who could never fully trust anyone, particularly a woman.

## The Characters

John Washington is drawn by David Bradley as a contemporary black man who has been assaulted by all the forces of a racist society at its most vicious and yet has managed to survive without being turned into a cipher or a demon. Bradley's first-person narrative places the reader close to Washington's heart and directly in his mind. Perhaps in an attempt to reject forever the slander that black men are intellectually inferior, Washington's intellect is especially impressive, and he has taken advantage of his educational opportunities to develop an analytical power that can penetrate the most complex conundrum or confidently confront any intellectual adversary. Because he fears that he will lose his mental descipline if he yields to his emotional impulses, he fails to understand the complete meaning of *anything*, although he has very ably covered this up, even to himself. At first, he seems distant, self-serving, and not very likable, but his sense of fairness, morality, and ultimate decency tend to compensate for his coldness. His intense interest in all of the things of the world and his dry sense of humor make him an interesting companion for a journey, and his tremendous desire to know and understand the circumstances of his life eventually overrides his limitations and carries the reader steadily closer to him (as Judith moves closer to him) as the narration progresses. By the time that John finally decides to sacrifice all his stratagems of defense and risk his soul to make it worthy, Bradley has carefully prepared the reader to share this experience with John and to rejoice at his success.

Still, the most interesting and bizarrely heroic character in the novel is John's father, Moses Washington. "Mose," in his son's words, is an "ex-moonshiner and murderer who has taken up philosophy, eccentricity, church-cleaning, marriage and fatherhood as retirement avocations." Bradley has created this character in a conscious effort to write into American literary history a black man who is unbreakable and in most endeavors unbeatable, who is a self-taught intellectual and a veritable poet of logic, who has the physical grace of an Olympic decathlon champion and a wicked gift for ghastly humor, which he directs at every form of villainy in American life. A victim of racism, he is not a racist himself, but he feels contempt for nearly everyone who is his inferior, regardless of race. He has a very stern sense of personal justice, which he delivers, in the absence of a social justice for most black people, with Old Testament severity. He is alive with passion but bereft of love, and although his exploits seem superhuman, it is Bradley's achievement to have made them completely plausible. Moses dominates the novel and dominates his son until John finally unravels all the clues his father left—an educational legacy to make his son even stronger than he was, but in a new form for a future time. Moses' suicide at the age of seventy is finally both a defeat and a symbol of the ultimate victory of a will that must control everything.

The other characters are dwarfed by comparison, but convincing. "Old" Jack is the last survivor of previous generations, the fabled storyteller of ancient cultures who is like the storehouse of collected wisdom of his tribe. "Uncle" Josh is a kind of natural man who would thrive in a fairer world but who is not cunning or clever enough for this one. John Washington's mother is a woman who has recognized what she must do in order to accomplish her goals and has turned all her strength and intelligence to these ends. Part of Washington's real education occurs as he learns that his contempt for her is misplaced and unearned, and that she has done admirably within the limits of the society to which she was tied. The mythic "C.K." Washington, legendary leader of a band of liberated former slaves, is an example of what careful planning, calculated resistance, and an incredible sense of mission can accomplish. Judith Powell, John Washington's best (possibly only) friend, is a straightforward woman whose complexity of character could easily justify a novel itself, but who functions here as a person of love, compassion, and common sense. She cares enough about Washington to stay with him through his mean times and believes enough in him to insist on accompanying him on his quest. His reluctance to accept her as a partner is overcome by her radiant spirit and her commitment to him (sometimes undeserved), and by his eventual realization that without her, he will forever be incomplete.

### Themes and Meanings

*The Chaneysville Incident* is David Bradley's attempt to compose an epic of black American male experience, in which the hero, as in traditional epic conception, is the epitome of a struggle to define, preserve, and extoll the values and virtues of a culture. In a bold diversion from classic epic form, however, his "hero" is twofold: twice born as father and then as son, eventually becoming unified in the hero's quest. To combat and vanquish the murderous stereotype of the ignorant black man, Bradley has composed a book whose gripping narrative is intertwined, as in Herman Melville's *Moby Dick* (1851), with a kind of lore and expertise that dazzles the mind and expands the scope of the action to cosmic proportions. To challenge the slander of the black man as a figure of violence and impulsive action, his hero is a man of contemplation, reflection, and philosophical invention. To reinvigorate the powerful black myth of "soul," his hero is akin to a figure from ballads, chants, and blues, whose humanity is universal and nonracial while his experience is specifically grounded in the customs, rituals, and patterns of the black community.

The structure of the book is controlled by language, location, and a search for knowledge which will reveal a greater or more complete self. The author's perspective is that of the trained historian, just as the mind of the epic poem is a concentration of the voices of history; his method of composition resembles the historian's painstaking sifting of evidence. His goal is a test of his training. Can he go beyond all he has been taught, employing the imagination to carry him to a conclusion unreachable by even the most careful and painstaking marshaling of the facts? Can he combine the accumulated technology of refined culture with an intuitive knowledge of the natural world? Can he combine two ways of knowing, or unite two separate societies, or reconcile two warring races? The meaning of Bradley's book is that antinomies are not necessarily always polar opposites.

*Critical Context*

*The Chaneysville Incident* was David Bradley's second novel. It was, as he notes in his acknowledgments, "ten years in the making." It received the prestigious PEN/Faulkner award as the finest novel of 1981 and, as various critics have claimed, it will take its place along with such books as Ralph Ellison's *Invisible Man* (1952) as a crucial part of American literary experience.

*Sources for Further Study*
Bradley, David. "Black and American," in *Esquire*. XCVII (May, 1982), pp. 58-60.
——————. "Christmas Vigil in Altoona, PA," in *The Nation*. CCXXXVII (December, 1983), p. 699.
——————. "My Hero, Malcolm X," in *Esquire*. C (December, 1983), pp. 488-490.
——————. "Telling the Black Woman's Story," in *New York Times Magazine*. January, 1984, pp. 24-37.
Holt, P. "Interview," in *Publishers Weekly*. CCXIX (April, 1981), pp. 12-14.

*Leon Lewis*

# A CHANGE OF SKIN

*Author:* Carlos Fuentes (1928-    )
*Type of plot:* Experimental
*Time of plot:* April 11, 1965
*Locale:* Mexico City, Xochicalco, and Cholula
*First published: Cambio de piel*, 1967 (English translation, 1968)

> *Principal characters:*
> JAVIER, a Mexican would-be writer
> ELIZABETH, his wife
> FRANZ, a Czechoslovakian émigré to Mexico
> ISABEL, his young Mexican lover
> FREDDY LAMBERT, the narrator

*The Novel*

Carlos Fuentes' *A Change of Skin* is a difficult novel when judged by almost any standards. At least part of its difficulty lies in the fact that it continually frustrates the reader's expectations of what a novel should be, and of how a novel should be constructed. The average reader expects the novel to "tell a story," to recount in some intelligible way events which at least could have happened in the "real world." The reader expects the novel, in a word, to be mimetic. Yet in *A Change of Skin*, Fuentes constructs a world that is absolutely and self-reflexively fictional and then deliberately destroys this world, causing it to collapse, like the Cholula pyramid of its final scene, under the weight of its own artifice.

The story of *A Change of Skin* is fairly straightforward. Javier, a frustrated Mexican writer, and his American Jewish wife, Elizabeth, are traveling from Mexico City to Veracruz to spend a holiday. They are accompanied by Franz, a Czechoslovakian who aided in the construction of the Nazi concentration camp at Theresienstadt and then fled to Mexico after the war, and his young Mexican mistress, Isabel. After leaving Mexico City, the couples stop to see the pre-Columbian ruins at Xochicalco and then continue to Cholula to see the pyramids. Their car is sabotaged and they are forced to spend the night in Cholula. There they are joined by the ubiquitous Narrator, who has been traveling to Cholula by the more direct superhighway in the company of a group of young beatniks who refer to themselves as "the Monks." At Isabel's suggestion, the two couples visit the Cholula pyramid at midnight. Here Franz, and perhaps Elizabeth, are killed in a cave-in, or, according to another contradictory version immediately following the first, Franz is murdered in the pyramid by one of the Monks to atone for his war crimes. The survivors then return to Mexico City. The story is thus in itself fairly simple. The complications and expansions that occur in the narrative presentation of this story (which include lengthy flashbacks, insertion of extraneous newspaper accounts and other real or imagined events) prolong these events, which take place in a single day, through a dizzying 462 pages and ultimately question the objective occurrence of any of the events and characters of the story by suggesting that the entire account may merely represent a demented delusion of the mad Narrator who last appears incarcerated in the insane asylum in Cholula.

*The Characters*

The artifice characteristic of *A Change of Skin* is particularly obvious in the portrayal of its characters, who represent doubles or paired opposites in continual conflict rather than fully developed, believable personalities. Ironically, Javier is first attracted to Elizabeth because he sees her as his opposite, as a person who possesses the strength he lacks. It is only during their idyllic honeymoon in Greece that, at least in Elizabeth's later reflections, their duality is briefly transcended. Their marriage later becomes a battleground where they play out their opposition in even the most trivial of gestures. As they enter the hotel room in Cholula, Javier draws the curtains, but Elizabeth immediately opens them complaining of Javier's obsession with darkened rooms.

The fragmentation and conflict in their lives cripple Javier and Elizabeth. Javier becomes the stereotypical artist manqué, incapable of producing any work of substance. Like her husband, Elizabeth too lacks the wholeness that would enable her to create. The child she aborts stands as the tragic sign of her failure. The couple's fragmentation and alienation is further manifested in the narrative itself as it records their disjointed conversations, which often degenerate into futile monologues or impossible dialogues between people who cannot hear each other.

While Elizabeth and Javier each represent the other's opposing double, Fuentes' doubling artifice extends to the other characters as well. Isabel is clearly Elizabeth's double. Fuentes underlines this fact by duplicating their names (Isabel is the Spanish equivalent of Elizabeth). Isabel seems to represent a younger Elizabeth, a sort of alternative possibility for her life. Javier is also Franz's double, but their relationship is far more complex. On one level they are opposites since Franz represents the active strength that the passive Javier lacks. Yet on another level, the two men are almost identical. Javier himself realizes that he is another Franz; his personality is simply latent, not yet fully realized.

The doubling of characters is further complicated by the fact that the characters continually change roles within the novel, Javier becoming Isabel's lover, and Franz making love to Elizabeth. This change is only one of the innumerable "changes of skin" the characters undergo as they search for the ultimate change of skin, the rebirth that would resolve the dualities that they have come to embody.

Fuentes frequently extends his obsessive doubling of characters to include the narrator himself, who undergoes several "changes of skin" in his relationship to his protagonists. The narrator first appears as an invisible witness who observes the characters entering Cholula and describes their actions. He later appears as a character himself and participates in the lives of Elizabeth and Isabel. Indeed, much of the content of the novel consists of the retelling of incidents which the two female characters have previously related to the narrator or vice versa. The intimate nature of the information the narrator recounts and his degree of knowledge of the women's lives combine to give the narrator at least the illusion of a limited omniscience in this role. Yet by the novel's end, the narrator again shifts posture and becomes personified as Freddy Lambert, who manipulates and attempts to control the lives of the four characters who appear merely as his puppets. The narrator appears ultimately as a composite of various narrative possibilities. This shifting narrative stance underlines the artifice inherent in the act of narrating and again points self-referentially to the artificiality of the fictional construct.

### Themes and Meanings

As might be expected in a novel based on the creation of deliberate fictional artifice, the themes and meanings of *A Change of Skin* are elaborately stylized and, like the novel's characters, its themes frequently split into a number of complementary doubles. Yet the most consistently developed theme equates the novel's action with a stylized re-creation of the Quetzalcoatl myth that was at the heart of pre-Columbian Mexican religion and philosophy. In pre-Columbian thought Quetzalcoatl represented the reconciliation of opposites, the union born of opposed dualities. This union was graphically represented in his chief emblem, the Plumed Serpent. In Aztec lore the serpent was associated with matter and the earthly realm while the bird denoted the opposite realm of heaven and the spirit. As God-King of the fabulous city of Tollan, Quetzalcoatl incarnated and reconciled these warring opposites. Quetzalcoatl taught his subjects the secrets of growing maize and the arts of weaving, and of working precious gold and feathers. He taught man the sacred calendar and the rites associated with its observance. He was in short the giver of all art and culture, and his kingdom in Tollan became idealized in later Aztec thought as a sort of indigenous Eden. Yet Quetzalcoatl was ultimately defeated by his dark double Tezcatlipoca, who caused him to succumb to the temptations of the flesh. Overcome by remorse, the God-King burned himself in sacrificial flames and was reborn as the Morning Star, the unified, pure spirit triumphant.

Many elements in the initial pages of *A Change of Skin* allude directly and indirectly to the myth of Quetzalcoatl and establish this myth as the work's central motif. The very fact that the novel's opening scene is in Cholula implicitly provides a background of Quetzalcoatl's lore, because pre-Columbian Cholula was primarily a ceremonial center dedicated to Quetzalcoatl, and the pyramid complex there terminated in a single great platform erected in his honor. The conquest of Cholula undermined the Mexicans' belief in Quetzalcoatl's power to deliver them from the conquistadores and contributed to the climate of terror and paralysis that later enabled the Spaniards to defeat Montezuma in Tenochtitlán and achieve the final conquest of Mexico. Fuentes calls up all of this historical background in the novel's opening sequence as he alternates descriptions of present day Cholula as it appears to the protagonists with passages from the chronicles which describe Cortés' entry into and destruction of the city. The juxtaposition of past and present emphasizes the contrasts between Cholula's past glory and its present squalor and poverty.

As the couples visit the church of San Francisco, a morality play is being presented to the Indians massed in the atrium. The play reenacts the Fall and loss of Eden. The parallels between the Spanish conquest and the biblical expulsion from the garden are obvious. As the chorus of the morality play sings, lamenting Adam's exile from paradise, the convertible carrying the Monks arrives, its radio blaring a pop song whose lyrics keep repeating "I'll give you back your time." This initial scene establishes the novel's basic theme: the quest for the Eden of plenitude where dualities will be reconciled and man will once more attain his original spiritual unity. In terms of the principal characters, this union would free them from their roles as opposed dualities and enable them to attain the spiritual wholeness that would allow them to live meaningful lives. The novel becomes a stylized rendering of the mythological quest genre in which Quetzalcoatl symbolizes the emblematic object of desire—the resolution of duality. The journey from Mexico to Veracruz introduces the "journey-as-quest" motif and again associates pre-Columbian culture with original plenitude, for the couples' journey retraces the route of the conquest in reverse.

Yet there is a significant departure from the traditional quest model. The union of opposites that the reader has been led to expect by the constant reference to the Quetzalcoatl myth never takes place. Precisely at midnight, the traditional time for enactment of primitive rituals of sacrificial renewal, Isabel leads her companions into the heart of the Cholula pyramid. There they face a pre-Columbian frieze decorated with locusts painted in colors symbolizing life and death. The locusts represent the expected fusion of opposites, the death which is a necessary prelude to rebirth. The desired union of opposites is acted out by Franz and Javier as they struggle in front of the frieze. At this point, however, the pyramid begins to cave in and Franz and Elizabeth are entombed. After the sacrifice of Franz and Elizabeth, the reader's attention shifts to Javier and Isabel as the source of anticipated renewal. Javier realizes, however, that there is no possibility of rebirth. He will only repeat the same destructive pattern with Isabel, converting her into a new Elizabeth. Unable to endure the repetition of the cycle of destruction, he strangles Isabel with Elizabeth's shawl.

Immediately after the narration describing the cave-in and Isabel's murder, Fuentes provides an alternative version of the pyramid sequence. In this version, Franz is ritually murdered by the Monks. After his death, Elizabeth and Javier remain alienated opposites, incapable of union. The attempt to return has failed; the rituals have lost their power and paradise remains forever lost. Javier and Elizabeth simply stuff Franz's body into the trunk of the Monks' car and return to Mexico City.

*Critical Context*

*A Change of Skin* is most noteworthy as Fuentes' best-known attempt to create an antinovel, a novel diametrically opposed to the traditional realistic novel. Everything about the novel points to its artifice, to its existence as a pure literary fiction with no relationship to the "real world." The novel's almost complete chronological disjunction is one obvious mark of artifice. Fuentes' exaggerated use of flashbacks and disjointed narrative sequences continually reminds the reader that what he is reading is a "story"—an artful, fictional construct which does not in any way attempt to imitate the normal, chronological flow of events. The narrative jumps back and forth, mixing what seem to be factual accounts of Franz's youth in Czechoslovakia with accounts of Javier's youth in Mexico, Elizabeth's childhood in New York, and events of their married life. Yet these "facts" are often impossible to distinguish from the "fictions" of the characters' imaginings or the pseudofacts of the newspaper accounts that are seemingly arbitrarily interpolated.

The shifting posture of the novel's narrator and the doubling of its characters are, as has been noted, still other ways in which Fuentes deliberately points out the total artificiality, the total fictitiousness of his tale. The two alternate endings are simply the ultimate rhetorical exaggeration and constitute the final parody of rhetorical technique and subversion of the mimetic principle. The reader is left with a sort of fictional model kit providing him with a number of possible characters, motifs, narrators and endings which he must structure in order to create his own version of the novel. It is finally this demand that the reader become creator/author that distinguishes *A Change of Skin* and makes it one of the most daring of the "new novels" of contemporary fiction.

*Sources for Further Study*

Duran, Gloria. *The Archetypes of Carlos Fuentes: From Witch to*

*Androgyne*, 1980.
Faris, Wendy B. *Carlos Fuentes*, 1983.

*Shirley A. Williams*

# CHEYENNE AUTUMN

*Author:* Mari Sandoz (1896-1966)
*Type of plot:* Historical realism
*Time of plot:* 1878-1879
*Locale:* The Great Plains, from Indian Territory to the Yellowstone Country
*First published:* 1953

> *Principal characters:*
> LITTLE WOLF, one of the Old Man Chiefs of the Northern
>   Cheyenne, bearer of the Sacred Chief's bundle
> DULL KNIFE, another Old Man Chief of the Northern Chey-
>   enne; captured at Fort Robinson, Nebraska
> LITTLE FINGER NAIL, a young warrior and artist
> RED CLOUD, Chief of the Sioux
> LIEUTENANT WILLIAM P. CHASE, a soldier, friend of the
>   Cheyenne
> CAPTAIN WESSELLS, an officer guilty of Indian atrocities
> BLACK COYOTE, a renegade Cheyenne

*The Novel*

Although based on intensive research, and supplemented by notes on sources, a map, and an index, *Cheyenne Autumn* is in fact an epic novel in which Sandoz employs dialogue and other fictional devices to re-create the historical event that is her subject. The novel recounts the fifteen-hundred-mile flight of the Northern Cheyenne in 1878-1879 from the Indian Territory back to their homeland in the Yellowstone Country. After the Cheyenne surrendered to General Miles in the spring of 1877, they were promised good treatment and an agency in their north country, but those promises were immediately broken, and they were told that they must resettle in the Indian Territory, far to the south: If they did not like it there, later they could return. The Cheyenne were refused all food and supplies until they agreed to go, so the starving tribe had no choice but to agree. The Northern Cheyenne were reunited with their Southern relatives at their new reservation near Fort Reno, in the Indian Territory, but that summer they were hungry and sick with malaria. The promised supplies never arrived, and finally Dull Knife and Little Wolf decided to lead their people north to the Yellowstone. A year earlier, they had brought two hundred warriors south, but starvation and disease had reduced their ranks to barely one hundred warriors, plus women and children.

On the night of September 9, 1878, the small troop set off on foot and horseback, slipping quietly past the army sentries under the veiled moon. They were pursued by Rendlebrock's cavalry from Fort Reno, with additional troops sent from Fort Dodge to intercept them. The Dog Soldiers, or warrior society men, defended the rear and kept the stragglers moving as the tribe wended its way through settled country.

The Cheyenne held off the first army attack at Turkey Springs on September 13 and 14, even though they were outgunned and outnumbered, by following Little Wolf's strategy of choosing a narrow ravine in which to ambush the approaching soldiers and hold them off while the tribe slipped away. These constant skirmishes were particularly hard on the women and children, already weakened by starvation and disease. As the Cheyenne moved, they lived on buffalo and wild game or on horse carcasses left behind after the fights, but it was still hard for the hunters to find enough meat for three hundred people. Young warriors had to capture wild horses or raid ranch stock to replenish their exhausted mounts. In Kansas, they were repeatedly harassed by cowboys and troopers, who killed women and children, until in revenge the Cheyenne began attacking white settlers. With guns and ammunition in short supply, the Cheyenne searched for army supplies after each skirmish or else brought back guns from their raids. The women dried meat and prepared skins in their temporary camps, but sometimes even these scant supplies had to be abandoned in the haste to escape from the cavalry. Always the Cheyenne kept to ravines, creek bottoms, and washouts to avoid detection. The newspapers exaggerated the size of the Cheyenne band and invented atrocities, whipping up anti-Indian hysteria among the cattlemen and settlers.

The Cheyenne crossed Kansas quickly, striking for the valley of the Arkansas River, which they crossed on the night of September 23. Colonel Lewis bragged in Dodge City that he would "wipe out those murdering redskins or leave his body dead on the ground." At the battle of Punished Woman Creek, Little Wolf laid a clever ambush for Lewis' soldiers, which was spoiled when a young warrior became overexcited and fired too quickly, revealing the Cheyenne position. The Indians held their fire, however, until the soldiers approached, and they brought down Colonel Lewis in the battle, causing the rest of the soldiers to retreat in confusion.

As the band approached the site of the Cheyenne massacre at the Sappa, on April 23, 1875, many in Little Wolf's band recalled the deaths of their relatives three years earlier, when soldiers and buffalo hunters had butchered almost 120 women and children, clubbing infants and throwing them on the fire. As the Cheyenne returned north, they were angered by the memory of the Sappa, and they began to raid the scattered settlements for guns and horses.

For more than a month, the ragged little band had moved more than five hundred miles north, crossed two railroads, and evaded several detachments of cavalry. Then they pushed northward to the valley of the Republican River, into the Nebraska Territory, and on to the Platte. There, soldiers of

General Crook and General Miles were awaiting them, and behind them came the troops of Mauck. With the route to their Sioux relatives at Red Cloud's and Spotted Tail's agencies blocked by troops, the two old chiefs quarreled for the first time about where they should go. Dull Knife argued for the Red Cloud agency at Fort Robinson, while Little Wolf insisted that the band should continue north to the Yellowstone. The two chiefs could not agree, and the Cheyenne split that night on White Tail Creek.

Winter arrived early that year, with the fall's first blizzard coming on October 23. Major Thornburgh and his cavalry pursued Little Wolf's diminished band across the sandhills toward the Niobrara. Meanwhile, Dull Knife's band pushed west toward the Red Cloud agency at Pine Ridge. The Cheyenne were short of meat and ammunition, and winter was upon them. Dull Knife's band tried to make a last run but was surrounded at Chadron Creek during a blizzard and forced to surrender to Colonel Carlton's and Captain Johnson's soldiers. The Cheyenne were forced to turn over their ponies and weapons and march back to Fort Robinson. There Dull Knife's band was held prisoner in the army barracks, while it was decided when to send the tribe back south to the Indian Territory.

At first the Cheyenne were treated well, but they were restless in their confinement and uncertain about their future. When Dull Knife refused to move back to the southern agency, Captain Wessells locked the Cheyenne in their barracks, without food, water, or fuel, and tried to starve them into submission. On the bright, moonlit night of January 9, 1879, the Cheyenne broke out of the barracks and fled across to the White River. The weak and poorly armed Cheyenne, numbering only 130, were pursued by five companies of cavalry and many civilians, the trigger-happy troops shooting women and children wherever they were found dug in the snow for protection. By January 22, the last of the Cheyenne had been captured, with only seventy-eight remaining, many of them severely wounded. There was widespread revulsion against the Cheyenne massacre, and Captain Wessells was investigated. Dull Knife and his family escaped to the Red Cloud agency, but the experience left him a broken man.

That winter, Little Wolf had eluded the troops and pushed north with his band of Cheyenne toward the Yellowstone. The strain of the winter created dissension among the warriors. By March, Little Wolf had reached the Yellowstone, only to be surrounded by Lieutenant White Hat Clark and his troops. Little Wolf was forced to surrender to Clark on March 25, 1879, thus ending one of the most remarkable exploits in the American West. The 114 Cheyenne remaining were brought into Fort Keogh and promised an agency of their own there. The Cheyenne found it a good, safe place, but there was nothing for them to do, and many turned to drinking and gambling. After a drunken argument, Little Wolf shot his friend Thin Elk and was afterward stripped of his chief's powers. He lived on for twenty-five years, keeping to himself and going afoot to visit relatives, often alone. He finally died in 1904, remembered by a few as the chief who had led his tribe back to the Rosebud.

## The Characters

Mari Sandoz tries to be fair in her presentation of both Indian and white historical figures, though her sympathies are clearly with the Cheyenne. While not romanticizing the Cheyenne as "noble savages," she is able to view their actions from the Cheyenne cultural perspective. She manages to avoid the archetypes and clichés of Indian characterization in depicting the individual personalities of a number of the Cheyenne.

Certainly, the most admirable figures in her novel are the two Cheyenne chiefs, Little Wolf and Dull Knife, and of these two, perhaps Little Wolf is the more interesting since his fate is the more tragic. The underlying strength and integrity of his character comes through in his forbearance toward the whites and his unwillingness to engage in unnecessary violence that would risk the safety of the women and children in his tribe. He tries to keep his word and to honor his promises, even in the face of the continual failure of the army and Indian Bureau agents to honor their agreements with his tribe.

The tragic dimension of both Little Wolf and Dull Knife emerges in their depiction as the leaders of a vanishing culture and a disappearing way of life. The Cheyenne were a nomadic people whose culture and land-use patterns conflicted with the American settlement of the Great Plains. Their eventual defeat was perhaps inevitable, but they fought so bravely against such overwhelming odds that they earned the respect of many whites.

Little Wolf was a particularly shrewd and capable leader, a brilliant strategist who was able to evade a succession of cavalry attacks, even when his small band seemed hopelessly outmanned. Little Wolf's tragic fate, after his surrender, in a sense represents the tragic fate of all the Plains Indians, a once-proud, nomadic people reduced to idleness and alcoholism. Dull Knife is perhaps a less interesting figure who serves as a foil to Little Wolf, demonstrating the wisdom of Little Wolf's decision to continue pressing northward, since "the Indian never caught is the Indian never killed."

Since Sandoz' novel is narrated from the Cheyenne point of view, the white characters are not as fully developed, with the exception of several of the army officers. By far the most sympathetic of these are the young Lieutenant Chase, who gives food and clothing to the Cheyenne out of his own pockets, and Lieutenant Clark, who permits Little Wolf to surrender with dignity. Many of the other army officers are depicted as cold and ruthless men, professional "Indian haters," or the unthinking agents of a genocidal policy.

*Themes and Meanings*

In her historical novel, Mari Sandoz tries to present a factual and care-fully documented account of the fate of the Northern Cheyenne after their escape north from the Indian Territory in 1878. Her novel was extensively researched, based on numerous interviews with Cheyenne who had actually taken part in Little Wolf's flight. Her childhood was spent near the Sioux reservation at Pine Ridge, and she heard many stories of the earlier years from both Indians and whites. Her intention in writing this novel was to tell the Cheyenne story from their own point of view, to tell how land greed and broken promises reduced "a free hunting people to sullen agency sitters" within a quarter of a century. She demonstrates that the official United States Indian policy from the 1850's onward was not accommodation but extermination of the Plains Indian peoples, with the enforced confinement of survivors on designated reservations, usually on the poorest and most unproductive land. The story of the Cheyenne's resistance in attempting to preserve their tribe and culture becomes a heroic account of a brave and determined people's struggle against overwhelming odds.

*Critical Context*

*Cheyenne Autumn* is the third in a series of six books in which Mari Sandoz tells the story of the settlement of the Great Plains, from the time of the earliest fur trappers and frontiersmen to the later Indian rebellions and immigrant settlements. Her theme is the epic pageant of the Old West, with its violence, beauty, bravery, hardship, and change. Other works in this series include *Old Jules* (1935), based on the life of her father, a Swiss pio-neer in western Nebraska; *Crazy Horse: The Strange Man of the Oglalas* (1942), the story of the famous Oglala chief; and *The Buffalo Hunters: The Story of the Hide Men* (1954). *The Cattlemen of the Rio Grande Across the Far Marias* (1958) and *The Beaver Men: Spearheads of Empire* (1964) depict the history of settlement in the Old West. Of these novels, *Cheyenne Autumn* is among the most powerful, evoking an elegiac mood in its account of the heroic flight of the Northern Cheyenne back to their ancestral home. A dedicated and prolific novelist of the Nebraska frontier, Sandoz employs an honest realism to re-create the annals of Western history. Her accounts of the Indians and the white settlers attempt to present the region both as it was and as part of the enduring American myth of the Frontier West.

*Sources for Further Study*

DeMarr, Mary Jean. "Mari Sandoz," in *American Women Writers*. IV, 1982.
Stauffer, Helen. *Mari Sandoz*, 1984.
_____ . *Mari Sandoz: Story Catcher of the Plains*, 1982.

*Andrew J. Angyal*

# CHILDHOOD'S END

*Author:* Arthur C. Clarke (1917-    )
*Type of plot:* Science fiction
*Time of plot:* The imagined 1950's and the twenty-first century
*Locale:* New York City, a Pacific island, and a planet orbiting the star
    NGS 549672
*First published:* 1953

> *Principal characters:*
>     KARELLEN, an alien being of a race known as the Overlords
>     RIKKI STORMGREN, Secretary-General of the United Nations
>     JAN RODRICKS, the only human being to reach another star, as
>         a stowaway
>     GEORGE GREGGSON, a stage director
>     JEAN MORREL, his partner, the most important human being
>         alive
>     JEFFREY GREGGSON, their son, the first child to make contact
>         with the Overmind
>     JENNIFER GREGGSON, "the Poppet," their daughter, a chrysalis
>         for a new evolutionary stage

*The Novel*

   *Childhood's End* is divided into three parts, "Earth and the Overlords," "The Golden Age," and "The Last Generation." All are concerned with the relationship between humanity and the Overlords, an immensely powerful but benign race of aliens whose spaceships appear suddenly in the sky, at some time in Clarke's imagined 1950's, to bring a halt to the Cold War, the arms race, and human scientific progress simultaneously. In the three parts, however, the attitude toward the aliens changes: from fear and distrust to passive acceptance, and finally, in a quite unexpected conclusion, to an alteration in the balance of power which sends the Overlords home but also destroys Earth and ends all humanity as it is known.

   There is some suggestion that the conclusion may not have been entirely expected by the author. *Childhood's End* sprang from a short story, "Guardian Angel," published in the British science fiction magazine *New Worlds* (1950), and this earlier work centers on the main surprise at the start of the novel's second section. In brief, the first section of *Childhood's End* deals with the relationship between the Secretary-General of the United Nations, Stormgren, and the chief of the Overlords, Karellen. These two beings like and trust each other. But as the Overlords refuse to show themselves, doubt and fear grow among those human beings most discredited by the aliens: nationalists, criminals, and religious fanatics. Stormgren in the end makes his own plan to see Karellen, by a trick— and succeeds. He goes to his grave, however, without admitting what he saw. Fifty years later, when the population of Earth is judged mature enough to stand the shock, Karellen does appear. He is not, however, a "guardian angel" as the *New Worlds* title suggested, but instead a picture-book devil: gigantic in size, with horns, leather wings, and barbed tail.

This amusing climax left Clarke, one feels, with the problem of explaining why an alien creature should correspond to a human myth. The explanation hinted at near the beginning of *Childhood's End* is that the races have met before, in some prehistoric disaster kept alive in human racial memory. This theory, however, is completely superseded by later events. In part 2, and even more in part 3, it becomes clear that the Overlords are not guides but midwives, come to usher humanity not to Utopia or to scientific advance but into a metamorphosis, during which all children under ten years of age suddenly acquire psychic powers, become part of a strange galactic "Overmind," and eventually destroy both Earth and what remains of their parents in their final rejection of matter. This process is not one which the Overlords themselves will ever reach. For all their material powers, they are psychically impotent, or barren, as they themselves regretfully recognize. One could well say that, like so many creatures of folklore, the Overlords have superhuman abilities, including near immortality; yet remain ultimately pitiable, for they have no souls.

Clarke's final explanation for the diabolic shape of Karellen and his colleagues, meanwhile, is not memory but premonition. Human psychic powers in some dim way foresaw the Overlords and associated them with apocalypse. This is a clever solution but, one feels, probably an afterthought, part of a general process of expansion from short story to novel.

## The Characters

Characterization is less important in *Childhood's End* than in any other major novel one cares to name. All the characters, human and alien, share similar temperaments, which furthermore closely resemble those of the authorial voice itself. They are cool, sensible, well-meaning, rational, irritated only by folly—perhaps a little bloodless. They also do not move very far from the social patterns of the British middle classes. Thus Clarke remarks, in "The Golden Age," that discovery of reliable oral contraceptives and an infallible method of determining paternity have swept away all trace of "the Puritan aberration." Yet one cannot help observing that though George Greggson and Jean Morrel do not get married, they still take out a "contract," and do not sleep together, apparently, until this has been done. Having marriage contracts for less than a lifetime seems as far away from Puritanism as Clarke was prepared (in 1953) to go.

Similarly, though the Greggson-Morrel marriage leads to the birth of the first "superchild," and is lived in great part on a revolutionary new island commune, it still conforms closely to the standard image of house, parents, two children and nursery, with a mother mainly concerned with her children and a father quietly distracted by affairs at work. One might even say that when Clarke attempts "characterization," he falls readily into stereotype. Perhaps *Childhood's End* lends support to the suggestion, often made, that science fiction is not a literature of characters, but a literature of ideas.

*Themes and Meanings*

It is indeed possible, and profitable, to see the characters in *Childhood's End* as in a sense diagrammatic, points on a graph or chart concerned above all with attitudes toward science. In such a scheme Karellen (and the other Overlords generally) figure as the extreme case of the development of material science. Their powers are godlike: They can travel between the stars, slow down subjective time, put out the sun. Yet all these powers, it is stressed, are scientific, subject to constraints already known, predictable to if not achievable by even the science of this century. The aliens cannot, for example, exceed the speed of light; their slowing down of time is a kind of stroboscopic paralysis; their extinction of the sun is only apparent, a trick of polarized light. In short, they may appear godlike, but they are in fact only very scientifically advanced. They represent an extreme case, but also a limit: There are things they cannot do.

Jan Rodricks, by contrast, seems to represent the furthest point human beings can reach along the aliens' materialistic road. He is a product of Earth's "Golden Age"—a rather dull product, it has to be said, for human scientific progress has slowed down as if in discouragement at the aliens' evident greater capacity. Karellen indeed tells an audience of journalists at the end of part 2 that "the stars are not for Man": Human beings do not live long enough, are not clever enough, are simply not built on the right scale for stellar travel. All Rodricks can do, significantly, is stow away on an alien starship, hiding in the life-size model of a sperm whale designed for an alien museum and putting himself in a state of hibernation. Human science, like Rodricks, can be summarized briefly as a hitchhiker on the science of the aliens, limited and constrained though even that science is.

Breach of these limits is achieved in *Childhood's End* another way, and it comes about through characters who appear, by contrast with Karellen, almost ironically ordinary. The first sign of "breakthrough" occurs during a party séance which could easily be written off as a sign of human decadence, a merely sportive response to boredom. In the séance, however, one clear piece of information is recorded: Jan Rodricks asks the name of the Overlords' sun, which they have always kept secret, and gets a true answer, derived apparently from the mind of Rashaverak, another Overlord standing by. Human beings, then, can read minds. As humanity trembles on the edge of its metamorphosis, other long-rumored but never-believed powers come into being. The infant daughter of the Greggson-Morrel pair discovers telekinesis. To this the children of Earth soon add teleportation, annihilation of matter, and direct contact with the Overmind of which the Overlords (as humans ironically call them) are only servants.

Rodricks and the Overlords represent, then, a false trail, or rather a clearly delimited one. Greggson, Morrel, and their frivolous mysticism-collecting friend Boyce represent a truer development. This antithesis is, however, strongly tinged with irony, in that the three characters named are all in themselves patently weak, and also in that the metamorphosis which comes about is one that they all bitterly regret, Greggson and Morrel above all because it deprives them forever of their children, whatever ineffable and incomprehensible stage these children have themselves reached. They do, in the end, accept their community's suicide, standing in the pathetic shell of what used to be their nursery.

The question that remains is whether Clarke means to endorse what appears as a rejection of science in favor of superstition, magic, mysticism, or whatever one chooses to call it. Could it be, for example, that the whole development of the story was triggered by the need to explain rationally that first beguiling image of the "guardian angel" who was in fact a devil, of the diabolic shape with human children crooked trustingly in each arm? It has to be said that Clarke's imagination is often strikingly pictorial, with the explanation, as it were, coming along later. Strongly visual sections of this book include the dreams of Jeffrey Greggson, in which he appears to wander among the stars, the world of the Overlords seen by Jan Rodricks, and its museum exhibits, including the tableau of sperm whale and squid responsible for Rodricks' presence. *Childhood's End* at times looks like a travelogue, and the overall cohesion of such works may be limited.

Clarke nevertheless seems in this novel to be attempting a definition of science, and his point is a double one. First, he argues that contemporary rationality is still capable of immense development, and that this ought to be encouraged (above all politically). Second, he accepts that there are areas which rationality cannot at present explain, and perhaps could not at any time explain. Science as at present understood is therefore a good answer to the problems of the universe—a better one than religion, for Clarke is no fundamentalist—but not the only one. Conceivably it needs to be redefined and extended.

### Critical Context

Like many science fiction novels, *Childhood's End* could be seen as a response to the Darwinian theory of evolution. It presents the appearance of a super-race, or rather of two: the aliens, who stand in relation to humanity rather as a tiger to a cheetah or a wolf to a terrier—namely, as the same kind of thing, but bigger and better. By contrast, the metamorphosed human children stand in relation to their parents rather as *Homo sapiens* to lemurs—namely, as a development of quite another order, with language, culture, and the ability to make and use tools instead of merely possessing longer arms or better teeth. As brain is to brawn, Clarke suggests, so psychic powers could be to reason: not a development but a change. The moral must be that evolution cannot be predicted.

*Childhood's End* may also be seen as a response to astronomical discovery and the now horrifying perceived scale of the universe. As in Clarke's famous *2001: A Space Odyssey* (1968), there is a sense that human beings simply cannot cope with this except (as in *2001*) by metamorphosing. The achievement of both novels is not to reconcile fear with hope, for Clarke does not entirely succeed in doing so. He does succeed, however, in transmitting a vision of awe and wonder to his readers, to which they must in the end construct their own reactions.

*Sources for Further Study*
Olander, Joseph D., and Martin H. Greenberg, eds. *Arthur C. Clarke*, 1977.
Scholes, Robert, and Eric S. Rabkin. *Science Fiction: History, Science, Vision*, 1977.
Slusser, George E. *The Space Odysseys of Arthur C. Clarke*, 1978.

*T. A. Shippey*

# THE CHOSEN and THE PROMISE

*Author:* Chaim Potok (1929-     )
*Type of plot:* Psychological realism
*Time of plot:* From 1944 to the mid-1950's
*Locale:* Williamsburg, Crown Heights, and other locations in Brooklyn, New
    York
*First published: The Chosen,* 1967; *The Promise,* 1969

> *Principal characters:*
> REUVAN MALTER, the narrator, son of a Talmud scholar
> DAVID MALTER, his father
> REB SAUNDERS, a Hasidic rabbi
> DANNY SAUNDERS, his brilliant son
> RACHEL GORDON, the niece of a Jewish philosophy professor
> MICHAEL GORDON, her cousin
> RAV KALMAN, Reuvan's Talmud teacher

*The Novel*

   *The Chosen* introduces the reader to two vastly different Jewish cultures, existing side by side in the Williamsburg section of Brooklyn. The world of the Hasid (pious one) is one of strict Jewish Orthodoxy. Each little Hasidic sect has its own synagogue and customs; Reb Saunders is the leader of a group of Russian Hasidim who are fiercely loyal to him.

   David Malter, instructor at a yeshiva (or Jewish parochial school), represents an Orthodox Jewish culture with a strong assimilationist mentality. *The Chosen* brings both cultures together suddenly and dramatically.

   The novel opens with a baseball game and a hit by Danny Saunders into the face of the pitcher, Reuvan Malter. With shattered glasses, Reuvan is taken to Brooklyn Memorial Hospital. There, an unlikely friendship is born between the Hasid Danny and the Orthodox Reuvan. Yet Danny does not act like a Hasid. He explains to Reuvan that he is being reared in silence by his father, Reb Saunders, in preparation for the day when Danny will inherit his father's position. Danny feels trapped; for months now he has gone to a library to read outside the prescribed works. He reads Ernest Hemingway, Sigmund Freud, Charles Darwin—books, it turns out, all suggested by Reuvan's father who has been meeting Danny at the library.

   During synagogue services, Reb Saunders plays a kind of game with his son: Reb Saunders' messages usually contain deliberate errors in citing Talmud (Jewish law) scholars, about which he quizzes Danny in public. Danny has a photographic memory and rarely misses. Reb Saunders also takes a liking to Reuvan, who has a facility in mathematics; in one synagogue meeting, Reuvan catches a numerology error in Reb Saunders' message.

Reb Saunders will not speak to his son except during such public times and during teaching sessions in the Talmud. He is aware of what his son has been reading in the library and feels confusion and pain.

With the end of World War II come the revelations of the German concentration camps. The news is shocking to Reb Saunders, but he believes that it must be accepted as the will of God. For David Malter, however, the matter does not rest with God. Jews in the United States must give the slaughter meaning, and a new Jewish homeland must be built in Palestine. In response to David Malter's Zionist activities, Reb Saunders forbids his son to speak with Reuvan.

Though both Danny and Reuvan attend the same college, there is a stony silence between them. Reuvan feels hate for the Hasidic and anti-Zionist factions in the college. Then, with the birth of the new State of Israel, the anti-Zionist pressure subsides. The ban is lifted and the two friends once again speak to each other.

The focus shifts to Reb Saunders and how Danny is to tell him of his plans to become a psychologist and not the leader of the Hasidic group. Reb Saunders invites Reuvan to his study, and there he and Reuvan and Danny have the conversation that is the climax of *The Chosen*. Reb Saunders pleads with Danny for understanding through Reuvan. The old Hasid explains to Reuvan that Danny's brilliance had to be tempered by compassion, and to force that compassion he had chosen to rear his son in silence. "He suffered and learned to listen to the suffering of others. In the silence between us, he began to hear the world crying." At last, with tears, Reb Saunders turns and speaks to his son as a father, not as a teacher. The leadership of the Hasidic group will pass to Danny's younger brother, Levi, and Danny will be allowed to pursue his secular studies. It is the time of the Israeli war of liberation, and for Danny Saunders, liberation has come as well.

Reuvan finishes his rabbinate studies in an Orthodox seminary; Danny, shorn of his Hasidic earlocks and beard, earns his doctorate in psychology from Columbia University. *The Promise* continues the story of Danny and Reuvan into their twenties, the start of their professional lives.

Reuvan has met Rachel Gordon at a party. A major in English literature, she is the niece of Professor Abraham Gordon, whose work in Jewish philosophy is disdained by the Orthodox at Reuvan's school.

One day at a county fair, Reuvan and Rachel stare in horror as Professor Gordon's fourteen-year-old son Michael explodes in anger. Cheated at a game table by an old Jewish man, Michael violently denounces the Orthodox of the world who have excommunicated his father for his antisupernaturalism and his questioning the literal truth of the Bible. Michael is taken to a residential treatment center where Danny Saunders works.

In absolute contrast to Professor Gordon is Reuvan's teacher Rav

Kalman, a Holocaust survivor. He rails against the Americanized version of Judaism. Reuvan's father publishes a book that criticizes the texts of the Talmud, and Rav Kalman is quick to condemn it in print.

Michael refuses to speak, and Danny proposes a new treatment: isolation. Rav Kalman accuses Reuvan of associating with an excommunicated Jew, Abraham Gordon. Rachel and Danny fall in love.

David Malter, frail after suffering through several heart attacks, remains the bedrock of Reuvan's life. Father and son drink tea and talk late into the night. Reuvan's father attempts to help his son view the strictly Orthodox with sympathy.

There is some question whether Rav Kalman will allow Reuvan to take the rabbinical examination. Eventually he relents, and Reuvan is welcomed as a rabbi—ironically, as a teacher at the same school where Rav Kalman teaches.

Silence has forced Michael to speak. Words of love and hate for his father tumble from his lips. He loves his father yet hates him for his writings—he feels branded by the same condemnation heaped upon those controversial books. Now that Michael has spoken, healing can come.

Danny and Rachel are married, the partnership of a brilliant man, fervently religious, with a worldly-wise woman, steeped in secularism.

## The Characters

The intelligent and mysterious Danny Saunders draws the reader into *The Chosen*. The title is a reflection of the traditional Jewish conception of the chosen people but also applies specifically to Danny. He has been chosen to succeed his father as leader of the Hasidim; yet his soul reaches beyond narrow Orthodoxy to a world of secular learning. For Danny, there is a kind of resolution in *The Promise*. As Reuvan observes, Danny had been so deeply rooted in Hasidism, had his soul so deeply knit with that of his father during those years of silence and pain that he could embrace the views of others (such as Freud and Darwin) and yet retain his rootedness.

Reuvan is challenged by the new secular learning and by his own father's textual studies in the Talmud. His Orthodox world will never be the same. Reuvan seems always to be fighting: the sectarianism of the Hasidim, the anti-Zionists, the teachers who reject textual criticism. In *The Promise*, Reuvan is unable to bring his two worlds together. He refuses to accept the insights of Professor Gordon and deny the faith, but he will not adopt his teachers' methods of Talmud study and commit intellectual suicide. He will again do battle with Rav Kalman, but next time it will be on an equal footing, as a rabbi from within the school.

Rav Kalman is an angry and impatient man, passionately criticizing what passes for Judaism in the United States. He is portrayed sympathetically: He asks forgiveness of a student whom he has embarrassed, and he is concerned about Michael Gordon's health, though he writes the severest critiques of Abraham Gordon's works. He is a man whose life tradition is being threatened, and he strikes back pointedly, sarcastically.

Events in *The Promise* swirl around young Michael Gordon. He sees in Reuvan an ally. If both have been branded traitors to Orthodoxy, at least both can take solace in each other. Michael is a symbolic lightning rod to which the contradictory forces inside Reuvan and Danny are drawn.

Though women appear in both books, they are uneasily handled. Even Rachel's relationship with Reuvan and later with Danny seems out of place. Rachel enjoys James Joyce and has grown up in an atmosphere of self-determination and sophistication. She muses that it is all a bit crazy that she should fall in love with Danny Saunders. Her personality seems tacked on, not radiating from within. Love here is talked about, never felt.

Fathers and sons demonstrate the real love in the novels. If Reb Saunders' tearful explanation of why Danny was reared in silence is not wholly plausible, there is a bond of love between this father and his son that is almost palpable. In *The Promise*, Danny finds himself wanting to live up to the freedom given him by his father. Danny is fearful of making a mistake and so violating his father's blessing.

Throughout both books, Reuvan's father is the (mostly) quiet voice of reason. David Malter is not a symbol; he is a breathing man who can rage against the anti-Zionists and crumble physically under years of controversy. He keeps the Commandments, but he is not of the old Orthodox order. His gentle sympathy with Rav Kalman helps Reuvan understand his teacher's fear of the new methods of Talmud study. After Danny's wedding, David Malter reflects on Reb Saunders and the Hasidim:

> He thanked me before the others for helping him to raise Danny. . . .He is a remarkable man. . . .They are remarkable people. There is so much about them that is distasteful to me. But they are remarkable people.

### Themes and Meanings

In *The Chosen*, David Malter tells his son that man must make his own meaning. While a life span is as nothing in the universe, what a man does with that brief moment is something indeed. That is the key to the sympathetic portrayal of those who strive to uphold the Hasidic and Orthodox traditions. Their strength, their rage have counted for something on the stage of history—have made it possible for the Jews to have a history at all. Meaning comes less in heroic choices than in the choices of ordinary life, about one's history and tradition, about faith and love. It is in those who have chosen to make their own meaning that the promise is realized. Yet for Chaim Potok, the creation of meaning is not *ex nihilo*; it comes as a life is able to encompass its past as well as its present.

Silence plays a significant role in these novels. In the silence of Reb

Saunders, the cry of the soul can be heard. In the silence of Danny's treatment of Michael, the voices of the soul drive Michael to burst with speech.

### Critical Context

An ordained rabbi (though not a pulpit rabbi) with a doctorate in philosophy, Chaim Potok has an unusual background for a novelist—a potential liability which he converted into an asset. While most contemporary American novelists avoid explicit engagement with ideas, Potok makes ideas come alive in the experience of his characters: Intellectual conflicts and their resolution are at the heart of his fiction.

*The Chosen*, Potok's first novel, was published when he was almost forty. It was a spectacular success, with sales of several hundred thousand copies in hardback and several million in paperback, and it remains his most popular book. (A film version of the novel appeared in 1982.) Its sequel, *The Promise*, was also a best-seller, and the two books are often read and taught together.

In *The Chosen* and *The Promise*, with their story of an Orthodox Jewish community in modern-day Brooklyn, Potok introduced countless readers to a fascinating new territory for fiction, at once distinctive and universal in its appeal. Both books are clumsy at times—Potok was still learning his craft—yet these flaws are transcended by the storytelling power and the intellectual passion that have made him a widely known and important novelist.

### Source for Further Study

Hochman, Baruch. "The Jewish Vogue," in *Commentary*. XLIV (September, 1967), pp. 107-108.

*Dan Barnett*

# CHRONICLE OF A DEATH FORETOLD

*Author:* Gabriel García Márquez (1928-    )
*Type of plot:* Mystery
*Time of plot:* Early twentieth century
*Locale:* An unnamed Colombian village on the coast of Caribbean
*First published: Crónica de una muerte anunciada*, 1981 (English translation, 1982)

*Principal characters:*
THE NARRATOR
SANTIAGO NASAR, the murder victim
CRISTO BEDOYA, his best friend and closest companion
ANGELA VICARIO, the bride whose loss of honor is avenged upon Nasar
PEDRO and
PABLO VICARIO, her brothers, identical twins, who murder Nasar
BAYARDO SAN ROMÁN, the groom who returns his bride to her parents when he discovers that she is not a virgin

## The Novel

The "chronicle" of the title is the attempt by the narrator to piece together events leading up to the murder of Santiago Nasar by Pedro and Pablo Vicario. He does so by drawing on his own memories as well as on the accounts of those who witnessed the murder and whom he sought out twenty-seven years after the event. Thus, the novel bears many of the trappings of a murder mystery, but it is hardly a conventional representative of that genre: The murderers had announced their intentions to everyone they met for hours before the event. What the narrator, and indeed all the characters need to learn, is how a murder so publicly announced could have occurred, with so many well-meaning people doing nothing to stop the Vicario brothers, who had little heart for carrying out the deed and who, by their open announcements, were in effect asking to be stopped.

As the novel begins, the narrator recounts Nasar's waking about an hour before his death and telling his mother his dream of walking in a drizzle through a timber forest. Although she is a renowned interpreter of dreams, she fails to recognize the ominous foreboding of death. Her failure is the first of many to come, culminating in her barring the door through which Nasar is about to escape from his attackers, when she hears the crowd approaching at the end of the novel, thinking her son already safe inside the house.

The narrator's reconstruction of the events of that morning is complicated by the varying accounts of people's whereabouts, their awareness of the brothers' intentions, and their feelings toward Nasar. They cannot even agree on the weather that morning, whether it was radiantly pleasant or oppressively funereal. The narrator objectively records all details, scarcely weighing them for consistency or import, possibly because he is attempting a purely journalistic account, and possibly because he resembles his mother in the way, as he notes, "she is accustomed to noting . . . superfluous detail when she wants to get to the heart of the matter."

Nasar is murdered by the Vicario brothers to avenge their sister Angela's dishonor. She had married Bayardo San Román the previous day, but after a day and a night of extravagant feasting by the village, the groom discovers that his bride is not a virgin and returns her to her home. Her mother beats her, and upon questioning by her brothers, Angela Vicario identifies Santiago Nasar as her "perpetrator." Their duty is clear. They take two of the knives they use in their trade of slaughtering pigs, sharpen them at another butcher's shop, then wait in Clothilda Armenta's milk shop, from which they can watch Nasar's bedroom window, until he goes out to see the bishop who is to come and bless the village. They carry out their simple plan, to butcher Nasar at his front door, and profoundly change the lives of everyone who has gathered to watch.

## The Characters

There is little attempt to represent the deep psychological dimensions of the characters, as has been prevalent in the novel in English since Henry James and Virginia Woolf. The characters are rather ingredients in Gabriel García Márquez' so-called Magical Realism, a Latin American offshoot of Surrealism, in which the fantastic is ordinary. These characters are like flowers in a small garden so exotic that the observer is astonished almost beyond understanding; they are more the inhabitants of folktale, myth, and legend, than of the twentieth century.

Even the narrator remains oddly unknowable, though he is clearly García Márquez' fictive alter ego (he tells how he proposed to his wife Mercedes, for example, and mentions her sister and aunt by name). He is a sort of wide-eyed, baffled observer, a student visiting home during the period of the novel, who simply likes his fellow villagers so much that he cannot find any wickedness in them—the forgivable sins of lust and drunkenness, perhaps, but not the malice that could produce the unthinkable murder of one of their own citizens in broad daylight, with practically the whole village as witnesses.

What the characters lack in psychological shading, they make up for in abundance of color. The groom Bayardo San Román arrived in town with silver decorating his saddlebags, belt, and boots, looking for someone to marry. He had "the waist of a novice bullfighter, golden eyes, and a skin slowly roasted by saltpeter." Magdelena Oliver could not take her eyes off him and told the narrator that she "could have buttered him and eaten him alive." He could swim faster, drink longer, and fight better than any man in town, and was far richer than any of them; every woman in town would have married him, except for the girl he wanted at first sight: Angela Vicario. He bought all the raffle tickets to win a music box for her, then bought the best house in town for her, though it was not for sale. (The sight of all the money he put on the table ultimately killed the owner.)

Bayardo's character may justly be said to be flat because he is little more than a vehicle for machismo, but such a stylistic choice enables García Márquez to portray his characters as victims trapped by the prevailing codes of their lives, as outmoded as they may be judged, which leads directly to the absurd murder of Nasar because he violated Angela, although no one is ever sure that he was guilty. Indeed, the reader will not find the characters divisible into categories of major and minor, but only find those who appear more often and those who appear less, and all contribute to the unlikelihood of the central action. Magdelena Oliver, who first reacts to Bayardo's male beauty, appears but once, and her comment stands not as her own opinion but as the ultimate consensus of the village. It is as though the village itself were the main character of the novel, speaking with many voices; in this reading, the murder itself becomes a ritualistic, cammunal suicide in which the forty-two characters who are named in the novel (and many more of their brothers and sisters and cousins) are helpless participants.

Thus, of the murdered man and the woman he allegedly wronged, the reader learns little more than of thc characters on the perimeter of the central drama: The lesser characters serve as a kind of moral reflection of the central ones. There is Maria Alejandrina Cervantes, for example, the elegant, serviceable woman who never sleeps and who, as the narrator attests, "did away with my generation's virginity," including that of Nasar, who dies for a crime that for the woman is a vocation.

Nasar is a fairly affluent young man, inclined to womanizing and drinking with friends. He dies not so much because his guilt is established, but because he is typical and therefore able to be presumed guilty. His public execution at the end of the novel is described as in slow motion and in precise detail, in more detail than any aspect of his life, because his death more profoundly affects the village than his life could. Until he dies, the characters are locked into the modes of action that will produce his death. Once that is accomplished, they are freed to pursue their individual lives again, though this time, haunted by a terrible memory.

*Themes and Meanings*

Where García Márquez' highly regarded novel *Cien años de soledad*

(1967; *One Hundred Years of Solitude*, 1970) has the large, episodic scope of a Greek epic, *Chronicle of a Death Foretold* has the concise brevity of Greek tragedy, and it shares with tragedy the theme of guilt and its purging through recognition of the truth:

> For years we couldn't talk about anything else. Our daily conduct, dominated then by so many linear habits, had suddenly begun to spin around a common anxiety. The cocks of dawn would catch us trying to give order to the chain of many chance events that had made absurdity possible, and it was obvious that we weren't doing it from an urge to clear up mysteries but because none of us could go on living without an exact knowledge of the place and the mission assigned to us by fate.

At the political level, the book is an allegory for tyranny made possible through uncritical obedience to established codes: No one is able to step out of the accustomed modes of behavior to stop the murderers. Indeed, the attempts to purge guilt through recognition meander through the inexactitudes of memory toward self-justification offered in terms of the original misjudgments that allowed the murder to take place. It takes place over and over, in the varying accounts of witnesses, in the narrator's conclusion, in the villagers' memories, and since no one has learned what is necessary to prevent its recurrence, it will continue to be obsessively replayed as ritual and as a mystery to which no solution can be found.

Most of the characters reason that affairs of honor exclude all but those involved, a circular logic that admits no intervention. The fictional narrative, however, points to a very active involvement by supposed bystanders. For example, Nasar's maid, Victoria Guzmán, wakens him as ordered at 5:30 in the morning but fails to warn him because she pays no heed to what she considers drunken boasts. In fact, Nasar had asked her to send her daughter Divina Flor, a nubile girl whom Nasar has repeatedly manhandled, to wake him, but Guzmán herself had suffered the advances of Nasar's father, and so goes in her daughter's place. While Nasar eats breakfast, she disembowels rabbits before him and throws the entrails to the dogs; at the end of the novel, Nasar's mother orders the dogs to be killed as they howl for his intestines. Though the narrator does not draw a conclusion, evidence is strewn through the book that Guzmán would sooner see Nasar dead than have him repeat his father's conquest and that she maliciously withholds the warning that would easily save his life. Her righteous disregard of drunken boasts plays into her maternal instinct and her secret loathing of her helplessness. While she cannot act on feelings she scarcely acknowledges, her inaction in not warning Nasar is fatally effective.

García Márquez challenges the reader to look more deeply than does the narrator at the pattern of chance that produces fate. The reader is prompted to reconsider the excuses, denials, and self-justifications that blind the narrator, who seeks through his chronicle of superfluous information to understand how a death so foretold could be allowed to take place.

*Critical Context*

Because many characters reappear in his works, because many of the works are set in Macondo (unnamed here, but recognizable as the fictional counterpart of his birthplace, Aracataca), and because of the persistently fabulous nature of his Magical Realism, García Márquez' novels and short stories may be said to constitute one grand fiction, of which *Chronicle of a Death Foretold* is a significant part.

García Márquez' treatment of isolation and solitude in previous work extends to this novel. Macondo's search for a way inland to other villages in *One Hundred Years of Solitude* is ended here with the coming of the railroad, on which many of the characters will leave following the murder. The novel also is linked by contrast with the short story "El ahogado más hermoso del mundo" (1972; "The Handsomest Drowned Man in the World," 1972), in which a drowned man is taken in by the inhabitants of a stagnant town after he washes up on shore, becoming a source of community pride. Care for the drowned man removes the villagers from their individual and collective solitude, as contrarily the community's witnessing the death of Nasar jolts its members out of their "linear habits" and into an obsession with their guilt. Where in *El otoño del patriarca* (1975; *The Autumn of the Patriarch*, 1975) the aging dictator is isolated by his tyrannical power, here the villagers are cut off from one another by their failure to use their power to prevent Nasar's death.

In interviews, García Márquez has often equated his fiction with journalism (he began his career as a journalist in 1948) and has said that the fantastic elements in his work are merely the reality of Latin America, faithfully transcribed. In *Chronicle of a Death Foretold*, he has written an investigative report of the circumstances of a murder. Yet he turns the genre of the mystery novel inside out in order to create his own convoluted, cyclical form of storytelling. It begins when the victim rises and ends one hour later with his death, but in between the narrator retraces the impossible labyrinth of circumstances and chance and the unwinding of its terrible consequences. Thus, the artist triumphs over the journalist, as García Márquez' humanity prevails in the foolish beauty of his unfortunates, and in their resilient good nature that struggles with fate to an outcome somewhat better than a draw.

*Sources for Further Study*

Buford, Bill. "Haughty Falconry and Collective Guilt," in *The Times Literary Supplement*. September 10, 1982, p. 965.
Gass, William. "More Deaths than One," in *New York*. XVI (April 11, 1983), pp. 83-84.

Rabassa, Gregory. "García Márquez's New Book: Literature or Journalism?" in *World Literature Today*. LVI (Winter, 1982), pp. 48-51.
Rodman, Seldon. "Triumph of the Artist," in *The New Leader*. X (May 16, 1983), pp. 16-17.
Rushdie, Salman. "Angel Gabriel," in *London Review of Books*. September 16, 1982, pp. 3-4.

*Robert Bensen*

# THE CITY AND THE PILLAR

*Author:* Gore Vidal (1925-    )
*Type of plot:* Social criticism
*Time of plot:* The late 1930's to the mid-1940's
*Locale:* Rural Virginia, Seattle, Beverly Hills, New Orleans, the Yucatán, and
    New York City
*First published:* 1948

> *Principal characters:*
> JIM WILLARD, a homosexual youth
> BOB FORD, his first lover
> RONALD SHAW, a Hollywood screen idol
> PAUL SULLIVAN, a disillusioned young writer
> MARIA VERLAINE, a rich, lonely friend of Paul Sullivan

*The Novel*

The subject of *The City and the Pillar* is Jim Willard's coming of age. The novel is an *Entwicklungsroman* reminiscent in some respects of Jean-Jacques Rousseau's *Émile: Ou, De l'éducation* (1762; *Emilius and Sophia: Or, A New System of Education*, 1762-1763) or Roger Martin du Gard's *Jean Barois* (1913; English translation, 1949). The crucial difference in *The City and the Pillar*, however, is that Jim Willard is homosexual, and the novel focuses on his growing sexual awareness, on his first sexual encounter, and on his leading a homosexual existence in a heterosexual world.

The book uses a frame technique. The protagonist is first introduced as he sits in a bar where he has been drinking for several hours. The last chapter of the book takes up where the first chapter left off, and the rest of the plot is developed through flashbacks which encompass Jim's life from age seventeen until now, when he is in his mid-twenties. In the course of the book, Vidal traces Jim's progress from small-town rural Virginia to Seattle, Beverly Hills, New Orleans, the Yucatán, and New York, where he has arranged a reunion with Bob Ford, his first lover.

Jim finds expression for his budding sexuality during a weekend that he spends in an isolated cabin with Bob Ford, a year his senior. The two fall into a sexual relationship spontaneously and naturally in the course of the weekend. Vidal portrays Jim not as the kind of homosexual whom most people would have thought prototypical in the 1940's, but rather as a quite virile, athletic type much like anyone else except for his homosexuality.

Jim does not get along with his parents, and as soon as he finishes high school, he leaves home and ships out as a cabin boy. When the ship lays over in Seattle, one of Jim's more worldly crew mates takes him to a prostitute. Jim is intrigued at first but then is repulsed by the female body, and he flees in such a state of embarrassment that he is unable to return to his ship and face his friends. Instead, he goes to Beverly Hills as a tennis coach at an exclusive hotel. Jim is invited to a party at the palatial home of Ronald Shaw, a film idol, who takes Jim in to live with him. The two have a prolonged affair.

When his affair with Shaw ends, Jim becomes the lover of Paul Sullivan, a writer who is attracted by Jim's masculine appearance and demeanor. The two have an affair, during which Jim comes more to grips with the idea of loving a man, something that he had considered unnatural in his relationship with Ronald Shaw.

When the two run into Maria Verlaine, a rich and sophisticated friend of Paul in New Orleans, she invites the two of them to go to the Yucatán with her. They accept, and Maria tries to involve Jim in an affair with her. Jim cannot respond, but the incident provides Paul, who is masochistic, with an opportunity to play the wounded one, which he enjoys. For his part, Jim is convinced, after his experience with Maria, that he is not like other men and that his homosexuality is ingrained to the point that he will never be rid of it.

With the entrance of the United States into World War II, Jim enlists in the army and Paul becomes a foreign correspondent. The two are separated. Jim, who does not like army life, becomes a physical training instructor but soon is mustered out because of arthritis.

Jim has learned still more about his sexual nature during his time in the army. Throughout his years of wandering, Jim has thought constantly about Bob Ford, his first lover. Before his discharge, while lying ill in an army hospital, Jim writes to each of the people with whom he has been involved: Bob Ford, Ronald Shaw, Paul Sullivan, and Maria Verlaine. Vidal relates the effect of Jim's letters on each person who receives one.

Significantly, Bob Ford's letter from Jim arrives on the day Bob is to be married to his childhood sweetheart. Bob is slightly discomfited by Jim's letter, which proposes that they meet in New York. He marries, however, and soon puts Jim and the letter from his mind. Bob does not answer Jim's letter, but Jim's mother tells him that Bob has married.

After a considerable time, Jim, visiting his family in Virginia, runs into Bob. They agree to meet in New York. When this happens, they sit in Bob's hotel room reminiscing and drinking. Jim has drunk so much that Bob persuades him to stay the night. After they are in bed, Jim advances on Bob, who repulses him cruelly, saying, "What are you doing, anyway? . . . You're a queer, you're nothing but a damned queer! Go on and get your ass out of here!" The two struggle, and in his drunkenness, Jim strangles Bob, leaving him dead in the room and going to the bar in which the novel opens and closes.

Recognizing that the novel was flawed by this melodramatic conclusion,

Vidal published *The City and the Pillar Revised* (1965), in which he tightened up the style considerably, reduced the moralizing, and changed the sensational ending so that Jim forces Bob into a sexual encounter on the night they meet, after which they go their separate ways; Jim is thus free of the hold that Bob has had on him through the years.

### The Characters

In *The City and the Pillar*, Vidal was not the master of characterization that he was to become in such later novels as *Julian* (1964), *Myra Breckinridge* (1968), or *Burr* (1973). Jim Willard, as the protagonist, is more multifaceted than are the other main characters in this novel, but even he is developed more through Vidal's omniscient presentation of him rather than by a well-constructed, consistent pattern of behavior.

In Jim, Vidal shaped a homosexual protagonist who did not fit the stereotype of the times. Handsome and athletic, Jim does not consider himself homosexual until well into the book. At first, he is able to dismiss his early affair with Bob Ford as being merely the adolescent experiment that Bob later labels it when he says, "that was awful kid stuff we did." The fact that he has lingering thoughts about Bob does not strike Jim as indicative of ingrained homosexuality.

Even during his affair with Ronald Shaw, Jim continues to regard himself as essentially heterosexual—in part because he does not fall in love with Shaw. Shaw is a less rounded character than Jim. He is proud, narcissistic, and given to self-pity and melodrama, as is evident in his parting words to Jim: "I admit I've been hurt, terribly hurt by you, but I don't hold it against you; that is probably the one quality I have that you will never find in anyone else: I could always forgive."

In Paul Sullivan, Jim finds another lover who indulges in self-pity and who manipulates situations so that they end up giving him pain. Vidal writes of Paul, "Pain, emotional suffering, finally became an end in itself . . . he opened himself wide to suffering and he was not disappointed." When the two meet Maria Verlaine in New Orleans and she suggests that they go with her to the Yucatán, Paul is quite willing, foreseeing that Maria will seduce Jim, who Paul still thinks is essentially heterosexual. Thus, Paul will experience the emotional suffering that he apparently finds necessary. Maria, portrayed quite sketchily, is necessary to the development of the novel only because she precipitates Jim's realization that he is quite thoroughly homosexual.

Jim's sexual exposure during his army experience is highlighted by Sergeant Kervinski, who wants to seduce Jim and whom Jim rejects, and by a young corporal, Ken Woodrow, whom Jim wants to seduce but who rejects Jim's one advance. Although there is a clutch of fairly obvious homosexuals on the base, Jim wants nothing to do with them. Instead, "He worked out in the gymnasium a great deal. Exercise had become a sexual release."

Bob Ford represents a fairly representative heterosexual type. There is no homosexual pattern in Bob's life, and he wants to forget his one youthful night of pleasure with Jim. His extreme reaction to Jim's advances when they meet many years later is motivated by fear: To acknowledge that he was capable of enjoying a homosexual encounter, even if that is not his primary inclination, would be to undermine his socially dictated sense of identity. In his own eyes, he would become a "queer"—a deviant, something less than a man.

### Themes and Meanings

In *The City and the Pillar*, Vidal explores the inroads that experience makes upon innocence. The sexual relationship between Bob and Jim is portrayed as spontaneous and natural. As Jim's sexual sophistication increases, sexual relationships become much more complex for him. As he realizes that the encounter with Bob was, for him at least, more than merely a casual release, he is forced to face his own homosexuality.

Vidal is saying essentially that homosexuality provides a reasonable but complicated sexual option and that one need not fit the stereotype of the homosexual in order to exercise that option. When Jim rushes out of the room to which he and his crew mate, Collins, have taken the two prostitutes, he hears Collins say, just as he is leaving, "Let the queer go; don't mind him." This remark festers, and when Bob, whom Jim has idealized for seven or eight years, calls him a queer, that catapults the drunken Jim into an action that results in his killing Bob. He is also killing the idealized vision that, in his own mind if not in actuality, led him into a homosexuality that he could neither accept nor overcome.

### Critical Context

*The City and the Pillar* was published at about the time the United States was undergoing a sexual reassessment if not an all-out sexual revolution. World War II had not been over long, and the war had brought with it a relaxation of conventional morality in the country. Alfred Kinsey had published *Sexual Behavior in the Human Male* (1948) in the same year, and in early 1949, *The City and the Pillar* headed *The New York Times'* list of fiction best-sellers while Kinsey's book was the nonfiction best-seller. Truman Capote's homosexual novel, *Other Voices, Other Rooms* (1948), was also a best-selling book of the same period.

*The City and the Pillar* was the precursor of a number of other homosexually oriented works of literature, most notably James Barr's *Quatrefoil* (1950), Alberto Moravia's *La disubbidienza* (1948; *Two Adolescents*, 1950), Arthur Anderson Peters' *Finistère* (1951), James Baldwin's *Giovanni's Room* (1956), Tennessee Williams' *Cat on a Hot Tin Roof*

(1955), and Edward Albee's *The Zoo Story* (1960). Vidal helped to bring a taboo subject out of the closet, and, despite the book's obvious stylistic inadequacies and mawkish melodrama, it helped to open the whole genre of gay literature.

*Sources for Further Study*
Dick, Bernard F. *The Apostate Angel: A Critical Study of Gore Vidal*, 1974.
Kiernan, Robert F. *Gore Vidal*, 1982.
Stanton, Robert J., and Gore Vidal. *Views from a Window: Conversations with Gore Vidal*, 1980.
White, Ray Lewis. *Gore Vidal*, 1968.

*R. Baird Shuman*

# THE COLOR PURPLE

*Author:* Alice Walker (1944-    )
*Type of plot:* Epistolary realism
*Time of plot:* Approximately the 1920's through the 1940's
*Locale:* Georgia and Africa
*First published:* 1982

> *Principal characters:*
> CELIE, a poor Southern black woman
> ALBERT, her husband
> NETTIE, her sister
> SHUG, the lover of Albert and Celie
> HARPO, Celie's stepson
> SOPHIA, Harpo's wife

*The Novel*

*The Color Purple* is composed of intimate letters from the protagonist, Celie, to God and, later, to her sister Nettie. Celie is a poor, uneducated black woman, whose letters represent her poignant attempt to make sense of her often tragic life.

Celie writes her first letter as a fourteen-year-old who is being sexually abused by her father. Characteristically, her main concern is for others as she tries to protect her younger sister, Nettie, from similar abuse.

Celie is married off to an older man and thereby begins her long and painful road to eventual self-awareness and to the experience of love. Initially, however, she has precious little of either, seeing herself as others treat her: ugly, uneducated, talentless—insignificant in every way.

Celie is seen as being victimized by men and by her own passive acceptance of their treatment of her. She accepts her role as a commodity—to be used for sex, labor, or scapegoating—because she can conceive of no other life.

The example of strong women eventually changes Celie's life. The most important is Shug, a former lover of Celie's husband, who is everything that Celie is not: confident, beautiful, sensual, and, most important, independent. Shug moves in with Celie and Albert, and the awakening process begins. Celie experiences love for the first time, slowly learning to value her body, her talents, and her spirit.

Another turning point for Celie is her discovery that Albert has been withholding for years the letters written to her from Africa by her dear sister Nettie. Nettie's letters record her struggles as a missionary in Africa in terms that parallel in important ways Celie's own experience. The discovery of these letters is the catalyst for a self-actualizing anger against Albert and against the restricted life that she has passively accepted.

Celie leaves Albert to live with Shug. She realizes not only that she is loved and can love, but also that she has creative talent. She makes unique, colorful pants, especially tailored to the personality and needs of those she loves. She makes money, earns an "address" (literally and figuratively), and finds a meaning in life that she never guessed before.

Because of her own healing and growth, Celie becomes an agent for healing in the lives of others. Albert learns to treat her as a valued human being and asks her to return to him. The relationships of other couples are restored on a more accepting and affirming level. The novel ends in celebration, with the return of Nettie and her family from Africa, Celie's reunion with her own children, and a general affirmation of life and of loving relationships.

### The Characters

The reader realizes Celie's strength of character long before she herself does. Her letters demonstrate her courage, adaptability, resourcefulness, and compassion even when she sees nothing in herself but ignorance, ugliness, poverty, and insignificance. The letters also create an air of poignancy as the reader identifies with a vulnerable woman who asks so little of life, yet receives even less.

Celie's development is, for the most part, believable and engaging, if somewhat programmatic. She marvels at women who are seemingly in charge of their own lives, only slowly realizing that the same is possible for her. Her attractiveness as a character depends, however, on her remaining for the reader a rounded human being, not a coatrack on which to hang a feminist ideology.

Other women in the book are engaged in similar journeys, either as guides or as learners or as both. Shug is a larger-than-life character who embodies a sassy sensuality and independence that largely frees her from male dominance. Her life revolves around men, in a sense, but on her terms and not theirs. Shug pays a price for her independence, earning the scorn of those in society who cannot abide the person, especially the woman, who steps beyond the normal boundaries.

Shug is not, however, merely an iconoclast; she is a celebrator. She teaches Celie to take pleasure in life—in her body, in the beauty and diversity of the natural world, and in loving relationships with others (even men).

Sophia is another strong woman, returning blow for blow during her husband's futile attempts to make her "mind." Sophia is stronger than she is wise, however, and in lashing out instinctively against any attempt to demean her, she breaks herself against entrenched prejudice and dehumanization. Her initial love for Harpo dies when she discovers that sex and marriage are euphemisms for male dominance, and the end of the book finds her a recovering but permanently scarred creature.

The remaining major female character, Nettie, follows a path different from that of the others, but the end result is nearly the same. Committed to traditional religion and values, she labors idealistically for the good of an African tribe. That labor comes to nothing as traditional religion is shown to be useless in saving the tribe from destruction by white, capitalist greed. Nettie, faced with a crisis of belief, takes refuge in the possibilitics of human love much as Celie does.

Initially, men in *The Color Purple* do not fare well. They are characterized as selfish, lazy, insensitive, and abusive. Albert does not even get a name until late in the book, referred to only as Mr. _____ by Celie, symptomatic of their impersonal relationship.

Younger men are generally shown as more humane, though greatly confused as to how to relate to women. Harpo genuinely loves Sophia, but he lacks a positive model on which to base his treatment of her. Eventually he comes to understand that the great suffering in her life is partially the result of his own ignorance.

A detached assessment of the characters in *The Color Purple* might suggest that they are, as a group, a little too neat. All the women end up strong and self-actualized, all the men end up chastened and more humane. It is a testimony to the power of the book, however, that one is only occasionally aware of this neatness during the actual reading of the novel itself.

### Themes and Meanings

*The Color Purple* is Alice Walker's attempt to embody her own particular vision of black feminism in a work that transcends ideology. She is searching for a basis for living that rejects dead orthodoxies and oppressive systems and which draws its energy from what it advocates, rather than from what it condemns.

On the surface, the novel displays a typical feminist analysis: Women are oppressed by males and by their own passivity, and will end that oppression only when they bond together in affirming their own self-worth and refuse to participate in the inhumane male system.

Celie's development follows the proposed feminist pattern. First, she learns from mentors, strong women, such as Shug and Sophia, who give her insight and courage to act. Second, she experiences true love and acceptance from other women. Through being loved and valued, she learns to love and value herself. Third, she learns the value of motivating anger. Her outrage at Albert for withholding Nettie's letters enables her to break out of a lifetime of resigned suffering. Last, she learns that she has skills, that she can do things, and her making of pants becomes an expression of who she is and of what she values.

In addition, there is also a rejection of traditional religious expression, though not necessarily a rejection of God. Walker rejects God as white and male, emphasizing instead Shug's vision of a spirit in the world that seems at the same time the Spirit of God, the spirit of nature, and the spirit of humanity. This quasi-pantheistic view, intentionally ambiguous, sees celebration, wonder, enjoyment, and mutual affirmation as the proper human response to this spirit.

*The Color Purple* escapes being a narrow, political tract in fictional clothing by its humility before life. This humility derives from Celie's own and is reinforced by the device of conveying the work through her letters. Written in the vernacular used by poor, Southern blacks, the letters convey, not a self-righteous parceling out of blame and judgment on Walker's part, but a genuine, empathetic search for love and for meaning in life. The values that Celie discovers and affirms are universal ones.

### Critical Context

Known first as a promising black writer, then as a black feminist, Walker became with *The Color Purple* a writer of national reputation. The winner in 1983 of the Pulitzer Prize for Fiction and the American Book Award, the novel earned for Walker a much wider hearing than she had previously enjoyed, and in 1985, it was adapted into a highly acclaimed motion picture.

It is clear from Walker's other writings, such as *In Search of Our Mothers' Gardens: Womanist Prose* (1983), that she believes that the "stories" of women and of the oppressed have been left untold. In telling Celie's story, Walker is telling the story of many who have had no opportunity to speak for themselves. She sees this as a moral as well as an artistic mission.

*The Color Purple* is important as a book which shows black feminism as compatible with good fiction. Rather than overpowering her writing and turning it into propaganda, her vision of the world becomes a source of power and insight.

### Sources for Further Study

"Alice Walker," in *Contemporary Authors: New Revision Series*, IX, 1983. Edited by Anne Evory and Linda Metzger.

Davis, Thadious M. "Alice Walker's Celebration of Self in Southern Generations," in *The Southern Quarterly Review*. Summer, 1983, pp. 39-53.

*Daniel Taylor*

# THE COMPANY OF WOMEN

*Author:* Mary Gordon (1949-    )
*Type of plot:* Psychological chronicle
*Time of plot:* August, 1963, winter, 1969-1970, and 1977
*Locale:* Orano, a small town in western New York State, and New York City
*First published:* 1981

> *Principal characters:*
> FELICITAS TAYLOR, a bright but sheltered Catholic girl
> CHARLOTTE, her widowed mother
> FATHER CYPRIAN LEONARD, a Roman Catholic priest
> CLARE,
> ELIZABETH,
> MARY ROSE, and
> MURIEL, the rest of the "company of women" centering on
> Father Cyprian Leonard
> ROBERT CAVENDISH, a radical Columbia University political
> science professor and Felicitas' first lover

*The Novel*

   *The Company of Women* is an initiation novel that follows its characters over a fourteen-year period in three jumps. Part 1 takes place in Orano, a small town in western New York where Father Cyprian Leonard has been living almost in exile. The "company of women" has known and loved "Cyp" since 1932, when, as a member of the Paracletist order, he inaugurated a series of weekend retreats for working Catholic women. Cyprian has long since left the order, in anger over its increasing liberalization, and now substitutes for sick or vacationing parish priests, but the six women have returned for the first three weeks of every August since 1959 to be together with him again. "When they all came together, they were something." The fourteen-year-old Felicitas, whose father died when she was still a baby, is surrounded by the love of no one under fifty, as she tells herself, but she is their hope for the future and for the future of their religion as well. No one loves her more strongly than Cyprian, who wants to mold her with his own "fiercely conservative" religious ideas and with his bitter view of "the whole sewer of the modern world."

   In the long second part of the novel, Felicitas replaces one authoritarian father figure with another. It is the winter of 1969-1970, and the sheltered Felicitas, now a sophomore at Columbia University, is about to make her break. She realizes how "bankrupt" and impoverished the lives of her mother and the other women have become and what a tyrant and hypocrite Cyprian is. Predictably, perhaps, she falls in love with her bright and handsome political science professor and, after a disastrous Christmas visit to Orano, moves into his apartment—only to discover that the other two women there also started as his lovers. The men and women circling around Robert Cavendish, however, offer her the opportunity to break from her mother and the women circling around Cyprian, and the naïve Felicitas grabs it. She does not realize that she has moved from one parochial and claustrophobic world into another. After a few months, Robert tires of her—at the same time she discovers that she is pregnant. Following a long and agonizing scene in the waiting room of an illegal abortion clinic, Felicitas flees back to the security of her mother's apartment.

As in many initiation novels, the last part of *The Company of Women* offers reconciliation and resolution; the thesis and antithesis of the first two sections of the novel become the synthesis in the third section in Orano seven years later. Here, also, the relatively objective third-person narration of the first two parts gives way to a series of first-person chapters, in which the major characters describe their lives in the present of 1977. The authoritarian Cyprian, readers discover, in the greatest surprise of all, had invited the women to Orano, where Felicitas gave birth to Linda and where they are all still living. Felicitas is about to marry Leo Byrne, the stolid, silent owner of the village hardware store; she has made her peace with Cyprian, and her large extended family is living in relative peace and happiness. The novel closes with a short, sentimental monologue by Linda, who has become the company's new hope for the future.

*The Characters*

The central character in this female novel of initiation is Felicitas, who grows from a sheltered fourteen-year-old into a responsible mother and (soon) wife. Yet Felicitas has paid a price for her rebellion and return: She is about to marry a man for his "silence" and for the "shelter" he represents, and her voice in this last part is blank and strained. Like all the women in this novel, she bears scars that will never heal.

If Felicitas' changes have been painful, the transformation of Cyprian has been truly miraculous. He confesses in the last part of the novel that he failed as a priest, as his vocation failed him. "The birth of Linda brought me back to life. And for the first time I had faith, the simple faith in God. . . ." Somehow Cyprian's pride and anger have been quelled; he has been redeemed by human love. Now, near death, he forgives his enemies and loves the women around him, truly for the first time. While Felicitas loses her God, Cyprian gains his.

The other characters in the novel are neither as fully sketched nor, for that matter, as important. The company of women includes distinctive personalities—the jealous Muriel, the solid Charlotte, the light-headed Mary Rose, the businesslike Clare, and the passionate Elizabeth—but they are less important as individuals than as a group, as a company of women who, in spite of their petty fights and hatreds, prove the power of their love and friendship over the long haul.

The characters in the long middle section of the novel—which balances, like a fulcrum, the two Orano sections at either end of this fictional see-saw—are not quite complete and are always in danger of becoming caricatures. Robert Cavendish is surely one of the most despicable characters to worm his way into contemporary fiction, and his Machiavellian machinations to manipulate those around him represent the worst excesses of a troubled decade. Here is a man who says that he agonizes over Vietnam but ignores his own children, a man whose greatest interest is his own ego and for whom the 1960's provide a great escape from moral restraints and responsibilities. Still, the other people in his casual collective are hardly better: The men mouth Marxist political slogans (including one who whispers "Fidel Castro" in orgasm), while the women seem doped or mindless.

*Themes and Meanings*

If there is a central idea to this harsh and painful initiation story, it is the redeeming power of human love. Like many contemporary novelists of varied religious backgrounds, Mary Gordon posits love as an antidote to the hopelessness of modern life. Yet, unlike Protestant writers (John Updike, for example) who can freely detail humanist ideas, or Jewish writers (Bernard Malamud, Saul Bellow) who can show the mystery at the heart of the mundane, Gordon seems left with the seed but not the husk of her religious message. She is a Catholic writer for whom the traditional symbols of the Church apparently no longer work but who still believes in religious meaning. There is no genuine sexual love or eros in the book, and certainly no transcendent spiritual love (the figure of Jesus Christ is curiously absent). What Gordon is left with is the agape of Christian friendship and the religious grace that it represents. Gordon wants her readers to believe that the survival of this company of women is the most important lesson of all. After the bitterness and hatred of Cyprian in the first part, however, and the manipulative maliciousness of Robert in the second, the resolution at the end seems a little false and forced. Felicitas' passive calm at the close of the novel seems appropriate, for her own initiation into adulthood is finally unconnected to the larger theme of faith, hope, and charity that Gordon is intent on teaching her readers.

A secondary theme involves the excesses of the 1960's. In the long and basically satiric middle section of the novel, Gordon details many of the failures of that decade. While people seem vaguely concerned with social issues here, their interpersonal lives are devoid of hope or love. The freedoms of the 1960's, coupled with the tragedy of the Vietnam War, appear to have poisoned the insides of people's lives. It is not a particularly positive picture of student life in New York City in the late 1960's, and Felicitas does not learn much about herself or her times in this section of the novel.

*Critical Context*

The Company of Women is one of an ever-growing number of novels about coming of age for women in American culture. Since at least Sylvia Plath's *The Bell Jar* (1963) and Erica Jong's *Fear of Flying* (1973), readers have experienced repeatedly the problems of growing up female in America. Like those earlier novelists, Gordon's central concerns are with women and their relationships to one another and to men: the subthemes of dominance and subservience, of control and manipulation, of parenting and being a child. The only problem with *The Company of Women* is that the men are so bad that the lessons are lost. Unlike Lisa Alther's *Kinflicks* (1976) or Marilyn French's *The Women's Room* (1977), two other feminist initiation novels of the 1970's, Gordon's book presents no positive men. In the characters of Cyprian and Robert, in fact, Gordon gives the reader two identical sides of the same masculine coin: the selfish father figure whose paternal power is softened by little love or understanding. The difficulties for a woman such as Felicitas growing up in a world dominated by such men are enormous. In the end, the reader has to fall back on the friendship of the women.

Gordon's version of this initiation story is tempered by her Catholicism: This is a novel not only about growing up in American society but also about growing up Catholic and trying to hold on to something from the relics of that religion. As in her first novel, *Final Payments* (1978), Gordon is writing in the tradition of Graham Greene and Evelyn Waugh; what distinguishes this novel from the other women's novels mentioned above is the constant possibility of grace or redemption. The institution of the Church is absent in *The Company of Women*, and there is little belief in the power of some personal Jesus, but what does remain from both traditions is the notion that human beings can be transformed, as Cyprian is, by their love for one another. It is a lovely lesson, and, if it does not quite work here, where both plot and characterization seem to work against it, Mary Gordon's courage in posing such an answer to the essential meaninglessness of contemporary life has been widely praised.

*Sources for Further Study*

Giantvalley, Scott. "The Company of Women," in *Magill's Literary Annual*, 1982.
Gunton, Sharon R., and Jean C. Stine, eds. "Mary Gordon," in *Contemporary Literary Criticism*. XXII, pp. 184-188.

*David Peck*

# A CONFEDERACY OF DUNCES

*Author:* John Kennedy Toole (1937-1969)
*Type of plot:* Epic comedy
*Time of plot:* The early 1960's
*Locale:* New Orleans
*First published:* 1980

*Principal characters:*

IGNATIUS J. REILLY, the comic protagonist, an obese, self-important, failed scholar in medieval studies and commentator on the deficiencies of the modern world

IRENE REILLY, his mother, a widow and closet drinker

MYRNA MINKOFF, his erstwhile girlfriend, who has continued to remain in touch with him through letter writing, now a radical in New York City

ANGELO MANCUSO, a comic policeman in search of "suspicious characters"

CLAUDE ROBICHAUX, Mrs. Reilly's elderly suitor, worried about Communists

LANA LEE, the owner of the Night of Joy bar, a part-time pornographer

BURMA JONES, a black porter at the Night of Joy, Lana's constant critic

DARLENE, a B-girl at the Night of Joy

GUS LEVY, president of Levy Pants, Ignatius' employer

MRS. LEVY, the dissatisfied wife of Mr. Levy

MISS TRIXIE, a senile employee at Levy Pants

## The Novel

The action of *A Confederacy of Dunces* blends such disparate elements as ribald farce, sophisticated intellectual and social satire, and realistic examination of the speech and customs of ethnic New Orleans. Binding these elements together is the magnetic figure of Ignatius J. Reilly, a grossly fat, thirtyish mama's boy and failed medieval scholar who is convinced of his own genius and of the fact that "the dunces are all in confederacy against him." Ignatius is eager to condemn any product of modern culture and technology for its "offenses against taste and decency," its "lack of theology and geometry," often while he is in the act of consuming it.

As the novel begins, Ignatius, a former graduate student whose one halfhearted attempt to secure a teaching position ended in a disaster that confirmed his low opinion of the modern world, is forced to go to work by his doting, alcoholic, weak-willed, but exasperated mother, who is fed up after years of supporting his "career" as a "writer." Having caused a public disturbance in the novel's first scene because of his outlandish dress and behavior, Ignatius bellows at the investigating patrolman, Angelo Mancuso, in his pompous diction, "Is it the part of the police department to harass me when this city is a flagrant vice capital of the civilized world?" His instinct is to shift blame in every circumstance and to retreat from modernity into his ivory tower—his smelly, disordered bedroom. There he is composing, on lined Big Chief tablets at a rate of "six paragraphs monthly," what he is sure will be "a magnificent study in comparative history" exploring how, "with the breakdown of the Medieval system, the gods of Chaos, Lunacy and Bad Taste gained ascendancy." Quick to condemn disorder and bad taste in others, Ignatius never sees them in himself. He hoots at sex, marriage, a career, industrialization, the profit motive, and *American Bandstand* as gross excrescences of modern culture, but of the lot he prefers *American Bandstand*, which he watches every afternoon, chortling at its offenses in a loud voice.

Yet, as Ignatius often says, "the *rota Fortunae*, or wheel of fortune," turned against him when his mother forced him to leave his room and seek work. With his retreat cut off, he goes on the attack. He takes a job as clerk for the failing Levy Pants company. There he performs his filing duties so easily (by throwing the documents in the trash) that he has ample energy to "improve" the company in other ways, all of which glorify Ignatius. Ultimately, in one of the novel's great comic scenes, he decides to prove his talent as a revolutionary to his former girlfriend Myrna Minkoff (who is in New York advocating sexual liberation) by leading the plant's unimpressed black factory workers on a "Crusade for Moorish Dignity" against the meek office manager, Mr. Gonzalez, using a stained bedsheet as their banner. The factory workers want wage increases; Ignatius wants violence for the fun of it. His exploit results in comic failure, and, after he is fired, Fortune's wheel sinks him a notch lower; he takes a job as a hot dog vendor.

Meanwhile, two other major (and several minor) lines of action have been set in motion. His mother, Irene, has developed friendships with Patrolman Mancuso, the officer who attempted to arrest Ignatius in the novel's first scene, and Claude Robichaux, an elderly but solvent suitor who finds Communists lurking behind every chair. These new friends, to the disgust of Ignatius, who exclaims, "It's not your fate to be well treated," succeed in getting his mother out of the house for the first time in years. They take her bowling and to films and in the process gradually convince her that Ignatius is crazy and that her path to happiness is to marry Robichaux, whom her son treats with contempt, and have Ignatius put away in an insane asylum.

The other major story thread in this novel full of such traditional devices of comic plotting as parallel action, coincidence, and mistaken identity involves the Night of Joy bar, where Ignatius and his mother fled after their early brush with the law. Lana Lee, the voluptuous but mean-spirited proprietress, is running a shady operation that relies on B-girls and watered-down drinks. Business is bad, and on the side she generates cash by selling pornographic pictures of herself to schoolboys. Working in the bar are Burma Jones, a black porter whom Lana cannot fire despite his stinging diatribes because he is working for a mere twenty dollars a week to avoid a vagrancy charge, and Darlene, a pretty and good-natured but dumb blonde whose one ambition is to be an exotic dancer. Ignatius is led into the bar by a chain of circumstances on the night of Darlene's dance-act debut. The result is the novel's climax, a comic debacle that finds Ignatius lying unconscious in the street while Patrolman Mancuso, under pressure to find "suspicious characters," makes a dramatic arrest of Lana Lee on vice charges. When the story and pictures hit the morning papers, an angry and humiliated Mrs. Reilly decides that she *must* have Ignatius put away. In the novel's final scene, however, one sees Ignatius escaping to fresh adventures with the lately returned Myrna Minkoff, while the wagon coming to take him away passes by. To the end he remains resilient, unshakably convinced of his own genius and the duncehood of others.

### The Characters

Ignatius, the undefeated, stands at the center of a matrix of comic failures. These are vivid, if flat, characters who escape being mere stereotypes because of Toole's genius for telling gesture and individualized dialect. Each character has learned about defeat in his own way, yet few have submitted to it. They are almost pathetic, but not quite. Mr. Clyde, the much put-upon owner of the understaffed Paradise Vendors (and Ignatius' future employer in the hot dog business), is bitterly aware that "nobody respects a hot dog vendor," and he describes his own product containing "rubber, cereal, tripe. Who knows? I wouldn't touch one of them myself." Yet when Ignatius tries to escape without paying, after wolfing down several Paradise franks, Mr. Clyde seizes a serving fork and, pressing it against Ignatius' throat, induces him, in lieu of payment, to come to work selling weenies. Almost all of Toole's characters will seize even a mediocre opportunity if it presents itself.

When Angelo Mancuso botches his first attempt as an investigator (instead of arresting Ignatius he is egged on by accusations of being a Communist to arrest the respectable Mr. Robichaux), his disgusted sergeant sends him to search for "suspicious characters" in ludicrous costumes (for example, a T-shirt, bermuda shorts, and long red beard) and forces him to endanger health and sanity by spending whole days on stakeout in public rest rooms, but Mancuso persists and finally triumphs.

The denizens of the Night of Joy bar are equally persistent, but the efforts of its proprietress, Lana Lee, are defeated by the very dishonesty and inhumanity on which she relies in her quest for success. An object of continual satire, she complains that "business stinks," but she is rude to customers and her bar is dark, dirty, and bad smelling. She will not pay her porter, Burma Jones, enough to motivate him to clean it really properly. As the B-girl Darlene complains,

> I only work on commission for how much I get people to drink. You think that's easy? Try to get some guy to buy more than one of the kinda drinks they serve here. All water. They gotta spend ten, fifteen dollars to get any effect at all.

Darlene, the novel's purest stereotype—the dumb blonde—aspires to rise from her form of servitude by becoming an exotic dancer. She works up a clumsy strip act involving her pet parrot that contributes to the comic denouement. Jones, one of the novel's funniest and freshest characters as well as its major black voice, is as notable for his intelligent anger as for the unschooled energy of his speech. Screened behind dark glasses and clouds of cigarette smoke, Jones takes savage delight in speaking his mind against a system that exploits and cheats him. "Hey!" he says, "I'm workin in modren slavery. If I quit, I get report for being vagran. If I stay, I'm gainfully employ on a salary ain even startin to be a minimal wage." Jones's cheerful efforts at "sabotage" help to destroy the evil Lana and ultimately lead both Darlene and himself to better jobs.

Irene Reilly is another character who seems to be beaten but who refuses to submit to defeat. When Mrs. Reilly at last recognizes that the cause of her poverty and unhappiness is her own son and that her only hope for a better life is to have her "boy genius" put away and marry the dim-witted but kind Mr. Robichaux, she reluctantly but firmly decides to do so (and the novel makes clear that she has made the right choice).

The only characters who have really given up are the ones with the least reason, Gus Levy, the affluent proprietor of Levy Pants, and his wife, Mrs. Levy. Gus has given up on the pants business because his father, when he was alive, would not try any of Gus's ideas. Now that his father is dead, Gus has chosen to get revenge by running the business into the ground. Mrs. Levy has given up on her husband and turned their daughters against him because of his deliberate business failure. She is a woman of causes, but her judgment is invariably misplaced. She sees Ignatius' ill-fated "Crusade for Moorish Dignity" as the act of a "young idealist," and she condemns Gus for firing him. She also insists on attempting to rejuvenate the vividly drawn Miss Trixie, the company's senile, oldest employee. Miss Trixie, whose only wish is to retire, symbolized the present senility of Gus's company. She must be replaced if Gus is to prosper, but Mrs. Levy, congratulating herself for her insight and kindness, will not let the poor woman quit.

It takes the machinations of Ignatius, who sends a hostile letter to Levy

Pants's best customer over Gus Levy's signature, a letter that occasions a potentially disastrous lawsuit, to shake Mr. Levy out of his lethargy. He ends the novel in a newly energetic frame of mind, ready to take his business in hand.

In the end, the good characters are rewarded and the evil punished through the workings of an intricate plot whose models extend back from P. G. Wodehouse to Molière and Geoffrey Chaucer to Plautus. Toole has created a very traditional comic structure. Despite its biting satire and its modern setting, the novel is in no sense a black comedy. Positive, traditional values are exemplified through the action of characters and the unfolding coincidences of the plot.

### Themes and Meanings

Ignatius' "worldview," which he is convinced is very original, embraces such standard ideas of medievalism as Boethius' wheel of Fortune, which in Ignatius' mind excuses laziness (all failures are already determined). It also includes most of the canards of modernism. His highly ahistorical vision of the Middle Ages as "a period in which the western world had enjoyed order, tranquility, unity, and oneness with its True God and Trinity" is a sort of bastardization of the vision of the Middle Ages developed by John Ruskin, Henry Adams, and T. S. Elliot. He echoes with comic hyperbole the standard modernist sentiment that contemporary technological society (symbolized in the mind of Ignatius by the Scenicruiser ride he took to Baton Rouge to interview for a teaching job) is "the vortex of the whirlpool of despair," and he glibly identifies himself with Marcel Proust's imaginative seclusion and with Kurtz in Joseph Conrad's *Heart of Darkness* when, during that one departure from New Orleans to search for a teaching position, "he was faced with the ultimate horror"—work. The novel's central theme is the necessity of individual effort, and Ignatius exploits references to despair in modern literature as excuses to reject industrial society because that society demands what Ignatius calls "the perversion of having to GO TO WORK." He gives his fundamental laziness away when, in explaining his preference for New Orleans, he describes it as "a comfortable metropolis which has a certain apathy and stagnation which I find inoffensive."

The novel's comedy depends repeatedly on the way Ignatius will expend almost unlimited energy, ingenuity, and low cunning to protect his sloth. The book is a send-up of the intellectual self-congratulation and readiness to despair that is promoted by what Saul Bellow calls "the *Waste Land* mentality," and, by contrast, it is a celebration of the diversity and crude comic energy that even an "apathetic" city such as New Orleans can contain.

Ignatius is ultimately spared the imprisonment and humiliation that he appears to deserve because his sloth is less powerful than his instinct for self-preservation. His willingness to depart from his room, that travesty of a

Proustian monastic cell, and to face adventure and risk in a larger world, symbolically justifies his continued life at large.

*Critical Context*

The story of the way Toole's novel came before the public is a strange one, involving frustration, tragedy, and posthumous triumph. Toole completed the book in 1963, but, after extended negotiations with one publisher came to nothing in 1966, he made no further attempt to publish it. In 1969, Toole committed suicide. Eventually, through the persistence of his mother, the novel was brought to the attention of novelist Walker Percy, who secured its publication in 1980. The book became a best-seller, an almost unanimous success with critics, a nominee for the PEN/Faulkner Award, and the winner of the 1981 Pulitzer Prize.

It has been praised for its comic structure, its brilliant use of dialogue, and its evocation of the setting and language of New Orleans. Most of all, critics have found it extremely amusing. They have hailed Toole as a comic genius, comparing his work favorably to that of the greatest comic and satiric writers, including Jonathan Swift, Henry Fielding, Charles Dickens, and Miguel de Cervantes. Critics have regretted that Toole's career was so tragically short. *A Confederacy of Dunces* has been recognized as a unique comic masterpiece, a book that successfully combines high and low comedy, realism and fantasy, with irresistible high spirits and sheer narrative drive.

*Sources for Further Study*

Adams, Phoebe-Lou. Review in *The Atlantic*. CCXLVI (July, 1980), p. 86.
Brown, Richard. "Tacky Vocations," in *The Times Literary Supplement*. July 18, 1980, p. 82.
Friedman, Alan. "A Sad and Funny Story," in *The New York Times Book Review*. LXXXV (June 22, 1980), p. 7.
Gay, Phelps. *The New Republic*. CLXXXIII (July 19, 1980), pp. 34-35.

*Thomas Travisano*

# A CONFEDERATE GENERAL FROM BIG SUR

*Author:* Richard Brautigan (1935-1984)
*Type of plot:* Comic fantasy
*Time of plot:* The 1960's
*Locale:* San Francisco and Big Sur, California
*First published:* 1964

> *Principal characters:*
> JESSE, the novel's narrator and chronicler of Lee Mellon's exploits
> LEE MELLON, the protagonist and self-styled descendant of a Confederate general
> ELIZABETH, a part-time prostitute and Lee Mellon's woman
> ELAINE, Jesse's woman and mainstay
> JOHNSTON WADE, a "crazy" insurance executive whom Lee Mellon dubs "Roy Earle," the Humphrey Bogart character in the movie *High Sierra*

*The Novel*

The very title of Richard Brautigan's novel emphasizes the unusual conjunction of events, characters, and places that distinguishes much of his fiction from conventional treatments of history and society. His characters are drawn to powerful figures, such as Lee Mellon, who define their own reality; fantasy, in other words, is related as fact—primarily because, in Brautigan's view, human beings make up their lives as they go along, regardless of what the history books and common sense seem to prescribe. The results of this flaunting of realism are usually comic and ironic and in the service of the novelist's perception that reality is not nearly so stable or so reliable as serious recorders of fact would have it.

Lee Mellon, for example, claims to be from the South, although he has no trace of a Southern accent. His great-grandfather was a Confederate general, he tells the narrator, Jesse, although on their trip to the library they find no General Augustus Mellon in the history books. Jesse, who admires Lee and takes on his propensity for rewriting history, begins the book by stating that Big Sur was the twelfth Confederate state. Both characters engender a sense of history that is true to their own situation—that is, as outcasts from the dominant culture, they have picked a time and a place that suits their identities; they have seceded, so to speak, from the mainstream and fashioned a counterculture.

As befits an unconventional novel, *A Confederate General from Big Sur* has no plot; rather, it follows a series of related adventures in which Lee and Jesse drop out of society. At first, however, Lee Mellon is a character (noteworthy for the great number of teeth he has lost) whom Jesse admires from afar as "a Confederate General in ruins." Lee has no army, but he does carry on a kind of assault against the status quo by illegally tunneling into and tapping the main gas line of the Pacific Gas and Electric Company and by taking up with Susan, the daughter of the "Freezer King of Sepulveda Boulevard."

Lee Mellon's battle with society, however, does not amount to much, and he retreats to Big Sur, building his own cabin like a latter-day Henry David Thoreau (1817-1862). He is hardly a self-sufficient model, even if he does manage to live without electricity. The five-foot-one-inch ceiling of his cabin, for example, is a poor affair and reflective of his impracticality. Yet this is his charm, and he succeeds in luring Jesse to Big Sur after the latter has lost Cynthia, the woman who has kept him in San Francisco.

Much of the rest of the novel details their meager existence at Big Sur. The men are short of food, and Jesse is troubled by a melancholia relieved on occasion by Lee's energetic imagination and resourcefulness and by the appearance of two women, Elizabeth and Elaine, who (along with "Roy Earle") create a weird, momentary utopia out of a culture of scarcity.

## The Characters

Although Lee Mellon is the "hero" of the novel, he is hardly an admirable character. He can be very cruel, calling the poor, demented "Roy Earle" a crazy man and keeping him in isolation from the others. When two teenagers are caught trying to siphon gas from Lee's truck, he elaborately creates a scene in which he debates with himself and Jesse over whether he should kill them. Even though his rifle has no bullets, Lee assumes an authority that is as impressive as it is frightening. In the right time, he probably would have made a vicious soldier.

Jesse is a puzzling character. He is obviously attracted to Lee and apparently is not discouraged by his partner's slimy ethics and mangy life-style. Jesse notes Lee's low-life characteristics but never editorializes—probably because he has no firm convictions himself. He is, in a manner of speaking, in Lee's tow. He is drawn to Lee's women—especially Elizabeth, who seems to be the sanest and most truly self-sufficient character in the book.

Elizabeth works part of the year as a prostitute, so that she can live the rest of the time as she likes. She is a professional and very good at pleasing men when she is on the job. If they want her to make them uncomfortable, she obliges. When she is not employed, however, she is sensitive and decent. She is obviously a woman of considerable self-confidence who copes with a corrupt society in order to get what she wants. Her sense of proportion is what makes her stand out from the other characters.

Elaine is Jesse's substitute for Elizabeth. Elaine comes from a wealthy background and surprises Jesse with her passion for him. He is unaccustomed to being able to attract and hold a woman. She makes him feel good about himself for a while, but by the end of the novel it is clear that her erotic ministrations will not be enough to pull him out of a severe depression.

"Roy Earle," whose real name is Johnston Wade, sees in Lee Mellon the reverse image of himself. Wade has been highly successful, a good provider for his family, but his dedication to business has driven him mad. Lee, on the other hand, lives as he likes with no thought of pleasing others, although he does, in fact, often make people happy—including Wade, who takes him home, much to the outrage of his family. While in some sense Lee is good for Wade, Lee does not try to hide his mixed motivations. On the one hand, he has been direct and sympathetic in a way that Wade values; on the other hand, his objective is to get Wade's truck. Furthermore, Lee romanticizes his greed by making this insurance man into "Roy Earle," although Wade, who is fat and balding, bears not the slightest resemblance to the film star Humphrey Bogart.

## Themes and Meanings

In the figure of Lee Mellon, Richard Brautigan satirizes the myth of the self-made man. Lee is self-deluded in claiming ancestry from a Confederate general, although his conceit has an ironic truth to it in the sense that Lee, like Robert E. Lee, is ultimately a loser. He loses grandly, and he loses ridiculously. Like the causes of death listed for the Civil War generals in the section that prefaces the novel, "Attrition's Old Sweet Song," Lee Mellon has suffered many different kinds of defeat. His illusions do give him a kind of power, though, that eludes the more conventionally successful Johnston Wade. Like his putative Civil War namesake, Lee Mellon thrives in people's imaginations, regardless of the fact that he has been, by several different measures, a failure.

What Jesse ultimately makes of Mellon is not entirely clear, although he recognizes the appropriateness of their names—outlaws both, they try to transcend their shortcomings in legendary, tall tale exploits, in episodes such as the one in which they buy two alligators to rid themselves of the noisy frogs that disturb their peace. Near the end of the novel, italicized passages portray the none too heroic adventures of Private Augustus Mellon. Evidently, Jesse has come to imagine, if not to admit explicitly, the absurdity of Lee Mellon's megalomania. The terse, documentary style of these Civil War scenes are a stunningly effective rebuke to the characters' fantasies.

## Critical Context

*A Confederate General from Big Sur* has had a mixed reception. It is usually not ranked as highly as Brautigan's masterpiece, *Trout Fishing in America* (1967) because the narrative point of view is somewhat clouded. Critics admire its comic inventiveness, however, and students have remarked upon its humor even when they are hard put to explain it.

Perhaps it is the unexpectedness of the connections Brautigan makes that delights some readers and dismays others. His similes and metaphors are often literally farfetched, seemingly awkward, and therefore subversive of literary conventions: "Elaine stared at the waves that were breaking like ice cube trays out of a monk's tooth or something like that. Who knows? I don't know." The inconclusiveness of the prose, the flatness of the style, can be irritating and boring. Yet the honesty inherent in forsaking smoothness and in admitting that all metaphors are only approximations, a part of the writer's search for appropriateness, is refreshing. The question in regard to this novel is whether Brautigan has balanced the opposing principles alive in all of his work: coherence and chaos.

A considerable poet as well as a novelist, Brautigan has favored writing in short units. Nearly all of his poems and short stories are quite brief, and the chapters of his novels rarely exceed five or six pages. A Brautigan novel seldom goes beyond two hundred pages. Yet there is a significant amount of monotony in his work that is the deliberate result of a casual, nearly self-negating style: "It is important before I go any further in this military narrative to talk about the teeth of Lee Mellon. They need talking about." For a different kind of writer, the second sentence would surely be superfluous, but for a Brautigan narrator there is almost a pathetic need to state the obvious. He has been called a "sweet" and a "gentle" writer because of this modest, apologetic way of imposing upon his readers.

Coupled to his assertions of the obvious is a bitterness and irony that is quite savage. Although it is masked by the cuteness of chapter titles such as "To a Pomegranate Ending, Then 186,000 Endings Per Second," Brautigan's sensibility seems at sea in a world that is disintegrating in narratives that barely hold themselves together. Thus, *A Confederate General from Big Sur* has five different endings plus a speedup of endings "until this book is having 186,000 endings per second." His world is essentially unstable, and he constantly attacks those who think life can be counted and measured. His lists of numbers and statistics are always parodies of the real thing, since the real thing, he believes, is always falling apart faster than it can be computed.

The instability of human character is what attracts Brautigan. He argues against everything that makes life static; history immobilizes human beings and novels ought to bring life back to the living and the dead, a point made by the conjunction of past and present in his title *A Confederate General from Big Sur*. Near the beginning of the novel, Brautigan demonstrates how literature is a form of renewal. Describing a Union assault on Confederate forces, Jesse remarks, "at the instant of contact, history transformed their bodies into statues. They didn't like it, and the assault began to back up along the Orange Plank Road. What a nice name for a road." On several occasions, Jesse exhibits a superb historical imagination, placing himself precisely in the past yet, as in this instance, remaining himself. As Edward Halsey Foster puts it, "the feeling that an individual should not be understood primarily as a function of time and place, as a psychological compromise between public and private needs, but rather as a self potentially and ideally independent of history underlies Brautigan's best work." That human beings are only "potentially and ideally independent of history" is what accounts for the melancholy strain and truncated achievement of much of the author's work.

*Sources for Further Study*
Chentier, Marc. *Richard Brautigan*, 1983.
Foster, Edward Halsey. *Richard Brautigan*, 1983.
Malley, Terence. *Richard Brautigan*, 1972.
Putz, Manfred. *The Story of Identity: American Fiction of the Sixties*, 1979.
Tanner, Tony. *City of Words: American Fiction 1950-1970*, 1971.

*Carl E. Rollyson, Jr.*

# THE CONFESSIONS OF NAT TURNER

*Author:* William Styron (1925-    )
*Type of plot:* Historical fiction
*Time of plot:* The early 1800's to November, 1831
*Locale:* Jerusalem and the surrounding region of Southampton County,
    Virginia
*First published:* 1967

> *Principal characters:*
> NAT TURNER, the narrator, a black slave and preacher
> T. R. GRAY, the lawyer who records Nat's confession
> SAMUEL TURNER, the slave owner who reared Nat
> MARGARET WHITEHEAD, a young white girl who is a friend of
>     Nat
> JOSEPH TRAVIS, Nat's last owner

*The Novel*

The Confessions of Nat Turner opens and closes in the jail cell in Jerusalem, Virginia, in November, 1831, where Nat Turner, a black preacher who led an uprising of slaves against the whites of Southampton County, awaits his execution. The entire action of the novel is filtered through Nat's tortured consciousness. In his jail cell and before his trial, Nat listens to the sparse detail of the confession which he had dictated to T. R. Gray as it is read back to him. Following his trial, Nat is left alone, and the narrative takes the form of a sequence of meditative flashbacks, providing an ironic counterpoint to the crude simplicity of Gray's document as Nat reflects both on his own origins and the events which led to the uprising of August, 1831.

Born the property of Benjamin Turner, Nat enjoys a privileged position for a slave. Selected by Samuel Turner to be the object of an "experiment" in educating blacks, Nat is introduced by Turner's wife, Miss Nell, and his daughter, Louisa, to reading, arithmetic, and the Bible. Drilled in "the serpentine mysteries of the Episcopal catechism," Nat becomes "a pet, the darling, the little black jewel of Turner's Mill." When Nat is eighteen, Samuel Turner tells him of his plans for him: At twenty-one, Nat is to be sent as a carpenter to work for an architect in Richmond for four years, at the end of which time, if he is given a favorable report, he will be emancipated. Nevertheless, Samuel Turner is not able to keep this promise to Nat. With the economic decline of Virginia in general and of Turner's Mill in particular, Samuel Turner can no longer afford his "experiment" in black emancipation. Most of the Turner slaves are sold, the mill passes into receivership, and Nat becomes the slave of the Reverend Mr. Eppes, a Baptist preacher, who, according to an agreement with Samuel Turner, is to arrange for Nat's eventual emancipation. Mr. Eppes, however, does not keep to the bargain, and in his charge Nat begins a decade-long initiation into the daily degradation and dehumanization that is the reality of a slave's existence. After numerous attempts at sexual relations with Nat, whom he overworks mercilessly, Mr. Eppes sells him to slave traders.

Nat spends the next nine years as the property of Thomas Moore, an illiterate and mean-spirited farmer. It is during this period of his life that Nat comes to know Mrs. Whitehead and, more important, her ingenuous daughter Margaret, an object of both his lust and, because of his commitment to celibacy, his hatred. It is also during this time that he comes to accept his "divine mission to kill all the white people in Southampton." Using his weekly Bible class to gather followers, Nat carefully plans for the uprising. He becomes part of the Travis plantation when, after Moore's accidental death, Moore's widow marries Joseph Travis. Although Travis is a kind master, on the Sunday night that Nat's uprising begins he and those in his house are the first victims. The massacre continues, and Nat finds it progressively more difficult to maintain discipline among his followers as they get drunk both on the early successes of their campaign and on looted applejack. Nat himself seems to lose his enthusiasm for his mission after he kills Margaret Whitehead, the young girl who, in the sincerity of innocence, had always been kind to him. After the destruction of the Whitehead family, Nat silently watches another young girl escape the slaughter at the Harris plantation. This girl survives to sound the general alarm. When Nat and his followers close in on a now armed Jerusalem, they are met by mounted troops. The uprising, which had lasted three days and three nights and resulted in the death of fifty-five whites, is put down. As Nat sits in his jail cell awaiting his execution and feeling estranged from God, he realizes that the campaign was a failure.

### The Characters

The strength of this novel lies in the characterization of its central figure. Styron undertook a bold experiment when he chose to present the story of the Southampton uprising through the words and mind of Nat Turner. Although such a strategy necessarily involved the surrender of certain traditional virtues of the novel form—for example, the inherent irony and degree of objectivity provided by a multiplicity of perspectives—it also allowed Styron to involve the reader more directly in Nat's sense of himself both as a man and as something of a public figure. What is sacrificed through Styron's decision to limit himself to the single point of view is more than offset by the subtlety and detail with which Nat's inner life is rendered. By presenting Nat from within, Styron offers the reader a dramatic portrait of the conflict between Nat and the society in which he lives.

This conflict is repeatedly foreshadowed in Nat's innermost feelings and thoughts long before it manifests itself in his behavior. Even after Samuel Turner is forced to break his promise to him about his emancipation, Nat continues to be a model worker. Yet Nat begins to brood over his sense of personal and racial betrayal. Becoming more assiduously religious, he begins to identify with the vengeful prophets of the Old Testament, particularly Ezekiel, Daniel, Isaiah, and Jeremiah, as he discovers what are for him undeniable analogies between the accounts of biblical bondage and the situation of his fellow slaves.

One of the consequences of Styron's use of a single point of view as the narrative center of the novel is that the novel's other characters become one-dimensional foils who merely reflect the various stages of Nat's spiritual development. One such character is the young slave Willis, who plays a brief but significant role in Nat's life as the unwitting instrument of the epiphany which forms the spiritual center of the novel. While at Turner's Mill, Nat befriends Willis, a boy two or three years his junior. When the boys' love for each other culminates in a homosexual encounter, the eighteen-year-old Nat is so deeply ashamed that he takes Willis with him into the creek in which they had been fishing and confesses his sin to God. In this act of confession, Nat realizes his vocation; after baptizing Willis, he declares his intention to be a preacher and then baptizes himself. It is not long after this event that Samuel Turner sells Willis to a slave trader. Although bitter at the loss of his closest friend and oblivious to what the sale of Willis augurs for his own future, Nat takes solace in Samuel Turner's promise of his freedom.

The primary function of Samuel Turner and Margaret Whitehead is to provide a dramatic focus to Nat's love-hate relationship with the nobler aspect of Southern white society. Encouraged by Samuel Turner's kindness, Nat comes to think of him as a father figure. Yet this man is also the author of Nat's greatest disappointments; when Nat is sold to the slave traders by the Reverend Mr. Eppes, he is overwhelmed by a hatred for Samuel Turner in which he earnestly wishes him dead and then dismisses him from his mind "as one banishes the memory of any disgraced and downfalled prince." Margaret Whitehead, whose innocently flirtatious character is derived from the tradition of the "Southern belle," treats Nat as an intimate, expressing both her disdain for slavery and her pity for those blacks abused by their white masters. Tortured by his desire for her, the puritanical Nat is silently enraged by her pity. She, however, is unaware of the repressed sexual desire that she stirs in him, and it is her incredible naïveté that both invites a greater intimacy and perpetuates the social system that prohibits it. The scene in which Nat pursues and kills Margaret is, predictably, cast in the imagery of a sexual consummation. Yet the scene is also highly symbolic. When Nat, a black slave, runs his sword into the body of this quintessential Southern belle, he is also symbolically defiling and destroying all that Southern white society holds dear.

*Themes and Meanings*

The universal themes with which *The Confessions of Nat Turner* deals—the quest for freedom, the torment of isolation, the desire for vengeance—are cast against the backdrop of a blighted Virginia landscape and given a local context by the novel's major historical theme: the curse of slavery. Judge Jeremiah Cobb, a once prosperous merchant whose decline in fortune and health is an image of the general decline of the South, sees clearly that Virginia has become a moral and economic wasteland. In Judge Cobb's lament, the evil of slavery is the objective correlative of Virginia's spiritual sickness; now a "monstrous breeding farm" supplying slaves to Mississippi, Alabama, and Arkansas, Virginia is cursed by Cobb: "ever damned in memory be the day when poor black men in chains first trod upon thy sacred strand."

It is this dehumanizing aspect of slavery which is the principal concern of Styron's novel. Certainly, it is this aspect of slavery which is at the root of Nat's loss of his humanity, of his sense of self. The world in which he lives deprives him of his birthright, namely to be respected as a sentient and thinking human being. The true horror of slavery for Nat is that in the face of its rigid division of the world into masters and slaves, he is reduced to less than a man; Nat is regarded as a chattel, albeit a chattel highly valued by his various masters. Yet Nat himself risks losing whatever humanity may be left him when, in his understandable desire to be free of the tyranny of his white masters, he becomes a slave to the remorseless logic of his program of emancipation, and he and his followers kill not only those cruel whites who would oppose them but also the gentle, the sympathetic, and the innocent. After he murders Margaret Whitehead, Nat is struck by the brutal paradox of slavery: He must purchase freedom at the cost of his humanity. As he awaits his execution in his jail cell, he realizes that although the uprising was necessary (and he feels no remorse for it), its promise of emancipation could never have been truly fulfilled precisely because its methods were cut from the same bloody fabric of dehumanizing violence and vengeance as that in which slavery itself had been so meticulously dressed by men such as T. R. Gray.

*Critical Context*

Based on Nat Turner's slave rebellion in 1831, *The Confessions of Nat Turner*, Styron's fourth novel, was completed in 1967 and parts of it were serialized in *Partisan Review*, *The Paris Review*, *Harper's Magazine*, and *Life* before it was published by Random House in October, 1967. Although early reviews were generally favorable, in 1968 the black intellectual community published an uneven collection of essays, *William Styron's Nat Turner: Ten Black Writers Respond*, in which Styron, a white liberal Southerner, is criticized for undertaking to tell the story of a black slave, and the novel itself is, for the most part, attacked as a symptom of an unconscious white racism. In that same year, Styron's novel was awarded the Pulitzer Prize.

*The Confessions of Nat Turner* is the logical development of the interest Styron displayed in his earlier novels in the figure of the rebel-hero and the moral implications of racial tension. Also, much of Styron's journalistic writing between the publication of *Set This House on Fire* (1960), his third novel, and the appearance of *The Confessions of Nat Turner* focused on the burdens of slavery and their consequences for the blacks of the 1960's. In his fictionalized account of the 1831 uprising, Styron presents Nat's struggle to understand the significance of his life in such a way that it implicitly touches on the racial tensions of his own era and explores the spiritual and moral consequences of violence as an instrument of the self-determination of oppressed peoples of all times.

*Sources for Further Study*

Casciato, Arthur D., and James L. W. West. *Critical Essays on William Styron*, 1982.

Crane, John Kenny. *The Root of All Evil: The Thematic Unity of William Styron's Fiction*, 1984.

Friedman, Melvin J., and Irving Malin. *William Styron's The Confessions of Nat Turner: A Critical Handbook*, 1970.

Morris, Robert K., and Irving Malin. *The Achievement of William Styron*, 1975.

Ratner, Marc L. *William Styron*, 1972.

*Richard Butts*

# CONVERSATION IN THE CATHEDRAL

*Author:* Mario Vargas Llosa (1936-    )
*Type of plot:* Social and political chronicle
*Time of plot:* The late 1940's and early 1950's
*Locale:* Peru
*First published: Conversación en la catedral*, 1969 (English translation, 1975)

> *Principal characters:*
> SANTIAGO ZAVALITA, also known as "SKINNY" and
>     "SUPERBRAIN," the protagonist of the novel, first a student
>     and then a newspaper reporter
> AMBROSIO PARDO, a servant, part black, at one time chauffeur
>     for Santiago's father
> TRINIDAD LOPEZ, a revolutionary who dies in the cause
> AMALIA, a servant, later wife of Trinidad Lopez, and then of
>     Ambrosio
> DON FERMÍN, Santiago's father, a wealthy businessman
> DON CAYO BERMÚDEZ, chief of security and right-hand man
>     of Peru's dictator, General Odria
> HORTENSIA, a wealthy prostitute and Don Cayo's mistress

*The Novel*

*Conversation in the Cathedral* is an ambitious novel. An epigraph from Honoré de Balzac claims that the novel written by a true novelist represents "the private history of nations"; Vargas Llosa is presenting a "private history" of Peru. The book is long, the social canvas broad. The major interest is the Zavalita family—Don Fermín the father, Doña Zoila the mother, and the three children: Santiago, his sister Tete, and brother Sparky. A vertical picture of Peruvian society is drawn by including the servants of the Zavalita household, Ambrosio and Amalia, who end up leaving the family to work for other employers with the narration continuing to follow their lives and adventures. The structure of the novel somewhat resembles the English television series *Upstairs, Downstairs*, alternating the story line between the "masters" or wealthy bourgeoisie and the disadvantaged servants; it is not, however, quite so schematic.

Near the beginning of the novel, Santiago accidentally meets Ambrosio, and they go to The Cathedral, a café for poor people, to talk, drink beer, and catch up on each other's activities. This conversation is the most forward moment in the chronology of the novel. What follows is a narrative reenactment in detail of the events they were only able to touch upon in the conversation. In the first scene of the book the reader learns that Santiago, the protagonist, is dissatisfied with his life, believing that somewhere he has taken a wrong turn. He has a good job, a relatively happy marriage, and what appears to be a comfortable middle-class life. Six hundred pages later, the novel returns to the same point in time. The reader knows much more about Santiago, Ambrosio, and a host of other characters—the "conversation" has been fleshed out, and Santiago's problem has been vividly dramatized: Time will continue to pass without change or hope for anything different, as long as Peruvian society remains enmeshed in corruption and gross inequities.

Although the bulk of the novel is set in the past, it has a remarkable forward drive. No answers or plot endings are revealed in the opening "conversation" (Santiago becomes partly drunk, Ambrosio is reticent), and thus each convolution of the narrative comes as a surprise.

Santiago's wealthy parents want their bright son to succeed in life; they hope he will go to the Catholic University, favoring it over the state university, San Marcos, like the rest of the Lima bourgeoisie. Santiago, however, who has lost his faith and dislikes priests, goes to San Marcos and soon joins a Marxist discussion group. He becomes ashamed of his own family, although his father in particular still treats him with great consideration. The group is arrested, and his father obtains Santiago's release through his political contacts. Santiago then leaves the university and goes to work for a newspaper, *La Crónica*, having broken completely with his family.

The rest of the novel is a detailed probing of South American history and politics. This is not done through Santiago's reportorial activities—when Santiago breaks with his family, he also breaks with politics. Instead, as noted above, there is an expansion of the plot and cast of characters, with a counterpoint developing between those who are wealthy and those who are trapped in poverty. Ambrosio, Don Fermín's chauffeur, becomes the chauffeur of Don Cayo Bermudez, the Minister of Security. Don Fermín is acquainted with Don Cayo, who turns against him, depriving him of government contracts. A plot is organized against Don Cayo, not by the poor or leftists but by a coalition of wealthy landowners—including Don Fermín, who plays a significant role in the group. The plot is discovered, yet it partly succeeds—Don Cayo leaves the country. His mistress, the prostitute Hortensia, is murdered, the criminal unknown (he turns out to be Ambrosio).

The question arises, then, why has Santiago broken with his family if his father is a basically tolerant man who even plays an important role in a plot against the military dictatorship? A full and satisfying answer is never given. Partial answers are suggested—Don Fermín is opposed to Don Cayo for business, not ethical, reasons; Don Fermín tolerates the prostitutes, thugs, and corrupt politicians who saturate Peruvian politics; Don Fermín turns out to be a homosexual. None of these, however, really justifies Santiago's break, which comes to dominate the father's life, torturing him until he finally dies.

It may be significant that Santiago's break with his family coincides with his break from all politics; perhaps these two actions have the same motivation, resembling that which fueled his original attraction to Marxism and subsequent repudiation of it. He was seeking a kind of purity, an immunity from corruption. The son tries to avoid the political system entirely while the father tried to work within it, preserving what honor he could. Is the Zavalita family so permeated by corrupt values of Peruvian bourgeois society that Santiago is compelled to make a total break with the family? Vargas Llosa succeeds in dramatizing the poignancy of Santiago's dilemma, but the question receives no satisfactory answer.

## The Characters

Vargas Llosa's success with his characters is, in like manner, mixed. Many readers will have difficulty in identifying with the protagonist Santiago, especially at the beginning. He is dissatisfied with his life, he believes that it is empty, yet he is privileged and comfortably middle-class, making him something of a spoiled brat. (It is true, however, that he has found a job and made his own way without paternal assistance.) In part, Santiago attributes his discontent to his family circumstances: His father turns out to be homosexual, his mother is cold and bigoted, his brother and sister are spoiled (like himself) and vapid. As the novel proceeds, Santiago tries to come to grips with his identity and that of his family. Minor revelations occur, but they remain minor—his father has business contracts with the dictatorial government; he plays a delicate cat-and-mouse game with the Minister of Security, Don Cayo; he lends money to Hortensia, the prostitute; he is known to the underworld of pimps and prostitutes in Lima as "Golden Ball" because of his wealth and his homosexuality. Yet these revelations have a certain forced character; they are asserted by the author and lack dramatic impact or a sense of inevitability. Indeed, the father remains the most likable member of the Zavalita family. Perhaps the family milieu was too close to the author; he revolted against it but was not able to deal with it objectively.

The servant Ambrosio is more successful as a character than Santiago; he is complex and explosive, always well intentioned yet capable of great violence. Like Santiago's father, he must make his way within the corrupt dictatorial system. He becomes the chauffeur of Don Cayo, threatens peasants and compromises himself, as does Don Fermín. Like Santiago, he tries to make his way in life and establish a family. He fails, and that failure is the most moving aspect of the book.

The other characters are always interesting. Vargas Llosa is especially successful with the poorer members of his cast of characters, who come from society's "downstairs."

The driver Ludovico, who becomes a policeman, is masterfully described, as are Trifulcio and other policemen. The senators and "Odristas"—members of the ruling party—are convincingly shown as they try to further their fortunes, plotting and counterplotting against one another, jockeying for power. Vargas Llosa depicts half-breeds, Indians, and the whole problem of race in Peruvian society with sensitivity.

## Themes and Meanings

The political and social meaning of *Conversation in the Cathedral* is unambiguous: A large part of the population of the country is trapped in a system of continuous exploitation, and most individuals, no matter what their origin, must adapt to the system and themselves become exploiters if they are to survive. Vargas Llosa clearly condemns this condition, yet in the novel he holds out little hope for change—it would seem that Peru is destined to continue in its underdevelopment, in the crudity of the exploitation of the poor by the rich. It is a misnomer to call the Peruvian bourgeoisie a "middle class," for it bears few resemblances to the post-World War II middle classes in North America and Europe. Vargas Llosa has spoken of Peru's "cultural apartheid," and the monied caste considers itself apart from the world of half-breeds, Indians, and blacks; they partly resemble the Southern whites in the United States before the Civil War.

Like Santiago, Vargas Llosa revolts against the monied caste, but he sees no way out of the spiral of exploitation. As a college student Santiago goes through a Marxist phase, but he soon sees that Marxism requires a leap of faith just as large as that required by religion—and he feels no spontaneous faith within, either for religion or for Communism. He is united with the other student revolutionaries by his sense of revolt and by his rejection of the only too conspicuous, Neanderthal-like injustices of the military dictatorship. Santiago must reject Communism for the same reason that he rejects priests: Both exploit blind faith and irrational obedience. The students' Marxist discussion group has a striking similarity to that described by the Polish Nobel Prize-winner Czesław Miłosz in his book *Rodzinna Europe* (1958; *Native Realm: A Search for Self-Definition*, 1968); in both countries—Peru with Vargas Llosa, pre-World War II Poland with Miłosz—existing social injustices cried out for a remedy, almost any remedy it seemed, that would obliterate the garish abuses. After joining the Communist government, Miłosz broke with it; similarly, in 1971, at a crucial stage in his career, Vargas Llosa repudiated the Cuban revolution and founded the magazine *Libre* with other Latin American and European writers. Vargas Llosa's political credentials are impeccable—a critic of both Right and Left, he has consistently spoken out in favor of social justice. His nonfictional writings in particular are a model of fairness and clarity.

Vargas Llosa has recognized the dangers to fiction of political commitment; art can easily be sacrificed on the altar of politics. Does this happen in *Conversation in the Cathedral*? To a certain extent, perhaps, it does. The revolt of Santiago becomes a matter of principle, and is shrill. His search for a family secret or skeleton in its closet—a "vice"—does not end in any new discoveries or knowledge. The brothel scenes, Don Fermín's "secret," the mindless and rather unattractive way in which the children of the wealthy are reared, are far less shocking than the details of real exploitation as they are presented in the lives of Ambrosio, Amalia, and others. The novel has a nineteenth century, sensationalist aura that seems commercial. If the worst criticism of Peruvian society is the fact that wealthy landowners, cabinet ministers, and army officers frequent brothels, then the country might be a very happy one. The ills, however, are much deeper. Other works by Vargas Llosa, in particular his nonfiction, have addressed these ills with greater clarity than *Conversation in the Cathedral*. Also, the characters are rarely seen from the inside. The density of consciousness, thoughts, feelings, or reactions is indicated rarely; instead, unflagging varied action is the main feature of the narration, probably its strongpoint. It is somewhat mysterious that a talented novelist who wrote a baccalaureate thesis on the Modernist Rubén Darío and a doctoral thesis on Gabriel García Márquez should write a novel that is technically so old-fashioned, the book's conspicuous devices— the lack of strict chronology, the crisscrossing fragments recalling Aldous Huxley's *Eyeless in Gaza*, and the constant references to the original conversation in The Cathedral—are only the superficial paraphernalia of Modernism. If, in part at least, the novel has been successful for the wrong reasons—for its sensationalism, fast-moving subplots, and mockery of easy targets—it is nevertheless impressive, with fine characterization and an evenhanded, profound, human vision of an entire society.

*Critical Context*

After writing *Conversation in the Cathedral*, Vargas Llosa's career skyrocketed. *Conversation in the Cathedral* was a pivotal book that made him known to a broad Spanish-speaking readership. Since that time, Vargas Llosa's concept of social and political justice has deepened and become, if anything, more acute. This is most evident in his novel *Historia de Mayta* (1984; *The Real Life of Alejandro Mayta*, 1985) and essays such as "Inquest in the Andes," "A Passion for Peru," and "In Nicaragua." The novel *La guerra del fin del mundo* (1981; *The War of the End of the World*, 1984) is a major effort, a polyphonic novel almost as long as *Conversation in the Cathedral*, yet, like the earlier book, it is peculiarly old-fashioned, owing much to Honoré de Balzac and nineteenth century realism. It is conceivable that this important, famous writer, who possesses a moral vision more profound than that of almost any other American writer, still has not found the style or genre that best suits him.

*Sources for Further Study*
Crain, Jane Larkin. Review in *Saturday Review*. II (January 11, 1975), p. 26.
Lernoux, Penny. "The Latin American Disease," in *The Nation*. CCXXI (November 22, 1975), pp. 522-527.
Levine, Suzanne Jill. Review in *The New York Times Book Review*. LXXX (March 23, 1975), p. 1.
Wood, Michael. Review in *The New York Review of Books*. XXII (March 20, 1975), p. 27.
*World Literature Today*. LII (Winter, 1978). Special Vargas Llosa issue.

*John Carpenter*

# CORONATION

*Author:* José Donoso (1924-    )
*Type of plot:* Social realism/expressionism
*Time of plot:* The 1950's
*Locale:* Santiago de Chile and Valparaiso, Chile
*First published: Coronación*, 1957 (English translation, 1965)

>      *Principal characters:*
>      ANDRÉS ABALOS, the protagonist, a neurotic middled-aged,
>           self-supporting bachelor who collects walking sticks as a
>           hobby
>      MISIÁ ELISA GREY DE ABALOS, a ninety-year-old demented
>           widow who controls the lives of all around her
>      ESTELA, a young servant at the Abalos household who cares
>           primarily for Misiá Elisa; she is the object of both Andrés'
>           and Mario's love
>      MARIO, Estela's boyfriend, a delivery boy who strives to rise
>           out of his social class.
>      LOURDES, a longtime servant of the Abalos family
>      ROSARIO, a longtime cook of the Abalos family

*The Novel*

Most of the action of the novel takes place in the Abalos mansion, occupied by Misiá Elisa Grey de Abalos and her three women servants, and in the working-class neighborhoods where Mario, who loves the young servant Estela, struggles to maintain his human dignity. The Abalos house represents the enclosed space of repressed characters; the outside constitutes that space where they would find liberation. *Coronation* consists of three parts; the first, "The Gift," introduces the characters who gather in the upper-class house to celebrate a birthday party. The guest of honor is Misiá Elisa, a demented lady in her nineties. Despite her old age and her confinement in bed, Misiá Elisa dominates all those who frequent the house, including Andrés, the orphaned grandson whom she and her husband reared. Still a bachelor in his fifties, Andrés lives comfortably on his inheritance and occupies his idle life by collecting fancy walking sticks and carrying on philosophical conversations with his lifelong friend Carlos Gross. Misiá Elisa also controls three women servants who live in the mansion: Estela, a young girl whose sole duty is to care for the aging lady; Rosario, who has cooked for the Abalos family for nearly half a century; and Lourdes, also an aging housekeeper.

The second section, "Absences" follows the fates of Andrés and Mario, Estela's boyfriend, as they both undergo a major crisis in their lives. Andrés is aroused from his complacency by the presence of Estela, the young, sensual servant just arrived from the country. Mario, the young delivery boy who aspired to lead an honest happy life with Estela, finds himself increasingly entangled in the world of his brother's illicit yet unprofitable dealings. While Andrés becomes obsessed with his newly found sensuality and a preoccupation with death, Mario seeks to escape the fate of poverty and crime that now encircles him. Both men feel persecuted and trapped, Andrés by his grandmother, and Mario by Estela; the women seem to have joined forces under the banner of morality and religion to find shelter from abandonment and solitude. This section develops the characters and signals the eventual disintegration of the men. At the end of *Coronation*, the men find a questionable deliverance from their fate as Andrés loses his mind and Mario steals Estela and disappears in the streets of the dark city. If the house represented the stage where the men felt confined, the assumption of a new space triggers a radical change in personal definition.

Having opened with the preparations for Misiá Elisa's birthday, the novel concludes with "The Coronation," a celebration of her saint's day. The guests never arrive; the house becomes a stage for the final phase of the already evident decay. In the final scene, the two old servants, now drunk and unmindful of the power that their mistress exerts upon them, crown Misiá Elisa in a grotesque pageantry that erases the boundaries between reality and fiction, decay seamlessly blending life into death. Donoso describes the downward moral path of the upper class by its decadence and the lower class by its degradation. Masters and servants coexist in the dilapidated old house, and both Andrés and Mario seek salvation through Estela, only to have their expectations crushed. By drawing a parallel between the two men, the novel goes beyond the issue of class conflict to evoke the universal quest for happiness. In José Donoso's world, the moment when dreams fail marks the passage into another, less clearly defined form of existence. In *Coronation*, flight leads the characters into madness and the unknown.

## The Characters

The characters in *Coronation* may be classified as those who experience inner anguish and undergo a significant change, and those who represent a prototype and serve to enhance the definition of the principal characters. The protagonist, Andrés Abalos, embodies the emasculated figure so prevalent in Donoso's work, who, aware of his inability to exert power over his life, translates that lack into a search for existential meaning and the creation of a fictional world to alleviate his suffering. Andrés is driven by two obsessions, sexuality and death. He fears both because they constitute an unattainable escape. The rebirth of his dormant sensuality together with the overriding morbidity of his grandmother's house drive him to seek refuge in his fantasy world of Omsk. Here he finds a faith in the harmony of life that he knows to be an impossibility for him. Unable to express his feelings or have them understood, Andrés escapes into a fulfilling madness.

The secondary characters of Mario and Misiá Elisa find justification in the novel as foils for the protagonist, Andrés. Like Andrés, Mario is oppressed by the social determinism that threatens to thwart his dreams. Mario, the Don Juan of his circle of friends, falls in love with Estela, only to find that the idyllic encounter leads to entrapment when she becomes pregnant and he loses his job. Mario acts on the desire that Andrés represses, yet he, too, finds reality unsatisfactory.

Misiá Elisa represents the past that is to become Andrés' fate. Like Estela, she lives at the fringe of a world populated by men. In her demented old age, she enjoys the power over the domain that she lacked as a young woman. She existed as the wife to be pampered and photographed by her husband, but she never shared, nor wanted to share, his intimate life. Her obsessions are a perverted sexuality and a self-consciousness in her own morbidity. Andrés inherits her fate in a more self-conscious way, and for him she serves as a transmogrifying mirror.

The two old servants observe the residents of the decaying house; they record and predict the repetitions in the family history, themselves remaining unchanged, always attending to every need in the family, undisturbed by the struggles within Misiá Elisa and Andrés. In the final coronation scene, they are like the Furies, avenging the social crimes of an upper class that dehumanizes its servants. As they make a grotesque caricature of their mistress' power by crowning her, they alone, of all the characters, are relatively untouched by the relentless forces of social determinism.

## Themes and Meanings

Images of madness and crowning reappear throughout the novel to signify a transcending of or escape from the lot of the characters' lives. In her madness, Misiá Elisa insists persistently that her family descends from the crowns of Europe and that she deserves to be treated as such. The aging lady fills the silence of the house with violent accusations against Andrés and Estela for being lustful and of dubious morality, while she, on the other hand, stands as a model of purity, a saint. It is no surprise that her maids, attentive to her every whim, crown her on her saint's day. The ancient lady contaminates her grandson with the same kind of madness. They become obsessed with perverse sexuality because neither has enjoyed sex in a meaningful way. Ironically, they constitute each other's only source of affection and love; since they are both incapable of feeling or giving love, their deprived existence expresses itself in a condemnation of precisely that which they desire most. For this same reason, Andrés—an emotional cripple—collects walking sticks. Misiá Elisa's obsession with being crowned indicates a need to flee her impoverished reality of isolation and immobility. This immobility propels her into a world where she reigns and controls her subjects. These two characters bear a cane and a crown as a caricature of their repressed obsessions.

When Andrés first feels the incongruity of his surroundings he creates the world of Omsk, where harmony rules all circumstance: Through madness, he escapes. Later, he assumes this madness in a very conscious fashion—he is conscious of the creative process and, hence, of his madness. When he feels rejected by his grandmother and Estela, he abandons his ties with reason and enters a domain where his own fictions blur with the reality of the house. Soon after the coronation scene, Andrés stages his own masquerade and convinces his doctor friend that he is mad, thus becoming a character in a world of his own invention. Once Andrés attains the coherence that he desires through a conscious assumption of madness, he then slips completely into his own world. The novelist portrays a social milieu of fragmented families and a decaying upper class. The characters who inhabit the novel escape that world by assuming madness. Likewise, Donoso transcends his Chilean reality by creating characters that repeat the liberating act of invention.

*Critical Context*

*Coronation*, Donoso's first novel, was awarded the 1963 Faulkner Foundation Prize as best postwar Chilean novel. Two years later, it was published in English. This first work repeats some of the themes developed earlier in short stories, but most important, it foreshadows some of the author's most marked obsessions. The metaphor of the boarded-up house to signify a world closing in on the character which becomes a dominant force in *El obsceno pájaro de la noche* (1970; *The Obscene Bird of Night*, 1973), already appears in *Coronation* as Andrés locks himself in the old mansion when he finds that Estela loves Mario. There is in this first novel great emphasis on the contrast between the outside and the inside of the house, representing internal, repressed forces and external possibilities for liberation, respectively. This play on internal/external spaces reappears in 1980 with *La misteriosa desparición de la marquesita de Loria* (1980). Similarly, the use of dramatically staged scenes such as that of the coronation at the end of the novel becomes the basic structuring model for *Casa de campo* (1978; *A House in the Country*, 1984).

The novel has been praised for its portrayal of the stratification of Chilean society and for its vivid incursion into a surrealistic world of dreams and the repressed unconscious. At a first reading, *Coronation* falls within the context of other novels written in Chile during the 1950's and following the trend of social realism. Donoso departs from this trend, however, by creating a self-referential work in which the characters invent their own worlds. In *Coronation*, Donoso writes about himself when he writes about Andrés. This complex vision finds its fullest expression in Donoso's masterpiece, *The Obscene Bird of Night*.

*Sources for Further Study*

Coleman, Alexander. "The Dictatorship of Senility: *Coronation*," in *The New York Times Book Review*. LXX (March 14, 1965), p. 5.
"*Coronation*," in *Times Literary Supplement*. July 1, 1965, p. 563.
Hicks, Granville. "*Coronación*," in *Saturday Review*. XLVIII (March 13, 1965), p. 27.
McMurray, George. *José Donoso*, 1979.

*Flora González*

# CORREGIDORA

*Author:* Gayl Jones (1949-     )
*Type of plot:* Psychological realism
*Time of plot:* From 1947 to 1969
*Locale:* Lexington and the surrounding small communities of Bracktown and
    Versailles in central Kentucky; Cincinnati, Ohio; and Brazil
*First published:* 1975

> *Principal characters:*
> URSA CORREGIDORA, the protagonist, a blues singer
> MUTT THOMAS, her first husband
> TADPOLE MCCORMICK, her second husband and the owner of
>     Happy's Cafe
> GREAT GRAM,
> GRAM, and
> MAMA, the Corregidora women to whom Ursa is both bio-
>     logically and psychologically bound
> CORREGIDORA, a Portuguese slave master and whoremonger,
>     the progenitor of the Corregidora women
> CATHERINE "CAT" LAWSON, a community hairdresser and
>     onetime friend and adviser, a lesbian from whom Ursa
>     recoils

## The Novel

The most immediate story in *Corregidora* is that of blues singer Ursa
Corregidora. For years, the central factor of Ursa's upbringing had been the
injunction to "make generations." Yet shortly after her marriage to Mutt
Thomas, an event occurs that causes her to lose her reproductive ability, the
source of her sexual being. Mutt, in a jealous, drunken rage, accidentally
causes Ursa to fall down a flight of stairs. The effects of the fall are
threefold: Ursa loses the child she was carrying; her womb must be
removed; she is left emotionally crippled. The forced hysterectomy severely
damages Ursa's sense of her own sexuality and her self-esteem. What disturbs her is that she can no longer bear children and thus, in her eyes, fails
in her commitment to her matrilineal line, fails to adhere to the command-
ment of her maternal forebears to make generations in order that the children may bear witness to and be the conscious reminder of slavery's legacy:
"The important thing is making generations. They can burn the papers but
they can't burn conscious, Ursa. And that what makes the evidence. And
that's what makes the verdict."

The psychic damage caused by Ursa's fall seriously affects her relationships with men. Filled with anger, hatred, and guilt, Ursa divorces Mutt as

soon as she recovers. Yet even their separation and alienation from each other remains charged by sexual tension and ambiguity. Mutt's voice echoes constantly in her dreams, memories, and reflections. He hovers consistently on the periphery of her consciousness. Later, at the novel's end (some twenty-two years later), when he returns to reenter her life, they are dramatically, and sexually, reconciled. Also at issue as a result of the fall are the underlying reasons for Ursa's sudden marriage to Tadpole McCormick, owner of Happy's Cafe where Ursa sings, and the complex reasons for which that marriage dissolves. A strong, perverse, psychosexual tension animates Ursa's alienation from men. This tension colors her estrangement from her husbands, or other men who approach her, and it colors as well her ambiguous feelings about her personal identity and the identity conferred upon her by virtue of her lineage.

Throughout the novel, Jones makes clear that Ursa's identity is intricately bound to and interwoven with the details of her family's history, a complex, horrifying history kept vivid and concrete through conscious oral recitation. The action within the historical past, which Jones deftly reveals through oral testimony, dream sequences, and psychohistory, dramatizes the sexual ambivalence in Ursa's family legacy. As the property of old man Corregidora, a Portuguese seaman resettled in Brazil, Ursa's great-grandmother endured sexual bondage to both her master and his wife. Her daughter, Ursa's grandmother, was fathered by Corregidora, as was *her* daughter, Ursa's mother. The pain of this collective history, the pain of her personal story, is the pain Ursa must surmount if she is to live her own life.

### The Characters

Jones's approach to characterization in *Corregidora* is improvisational and borrows heavily from three strong traditions within Afro-American culture: the blues, black urban folk culture, and the oral tradition. Just as Jones tells Ursa's story in mosaics which eradicate linear time by blending past and present, uniting collective memory, dreams, and recollections to current realities, so, too, must readers be conscious of these methods when probing for Ursa's true character.

Ursa tells her story herself. The autobiographical or first-person narrative structure permits Ursa to conceal or reveal as much about her life as she chooses. It also permits readers to follow her closely as she engages, consciously and often subconsciously, in self-exploration. What Ursa must first explore is how she feels, what she feels, about her new barrenness. Initially, what she feels is an emptiness, that "something more than the womb had been taken out." What readers subsequently see is a remarkable evocation of an injured woman engaged in the struggle to regain her psychological balance. Jones shows a blues singer bent but not broken by the weight of her blues; a singer whose experience gives her voice an added quality; a singer who uses a blues sensibility to give voice to who she is; a woman who sings the blues to help her explain what she cannot explain.

Jones employs voice to indicate character. Because of the narrative structure of the novel, other characters are illuminated as they come into contact with Ursa and, principally, by what they say or do not say to her. The Corregidora women preceding Ursa can best be seen by listening to their testimony; readers develop a sense of their fierceness, their stature, through hearing their collective voice. While old Corregidora himself never speaks in the novel, his deeds speak for him. Tadpole declares his love for Ursa, but he does not articulate what he wants or needs from their union. Since neither he nor Ursa communicates openly, their marriage fails. Sometimes exchanges in the novel are taut, terse, elliptical; at other times they are rhythmic, poetic renderings of oral speech. Catherine "Cat" Lawson emerges as a blunt, straightforward adviser and friend at the beginning of the novel. Nevertheless, once Ursa discovers her lesbianism, after overhearing an exchange between Cat and her young lover, she can no longer hear anything Cat says, and Cat is effectively muted.

Although Ursa's relationships with men are strained, a palpable sexual tension, couched in the blues idiom, remains a constant. As a character, Mutt Thomas is physically absent for much of the novel, yet his voice, their verbal exchanges in Ursa's dreams and memories, serves as a poetic recapitulation of the urban folk idiom and a ritualized version of the blues. Despite repeated interspersed rejections (Ursa continually says "Naw"), Mutt demands of her: "Come over here, honey. I need somebody. I won't treat you bad. I won't make you sad. Come over here, honey, and visit with me a little. You got to come back to your original man."

*Themes and Meanings*

*Corregidora* treats four major themes with sensitivity and compassion. Foremost among these is the living charge given Ursa to "make generations," to reproduce children who will bear witness and testify to the legacy of slavery. A second theme evolves from this, asking how a woman without a womb is to fulfill her commitment to her forebears. As Jones allows Ursa to work this problem out in context, one sees a third theme arising from Ursa's efforts to adapt to a new responsibility, the restoration and reenergizing of her spirit, the care of her own life. Yet, Ursa must confront the past, probe it, read its messages and its silences before she can let it go and allow the psychic wound to heal. Finally, Ursa must confront the sexual and psychosexual tensions which are the result of both her heritage and her immediate personal relationships.

Readers coming to the novel for the first time quickly note the unusual frankness with which Jones treats her subject matter; her use of explicit detail and concrete, realistic dialogue set the novel apart. Because of the painful sexual tension between Ursa and her husbands, some readers have seen the novel as a strident feminist piece attacking black men. A more balanced reading indicates that because of her historical legacy, because of the living witnesses who tutored her, because of the psychosexual indictments against men, as personified by Corregidora, embedded in her consciousness, Ursa Corregidora was bound to feel ambivalent about men. Such ambivalence was inevitably heightened after her fall. *Corregidora* is a story of lust and love, of failing and caring, of love and hate, of violence and tenderness, of love lost, of the pleasure and the pain involved in the blues.

### Critical Context

As a first novel, Gayl Jones's *Corregidora* made a dramatic entry into the literary world. It was highly praised for its daring approach to a sensitive subject and its innovative approach to narrative form and language. *Corregidora* asserts unequivocally that the past has a marked impact on both the present and the future. *Corregidora* is also avowedly a blues tale, adhering to a blues motif and illuminating a blues aesthetic. The novel's complex adaptation of this black music form makes it all the more striking.

*Corregidora* is an important novel because it addresses large political issues—racism, sexism, sexual exploitation, and sexual ambivalence—not as issues but as human problems. The novel humanizes the impersonality of such large topics by showing their disruptive effects on intimate human relationships, human values, and traditions. In *Corregidora*, Jones confronts powerful subject matter, treats it with sensitivity, and does so gracefully and skillfully from the perspective of a black woman, the blues protagonist. No omniscient authorial voice intrudes in or interprets the story of the Corregidora women. Jones permits them to tell their multilayered story themselves, in their own voice. What emerges from this stance toward storytelling is less emphasis on fiction as conscious craft and more emphasis on storytelling, as distinct from fiction-making, or orality in a story. Clearly, the strongest models and influences informing Jones's work come not from the strictly literary tradition but rather from the oral traditions of the Afro-American community.

While *Corregidora* does not purport to be a manifesto of any kind, there is present a strong affirmation of female experience, the female voice. The women in this novel speak with a collective voice about the violence and the passion in their lives. Yet each women is clearly individualized and each guards protectively her own uniquely personal experience. *Corregidora* is a passionate novel examining sexual identity and sexual exploitation, the roles played by heritage, ambiguity, and the blues in human relationships.

### Sources for Further Study

Bell, Roseann P. "Gayl Jones Takes a Look at Corregidora—An Interview," in *Sturdy Black Bridges: Visions of Black Women in Literature*, 1979. Edited by Roseann P. Bell, Bettye L. Parker, and Beverly Guy-Sheftall.

Byerman, Keith E. "Gayl Jones," in *Afro-American Fiction Writers After 1955*, 1984.

Dixon, Melvin. "Singing a Deep Song: Language as Evidence in the Novels of Gayl Jones," in *Black Women Writers (1950-1980)*, 1983. Edited by Mari Evans.

Harper, Michael. "Gayl Jones: An Interview," in *Massachusetts Review*. XVIII (Winter, 1977), pp. 692-715.

Jones, Gayl. "About My Work," in *Black Women Writers (1950-1980)*, 1983. Edited by Mari Evans.

*Sandra Y. Govan*

# THE COUP

*Author:* John Updike (1932-    )
*Type of plot:* Political satire
*Time of plot:* 1973, with flashbacks to 1954-1958
*Locale:* The fictional African country of Kush and the fictional town of Franchise, Wisconsin
*First published:* 1978

> *Principal characters:*
> COLONEL HAKIM FÉLIX ELLELLOÛ, the protagonist, president of Kush
> KADONGOLIMI, his first wife
> CANDACE (CANDY), his second wife, an American
> SITTINA, his third wife
> SHEBA, his fourth wife
> KUTUNDA, his traitorous mistress
> MICHAELIS EZANA, his political rival and Minister of the Interior of Kush
> EDUMU, the deposed king of Kush
> DORFÛ, Ellelloû's successor

## The Novel

To the benign dictator of Kush, his country is more a state of mind than a true nation. *The Coup* also shows that Colonel Hakim Félix Ellelloû sees himself in much the same way. Writing his memoirs while in exile in the south of France, Ellelloû attempts to understand both his native country and himself, alternately writing in the self-justifying first person and the more censorious third.

For the bulk of *The Coup*, the forty-year-old Ellelloû wanders in Kush, "this remotest and least profitable heart of Africa," in various guises, trying to discover some mystical explanation for the deadly drought which has plagued his five-year regime. He has resisted all foreign efforts to help alleviate the suffering of his people, ordering a mound of sugarcoated breakfast cereals, potato chips, and other useless food sent by the inevitably eager-to-help Americans burned and the accompanying American diplomat shot. Ellelloû sees his sub-Saharan nation as an extension of his mind and soul, and he jealously guards it against potential violators. Despite basing his political system on an Islamized Marxism, he fears and distrusts the Soviets. Despite his nostalgia for his days at McCarthy College in Franchise, Wisconsin, in the 1950's, the colonel hates the idea of American interference even more.

During his undercover travels, always followed by two bodyguards in his

Mercedes, Ellelloû, who already has four wives, acquires a peasant mistress, Kutunda. Returning to the capital with her master, this "smudged whore" quickly transforms herself into a sophisticated, though still illiterate, modern woman and an efficient bureaucrat. Ellelloû's downfall begins when he allows Kutunda to convince him to execute his mentor, the deposed king, Edumu. Kutunda is soon conspiring with her lover's main political rival, Michaelis Ezana, who longs for American aid. Ellelloû returns from another trip to find that the quietest of coups has occurred and that he has been replaced by a nonentity. Calling himself Dorfû, the new ruler, who also sees his role as a mystical one, is a caricature of Ellelloû who allows Ezana and the Americans to begin the modernization of Kush.

As a result of discoveries which he makes during his travels, Ellelloû's loss of power comes as no surprise. In his college days, he had decided that "government is mythological," and his wanderings reveal that both he and Kush are mythological concepts to the poor inhabitants of his land, his rule the most ephemeral of whims. He also learns that Ezana has caused to be created in the middle of the desert a green junk-food parody of an American industrial town whose residents wear miniskirts and chew bubble gum, whose jukeboxes play the same pop tunes that the colonel heard in Wisconsin almost twenty years earlier. This travesty of everything in which he believes is named Ellelloû, complete with a statue of its namesake.

Intermingled with Ellelloû's travels are past and present meetings with his wives and memories of McCarthy College, where he met Candace, his blonde, all-American second wife; rediscovered Islam through Oscar X, a Black Muslim; began his love-hate relationship with America; and evolved his dream of Kush. That this dream is doomed to failure adds pathos to Ellelloû's mostly comic tale.

*The Characters*

*The Coup* is primarily a portrait of the many sides of the complex, contradictory Ellelloû. Even his name, chosen because it means freedom, is a mask. He is not only on a quest for the source of the drought, for the mystical essence of Kush, but also for the identity of the traveler himself. It is appropriate that he assumes such roles as orange seller, government messenger, parking attendant, and singing beggar, since he has no clear idea of who he is. To Kadongolimi, his first wife, who has known him all his life, he will "always be a child who had just left his mother's hip." Candace, who nicknames him Happy, greets him after a long absence, "Holy Christ, look who it isn't," and what he is not may be more obvious than what he is. Candace tries to explain her husband to himself: "You don't know what you are, you poor little spook. You are the most narcissistic, chauvinistic, megalomaniacal, catatonic schizoid creep this creepy continent ever conjured up."

Ellelloû, the lover of French poetry, the devoted follower of Islam, cannot remember the names of his children and orders a group of tourists beaten, raped, and machine-gunned. (His soldiers ignore the last order.) He cares about his people and wants to end their poverty yet offers little but revolutionary clichés. While Ezana wants to transform the country with no regard for what would be lost, the colonel wants to revolutionize a place with no resources but its diseases. He seems to revel in its barrenness, preferring Kush, the state of mind, to any realities it might become. That the drought ends when he is overthrown is a damning commentary on the selfishness of his vision.

Ellelloû's wives serve mainly to fulfill his needs. Wise Kadongolimi is motherly; Sheba, the only one shorter than he, is sexy; Candace, the vulgar American with the powdery white skin, is exotic. Fittingly, Ellelloû is accompanied into exile by the Westernized, artistic Sittina, the wife most like him. Each wife understands Ellelloû much better than he is capable of understanding himself.

### Themes and Meanings

Global politics are satirized in *The Coup*. Ellelloû vaguely hopes for some kind of uniqueness or purity for Kush but is confronted by the encroachment of international sameness. The main transgressors are the Americans, who wander "everywhere like children, absurdly confident of being loved." The American diplomat whose execution Ellelloû orders explains his country's point of view: "There cats are *starving*. The whole world knows it, you can see 'em starve on the six o'clock news every night. The American people want to help"—and help they will, regardless of whether their aid is wanted or will truly be beneficial. The absurdity of the colonel's efforts at isolationism is underscored when the logical Ezana masterfully explains how the American physical-fitness craze could lead to even greater poverty in Kush, whose major export is peanuts.

Ezana even sees Ellelloû as American. The leader of Kush considers himself above the corrupting influences of the West, but Candace tries to bring him back to earth: "Don't give me any of this Kismet crap. I knew you when you couldn't tell the Koran from the Sears Roebuck catalogue." Ellelloû accepts this reality during his McCarthy period when he explains to Mr. Cunningham, Candace's father, "In the less developed quarters of the world, the power politics of the West can be brushed aside, but its culture is pernicious." On Edumu's walls are posters of Elvis Presley and Marilyn Monroe, and when Ellelloû sees a camel, he is struck by its "Disneyesque eyelashes." He will not become reconciled, however, to living in a country where prayers from the Koran are drowned out by rock and roll. His nation wins its independence from France in 1960 and changes its name from Noire, yet Kush's leader ends up in France wearing NoIR sunglasses.

Such a pun is appropriate, since language, even more than politics and culture, is at the center of *The Coup*. The inhabitants of Kush speak twelve languages, and when Ellelloû and the king converse in Arabic and French, they are uncomfortable since neither is the language taught by their mothers: "All the languages they used, therefore, felt to them as clumsy masks their thoughts must put on." In his narrative, the exile alternates between an effusively mystical style and "the rhetoric of 'Poli Sci.'" Since he is unable to fill the vast emptiness of Kush with the reality of his dream, he fills blank pages with words: These are his only weapons for striking back at those who have robbed him of his dream. Updike implies that art is the only true form of control or power for the inspired, visionary individual.

*Critical Context*

Much of the critical commentary on *The Coup* has focused on how different it is from Updike's other fiction. Updike has written extensively about the morality of suburban America and the various crises of middle age. Too readily categorized by some as the quintessential WASP novelist, he is not content to revisit the same milieu over and over. His desire for diversity can be seen in the Gothic convolutions of *The Witches of Eastwick* (1984) and especially in the two books that feature the globe-hopping Jewish writer Henry Bech: *Bech: A Book* (1970) and *Bech Is Back* (1982); Africa briefly appears in the latter.

*The Coup* is in keeping with the Anglo-American tradition of African novels by outsiders. Updike follows—and may be influenced by—Joseph Conrad, Evelyn Waugh, Joyce Cary, Graham Greene, Saul Bellow, Paul Theroux, and others; T. Coraghessan Boyle and William Boyd have continued the tradition since *The Coup*. Africa is the perfect place, as Conrad and Greene in particular have shown, for exploring the complexities and ambiguities of life, subjects Updike examines in less exotic settings elsewhere in his fiction.

Also notable is the novel's black humor, as when Ezana offers a lengthy analysis of Richard M. Nixon's Watergate woes: "What more poetic and profoundly satisfying psychotherapy... than the evisceration of a President, out of whom tumble in majestic abundance tapes, forgeries, falsified income taxes, and mealy-mouthed lies? This is theatre in the best African tradition, wherein the actor is actually slain!" In the novel's most striking episode, Russians steal Edumu's head after Ellelloû severs it, install elaborate electronic equipment in it, and have it appear to talk to tourists, denouncing Ellelloû's regime before reminding the audience, "For your further entertainment a slide show depicting the Kush national heritage will be shown on the wall behind me."

The Soviet in charge of this exhibition is named Sirin, a pseudonym that Vladimir Nabokov once used. The Nabokov allusion is Updike's acknowledgment of his debt to that master of the self-conscious, ornate style, whose fiction also explores the ambiguities, both dark and comic, lurking behind our many masks. Like the best of Nabokov's fiction, *The Coup* manages to be experimental, ironic, and lyric all at the same time.

*Sources for Further Study*
Detweiler, Robert. *John Updike*, 1984.
Greiner, Donald J. *John Updike's Novels*, 1984.
Macnaughton, William R., ed. *Critical Essays on John Updike*, 1982.
Uphaus, Suzanne Henning. *John Updike*, 1980.

*Michael Adams*

# COUPLES

*Author:* John Updike (1932-    )
*Type of plot:* Erotic realism
*Time of plot:* The summer and autumn of 1963 and the winter and spring of 1964
*Locale:* Tarbox, Massachusetts, a fictitious town in Plymouth County, southeast of Boston along the Atlantic coast
*First published:* 1968

> *Principal characters:*
> PIET HANEMA, born of Dutch immigrant parents, a builder and a lover
> ELIZABETH "FOXY" WHITMAN, the pregnant wife of Ken and also Piet's lover, later his wife
> ANGELA HANEMA, Piet's wife and the mother of his two children
> RUTH HANEMA, the eldest daughter of Piet and Angela
> KEN WHITMAN, a research biologist and Foxy's husband
>
> *The Couples*
> FREDDY and GEORGENE THORNE: he is a local dentist; she is one of Piet's lovers
> MATT and TERRY GALLAGHER: he is Piet's partner; she is a potter and a musician of sorts
> ROGER and BEA GUERIN: he is independently wealthy; she is barren and is also Piet's lover
> FRANK and JANET APPLEBY and HAROLD and MARCIA SMITH (THE APPLESMITHS), couples who trade partners
> EDDIE and CAROL CONSTANTINE and BEN and IRENE SALTZ (THE SALTINES), involved in partner swapping but with homosexual overtones
> JOHN and BERNADETTE ONG: he is a Korean nuclear physicist; she is his American-born wife and Piet's lover

## The Novel

The story of *Couples* is relatively simple, but the plot is extraordinarily convoluted and complex. At the beginning of the novel, nine middle-class or upper-middle-class couples, mostly in their thirties, with mortgages, children, pets, and professions, live in an interconnected social world in the fictitious bedroom community of Tarbox, located slightly south of Boston in Plymouth County. The appearance of a young couple who move to Tarbox from Cambridge causes a series of realignments within the group and finally, by the novel's end, two divorces, and precipitates the action of the story. Ken Whitman and his pregnant wife, Foxy, buy an old beach house and hire Piet Hanema to renovate the property. Piet, already a restless husband and lover, breaks of his current affair and takes up with Foxy, continuing their sexual liaison after her child is born. She becomes pregnant again, only this time by Piet. The lovers arrange an abortion with the aid of the local dentist, Freddy Thorne, who insists that as payment he be allowed to sleep with Piet's wife, Angela. Georgene, Piet's former lover and Freddy's wife, in a fit of jealousy tells Ken Whitman about his wife's affair and abortion, causing the Whitmans to separate and eventually divorce. Angela and Piet have also separated and divorced, and the novel concludes with Piet and Foxy getting married and starting their lives over again in another community away from Tarbox.

This bare-bones sketch of the tale of *Couples* reduces both the scope and the significance of the novel to a minimum. The fascination of the novel comes from the delicate interworkings or interconnections among the various couples and not from the question of whether Piet and Foxy will run off together to get married.

*The Characters*

The central character is Piet Hanema, a local builder who values old-fashioned style and construction techniques, much to the dismay of his partner. Piet is also a lover who searches for a release from his fears of death in the sexual encounters that he shares with his neighbors' wives. Traumatized by the early death of his immigrant parents in an automobile accident, Piet is losing his once-vital Christian faith, finally abandoning it altogether in favor of salvation through the flesh in his new marriage to Foxy. It is Piet's quest for personal meaning which forms the core of the plot and not the more highly sensational sexual antics of the Tarbox ménage.

Over against Piet are placed the two central female characters: Angela, Piet's wife and the mother of his children, and Foxy, his lover, future wife, and, one presumes, future mother of more children. Angela, as her name implies, represents for Piet something spiritual and therefore unattainable. She accepts life and death as part of a natural cycle and does not share either Piet's fears about his mortality or his search for a meaning in life. The very anxieties to which she does not respond, however, provide the attraction which draws other women into trying to comfort Piet's sense of loss. Portrayed as possessing a diminishing sensuality, Angela becomes increasingly distant, both as a wife and as a symbol for Piet, thereby opening the opportunity for the affair with Foxy, who is sexually willing and who becomes symbolic of the object of Piet's quest for meaning. As Piet turns away from the orthodox beliefs of the Church and increasingly abandons his marriage bed and his unattainable wife, he turns more and more toward

Foxy and his carnal worship of her. Celebrating her procreative nature—in contrast, Angela will not have any more children—he settles for temporality instead of transcendence: He stops reaching for the angels and opts for the animals.

The other women and men in the novel function as variations of these three basic characters. Indeed, as one critic has pointed out, the couples form *in toto* one composite character who displays numerous individual traits divided among the figures of the fiction. Freddy Thorne is the exception to this amalgam because Freddy becomes a spokesman for the hedonistic mob formed by the couples and so becomes a master of revels, the high priest of the new religion of sex. Much has been made of his character and its place as a counterfoil to Piet. Where Piet is treated seriously and his fears and anxieties taken as genuine, Freddy is satirized and his solutions mocked and deflated. Just as Freddy cannot consummate his desire for Angela when he has the chance, so his worship of sex is ultimately seen as a pose. He is a priest who does not really believe in rituals over which he presides.

Whether one reads Piet as a variation on Don Juan or Tristan, as several critics have, or merely understands him as a man who seeks the mysterious power of women as a defense against death, the novel accords him the central and significant role.

### Themes and Meanings

Updike has been quoted as saying that *Couples* is about sex as an emergent religion, and indeed the novel does chronicle the practices and consequences of the near worship of sex in contemporary American culture. Yet the book also contains a criticism as well as a celebration of the new sexual morality which has replaced moribund religious beliefs that no longer seem relevant. The substitution of a natural experience, sex, for a supernatural one, religion, also coincides with prevalent modern attitudes about the diminishing role of the Church in the world. Piet is a victim of his need for a belief in something beyond the world and for physical comfort against the fears that he harbors about death and corporal nothingness. His prayers, which provide little solace, are gradually replaced by the worship, literally, of the body and its temporality. He finally comes to abandon his need for the spirit and accepts his mortality by immersing himself in his own finititude, accepting the transitoriness of the joys of the flowers and of the flesh.

His abandonment of Angela and of his spiritual need or search takes its toll on Piet, and his acceptance of Foxy is a fall, not simply a realignment of relationships or a change of wives. When he surrenders himself to Foxy, he also commits a kind of spiritual suicide, partly because Foxy's physical need for him is suffocating in a way that Angela's lack of need was not, and also because such a consuming desire overwhelms his religious impulses while smothering his spirit. It is instructive that Piet embraces his fall with such fervor. Updike has said that his character at the end of the novel both becomes a satisfied person and dies at the same time.

*Couples* is not a fairy tale for all of its mythical qualities; the tale is not a simple one in which the boy gets the girl in the end. Indeed, Foxy and Piet do marry, but they are expelled from whatever kind of postpill Eden that Tarbox had become. As he was expelled from his parents' greenhouse in his childhood, Piet is again thrown out into the world by death, this time his own spiritual death, leaving the reader to wonder about the permanence of this new relationship. In the end, *Couples* promises very little for the future.

*Critical Context*

The sensation caused by the publication of *Couples* in 1968 not only placed the novel on *The New York Times'* best-seller list for a number of weeks but also promoted Updike into the ranks of the popular writers. His name, somewhat restricted to the serious reader, became widely known to the broader book-reading public. The reviews, predictably enough, reflected the critics' sense of lost proprietorship and complained loudly that Updike had sold out to the meretricious contemporary mass cult. The novel was too sexy and too sensational to be considered a serious work of fiction. It was a large book (450 pages), if not the large book which the reviewers had expected of Updike and had chided him for not writing, but subsequent readings of the novel, removed from the hysteria of the period, have revealed depths overlooked in the initial responses. Few critics now would describe the book as cheap and trashy and a waste of Updike's considerable literary talent.

The novel not only provided Updike with financial security but also reflected a sense of historical presence which was new in his longer fiction. The explicit treatment of the subject of sex was a reflection of the times as well and cleared the way for other "serious" novelists to take advantage of the new permissiveness. Whether *Couples* will ultimately be adjudged one of Updike's best novels remains to be seen; that it is a challenging and provocative novel, one which engages the mind as well as the senses, cannot be denied.

*Sources for Further Study*

Detweiler, Robert. *John Updike*, 1972.

Hunt, George W. *John Updike and the Three Great Secret Things: Sex, Religion and Art*, 1980.

Markle, Joyce B. *Fighters and Lovers: Themes in the Novels of John Updike*, 1973.

Uphaus, Suzanne Henning. *John Updike*, 1980.

Vargo, Edward P. *Rainstorms and Fire: Ritual in the Novels of John Updike*, 1973.

*Charles L. P. Silet*

# THE CRYING OF LOT 49

*Author:* Thomas Pynchon (1937-    )
*Type of plot:* Philosophical satire
*Time of plot:* The early 1960's
*Locale:* Primarily San Francisco
*First published:* 1966

> *Principal characters:*
> PIERCE INVERARITY, the late, unlamented mogul whose presence in the novel is realized as a controlling force
> MRS. OEDIPA MAAS, the central character, an intelligent woman
> METZGER, a lawyer and coexecutor with Oedipa of Inverarity's will
> MUCHO MAAS, Oedipa's pathological husband

*The Novel*

At first reading, *The Crying of Lot 49* is a surrealistic portrayal of life in America in the 1960's—a time of self-doubt, frustration, and alienation. Scenes of California life-styles and of characters such as Dr. Hilarius, Oedipa's psychotherapist who is himself mad, combine with such surrealistic details as human bones being used to decorate the bottom of swimming pools and the inane plots of old films which Oedipa and her lawyer and would-be seducer, Metzger, watch on television.

Such satiric elements fuse elegantly with the novel's plot—a mystery story centering on Oedipa's attempt to sort out all the details involved in the will of her late former lover, California real-estate mogul Pierce Inverarity. As coexecutrix of his estate, Oedipa finds herself journeying through several California cities in an attempt to discover the full implications of Inverarity's bequest. Though dead, Inverarity is the controlling force of the action. His own name, for example, suggests the nature of the action on which Oedipa embarks. The root "vera" denotes "truth" or "certainty," and the meaning of "Pierce" is obvious. Oedipa must pierce the truth, or, indeed, pierce the untruth. She must, in any case, come to certainty, clear up the mystery of his bequest.

The most mysterious aspect of Inverarity's will seems to be the mogul's involvement in Tristero, a secret, underground communication system which refuses to use the United States mail and which relies on its own franking mark, the post horn. After taking leave of her husband, Mucho, a used-car salesman besieged by guilt about his profession, Oedipa strikes out by car, visiting first San Narciso, a fictional locale whose name suggests the self-love and introspective narcissism of a whole generation during the 1960's.

Here Oedipa spends the night in a motel room with Metzger, drinking and watching old films on television. Metzger tries to seduce her, but she eludes him by dressing in several layers of clothing so that Metzger quickly gets bored and fatigued in trying to remove them all.

The scene is comically symbolic, for soon afterward Metzger drops out of the action, unable to continue "unravellng" the layers of mystery behind Inverarity. Oedipa continues her journey alone. She has not given in to the narcissism of the body, and in subsequent scenes she repudiates as well the mind-distorting drugs of those whom she meets during her travels.

Her quest takes her at last to San Francisco, where she becomes obsessed with finding the truth. In the key scene of the novel, Oedipa walks the streets at night, seeing, or imagining she is seeing—for Pynchon is purposely ambiguous here—the post horn symbol of Tristero inscribed everywhere in the city, like some wild or passionate graffito. As insignia it is worn by scores of people, particularly by the sick, the poor, and the dispossessed. The scene is hallucinogenic, suggesting the drug culture of 1960's San Francisco and paralleling Oedipa's quest for an almost hallucinatory symbol.

The meaning of it all, the solution to the mystery, finally eludes her. By novel's end, Oedipa's quest has taken her to an auction where Tristero's post horn stamp is to be sold in a collection. Here she waits impatiently for the auctioneer to "cry," that is, to sell, the collection, cataloged as lot #49.

The seemingly inconclusive ending in which Oedipa is still awaiting the auction to begin suggests a deeper reading. Aside from the obvious satire on California and on American cultural totems, the book is really a novel of ideas. The plot, for example, seems to parody itself: The mystery story style, the concise, swiftly moving narrative, both serve as foils to a more profound, philosophical meaning. Oedipa's search for the truth is not merely physical, as in a mystery story, but metaphysical, as in a Platonic dialogue. Her groping toward a solution can be viewed as a symbolic presentation of a human being's search for the ultimate reality. Does Tristero really exist? Oedipa acts existentially—that is, as if it does.

Even while pursuing Tristero, Oedipa is plagued by uncertainty, haunted by doubt, by what she calls her "paranoia." That Tristero is an order whose essential purpose is communication and yet whose existence is at least covert and at most problematic gives the novel its philosophical tension. Meaning in Oedipa's life is not possible without Tristero, yet Tristero's own existence is in doubt. Tristero as a communication system, real or imaginary, has become somehow problematic. Oedipa and all the minor characters are unable to communicate; they are alone, isolated, wandering in their own private night-towns in search of meaning, compassion, and love.

*The Characters*
Like the eyes of Dr. T. J. Eckleburg in F. Scott Fitzgerald's *The Great*

*Gatsby*, the figure of Pierce Inverarity broods over the action as would some malevolently indifferent diety. As the characters in *The Great Gatsby* traveled through the ash heaps midway between their country estates on Long Island and the city of New York, ash heaps presided over by the abandoned sign of the eye doctor, still flashing in vacant desolation, so, too, Pierce Inverarity presides over the characters in search of the full meaning of his bequest. In this respect, none of the characters has a flesh-and-blood personality. Rather, each represents, in parable fashion, a particular aspect of a relationship to Inverarity, the presiding deity.

Some, like Mucho Maas—whose name suggest pure physical existence—ignore the Inverarity bequest. Mucho is caught up in his own shame at being a used-car salesman. He does not care about Inverarity, but only about his own salvation through sexual relationships with teenage girls. He is a pathological sufferer, flagellating himself with guilt and sexual misprision.

Some, like Metzger, start out seriously enough in search of the truth but soon fall away, bored or weary. Like Mucho, Metzger is essentially a comic figure. His interest in the Inverarity bequest is strictly business, for he does not share his coexecutor's passion for the truth. He, too, is addicted to the banalities of civilized life. As Mucho's "redemption" takes the form of dalliance with teenagers, Metzger's preoccupation is with the plots of old films, in some of which he claims to have starred. In the motel with Oedipa, just before his attempted seduction of her, Metzger rhapsodizes over the plots, litanylike, as if each detail were a great moment in the intellectual history of man. When his seduction fails, he ends in befuddlement and drops his interest in the Inverarity adventure.

Only Oedipa has the fortitude, the seriousness, the wit to continue. Oedipa's name is itself indicative of both her personality and her predicament as a human being. Like her Sophoclean namesake, Oedipa is virtually obsessed with finding out, bringing to light, sorting it all out. Like that of Oedipus, too, Oedipa's predicament is ironically the result of her attempts to solve a riddle. In the ancient myth, Oedipus answers the riddle of the Sphinx, saving the city of Corinth and being rewarded as its savior by marriage to its queen, who, unknown to him, is his true mother. Oedipus' fate is thus tied to his own intelligence, his own cleverness as a finder of truth. Oedipa is also clever and intelligent. Her repartee with her husband, Mucho, and her parrying with Metzger in the motel room show her to be witty and shrewd. It is this intelligence that drives her. She calls her quest a kind of "paranoia," and the reader tends to agree, just as the audience sees the ultimate disaster of understanding which awaits Oedipus.

Unlike Oedipus, however, Oedipa Maas is not a realistically portrayed character. Oedipus showed his passion, his hotheadedness, his pride, the classical hubris regarded as mankind's cardinal sin. Oedipa, by contrast, is more the author's projection of an idea than a creature of flesh and blood.

Oedipa represents the existential middle way, the philosophical compromise between faith and despair, knowledge and ignorance. That her quest is inconclusive only supports her position as intermediary between two extremes. She doubts yet she goes on. She never learns completely, never fully understands Meaning, or if, indeed, Meaning itself exists.

## Themes and Meanings

Oedipa's search to find the meaning of her legacy is not only a quest for a philosophical explanation of existence but also a search for a valid social, national ethos, for values that clarify, for better or for worse, "the legacy that was America." That legacy is not necessarily one of despair.

Though Oedipa's quest takes her through an American society of the maladjusted, the fantasy-ridden, the dropped-out, the "intellectual," and the materialistic, this stream of humanity does not provide Oedipa with a solution to the meaning of things. Even though a large segment of the disinherited seems to communicate by depositing letters in boxes marked WASTE (We Await Silent Tristero's Empire), even though the social fabric seems tottering on the verge of anarchy—an entropy of both body and mind, a paradigm of the modern scientific notion of the entropy of nature—and even though Tristero's own name seems to connote a universal "triste," a sadness, it is the very uncertainty of a solution that holds out for Oedipa some random hope, a hope symbolized at the novel's end by Oedipa's waiting for the auction to begin. Indeterminacy is hope.

In Charles Dickens' *A Christmas Carol*, Scrooge asks the ghost of Christmas future, "Are these the things that will be, or only the shadows of things that *may* be?" Similarly, Oedipa's discovery of America is ghostlike—a specter of what is, and yet possibly only a shadow, a hallucination, a paranoia.

## Critical Context

Of Pynchon's novels, *The Crying of Lot 49*, his second, is the most suitable introduction to his work. Certainly it is more concise and verbally controlled than its predecessor, *V.* (1963), and the social satire and parody are more clearly directed at recognizable cultural idols—the California scene being in effect the metonymic representative of America itself.

*The Crying of Lot 49* is also more traditional than its innovative, diffuse, almost encyclopedic successor, *Gravity's Rainbow* (1973). If it lacks the later novel's exuberance and daring, *The Crying of Lot 49* is also less arcane, more classically disciplined as a novel.

In spite of the book's deceptive simplicity, or perhaps because of it, *The Crying of Lot 49* is the fulcrum of Pynchon's work—the balancing point between the diffuse experimentation of *V.* and the hermeneutical gigantism of *Gravity's Rainbow*. At the same time, *The Crying of Lot 49* deals with a central idea inherent in all of Pynchon's work: the indeterminacy of meaning and the frightening possibility of the cosmic disorder that is at the heart of reality.

Thomas Pynchon himself has remained obsessively private. His public inaccessibility and the dearth of any personal comments about his own work have made his novels virtually the only source of understanding the artist himself. This is, perhaps, as it should be. Given the importance of Pynchon as a writer, and the hieroglyphic nature of his work, *The Crying of Lot 49* may aptly be regarded as a Rosetta stone.

*Sources for Further Study*
Hite, Molly. *Ideas of Order in the Novels of Thomas Pynchon*, 1983.
Mendelson, Edwin, ed. *Pynchon: A Collection of Critical Essays*, 1978.
Pearce, Richard. *Critical Essays on Thomas Pynchon*, 1981.

*Edward Fiorelli*

# DANGLING MAN

*Author:* Saul Bellow (1915-    )
*Type of plot:* Psychological realism
*Time of plot:* 1942-1943
*Locale:* Chicago
*First published:* 1944

> *Principal characters:*
> JOSEPH, the protagonist, whose diary entries while awaiting
> World War II induction constitute the novel
> IVA, his wife
> KITTY DAUMLER, his former mistress

## The Novel

*Dangling Man* takes the form of a journal kept by the protagonist, Joseph, between December 15, 1942, and April 9, 1943. All the action is retrospective, filtered through the troubled mind of Joseph, and committed to his journal. Introspective and tentative, the entries record Joseph's increasingly desperate quest for self-knowledge.

As the novel opens, seven months have passed since Joseph resigned from his job at the Inter-American Travel Bureau to await army induction. Because of snarled bureaucratic red tape, he dangles between civilian and military life. A sort of scholar manqué, Joseph had imagined that leisure would allow him to devote himself to study, but he finds himself unaccountably unable to read. Supported by his uncomplaining wife, Iva, in a desultory room in which they have lived since giving up their flat, Joseph grows heavy and dispirited. Continued errands and aimless wanderings signal a paralysis of will that takes the form of obsessive self-absorption. Joseph feels himself changing, becoming suspicious and ill-tempered in his relations with others; he begins to refer to his "older self," as if he were once a different person. It is this identity crisis underlying Joseph's journal entries that forms the true subject of *Dangling Man*.

While the device of the journal imposes an overall chronological pattern on the novel, several of the most important entries are devoted to Joseph's extended accounts of prior events, some of which took place before his writing began. Perhaps the most crucial of these flashbacks, the one that goes furthest toward explaining how the old Joseph became the diarist, concerns the Servatius party of the previous March. At the party, Joseph is shocked by the defects in friends whom he had glorified as a "colony of the spirit." Their petty cruelties, culminating in the sadistic treatment of the hypnotized Minna Servatius by Morris Abt, disillusion Joseph, who henceforth thinks of his friends as having failed him. The episode marks the onset of Joseph's growing sense of alienation. Succeeding episodes trace his disaffection from his brother, Amos, whose money he refuses and whose spoiled daughter he spanks when she calls him a beggar; from his in-laws, the Almstadts, whose solicitousness he regards as phony; from his mistress, Kitty Daumler, who "betrays" him with another man after he neglects her; from his wife, Iva, who resents the role he imposes upon her; and, most critically, from himself.

Joseph's alienation stems from his fatal inability, first revealed to him at the Servatius party, to answer the question, "How should a good man live; what ought he to do?" In the first of the two imagined conversations with an invented Spirit of Alternatives, Joseph thrashes about in a hopeless effort to close the gap between the ideal construction and the real world. Apparently one requires an ideal construction—God, art, money—as proof against chaos. Unfortunately, none of them suffices. Believing in the efficacy of reason yet haunted by a failure of vision, Joseph wallows in a sea of alternatives, obsessed by a seemingly insoluble dilemma. He begins his second conversation with the Spirit of Alternatives by returning to the question of how a man should live, arguing strongly that self-knowledge is a prerequisite for freedom, without which man can never attain the ultimate goal of governing his own destiny. "Then only one question remains," replies the Spirit of Alternatives, ". . . whether you have a separate destiny." Joseph pales, unable to answer the question posed by his alter ego.

With the coming of spring, Joseph's despair deepens as he comes to realize fully that freedom, unaccompanied by comprehension, is meaningless. One dreary and drizzly night, having quarreled with Iva and noisily vilified their neighbors, Joseph rushes from the house, to stalk the streets aimlessly. Oppressed by images of dissolution—a scurrying rat, a torn umbrella, a stagnant puddle—Joseph takes the decision to surrender. Heading directly for the draft board, he writes out a request to be called up "at the earliest possible moment."

The scene at the draft board is the climax of Joseph's quest for self-knowledge and, therefore, of the novel. No longer dangling, Joseph has answered the question posed by the Spirit of Alternatives in the negative: He has no separate destiny. Henceforth, he will be defined as a soldier, a member of a group which confers that identity upon him which he could not achieve in solitude. Written on his last day as a civilian, Joseph's final journal entry expresses only relief from the burden of self-determination and freedom: "Hurray for regular hours! And for the supervision of the spirit! Long live regimentation!"

## The Characters

Because *Dangling Man* is a journal, it is inevitable that its protagonist, the diarist, dominates the novel. Like Saul Bellow at the time of the book's

action, Joseph is in his late twenties, Canadian-born, the son of Russian immigrants who relocated to Chicago during his boyhood. Yet Joseph—his
surname is conspicuously omitted—is less an autobiographical character
than a kind of 1940's American Everyman. In his state of dangling between
civilian and military life during a period of historical crisis, Joseph, with all
the young men of his generation, awaits war and future uncertainty. This
tenuous limbo, rendered increasingly absurd by the length and unpredict-
ability of its duration, triggers the obsessive introspection that produces his
journal. An eighteenth century aficionado as a college history major, a former Communist, a lover of classical music, Joseph sprinkles his entries with
references to figures as disparate as Denis Diderot, Karl Marx, and Joseph
Haydn as he gropes toward self-understanding. Unwilling to accept either of
the fashionable modern shibboleths—unreason or nihilism—Joseph at first
welcomes his enforced freedom as an opportunity to discover how a good
man should live. Paradoxically, however, he is undone by the very moral
idealism he espouses. Racked by guilt, beset by dreams of death, increasingly at odds with friends and relatives, he grows masochistic and misan-
thropic in his deepening isolation. Whether his ultimate failure is a paradigm of human frailty or merely a result of personal inadequacy, Joseph's
attempts to answer the big questions, no matter how often they misfire,
lend status to his characterization.

The progress of Joseph's alienation can be traced in his worsening relations with friends and relatives. Nearly every human contact is designed by
Bellow to reveal aspects of his hero's trauma. Myron Adler, Morris Abt,
Minna and Harry Servatius, old friends and members of Joseph's "colony of
the spirit" are suddenly found wanting. Myron, who tries to find Joseph a
job, is accommodating, Mavis cruel, the Servatiuses tasteless. His brother's
family and his in-laws fare no better. Amos' repeated offers of money and a
job evidence a sense of superiority rather than brotherly concern. Amos'
wife, Dolly, is suspicious and patronizing; their daughter Etta spoiled and
hateful. Joseph's in-laws, the Almstadts, are despised—she for her foolish-
ness and apparent malice, he for his unquestioning stolidity.

Joseph is at his most unattractive, however, in his dealings with the two
women in his life. With his wife, Iva, he is supercilious and domineering.
Perhaps because she is generally uncomplaining and self-effacing, and exists
chiefly as the locus of Joseph's guilt feelings for his bad behavior, her characterization seems perfunctory. While long-suffering, however, she is not
spineless. Her deliberate drunkenness at the Servatius party and her frequently sharp rejoinders to Joseph's browbeating constitute refusals to conform to the pattern that he tries to impose upon her. Also, her unwavering
love in the face of Joseph's negligence and nasty moods shows up the poverty of his affections. Joseph's relationship with his mistress, Kitty Daumler,
is no more satisfactory. Vivacious and faintly exotic, Kitty, in her frank sen-

suousness, is a welcome contrast to Joseph's characteristic indecision and guilt. Although he is flattered by Kitty's love, his feelings for her, like those for Iva, seem tentative and partial, and he is mostly relieved when the affair ends. As different as Kitty and Iva appear to be, they serve identical purposes in *Dangling Man*: to throw Joseph's self-absorbed alienation into high relief.

Sharply drawn minor characters interact with Joseph to round out Bellow's portrayal of his troubled hero. Vanaker, who lives down the hall, uses the bathroom noisily and leaves its door ajar, throws a great many empty whiskey bottles into the yard, and even steals Joseph's socks. Joseph's increasing hostility to a man he once regarded as a harmless loon traces the downward curve of his despair, and his subsequent shame at his treatment of Vanaker signals his "adjustment" after he receives his induction notice. Alf Steidler, an extravagantly theatrical acquaintance of long standing, and a sickly and shabby middle-aged woman peddling Christian Science tracts, represent competing solutions to the problem of living. Alf's pathetic flashiness, ubiquitous cigars, and interminably predictable stories comprise a lifestyle based upon gestures, trivial though consistent. The anonymous woman rapidly whispers her memorized sales pitch through "lips come together like the seams of a badly sewn baseball." Hers is the religious solution, its heartfelt sincerity evident in her clumsiness. Neither Stadler nor the woman offers "ideal constructs" acceptable to Joseph; both embody the frustration of an impossible quest which eventually leads Joseph not toward but away from freedom.

### Themes and Meanings

The principal theme of *Dangling Man* involves the age-old search for values by which one can live in the world. For Joseph, this quest for ultimate meaning is necessarily preceded by self-knowledge: "But I must know what I myself am." Against the backdrop of World War II and its attendant death and determinism, Bellow poses the alternative of human freedom and self-determination. The war itself exists chiefly to dramatize the starkness of the choice between freedom and surrender and to add urgency to Joseph's quest. Beginning his journal as a "record of inward transactions" that will lead to self-definition, Joseph assumes that, given the leisure necessary for self-examination, some such definition is possible. After five months of growing frustration, during which he succeeds only in making himself and others miserable, he abandons the struggle and requests induction. The reasons for Joseph's failure and the meaning of that failure form the substance of *Dangling Man*.

A compulsive dualism lies at the heart of Joseph's failure. His many ideal constructions represent unsatisfactory solutions to the problem of reconciling the self to the world. As the gap between self and world widens, he turns increasingly inward, seeking self-definition divorced from its social context. In so doing, he ironically explodes the very impulse—to solve the problem of living in the world—that underlies his quest. When his isolation deepens and the outside world recedes, Joseph is forced to root his search for values in an autonomous self. His subsequent failure to define that self apart from its social actions is tantamount to an admission that the self has no independent existence. Since freedom is therefore an illusion, man can only be defined in external or historical terms; Joseph's request for induction embraces that very social determinism he set out to demolish. His acquiescence is signaled by a seemingly trivial incident near the end of *Dangling Man*. Attempting to cash Iva's paycheck at a bank, Joseph is refused because he has no job. In the eyes of the bank president whom he confronts in an embarrassing scene, Joseph has simply ceased to exist. Completely isolated, Joseph has forfeited that identity which only society can confer.

To read *Dangling Man* merely as a broadside against self-autonomy, however, is grossly to simplify the novel. While it is true that Joseph's quest for the self is unsuccessful, his attempt can be interpreted as a triumph of sorts. Perhaps his request for induction is an affirmative decision: By joining the army, he rejoins the society he disdained. Accepting human limitations, Joseph loses the sense of strangeness that marked his divorce from the world. His sudden ability to read again, his reconciliation to other people, and his general feeling of relief may indicate a sensible rapprochement with the world that human nature demands. To be most fully human is to forswear the chimera of a transcendent self. Indeed, transcendence itself may be merely another of those "ideal constructions" which Joseph so contemptuously rejected in his first talk with the Spirit of Alternatives. Tacitly imagining himself superior to others, Joseph's failure might illustrate the maxim that pride goeth before a fall. No better than his fellow human beings, Joseph must seek his identity among them. In this sense, *Dangling Man* can be read as a plea for human community.

Joseph's inability to function apart from society does not, however, invalidate the cultural criticism that fills his journal entries. As an outsider, keenly observing rather than actively participating in the life around him, Joseph is an ideal mouthpiece for Bellow's social critique. A disillusioned former Communist, Joseph approves of the war only because he prefers "our" imperialism to "theirs." Capitalistic society, driven by blind acquisitiveness, has long since lost its sustaining vision. The many ideologies he calls ideal constructions testify to an absence of shared belief as they wage their fearful battles for supremacy. Lacking a true sense of community, people band together in groups such as Joseph's "colony of the spirit" which, as the Servatius party reveals, are symbols of modern corruption. While it is undeniable that Joseph's attempt to locate values in the autonomous self is a failure, his yearning for transcendence may be a valid response to the fallen world of *Dangling Man*.

If Joseph is seen as a victim of a corrupt society, then his self-absorption is less a result of misplaced belief than a refusal to accept a social identity poisoned at its source. While it appears that man cannot cast off his social burden and that Joseph's quest was foredoomed from its inception, his very struggle is not without nobility. In seeking to assert the primacy of human reason and imagination, Joseph wages a valiant, albeit losing, fight against the chaos that he perceives around him. Even if his grim view of society is mistaken or merely self-serving, he has freely chosen his own fate. Whether his induction request is an affirmation of social bonding or a defeat for the unaided human intellect, Joseph has made a conscious decision to give up his freedom. Moreover, his failure need not invalidate the urgency of the quest. Joseph may lack the moral or intellectual weapons to attain a self-sufficient rationality. Yet his very insistence on rationality and his refusal to surrender to meaninglessness embody Bellow's theme: that the struggle toward moral order is a necessary human enterprise.

*Critical Context*

An immediate critical success, *Dangling Man* was a first novel that pointed not only to the direction of its author's later work but also to that of American fiction itself. Encapsulating the psychology of the 1940's, it simultaneously looked ahead to the fiction of the 1950's. On the first page of *Dangling Man*, Bellow speaks disparagingly of the "hard-boiled": "They are unpracticed in introspection, and therefore badly equipped to deal with opponents whom they cannot shoot like big game or outdo in daring." This scarcely veiled reference to Ernest Hemingway contains Bellow's rejection of externalization and his intention to create a fiction of the inner life. His Joseph, introspective and flawed, is the model for all the later Bellow heroes who struggle mightily to understand and to find salvation through reason. The many alienated figures whose introspections crowd the pages of contemporary American fiction are Joseph's descendants.

In its style and aims, no less than in its characterization, *Dangling Man* has pointed toward Bellow's future work. Tersely reported evocations of grim urban landscapes relieved by sporadic metaphysical flights, all filtered through a troubled central consciousness, established a narrative mode that Bellow has never abandoned. Later protagonists, older and more sophisticated than Joseph, act on a wider stage and philosophize more abstrusely. Yet their struggles, essentially similar, are expressed by similar means. At the outset of his career, Bellow found, in Joseph's dangling, a metaphor for the human condition. All of his future protagonists would dangle, sifting alternatives, searching for the proper means of carrying on their lives. Beginning with Joseph, these free agents, morally aware and hungry for values, have done battle against the forces of nihilism and unreason. For Bel-

low's is finally a fiction that is dedicated to the celebration of human poten-
tialities.

*Sources for Further Study*
Clayton, John J. *Saul Bellow: In Defense of Man*, 1968, 1979.
Malin, Irving. *Saul Bellow's Fiction*, 1969.
Opdahl, Keith M. *The Novels of Saul Bellow: An Introduction*, 1967.
Tanner, Tony. *Saul Bellow*, 1965.

*Lawrence S. Friedman*

# DAUGHTER OF EARTH

*Author:* Agnes Smedley (1890-1950)
*Type of plot:* Social autobiography
*Time of plot:* The 1890's to the 1920's
*Locale:* The American Midwest, Southwest, and New York City
*First published:* 1929

*Principal characters:*
> MARIE ROGERS, the main character, a student, teacher, writer,
> and political activist
> MARIE'S FATHER, an uneducated laborer
> MARIE'S MOTHER, a dispossessed farm woman and menial
> laborer
> HELEN, Marie's aunt, an attractive woman who becomes a
> prostitute
> BEATRICE ROGERS, Marie's sister, hardened by a difficult life
> KNUT LARSEN, Marie's first husband, a Scandinavian
> intellectual
> ANAND MANVEKAR, Marie's second husband, an Indian
> nationalist

*The Novel*

*Daughter of Earth* is a chronicle of the life of Marie Rogers, a woman who, like the people for whom she worked and sacrificed her life, was "of the earth" and whose "struggle is the struggle of the earth." Spanning the first thirty or so years of her life, the account is an attempt to resolve personal and political issues. Searching her earliest childhood memories, Marie traces the development of a political awareness which grew as a reaction to the tragic consequences of poverty and discrimination.

Marie's story begins with her family's journey as they leave the meager but stable sustenance of a farming life to look for success by engaging in what they find to be the wearisome and unending toil of a disenfranchised proletariat. Their situation illustrates on an individual level the circumstances of all workers who fruitlessly struggle for financial success. In the same way, the situation of Marie's mother is emblematic of the lives of women who have no choices once they are committed to a marriage in poverty. The real and threatened violence which Marie's father inflicts on his wife and children expresses his frustration in never getting ahead.

As Marie's family drifts from one company mining town to the next, and as their economic status and family cohesiveness deteriorate, an awareness of the all-pervasive systems of class and gender oppression dawns in her mind. She commits herself to the goal of becoming educated, hoping to extricate herself from the inevitabilities of poverty—and of marriage. When young Marie glimpses the relationships between husbands and wives, she sees the threat of ultimate demoralization for herself. Sex becomes for her a cruel exchange in which women trade their bodies for the doubtful economic security of marriage. The legitimacy of married women is, for Marie, less honorable than the lives of women such as her aunt Helen, a prostitute, for at least Helen's circumstances tell the truth about sexual relations. To Marie's immature mind, the responsibilities of marriage are naturally repugnant. A cowhand's proposal is refused because Marie "won't have nothin' to do with dooties! . . . some things make me sick!"

Reflecting upon the incidents of her life, Marie attempts to understand her damaged sexuality. A brief, early marriage ends in pain for both Marie and Knut Larsen, her gentle, uncomprehending husband, when she realizes that she cannot compromise in her deep aversion to the implications of any marital situation. Marie's inability to understand and express her conflicting feelings, as well as the loss suffered when she undergoes two abortions, causes her to withdraw in despair and confusion from the relationship.

As Marie works and sacrifices to gain an education, she begins to understand on an intellectual level what she has always sensed emotionally—the necessary fight for survival of both the working classes and women. In a struggle to better the quality of her own life, Marie finds it necessary to turn away from the demands of her young siblings, who, after the death of their mother, expect her to take over the maternal, self-sacrificing role. When Marie's brother, working at manual labor, is crushed by a collapsing ditch, the guilt over leaving her family deepens. Ultimately, Marie comes to see the choice of an independent life over a life like her mother's as a political necessity—the only way to live meaningfully becomes to strive for knowledge and work for change on a mass scale.

Living in New York City, distanced from the scenes of her childhood, Marie finds spiritual and political satisfaction through working with the Indian nationalist movement. Incarceration as a suspected spy in the fearful atmosphere of World War I America marks her as a committed activist; she is accepted by the Indians despite being both a Westerner and a woman. Marie falls in love with, and promptly marries, Anand Manvekar, a native Indian also working for independence. Although more satisfying than her first marriage, Marie's marriage to Anand is clouded by her sexual past. She watches helplessly as their marriage is destroyed in a clash of sexual politics and personal integrity. When a previous sexual encounter of Marie becomes a weapon to destroy the couple's political credibility, the destructiveness of self-righteous morality and double standards is exposed as ultimately responsible for the failure of the marriage.

When Marie leaves Anand, she is brought to the point at which her story begins—she is alone and trying to integrate the events and emotions of her life with a committed political identity.

## The Characters

Marie, as the narrator of her own story, is unremittingly honest as she explores the memories of a bleak childhood and her struggle to persevere and forge a decent life for herself. The process she undergoes requires a critical eye and a frank appraisal: She is trying to become a whole person in a fragmented and destructive world. Marie finds explanations for her own behavior and that of others in the conditions of life which they experience. If people are wanting, it is an effect of circumstance and not a lack of human impulse.

The failure of Marie's mother to rebel against the brutality of her husband is not a result of a weak will; rather, she has been rendered powerless to change her situation. In one rare instance, she refuses to let him control her and will not reveal how she voted; as a consequence, he leaves her. Any sense of autonomy that she might have derived from the coming of women's suffrage is completely negated by the fact that, once her husband leaves, she is even less able than before to meet her family's basic needs. Her triumph becomes a failure as it reveals her economic powerlessness.

Marie's father, unlike his wife, continues to believe that he can take some control over his desperate situation. He lives in dreams and stories and persists in believing that success will come in the next mining camp or business venture. His descent into alcoholism and delusional thinking is a result of his inability to overcome the powerful socioeconomic structures which dictate his lack of success.

Smedley illustrates a gender-based difference in the way that responsibilities are handled. When Helen, Marie's aunt, becomes a prostitute, she does not question the need to help support her sister's family, while their father frequently drinks all of his wages and fails to provide for the family. The hypocrisy of his condemnation of Helen's immoral behavior, when held up against his own, makes the point that integrity can be judged, not by social convention, but by the willingness to give unstintingly and at great personal cost.

For Marie, the lives of those who have known ease are even more mystifying than the lives of the suffering. The calm pleasure which her first husband, Knut Larsen, and his sister Karin find in living is beyond the scope of her understanding and experience. She is unable to trust the unaffected emotions which go along with it. When Knut speaks a few sharp words to Marie, she amplifies their cruelty because "there was a merciless war being waged . . . between my need and desire of love, and the perverted idea of love and sex that had been ground into my being. . . ." Marie's analysis of reactions and attitudes such as this are part of her determined effort to create a whole self and to understand the skewed justice of the world.

It emerges that the thing to be valued by both Marie and Smedley is the inherent dignity of human nature. Despite the crippling effects of a base existence, Marie and many of the people around her manage to sustain a spark of human generosity. These individuals, who endure despite "the darkness of not-knowing—who can realize what that means unless he has lived through it!" and who "reacted instead of thinking," are held up by Smedley as an article of faith. Marie finds her motivation in this spirit of endurance. By blaming conditions and not individuals, Marie locates the cause of her anger; she creates a sense of purpose in attempting to change that source.

## Themes and Meanings

Marie's journey of healing focuses on her desire to abolish injustices experienced by women and by the poor. She comes to accept the necessary stance for her struggle: "I belong to those who do not die for the sake of beauty. I belong to those who die from other causes—exhausted by poverty, victims of wealth and power, fighters in a great cause." Yet Marie's commitment is not one that requires complete self-denial. Smedley recognizes that to undertake such a work as Marie's, one must overcome psychological oppression as well. The same power structure which creates inhumane living conditions also thwarts the emotional needs of those subject to it. An unending round of labor which requires the repression of all needs except hunger reinforces the social control exercised by the economic system.

The system of sexual oppression is at the core of economic control and ultimately upholds it. Because a laborer's value resides in earning capacity, and conventional marriage makes a woman's earning ability that of her husband, she is valued only as a supplement to his potential. Once the forces of childbirth and motherhood begin to take effect in a woman's life, she becomes an object of total submission under the guise of her husband's "natural dominance," regardless of whether his actual protection is also included therein. For Marie, the horror of the situation is bound up with sex and the guilt of participating in her own subjugation. Marie's second marriage fails, and she is divided from her beloved work in the Indian movement, when an incident in her sexual past is used against her. These events dramatically illustrate that no movement of human struggle can succeed while men and women are divided by sexual politics which place them in unequal positions of power with disparate standards of behavior.

Marie's bout with emotional illness and her sense of a loss of control bring her to a point of decision—to accept the pain of life as the price exacted in a struggle to better the quality of life. To recognize her status of victim, while no longer allowing herself to be victimized, is possible only when she is armed with the knowledge of experience.

*Critical Context*

   *Daughter of Earth* differs from much of Smedley's other work, not because it chronicles personal experience but because it does not focus on her experiences in the Chinese revolution, to which she ultimately devoted her life and writing. In many ways, the incidents in the life of Marie Rogers mirror those in the life of Smedley and probe deeply into the psychological structures which motivated her. An intense work of personal passage and liberation, *Daughter of Earth* is largely a cathartic exercise for Smedley, allowing her to exorcise the ghosts of her past and embrace more fully her commitment to the universal plight of workers, women, and all the oppressed.

   That *Daughter of Earth* has endured and is available to contemporary readers is a benefit of the current interest in reprinting works which have been lost through political and social disfavor. Smedley's absence from the canon of American literature dates from the McCarthy years. Branded as a dangerous "Red" for the time that she spent working in China during its revolution, she was harassed by government agents and shunned by the literary establishment, and her books were removed from public circulation.

   The reprinting of *Daughter of Earth* and other of her works encourages Smedley's reception into the American canon. Her portrait of the soul of America—the dreams and struggles of unempowered workers and women—is lovingly and respectfully executed and deeply moving for its refusal to accept the limits of adversity.

*Sources for Further Study*

Ickes, Harold L. "Death by Association," in *The New Republic*. CXXII (May 29, 1950), pp. 16-17.

MacKinnon, J., and S. MacKinnon, eds. "Agnes Smedley's 'Cell Mates,'" in *Signs*. III (Winter, 1977), pp. 531-539.

Milton, Joyce. *A Friend of China*, 1980.

Smedley, Agnes. *Battle Hymn of China*, 1943.

_____. *Portraits of Chinese Women in Revolution*, 1978. Edited by Jan MacKinnon and Steve MacKinnon.

*Mollie A. Brodsky*

# THE DEAN'S DECEMBER

*Author:* Saul Bellow (1915-    )
*Type of plot:* Comic realism
*Time of plot:* Approximately the 1970's
*Locale:* Bucharest, Chicago, and California
*First published:* 1982

> *Principal characters:*
> ALBERT CORDE, a professor of journalism and a dean at a
>     university located in Chicago
> MINNA, his Rumanian-born wife, a professor of astronomy at
>     the same university
> VALERIA RARESH, Minna's mother, who is dying in Bucharest,
>     a former Communist Party member and Minister of
>     Health
> ELFRIDA ZAEHNER, later SOROKIN, Corde's sister
> MASON ZAEHNER, SR., Elfrida's deceased husband
> MASON ZAEHNER, JR., Elfrida's son and Corde's nephew
> ALEC WITT, the provost, Corde's superior at his university
> DEWEY SPANGLER, a famous journalist and Corde's boyhood
>     friend

## The Novel

Most of *The Dean's December* takes place in Rumania; only the last thirty pages are set in the United States, and these are divided between Chicago and California. At the opening of the novel, Albert Corde and his wife, Minna, have just arrived in Bucharest, where Valeria, Minna's mother, is dying. They have come—in December—to be with her during the last days of her life. The bulk of the novel describes these last days and the efforts by Corde and Minna to communicate with Valeria. She is partially paralyzed and in intensive care; they want to be with her as she dies. This is no simple task. Valeria is in a Party hospital, and visits are strictly limited by a colonel in the secret service. A minor duel of wits, or influence, ensues, Corde pulling strings with the American ambassador and a famous journalist in an attempt to circumvent the colonel and see Valeria. Even after Valeria's death, this "duel" with authorities continues over the arrangements for Valeria's burial.

Another significant series of events is taking place in Chicago, thousands of miles from Bucharest. These events are recounted by means of flashbacks, mail arriving for Corde in Bucharest, and encounters with Americans such as the ambassador and the influential journalist mentioned above, Corde's boyhood friend, Dewey Spangler. A student at Corde's university has been killed; a black man is on trial for the murder. Corde follows the trial closely—he has personally posted a reward for information leading to conviction. The provost opposes Corde's involvement—and that of the university—in the trial. Corde's nephew Mason also opposes it; he is a friend of the black man accused of the murder, and he attacks Corde for having no real understanding of the Chicago underworld. In addition, Corde's own cousin Max Detillion, a flamboyant and corrupt Chicago lawyer, is defending the accused killer.

The novel thus establishes a counterpoint between events in Rumania and different (yet similar) events in Chicago. These events are less important, however, than Corde's speculations about them. To a large extent *The Dean's December* is a novel of ideas. Corde has a restless, impatient, questing mind, and he constantly attempts to explain the actions in which he is caught up, drawing conclusions from them. Approximately the first half of the novel is "about" a comparison between Communism and Chicago politics. This comparison slowly breaks down for a variety of reasons. The personality of the dean—full, "round," entirely believable—comes to occupy center stage, and the Rumanian setting, although concretely described, becomes shadowy, and the Communist Party mechanism is invisible. Although Corde theoretically compares the Communist "jungle" to that of Chicago, he has no real access to the Rumanian "jungle," and his presence in Bucharest is that of an American tourist. The comparison is an excellent idea. Tocqueville made a different yet analogous comparison more than a hundred and forty years ago; it remains very much a part of American culture and contemporary consciousness. Bellow starts the novel with an ambitious analogy between a Rumanian colonel in the secret service and his counterparts in the Chicago political machine. Yet as the novel progresses, this promising parallel retreats far into the background. The colonel disappears; Chicago concerns come to the fore even in Bucharest, via the mail. When Corde and Minna return to the United States, interest in Rumania and Communism has long since ceased to engage the reader. The strong-minded Valeria is no more, and in practical terms the same holds true of the colonel—the author's available material seems to be exhausted.

## The Characters

It is not fair to discuss *The Dean's December* only in terms of what "happens" in the book. It is a novel of ideas or, to be more exact, of speculations. The person who constantly speculates, trying out new theories and coining witty phrases, is the dean, Albert Corde. Who is he? The title of the book notwithstanding, Corde is not really a dean. Although a college dean holds great prestige and power over people, the reader quickly learns that Albert Corde does not fit this mold. He has many insecurities. He regrets that he is not a "hard" scientist, and it turns out that he does not even have a Ph.D.—he is an "outsider" to academia, having made his reputation as a journalist for the *Herald* in Paris. It appears that diplomacy is not his forte, and this is one of his endearing characteristics; he has written several speculative, emotional articles for *Harper's Magazine* about Chicago and has offended many people.

This notion of an "outsider dean" (some of his relatives call him the "dud dean") lacks verisimilitude—Bellow never explains how or why Corde was appointed, and it would seem his university either lacked evaluative controls or acted suicidally. (Perhaps Bellow was imagining an analogy with his own unique position as a writer in a university.) Nevertheless, by the novel's premise Corde is a dean, and a highly interesting one at that: humorous, given to theorizing, emotional, and apocalyptic, with a real gift for words. His background is French and "Huguenot-Irish-Midwesterner and whatever else," and he is in his early fifties, very much in love with his Rumanian, "hard scientist" wife. His mind is the novel's center of interest: fully sympathetic, vulnerable yet carrying the world on his shoulders, he is everything for which a reader of fiction could reasonably ask—except that he is not a credible dean. The speculations and ideas of the novel are convincingly Corde's. They have real urgency and centripetal force—occasionally the reader is tempted to wonder if these ideas, with their driving momentum, are also those of the author. Sometimes, no doubt, Corde acts as Bellow's stand-in or mouthpiece. Critical opinion is divided on this topic, but Corde is very likely an authentic, relatively independent creation. Unless the reader knows Bellow's work extremely well and inevitably finds numerous echoes, Corde, the unconvincing dean, stands on his two feet as a character, the novel's most successful creation.

Corde's wife, Minna, who is generally obliging and lost in the clouds of her vocation, is attractively drawn but is a rather flat character. Minna's mother, Valeria, is supposed to be a strong, warm, and sterling woman, greatly respected and wielding considerable influence over others. The reader must accept this image of Valeria largely on faith—she is incapacitated during most of the book and is largely seen reflected in other people's opinions. It is claimed that

> she had loved her husband, that was why she became a Communist militant: she had loved her husband, loved her daughter, her sister. Then for thirty years she had made up for the Marxism, for the sin of helping to bring in the new regime, by a private system of atonement, setting up her mutual-aid female network.

She was even at one point Minister of Health, yet she "fell in disgrace" or resigned. The reader can accept her former militancy, her Party membership, but the claim that she was Minister of Health would put her in an entirely different class and milieu and defies credibility, just as Corde's deanship defies it. Perhaps the author felt the need to add these vocations because there are so many speculations about the nature of power in the novel.

The other characters are all substantial, although less important to the design of the book. Corde's sister Elfrida is finely rendered. Elfrida's deceased husband and her son, Mason, Jr., are flat characters and somewhat crudely drawn, yet believable. The blacks Rufus Ridpath and Toby Winthrop are sensitively sketched, although sometimes Bellow has difficulties with the rhythms of black vernacular.

### Themes and Meanings

*The Dean's December* is about power and the nature of reality. Corde, for many years a journalist based in Paris, returned to Chicago because "for me it's more like the front lines. Here is where the action is." The entire novel can be seen as an attempt to locate this "action." Relationships are constantly tested in terms of relative or effective power. When he is in Rumania, Corde constantly tries to pull strings. Indeed, throughout the novel, Corde is dealing with power-savvy realists: the colonel, the provost, Zaehner, and, as it turns out, Dewey Spangler. The ineffective, theory-spinning Corde—and here he is not alone among academic liberals—admires toughness. He is fascinated by power, and he realizes that it is power, not ideas, that moves the world. He grudgingly admires his brother-in-law Zaehner (who despises him) because he is forceful, smart, political, cynical, and rich, "a Lyndon Johnson type of bully." Chicago, the "Cloaca Maxima," rivets his imagination with its "wild, monstrous setting of half demolished cities" where the only choice is "between a slow death and a sudden one, between attrition and quick destruction."

The book's best descriptions are of the Cook County hospital and the county jail, where the younger lawyers "were built like professional athletes, flashy dressers who went to hair stylists, not to barbers. Beautifully combed, like pretty ladies or dear small boys in Cruikshank's Dickens illustrations, they might have been either thugs or bouncers." Corde is equally fascinated by the criminals:

> Dope pushers, gun toters (everybody had a gun), child molesters, shoplifters, smackheads, purse snatchers, muggers, rapists, arsonists, wife beaters, car thieves, pimps bailing out their whores. People were all dressed up.

There follows a long, lively description of the various outlandish types of dress of Chicago's underworld. Corde is fascinated by the colorful characters, and the vigorous passage is one of the high points of the novel, recalling Charles Dickens' interest in similar types of characters and institutions.

When Corde's nephew and others criticize him for being "out of it,"

Corde agrees; he is far more attracted than repulsed by the *de facto* cynical power of the Chicago "jungle." A similar impulse lies at the source of his fascination with Communism and the colonel:

> No outsider could understand these multiple roles and Chinese intricacies. It was beyond Corde, certainly. It was not the American kind of loyalty-duplicity; in America the emotions were different somehow, perhaps thinner. Here you led a crypto-emotional life in the shadow of the Party and the State.

The moral condemnation of Communism is not for Corde (perhaps not for his creator), and the colonel in the Rumanian secret police is no worse than the corrupt Chicago judge. Corde's attitude about Communism curiously echoes the attitude of George Kennan, who wrote in *Encounter* (September, 1976): "Show me first an America which has successfully coped with the problems of crime, drugs, deteriorating educational standards, urban decay, pornography, and decadence of one sort or another, only then I will tell you how we are going to defend ourselves from the Russians."

What does Corde do with these sources of power once he has identified them? In his quixotic way he tries to test them, to provoke them and see how far they can be pushed. The ending of the book, however, is completely ambiguous. Whether Corde's increasing number of enemies is caused by his concern for the truth, or by his own subconscious desire to make enemies— to antagonize people—is unclear. The book concludes inside the Mount Palomar Observatory in California, Corde literally coming down from the stars in an elevator and finding that he dislikes the return to Earth. The ending is both humble and ironic.

*Critical Context*

The critical reception of *The Dean's December* was mixed. No one has claimed for it the excellence of *Herzog* (1964), *The Adventures of Augie March* (1953), or *Henderson the Rain King* (1959). Some critics have claimed that the novel is a failure. In John Updike's felicitous phrase, Bellow is not simply a good writer, "He is one of the rare writers who we . . . feel to be taking mimesis a layer or two deeper than it has gone before," yet *The Dean's December* lacks "a firm, simple center." Some critics have admired Bellow's descriptions of Bucharest, yet there is a consensus that the descriptions of Chicago are even more effective. Most critics and readers have felt that the Tocquevillian comparison of the Communist system with that of Chicago does not work. There is more disagreement about the second major criticism of the novel, the figure of Corde. Although an unconvincing dean, he is nevertheless a substantial, contradictory, fascinating character. As Robert Towers pointed out, even more than in *Herzog* Bellow has staked everything upon the personality, reflections, and speech of his central character. This daring is not without interest and rewards. *The*

*Dean's December* is certainly a problem novel—it is far from an aesthetic success—but in it Bellow has revealed some of his most intimate, intriguing personal concerns.

*Sources for Further Study*
*Contemporary Literary Criticism*, XXV, 1983. Edited by Jean C. Stine.
Fuchs, Daniel. *Saul Bellow: Vision and Revision*, 1984.
Towers, Robert. "A Novel of Politics, Wit and Sorrow," in *The New York Times Book Review*. LXXXVII (January 10, 1982), p. 1.
Updike, John. "Toppling Towers Seen by a Whirling Soul," in *The New Yorker*. LVIII (February 22, 1982), p. 120.

*John Carpenter*

# DEATH OF THE FOX

*Author:* George Garrett (1929-     )
*Type of plot:* Historical novel
*Time of plot:* The English Renaissance, from the last days of the reign of
   Henry VIII to the early days of the reign of Charles I
*Locale:* The British Isles, continental Europe, and the oceans of the world
*First published:* 1971

> *Principal characters:*
> SIR WALTER RALEGH (1552-1618), who is self-described as "a
>    seafaring man, a soldier and a courtier"; also a poet, his-
>    torian, and adviser to Queen Elizabeth I
> ELIZABETH TUDOR, the Queen of England from 1558 to 1603
> JAMES STUART, the King of England from 1603 to 1625

## The Novel

In late October, 1618, Sir Walter Ralegh, known as "The Fox" to the citizens of England and author of, among other works, an unfinished "History
of the World" and some very popular short poetry, was tried for treason for
the second time and condemned to death. George Garrett's novel *Death of
the Fox* concentrates on the events of the day before Ralegh's execution and
the morning of his death and, by focusing on Ralegh's thoughts and reflections during that time, re-creates the crucial moments of his life and sets
them in the context of a very turbulent and enthralling time in the history of
the British Isles. The absolute accuracy of Garrett's account can never be
determined, but through the accumulation of a multitude of particulars
based on very thorough historical research and through an act of empathetic
imagination that makes the character of Ralegh vibrant and compelling,
Garrett has made a life and era both vivid and convincing.

Garrett's task is that of any serious historical novelist. He must work with
a vast amount of recorded historical data, select what is crucial to understanding an epoch, present it so that it provides what Leo Tolstoy called the
"life of the facts," and then show how his protagonist is intricately involved
in the shaping of the sensibility of the times. To avoid being overwhelmed by
a sheer list of events, causes, names, and places—that is, the undigested
mass of material cataloged with no guiding principle by stolid scholars—
Garrett has developed a method for combining information and narration
that depends on the specific, singular voice of an observer/participant who is
known as an interesting if minor character in the larger drama. With these
people as anchors in the great sea of Elizabethan life, Garrett is able to
navigate a course which locates the reader on one island of data after
another until the sea itself becomes familiar. Then the course can proceed

as Ralegh himself becomes the source and impetus for the continuation of the voyage.

The first voice one hears is that of Henry Yelverton, the king's attorney general in 1618, who is preparing for his presentation of the case against Ralegh. In his desire to avoid the embarrassment which his predecessor, the very gifted jurist Edward Coke, suffered as the victim of Ralegh's wit in the trial of November, 1603, Yelverton is seen carefully studying the documents of that case as the narrative begins. In this way, Garrett can bring to the reader's attention the facts of Ralegh's fall from glory in the court of Elizabeth I and his subsequent residence in the Tower of London for most of the next fifteen years. An interesting symmetry is established, since the fifteen years preceding the first trial, spanning the time from the destruction of the Spanish Armada in 1588 to the death of Elizabeth I in 1603 mark the high point of Ralegh's power and influence in court life. Through Yelverton's review of the case, the court of Elizabeth I is described and contrasted with the court of James I. The narrative scope widens as Garrett then shows both King James and Ralegh through the process of their thoughts as they awaken on the same day. While this is the initial view of Ralegh, he is shown primarily in contemplation of the king's motives, so that it is James I, Ralegh's adversary, who is examined next—his vision of himself as king, his plans for England, his struggles with his enemies within and beyond the realm, and the economic difficulties at the heart of his statecraft are presented. As the measure of a heroic combat is the mettle of the adversaries, it is necessary to give James I the substance which would make his conflict with Ralegh a clash of titans. Once this has been done, the scene is set for the final trial that will determine Ralegh's fate, and Garrett is ready to describe the events of the extraordinary life which have shaped his character and destiny to this point.

The pattern of the narrative is to move steadily closer to Ralegh, and Garrett's technique here is to relate the history of the man in chronological order, beginning with his arrival in London as a callow west country lad, innocent and eager, unformed but already recognizable. The narrative perspective shifts from Ralegh's own developing consciousness to the accounts of several men whose lives touched his in some significant fashion. Through Ralegh's eyes, the reader sees London in mid-century, growing toward greatness as a world capital. Then, after a brief sojourn at Oxford, there are three extended set pieces, each composed with appropriate typological invention, in which Ralegh's strengths as a young man emerge. An army veteran, a captain whose bluff manner expresses the soul of the English army regular, speaks of Ralegh's daring, courage, determination, and inspiring leadership. A seafaring man who is the spirit of the British sailor depicts Ralegh as an ingenious, persistent, and intrepid explorer who ranks with Sir Francis Drake and Sir Martin Frobisher in nautical annals. An anonymous courtier, whose cynicism, weary sophistication, and self-regard define the decadence of court life, describes the magnetism, daunting style, and astonishing wit of a Ralegh radiant as the queen's favorite. It is clear from these accounts why Ralegh inspires such devotion and loyalty from the men he leads, and why he has also drawn such hate and envy from rivals confounded by his ability and self-possession. When James I assumes the throne, it is not surprising that a cabal of lesser men can convince him that Ralegh—implacable enemy of Spain, suspected atheist, confidant of the already legendary Elizabeth I—must be condemned as a traitor and put to death.

As Ralegh prepares for the second trial, the narrative focus narrows still further, often moving on a track parallel to Ralegh's mind. Until this stage in the narration, he has been a fascinating but forbidding figure. Now his humanity is established to complement and enhance his heroic image. Except for an unsuccessful maritime expedition to Guiana, he has been living in the tower for more than a decade, and he is weakened by his wounds and disappointments. Still fully conscious of the world to which he has been denied full access, he is now occupied with thoughts of his family and the effect of his life on those who were close to him. There is a sadness in his recollection of his wild son Wat, dead in battle, and his younger son Carew, almost unknown to him. There is a deep poignance in his concern for his wife, Bess Throckmorton, formerly a maid of honor in the court of Elizabeth I, who lost her valued place there when she married Ralegh. There is a rueful sense of friendship unfulfilled in his recollections of his pleasure in discourse with Thomas Harriot, a scholar and naturalist. The novel concludes as Ralegh prepares for, faces, and then literally commands his own death on a cold, clear autumn morning, and it offers, paradoxically, a vision of singing life as Ralegh's own life span comes to an end.

## The Characters

George Garrett is constrained in the development of the characters in *Death of the Fox* by the historical information that is available about each of them, but he has turned this difficulty into an advantage by using what is known, including portraits, descriptions, and the extant writing of these people as a foundation, and then extending what has been into what could be. James I and Elizabeth I are figures familiar in British history, but Garrett makes them fresh and alive in the narrative by a thorough understanding of their recorded behavior, which he traces back to an artful reconstruction of their thoughts. James I, in particular, emerges as a man who, if not quite sympathetic, is completely comprehensible. His ideas on the divine right of monarchs to rule are an enlightening example of a worldview that is hard to understand today. Both James Stuart, the man, and James I, the king, are interesting beyond the facts listed in conventional histories. Elizabeth I is much more famous and needs less explanation, but Garrett, with quick, deft touches, reinforces the strength of the myth by demystifying the person. He shows how truly regal she was in action for one so thoroughly human in emotions and instincts.

Less is actually known of Walter Ralegh than either monarch, but what remains of his writing mixes with stories of his adventures as an intriguing inducement to understand the man. The questions of why Elizabeth I "loved" him, why James I admired and feared him, and why he has become a kind of folk hero despite his intellectual accomplishments all demand an imaginative explanation. Garrett provides it by demonstrating Ralegh's greatest gifts in their fullest expression and then analyzing them from their conception.

Although Ralegh is a man of energy and sinew *par excellence*, whose exploits and visions of exploration are the essence of inspiration to action, his greatest strength is his mind. He is a man of exceptional mental activity, and how he perceives himself is the key to the way that the world perceives him. Garrett contends that he attracts Elizabeth I through the *style* of his service, which surpasses even the principles upon which it is based. This is crucial to his character, because his dedication to law, religion, and proper moral conduct represent the best of English culture and custom. At the same time, he exhibits the gravity, complexity, and subtlety characteristic of the finest products of Renaissance thought. Because they have been involved in his life, his friends, family, enemies, and even servants glow for a moment in history by reflection of his dazzling light—a light generated by an awesome mental energy.

*Themes and Meanings*

The meaning of Walter Ralegh's life coincides with the meaning of the book. Those things he loved remain as a tribute to him, their continuance in history partially sustained by his participation. Shifting personal allegiances, duplicitous national alliances, and immense governmental corruption marked the turbulent, chaotic era in which he lived. To counteract these forces for disorder, Ralegh was drawn to the law as a means of creating substance and certainty and was expert in its ways although never a formal practitioner. The age's woeful record of fratricide, homicide, and regicide drew Ralegh to a thorough philosophical examination of the nature of God as a source for justice and mercy, although he was accused of atheism at his trials. The limitations and confinements of a class-ridden, power-crazed, ego-dominated social structure, not to mention actual incarceration, drew Ralegh to fields of fire, on land and sea, and to new and unknown territories in an attempt to find uncluttered arenas for freedom and fantasy. Most significantly, out of a desire to transcend all of the limits of his life, Ralegh chose language as his ultimate weapon in his attempt to establish something permanent in an age when men's fortunes, as ever, were subject to time and chance. As he wrote to his son, "Words fail and falter often, but they are the best servants we have."

The importance of language and literature for Ralegh is emphasized by Garrett's inventive use of language to create the ethos of the Elizabethan cosmos. In a sense, the setting of the book is one of the major "characters" of the novel, and Garrett is both eloquent and poetic in his descriptions of the British countryside and in his evocation of the life of the city's taverns, streets, waterways, and markets. The voice which Garrett uses for those sections when he is operating as an almost omniscient narrator is an interesting amalgam of the descriptive style of Joyce Cary's Gulley Jimson (from *The Horse's Mouth*, 1944) combined with Dylan Thomas' syntactic strategy of loading a line with adjectives and placing the subject at the end of an adjectival chain. Other touches from recent modern poetry are employed as well, such as the frequent removal of the definite article to achieve an effect of immediacy. The result of this linguistic creativity is to include images, figures, conceits, and phrases from the canon of Elizabethan literature in a context that is appealingly crisp and contemporary. The achievement of this style is to make Ralegh's speech and thought authentic and relevant without being dated—in other words, an image from the Elizabethan world placed in a modern frame. The rhythms and metaphors of Renaissance England have been carried intact to live in a twentieth century American novel, and a hero of that ancient time has been brought to life again in a future age.

*Critical Context*

*Death of the Fox* is a complete success as a historical novel because, upon reading it, one cannot imagine the times it describes to have been at variance to the picture it presents. It does a superb job of capturing the tone of a time through its combination of careful, thorough research, imaginative writing, and poetic writing. While *Death of the Fox* may not be on the same level of achievement as *War and Peace*, the fact that Tolstoy's masterpiece even comes to mind is a testament to its excellence.

Readers who have enjoyed *Death of the Fox* will be glad to know that Garrett, a poet, story-writer, and biographer as well as a novelist, has produced another powerfully imagined work of historical re-creation, not strictly a sequel to his book on Ralegh but a companion volume: *The Succession: A Novel of Elizabeth and James* (1983).

*Source for Further Study*

Robinson, W. R. "Imagining the Individual: George Garrett's *Death of the Fox*," in *The Hollins Critic*. August, 1971.

*Leon Lewis*

# DEMOCRACY

*Author:* Joan Didion (1934-      )
*Type of plot:* Domestic tragedy
*Time of plot:* The mid-1970's
*Locale:* Hawaii and Southeast Asia
*First published:* 1984

>  *Principal characters:*
>  INEZ CHRISTIAN VICTOR, the protagonist, a native of Hawaii,
>      the wife of a liberal Democratic senator from California
>  HARRY VICTOR, Inez's husband who narrowly lost the 1972
>      Democratic nomination for president
>  ADLAI VICTOR, the dull-witted son of Harry and Inez
>  JESSICA VICTOR, Adlai's twin sister, a heroin addict
>  JACK LOVETT, a right-wing rogue and "information specialist"
>      who is Inez's one true love
>  PAUL CHRISTIAN, Inez's father, driven to insanity by the de-
>      mise of the feudal aristocracy
>  DWIGHT CHRISTIAN, Inez's uncle, the current head of the
>      family
>  BILLY DILLON, Harry's tough-minded but tenderhearted
>      press secretary
>  JOAN DIDION, the author who tells the story and occasionally
>      appears as a character

*The Novel*

   *Democracy* is the story of Inez Christian Victor, the daughter of a once-prominent Hawaiian family and the wife of a liberal Democratic senator from California. Essentially alienated from her husband, Inez maintains a lifelong love affair with a mysterious "information specialist" who operates on the fringes of the CIA and the military-industrial complex. She follows this man, whose name is Jack Lovett, to Southeast Asia, where, as South Vietnam is falling to the Communists, he rescues her daughter Jessica, who has drifted to Saigon because she has heard that job opportunities are good there. While in Southeast Asia, Inez sees Jack drown in a hotel pool in Jakarta and brings his body back to Hawaii to be buried under a jacaranda tree at Schofield Barracks. Disillusioned with life in the fast lane, she returns to Kuala Lumpur to work with refugees.

   Somewhat on the periphery of Inez's story is the public chaos of Indochina and the more private tragedy of the murder of her sister Janet Christian Zeigler by their father, Paul Christian. The circumstances of this murder are shrouded in ambiguity. The reader knows that at the time of the shooting Janet was entertaining Wendell Omura, a congressman of Oriental descent, and that Paul Christian is a genteel racist of the old feudal aristocracy. The suggestions of an interracial affair and of the conflict of cultures seem to be vestiges of the more specifically regional Hawaiian novel which Didion says that she tried to write. What she actually produced is a blend of current history and domestic tragedy that starts as a brilliant satire of political manners and blossoms into a strangely compelling romance. *Democracy*, in short, is a rich but hybrid novel.

### The Characters

Like the deracinated women in Didion's earlier novels, Inez Christian Victor is a long way from the home of her youth. The glimpses that Didion provides of that home (feudal Hawaii) suggest that it is modeled on the stable agrarian culture of Didion's own Northern California childhood. Inez is caught up in a jet-set life-style that she cannot stand but does not know how to escape, trapped in marriage to a man she does not love, and saddled with two children who seem beyond redemption. By having Inez make a commitment to the refugees in Kuala Lumpur, Didion may be trying to give her protagonist a moral strength lacking in the women of her earlier novels. (She has been frequently criticized for depicting women weaker than herself.) What connects Inez most obviously with earlier Didion women is the fact that she is torn between two very different kinds of men.

Didion reveals Harry Victor's personality to the reader by allowing Harry to condemn himself with his own clichés. He is the author of such memorable tracts as "Justice for Whom—A Young Lawyer Wants Out" and *The View from the Streets: Root Causes, Radical Solutions and a Modest Proposal*. When he makes a human rights junket to a Third World trouble spot, he refers to the anarchy and bloodshed as "the normal turbulence of a nascent democracy." Mary McCarthy writes: "At times Harry Victor seems meant to recall one of the Kennedys (most likely Bobby) or all of them. There is a hint of Jack's womanizing, and the suggestion that Inez Victor may have a 'drinking problem' brings to mind Teddy and Joan."

If Harry Victor is the most contemptible male character in Didion's fiction, Jack Lovett is probably the most admirable. He combines vitality and realism with compassion and sentiment. He may even be a closet romantic, a latter-day Rhett Butler. As the professional rogue with a heart of gold and an unrequited passion, Jack Lovett is not only more attractive but also more interesting than the numbingly predictable Harry. If Harry is correct in calling him a "war lover," that is of little consequence. Jack's virtues have more to do with personal character than with ideological commitment. He possesses sufficient moral responsibility to go to Vietnam and rescue Inez and Harry's drug-addicted daughter from the ruins of a war that Didion believes was spawned by liberal self-delusion. Significantly, Jack entices Jessica into his custody by promising to take her to a John Wayne film.

From a purely technical standpoint, the most controversial character in this novel is "Joan Didion" herself. Departing from the more conventional narrative techniques of her earlier novels, Didion inserts herself into *Democracy* and claims to have been personally acquainted with her characters. Although this may appear to make Didion's tale a postmodernist novel about novel-writing, it also places her in the decidedly premodernist company of George Eliot and William Makepeace Thackeray, both of whom inserted themselves into their fiction. By telling the reader about her problems in writing this book and by treating the characters as if they were as real as the figures in her journalism, Didion may be trying to collapse the distinction between fiction and nonfiction narrative. If the new journalism brings the techniques of fiction to the writing of fact, this novel brings the illusion of fact to the writing of fiction.

## Themes and Meanings

Joan Didion is well-known for her acute sense of place and for her fascination with the American West. These twin aspects of her muse have long been evident in her writings about her home state of California; she has, however, occasionally cast her glance farther westward to Hawaii. In *Slouching Towards Bethlehem* (1968), she wrote: "I sat as a child on California beaches and imagined that I saw Hawaii, a certain shimmer in the sunset, a barely perceptible irregularity glimpsed intermittently through squinted eyes." In a column for *New West* magazine written more than a decade later, she revealed that she now kept a clock in her bedroom in Los Angeles set to Honolulu time.

When Didion tried to write a novel about feudal Hawaii (originally entitled "Pacific Distances"), however, she produced a book that is only peripherally about that subject. In *Democracy*, Hawaii is less important as a society in transition than as a way station between the Mainland and America's ultimate Western frontier—Southeast Asia. (In *Slouching Towards Bethlehem*, Didion speaks of sailors who got drunk in Honolulu because "they were no longer in Des Moines and not yet in Da Nang.") As Walt Whitman proclaimed more than a century earlier in his poem "Passage to India," the roundness of the Earth leads one not to some apocalyptic West but back east whence one came. America's manifest destiny, however, has produced not a mystical passage to India, but helicopters lifting off the roof of the American embassy in Saigon during the final days of the only war that the United States has ever lost.

After Jack Lovett dies, Inez is Didion's only decent survivor. She vows to stay on that last Pacific frontier, caring for the casualties of war, "until the last refugee was dispatched," something that Didion thinks is unlikely to happen in "Inez's or my lifetime." Her stance, then, reflects neither the liberal hubris of Harry Victor nor the conservative realism of Jack Lovett so much as Christian charity. As Mary McCarthy has noted, Inez makes "the choice of Guinevere: to take the veil. Kuala Lumpur is her Almesbury." When all external frontiers have been traversed, the only remaining refuge is the West within. In one particularly evocative passage, Inez describes "the Singapore Airlines flight that leaves Honolulu at 3:45 A.M. and at 9:40 A.M. one day later lands at Kai Tak Hong Kong" as "an eleven hour dawn, . . . exactly the way she hoped dying would be."

*Critical Context*

In this imagistic, elliptic novel, much is left to conjecture. More than in any of her previous works Didion has helped to fuel this conjecture by an almost compulsive literary allusiveness. Certainly the most significant allusion is to Henry Adams, who in 1880 published a novel entitled *Democracy*. Although McCarthy makes nothing of the two novels' having the same name, Thomas R. Edwards sees both Didion and Adams as displaced aristocrats who with "irony and subtlety confront a chaotic new reality that shatters the orderings of simpler, older ways." Perhaps an even more instructive link can be drawn between Didion's novel and *The Education of Henry Adams*, particularly its most famous chapter—"The Dynamo and the Virgin."

The thesis of this chapter is that over a period of six hundred years, Western civilization has moved from thirteenth century unity to nineteenth century multiplicity, from the age of the virgin to that of the dynamo. While this development represents progress to many, those of a traditionalist sensibility (such as Didion, Adams, and T. S. Eliot) realize that there is a dark side to progress, that another name for multiplicity is fragmentation. That we now live in an age when the ultimate fragmentation is prefigured in nuclear fission and that such an age represents an "advance" even beyond the dynamo occurred to Didion when touring Berkeley's nuclear reactor in Etcheverry Hall in 1979. Writing in a column for *New West*, she recalled that experience:

> In my Modern Library copy of *The Education of Henry Adams*, a book I first read and scored at Berkeley in 1954, I see this passage underlined: ". . . to Adams, the dynamo became a symbol of infinity. As he grew accustomed to the great gallery of machines"—he is talking about the machines at the 1900 Paris Exposition—"he began to feel the 40-foot dynamos as a moral force, much as the early Christians felt the Cross." After I had left the TRIGA Mark III reactor in the basement of Etcheverry Hall I wondered for a long time what Henry Adams would have made of the intense blue of the Cerenkov radiation around the fuel rods, the blue past all blue, the blue like light itself, the blue that is actually a shock wave in the pool water and is the exact blue of the glass at Chartres.

Significantly, *Democracy* begins with Inez observing the light at dawn during nuclear tests in the Pacific. At the end, when the narrator, Joan Didion, asks Inez for four reasons why she is in Kuala Lumpur, she replies: *"Colors, moisture, heat, enough blue in the air."*

*Sources for Further Study*

Edwards, Thomas R. "An American Education," in *The New York Review of Books*. XXXI (May 10, 1984), pp. 23-24.

McCarthy, Mary. "Love and Death in the Pacific," in *The New York Times Book Review*. LXXXIX (April 22, 1984), p. 1.

Mallon, Thomas. Review in *The American Spectator*. August, 1984, pp. 43-44.

*Mark Royden Winchell*

# THE DHARMA BUMS

*Author:* Jack Kerouac (1922-1969)
*Type of plot:* Spiritual quest
*Time of plot:* From 1955 to 1956
*Locale:* The California coast, San Francisco, Berkeley, the California Sierra,
    North Carolina, Marin County, and the Washington Cascades
*First published:* 1958

> *Principal characters:*
> RAYMOND SMITH, the first-person narrator, an author and
>     wanderer, based on Kerouac himself
> JAPHY RYDER, an outdoorsman, Buddhist, scholar, and poet
>     who becomes Smith's friend and mentor, based on Gary
>     Snyder
> CODY POMERAY, an old friend of Smith, based on Neal
>     Cassady

*The Novel*

Like most of Jack Kerouac's novels, *The Dharma Bums* is an autobiographical fiction in which a particular period in its author's life is dramatically heightened and given coherent shape. The book focuses on the friendship between its first-person narrator, Raymond Smith (based on Kerouac himself), and Japhy Ryder (based on Gary Snyder), and on the ways in which Japhy inspires Ray to lead a more spiritual, self-sufficient life.

The novel begins, however, not with the first meeting between Ray and Japhy, but with a freight train ride from Los Angeles to Santa Barbara, during which Ray is delighted to meet a little bum who carries a prayer by Saint Teresa. This tramp, whom Ray takes to be a religious wanderer, is less important in himself than as a precursor of Japhy Ryder, who comes to represent the ultimate "Dharma bum" in Ray's rapturous eyes. From their first meeting, Japhy is seen as an exemplary pilgrim who travels the world "to turn the wheel of the True Meaning, or Dharma, and gain merit for himself as a future Buddha (Awakener)."

Though Kerouac does not group his thirty-four chapters into sections, the novel does, under close scrutiny, reveal a symmetrical tripartite form. In each of its three parts, Ray moves from stressful encounters in civilization toward epiphanies in nature—epiphanies which he either experiences with or associates with Japhy.

In the first section, Ray enjoys certain aspects of his new friendship with Japhy in San Francisco and Berkeley, but it is their trip to the High Sierra that takes him to his first major "peak" experience of the novel. Kerouac dramatizes the historic group reading at the Gallery Six which launched the

San Francisco Poetry Renaissance in October, 1955, but he relegates Allen Ginsberg's breakthrough chanting of "Howl" (here Alvah Goldbook's recitation of "Wail") to the background, preferring instead to concentrate on Snyder/Japhy's reading, which Ray considers more "pure," "hopeful," and reminiscent of "oldtime American heroes and orators." In Berkeley, Ray admires Japhy's simple life-style and ability to attract women, but he finds his own commitment to sexual abstinence disturbed by Japhy's voracious lover Princess, and Ray is thus relieved when he, Japhy, and Henry Morley (a character based on John Montgomery) leave for the mountains.

The backpacking excursion into the High Sierra is the most exhilarating episode in the novel. Finding themselves alone for the major part of a day, Ray and Japhy hike along the "immortal" trail, singing out haiku and dancing over boulders on their way up to California's Matterhorn. Though Kerouac's innovative "spontaneous prose" style is less prevalent in this novel than in many of his others, there are a number of passages, particularly in this episode, that richly demonstrate his talent for expressing a simultaneous rush of sensations and ideas through unorthodox diction, syntax, and sentence rhythms:

> Pretty soon we got to a bend in the trail where it was suddenly gladey and dark with shade and a tremendous cataracting stream was bashing and frothing over scummy rocks and tumbling on down, and over the stream was a perfect bridge formed by a fallen snag, we got on it and lay belly-down and dunked our heads down, hair wet, and drank deep as the water splashed in our faces, like sticking your head by the jet of a dam.

In the second third of the novel, immediately after their return to Berkeley, Ray enjoys hearing Japhy generalize their backpacking experience into a vision of a "great rucksack revolution" in which millions of youths will forsake the dominant consumer culture and roam freely through the vast American wilderness. Yet civilization in the Bay Area soon becomes intolerable for Ray once again, when his old friend Cody (based on Neal Cassady) asks him to look after his paranoid girlfriend Rosie (based on Natalie Jackson), and she commits suicide while Ray sleeps. Ray then travels to North Carolina to be home with his mother and sister's family at Christmas. Though dependent on his sister's husband for grudging support, Ray stays until April, spending most of his time meditating in the woods. There he attains visions of himself as a Buddha, which he wants to share with Japhy, and he therefore returns to California.

At the beginning of the final third of the novel, Ray feels that he is in "paradise," for he is allowed to share a shack with Japhy near a hospitable Buddhist family in rural Marin County, just north of San Francisco. By the end of the summer, however, both he and Japhy tire of the family's drunken parties, and the two abandon Japhy's farewell party to hike over to Mount

Tamalpais for a final backpacking trip before Japhy leaves for Japan. Following Japhy's advice, Ray takes a summer job as a lookout on Desolation Peak in the Washington Cascades, and he attains a final ecstatic vision of "the freedom of eternity" before heading down the mountain as the summer and the novel end.

## The Characters

The Dharma Bums follows the pattern of many of Kerouac's other novels in concentrating mainly on two characters: a first-person male narrator based on Kerouac himself, and a larger-than-life male hero who inspires the narrator's admiration and allegiance. This pattern has a long tradition in American literature, including such important works as *Moby Dick* (1851) and *The Great Gatsby* (1925), but Kerouac's use of the pattern raises interesting new issues because all of his heroes were based on close friends, usually writers themselves, who sometimes had strong reactions to Kerouac's fictional use of them. Gary Snyder, for example, was initially angered by the image of an irrepressible extrovert and womanizer that *The Dharma Bums* imposed on him. Years later, however, Snyder praised Kerouac for his talent as a mythographer—for synthesizing the values that he wanted to promote in his archetypal characters.

Kerouac's characterization of Ray and Japhy has much to do with his personal and professional situation at the time that he wrote the novel. In the year between the experiences chronicled in *The Dharma Bums* and the time of its writing, Kerouac's most famous novel, *On the Road* (1957), was published, and he was unsettled by the glare of publicity and deeply troubled by the outraged vituperation of critics, who denounced the activities of Kerouac's hero Dean Moriarty (based on Neal Cassady) as depraved and subversive. Thus in November, 1957, through the haze of an increasing drinking problem, Kerouac wrote *The Dharma Bums* in an attempt both to hold on to the positive aspects of his life from just a year earlier, and to embody those aspects in a hero whose associations with the American frontier tradition would allow Kerouac's critics to see his visionary intentions in a more positive light.

Like all of Kerouac's first-person narrators, Ray Smith is a man of immense inner conflicts. Though it is one of Kerouac's weaknesses as a writer that he does not always seem aware of these conflicts, his great strength is the openness with which he allows these conflicts to express themselves—often in disconcerting or humorous juxtaposition. An episode in the first chapter illustrates several of these conflicts in Ray: between the freedom of wandering and the longing for a home, the exultations of solitude and the trials of loneliness, the sensual pleasures of the world and the inescapability of suffering. When Ray hops off the freight train in Santa Barbara, he enjoys an ecstatic evening on the beach. "You've done it again," he congratulates himself. "Happy. Just in my swim shorts, barefooted, wild-haired, in the red fire dark, singing, swigging wine, spitting, jumping, running—that's the way to live." Later, however, he wakes up in the middle of the night, and says to himself, "'I be as hard and old as a conch shell.'" He thinks of himself as "lonely man alone on the beach" and dreams "of home long ago in New England." Waking once more, he finally falls back to sleep, saying "It's all the same thing," thus reassuring himself of a Buddhist truth which in fact becomes his major goal in the novel: to sustain some unity—not only on an intellectual but also on an emotional and spiritual level as well—among the conflicting sides of his character.

For Ray Smith, Japhy Ryder represents a hero who can show him the path to just such an integrated self. Paradoxically, Japhy seems most at home when he is wandering in the wilderness, for he was reared in the woods of eastern Oregon and has spent most of his life working or hiking there. Also, Japhy's studies have enabled him to draw together American literature, native American mythology, and Oriental religion, thus integrating whole cultures in his personality, while Ray is still struggling with the discontinuity between the East and West Coasts. Though Japhy's heroes are such men of solitude as the American naturalist John Muir and the Chinese mountain poet Han Shan, he also enjoys sharing the wilderness with other people. In the way that Japhy seems to shift effortlessly from serious to ecstatic moods, in the way that his monastically austere dwelling places can quickly become the scene of abundant talkfests or orgies, and in the way that he practices Buddhism through both strenuous physical activity and anarchic "Zen lunacy," he seems to enjoy a consistent peace of mind. Ray, on the other hand, with his unaccountable mood swings from joy to sorrow, his struggles to curb his sexual desire and his alcoholism, and his more static practice of "do-nothing" Mahayana Buddhism, never seems able to sustain the level of enlightenment that he sometimes feels. Japhy is not, however, portrayed as a perfectly beatific saint: He has his moments of doubt about his life, he argues with Ray, and he suffers and causes suffering when he tries to juggle too many love affairs. Yet to Ray he remains a model of self-reliant conduct and a luminous source of spiritual inspiration to the very end of the novel.

*The Dharma Bums* also present vignettes of many other people who passed through Jack Kerouac's life during the year from September, 1955, to September, 1956, from "the little bum of Saint Teresa," to the garrulous Bay Area writers and bohemians, to the lonely truck drivers who give him transcontinental rides, to the gruff forest rangers in the Washington Cascades. Momentarily fascinating as some of these minor figures are, however, in general they are developed only sketchily, with thumbnail descriptions and dialogue that often seems barely differentiated in its voices. An exception to this prevailing sketchiness is Henry Morley, whose personal disorganization and brilliantly inane manner of speech add considerably to the comedy of the High Sierra excursion. Kerouac's treatment of women, on the other hand, is especially superficial: Though Ray observes a number of women with interest and sympathy, he never gains much insight into their characters.

## Themes and Meanings

The major goal of Ray Smith as discussed above—the achievement of a sustained unity among the many conflicting sides of his personality—is also the major theme of the novel as a whole. A consideration of all the important conflicts in Ray's character, and of all those moments in which he perceives ways of resolving them, would easily fill a book. Yet what is most interesting and feels most true about *The Dharma Bums* is that the novel as a whole expresses something that Ray never recognizes, and in fact tries to deny at the end: that such a euphoric state of sustained enlightenment is beyond him. Coming down from Desolation Peak, where Japhy had also worked as a lookout, Ray tries to believe that in taking Japhy as a model he has finally attained the state of permanent blissful enlightenment that he has been seeking: "The vision of the freedom of eternity was mine forever." For the reader, however, who remembers many similar moments in the novel, it is hard not to view this overly optimistic finale with some skepticism.

Like many other wondrous characters in American literature, Japhy Ryder represents a myth into which the first-person narrator ultimately cannot enter, a limit that he cannot achieve. What is even more interesting than the wondrousness of the mythical hero in *The Dharma Bums*, as in many other American novels, is the curiosity and resilience of the earthbound narrator. Though he repeatedly lapses from what he thinks should be permanent enlightenment, Ray Smith never ceases to explore large questions in a way that compels the reader to accompany him on his quest.

## Critical Context

Jack Kerouac was the primary spokesman for the Beat writers—a romantic group of poets and novelists who in the 1950's rebelled against the conformist, consumer orientation of American society. In this role, Kerouac endured the brunt of the cultural abuse that was heaped on the Beats, and in the years since he wrote his books, his work has not received the serious critical attention from the literary establishment that it deserves. Though *On the Road* remains his most famous book, *The Dharma Bums* is perhaps his most enduringly significant one. While *On the Road* presages the immense cultural changes, involving automobiles, drugs, sex, and uninhibited music, that reached a peak in the 1960's, the "rucksack revolution" prophesied by *The Dharma Bums* led to the environmental movement, which may help ensure the very survival of the planet. Thus, the spontaneous energies which remain chaotic in *On the Road* find a direction in *The Dharma Bums*; the latter book has led the way in providing youthful rebels with a compelling cause.

*Sources for Further Study*

Gifford, Barry, and Lawrence Lee. *Jack's Book: An Oral Biography of Jack Kerouac*, 1978.
Montgomery, John. *Kerouac West Coast: A Bohemian Pilot, Detailed Navigation Instructions*, 1976.
Nicosia, Gerald. *Memory Babe*, 1983.

*Terry L. Andrews*

# DIARY OF THE WAR OF THE PIG

*Author:* Adolfo Bioy Casares (1914-     )
*Type of plot:* Social satire
*Time of plot:* The near future
*Locale:* Buenos Aires
*First published: Diario de la guerra del cerdo*, 1969 (English translation, 1972)

> *Principal characters:*
> DON ISIDORO VIDAL, the protagonist, an elderly widower
> ISIDORITO, his son
> NÉLIDA, the young girl who falls in love with Don Vidal
> ARTURO FARRALL, the chief of the "Young Turks," whose pro-
>     gram instigates the repression squads aimed at the senior
>     citizens
> NÉSTOR LABARTHE, one of Vidal's elderly friends
> LEANDRO REY, an elderly friend of Don Vidal
> JAMES NEWMAN (JIMMY), a sixty-three-year-old member of
>     Don Vidal's group
> DANTE RÉVORA, a member of Vidal's group who attempts to
>     appear young by dyeing his hair
> LUCIO ARÉVALO, yet another member of Vidal's group of
>     cronies

*The Novel*

A nightly card game in a Buenos Aires café opens the action of the novel. Here, members of an elderly group discuss the topic that dominates the ensuing narrative: Members of a youth movement are exterminating old people. On their way home from the game, Don Vidal and his friends witness an encounter with one of the repressive squads of youths. In an alleyway, amid the turmoil of yelling and brutal sounds of sadistic aggression, they discover the body of the old newspaper vendor, Don Manuel. This nightmarish experience is repeated throughout the story as Don Vidal slowly discovers his precarious position in this absurd war of the pigs; that is, of the elderly.

Soon, Don Vidal feels the threat of his own extinction as the warring bands of youths raid the squalid tenements. After the death of Señor Huberman, the neighborhood upholsterer, the youth organization attacks members of Vidal's own group of cronies. First, Néstor Labarthe is killed while attending a soccer game with his son. His brutal murder, in the presence and by consent of his own son, bitterly divides the group into those who try to avoid the danger by conforming and those who try to rebel against the harassment of the youth-oriented society. The second tragedy caused by the juvenile squads sends Dante Révora, another elderly gentleman in the group, to the hospital.

In the midst of all these devastating events, Don Isidoro Vidal finds refuge from his frustration in the arms of Nélida, a beautiful and young neighbor who falls in love with the middle-aged protagonist. This erotic adventure becomes a turning point in the novel, for it provides the background for the examination of the polarization of the old people and their delinquent enemies, an antagonism which is developed from the outset: "It was as if with her beside him he would be safe, not from the young people—this threat had almost ceased to alarm him—but from the contagion to which he was clearly susceptible (given the sensitivity he felt for his environment), the insidious and terrible contagion of old age."

Love, then, becomes the catalyst which neutralizes the protagonist's pessimistic response to the biological, if not spiritual, process of decay, of aging and ultimate death: "Young people cannot understand how having no future to look forward to eliminates everything that is important in life to an old person. *The sickness is not the sick person*, he thought, *but an old man is old age, and there is no other way out but death*." More than simply providing a happy conclusion to an otherwise fantastic tale of tragic dimension, the love motif between the middle-aged Vidal and the young Nélida treats the stock literary convention of the power of love with such subtlety that it becomes a modern parable of frustrated desire.

### The Characters

Like most of Adolfo Bioy Casares' characters, Don Isidoro Vidal represents the enigma of the individual faced with the problems of modern society (such as overpopulation). The classic portrait of Don Vidal is destined to become one of the most well-defined character studies of twentieth century fiction. With astute psychological insight, the author reveals the inner conflicts produced by this middle-aged man's fear of growing old. Interior monologue is frequently used to express Vidal's complex and frustrated desire for youth and the passion of young love, the " . . . hopelessness of bridging the two generations." Don Isidoro often remarks that his world appears to be that of a dream in which reality dissipates before the demands of a fanciful society, ready to condemn and exterminate the outcast. These deeply rooted sentiments of persecution lead Don Isidoro to a sadly ironic vision of life: "*I've been left behind*, he thought. *And now I'm old, or getting ready to be*."

Similar to other characters that populate Adolfo Bioy Casares' fiction, Don Vidal represents the pain and suffering of existential isolation, as the individual is caught in the absurd trap of an enigmatic society. The fantastic (although entirely plausible) world of persecution in which Don Vidal and his friends are engaged is set within a realistic framework. The novelist is thus able to attenuate the nonrealistic dimension of the story through specificity of detail and psychological depiction of character.

## Themes and Meanings

Adolfo Bioy Casares' unique interpretation of the problem of aging serves as the basic motif for a much more important and universal theme of the novel: death. The author exploits the polarization of the young and the old in an attempt to decipher the meaning of life as it draws near its termination.

In the abstract and fanciful game played by the characters of the novel, the reader quickly notes the morbid symptoms of a youth-oriented society. In this fantastic world of persecution, everyone is a victim. Even the young, as Dr. Cadelago explains to the protagonist, " . . . come to understand that every old man is what one young man or another will someday become." This fatalistic notion, in turn, provides the motive for the persecution, for in the intricate campaign to annihilate the old people, the juvenile members of this inhuman society become self-destructive. Dr. Cadalego further explains the hostile obsession of the young when he clarifies the problem: " . . . killing an old man is a kind of suicide."

Furthermore, in this oppression of the old by the young, the author delineates a universal pattern for persecution. Author D. P. Gallagher notes that the reader of this novel observes "the volatility of crowds, the persuasive power of demagogy, the problem of the divided family, the dilemma of those who believe they are not one of the victims (the old man who believes he is not yet old, like the Jew who believes he isn't a Jew), or of those who try to alter their appearance in order not to look conspicuous (the old man who dyes his hair, like the Jew who alters his nose)."

## Critical Context

Adolfo Bioy Casares' *Diary of the War of the Pig* brought almost immediate national and international acclaim to its author. Often dismissed as merely a disciple of and collaborator with Jorge Luis Borges, he has suffered greatly from a lack of critical attention. It was shortly after the publication of *Diary of the War of the Pig*, however, that Bioy Casares began to be recognized for his highly original contribution to the Latin American "boom" in literature. Evidence of the author's growing international popularity can be seen in the many translation of this novel into English, French, Italian, German, Portuguese, and Dutch.

Although Bioy Casares' contribution to the type of literature known as "magical realism" is weighty, especially after the 1940 appearance of *La invención de Morel* (*The Invention of Morel*, 1964) in *Diary of the War of the Pig*, he deemphasizes the magical elements of his previous writing. Indeed, in its indirect satirization of social corruption and its effect on man,

*Diary of the War of the Pig* finds its most poignant message of societal reform.

*Sources for Further Study*
Gallagher, David P. "The Novels and Short Stories of Adolfo Bioy Casares," in *Bulletin of Hispanic Studies*. LII (1975), pp. 247-266.
Villordo, Oscar Hermes. *Genio y figura de Adolfo Bioy Casares*, 1983.

*René P. Garay*

# A DIFFERENT DRUMMER

*Author:* William Melvin Kelley (1937-    )
*Type of plot:* Impressionistic realism
*Time of plot:* 1931-1961
*Locale:* A fictitious East South Central State in the Deep South
*First published:* 1962

Principal characters:

TUCKER CALIBAN, the novel's protagonist, the "different
drummer"
BETHRA, his wife
MISTER HARPER, the town philosopher who tells the story of
"the African," Tucker Caliban's black ancestor
HARRY LELAND, a poor white who is sympathetic to Tucker
Caliban
MISTER LELAND, Harry's son, who befriends Tucker Caliban
DAVID WILLSON, a liberal descendant of Dewey Willson, who
was a Confederate general and the state's governor in 1870
CAMILLE WILLSON, David's wife
DEWEY WILLSON III, David's son
DYMPHNA WILLSON, David's daughter
BENNETT T. BRADSHAW, David's black college roommate who
is active in the civil rights movement

*The Novel*

   *A Different Drummer* begins with "an excerpt from THE THUMBNAIL
ALMANAC, 1961 . . . page 643" describing a fictitious Southern state,
admitted to the Union in 1818, the home of Confederate General Dewey
Willson, who was born in Sutton, a small town twenty-seven miles north of
the Gulfport city of New Marsails. Willson was a brilliant military commander and the dominant figure in state politics after the war, and his
descendants have controlled the government and the economy for generations. Yet a brief notation in the Almanac under the heading "Recent History" refers to the mysterious departure in June, 1957, of "all the state's
Negro inhabitants." This dramatic juxtaposition of whites and blacks, of the
governors and the subjects of society, provides the central focus for *A Different Drummer*. Somehow a whole people has heeded Henry David
Thoreau's powerful words of dissent which serve as an epigraph to the
novel. Blacks have left the state hearing a "different drummer" and stepping
to the "music" created by Tucker Caliban's destruction of his farm and
abandonment of the state.
   In the first chapter, "The African," men gather on the porch of

Thomason's Grocery Company to hear Mister Harper tell the story of Tucker Caliban's ancestor, the giant African chief brought in a slave ship to New Marsails, where he was bought by the general's father, Dewitt Willson. Only Mister Harper understands that his tall tale will help explain the reasons for the black exodus from the state. Because Harper exaggerates the African's strength and the inability of the whites to control him, the men on the porch, especially Bobby-Joe McCollum, question the relevance of this tall tale to the present.

Mister Harper, however, does not claim to be wholly accurate; indeed, he suggests the story's explanatory power depends on its exaggeration, as if that is the only way people will remember the truth. In effect, he is invoking the power of all myths that have less to do with literal facts than with the reality of people's feelings. In this case, Mister Harper (although he does not put it this way) is describing the myth of black resistance to white subjugation. "The African" may not have been so superhumanly powerful, but he is an example of the independence exemplified in Tucker Caliban's decision to own and then dispossess himself of the land that whites have created for him and his family. Thus the story of the African serves two functions: It is a parable that explains how a people have been made slaves against their will, and it is a prelude to the final act of violence committed against Bennett T. Bradshaw by Bobby-Joe McCollum and the other whites on the porch during Mister Harper's absence.

## The Characters

Each chapter of *A Different Drummer* concentrates on a unique point of view, so that the history of the state, of the Willsons, and of the Calibans is intricately pieced together by seeing how individuals have discovered and dealt with the relationships between blacks and whites. Tucker Caliban, for example, is approached obliquely—first through the story of his African ancestor, and then through the Lelands, father and son, who give a sympathetic but somewhat removed view of Caliban, a view that is available to the community but which it does not share because intimacy between the races is discouraged.

David Willson, the great-grandson of the general, gradually becomes the novel's chief interpreter of Tucker Caliban's actions. He has grown up with Tucker, seen an uncomplaining Tucker take a beating because he stayed out too late helping David learn how to ride a bike. Willson's diary, covering the years from 1931 to 1957, reveals how he has tried to surmount the limitations of his Southern background. At college, he has befriended the radical Bennett T. Bradshaw, espoused Socialist causes, equal rights for blacks, and then come home to compromise his ideals when it becomes clear that he will not be able to support his family otherwise.

In many ways, Willson reflects his family's ambivalent history. In "The

African," Dewitt Willson seeks to own the defiant black, but the master also admires the slave's independence. Similarly, David is alternately respectful and condescending with Tucker; he is caught up in the complex of conflicting emotions which his family and his people have never been able to resolve.

David's wife, Camille, is hurt by his inability to accept the full faith that she has in him, and their marriage is nearly ruined by the attenuation of his convictions. His son, Dewey, does not realize how his father has relinquished his youthful ideals and sees only a lack of generosity and an unwillingness to communicate. David's daughter, Dymphna, provides interesting insights into the marriage between Bethra and Tucker and thereby unwittingly reveals the sources of trouble in her parents' marriage. Tucker and Bethra have worked out their differences in temperament and background, and it is their marriage and their decision to leave the state together that makes possible the redemption of David and Camille's marriage.

Tucker Caliban leaves the state because it is the only way that he can free himself. By David Willson's own account, the efforts of Southern liberals have failed, and only Caliban's "primitive act" of salting his fields and burning his farmhouse has freed both himself and the Willsons. Caliban, like the African, has not depended on any organization, white or black, to assert his rights as a human being. Indeed, he has rejected his educated wife's faith in civil rights organizations, for he has concluded, in David's words, that he must act "individually."

*Themes and Meanings*

The quest for freedom—the main theme of *A Different Drummer*—has to be the individual's responsibility. This is why the spirit of Henry David Thoreau's insistence on self-reliance in *Walden* (1854) pervades the novel. It is his argument that only individuals change history, and that the powerful actions of a single person can mean more than any collective force or government.

Tucker Caliban says remarkably little in this novel and does not, like the other principal characters, have a chapter that expresses his point of view. Much of what he thinks is embodied in his actions, in his brief conversation with David Willson, and in "The African." He is meant to be a somewhat mysterious character and to have mythic properties. In a sense, the novel's separate chapters—each expressing a point of view—all go to sum up what Caliban knows intuitively: His strength is self-generated and stems from relying on his own counsel and not on the forming of alliances and on the politicking that distinguishes the Willsons and educated blacks who have participated in civil rights organizations.

*A Different Drummer*'s ending, which contrasts the lynch-mob psychology of the men on the porch with the indelible impression that Tucker Caliban has made on the mind of Mister Leland, the poor white boy, preserves the tensions between individual and collective psychology that make up the dynamic of the novel.

### Critical Context

As many readers have noticed, William Melvin Kelley's first novel suggests a black writer's mature response to the work of the South's greatest novelist, William Faulkner (1897-1962). Like Faulkner's Yoknapatawpha County, Kelley's fictional Southern state with its history of interrelated black and white families provides him with a way of crystallizing the meaning of Southern history. General Dewey Willson's historic example is like that of Colonel John Sartoris in Faulkner's novel *Sartoris* (1929; revised as *Flags in the Dust*, 1929). Both writers share, moreover, a basic concern with the theme of freedom and with the way slavery has demeaned both blacks and whites.

Kelley has been influenced by Faulkner not only in terms of themes and characters but also in the way that he handles point of view and chronology. Like Faulkner in *Go Down, Moses* (1942), Kelley begins in the present and moves rapidly into the past. Separate chapters of *A Different Drummer* reflect different periods of time and points of view, as is true in much of Faulkner's fiction. Both writers withhold crucial information and force readers to assemble history in the fragments of evidence offered in widely separated chapters. In this way, not only is considerable suspense and mystery generated but also readers are forced to take individual responsibility for making the narratives of the novel cohere.

A comparison between these two writers should not obscure, however, Kelley's originality. It would be more proper to say that he takes on the methods of one of America's greatest writers to embody an original vision. For example, Tucker Caliban's act of renunciation in *A Different Drummer* has a far more powerful impact on society than the white Ike McCaslin's relinquishment of his inheritance in *Go Down, Moses*, where he is relegated to the status of ineffectual idealist. Unlike Lucas Beauchamp, the head of the black branch of the McCaslins, who decides to stay on the land his white ancestors first farmed, Tucker acknowledges his bond with the Willsons, but he can no longer let them set precedents for his own actions.

The twenty years that separate *A Different Drummer* from *Go Down, Moses* reflect changes in Southern society and in political thinking that Faulkner's conservatism did not anticipate. As a contemporary black writer, Kelley places great emphasis on Caliban's carrying on the tradition of the African, although Kelley's white predecessor also used parables to show the resistance of blacks to white superiority. The difference between them is perhaps most clear in Kelley's sense of the future, for he concludes *A Different Drummer* with Mister Leland imagining Tucker Caliban's return. The white child would ask the black man why he returned, and "Tucker would say he had found what he had lost" thus clearing up the boy's confusion about something Tucker told him before he left. The two would be together laughing and eating food Tucker had brought home. Tucker's act of renunciation, the novel implies, has left a gap in Southern identity, a gap even the white bigots in the novel uneasily sense, and it will only be when Tucker returns, with his own identity intact, that the South will be made whole.

*Sources for Further Study*

Bone, Robert A. *The Negro Novel in America*, 1958, 1965.
Bruck, Peter, and Wolfgang Karrer, eds. *The Afro-American Novel Since 1960: A Collection of Critical Essays*, 1982.
Rosenblatt, Roger. *Black Fiction*, 1974.

*Carl E. Rollyson, Jr.*

# DINNER AT THE HOMESICK RESTAURANT

*Author:* Anne Tyler (1941-    )
*Type of plot:* Family chronicle
*Time of plot:* 1924-1980
*Locale:* Baltimore, Maryland
*First published:* 1982

> *Principal characters:*
> PEARL CODY TULL, the matriarch and protagonist, whose
> entire life in relation to her family is the subject of the
> book
> BECK TULL, Pearl's husband, a salesman who abandons his
> family in 1944
> CODY,
> EZRA, and
> JENNY, their children

*The Novel*

Pearl Tull, age eighty-six, lies dying as the book opens, and her mind ranges, chronologically disconnected, over her entire life. Through her memories, reflections, dreams, and occasional brief conversations with her son Ezra, she recalls, but not in chronological order, Beck Tull's courtship just as she was beginning to accept spinsterhood, their impulsive wedding, the births of their three children, Beck's totally unexpected announcement that he was leaving her, the various stages of the children's growing up, their "trademark flaws," her own failings, and her surprised realization of approaching death.

As she "skids through time," she recalls some of the incidents that form the "plotlessness of life"; these small events include a visit to the beach and an outing in the country during which one of the boys (it is never certain which one) accidentally shoots an arrow at her and wounds her slightly. By the time this first chapter ends, the reader knows what Pearl and the members of her family are like and much about the kind of lives they have led.

Each of the succeeding nine chapters has as its heading a phrase taken from the chapter itself, developing and expanding the story that has been brilliantly suggested in the first chapter, entitled "Something You Should Know." A particular member of the family is the central figure of each chapter: The focus is on Cody in chapters 2, 5, and 10; Jenny's story is told primarily in chapters 3 and 7; Ezra is the main subject of chapters 4 and 9; Pearl is again the central figure in chapter 6; and Luke, Cody's son, the only member of the third generation to have a chapter of his own, adds a different dimension in chapter 8.

The story is as simple—and as complicated—as that of any family. Beck and Pearl meet in 1924, marry shortly thereafter, and separate when Cody is fourteen, Ezra eleven, and Jenny nine years old. Cody goes to college, becomes a successful businessman, marries Ezra's only love, Ruth Spivey, and they have one son, Luke. Ezra rejects college in order to work at Scarlatti's, an elegant restaurant, serves a short stint in the army and is discharged for sleepwalking (a nice ironic touch), takes over the restaurant and eventually remodels it into the Homesick Restaurant, and continues to live at home with his mother in the Calvert Street row house. Jenny goes to college, then to medical school, suffers and recovers from a breakdown, becomes a pediatrician, is married three times, and has one daughter, Becky, and six stepchildren. While Cody catalogs his grievances against his mother and Jenny learns to "make it through life on a slant," Ezra tries repeatedly to pull the family together by arranging celebratory dinners at his restaurant, dinners that are never finished because they always end in quarrels, angry accusations, and sudden departures.

The final chapter describes Pearl's funeral, which Beck Tull attends, appearing to his children for the first time in thirty-five years. Once more Ezra tries to get his family to finish a meal together. Seated around the table are fourteen persons, including the children. Beck is impressed by this crowd, which seems to him to be "one of those great big, jolly, noisy, rambling . . . why, *families!*" Cody tries to correct this impression in his usual fashion: "You think we're some jolly, situation-comedy family when we're in particles, torn apart, torn all over the place, and our mother was a witch." Ezra denies this, trying to set the record straight. The dinner is further disrupted by the unobserved departure of Beck during a momentary crisis involving a choking baby. Everyone rushes off to look for Beck; Cody finds him, and for the first time learns Beck's side of the story.

The book ends with the rest of the family coming up to Beck and Cody, who feels pulled toward them. He leads his father back to the others, and as he does so, he recalls the family outings of his boyhood, especially the archery trip, and sees his mother as she was then: young, calm, and lovely. In a characteristic embellishment, one of poignant beauty, Cody thinks that he also recalls "a little brown airplane, almost motionless, droning through the sunshine like a bumblebee."

### The Characters

The characters of the story are not unusual, but they are in no sense simple. They all see themselves and one another in highly individualized ways colored by faulty memories and reluctance to face certain realities.

Pearl Tull, as the central figure, has the most facets, partly because her long life has enabled her character to develop most fully, and the years have given her a measure of wisdom. She has a considerable amount of insight, calling herself "an old maid at heart," but the blindness that afflicts her in the end and her proud refusal to acknowledge it are both metaphors of her personality. Competent and strong-willed, she is also hot-tempered and compulsive. She cares deeply for her children but is unable to express her love except in what she does for them. She is highly critical, "an angry sort of mother," and fears weakness in herself more than anything else.

Cody, the firstborn, suffers most from his father's abandonment, his mother's cruel outbursts, and what he regards as her preference for Ezra. Obsessively jealous, he is a mischievous and contrary child, constantly playing malicious tricks on Ezra in a one-sided rivalry that culminates in his marriage to the only woman Ezra ever loved. Successful in his profession, he is nevertheless restless and unsatisfied, and he fails to build the kind of relationship with his son, Luke, that he so badly missed having with his own father.

Ezra is a dreamy, accepting person, sweet-tempered, unaggressive, patient, sensible. His temperament and his talents manifest themselves in his devotion to Pearl, Cody, and Jenny, and in his skill in providing what people need, symbolized by his restaurant, where you can get "what you long for when you're sad and everyone's been wearing you down." His dogged determination to get the family together for a whole dinner never succeeds, but he persists in his efforts.

Jenny, who believes that "you make your own luck," changes from a sad, confused, superconscientious girl to a brisk, detached, skillful professional woman. She adopts a whole family of children after bearing one of her own, Becky, who suffers from anorexia nervosa, as did, probably, Jenny. To Pearl's dismay, Jenny sees everything as a joke, having deliberately lost the intensity that more than anything else characterizes her mother.

There is also a whole gallery of minor characters, some of whom only make one appearance, as in Luke's chapter, while others come in and out of the story because of their importance to a particular character, such as Cody's wife, Ruth; Mrs. Scarlatti, the original owner of the restaurant; and Josiah, the gentle giant whose only friend is Ezra.

### Themes and Meanings

As its title suggests, *Dinner at the Homesick Restaurant* is about longing. Its characters yearn for the familiar and the comfortable, the imagined ideal, never known but constantly sought. As a metaphor of this hunger, food is occasionally mentioned throughout the book to suggest its significance in different ways. It is Cody who reflects on "its inexplicable, loaded meaning in people's lives." He realizes that his mother's attitude toward food revealed her disapproval of neediness, and he recalls how family arguments usually started at the dinner table.

The meanings of the theme are revealed primarily in dialogue, each person speaking naturally in his own characteristic voice rather than in interior monologues. Self-deception, pretense, misery, humor, courage, tolerance, impatience—all are present, and most of all in Pearl, who at the end of her life is still discovering her children and trying to understand them. Finally, she has learned to drift, and surprisingly but satisfyingly, her memories are pleasant ones, perfect in their simplicity and ordinariness—a summer wind, the weight of a sleeping baby, the privacy of walking in the rain under one's own umbrella, a country auction, a day on "sunlit sand."

*Critical Context*

Anne Tyler's ninth novel was her first best-seller. Since the appearance of her first novel, *If Morning Ever Comes* (1965), published when she was in her early twenties, she had been highly regarded by the critics, and with *Dinner at the Homesick Restaurant* she gained a wide readership as well—a popular success continued with her subsequent novel, *The Accidental Tourist* (1985).

*Dinner at the Homesick Restaurant*, like many of Tyler's novels, explores the ways in which being part of a family defines each of its members. The book is not a psychological case study, though it is acute and sensitive in its insights; it is an artistic study, carefully crafted, of a group of people who happen to be related to one another and who therefore all contribute in one way or another to what they eventually turn out to be. It is artistic because it is imaginatively created, yet its resonances strike responses in every reader, no matter what his own experiences within a family have been.

*Sources for Further Study*

Brooks, Mary Ellen. "Anne Tyler," in *American Novelists Since World War II*, 1980. Edited by James E. Kibbler, Jr.

English, Sarah. "Anne Tyler," in *Dictionary of Literary Biography Yearbook: 1982*, 1983. Edited by Richard Ziegfeld.

Evans, Elizabeth. "Anne Tyler," in *American Women Writers*, 1982. Edited by Lisa Mainiero.

Gibson, Mary Ellis. "Family as Fate: The Novels of Anne Tyler," in *Southern Literary Journal*. XVI (Fall, 1983), pp. 47-58.

Shelton, Frank W. "The Necessary Balance: Distance and Sympathy in the Novels of Anne Tyler," in *The Southern Review*. XX (October, 1984), pp. 851-860.

*Natalie Harper*

# THE DISPOSSESSED
## An Ambiguous Utopia

*Author:* Ursula K. Le Guin (1929-      )
*Type of plot:* Utopian science fiction
*Time of plot:* Centuries in the future
*Locale:* The planet Urras and its moon Anarres, in the solar system of Tau Ceti
*First published:* 1974

> *Principal characters:*
> SHEVEK, the central character, a physicist
> TAKVER, his permanent sexual partner
> RULAG, his mother and political opponent
> SABUL, a senior physicist, his rival and antagonist on Anarres
> DR. ATRO, a senior physicist, Shevek's competitor and sponsor on Urras

*The Novel*

*The Dispossessed* is a novel of double disillusionment. In one half of the book, its central character, the physicist Shevek, discovers that for all of its apparent freedom, his native world, the moon Anarres, will not allow him to complete and publish his major work on a general theory of time—a work which would lead to breakthroughs in faster-than-light communication and even travel. With a mixture of hope and despair, Shevek leaves Anarres for the planet of Urras (a world more like Earth), from which his ancestors were exiled for their beliefs several centuries earlier. On Urras, however, he finds that although he can complete his work, and is indeed given every encouragement to do so, once it is completed it will be taken from him and used in ways which he cannot tolerate. He decides in the end to give his work to the embassy of Earth, so that it can be freely communicated to all, and to return to Anarres, in a sense to stand trial by those whom he has rejected.

A large part of the power of *The Dispossessed* comes, however, from the fact that the two "halves" of the book mentioned above are not presented in simple sequence, one after the other, but continuously interact with each other. The first and last chapters of the book deal respectively with Shevek's journeys from Anarres to Urras and then back from Urras to Anarres. In between, the even-numbered chapters follow Shevek's life on Anarres from birth to exile (and so lead up chronologically to the first chapter), while odd-numbered chapters describe his experience on Urras after he has been exiled and so culminate naturally in the last. This narrative structure on one level reminds one of Shevek's work as a physicist, which could be described as the reconciling of two opposed theories about time, those of "simultaneity" and of "sequency." At another level, though, it makes the reader follow Shevek twice from a period of high hopes through increasing difficulty to an abrupt solution; there is a kind of symmetry in his double descent. Finally, a major function of the novel's unique structure is to bring into opposition two contrasting societies, those of the planet Urras (or rather of the nation A-Io on the planet Urras) and of the moon Anarres.

*The Characters*

On Anarres, individuality is strongly suppressed. Children do not live with parents. There is no such thing as marriage. Even partners who wish to stay together may be separated by job postings. People eat communally and often live in dormitories. In every way, the individual is taught to subordinate himself to the needs of the community. Even names are generated by computer, and all (Sadik, Bedap, Tirin, Sabul, Rulag, and so on) sound rather like one another. In these conditions one might well expect to find no memorable, or recognizable, characters. A basic question of *The Dispossessed* is whether human nature can be changed, or tamed, by social engineering.

In fact, many of the characters on Anarres are seen as familiar human types struggling against their environment. Sometimes the familiarity is an unpleasant one. The whole structure of society on Anarres is dedicated to preventing the growth of private property, whether this is counted in possessions or money or rights over other people. Nevertheless the urge to possess and to dominate is shown welling up through all discouragements in such figures as Sabul, the senior physicist to whom Shevek is sent for early instruction. Unlike a professor at, for example, a modern American university, Sabul has no official power over Shevek, to fire him, terminate his research grant, or cut him off from money. Yet in convincingly roundabout fashion he manages to block Shevek's career and to compete with him for one "commodity" which even Anarres has not managed to outlaw: credit, reputation, having one's name on the cover of a book. In a convincing scene, Shevek reflects that in a world where even the words "buy" and "money" are unknown, and where the worst insult is to call someone a "profiteer," he has nevertheless been forced to "bargain" and has in the end himself been sold.

Equally interesting, and perhaps even less predictable, are the two major female characters of the book, Shevek's mother, Rulag, and his partner Takver (on Anarres there is no such thing as a "husband" or "wife"). Both seem to suggest that in the rational, artificial society of Anarres there is something missing, and that something is emotional security, the tie of one individual to another, not as two members of a larger community, but tighter, more possessively, one to one. Very early in his life, Shevek's mother, Rulag, breaks connection with his father and leaves her child to be brought up communally. On Anarres she has every right to do this, and even in the real world many would say that a woman with work to do should not be forced by social expectation to sacrifice herself to her child. Nevertheless, Rulag leaves a gap in Shevek's life which seems to contribute to his later unhappiness. It is one of the major criticisms of Anarresti society that later, even when Shevek and his partner Takver try to stay together with their children, they are split up, as if to repeat Rulag's previous choice, but this time by compulsion. Rulag reappears in the story, furthermore, as Shevek's bitter political rival, a more honest but more fanatic counterpart to Sabul in the stifling of Shevek's development; she represents the dark side of Anarresti liberation.

The characters on Urras, meanwhile, though not computer-named, are paradoxically less individualized and more easily defined in terms of social roles. Shevek finds it difficult to understand the senior Iotic physicist Dr. Atro, who is simultaneously a convinced supporter of Shevek's physics and a thoughtless opponent of his politics. Yet this mixture of intelligence and inexperience carries no surprises for the reader, approximating indeed the stereotype of the naïve or absentminded professor (a stereotype which Shevek strongly rejects). At the opposite extreme of Urrasti society is Shevek's manservant Efor, streetwise, underprivileged, subservient, secretly in sympathy with the anarchist underworld. It is through him that Shevek escapes from his undeclared imprisonment to make contact with the embassy of Earth.

## Themes and Meanings

At the heart of *The Dispossessed* lies the question of whether virtue can be made compulsory, or, to put it another way, of whether vice is, as so many have thought, the result of society's failings rather than the individual's. At first sight, Le Guin appears to be taking a strongly anticapitalist or liberal-egalitarian line. On Anarres, she tells the reader (and indeed she makes the reader believe), rape, robbery, and violence are all, not unheard of—for that would involve a total alteration of human nature—but pointless, profitless, and difficult to achieve. Where no one has money, private possessions, or a place to hide private possessions, and where everything available is free, theft never gets beyond the mildly comic "jackdaw" level. The motivation for rape is meanwhile defused by complete sexual freedom and openness, while violence is kept down to occasional scuffles and fistfights by the fact that there are no weapons and few material things for which to fight.

Does this imply, then, that people can be made to be good? Le Guin's answer is significantly less optimistic than that. *The Dispossessed* implies that people can be given little opportunity to be bad. Yet their motivations may not change, so that Sabul, for example, translates the desire for domination into credit rather than cash, while at other moments natives of Anarres seem spontaneously to reinvent, for example, imprisonment, manslaughter, and psychological tyranny. Furthermore, the egalitarian social organization which makes theft so difficult seems to create a corresponding fault of its own, which is envy or jealousy, the desire to hold everyone down to one level. Can such a society cope with excellence? The case of Shevek seems to argue that it cannot; Shevek gives due credit to Urras, when he arrives there, both for its encouragement of "splendor" and for its demonstration of the power of the profit motive. A minor joke about Anarres is that all the characters (without realizing it) are rather lazy. To them an eight-hour day is quite exceptional; their poverty, and the wealth of Urras, may not come entirely from disparities in natural resources.

The *Dispossessed* accordingly asks questions about human nature and about the nature of society, to which it returns subtle and disquieting answers, very liable to misinterpretation. Marxist critics, for example, tend to see Anarres as ideal and Urras as an aggressive parody of the United States, while others have replied with the suggestion that the whole organization of life of Anarres is impractical, if not impossible. Few have noted, however, the deep interest of *The Dispossessed* in corruption and modification. It is extremely rewarding to observe the way in which the different languages of the novel, Pravic and Iotic, are brought into contrast with each other. At first sight Pravic (the language of Anarres, an entirely artificial one) is an ideal: In it insults such as "bastard" have no meaning, euphemism is impossible, notions such as "class" and "status" have been abolished. As time goes by, however, one realizes that the demons expelled by one door have returned through another: "Profiteer" is used in Pravic as meaninglessly as "bastard" in Iotic, while such opposites as "functional/excremental" are continually redefined for tactical purposes. "Human nature is human nature," says one character in Urras, and at the time he seems stupid and pessimistic with his implication that it cannot be improved. The nature of language in *The Dispossessed* implies, though, that he is half right; though he may be wrong in thinking that the struggle for improvement should therefore be abandoned.

### Critical Context

The *Dispossessed* is very clearly in the tradition of Sir Thomas More's *Utopia* (1516), a work which it echoes and in several places answers. It is a surprise to find such a work written in 1974, after many decades in which social ideals of any sort appeared to have given way to "Dystopias," or socially engineered nightmares, such as Aldous Huxley's *Brave New World* (1932) or George Orwell's *Nineteen Eighty-Four* (1949). Le Guin has received much praise for standing out against this trend, for contributing a major document on sexual liberation, and for translating Utopian themes into a classic science-fiction setting, an achievement recognized by both Hugo and Nebula awards to *The Dispossessed* as the Best Science Fiction Novel of 1974.

Yet the main achievement of *The Dispossessed* lies in its modernization of ancient questions. Sir Thomas More could not have imagined a technologically sophisticated community which could afford to operate without slaves or hangmen; even later writers worked without the hopes born from sociology or the doubts created by animal ethology. Le Guin has succeeded in integrating insights from both fields, and from many others, including physics and linguistics, and has expressed them all with unflinching intellectual honesty. *The Dispossessed* will certainly remain a classic, and together with her earlier *The Left Hand of Darkness* (1969) makes her perhaps the leading novelist of political ideas in America today.

*Sources for Further Study*
Myers, Walter E. *Aliens and Linguists*, 1980.
Olander, Joseph D., and Martin H. Greenberg, eds. *Ursula K. Le Guin: A Critical Study*, 1979.
Slusser, George E. *The Farthest Shores of Ursula K. Le Guin*, 1976.
Spencer, Kathleen. "Exiles and Envoys: the Science Fiction of Ursula K. Le Guin," in *Foundation*. XX (1980), pp. 32-43.

*T. A. Shippey*

# DISTANT RELATIONS

*Author:* Carlos Fuentes (1928-    )
*Type of plot:* Fantastic narrative
*Time of plot:* The early 1980's
*Locale:* Paris, Mexico, and the Caribbean
*First published: Una familia lejana,* 1980 (English translation, 1982)

> *Principal characters:*
> THE COMTE DE BRANLY, an eighty-three-year-old French
>     aristocrat
> THE NARRATOR, a Latin American friend of Branly who has
>     taken France as his adopted country; only at the end of the
>     novel is it revealed that his name is Carlos Fuentes and that
>     he is living out an alternate destiny to that of the author
> HUGO HEREDIA, a distinguished Mexican archaeologist
> VICTOR HEREDIA, his twelve-year-old son
> THE FRENCH VICTOR HEREDIA, a mysterious man who traces
>     his family back to nineteenth century Cuba and Haiti; he
>     may be a phantom, or someone who was never born
> ANDRÉ HEREDIA, the young son of the French Heredia

## The Novel

Most of *Distant Relations* takes place during one long afternoon in Paris, but the events that it recounts take place in Mexico and the Caribbean as well as France and extend two centuries into the past. The title refers not only to the familial connections between the characters in the novel but also to the historical relationship between the French and Spanish-American traditions. Fuentes puts particular emphasis on a series of French writers born in Spanish America—writers who, to a greater or lesser degree, bridge the distance between the two cultures. A poem by Jules Supervielle (1884-1960), a French poet born in Uruguay, is recited by one of the characters and serves as a leitmotif for the entire novel. The poem, "The Adjacent Room," refers to the notion, central to the plot of the novel, that there is an infinite series of contiguous possibilities for each historical event and for every personal destiny. This fantastic premise allows *Distant Relations* to be read as an entertaining and compelling ghost story. At the same time, by replacing a stable vision of the past with a precarious one in which alternate possibilities struggle to exist, it permits Fuentes to carry out a critical and imaginative interrogation of history.

Although the structure of *Distant Relations* is complex, it consists primarily of one long conversation between the Comte de Branly and the narrator, who then reports the exchange to the reader. Branly, a cultured and cosmopolitan French aristocrat, has been deeply shaken by his recent involvement with the Heredia family, and by an experience which culminated in the mysterious disappearance of twelve-year-old Victor Heredia. Branly explains that he met the Mexican archaeologist Hugo Heredia and his young son Victor while visiting the Toltec ruins of Xochicalco in Mexico. Branly was impressed by the father's universal grasp of culture and love for the Indian past, and intrigued by the son's "imperious innocence" and childish games. Branly explained the closeness of the two by the recent deaths of Hugo Heredia's French wife and older son in a plane crash, and excused their arrogance when they appropriated a valuable, if broken, artifact that Victor found among the ruins.

Several months later, when the Heredias accepted his invitation to come to Paris, a series of events made Branly an unwilling guest in the suburban home of another Victor Heredia, a rude and resentful Frenchman who appeared in Branly's room only at night. For several days, while the Mexican boy played with the French Heredia's son André, Branly was forced to recall forgotten details of his own life and listen to the chaotic and incoherent family stories of a man whom he finally realized never existed. The inconsistencies in Heredia's stories of the changing fortunes of his family in the nineteenth century Caribbean are never resolved, but they do show that in some way, Branly's destiny is intertwined with that of the Heredias.

This explanation of the French Heredia's raging insistence on the forgotten injustices of the past also accounts for his desire to bring about the birth of a new being, one that was previously denied existence, by joining his son and the Mexican boy. Before leaving Heredia's house, Branly tells the narrator, he witnessed the union of the two boys, each of whom brought one-half of the artifact from Xochicalco to form a whole; Branly was shocked to learn that Hugo had agreed to surrender his son to the French Heredia.

Despite this disturbing experience, Branly is somehow satisfied personally by the interrogation of his own past that he has carried out twice: once at the home of Victor Heredia, and once in the presence of the narrator. Branly, who is childless, leaves the story of the Heredias as a legacy to the narrator, who accepts it reluctantly. The narrator is someone who has refused the legacy of the past by turning his back on his Latin American roots. The reader learns in the last two chapters that he is an alternate destiny of Carlos Fuentes, but that the other Fuentes is constantly at his side, refusing to allow him to forget the legacy of the past. In the striking last scene of the novel, Fuentes is escorted by his phantom presence to the pool of the Club, where he sees a vision of the American jungle and also of the two boys, floating in the pool, oblivious of time. Their mystery is not explained, but Fuentes realizes that the destiny of the Heredias has included him as well.

*The Characters*

Each of the major characters in *Distant Relations* carries the burden of representing an era, a nationality, or an attitude toward the past. Rather than shy away from this symbolic tendency, Fuentes indulges it by letting the characters make elegant pronouncements about themselves and one another. *Distant Relations* is as much a work of cultural criticism as it is a gothic fantasy, and the reader never forgets that the conversation he is reading takes place in Paris between two cultured and erudite men enjoying a leisurely lunch.

The Comte de Branly is responsible for the encyclopedic quality and tone of the novel. Knowledgeable in literature, painting, film, and music, he represents the high achievements of French culture, with its emphasis on order, reason, and refined manners. When he recites the poem by Supervielle, he is "exercising the supreme gift of selection, synthesis, and consecration that France has reserved for herself through the centuries." Although he traces his family back nine centuries, his father's early death cut him off from his immediate past, and he identifies himself more with twentieth century culture than with the French historical tradition.

Hugo Heredia is a more complex character. A Mexican whose family goes back to the sixteenth century, Branly sees him at first as a universal man of the century of the founding of the New World. His arrogance, however, reveals the presence of a patriarchal authoritarianism that his son Victor seems to have absorbed all too zealously. Hugo Heredia has the archaeologist's veneration for the past and believes that the "present is incomprehensible except within the context of the past." On the other hand, after the death of his wife and older son, he must acknowledge the fact that what he and his surviving son share is "scorn for men, respect for the stones." At the end of the novel, having lost his wife and both of his sons, he says to Branly, "I am sorry to have deceived you. I am not a universal man from the century of discoveries. I am only a slightly resentful Mexican Creole, like all the rest of my compatriots marked by mute rage against their inadequacies."

Given this gloomy conclusion, it is interesting that when the narrator speculates about what he might have been had he stayed in Mexico, he proposes himself as the friend that Hugo Heredia never had. Although the Carlos Fuentes who chose to live on the margin of French culture rather than stay in Mexico does not talk about his activities or personal life, he paints an "alternative portrait" of himself as a lover of French culture that is a salute to the civilization that has been adopted by so many American artists and writers. By inscribing his "Mexican" destiny in the plot of the novel, however, Fuentes suggests himself as "the reluctant phantom that appears to tell us: this is what you were, this is what your people were; you have forgotten."

## Themes and Meanings

*Distant Relations* can be read on several levels—as a mystery, as a fantasy or metaphysical speculation, as an essay about the literary and historical relationship between the Old World and the New. The archaeologist Hugo Heredia says at one point: "If you want me to summarize the most profound lesson of Mexican antiquity, it is this: all things are related, nothing is isolated; all things are accompanied by the totality of their spatial, temporal, physical, oneiric, visible and invisible attributes." In looking at French culture and history in relation to Spanish America, Fuentes shows a desire to find equilibrium and balance—in the perfect spherical object from Xochicalco, in the phantom presence that lives beside us, and in the order and reason that Branly tries to bring to the telling of his story. Yet this sense of balance seems to elude him: The story remains incomplete, and the symmetry of the Mexican temples is the "fearful symmetry of [William] Blake's tiger in the night."

This preoccupation with memory and inheritance animates all of Fuentes' works. In elaborating a genealogy of the New World, Fuentes struggles to discover how the past determines the identity of a nation. The uneasy and often violent legacy of the New World is a difficult one with which to come to terms.

## Critical Context

Carlos Fuentes is without a doubt the most widely read Mexican writer on the international scene. As Branly says in *Distant Relations* when he suggests that the narrator might have chosen to stay in Mexico instead of going to France, "You write about Mexico, about Mexicans, the wounds of a body, the persistence of a few dreams, the masks of progress. You remain forever identified with that country and its people." Indeed, Fuentes is a prolific writer who is both cosmopolitan diplomat and erudite professor. He is well known for his essays on contemporary Mexico as well as for his literary criticism.

In many of Fuentes' earlier novels, he discusses present-day Mexico by looking at its relationship to its violent and often brutal past. In later novels, he has looked at Mexico in relation to other nations and cultures, without ever abandoning the historical question. In *Terra Nostra* (1975; English translation, 1976), a massive and encyclopedic novel, he examines Mexico's relationship with Spain. In *El gringo viejo* (1985; *The Old Gringo*, 1985), he looks at Mexico's relationship with the United States. In *Distant Relations*, Fuentes pays homage to French culture and literature, to what he calls "that strange love for France which supposedly saves us Latin Americans from our ancient subordination to Spain and our more recent subordination to the Anglo-Saxon world."

*Sources for Further Study*
Brody, Robert, and Charles Rossman. *Carlos Fuentes: A Critical View*, 1982.
Faris, Wendy B. *Carlos Fuentes*, 1983.
Guzman, Daniel de. *Carlos Fuentes*, 1972.
*World Literature Today*. LVII (Autumn, 1983). Special Fuentes issue.

*Marisa Moolick-Gutiérrez*

# DOG SOLDIERS

*Author:* Robert Stone (1937-    )
*Type of plot:* Social morality
*Time of plot:* The early 1970's, the beginning of the end of the Vietnam War
*Locale:* South Vietnam and California
*First published:* 1974

> *Principal characters:*
> JOHN CONVERSE, the protagonist, a journalist and cynic
> RAY HICKS, a drug smuggler and self-taught mystic
>     philosopher
> MARGE, Converse's wife and Bender's daughter, a drug addict
> DIETER, a guru
> ELMER BENDER, a former Communist press baron
> ANTHEIL, a crooked lawman, director of the drug hunt, and
>     Converse's chief tormentor

*The Novel*

In terms of its action, *Dog Soldiers* may be considered a thriller. Its plot, however, is merely a vehicle for an elaborate superstructure containing a mordant, satiric, despairing meditation on the manner in which the experience of Vietnam invaded the American consciousness.

The plot tells of John Converse, a weak though talented journalist, and his scheme to smuggle three kilos of pure heroin from Vietnam to the United States. He has been sent on assignment to Vietnam by his father-in-law, Elmer Bender, the ruthless publisher of a sensationalist scandal sheet. The idea to smuggle the heroin is an expression of the increase in Converse's amorality and confusion resulting from his exposure to America at war in Vietnam.

To assist in the smuggling, Converse enlists Ray Hicks, a former Marine Corps friend, and, to Converse, "probably a psychopath." Hicks completes the task with ease. Then, as directed, he contacts Converse's wife, Marge, who sells tickets at a pornographic cinema and lives on tranquilizers. At this point, however, everything begins to go dreadfully wrong, as though to confirm Hicks's earlier perspective: "It's gone funny in the states."

Almost as soon as Hicks meets Marge, he is waylaid by hoodlums, and he and Marge are forced to flee. This flight across Southern California, and Converse's subsequent pursuit of them, is the mainstay of the plot. The flight takes the characters through a generally unstable and often nightmarish social landscape. Among the characters whom Hicks and Marge meet is Eddie Peace, a sleazy Hollywood hanger-on, to whom Hicks unsuccessfully tries to sell the heroin. Shortly thereafter, Marge becomes addicted to heroin. Converse, on the other hand, is forced to pursue the heroin by some extremely unsavory lawmen, led by a certain Antheil. The differences between law and disorder are shown to be insignificant.

The flight ends in the mountains near the Mexican border, where Hicks visits his "alma mater," an encampment run by Dieter, a guru of the Apocalypse. Here Converse and the lawmen corner them. Hicks, however, decides to make for Mexico with the heroin, but he dies of a gunshot wound, exposure, and exhaustion on the way. Converse, now reunited with Marge, finds Hicks but is too late to do anything to help. He decides to jettison the heroin, leaving it for the thuggish lawmen.

The novel's action is accompanied by heavy symbolic and intellectual overtones. Characters exemplify a variety of philosophical and ideological emphases. Elmer Bender, for example, is a former Communist who served in the Spanish Civil War as a member of the Lincoln Brigade. Now he is a malevolent cultural shyster, a remorseless manipulator of public taste and gullibility. On Dieter's mountain, the action temporarily stalls to allow the guru to recount the commune's history of drug-induced orgies of visionary overload masquerading as cosmic overview. In the context of these two embodiments of compulsive distorting, three kilos of heroin may seem to be a comparatively trivial matter.

Heroin, however, is a means of linking America at home with America in Vietnam. It unites the characters by revealing that, in the name of the drug, their behavior is distorted. Converse, having witnessed a United States Army drive to stamp out elephants—"enemy agents because the NVA used them to carry things"—reflects: "As for dope . . . and addicts—if the world is going to contain elephants pursued by flying men, people are just naturally going to want to get high. So there, Converse thought, that's the way it's done. He had confronted a moral objection and overriden it." His thoughts anticipate Hicks's remark to Eddie Peace: "I'm just doing what everybody else is doing."

*The Characters*

The three main characters of *Dog Soldiers* are Converse, Hicks, and Marge. Although he initiates the action, Converse is unable to control it. As a result, he is the main focus for the author's view of America as the self-incriminating victim of its own ignorance and self-deception regarding Vietnam. Converse's verdict on the Vietnam experience applies with equal validity to his own attempt to authorize a specific course of events: "Nobody knows. . . . That's the principle we were defending over there. That's why we fought the war."

In terms of individual experience, however, such ignorance is the basis of Converse's extreme vulnerability and hapless impotence. Those two aspects of his condition are confirmed by his falling afoul of the law. His actions reveal rather than overcome the element which "morally speaking . . . was the basis of his life": fear. "It was the medium through which he perceived his own soul, the formula through which he could confirm his own existence." The impoverished quality of his actions also confirms what he experienced under fire in Vietnam: "Existence was a trap; the testy patience of things as they are might be exhausted at any moment."

Nevertheless, when faced with the choice of whether to enter the trap, Converse decides in the affirmative. Thus, he becomes "the celebrated living dog, preferred over dead lions." He chooses "to begin again from nowhere . . . to soldier on. Living dogs lived. It was all they knew." Converse's choice, and the survival which eventually results from it, is, in the poisonous atmosphere of the novel, a triumph of a kind, one which is commemorated in the novel's title.

In contrast, the "dead lion" is Ray Hicks. A devotee of Friedrich Nietzsche and Zen, he is enamored of a heroic, transcendent vision of himself. As Dieter says of him: "He's trapped in a samurai fantasy—an American one. He has to be the Lone Ranger, the great desperado—he has to win all the epic battles single-handed. . . . It may not be an original conception, but he's quite good at it."

His willingness to smuggle the heroin is the first of many examples of Hicks's relish for risk and his amoral indifference to consequences. The contradictory ethic of arrogant stoicism which he embodies receives its final expression in the abortive mountain trek to Mexico, the principal feature of which is Hicks's delirious philosophizing about the possibility of overcoming his own death. Hicks's intellectual inclinations produce in him a species of moral idiocy—the spirituality of hicks. The pun seems admissible in a novel in which names carry moral overtones—Converse, Bender, Peace, Antheil, which may be pronounced "anthill."

Marge is caught between Hicks and her husband and suffers as a result of their weaknesses. She also suffers a type of emotional deracination through being the daughter of Elmer Bender. When the career of Senator Joseph McCarthy was at its height, Marge's left-wing mother killed herself together with her lover. Not surprisingly, Marge is the novel's most complete victim. Her survival is not the success, however partial and unglamorous, that is Converse's. On the contrary, it seems merely the fortuitous outcome of her helpless sense of dependence, a sense symbolized by her heroin addiction. Reared in an atmosphere of psychic suffocation and ideological bitterness, Marge has been unable to conceive of an adequate reality for herself. This inability is exaggerated and exploited by the novel's action, so that Marge emerges as a portrait of terminal weakness. Here again, the author seems to ask the reader to listen to the character's name: Marge, as marginal.

The bonds which unite the three main characters strongly implicate each of them in the others' destinies. As a result, the minor characters seem remote and one-dimensional, menacing figures in a pitiless, barren landscape. In general, the minor characters make inescapable the novel's vision of the human as being merely synonymous with fear, lovelessness, greed, violence, and self-deception. Yet it is such a vision of a fallen and corrupt America which enables the novel to contemplate with largeness and purpose a world devoid of both.

## Themes and Meanings

A statement of the main theme of the novel is contained in its epigraph, which is taken from Joseph Conrad's *Heart of Darkness* (1902). In it, the emphasis falls on "a flabby, pretending weak-eyed devil of a rapacious and pitiless folly." Undoubtedly, "folly" sums up the waste, confusion, and fear which is depicted in *Dog Soldiers* as representative of both America in Vietnam and the moral price paid on the home front for that involvement.

In order to make this representative portrayal persuasive, however, the novel sustains its symbols and motifs with a virtually allegoric consistency. Here, as in the matter of the main characters' names, the author resorts to the seemingly fundamentalist imaginative strategies of a medieval morality play.

The primary symbol is heroin. It arbitrarily generates a chain of events which nobody can control. Its existence in the lives of the three main characters makes their destiny synonymous with chaos, at least for a time. The drug's power to corrupt and destroy is directly related to its purity. Such an unnerving paradox may be seen as the novel's despairing assessment of American activities in Vietnam.

Ironically underscoring the entrapment which heroin symbolically connotes are numerous motifs concerning freedom. Some of these are intellectual, combining features of watered-down existentialism with high-octane millenarianism, characterized by Dieter as "that flash." More substantially, the form of freedom which Converse asserts—a combination of a naïveté and desperation, leading him to attempt to do whatever he pleases—is a symptom of the times, not an escape from them.

The resulting moral confusion makes explicit the "folly" at the heart of this novel's darkness. If, as is stated, "the mind is a monkey," that beast is not about to relinquish its position on the backs of the characters in *Dog Soldiers*.

## Critical Context

*Dog Soldiers* was Robert Stone's second novel. His first, *Hall of Mirrors* (1967), received the William Faulkner Award for Best First Novel, while his third, *A Flag for Sunrise* (1981), was nominated for the American Book Award and the PEN/Faulkner Award.

In the impressive and extensive fiction about the Vietnam War era, *Dog*

*Soldiers* occupies a prominent place. Part of its significance derives from the fact that it does not portray combat. Rather, it concentrates on the conflict's impact on civilian America. Here, too, however, it avoids the obvious for the most part by not portraying student revolutionaries, "peaceniks," and the like.

Instead, the novel dwells on the shadowy and disturbing antitheses to all such well-documented features of the period. It presents characters who are trapped in a psychic fire fight. It dwells at great length and with unnerving dramatic effect on the relationship between action and consciousness. On a different plane, *Dog Soldiers* established its author as an important voice, one capable of addressing American experience as a totality at a specific historical moment, one capable of mustering a degree of ambition and commitment uncharacteristic of many of his artistic contemporaries. *Dog Soldiers* won for Stone the National Book Award for Fiction in 1975. It was also filmed as *Who'll Stop the Rain?* in 1978.

Despite its range and its status among works dealing with similar material, *Dog Soldiers* is hampered by a rather didactic plot and a scheme, rather than a cast, of characters. Moreover, its conclusion is reached more by attrition than by insight. Nevertheless, *Dog Soldiers* bears crucial witness to one of the decisively influential American experiences of the century.

*Sources for Further Study*

Epstein, Jason. "Robert Stone: American Nightmares," in *Plausible Prejudices: Essays on American Writing*, 1985.

Sale, Roger. "Robert Stone," in *On Not Being Good Enough*, 1979.

*George O'Brien*

# THE DOLLMAKER

*Author:* Harriette Arnow (1908-    )
*Type of plot:* Social realism
*Time of plot:* Late autumn, 1944, to late autumn, 1945
*Locale:* Appalachian Kentucky, then Detroit
*First published:* 1954

> *Principal characters:*
> GERTIE NEVELS, the dollmaker, a big, strong-spirited moun-
>     tain woman
> CLOVIS NEVELS, her well-meaning, mechanically inclined
>     husband
> CLYTIE, their daughter, aged fourteen, who adjusts to Detroit
> REUBEN, their son, aged twelve, who returns to Kentucky
> ENOCH, their son, aged nine, who also adjusts to Detroit
> CASSIE, their daughter, aged five, who is killed by a train
> AMOS, their son, aged three
> CALLIE LOU, Cassie's imaginary playmate
> HENLEY KENDRICK, Gertie's brother, who is killed in the war
> GRANMA KENDRICK, Gertie's mother, who is sickly, complain-
>     ing, and religious
> VICTOR, a kind Detroit neighbor who is Polish American
> MAX, Victor's attractive young wife, who leaves him
> SOPHRONIE, another friendly Detroit neighbor, originally
>     from the South
> WHIT, her husband, who is also from the South
> MR. DALY, an obnoxious Detroit neighbor
> MRS. DALY, his long-suffering wife, the mother of ten
> JOE, the friendly vegetable man, a Sicilian American
> JOE'S NEPHEW, an illegal immigrant who is killed by Clovis in a
>     labor dispute

## The Novel

*The Dollmaker* is the story of an Appalachian family's migration from Kentucky to Detroit during World War II. Uprooted from the land, the Nevelses in Detroit become culturally displaced persons and economic pawns, able to survive, if at all, only by denying their sense of identity and adjusting to the system. Yet they are not alone: The millions of other workers, coming from numerous ethnic backgrounds and crowded into Detroit's industrial melting pot, suggest that the Nevelses' experience is a familiar one, with variations. In Detroit, human beings are reduced to economic integers. Thus, unfolding in slowly building, realistic detail supported by powerful unifying symbols, *The Dollmaker* is ultimately a damning critique of the American industrial order.

The story begins during late fall in the Kentucky Cumberlands, where Gertie and Clovis Nevels and their five children live a poor but close-knit life on a tenant farm. By selling eggs and other farm produce, Gertie has hidden away money for fifteen years to buy their own farm. When her brother, Henley, is killed in the war and her parents give her the government's compensation payment, Gertie finally has enough money to buy the old Tipton place. A home and an independent livelihood seem within reach.

Clovis, however, unaware of Gertie's secret plans, has other ideas. He has long been unhappy that he could not provide better for Gertie and the children. He has earned a little money by hauling coal in his old truck, but now, with the miners off at war and gas rationed, even coal hauling is down. Advertisements for war workers in Oak Ridge and elsewhere are enticing. When he goes to Lexington for his army examination and the army indefinitely postpones his call-up, he continues north to Detroit. In Detroit he gets work, sells his truck, and sends money home.

Gertie proceeds with plans to buy the old Tipton farm, but her scandalized mother, believing a wife's place is with her husband, blocks the sale. When Clovis sends for Gertie and the kids, Gertie's mother spends the Henley money on clothes and train fare for Detroit. The family's horrifying train ride—steerage on rails—is a prelude to Detroit itself. The first thing that Gertie hears when they arrive is the slur, "Hillbilly," and the first things that she feels are Detroit's blowing snow and paralyzing cold. Taking the mountain family on a winding ride through the Dantesque industrial hell, the taxi deposits them on a garbage-strewn street before a row of connected gray-green sheds just across the railroad tracks from a blast furnace. This is Merry Hill, their new home.

Gertie and the children are stunned by the urban environment—the ugliness, the overcrowding, the noise, the strange Detroit accents. Some neighbors are friendly and helpful, but others mock the Nevelses' dislocation. The Nevels children are beaten up in the alley and told in school to "adjust." Wanting to be accepted, Clytie and Enoch do adjust at an alarming rate: Within a year, they have even learned to laugh at cartoons of "Hillbillies." Reuben, his pride repeatedly hurt, stubbornly resists adjustment; he finally becomes so unhappy that he runs off back home to Kentucky, to his grandparents. The bright, elfin Cassie, also highly sensitive, withdraws into conversations with Callie Lou, her imaginary playmate. When the alley kids call Cassie "cuckoo," Gertie denies Callie Lou's existence. Yet Cassie retreats further with Callie Lou—to the railroad tracks, where, in a gruesome, heartrending scene, a train cuts off Cassie's legs and she bleeds to death. Gertie uses her hidden money, saved to buy a farm, to bury Cassie.

After the war is over, things become even worse in Detroit. The manufacturing companies lay off workers and try to break the unions, and management-labor disputes, always common, escalate into industrial warfare. When Clovis is laid off, the Nevelses are deeply in debt, Clovis having bought the furniture, the car, and the Icy Heart refrigerator on time. Gertie, who has been making a little money by whittling out dolls and crucifixes on special order, is forced to mass-produce the objects to which she had devoted an artist's care. A factory system evolves within the home: Clovis roughs out the items on a jigsaw, Gertie adds the finishing touches, and the surviving kids hawk the product in the streets.

The nadir is reached when Clovis, fighting for the union, kills a man. In street battling, a young "goon" hired by management beats Clovis about the face with a lead pipe, leaving scars, but Clovis tracks the man down and takes revenge, using Gertie's whittling knife on him. Unhappily, Gertie knows the young man as more than a "goon": He is an illegal Sicilian immigrant, the nephew of Joe, the friendly vegetable man who brings his produce truck around and gives Gertie credit. Gertie is afraid to ask Clovis for details, and Clovis is afraid of being recognized by the police, so he stays inside during the day, and more of the family's economic burden falls on Gertie.

When Gertie receives a big order from Grosse Pointe for dolls and crucifixes of high-grade wood, she makes her symbolic sacrifice—a huge chunk of cherry wood which she brought all the way from Kentucky and on which she has been carving the upper torso and head of Christ. Followed by a procession of her neighbor's children, Gertie hauls the chunk of wood to a lumberyard to be split. All along, Gertie has had trouble finding the right face for Christ, so the statue remains faceless. Now, however, as she drives an ax into the statue's head and listens to the wood groan, she tells the lumberyard owner that "millions an millions" of faces would have done, including the faces of some of her neighbors.

## The Characters

*The Dollmaker* is a woman's story, expressing a feminist outlook in the days before feminism, with Gertie as the prototypical feminist heroine. Her heroic credentials are established in dramatic fashion in the very first chapter, where, riding her prancing mule, Gertie waylays a military car to take her choking baby to a doctor. The officer protests and threatens to draw his revolver, but he faints away when Gertie draws her knife and performs a little surgery on Amos' throat, letting out the pus. Gertie continues to show the same indomitable spirit throughout the novel, yet she is also a victim in a man's world, particularly of the notions that a wife must quietly obey and must sacrifice her dreams for her husband's.

Using a limited omniscient point of view, Harriette Arnow tells the story from Gertie's perspective. Drawn into this perspective, the reader is encouraged to identify with Gertie and to share her opinions. The point of view allows a close study of Gertie and gives the novel a powerful emotional unity, but it might also be the novel's main flaw. Gertie and her observations dominate the story: The cards seem stacked against Clovis, Detroit, the military-industrial complex, and established religion.

Clovis is depicted as Gertie's foil, a well-meaning but basically no-account man: He cannot do anything right. Mechanically inclined rather than a farmer, he lets Gertie and the children struggle with the farm work in Kentucky while he occupies himself with what Gertie calls "tinkering." She cannot tell him about the money she has saved, or he would spend it on his truck. On top of this, he is a petty complainer, complaining about the food that she puts on the table and about almost everything else that she does, such as working too hard. It is not surprising that a man so insensitive to his wife's needs should become a vengeful killer, hardly more than an extension of the military-industrial complex.

The reader may question the fairness of Arnow's characterization of Clovis, and in this connection Gertie's remark about his "tinkering" is significant: It reveals a basic split between Gertie's image of Clovis and Clovis' image of himself. She never recognizes that Clovis' "tinkering" is as important to him as her "whittling" is to her, or that he deferred his dream for years while she kept him tied down on the farm; instead, she merely belittles him. No wonder these two, despite fifteen years of marriage and five children, communicate with each other so poorly. Although Arnow seems unaware of any failings on her heroine's part, Gertie's own insensitivity and complaining tend to draw her perspective in the novel into question. Gertie begins, at times, to sound a bit like her carping mother (Gertie's mother, a truly vicious character, and the obnoxious Mr. Daly of Detroit are extreme representatives, respectively, of the Protestant and Catholic religions).

The Nevels children reflect, to a great extent, the split between their parents. Taking after their father, Clytie and Enoch adapt to Detroit ways; despite this, they are good children. Eventually their adaptation proves beneficial in selling the dolls about the streets (Gertie tries hawking the dolls once but immediately gives up in embarrassment), and they help ease their mother into Detroit life. Reuben and Cassie take after their mother, even symbolically representing different sides of her. The stubbornly resistant Reuben, who returns to Kentucky, represents the part of Gertie that will not stop dreaming of down home. Cassie, with her folkloric imagination, represents Gertie's artistic side. When Gertie denies Callie Lou to Cassie, Gertie is also denying her own deepest self, with consequences symbolized by Cassie's death.

After Gertie has experienced her suffering, she begins to understand more about the suffering of her neighbors in Detroit: Sophronie, who must leave her children and work a night shift in a factory; the kindhearted Victor, whose young wife leaves him; Joe, the friendly vegetable man, who did not come to America to like it; Joe's nephew, with his roving eye for pretty girls and cars; Mrs. Daly, mother of ten, crying at her ironing board. These are only a few of the many people who help Gertie see the vision of the crucified Christ in Detroit.

*Themes and Meanings*

As stated earlier, *The Dollmaker* is a damning but onesided critique of the American industrial order (depicted in the novel as a vast, perverted system based on the machine), a monstrosity that consumes human beings by the millions. People must fit themselves to serve the machine, living within its inhuman environs and serving at the times of its bidding; what is extraneous to this purpose, such as aesthetic and spiritual values, must be stripped away. What is stripped away can then be replaced with commercial values, which create artificial needs for those shoddy, expensive products of the machine. The industrial order thus becomes a mindless parody of its utilitarian beginnings (presumably, it was created to serve human needs); even worse, it becomes a paradigm for political and social order: Little children are told in school to "adjust" to the American way, and the family is structured after a factory model. This erosion of American values—artistic, religious, familial, and democratic—benefits only a few people who live at the top of the pyramid: those who live (and the name is significant) in Grosse Pointe.

This "death" society, as D. H. Lawrence termed it, especially suffers in comparison with the older, Jeffersonian version of America which the Nevelses leave behind in Appalachian Kentucky. In the Cumberlands, the Nevelses, though mere tenant farmers, have plenty to eat and the freedom of the mountains. They "belong" to a culture and a community in a much different way than they do in Detroit. The structure of *The Dollmaker* relentlessly drives home the contrast, with the earlier chapters establishing the Appalachian ethos and later chapters recalling it through Gertie's reveries. Autumn on the land is contrasted to autumn in Detroit with a strike on and winter coming on. Most powerfully, the Appalachian ethos is embodied in Gertie's perspective, where the critique of American society becomes not an abstract theme but a personal cry from the heart.

*Critical Context*

In a 1971 commentary, the novelist and critic Joyce Carol Oates, who has some experience of Detroit, called *The Dollmaker* "our most unpretentious American masterpiece." Most readers of the book would agree with her, and through the years appreciation for the work has grown, though proper recognition has never been given Harriette Arnow. *The Dollmaker* was nominated for a Pulitzer Prize but lost out to William Faulkner's *A Fable*

(1954). In 1984, the novel was made into a television film starring Jane Fonda.

Possibly Arnow's Appalachian origins and subjects have caused the literary world to underestimate her. In actuality, qualifying as "our contemporary ancestors" gives Appalachian writers a rather distinct vantage point from which to examine America. So far, no one has demonstrated this better than Harriette Arnow in *The Dollmaker*, and her example has inspired such younger writers as novelist Gurney Norman in *Divine Right's Trip* (1972) and poet Jim Wayne Miller in *The Mountains Have Come Closer* (1980).

*Sources for Further Study*

Eckley, Walton. *Harriette Arnow*, 1974.

Hobbs, Glenda. "A Portrait of the Artist as Mother: Harriette Arnow and *The Dollmaker*," in *The Georgia Review*. XXXIII, no. 4 (Winter, 1979), pp. 851-866.

Lee, Dorothy H. "Harriette Arnow's *The Dollmaker*: A Journey to Awareness," in *Critique: Studies in Modern Fiction*. XX, no. 2 (1978), pp. 92-98.

Oates, Joyce Carol. "Harriette Arnow's *The Dollmaker*," in *Rediscoveries*, 1971. Edited by David Madden.

*Harold Branam*

# DON GOYO

*Author:* Demetrio Aguilera Malta (1909-1981)
*Type of plot:* Realism and fantasy
*Time of plot:* Undefined
*Locale:* A group of islands on the coast of Ecuador, near Guayaquil
*First published:* 1933 (English translation, 1942)

> *Principal characters:*
> Don Goyo, the legendary protagonist, a 150-year-old man
>     whom everybody in the region obeys and respects
> Cusumbo, a young highlander who becomes a fisherman and
>     mangrove cutter after misfortune befalls him
> Gertru, his love interest and future wife
> Don Carlos, an archetype of the white man who exploits the
>     islands and the *cholos*
> Don Leiton, the leader of the mangrove cutters and the op-
>     position to Don Goyo
> Ña Andrea, Don Goyo's last wife

*The Novel*

This work combines the realism of the life of the *cholos* in the coastal areas of Ecuador with the fantastic elements of the legends that prevail in those tropical regions. The action evolves around two central characters, Don Goyo and Cusumbo. The former is the patriarch of the island region and of the town of Cerrito de Morreños, which he founded after leaving his native town and which he helped develop into a peaceful and harmonious community. During the action of the novel, Don Goyo, nearly 150 years old, is still the virile man and the authority figure that makes the inhabitants listen and obey. He is admired for his manly qualities, which have yielded for him many children. He has stood up to the white man and has prevented him from abusing his people, cohabiting with him side by side in a cordial but uncompromising relationship. Misfortunes come to the region, however, when, after having a vision in which a mangrove tree tells him that the white man will ultimately ruin and own the land, Don Goyo orders the mangrove cutters to turn their livelihood to fishing. This proves to be disastrous since they do not have the skills or the interest to succeed. When they disobey and go back to cutting, the largest and oldest mangrove tree falls to the ground, and Don Goyo is found tangled among its branches.

Cusumbo, the other main character, is Don Goyo's counterpart, in that he represents the average man of the region. When the novel begins, Cusumbo reminisces about his life in the highlands before he emigrated to the islands. There, after inheriting his drunken father's never-ending debt to the white man, he had become a drunk himself. Rehabilitated by Nica, his wife, he had gone back to work, only to realize that he would never pay his debt in full; the white bosses cheat the workers mercilessly, taking advantage of their illiteracy. The final blow came when he found his wife in bed with a white man; killing them both with his machete, he fled to the islands, where he settled as a fisherman. In the course of the novel, he falls in love with Gertru, Don Goyo's daughter, and decides to become a mangrove cutter, only to go back to fishing on Don Goyo's orders. At the end of the novel, Cusumbo sees the specter of Don Goyo at the exact time the dead man's coffin, which the men transport in a canoe, falls in the river. Although it is clear that Cusumbo will never achieve the old man's legendary status, he will carry on his traditions as well as his line, since the reader is led to believe that he and Gertru will marry.

## The Characters

The novel is an interplay of the two main characters, Don Goyo and Cusumbo. The old man, besides being a mixture of fantasy and reality, represents all the qualities of the Latin American myth of the natural man. Don Goyo, who fears no man and stands up to the white man to defend his people, is humbled before nature. When the mangrove tree speaks to him in a vision, he immediately proceeds to take action. The men's defiance and refusal to defer to his vision for the future of the land makes him an alien to the things he has always known how to control. His death, it appears, comes from this alienation, since nature becomes vengeful and tears at his flesh.

Although Don Goyo is portrayed as a flesh-and-blood man, lusty and virile, solitary and taciturn, he is elusive and difficult to visualize. At the beginning of the novel, he is seen almost as an apparition who emerges from the lush, tropical settings at odd times. It is not until the last chapter that he is described fully as a man, with flashbacks depicting his arrival and the founding of Cerrito. The significance of this late introduction is that Aguilera Malta very clearly wanted to establish Don Goyo's mythic status before portraying the man himself. As an impressionistic force who permeated the life of the region, Don Goyo is as vital to its inhabitants as the natural elements that surround them.

Cusumbo, in contrast, is developed from the beginning as a hot-blooded, physical, young coastal inhabitant. Forced to violence by tragic and deterministic circumstances, Cusumbo, nevertheless, remains a pure and uncorrupted example of the common man. His development, poeticized by a lyric style, elevates him from the lowly circumstances in which he lives. Not clearly distinguishable from the other men in the village, he nevertheless displays a sensitivity that belies his origins and his environment. His relationship with Don Goyo and his belief in the old man's qualities make the myth come alive. In Cusumbo, moreover, one sees the rites of passage of a young man in any society, from birth to nascent sexuality to first love. Although there is not great depth in the characterization of Cusumbo, Aguilera Malta communicates with poignancy a young man's struggle to survive in a difficult environment.

Because the islanders' society is centered on the most rudimentary elements of human life (men work, eat, drink, and seek sexual gratification), the rest of the characters have little development. The white man is seen as a stranger who demands much and gives nothing, an alien who speaks an unknown language and whose presence serves only one purpose: to exploit the region and its inhabitants. The *cholos* are hardworking, illiterate men who allow themselves to be abused and who seek only to have food on the table and a woman on their deerskin bed. The women characters are portrayed only as the creatures who provide that food and who fulfill the men's desires with their ripe bodies.

The secondary role of character development in this novel, however, rather than being a flaw, serves to enrich the impact of the poetic qualities of the regional lore. By deemphasizing the psychological traits of his characters, the author stresses the importance of myth to the islanders. He reminds the reader that there are some phenomena that can never be explained and that the people are subordinate to the magical qualities of their reality.

### Themes and Meanings

*Don Goyo* treats social-protest themes with a unique approach. The central element of *cholo* life in all of its facets is portrayed realistically as well as poetically. The true-to-life descriptions of the action and local customs, as well as the authentic dialogue, convey an accurate picture of the Ecuadorian coastal region. The style of the novel, however, gives the narrative a lyric quality, a technique that brings about the creation of an emotive reality, one that transcends its limitations. The characters are not so poetic, however, that they are mere abstractions. Aguilera Malta's world is imbued with magical qualities while it maintains its firm footing in reality.

At the same time, *Don Goyo* is a socially conscious and committed novel which denounces the disappearance of *cholo* life, with its reliance on nature and simple things, and the emergence of white society. The white man, Aguilera Malta says, is only interested in exploiting those whom he considers his inferiors. Even though he respects Don Goyo, Don Carlos has no sense of community or sympathy for his neighbors. In Cusumbo's early life, another white landowner transfers the father's unpayable debt to the son, thus keeping him in chains. When Cusumbo murders him and his own adulterous wife, there is no retribution nor any indication that Cusumbo is a fugitive from justice or that he feels any remorse. The white man's abuses seem to justify both the murders committed by Cusumbo.

The love theme is represented by Cusumbo's relationship to two women, Nica and Gertru. The former is mentioned as the embodiment of the betrayer and the reason for Cusumbo's exile. She is the unfaithful wife who deserves no pity. Gertru, on the other hand, is the humble, naïve girl who gives herself to Cusumbo in spite of her fear of losing him. Ña Andrea, Don Goyo's wife, is the faithful spouse who obeys her man and makes coffee for the men. Overall, love is a simple thing to the people in those regions, says Aguilera Malta. It is based on sexual attraction and loyalty to one's mate. Unfaithful spouses deserve to be killed. In the world of the *cholo*, there are no gray areas, love being no exception.

Finally, nature plays a very important role in *Don Goyo*. Not only are all the characters intimately bound to their environment, but they also believe in its magic qualities. From the beginning of the novel the fishermen are described like water creatures: "Now they were naked again. Deep in the water, swimming—more fish than men—they raised the nets above the level of the water." Don Goyo is the embodiment of this symbiosis between man and nature. As he obeys the commands of the mangrove, the charcoal-giving tree, to stop the exploitation and the destruction for the benefit of man, he demonstrates the relationship that all the inhabitants of the islands have with their surroundings. The fact that they do as he says reinforces their beliefs in nature's powers. Moreover, as the men escape to Guayaquil in their frustration, they see the ugliness of the city, which they say should be called "Guayastink." At the end of the novel, the men defy Don Goyo and go back to cutting trees, but they learn a lesson as the old man dies. With this novel, Aguilera Malta reminds his countrymen and those outside Ecuador that the exploitation of their natural resources ultimately destroys its inhabitants as well and that as the countryside falls to the city, the soul of the nation dies.

*Critical Context*

*Don Goyo* was one of Aguilera Malta's early novels in a career that spanned four decades. Representative of the works of a group of writers of the 1930's, the Guayaquil Group, to which Aguilera Malta belonged before leaving Ecuador for Mexico, *Don Goyo* also bears many typical characteristics of the writer's style. It is a short, impressionistic work which seeks to convey a powerful message through understatement. The absence of anecdotal detail, the precise descriptions of the region, and the social message placed Aguilera Malta with his group stylistically and politically.

While drawing attention to their country's social problems, the writers of the Guayaquil Group also wanted to preserve the characteristics of their native region in detailed and precise descriptions of flora, fauna, and native customs. In this sense, *Don Goyo* fulfilled its mission but ultimately stood out among the rest, as it is the best-known work of the entire group's production.

*Sources for Further Study*
Brushwood, John S. *The Spanish American Novel*, 1975.
Fama, Antonio. *Realismo mágico en la narrativa de Aguilera-Malta*, 1977.
Rabassa, Clementine. *Demetrio Aguilera-Malta and Social Justice: The Tertiary Phase of Epic Tradition in Latin American Literature*, 1980.

*Stella T. Clark*

# DONA FLOR AND HER TWO HUSBANDS
## A Moral and Amorous Tale

*Author:* Jorge Amado (1912-    )
*Type of plot:* Social morality
*Time of plot:* The 1960's
*Locale:* Salvador, in the state of Bahia, Brazil
*First published: Dona Flor e seus dois maridos*, 1966 (English translation, 1969)

*Principal characters:*
> DONA FLOR DOS GUIMARÃES/FLORIPEDES PAIVA MADUREIRA, a teacher of cooking, a lovely young woman, decent, kind, and sensual
> WALDOMIRO GUIMARÃES/VADINHO, Dona Flor's first husband, a lover of life, gambling, and the night life
> DR. TEODORO MADUREIRA, Dona Flor's second husband, a pharmacist by profession and an avid amateur bassoonist

*The Novel*

As the novel begins, it is the first Sunday of Carnival in Bahia, and Waldomiro Guimarães, known by everyone as Vadinho, husband of Dona Flor, has just died while dancing the samba, dressed as a woman, with a large cassava tuber tied under his skirt. With this beginning, Amado introduces the reader to a rollicking, bawdy world inhabited, it seems at times, by the entire population of Brazil.

The novel is divided into five parts, each part chronicling a segment of Dona Flor's life, the first dealing with Vadinho's death, wake, and burial, and the stirring of Dona Flor's fears of life without her husband. The wake is a great success, with people streaming in and out to pay their respects; everyone, it seems—from politicians to members of the exalted professions and the inhabitants of gambling parlors and houses of ill repute—has a story to tell of Vadinho and his deeds. Yet if Vadinho's wake is a success, it pales in comparison to his burial procession. In the opinion of one observer, it seems as if half the population of Bahia is there, more than any of the Carnival parades draws—proof, if any is needed, that Vadinho, gambler, rascal, and unfaithful husband that he was, knew how to make friends.

For Dona Flor this is small solace. With Vadinho's burial, the reality of his absence becomes more pronounced, and Dona Flor struggles through a period of deep mourning. Through flashbacks (and certain pertinent digressions by the author), her life as a young girl, her whirlwind courtship, and her subsequent marriage to Vadinho is recounted. The memories of her life with Vadinho haunt her at every turn. To be sure, not all of her memories are happy ones. Vadinho, being Vadinho, had carried her through life, its highs and lows, sorrows and disappointments—all of its aspects. Now, with Vadinho gone, it seems as if she lies buried with him, and only the shell of Dona Flor remains, going through the motions of living. Not until she has pushed these memories aside, plunged them deep into the bottom of her consciousness, is she able to resume her life. In a symbolic gesture at Vadinho's grave, she lays a bouquet of flowers and at the same time buries desire, love, things of the bed and the heart, in order to take up life again, the life of a decent, respectable widow.

Dona Flor settles into a routine that is slowly broken up by the insistent talk of matchmaking, marriage, men, and sex that her friends and neighbors continuously conduct in her presence. Though outwardly a respectable, upright woman, inwardly and at night, alone with her dreams, she is consumed by desire, by matters of the flesh. Even the most innocent of novels provokes in her all the desires she thought she had buried with Vadinho. Into her life at this time—when Dona Flor knows that to remain in this state may lead to insanity, while to do anything else would mean a loss of respectability or, worse, total ruination—comes Dr. Teodoro Madureira, the local pharmacist.

To Dona Flor, and indeed, all the women in the neighborhood, this comes as a shock, since in all the talk of matchmaking not one of them has mentioned Dr. Teodoro as a possibility. Yet once the possibility is entertained, everyone agrees that he is perfect for Dona Flor, a man of standing, respectable, and a fellow known within his profession—a profession, not merely a job, a profession with university credentials.

Dona Flor finds him acceptable, and a courtship, very different from her first one, ensues: a formal, proper, and respectable courtship, in which they walk, talk of their future, and make preparations for their wedding. At the wedding, everyone agrees that this time Dona Flor has achieved her deserved status, that finally she will have the happiness she deserves.

Dr. Teodoro and Dona Flor settle down to a life of respectability after their honeymoon, a honeymoon which Dona Flor finds a little disconcerting. She expects blazing lights and a night of complete abandonment, something of what she has known before; instead, it is a night of restraint, modesty, and discreetness. To everyone who knows them, Dr. Teodoro and Dona Flor are a happy couple, he busy with his pharmacy, she with her cooking school. On occasion, Dona Flor attends conventions of pharmacists, where Dr. Teodoro reads learned speeches railing against the giant pharmaceutical companies, and where Dona Flor struggles to stay awake. At other times, she is host to the amateur orchestra, in which Dr. Teodoro is a featured bassoonist. So Dona Flor's life goes, with the unexpected never happening, with no tears or sorrows, until, on the night of the first anniversary of her marriage to Dr. Teodoro, she walks into her bedroom and sees Vadinho lying in her bed, nude.

From this point, the struggle that Dona Flor has been conducting within herself since Vadinho's death becomes a full-scale battle between order and disorder, between love as represented by Dr. Teodoro and love as represented by Vadinho, a struggle which, before it is over, turns the entire society of Bahia upside down, involving everyone from the poorest ragamuffins to the richest social and political circles, and even the entire pantheon of Bahian gods.

### The Characters

In the figure of Vadinho, Amado has fashioned a remarkable character, a rogue of epic proportions, a man roaring through life, gobbling it up before it gobbles him up, which is exactly what happens. As the autopsy report indicates, Vadinho could have expired at any moment; his heart, that great heart that propelled him through the streets of Bahia, was useless; his liver, that liver that had filtered tremendous amounts of rum and other manner of spirits, had ceased to function, and his kidneys had worn out.

To his friends of the gaming tables, the whorehouses, and other such pillars of Bahian nightlife, Vadinho is a generous man, a stand-up fellow. To Dona Flor's friends and neighbors, the women of the neighborhood, Vadinho is a wastrel, a scoundrel, and, what to them is worse, a bad, unfaithful husband. The leader of this chorus of boos, Dona Rozilda, Dona Flor's mother, when she hears of Vadinho's death, boards the first ship to Bahia; even before the ship has safely docked, she is heard railing against Vadinho and praising the saints and anyone else concerned for ending his life. Dona Rozilda is a veritable virago, and Amado, in sure, deft strokes, paints her as one. In recounting the death of Dona Rozilda's husband, Amado intimates that he died of a low grade of pneumonia, a slight cold, so desirous was he of departing for Heaven, or anywhere away from his wife, that he was not willing to wait for something serious. There are two other references to her that require no elaboration: In one, Amado writes that Dona Rozilda was "born to be a stepmother, devotedly doing all she could to fulfill her vocation." In the second, her son-in-law refers to her as an Ash Wednesday—the end of Carnival, the end of happiness.

It is with Dona Flor that Amado truly shines in delineation of character. Portrayed as pretty, more than pleasant to look at, with bronzed skin, black, almost bluish hair, and eyes and lips that belie her calm and easy nature, she is capable of giving free rein to her emotions and desires when truly aroused. With Vadinho, she scales the heights of sensual pleasure and endures the sorrows and disappointments of life. With Dr. Teodoro, she gains the respectability she yearns for and endures the lack of excitement that Vadinho provided. Intelligent, aware of her inner and outer selves, she struggles to reconcile the two in a society that hypocritically demands that she choose one or the other, with damning results on the one hand, torment and unhappiness on the other. What Dona Flor wants and needs is a balance that would consist of a fusion of Vadinho's and Dr. Teodoro's characters. That she gets both is a cause for rejoicing.

Dr. Teodoro's character is not as appealing as Dona Flor's or Vadinho's; where Vadinho is fair, gay, and dashing, Teodoro is dark, brooding, and reserved. Where Vadinho is generous and abandoned in his lovemaking, Teodoro is decorous and makes love only on Wednesdays and Saturdays, with a possible encore on Saturdays, if requested. Kind, industrious, generous, and eminently respectable, he lacks the spark, the spontaneity so abundantly present in Vadinho.

### Themes and Meanings

Though the style is comedic, the novel deals with serious and thought-provoking themes. It is a story of two worlds; of a clash between good and evil, where good and evil are not so sharply defined that a person can easily distinguish them; of love in all of its forms; of the meaning of happiness and respectability; of a battle between spirit and matter. Above all, however, it is a celebration of life.

By embodying the struggle between good and evil, between spirit and matter, in the character of Dona Flor, Amado is better able to point out and attack the hypocrisy of a society that makes such a struggle necessary. Dona Flor finds it necessary to bury desire, love, the things of the bed and of the heart when Vadinho dies, in order not to be tempted by that part of her that Vadinho so generously satisfied. She does so because if tempted, she might succumb, and if she succumbs, outside the institution of marriage, she loses (in the eyes of her neighbors, that is) the other side of herself—the decent, honorable, respectable side. In the society that she inhabits, it is the outward appearance of these qualities that counts more than the actual possession of them.

For Vadinho and Dr. Teodoro, no such problem exists. For Vadinho, a child of the street, illegitimate, there are no restraints whatsoever. He knows at first hand the hypocrisy that exists in the world, and he will have no part of it. Generous to a fault with his love (physical) and prodigious in his excesses, he suffers no disgrace, not only because he is a man but also because, unlike Dona Flor, he has nothing to protect.

Dr. Teodoro, Vadinho's exact opposite, is a very respectable gentleman, and in everyone's mind (including Dona Flor's) he confers his respectability on her when they marry. Yet before he marries, he tarries with prostitutes without inflicting damage on his reputation. There is no doubt that he is decent, honorable, and respectable, but he embraces these traits so tightly to him that spontaneity and unbridled joy have no room to penetrate. Where

Vadinho has no restraints whatsoever, Dr. Teodoro has too many, and it is to Dona Flor's sorrow that he brings his respectability to bed with him. Even in their food preferences, Vadinho and Dr. Teodoro are opposites—Vadinho will eat anything, the more exotic, the better; Dr. Teodoro has no taste for spiced foods.

Dona Flor's nature encompasses both of these extremes—indeed, she has need of them in order to survive—but she must have them in balanced measures, not in extremes. Because of this, Vadinho and Dr. Teodoro are both good and evil, life and death. To choose the unbridled passions of Vadinho means death to the decent, honorable side of her; to choose the monotonous happiness of the respectability and security of Dr. Teodoro means death to her spirit, or, given her character, death to her decent, honorable, respectable nature, because sooner or later she would seek out, with one or another or many, the passions represented by Vadinho.

Amado expresses these themes not simply with his characters but with his skillful use of narrative structure and clean, graceful, poetic language. In the recounting of Vadinho's escapades and his life with Dona Flor, the story moves with the rhythms and sounds of Bahian popular music (Vadinho's music), then slows with respectability before and during Dona Flor's marriage to Dr. Teodoro, in tune with his amateur orchestra, Vadinho's music submerged just beneath it.

During the climactic struggle of the novel, the mood is discordant and chaotic, with no sense of rhyme or reason. When Dona Flor emerges victorious, at peace with herself, in balance, walking down the street to the seashore, arm-in-arm with her two husbands, the mood, the sense of sound is harmonious, in balance.

*Critical Context*

In the beginning of his career, Jorge Amado concerned himself with the themes of social justice and class struggle. It was not until the appearance of *Gabriela, cravo e canela*, (1958; *Gabriela, Clove and Cinnamon*, 1962) that this emphasis shifted and Amado began to explore and expand the rich, comic literary territory that he pursues in *Dona Flor and Her Two Husbands*. Yet Amado has not abandoned the themes of social justice and class struggle; they are still present in *Dona Flor and Her Two Husbands*, where the discerning reader can pick them up.

As Amado's themes have become universal, he has moved from a regional or Brazilian writer to one of international stature. With *Gabriela, Clove and Cinnamon*, *Dona Flor and Her Two Husbands* is among the most widely read contemporary novels from Latin America; its wide appeal can be gauged by the fact that it has served as the basis for a successful Broadway play, *Sarava* (1978), and two films, *Dona Flor e seus dos maridos* (1977), a Brazilian production, and *Kiss Me Goodbye* (1982), an American film in which the story is shifted from Bahia to New York City, undergoing a number of changes in the process but retaining the basic premise.

*Sources for Further Study*
"Dona Flor and Her Two Husbands," in *Negro Digest*. XIX (February, 1970), p. 88.
Fernández, Oscar. "Dona Flor and Her Two Husbands," in *Modern Language Journal*. LIV (May, 1970), pp. 386-387.
"Notes on Current Books," in *Virginia Quarterly Review*. XLVI (Spring, 1970), p. xliv.
Reynaldo, Stanley. "Courage and Blood," in *New Statesman*. LXXX (July 17, 1970), p. 63.

*Ernesto Encinas*

# DÔRA, DORALINA

*Author:* Rachel de Queiroz (1910-     )
*Type of plot:* Psychological realism
*Time of plot:* The 1930's to the 1940's
*Locale:* Brazil, including the Northeastern state of Ceará, towns and cities in the interior, and Rio de Janeiro
*First published:* 1975 (English translation, 1984)

> *Principal characters:*
> MARIA DAS DORES (DÔRA OR DORALINA), the protagonist, an actress and eventually mistress of Soledade Ranch
> SENHORA, the widowed mother of Maria das Dores
> LAURINDO QUIRINO, the husband of Maria das Dores, a surveyor
> ASMODEU LUCAS (THE CAPTAIN), the lover of Maria das Dores, a riverboat captain and smuggler
> RAIMUNDO DELMIRO, an old man who lives on Maria das Dores' land, formerly a bandit
> BRANDINI, an actor and the director of the Brandini Filho Company of Comedies and Musical Farces
> DONA ESTRELA, the wife of Brandini and the lead actress in his theater company

## The Novel

The action of *Dôra, Doralina* is located in the consciousness of the protagonist Maria das Dores (nicknamed Dôra or Doralina) who broodingly remembers the pleasures and pains that she has experienced as a daughter, a wife, and an actress.

The novel's first section revolves around Dôra's bitter struggle with her mother, whom she always formally calls Senhora. A beautiful widow, Senhora tyrannically manages the family ranch, Soledade, while showing no love toward her daughter, and the depth of Dôra's alienation is evidenced in many ways: through her deep sense of loss over the death of her beloved father, through her belief that she is her mother's slave and that she has been dispossessed of her inherited share of the ranch, and through her desperate need to be loved.

This desire for love, however, seems to be realized when Laurindo Quirino, a handsome surveyor, enters Dôra's life. Investing him with the aura of a film star, she sees Laurindo as a release from her emotionally stunted life on the ranch. Moreover, he becomes a way for Dôra to defeat her mother, especially since Senhora is also attracted to him. Thus, Dôra gloats: "I was twenty-two years old, she was forty-five—Laurindo married me." This joy, though, soon sours as she realizes that he is a violent, morally hollow opportunist; the climax of this section occurs when Dôra discovers that he is having an affair with her mother. Dôra is shattered by this revelation, and her sense of imprisonment deepens—only lessening when her husband is killed in a mysterious hunting accident. Although Queiroz never completely explains this mystery, she implies that Laurindo is murdered by Raimundo Delmiro, a former bandit now living on the ranch and devoted to Dôra because she once saved his life.

No longer able to tolerate her mother, Dôra leaves the ranch and moves to the city. The second section of the novel describes how she increasingly escapes her haunted past. Whereas the claustrophobic first section is filled with images of death, imprisonment, and alienation, this part is a picaresque affirmation of the human spirit, especially after Dôra joins a ragtag theater group as a fledgling actress. For the first time, as the company travels back and forth across Brazil by ship, train, and truck, Dôra begins experiencing the larger world. Just as important, the company gives her the sense of family that she has always desired. Brandini, the vital Falstaffian director of the group, and Dona Estrela, his commonsensical wife, love and protect Dôra as she becomes more independent, as she tests her society's mores by coming to the realization that "my body was mine, to keep or to give, as I wished. . . . This change made a tremendous difference to me. . . ." Eventually, three years after Laurindo's death, this section reaches its fullest expression when Dôra meets the man who fulfills her dreams: Asmodeu Lucas, a handsome, volatile, "macho," even demonic river captain. The two grow more intimate as they travel down the São Francisco River, and finally they "marry"—neither worrying about obtaining any legal sanction for their union.

Their relationship is the heart of the novel's final section. When the pressures of World War II force the theater group to disperse, Dôra and the Captain begin to live together in teeming Rio de Janeiro. Queiroz initially depicts the idyllic nature of their everyday life, which, as Dôra stresses, "centered around just the two of us. But it wasn't a prison; it was more like a hedge protecting a garden, which made it fun." In contrast to her marriage with Laurindo, she gives herself to the Captain not out of duty, but out of love. Thus, she feels free, even though the demands of their relationship cause her to abandon her theater career, to accept his occasionally violent behavior, to acquiesce to his jealousy, and to close her eyes to the dangers of his new profession: smuggling. In short, she makes him a god whom she wants to possess totally, and as she says: "That could have been a mistake, I don't know. In the end love is like that: We get a man or a woman just like all others, and endow that creature with everything our heart wishes."

Their Edenic existence, however, is very precarious. This becomes increasingly apparent as one shadow after another begins haunting Dôra. Besides the Captain's violence, which always threatens to destroy him, memories of Dôra's past begin to stalk her again. Her mother dies, leaving the responsibilities of the ranch to her, and Delmiro is gruesomely killed, thus bringing the death of Laurindo to the forefront of her consciousness. Finally, the novel climaxes with the Captain's death from typhoid—a disaster that makes Dôra, for the rest of her life, see the world as "one vast nothing." Unable to cope with her grief in Rio, she returns to the more familiar solitude of the ranch and becomes the new Senhora. Now the novel has come full circle as Dôra, again in prison, tries to endure by rebuilding the deteriorating homestead.

## The Characters

Maria das Dores is a complex protagonist because her passionate nature expresses itself in so many ways. During her life at Soledade, it rests behind her bitter, competitive relationship with Senhora, her persistent yearning for maternal love, her refusal to forgive the unworthy Laurindo, her single-minded desire to protect Delmiro, and her idyllic vision of the lost father who tenderly called her Doralina. Later, it leads to her becoming an actress, to her challenging the morality of her culture by living with the Captain, to her celebrating their tender moments together, and to her feeling jealous toward anyone who receives affection from him. At its most dangerous, her passionate nature luxuriates in the Captain's occasionally very violent, bullying behavior: Being with him gives her the freedom to act irresponsibly, to feel "delight in the taste of power, provoking everybody who was afraid to respond." When she behaves like this, Dôra realizes that she is indeed the strong-willed Senhora's daughter. Finally, this will to power helps Dôra survive the Captain's death, for it leads her back to the ranch, which is now her possession: "A king dead is a king deposed. The Sinhá Dona had died and I had arrived. . . ."

While Dôra is the novel's most dynamic creation, Queiroz also successfully draws Senhora, Laurindo, the Captain, and Brandini—all these characters being colored by the protagonist's passionate attitude toward them. Senhora initially seems to be a monstrous maternal figure as she controls her ranch, her daughter, and herself with an iron hand. She is, as Dôra stresses, the "man of the house," who renounces the tender side of her nature in order to step over all obstacles threatening her authority. Thus, Dôra's alienation is well justified. Yet Queiroz tries to be fair to Senhora, as well. She indicates that this woman, like Dôra, has been the victim of a terrifying, often senseless world. In fact, as Dôra faces the Captain's death, Queiroz makes her increasingly reflect on the woman whom she has so long hated. She has the same look of outrage, the same faith in the land, the same desire for solitude; and these similarities cause the reader to entertain the possibility that Senhora's behavior was an outgrowth of the death of her husband—whom she loved as Dôra loves the Captain.

Just as Queiroz reveals the complexities of Dôra and Senhora by comparing and contrasting them, so she dramatically examines the ambivalent ideal of the "macho" man by playing Dôra's lovers, Laurindo and the Captain, off each other. The men, on one level, seem quite similar. Both are physically attractive, and this draws the romantic Dôra to them. Both see themselves as "the beloved man, the dear master" whom women are born to serve. Also, both have an irresponsible violent streak linked to their need to assert their masculinity. Yet Dôra comes to detest Laurindo, even before she discovers his relationship with her mother, while her love for the Captain grows increasingly stronger. These different responses stem from her attraction to the Captain's passionate interest in life, so unlike Laurindo's shallow, hard impersonality; from her realization that the Captain—despite his moments of insensitivity—has intuitively understood her deepest needs; and from her sense that he, in contrast to Laurindo, has never been "one of those who hides love or is ashamed to love." Therefore, she continues to endure his more diabolical actions (he has been appropriately named Asmodeu, after the devil in the Book of Tobias) long after they cease to be exciting to her.

Finally, there is Brandini, the comic soul of the novel's second section. He is an impudent, spontaneous, crafty, thoroughly romantic, and always curious life force, whose unfettered imagination is usually filled with grandiose future schemes as his theater company stays one step ahead of his creditors. As Dôra notes, everyone seems to bask in his vitality. Certainly he helps her experience life more fully, for he becomes her surrogate father when she joins his company. Striking a perfect balance in this role, he not only protects her, but he also encourages her to become an actress. Brandini thus gives Dôra the opportunity to express the artistic side of her personality, which has been so oppressed during her life with Senhora. Considering his love of life, it is not surprising that Brandini, of all the characters, has the greatest fear of death—a fear evident in his plaintive response to the news that Senhora has died: "That's the way it is. People die!"

*Themes and Meanings*

In the striking first paragraph of the novel, Queiroz introduces the tragic vision which will color much of Dôra's story: "And so, as the Captain used to say, it's natural to be in pain. I was always in pain. Pain always hurts, and the only time it doesn't is when you are dead." This statement points to Dôra's realization that she, like all human beings, has been doomed to suffer and to die in a harsh, mutable world. Dôra, in fact, sees the effect of time everywhere; for life, to her, is like a rock gradually crumbling to nothingness. She sees this truth through the deaths of the Captain, Senhora, Laurindo, her stillborn daughter, and Delmiro; through the perpetual changes of nature; through the slow deterioration of her ranch; through the deterioration of human beings from old age; and through the dissipation of human emotion, whether it be anger, hate, friendship, happiness, or grief. Her obsession with time is rooted in the everyday reality which Queiroz so successfully creates through her episodic, extremely concrete narrative.

Yet Queiroz' artistic vision resists morbidity because it also depicts, with the same vivid detail, the characters' deep-seated need to struggle against time. This struggle enlivens the novel, especially since Queiroz plays the comic second section off the tragic first and third parts. Dôra's love for the Captain, Brandini's vitality, and the Captain's bristling masculinity are attempts to challenge the horrors which inevitably come. Even more important, throughout the novel, there is a kind of tragic exultation in Dôra's persistent, unsparing, and honest attempt to remember and to confront her everfading past. By trying to rescue her memories—an act which brings more pain to her already desolate existence on the ranch—she rejects the temptation to give in to time. Thus, she keeps the rosebud that the Captain once gave her: "I still have it pressed between the leaves of the dictionary; and even if it turns to dust and disappears, the impression that it made on the pages of the book will never leave."

*Critical Context*

Critics have associated Queiroz with a group of writers (including José Lins do Rego, Jorge Amado, and Graciliano Ramos) who were bred in the remote Northeastern areas of Brazil and who burst onto the Brazilian literary scene in the 1930's to create what has been called "the novel of the Northeast." As Fred P. Ellison explains, this genre of the Brazilian novel is "characterized by its interest in man in his regional environment, by its implicit (and sometimes explicit) note of social protest, and by its endeavor to discover psychological truths in man, no matter what his walk of life. . . ." *Dôra, Doralina* can be seen as a late and interesting addition to this genre. The novel begins and ends with graphic descriptions of Dôra's life in the Northeast as she is both repulsed by and drawn to her family's ranch. Moreover, through Dôra's struggle to find individual freedom, Queiroz once again explores a social issue that is in all of her novels: the degrading secondary status of most women in this region.

Yet *Dôra, Doralina*, which has rightly been called Queiroz' most ambitious and accomplished novel, goes far beyond being merely a regional work. It contains her broadest vision of Brazilian society, as Dôra travels to many cities when she is with Brandini's company before settling in Rio de Janeiro with the Captain. In addition, it continues Queiroz' movement from the sociological emphases of her earliest works toward the psychological realism of *As três Marias* (1939; *The Three Marias*, 1963). Thus, with un-flinching honesty, Queiroz reveals the subtleties of Dôra's character and in the process—with more depth than ever before—develops some of the prevailing themes within her fiction: the ambivalent nature of memories, the human need for nurturing maternal love, the difficulties and beauties of male-female relationships, and the individual's painful existence in a universe where the "good things in life occur less often, the evil ten times more."

*Sources for Further Study*
Ellison, Fred P. "Dôra, Doralina," in *Hispania*. LIX (1976), p. 963.
————. "Rachel de Queiroz," in *Brazil's New Novel: Four Northeastern Masters*, 1954.
Laus, Lausimar. "O romance em Rachel de Queiroz," in *Minas gerias, supplemento literario*. XI (October 11, 1975), p. 11.

*James Grove*

# THE DUNE TRILOGY

*Author:* Frank Herbert (1920-1986)
*Type of plot:* Science-fiction epic
*Time of plot:* The remote future
*Locale:* Several planets in the galaxy, principally Arrakis, also known as Dune
*First published:* 1979 (as *The Great Dune Trilogy*): *Dune*, 1965; *Dune Messiah*, 1969; *Children of Dune*, 1976

> *Principal characters:*
> DUKE LETO ATREIDES, the head of an aristocratic Imperial family
> JESSICA, his concubine, a member of the Bene Gesserit
> PAUL ATREIDES, their son and heir
> ALIA, their daughter
> CHANI, a Fremen girl, later Paul's concubine
> LETO II and
> GHANIMA, the twin children of Paul and Chani
> BARON VLADIMIR HARKONNEN, head of an aristocratic family feuding with the Atreides
> STILGAR, the leader of a tribe of Fremen, natives of Dune
> DUNCAN IDAHO, a liegeman of Duke Leto
> DOCTOR YEUH, the Atreides' doctor, who betrays them

*The Novels*

Ever since the publication of *God Emperor of Dune* in 1981, it has been inaccurate, strictly speaking, to refer to the "Dune Trilogy," and subsequent books in the series have given the term even less validity. Nevertheless, there is one sense in which these first three works may be thought of as a unit. *Dune, Dune Messiah*, and *Children of Dune* show a unity of time and characters that makes it appropriate to group them as a single story; it is a story which is continued, to be sure, but one whose next installment takes place thousands of years after all but one of the characters of these three works have become dust. In that sense, then, a "Dune trilogy" still exists. Although a changed Leto II appears in *God Emperor of Dune*, that book has new characters, new concerns, and new themes.

It is difficult to summarize the intricate plot of the first three books, for if science fiction has an epic, this is it. The story moves with the grandeur of history and paints large pictures on a canvas crowded with characters and incidents. Yet all of those incidents revolve around a single commodity and its possession—the spice melange. Millennia from now, an empire of thousands of worlds is held together only by a network of spaceships that fly faster than the speed of light. For navigation at those tremendous velocities, human reactions are too plodding and, because of a religious war thousands of years in the past, computers are forbidden.

In order to navigate their ships, the members of the Spacing Guild, which has a monopoly on the piloting of interplanetary craft, ingest melange in order to extend their senses and, in a way, read the future. Yet of all the worlds of the Imperium, only the planet Arrakis, which is also called Dune, produces the spice, as the by-product of giant creatures known as the sandworms. Whoever controls Dune, then, will eventually control the empire.

As the story opens, Duke Leto Atreides, hereditary ruler of the planet Caladan, has recently gained a signal victory in his family's carefully regulated feud with another noble house, the Harkonnens: The Atreides have gained possession of Dune. The Emperor, however, aware of Leto's popularity, judges him too dangerous a figure to control the spice planet; consequently the Emperor arranges with the Harkonnens to have Leto betrayed and murdered soon after Leto's family arrives on the planet.

Leto's son Paul and Paul's mother Jessica escape to the vast deserts that almost cover Dune. Neither mother nor son is ordinary. Jessica is a member of the Bene Gesserit, an organization of women dedicated to a single purpose: the breeding of a god. For centuries the Bene Gesserit have possessed a kind of extended awareness that allows the Reverend Mothers access to the consciousnesses of all their predecessors. Through selective, if secret, breeding, they have tried to produce a male capable of the same kind of consciousness. Jessica, supplied to Leto as a concubine, was part of the plan.

The Bene Gesserit have staggering powers, among them the ability to decide the sex of their children. To enhance their plan, Jessica was to bear a female child by Leto, but the plan failed when Jessica fell genuinely in love with Leto and gave birth to Paul instead. Paul therefore has had the benefit of Bene Gesserit training from his mother, and, when his latent abilities are unlocked by a massive dose of spice, he becomes the messiah that the Bene Gesserit had hoped to produce, yet one outside their control.

The Fremen, independent and fierce dwellers in Dune's harshest regions, become the fitting tool for Paul to use. At their head, he leads them from the desert, defeats the elite troops of the Emperor and forces his abdication, and becomes Emperor himself, an event with which the first book, *Dune*, concludes.

*Dune Messiah* shows a much different Paul, however, one aghast at the effects of his rule. The Fremen have conquered the empire for him, but at a cost of millions of lives. With the vision of alternative futures that his prescience gives him, Paul is tempted to try to decide the best course for humanity. This choice he refuses to make. He becomes blinded by a conspiracy against his rule; he leaves his infant son and daughter, Leto and Ghanima, in the care of his sister Alia, and goes off into the desert to die.

Some critics have argued that *Children of Dune*, the third part of the story, warns of the dangers of following a charismatic leader, even one as personally appealing as Paul. The story begins nine years after Paul's disappearance. His sister Alia, ruling as regent for Paul's children, has nearly destroyed the old Fremen ways. Her mother, Jessica, took a large dose of melange while pregnant with Alia, and as a result Alia gained access to her ancestors' awareness while still in her mother's womb. Throughout her life she has been struggling against the attempts of those personalities to take control of her in a kind of demonic possession; as the story opens, she fails in the struggle. The personality of Baron Harkonnen takes control of her, and she establishes an oppressive religious tyranny.

Leto recognizes the threat that he represents to "Alia" and, like his father before him, escapes to the desert for a time of testing. There he gains an awareness of the future outstripping even Paul's. Under Paul's ecological programs, Dune has flowered into a green planet. Yet Leto foresees that humanity's choices will narrow to a chilling few unless he acts. His only choice is to choose the "Golden Path," to transform himself into an inhuman monster who will live for thousands of years, to rule his empire pitilessly until humanity becomes so independent that each man and woman will no longer need leaders at all. This is the path that he chooses. With inhuman strength, he destroys the irrigation systems that have brought prosperity to Dune and sets his foot on the road that will lead him to empire.

*The Characters*

This massive work is filled with scores of memorable characters, each distinctively created by an author skillful at his work. The sheer number of characters does not tax the reader's memory because of a schema that Herbert adopts: He divides the characters into sets along political lines, and each set is made up of characters who stand in a parallel relation to the other characters in the other set. For example, Duke Leto heads House Atreides, Baron Harkonnen heads his own house, and so on. Each of these leaders employs a mentat—a human computer: Leto's is Thufir Hawat, Harkonnen's is Pieter de Vries. Each has a war leader: Duncan Idaho for Atreides, "Beast" Rabban for Harkonnen. Each has a scion: Paul among the Atreides and Feyd Rautha among the Harkonnens. When Paul becomes the leader of the rebel Fremen, the set of characters who surround him will come to occupy almost the same positions: Paul can serve as his own mentat, but in the Fremen Stilgar he will find his battle leader, and from his love of Chani will come his heirs, Leto II and Ghanima.

Each of the great power blocs also has a character more mystical than mental, serving as adviser to (and sometimes manipulator of) the bloc. The Emperor Shaddam has a high-ranking member of the Bene Gesserit, the Reverend Mother Helen Gaius Mohiam. She analyzes his enemies for him, depending on her more-than-natural powers to be of service. Within Duke Leto's circle, Jessica, his concubine, has been trained by the Bene Gesserit and possesses the same kinds of powers. There is, however, a similar class of "witch-women" within the Fremen, their own Sayyadina. After her flight into the desert with her son, Jessica will add the powers of the Sayyadina to the training provided by the Bene Gesserit and serve Paul in a much more profound way than she had been able to aid Leto.

Herbert's Galactic Empire has no alien races as such, but some of the "humans" have been so changed that they are scarcely recognizable as human beings. These groups are nevertheless composed of memorable, recognizable individuals. One such group is the Spacing Guild, whose consumption of large amounts of spice has made their chief navigators unfit for a normal human environment. One of them appears early in *Dune Messiah*, swimming in something like a gigantic fishbowl, surrounded by the clouds of melange-laden gasses without which he can no longer survive.

Another group of "aliens" are the Face Dancers—skillful impersonators and athletes from the planet Tleilax. They have been severely modified both by genetics and by surgery to fit them for the overt role of entertainers and the covert one of spies. They illustrate well that even those characters who play relatively small roles have an unforgettable uniqueness about them.

Each reader may well favor a different character from the rich offering that Herbert has presented. Especially in *Dune*, Herbert surrounds the young Paul with a brilliantly drawn cast of mentors: the musician and swordmaster Gurney Halleck; the battle-wise Duncan Idaho; the Fremen leader Stilgar; even the traitor, Doctor Yeuh. Each of them is as individually marked as are the major characters; there are no cardboard characters in *Dune*.

### Themes and Meanings

This very sketchy outline of the first three *Dune* books has largely omitted those themes that stand in the foreground of the individual works. On its publication, *Dune* was hailed as a bible of ecological awareness. The central theme of the work is that actions have consequences throughout the ecosystem, and the reforming of a whole planet over centuries of labor seemed to offer the kind of vision so desperately needed in a nation just becoming aware of pollution and its problems. Yet if *Dune* concentrated on the goal, *Dune Messiah* and *Children of Dune* examined the means used to get there and rejected them.

Herbert had in fact turned the tables on his readers, many of whom did not enjoy their new seats at the later courses he served. Several arguments are made in the later two books that repelled some readers. First, the Fremen who have been liberated by Paul become conquerors in their turn, subjecting the galaxy to a jihad, or holy war, repeating the barbarians' invasions on a grand scale. Next, when the planet Dune becomes a place of greenery, a place hospitable to human life, one finds two results: The Fremen gradually begin to lose their admirable qualities—independence, hardiness, honesty—and become sycophantic. Herbert clearly accepts the dictum that the history of human warfare is the history of hobnailed boots going upstairs and silken slippers coming down. Yet Paul seems almost immediately helpless to stop the jihad and later to prevent the degeneration of the Fremen. An inertia grasps him, explained in part in the text by his ability to see future alternatives for human history. It is Paul's judgment that the slaughter of millions in the jihad and the destruction of all that is good in the Fremen is the least evil of possible outcomes.

The greening of Dune has a second consequence: As Arrakis blooms, the very conditions that make the planet habitable for humans make it uninhabitable for sandworms. They begin to die off, and since the production of melange is part of their life cycle, interstellar communication and transport is threatened. The change in the planet, the life's work of characters such as the planetologist Liet-Kynes and countless Fremen, has led to unforeseen and unacceptable consequences. This reversal of plot in particular seemed to readers a betrayal by Herbert of the honor they had awarded him as an apostle of ecology.

Paul's son, Leto II, exceeds his father in his ability to read the future, and he chooses what he calls the "Golden Path," to make himself into a dictator so odious and at once so long-lived that the human race will by his lesson never again be tempted to follow a messianic leader.

A deep suspicion of popular leaders shows up in the two later works, which put forward the thesis that it is always dangerous to turn over one's destiny to another, no matter how capable or well-meaning that other may be. Yet when the reasonableness of this view is granted, it is still hard to agree with the methods of the third book, *Children of Dune*. The reader must first accept that Leto's medicine is in fact needed, and that no other cure will serve. Here Herbert is less than successful, since he gives the reader no reasons whatsoever to agree with Leto. One must accept Leto's judgments on faith, an acceptance which appears to be the very thing against which Herbert is arguing.

The themes of the Dune Trilogy are several, and not always obvious. Surely the overriding theme is the necessity of knowing the consequences of one's actions; ecology is only a subtheme of the larger one. A warning against the blind tendency of humans to follow a charismatic leader is another. Yet beyond those two, agreement ceases.

### Critical Context

As one might expect, those readers who had lionized Herbert for what looked like advocacy of the ecological movement reacted with coolness to the sabotage of their vision in *Children of Dune*. Yet in fairness to the author, Herbert can hardly be blamed for not writing the book that someone else wanted to read. If readers of the first part mistook his theme, it needs to be stated that Herbert did not originally separate the work into three volumes but saw it as a single story. A second objection is harder to explain away: To the claim of the book's admirers that it illustrates Herbert's constant rejection of easy answers to human problems, one might reply that the reclaiming of Dune was no easy answer.

The religious themes of the book, the tensions between prophets and the religions that grow up around them, have been a second center of critical discussion. The books never show institutionalized religion (or governments, for that matter) in a favorable light. Throughout the works runs a distrust of anyone conceding responsibility and decision making to another. One wonders, however, if this suspicion is valid, given that nowhere in any of the books is a representative or elected government shown.

Even the figure of Paul provoked some readers, among them John W. Campbell, Jr., the editor of *Astounding Science Fiction*. Although Campbell had published *Dune* in serial in his magazine, he rejected the later parts of the story, complaining mainly about the change in the character of Paul. Whereas Paul had been an agent in the movement of the plot of the first book, he decides in the second and third that he does not like what he has done, and passively retires from power, accepts a preventable blinding, and flees into the desert from the society that he has made. Those who, like Campbell, prefer activity to passivity found an unexpected change.

Nevertheless, the popularity of the Dune series shows no sign of lessening. Subsequent volumes have been best-sellers, although their action is far different from that discussed here. It may well be that today's readers (and many future ones) will turn to *Dune* and its sequels for the same pleasures that its first readers found there: a sweeping story of action on a galactic scale, with a cast of characters both large and colorful, both heroic and thoughtful.

*Sources for Further Study*
Allen, L. David. *Herbert's Dune and Other Works*, 1975.
Miller, David M. *Frank Herbert*, 1980.
O'Reilly, Timothy. *Frank Herbert*, 1981.

*Walter E. Meyers*

# 1876

*Author:* Gore Vidal
*Type of plot:* Historical chronicle
*Time of plot:* 1875-1877
*Locale:* New York City and Washington, D.C.
*First published:* 1976

*Principal characters:*
> CHARLES SCHERMERHORN SCHUYLER, the novel's narrator, a
> journalist and historian
> EMMA, Schuyler's daughter, who was reared in Europe and is
> visiting America for the first time
> JOHN DAY APGAR, Emma's suitor
> JAMES BENNETT, Schuyler's newspaper publisher
> WILLIAM CULLEN BRYANT, a renowned American poet and
> newspaper editor
> CHARLES NORDHOFF, a journalist
> WILLIAM SANFORD, a millionaire dabbler in politics
> DENISE SANFORD, William's wife and a close friend to Emma
> ROSCOE CONKLING, a prominent Republican politician and a
> presidential aspirant
> JAMES G. BLAINE, Conkling's Republican rival
> PRESIDENT ULYSSES S. GRANT, who is serving his second term
> SAMUEL TILDEN, the Democratic candidate for President
> JOHN BIGELOW, Secretary of State in New York and Tilden's
> supporter
> JAMES GARFIELD, a Republican congressman

## The Novel

*1876* is written in the form of a journal that Charles Schuyler is keeping for himself. After a more than thirty-year absence, he is returning with his daughter to the United States, which is on the eve of its centennial year. The panic of 1873 (a monetary crisis initiated by the passage in that year of the Silver Act, which ended the coinage of silver and thus reduced the amount of currency in circulation) has wiped out his capital, and he is forced to solicit journalistic assignments and to secure a wealthy husband for his widowed daughter. His main aim is to help Samuel Tilden, governor of New York, get elected president, for which Schuyler hopes to be rewarded with a diplomatic post in France.

Schuyler is a self-described "Rip Van Winkle" who is awakening to what is, for him, a new country. Thus his journal is filled with commentary on the manners and morals of the populace, on the way that Americans speak, dress, neglect to bathe frequently enough, and so on. He is a Europeanized American who is alternately amused and irritated by the crudeness of the cultural and political climate. Mark Twain, for example, is viewed as a kind of professional roughneck whom Schuyler detests. Twain has "cunningly" played "the fool" for his own enormous profit and popularity, but in Schuyler's view, Twain has also "come to hate himself, but lacks the courage either to crack the mirror or to change, if he could, that deliberately common face which it so faithfully reflects." Corrupt politicians and businessmen conspire to defraud the public of millions, and thus Schuyler is confirmed in his support of Tilden's candidacy as a reformer and as one of the few men in public life who is not afraid to expose corruption.

At the same time, Schuyler's critique of America is tempered by his awareness of his own connivance in corruption. After all, he assiduously courts well-to-do New York families, such as the Apgars, who have eligible sons who might marry his daughter. He is troubled by his role as journalist, since that also means kowtowing to the powerful in order to gather information and commissions for more work. He prefers the guise of the historian who can afford to take a more impartial and objective view of politics and society. He is best known in Europe for his book, *Paris Under the Commune.*

As the illegitimate son of Aaron Burr (Schuyler is also the narrator of Vidal's *Burr*, 1973), as a writer who has covered nearly a half-century of American and European history, and as a partisan deeply involved in the upcoming election, Schuyler is in a perfect position to bring a very complex consciousness to his descriptions of personalities and issues. Having compromised some of his own principles for money, Schuyler can tolerantly record the schemes of politicians such as James G. Blaine and show how they fit into a nation bent on efficiently consolidating its power and prosperity. As Schuyler says of Cornelius Vanderbilt,

> it must be said in the old villain's favour that before he managed through theft, violence, and fraud to put together his railroad empire, a passenger from New York City to Chicago was obliged to change trains seventeen times during the course of the journey.

Schuyler is hardly an apologist for capitalism, but he cannot gainsay the service that Vanderbilt has provided to the public any more than he can overlook "such a vast floating criminal class" and the "grinding poverty in grisly contrast to the awful richness of the sort of people" he has been seeing in New York. If he is not as fiercely dedicated to reform as his journalist colleague, Charles Nordhoff, Schuyler is a more aloof and therefore a more reliable observer of politics.

As the nation heads indifferently toward electing a new president, Schuyler and his daughter alternately court and criticize society. Emma is something of a Bonapartist and is attracted to politicians such as Blaine who are not bothered by the brokering of principles as long as they advance to higher offices of power. Schuyler, on the other hand, is allied to the legalistic Tilden, who would do more for the poor and bring order to the slipshod procedures of President Ulysses Grant's corrupt government. Father and daughter, in other words, are excellent exemplars of the conflicts and contradictions that beset mid-century America.

## The Characters

As is the case with all of Vidal's historical novels, characters are vividly described and balanced carefully against one another. The women exhibit considerable wit and shrewdness. Emma is every bit as sly as any of the politicians in the book, withholding information from her father when she believes that it will hurt him and treating her fiancé, John Apgar, tactfully even when it is clear that she is receiving this unimaginative man's attentions for the sake of relieving Schuyler's anxiety over her security. Similarly, Denise Sanford becomes Schuyler's dear friend and confederate and Emma's closest companion, for Denise has a subtle feel for the politics of human relationships that surpasses the rather dull or comic conventionality of most of the Americans Schuyler meets. Complicating the friendship of Denise, Emma, and Charles is the presence of William Sanford, an opportunist and intriguer whom Schuyler despises and yet must tolerate when it becomes clear that Emma's happiness depends on the favors of Denise's husband. Once again, the compromises of private life and politics are skillfully intertwined in Vidal's fiction.

The historical figures, particularly James Garfield, stimulate Schuyler's perplexity over American politics. On the one hand, Garfield is well educated in the classics, argues from the standpoint of clearly articulated principles, and seems able to balance private and public interests. On the other hand, he is a part of the crass maneuvering that secures the presidency for Rutherford B. Hayes even though Tilden wins the popular vote by 250,000 votes.

As in *Lincoln* (1984), Ulysses Grant is something of a mystery. He appears deliberately to conceal his true nature. Thought to be inept by some, regarded as fundamentally uninterested in politics by others, Grant is, in Schuyler's estimation, far from being the fool that others take him to be. On the contrary, while Grant practices politics and is probably aware of the corruption of his colleagues, he does not commit himself to any kind of public positions that would make him accountable for the failures of his administration.

James G. Blaine is Grant's opposite, for he shamelessly courts popularity, makes deals with those who hold incriminating evidence against him, and wins an enormous following by ostentatiously exercising his forceful personality. Whereas Blaine ultimately fails to secure his party's nomination for president because he has been involved in more financial scandals than even he can finesse, his rival Roscoe Conkling is denied the nomination because of his affair with a senator's wife. Conkling is too much the preening politician to prevail in a Republican party that finally settles for a more demure, if obscure, candidate.

## Themes and Meanings

*1876* finds its truest and most exciting theme in the presidential election, for what is at stake is nothing less than what kind of country America will become. Will it continue to be "this vigorous, ugly, turbulent realm devoted to moneymaking by any means"? Or will the forces of reform, under Tilden's leadership, reassert the principle of the public interest? Tilden, at one time an attorney for the railroads, has helped to build the very capitalist system that he now would like to restrain. Yet, like the Aaron Burr whom Schuyler served in *Burr*, Tilden will not grab for power even though he has significant popular support. He will not engage in the bribery that ultimately puts Hayes in office.

Throughout Vidal's historical novels, the most successful politicians are opportunists and hypocrites, men and women who realize that power is built upon the leverage acquired by shaping principles to fit the requirements of political office. It is not that principles count for nothing; rather, as Garfield (a man who knows the value of principles) puts it, "when you are dealt the cards, you play them." Schuyler's bitter but realistic conclusion is, "So Caesar must have sounded when he set aside the old republic."

## Critical Context

*1876* is one of a series of novels by Vidal that provide a lively and incisive history of the American republic. It is less exciting than *Burr* and *Lincoln* because it lacks a dominant historical figure about whom events and themes naturally cluster. Yet Schuyler is a thoroughly convincing narrator, and his account of the election provides an exciting and instructive denouement of the novel. Although it is a historical fact that Tilden lost the election, and therefore it would seem impossible for there to be any suspense in a detailed recounting of his campaign, Vidal manages to devise a plausible, almost day-by-day, rendering of how Tilden almost won.

This devotion to the 1876 election is characteristic of Vidal's effort as a historical novelist to show history in the making, to identify those moments when the past nearly turned in a direction different from its eventual outcome. There is, in other words, nothing inevitable about how history has developed. It might easily have been otherwise, Vidal implies, when he has Schuyler speak of Tilden's "chance" to reject legalistic maneuvering in determining the winner of the presidential election. Tilden's failure to act as the leader of his party and his reluctance to appear to be intervening with the legislative branch's authority to determine who won the disputed election cost him all of the twenty disputed electoral votes—only one of which he needed to become president.

Without question, Gore Vidal is America's premier historical novelist. He has adhered to the documentary record while debating the meaning of that record and the motivations of those who have promulgated the official history of the republic. As a result, there is in his historical novels a constant dialectic between fact and fiction that dramatizes history as a dialogue which is never finished, never definitive. Vidal's work is the perfect antidote to pious versions of American history; it is impossible to become complacent about the idea of America as a fact of life, Vidal implies, when so much of it is a construct of the imagination.

*Sources for Further Study*
Dick, Bernard F. *The Apostate Angel: A Critical Study of Gore Vidal*, 1974.
Kiernan, Robert F. *Gore Vidal*, 1982.
Stanton, Robert, ed. *Gore Vidal: A Primary and Secondary Bibliography*, 1978.
Stanton, Robert, and Gore Vidal. *View from a Window: Conversations with Gore Vidal*, 1980.

*Carl E. Rollyson, Jr.*

# THE EIGHTH DAY

*Author:* Thornton Wilder (1897-1975)
*Type of plot:* Family saga
*Time of plot:* 1880-1905
*Locale:* Chicago, Illinois; Coaltown, Illinois; Hoboken, New Jersey; and
Chile
*First published:* 1967

Principal characters:
JOHN ASHLEY, a mining engineer and fugitive after a murder
conviction
BEATA ASHLEY, his wife, an operator of a boardinghouse
ROGER ASHLEY, their son, a prominent young journalist
LILY ASHLEY, the eldest Ashley daughter, a concert singer
SOPHIA ASHLEY, the second Ashley daughter, her mother's
chief support
CONSTANCE ASHLEY, the youngest daughter, a social reformer
BRECKENRIDGE LANSING, John Ashley's friend and employer
GEORGE LANSING, the murderer of his father, Breckenridge

## The Novel

In a prologue, Thornton Wilder sets forth the external facts of the
conviction of John Ashley in 1902 for the murder of Breckenridge Lansing,
his subsequent rescue by five masked men shortly before his scheduled execution, and his escape to parts unknown. Then, in six long chapters, the
novel moves backward and forward in time to explore the background of the
Ashley and Lansing families, their relationships to the community, and their
reactions to these bizarre events.

The Ashleys and Lansings live at opposite ends of the main street of a
depressed southern Illinois coal-mining town. By hiring Ashley, a creative
tinkerer, Lansing props up the faltering mine, which he has been incom-
petently managing, and leaves himself free for the social life which interests
him more. At a weekend get-together of the two families, while the men are
practicing with rifles, a bullet kills Lansing. Unjust town gossip linking Ashley and Eustacia Lansing in an affair and the absence of any other plausible
suspect creates an atmosphere prejudicial to Ashley. Following his conviction and mysterious rescue, the novel details Ashley's flight down the Mississippi River to New Orleans and eventually to South America. Knowing
that copper-mining engineers are needed in Chile, he acquires a new identity as James Tolland, a Canadian engineer. In South America, he establishes a reputation as a hard worker and active humanitarian. When, three
years after his escape from the law, a bounty hunter succeeds in identifying

him, Ashley flees, and shortly before the middle of the book the fugitive drowns at sea.

The novel then traces the same period in Coaltown and in Chicago, where Roger Ashley goes to work in anonymity to help support his mother and sisters. The middle daughter, Sophia, encourages her mother to convert their home to a boardinghouse, which gradually prospers despite the obloquy of their situation as the family of an escaped convict. After energetically pursuing many humble jobs, Roger finds his métier in journalism, and his sister Lily discovers hers on the concert stage. Eventually, both succeed well enough to shed protective pseudonyms and proclaim their identity as children of the notorious Ashley.

After bringing both the Chilean and Illinois events forward to 1905, John Ashley and his family remaining mutually ignorant of one another's circumstances, Wilder reverts to the year 1883, in New Jersey, the scene of Ashley's courtship of Beata Kellerman, daughter of a prosperous Hoboken brewer, their elopement, and their later settlement in Coaltown. Before resolving the mystery, however (Wilder contrives that the reader suspects the identity of the killer long before the Ashleys do), another lengthy flashback describes the formation of the Lansing family, Breckenridge's deficiencies as husband and father, and the consequent plight of the three Lansing children, especially George's as the only son. This chapter tends to create sympathy for the Lansings, who are all victims in one way or another.

In the final chapter, dotted with brief anticipations of the subsequent lives of the two families, George, who had disappeared from home around the time of the murder and later fallen from a train and spent time in an insane asylum, returns and confesses to killing his father in defense of his afflicted mother. A sympathetic Russian-born neighbor, Olga Doubkov, arranges for George's written confession and his escape to her own native land. Finally, the deacon of a small religious sect informs Roger that members of his congregation had daringly rescued his father to express their gratitude to the man who had helped them build their church.

The mystery surrounding Ashley is less important than Wilder's conviction that the truth is complex, contrary to external appearances, and discoverable only in time. Thus, he organizes the novel to create in the reader not suspense but progressive insight into the minds and hearts of its characters, who themselves are following the path of discovery.

## The Characters

The reader senses a tinge of irony in Wilder's frequent references to John Ashley as "late-maturing" and "unreflective." Ashley is a man uninterested in the goals of most people who are considered mature: the making of money, advancement on the job, community acknowledgment. He happily allows Lansing the credit for his own work in the Coaltown mine. He would rather invent useful devices than patent or sell them. Even his family knows little or nothing of his charities, which typically take the form of deeds rather than of donations. He is "unreflective," for example, in his failure to see the good in making his inventions and services available to the world at large. No abstract philanthropist, Ashley wishes only to help people within his ken. Nor do discriminations of rank, wealth, race, ethnicity, and religion mean anything to him. He restricts his thinking to the solution of practical problems and the assistance of neighbors.

Wilder draws Beata Ashley in the broadest of descriptive strokes. She is a colorless character completely devoted to her husband; as wife of a supposed murderer, she stands proud, silent, aloof. The children, especially Roger and Sophia, resemble their father in their energetic and resourceful approach to pressing problems, although as social outcasts with their usual source of income cut off, they are more cunning and calculating. Roger's rise to eminence in Chicago journalism before he is out of his teens is less credible than Sophia's labors to establish the boardinghouse that her mother would have been too proud to initiate and too distant to maintain alone. Both Lily and Constance, the youngest daughter, resemble their parents in daring to be different. Lily informs Roger that she intends to have a dozen children by a dozen different men, all of whom she will love without marrying. Constance, the least well-developed Ashley character, will live the life of an international social reformer.

As the unhappy son of an autocratic father, Breckenridge Lansing duplicates his father's folly. A hearty man with the knack of making a strong initial impression, Breckenridge wins the heart of a beautiful girl of mixed Creole and English parentage. Although an able assistant in her father's store, she nevertheless desires neither more nor less than to be a wife and mother. Learning of her husband's weaknesses too late, Eustacia Lansing watches him try to "make a man" of George by subjecting the boy to stringent and disheartening exercises, refusing to acknowledge his achievements, and always setting a standard beyond his capacity. One of John Ashley's charitable deeds is the befriending of this severely maladjusted boy, who later shoots his father and (inadvertently, it would appear) brings on Ashley's murder conviction. Wilder never shows Lansing outside his family circle; as his childhood is reported only summarily, his back-slapping, lodge-joining aspect only briefly, Lansing emerges as a rather sinister figure, and it is difficult to imagine Ashley choosing to socialize with him on weekends.

Ashley, however, is a character more mythic than realistic. At one point, Wilder compares him to an apostle, at another a Chilean fortune-teller insists that he is especially beloved of God. The manager of the Chilean mine, Dr. MacKenzie, tells Ashley about Greek mythology and raises the question—which he does not presume to answer—as to what sort of hero "Tolland" is. Ashley displays a number of the traits of Homeric heroes, particularly Odysseus. He makes periodic descents to the "underworld" of mines, though he normally conducts his work on the surface. Very Homeric are his periodic rejuvenations, as though touched by a friendly deity, which allow him to pass as a much younger man (he is actually in his early forties during his exile) and escape detection by a swarm of international bounty hunters. He is most Odyssean in his never being at a loss. Yet he does not return to his patent "Penelope," and his "Telemachus" must fight the battles of maturation without his father's assistance. In his attitude toward his accusers, he is more apostolic than Homeric: Revenge never enters his mind.

## Themes and Meanings

Ashley, Wilder reiterates, is a "man of faith"—endowed also with substantial funds of hope and charity. A sharply contrasting fellow townsman, Dr. Gillies, proclaims the inevitability of a continued "eighth day" development of man and the human community in the new century—but without believing it himself, for he considers it the duty of the old to deceive the young. Ashley, however, embodies hope. Although he accepts his temporary role as Tolland, he clearly expects to return someday in honor to his family; his family is imbued with the same hope. Meanwhile, he gains strength by overcoming deprivation, by a generous giving of himself and his talents to others who are also in some way deprived. Along the way he meets and benefits from other positive thinkers, including Dr. MacKenzie and Mrs. Wickersham, a founder of Chilean orphanages and hospitals. Back in Coaltown, a few souls shine forth: Porky O'Hara, a cobbler who quietly assists the young Ashleys, and Miss Doubkov, the dressmaker who supports George Lansing in the depths of his despair. Wilder presents such people as strengthening and confirming the character of their beneficiaries as well as helping them over the rough spots.

The real "eighth day" of continued creativity is the work of a choice few in a world that practices little faith, hope, and love. Successes are ironically qualified. Ashley dies without learning that his name has been cleared; Sophia restores the family to solvency but lapses into insanity in later life; Roger reconciles the two families and marries one of the Lansing daughters, but their son turns out to be hostile and self-destructive. The author provides no glib answer to the questions his novel raises—why, for example, innocence suffers while ignorance, greed, and prejudice flourish. Taken as a whole, however, *The Eighth Day* modestly affirms that the struggle to live decent, caring lives, regardless of whether the effort receives acknowledgment, gives life its meaning.

## Critical Context

Common threads run through many of Wilder's plays and novels. In *The*

*Eighth Day* as in *Our Town* (1938) and *The Skin of Our Teeth* (1942), his imagination focuses on family relationships—both the loyalty and the conflict of close families. The same fondness for editorial comment and omniscience that created the character of the Stage Manager in *Our Town* (a role that Wilder himself played for two weeks on Broadway) breaks forth in *The Eighth Day*. As in *The Bridge of San Luis Rey* (1927), published forty years earlier, this novel begins with sudden death and proceeds to scrutinize its meaning and effects. Like *The Ides of March* (1948), *The Eighth Day* develops its story of a murder by moving back and forth in time. There are many other thematic and technical similarities to other Wilder works.

While Wilder's best plays are highly innovative, his novels are more conventional, and the narrative technique of *The Eighth Day* works against its theme to some extent. Like Joseph Conrad and William Faulkner before him, Wilder uses chronological shifts and dislocations to develop the sense of an unfolding truth, but he undercuts the effect with fussy references to this technique ("as we shall see," "as I shall have occasion to say"). Such disparities seem to reflect an unresolved tension in Wilder between his receptivity to highly original minds and talents (for example, his intimate knowledge and love of the work of Sigmund Freud, Gertrude Stein, and James Joyce) and his conviction that the old-fashioned values and virtues of Protestant Christianity remain adequate to guide men in the twentieth century. As a result, this highly intellectual and sophisticated man often wrote in the manner of a nineteenth century novelist who feels free to hold forth comfortably as though unaware of modern doubts and skepticism. In *The Eighth Day* much more than in *The Bridge of San Luis Rey* or *The Ides of March*, the reader senses his manipulating of his characters and situations.

*The Eighth Day* stands as the longest and most ambitious novel of a man whose dual achievements in the novel and drama are unequalled by any other American writer. Because of its lapses into didacticism and authorial self-indulgence, it cannot be considered a complete success. Yet if it fails to capture the essence of the American experience, it remains an impressive testament to the possibility of familial solidarity in an unstable and largely faithless world.

*Sources for Further Study*
Burbank, Rex. *Thornton Wilder*, 1961, 1978.
Kuner, M. C. *Thornton Wilder: The Bright and the Dark*, 1972.
Papajewski, Helmut. *Thornton Wilder*, 1968.
Stresau, Hermann. *Thornton Wilder*, 1971.

*Robert P. Ellis*